" Love begins by taking care of the closest ones — the ones at home." ~ Mother Teresa. Hope this gives you & your family empowerment.

♡ Jennifer Lue

Billionaire Parenting
Give Your Kids The World

Jennifer Luc

Dr. Stéphane Provencher

iUniverse LLC
Bloomington

BILLIONAIRE PARENTING
GIVE YOUR KIDS THE WORLD

iUniverse books may be ordered through booksellers or by contacting:

iUniverse
1663 Liberty Drive
Bloomington, IN 47403
www.iuniverse.com
1-800-Authors (1-800-288-4677)

Because of the dynamic nature of the Internet, any web addresses or links contained in this book may have changed since publication and may no longer be valid. The views expressed in this work are solely those of the author and do not necessarily reflect the views of the publisher, and the publisher hereby disclaims any responsibility for them.

Credit: *From the book A 3rd Helping of Chicken Soup for the Soul by Jack Canfield and Mark Victor Hansen. Copyright 2012 by Chicken Soup for the Soul Publishing, LLC. Published by Backlist, LLC, a unit of Chicken Soup for the Soul Publishing, LLC. Chicken Soup for the Soul is a registered trademark of Chicken Soup for the Soul Publishing, LLC. Reprinted by permission. All rights reserved.*

Any people depicted in stock imagery provided by Thinkstock are models, and such images are being used for illustrative purposes only. Certain stock imagery © Thinkstock.

ISBN: 978-1-4917-3457-5 (sc)
ISBN: 978-1-4917-3458-2 (e)

Library of Congress Control Number: 2014909285

Printed in the United States of America.

iUniverse rev. date: 05/23/2014

Disclaimer

This book has the opinions and thoughts of its writers and is complimented with compilations of current and earlier research from the Internet and from research journals, and books within the scientific fields of neuroscience, psychology, energy psychology, educational psychology, prenatal psychology, energy medicine, kinesiology, neurology, chiropractic Craniopathy, chiropractic, epigenetics, physics and other scientific disciplines.

This book is not intended to offer professional services or medical advice and is written for educational purposes only. The writers' claim no responsibility or liability for loss or risk incurred as a result of the use or application of any of the contents of the book. We encourage anyone that is looking for a brighter perspective on health and educational reform to read this book from cover-to-cover.

We have gathered information here so that you can make an informed decision as a consumer but most importantly as a parent, grandparent or someone that cares within the community. It truly takes a community to raise a child. We would like to welcome you to the "Billionaire Parent Community" (www.billionaireparenting.com) and we are thrilled to have you become a part of the family.

We will share our personal experiences and insight within the book to substantiate the proven research theories. Since there are varying perspectives and outlooks surrounding the information saga, before ingesting any information, you need to ask yourself this simple question: "Who do you listen to?" As

Tony Robbins says, "Successful people ask better questions, and as a result, they get better answers."

Knowledge is power; however, in this information age of overload, it is imperative for you as a consumer to become selective, you truly deserve the best for your families. Successful people listen to two types of people only: "someone that has been in your shoes because nothing beats real-life experiences" or "someone that you aspire to become in the future." This is why Oprah Winfrey, Dr. Wayne Dyer and Anthony Robbins have such credibility, they are walking the talk.

The book encompasses the best resources in the fields of education and healthcare and combines them into an innovative concept (The Whole-Listic Children's Hospatal) for the future generation. This is why the compilation of this book contains proven theories from experts within their fields. Our philosophies are to not reinvent the wheel but to unite the resources into a more powerful tool for healing and educating our children.

It truly takes a community to raise a child and as such we wanted to bring you a book that was carefully researched with proven success within the educational and health industries. Bill Gates used this same concept to bring you Microsoft and it has provided value for the computer information age. We hope that you will find this book to be as comparable for the information parenting age. In an age where parents and children are more stressed than ever, our hopes was to provide a resource guide that touched upon the decisions that parents faced on a daily basis and give them hope for the next generation.

Many of these concepts, products, and services were designed without the true inventor even realizing its' own maximum potential and how it plays an integral role in the development of the "Whole-Listic" child. As humanity, we are all interconnected. It is time to truly unite all the resources within a community that can help the next generation not only succeed but become the true Leaders that the World desperately needs. Governments and corporations are merely composed of people; we must prepare the next generation to fulfill their destined roles in society.

Jennifer will share her personal story that is highly unusual but all non-fiction, but one that provides a compelling reason for mothers to be attuned with their emotions and thoughts during pregnancy. As painful as the experience was to her, it provided an opportunity to truly appreciate all the scientific research done within the prenatal psychology and epigenetics fields. She is grateful to be able to finally have an opportunity to share her story with others where it would truly bring value instead of just empathy.

Jennifer's goal is that if she can help one mother avoid what she went through during her pregnancy, especially a first-time mother or someone that has experienced infertility challenges to become a mom, it will be worth the effort and sacrifices it took to write this book. Jennifer has a unique ability to recognize the innate "gifts" in others and wants to help others recognize it too. When Jennifer stared into the eyes of Doreen Virtue, Doreen at once knew that this soul had the opportunity to uplift humanity with her experience and this is why her story is being shared with the world.

Coupled with Dr. Stéphane's medical and research ability, this book provides a psychological, sociological and medical perspective for the consumer to consider when making choices for their kids. This book might be thought-provoking but it truly allows you to become empowered and accountable for the decisions you make for your children. As

Tony Robbins' states, "It's never too late to have a happy childhood."

Medical Advice

The information, ideas, and suggestions in this book are not intended as a substitute for professional medical advice. Before following any suggestions contained in this book, consult your physician. Neither the writers nor the publisher shall be liable or responsible for any loss or damage allegedly arising as a consequence of your use or application of any information or suggestions in this book.

Psychological Advice

The information, ideas, and suggestions in this book are not intended as a substitute for professional advice. Before following any suggestions contained in this book, consult your physician or mental health professional. Neither the writers nor the publisher shall be liable or responsible for any loss or damage allegedly arising as a consequence of your use or application of any information or suggestions in this book.

Diet/Exercise Regimens

You should not undertake any diet/exercise regimen recommended in this book before consulting your physician.

Neither the writers nor the publisher shall be responsible or liable for any loss or damage allegedly arising as a consequence of your use or application of any information or suggestions contained in this book.

Dedication

This book is dedicated to Anthony and Sage Robbins. Huge thanks to Tony for helping us find our voices and inspiring us to become true leaders.

A Soul that …
T ouches so many lives by
O pening his own heart and empowering others with this gift: You
N otice and appreciate but mostly inspire,
Y et another generation

A Soul that …
S ees beauty and hope in others and
A sks nothing in return; she
G enerously shares her love (Tony) with the world. Behind every OUTSTANDING man there MUST be an
E ven stronger (caring) woman

Thank you both for sharing your energy and time with the world! You are both an inspiration for the next generation! As the saying goes; when the student is ready, the teachers appear.

Jenn's Muses

Alexander Doan: thank you for enduring all the emotions during your prenatal months to share this lesson with the world and thank you for providing me with my dream job as "Mommy."

Benjamin Otto: your early departure from this world due to medications inspired me to dream a vision where medications would no longer take little souls prematurely. Your light was such an inspiration to all that came across your path and your legacy will continue on this Earth.

Dr. Stéphane's Muses

Near or far, you will always be the inspirations in my life and I hope that someday you will continue the legacy to inspire and help others. The time sacrificed was well worth it to give you all a more hopeful future. As Tony says, "It is not what we get. But who we become, what we contribute that gives meaning to our lives." You will be my Princesses and Prince:

Sébastian Lai-Provencher, Sophie Lai-Provencher, Sarah Lai-Provencher

A special gratitude to our Editors: K. Raichelle Smith, Heather Fellows and Robyn Moncure who spent countless hours bringing this story to life.

Contents

From Jenn's Heart to Yours ... In Gratitude

"Do not wait for leaders; do it alone, person to person."

–Mother Teresa–

I am grateful foremost to the role models in my life, without their footprints to follow it would be difficult for me to attempt such a big dream. Mother Teresa, Princess Diana and Anthony Robbins are true inspirations to my core; they epitomize the essence of humanity. One look into Anthony Robbins' eyes and he is able to absolve away your pain, I experienced it first-hand. That is the level of empathy that should be taught to our kids and grandkids.

During the darkest nights my soul, there were messengers that were sent to guide me back to the light. Some accompanied me for longer periods of time such as: Jonathan Foust, Penelope (my yoga teacher), Laura S., Aunt Yen, Shalini M., Kenneth S., June B., and Gary and Patricia O., of which I would not be here today to share my stories if you had not pulled me out of the trenches. While others were sent to inspire me for a brief encounter but left a lasting impression as a muse: Ellen Carroll, Ms. K, Karen B., and Alicson Knowland which I owe my deepest gratitude for gracing me with your presence.

To look into someone's eyes and truly know the essence of their soul, takes a true guru in their field. Dr. Doreen Virtue, thank you for seeing the truth and knowing the capabilities within me, your words of encouragement and your book about Assertiveness provided the foundation for this book. Donna Eden, when I looked into your eyes, I could tell there was a kindred spirit. I have often been told I tend to be naive, but I would rather believe that the deep-down goodness buried in a person is still alive, rather than to judge them by their superficial wounds. You and David are true inspirations to the Energy Medicine and Psychology fields. Who would have guessed that one seminar could make a difference in this world! Also, I would like to acknowledge the designer of Your Wish Is Your Command while sending him a huge thank you for sharing his knowledge with the world and being a true Advocator.

I have high standards for the medical profession, especially doctors because I had strived to become a healing agent for the world's pains so I unconsciously was seeking the best to model from. The doctors that are in my 2% exhibit characteristics that is beyond credentials. My OB/GYN is the Chief of Staff; however, he is so humble and modest that it brings true joy to my heart.

My son's pediatrician created orphanages overseas with the proceeds from his practice. Dr. Bart Rademaker specializes in making females feel beautiful, but his innate abilities to bring out their internal beauty, is what characterizes a doctor's true healing powers. He is another doctor that will transform the health care industry. Dr. Stéphane Provencher has an innate gift of healing because he truly has a humanitarian heart that can provide the best healing medicine. I would like to thank Dr. Stéphane for spending countless resources and time to help heal my family and for being the catalyst for my healing needs.

Special thanks go to my Business Partners, K. Raichelle Smith and Dr. Stéphane Provencher for believing in my Leadership abilities and encouraging me to tap into my talents to bring hope and healing for the world. I could not have asked for a better team, without both of you this dream would not be possible.

Finally, I would like to thank the immediate Doan and Luc families for all their support during the hours that I was away from my son delving into the research and writing of this book. My husband Kevin deserves a medal for his unquestioning support for me to chase after a dream. Lastly, I would like to thank all the experts in their field for the products and services that are presented in this book. Our goal was not to reinvent the wheel but to unite these resources so that they can better empower parents.

♡♡♡ From Dr. S' Heart to Yours ...
In Gratitude

First and foremost I would like to personally thank Anthony Robbins, Denise Makus and Dr. Bart Rademaker for making this, part one, of our dreams a reality. Thank you all for your encouragement, support and guidance throughout this project. Your strategies helped empower my commitment to life's endeavors and understand the importance of what this would mean for my children and children all around the world. Just wait for part two...Tony sets high standards to follow but if you want to be the best, you have to learn from the best.

Thank you to all of my chiropractic colleagues past and present, here in the United States and around the world, who are working to develop and spread the greatest healing art in the world. Special thanks to the following chiropractic physicians, who have shared their knowledge and enthusiasm with me:

Joseph F. Unger Jr. DC, FICS	Suzanne A. Seekins, DC, DICS
Mary Unger-Boyd, DC, DICS,CACCP	Dr. Jonathan Howat FICS
Stephen Williams DC, FICS, FRCC (paeds), FRCC (cranio), FBCA	Nelson DeCamp DC, FICS, DACAN
Skip Skibstead DC, FICS	Patrick Montgomery DC
Marc Hartsuyker	John Demartini DC
David Seaman DC	Curt Budding DC
John Crescione DC, DICS	Jeanne Ohm DC
Skip Skibsted DC, FICS	Gregory Plaugher, DC
Jeanne Ohm DC	Ted Koren DC
Alan W. Fuhr DC	Luc Roberge DC
Thomas Hyde DC	Steven D. Roffers DC
Gilles Brunelle DC	André Provencher DC. (my 1st role model)

Extra special thanks goes to Dr. Pamela Peeke, MD, MPH, FACP and Bruce Lipton PhD whom also provided support and wished us best of luck with the endeavors but due to the short-turn around they were not able to provide further feedback for this edition. Dr. Sherri Tenpenny DO, AOBNMM who was a mentor and a highly regarded colleague within the expertise of vaccinations provided much insight to enhance my knowledge in this arena.

I am also grateful to my staff at Gainesville Holistic Health Center in Gainesville, Virginia, including Cindy Jones, Kirsten Donica and all my former and present practitioners for their enduring support of my dreams for the Center and the hospital. Special gratitude goes to Dr. Greg Nash, Michelle Emerson, Rob Pritchard, Sky Wolf and Gina Phelps for complimenting the healing that clients receive.

This book would not be possible without the countless hours that were put in refining the content from an editorial perspective. Special gratitude also goes to the Kroboth family for their editorial support.

Very special thanks to my business partners K. Raichelle Smith and Jennifer Luc. They have provided inspiration, encouragement and motivation for this project. Behind every successful man, there is an even stronger team of women behind the scenes. This book would not have been possible without the support from my wife who endured countless hours of me working at the office to research and share knowledge to empower other families with prospects of health and to provide them with added value.

My hope is that someday my children will serve as role models for others and share their gifts with humanity as their father is attempting to do. It is with great love and appreciation that I extend the warmest thanks to all of my family, patients and friends for their whole-hearted support; without you, this book would not have been possible.

About Jennifer Luc

Jennifer Luc has a diverse background that has provided her with myriad exposure to the forms of physical, emotional and energetic healing realms. She double-majored in Psychology and Sociology in her undergraduate studies focusing on sub-specialties Organizational Developmental Psychology, Industrial Organizational Psychology, Developmental and Abnormal Psychology and the Sociology of Death and Dying. She knew her passion was to alleviate pain and suffering from people's lives and wanted to understand the intricacies of the human psyche and its interrelationships to things and processes.

She has extensive hands on experience volunteering in pathology, cardiology, physical therapy and pediatric departments in private practices and renowned Hospitals. Jennifer has also spent the last two years volunteering at the Gainesville Holistic Health Center to practice the Energy Medicine principles she acquired. Additionally she has a combination of 17 years of experience in the business-technical arena of both private and public organizations and worked for the Big 5 firm Accenture. She also operated a small graphic design business.

Jennifer broadened her educational perspectives and graduated Suma Cum Laude with an MBA and Magna Cum Laude with a Masters in Information Technology. Her passion is in International Business with a Marketing sub-specialty which allows her to use her innate gifts of innovation and creativity.

Jennifer is a Visionary Leader who combines psycho-business trends to guide her decision making process and leadership. She is the President of the Whole-Listic Children's Foundation and is working tirelessly on building the dream of the Whole-Listic Children's Hospatal to serve the next generation's needs for total wellness from a mind + body + energized spirit perspective.

Jennifer enjoyed mystery novels when she was younger, and read each entire Hardy Boys, Nancy Drew and Bobbsey Twins' series. Her favorite books were ones that taught her the skills of creativity; the Choose Your Own Adventures were ingenious to her. Therefore, Jenn invites you to read the Last Chapter in the book first to figure out all the clues from her persona. Jennie was the name she was called as a child and Jenn is her grown-up persona.

Jennie's Story

I am a child of the orients.
A light-skinned child of many Diasporas assimilated into this continent.
A product of the rice fields of Vietnam I have long forgotten.
An immigrant and the daughter and granddaughter of immigrants that survived and thrived;
I speak English with passion: it's the tongue of my consciousness,
Where words are used to inspire, uplift and heal
Highlighted ripples from my hair, slants in my eyes accent my figure:
The healing language of Qigong and acupuncture and the foods fish and rice are ingrained in me,

I am an Asian American, rooted in the history of my continent:
I speak from that body and express my distinction in the art of dance.
I am not Vietnamese. Vietnam is in me, but I cannot return.
I am not Chinese. China lives in me, but I have no home there.
I am not French. French is in my ancestry and resonates within my DNA.
I am new. History made me. My first language was *ching-lish* (Chinese and English.)
I was born at the crossroads and I am NOW whole.

Who Is Jenn?

On the surface, she appears to be a quiet leader, deeply introverted; however, you can be the ultimate judge after reading Chapter 16. Can you judge a book by its cover, or will you see her true identity? Like the majority of people, she has forgotten her own true identity and learned to assimilate behind a facade of cultural and social constraints. In Chapter 16's Identity Blueprint, you will find more of Jenn's gifts and talents to share with the world, once she learns to unleash her power within.

- She is a Pioneer with the traits of natural leadership, courage, strength and firmness.

- She is a Helper with the traits of cooperation, compassion, sensitivity and empathy.
- She is a Strategist with the traits of innovation, breadth of view, planning and versatility.
- She is a Transformer with the traits of imagination, gracefulness, peace maker, and harmony.
- She is a Specialist with the traits of analyzing, objectivity, knowledge and discipline.
- She is an Advocate with the traits of energetic, passion, devotion and optimization.
- She is an Organizer with the traits of coordination, facilitation, elegance and designing capabilities.

A lasting impression to ponder over:

"You must not lose faith in humanity. Humanity is like an ocean; if a few drops of the ocean are dirty, the ocean does not become dirty."

–Mahatma Gandhi–

As cruel and inhuman a treatment as Jennifer received during her pregnancy, she is choosing to share this story with the world in hopes that they do not view the Military or Special Ops with this impression. In truth, Military personnel are altruistic souls who put their lives and their family's lives second for the sake of humanity. How many people would send their brothers/sisters, sons/daughters or husbands/wives to help defend the love of humanity and its principles of freedom and justice. A Government or an Organization is merely comprised of people, it is not the individual entities that are problematic but the people leading their mission; this is why Tony Robbins emphasizes it is time to be a Leader and not a follower.

Once upon a time, a little girl came on Earth, and wondered why we couldn't have Peace on Earth. I have met so many beautiful souls that have tolerated many hurts and disappoints in life and when I look into their eyes and asked why we couldn't have peace on Earth, they tell me it is a mere illusion. I refuse to believe this as truth; because if the entire world dreamed the same dream, reality would shift. How wonderful would it be to award your children or your grandchildren the gift of peace: a legacy with a lasting impression? As Martin Luther King Jr. stated, "I have a dream" where all our children will learn to play together from childhood to adulthood in …

P eople
E verywhere
A lways
C aring about
E ach other

About Dr. Stéphane Provencher

Dr. Stéphane is the founder and owner of Gainesville Holistic Health Center (GHHC) in Gainesville, VA, where integrative holistic treatments are offered to rejuvenate energies of the mind, body and spirit.

Stéphane Provencher, DC, CC, CKTP was born in Québec, Canada and speaks English and French. He received his B.S. Degree in Medical Biology from the University of Québec. Dr. Stéphane went on to attend Logan College of Chiropractic, where he earned his Doctor of Chiropractic degree with honors. He possesses multiple advanced certifications and is currently pursuing a Doctoral in Energy Medicine.

While at Logan College, Dr. Provencher's numerous honors included the Dean's List, the Health Center Achievement Award, the Clinical Assistant Award and Who's Who among students in American Universities and Colleges. Dr. Stéphane was named Researcher of the Year 2009 by SORSI, America's Chiropractors of the Year 2009, 2011 and 2012 by the Consumer Research Council of America and Presidential Appreciation award by SORSI in 2010. He was awarded the Talk of the Town Award from Haymarket, VA in 2013 and 2014.

Dr. Stéphane is an avid researcher, having completed more than 11 senior research projects at Logan College, including research on SOT° Methods, which he currently utilizes in his practice. He has published one article in the scientific journals JVSR in 2009 and presented in multiple research conferences including the Society of Neuroscience, Neuroscience Brain Research Conference, in Chicago in 2009.

In collaboration with Dr. Joseph F. Unger, Jr., he developed information on ADHD/ADD and Autism for use by chiropractors and their patients to learn more about natural therapies. Dr. Stéphane is also the chairman of research for SORSI. He is the Co-founder and primary developer of the SORSI-EBRN (Evidence Based Research Network) and automatic online case reporting system to improve Chiropractic research.

Dr. Stéphane is a renowned instructor and speaker in pediatric chiropractic, chiropractic Craniopathy, energy medicine, and Whole Foods nutrition.

Dr. Stéphane is the Vice President of the Whole-Listic Children's Foundation and preaches and practices promoting healthier lifestyles on a daily basis. He incorporates various healing modalities to ensure the most effective and efficient means of achieving total healing (mind + body + spirit) for his clients. With the science and art of combining chiropractic, chiropractic Craniopathy, and energy medicine, coupled with the latest scientific diagnostic tools available, a treatment at GHHC is truly a unique experience with ever-lasting healing results.

A Roadmap for This Book

As parents and grandparents, we are often given so much advice and yet there are many differing viewpoints that lead to ambiguity. The goal of this book is not to usurp your authority as a parent or grandparent; on the contrary it is designed to empower you with resources that are available on a global scale so that you may choose to incorporate into your family's lifestyle. You are the best judge of what is needed for your kids and as such we are hoping that you will become empowered consumers for all of your future products/services.

We recognize the cliché phrase "to reinvent the wheel" as a reference for duplicating a method that has already previously been created or optimized by others. But what if you completely re-imaged the wheel and its very functionality by putting all the pieces together into a new lifestyle called the Billionaire Parenting revolution? The resources introduced in this book are merely pieces of the puzzle that may enhance your masterpiece called "Life."

Our International Business Arena has expanded globally and as such this is truly an era where everything and anything can be re-imagined. As such, it would be pretentious for us to claim that we are leading authorities within all the fields that this book attempts to cover. The credibility for these concepts has been found to be effective in its industry; however, the missing component was how it could be applied on a larger scale and complimented with other sources. What we are offering is a unique concept for bridging all these services/products together under one "book" and will be practically demonstrated under one "roof" at the Whole-Listic Children's Hospatal.

Innovation is not just about original creation; it is about optimizing the fullest potential in any product/service. Therefore, the book provides a brief overview of existing products/services; however, we encourage you to research and learn more about each of the resources because nothing beats hearing it from the originators themselves.

This book was designed to serve a humanitarian purpose, illustrating the potential that unity and collaboration can create. We purposely researched for resources on a global scale so that you can recognize the significance of how we can truly learn from every culture. For beneath the layers of flesh and bones we all have the same blood coursing through our veins and the same desires of wanting to be understood, appreciated and loved. The ultimate goal of any parent or grandparent is to provide the best for their children's well-being.

Foremost, we believe it is vital to unite all the resources that have been gifted to this world. Everyone has a unique talent and gift (s) to share with humanity and if we recognize the ability to put all the pieces together instead of trying to compete for resources, we would be able to assemble a world filled with **love**, **hope** and **peace** for our **children** and **grandchildren**. This is truly everyone's legacy.

We hope that you will approach the reading of this book with an open-mind frame. It is not designed to promote more controversy or distress, but rather a feeling of empowerment because knowing is truly half the formula of success. We will continue to provide guidance for the Billionaire Parenting family on our website and guide you along this special journey to bring out yours, your children's and your grandchildren's fullest potential. We want to thank you for investing your time and energy on the most important resources on this planet – your kids and grandkids!

"BeKind Whenever Possible. It is always possible."

–Dalai Lama–

1
Billionaire Parenting

What is Billionaire Parenting?

To be a billionaire is described as having an abundance of, being wealthy, elite, rare, and sometimes prestigious. The lifestyle of a billionaire is observed as extravagant and luxurious. The ability to live a life of abundance, wealth, and luxury is one that every parent, guardian, and care-taker wants to afford for their children or the essence of providing this comfort. Being a billionaire parent is having the knowledge necessary to assist your child in the ultimate development of their richest, fullest life.

Every child is born a billionaire. That is, they are born with 100 billion brain cells. It is the goal of every parent to raise their child the best they can. Part of the upbringing should include finding strategies that will fully develop all those brain cells. When done correctly their child will be able to meet their full physical, emotional, mental and soul's potential. Keep in mind that the brain is not fully developed until the child is in the late teenage years of their life. In the mid-twenties, the brain cells continue to grow or they wither away due to non-usage.

The structure of the human brain begins at conception. From that point on, it is constantly changing, usually in an expectable process. Infants have numerous neurons in their brains. Some of them are connected to others, and some are not. Repeated experiences and the lack of experiences will determine which of these neurons connect to others. The experiences (or lack of) will have good or insufficient lifelong ramifications.

Bonding with your baby occurs intra-uterine. This prenatal bonding develops a sense of trust, unconditional love, acceptance and safety. In return the baby feels safe and loved which builds their self-esteem and self-confidence from the moment of birth.

It has been said in some cultures that if you talk about ugly or unattractive people then your child will also be ugly or unattractive. If you eat too much pizza then your baby's birthmark will be in the shape of a slice of pizza. Here's a good one, don't look at a mouse when you're pregnant-if you do, your baby will be born with a hairy birthmark. Although these are no more realistic than cartoons that portray getting hit in the head producing stars, there are some that are true. It is not just some 'old wives' tale' that your baby feels what you feel, it is actually true.

There is no questioning how strong the connection is of the mother and child during pregnancy. They can sense each other's emotions. Therefore it makes a huge difference if the conception was wanted or not. The development of the baby begins with a feeling of love or a lack of unconditional love. It is important that the mother has a calm, stable, healthy pregnancy supported by friends and family to provide an emotional well-being for the baby.

Parents' lives are turned completely upside down when a baby enters their life. They have new challenges never thought of before. Since instruction manuals are not issued in the delivery room, new parents need to rely on the tips and tools of those that have been on the journey of parenthood and often this brings about varying parental advice that may lead to ambiguous feelings.

Wouldn't it be great, however, if there was an instruction manual to come with each child, one that was made specifically for that child? Let's think about it, on the front of each manual there is a picture of the final product, you know exactly what to expect when you successfully complete all given instructions. This also will allow you to see if you've missed something along the way so you can go back and redo it before you get to the end and all is still well, nothing's lost. Each step is set out for you, all plans numbered and lettered and validating your accomplishments as you go and ensuring you are on the right track.

Unfortunately parenting is not that easy, nor is it that cut and dry. The manuals that we often use are those that are from instinct, previous experience, advice from friends and family and authors. Oops, did we just cliché ourselves? Well we accept the challenge.

Billionaire parenting is not an exact science, yet it is an accumulation of results proven practices that have been implemented, tested, and pioneered over hundreds of years. There is no reason to reinvent the wheel and we have no intention to. We are improving the wheel by taking the best of the best (in natural and holistic areas) in each category (health, education, and spa) and combining them to give an instructional manual of sorts that will help you to individualize it for your children, each of them.

If a billion dollars was just deposited into your bank account, how much time and energy would you use to make sure you get the highest return on investments? This is what you have been given each time you have a child. As previously mentioned infants have the potential to access and utilize their billions of neurons.

These neurons could make them into genius. Are your actions diminishing their truest potential? Are you allowing society and culture to pre-label them, over medicating them because their imagination and beliefs are not conforming to so-called standards of conduct? Each child deserves the best in life. If you don't believe in your own child, who will?

The children of today are our leaders of the future, yet they are teachers from the moment they step foot on Earth. Children will take on their parents' positive qualities, but also their negative qualities. The patterns can continue to generations unless the pattern is altered. This is why it is important to make the best choices for how we raise our children up-front. Their genetics, family and friend relationships, experiences and schools all influence their development.

All children need time to explore, to experiment, learn from their mistakes, discover, dream and wonder. These are lifelong skills that cannot be measured. Our culture usually determines what we value the most. These values determine what we want for our children. If the parent isn't fully attuned to their child, they will not be able to fully meet the child's needs. The parents may also respond in an inappropriate way. Both situations will result in poor experiences for the child to role model after.

Children are like sponges absorbing everything around them. The largest amounts of absorption come from the parents, the home environments, and the people that they are in contact with most. Because of this, it is imperative that parents are aware of the example they set for their children. We must be very conscience of what we say to them. Not only what the caregivers say about their children but what they say about themselves needs to also be closely monitored. All of these experiences will influence how they view themselves as they grow up. When parents are synced, they will be able to make positive influences on their child. They will be healthier emotionally. Although it is impossible to be the perfect parent, reflection will make our children's lives better.

Children are always learning and need help managing their feelings and actions. The adults in their lives are learning as well. We are learning how to manage stress, and responsibility, the ever changing demands that need to be met along with the needs of a little person that is also depending on us, in addition to coping with the child's needs. This could actually turn into a 'Molotov cocktail' if not handled properly. As both the parent and child are learning it is easy to react instead of predict as some things just aren't very predictable. It is also very easy to lose your temper or your patience in this instance as both are agitated.

Parenting can be fairly easy when you and your child have the same desires. However, it can become more difficult when you want different things. Have you ever found yourself bribing or threatening your children to make things happen? Have you found yourself just giving in or just complying to experience some moments of peace? Do these encounters make you feel like a good caretaker? What separates billionaires from the average person is their refusal to give up.

Every child will experience fear, anger, and frustration. That is a fact of growing up. Although we don't always have the answers, children turn to parents for answers and advice. Even though we want the best for our children, we must assist them to realize their own potential. By 'assist' we don't mean to plan it out and determine it for them. Be the catalyst in their journey to find out who they are and what they desire. Naturally parents want to pre-determine all that their children will do, be, dream, and aspire without giving them the power to choose on their own without the emotional manipulation of the parent.

Children come to terms with their own uniqueness and talents. We must allow our children to flourish and not allow society and cultural standards to label them. There are some indicators that will show if a child is considered gifted, genius, remedial, have learning disabilities, or even personality complexes. All children are a unique gift and every child is different. Some children are misdiagnosed and are labeled with ADD, depression and autism. It is important for parents to take the time to truly research these labels and obtain second and third opinions on the diagnosis. It is time to rethink the labels of autism, depression and ADHD. Did you know that if you utilize the free services such as The Early Intervention Program; the records are automatically transferred to your child's school when they enroll in kindergarten and these children are pre-determined as possessing learning difficulties before they even enter the foundations of the school system?

Many parents may not seek help for their child until their problems have gotten out of hand instead of seeking prevention and early intervention. How much money would be saved if early intervention was sought? How much better off would the child be? The future of the world depends on fostering healthy development of our children.

Parents have fought and are fighting against their child being labeled, especially learning disability labels. However, nowadays, instead many are reverted to these labels to seek educational entitlements that may provide learning disabled children extra accommodations in class due to their designated labels. They even go the extent to get treatments that only insurance will reimburse so they comply with classification tactics.

Jenn's Insights

This book is a culmination of research from leading experts in their field; however, we believe that it would not do justice to simply present facts/theories without sharing real-life experiences and insight. There are numerous parenting books out there; however, there is none that truly touches upon the emotions from a child's perspective and the retrospection as an adult and what changes if any would be implemented for your own kids.

As such, throughout the book, after the facts/theories are described, Dr. Stéphane and I will be sharing some of our deepest thoughts about the discussed topics to provide more of a personalized viewpoint.

My thoughts will be organized from the viewpoint of what I felt as a child, in hopes that you can gain some insight into the minds of the nonverbal communications your child might not be able to express to you. Optimistically these sections will provide you with insight as to what a child is able to truly recall and learn from their first role models, their parents. Especially if you are a parent of an empath or a sensitive child, it will provide you with an example of their train of thought coming from the experience of someone that has walked those shoes. This will be categorized in the form of (Jennie's Insights.)

Then, as a mom, I want to share my story with you, so that you may gain a better understanding as a mother to what types of emotions and life lessons that you may be indirectly teaching your children. This section will hopefully provide some seeds of thoughts to ponder over. These insights will be categorized in the form of (Jenn's Insights.)

Many of these insights are so deeply internalized in me that I had to truly reflect to write this book. I am honored to be able to share these thoughts with you. In the last two years, I have lived my life in the mere existence of a shadow form. This is because my parents had taught me it is better to just blend in and slowly lose your identity along with your voice.

Having gone thru so many traumas and betrayals in my life, I adapted a lifestyle based on fear and guilt/shame of not being able to repay my parents for their sacrifices. I imposed upon myself a life imprisonment of silence and solitude from my friends and family because I did not know who I could trust and doubted my own abilities.

The topic of Epigenetics is a hot topic in the Parenting World with extensive research being applied; however, I believe that the best case study that can help one understand the importance of their emotions and how it is transferred intrauterine to a child would be my own life story.

I was a mom that underwent 5 surgeries just to be able to finally conceive, but I was robbed of the joys of my own pregnancy. I hid my pregnancy from the world for 8 months in fear of me and my unborn child being killed. I was subjected to psychological warfare from Special Ops, but the irony was that I was a Civilian. With their psychological profiling, I was told that my weakness was my "altruism" and as such, I decided to turn this into my strength and write this book for humanity.

They used every one, my colleagues, my friends, some family members, entrusted doctors and lawyers to carry out their inhumane acts towards a pregnant woman and her unborn child. I am forgiving and I am releasing all those that voluntarily or involuntarily participated in these inhumane acts. I just pray that your souls will someday seek out the truth because I learned the truth is the only thing that truly sets you free.

What Jason Bourne or Edward Snowden went thru pales in comparison to what my prenatal and post-natal emotions endured? However, after two years, I finally realized that I had to be the lucky candidate to experience this so that the world can finally wake up and realize what they are doing to their children and their grand-children if we continue to claim that this is not "my issue."

In performing the research for this book, I realized that as scary as it is to find my voice, it was needed for my son. Since children are absorbing and indirectly learning up to age 7, what lessons am I teaching my son by hiding the truth from the world? My son already knows the truth; unfortunately he lived all these memories with me intrauterine.

To this day, my son does not speak and his teachers believe that he needs speech therapy. As a mom, I know that he has not spoken because throughout his pregnancy, I asked him to stay quiet. I told him every night, that if you kick or make a sound, that mommy and you can both be killed. So how can I subject my son to more mistreatment and mis-diagnosis of so called learning abilities?

He has not spoken because he has not connected that it is safe for him to be seen in this world? Unfortunately, he listened to the message too intently that mommy had sent him in the womb. I knew after I had the conversation with the therapist that I needed to take responsibility and to find my own voice and show my son that it is safe now to tell the truth. I knew that my son was going to learn indirectly from me, so I am very grateful for Tony Robbins and others in helping me find the courage to find my voice again.

 Jennie's Insights

Once upon a time in a country far away, there lived a little girl that was born in a third world country amidst a civil War that was breaking out in her homeland. I was born in what was known as Ho Chi Minh City, better known as Saigon, Vietnam. The irony was that I never felt like I had a nation to call my own until I came to America. My ancestors came from China but when they immigrated to Vietnam, they were still seen as foreigners.

Many of the Chinese that came to Vietnam went there to do business and as such the locals were not too fond of their wealth prospects. Growing up in that land, the Vietnamese community never considered our family as being Vietnamese.

And the Chinese community didn't consider us to be "Chinese" enough since we were not born in the homeland nor spoke the mandarin dialect. We were to them not authentic enough. We spoke Cantonese, but since we were born in Vietnam instead of Hong Kong or Singapore we were considered a sub-class. It is sad to me how society has become so divided even amongst its own ethnicity there is discrimination. People feel compelled to compete when they can simply cooperate and achieve even more by seeing goodness in others instead of threats.

My parents lived in what was known as Cholon (China Town) and by the end of the war my father who had a tough childhood was finally in the ranks of the elite business world. Our home was surrounded by marble. My mom had a private doctor that graduated from America. I grew up with a nanny and tailored outfits that were all ready for me before I was even born. I felt like a Princess at-heart and felt that anything was possible for this world, even amongst the war-torn country.

The context of my up-bringing is shared so that you can gain a better understanding of what it felt like to lose everything as a child, your home, your identity, and your loved ones. Many of the immigrant parents that came to this country led influential lives but they came in hopes that freedom and education would be something that no other nation could provide their children.

My mother worked at the USA Embassy but retired early because she did not want to deal with the corruption that occurred there. While my mother was pregnant with me, I was a very weak fetus, so much in fact that my mom was told that if she did not stay in bed rest that I might be lost.

Instead of embracing the gift of fertility, my mom felt that it was more of a burden to have something imperfect in her. My mom told the doctor that if this fetus is not strong and perfect enough then maybe it would be better just to get rid of it. So from Day 1, intrauterine, I felt that I had tough shoes to fill, and that if I was not perfect enough that I would not be wanted or accepted in this world. It's ironic how I often am criticized for my perfectionism mentality.

My mom had unconsciously learned this lesson from my grandmother. Without ill intentions, she saw how my grandmother had 4 sets of twins that all died prematurely. So my mom was scared of having weak children. My grandmother was so distraught with her kids' deaths that she internalized all the emotions. She ended up having Alzheimer's at the end, which is a dis-ease with a deep-rooted seed of internalized depression.

My grandmother saw herself as being a failure, so much that she was afraid to touch or care for any of her children. Consequently, that was the lifestyle that my mother grew up with and the epigenetics she inherited. Out of 12 children, only 3 survived and my mother was the middle child, who had the least attention and consequently this was the parenting style she learned to adopt and practice when she became a mom. My hope is that other parents can truly understand the impact that their words and emotions can have on their children and grandchildren.

♡◯◯ Dr. S' Insights

I can still recall the stories that my father told about how he had helped children and adults with their health issues. My little eyes were so mesmerized and I began to dream of the day that I would be helping others.

My father was a Chiropractor and when I first heard these stories I knew that I wanted to follow in his foot-steps some day and make as much of a difference in the world. He was an early role model that helped shape my future. It was destiny for me to be a Chiropractor, my mind was made up at an early age; I had found my idea of a hero.

I still can recall that my parents never vaccinated me and when we were sick, my dad would adjust me. He often used chiropractic adjustments to help restore my nervous system so that it could innately use its healing powers. As a child we did not use a lot of medications, only an occasional Tylenol or Advil so I did not deem that my body was toxic.

However, what were not properly addressed were my eating habits. I can still recall my eating lifestyle; it consisted of canned soups with Kraft microwave dinners and washing it all down with 2 liter Pepsi bottles. Looking back it was ironic because as a Chiropractor I knew my father was not sending these same nutritional messages to his clients.

Due to my eating habits, I was rushed to the hospital at age 13. It started with a racing sensation of the heart and soon I lost total consciousness and blacked out. I was covered in monitors and both the Medical Doctors and the Specialists could not explain the source of the problem. I even had to spend the night at the Hospital and of course it gave my parents a scare.

Unfortunately, this was not a single incidence, multiple times during high school, college and at university and even during my time in Chiropractic College it occurred again some at even more intense levels. Between these episodes I frequently had emergency visits to the hospital but no technology or medical personnel could explain the real issue to me.

I can still remember speaking to my mother on the phone when I was at school in Québec Canada, during my Bachelors education. I started having an attack during the conversation but fortunately I was able to control it after 20 minutes. Imagine as a mother how scared you would be for your child that was 1.5 hours away from your care.

She felt utterly helpless and I knew she was my biggest supporter. She was the perfect role model for unconditional love. I can still recall every time I was in a car accident, she was more concerned about my well-being and never yelled. Her response was that a car could be repaired, but as long as I was safe, everything else was a learning experience and not as important to fret over.

You are often told that in life you gain experiences for a purpose and that we are all here for a reason, mine was to live thru those experiences and to be able to share with others the importance of what eating unhealthy foods (junk foods) and sugar could do to your body. Even though our family was in the health care industry, my parents were not practicing what they were preaching.

We consumed junk food, microwave food, canned food and drank tons of soda and often ate tons of sugar that was loaded in the candies and cereals. Even though I did not get vaccinated, I had enough toxins alone from the food elements. When I was going thru my chiropractic studies and spent extra hours including the nutrition curriculum (appreciatively 1400 hours,) I finally came to the epiphany of why these toxins had contributed to my heart issues and how stress was the trigger that often exacerbated the condition.

The source of my tachycardia (extreme heart racing) was due to an extreme acidity in my body. Apparently all the sugar intakes over the years created a stress to the heart. The so-called symptoms of the heart racing occurred when the body was trying to abruptly take off the sugar overload out of my body.

This makes me wonder how many other heart-racing or heart attacks are being caused in this nation and around the world because parents did not have this knowledge about sugar and its side effects. This is why I am so upset when sugar is fed to my own kids, I just do not want them or any other kids to have to go thru what I did.

This is the primary reason why I have dedicated so many hours into research and the writing of this book and it was done after-hours so much of the time was sacrificed away from my children. But I knew *they would understand the importance and hopefully be able to share this knowledge with their own kids. Can you imagine how many parents would avoid feeding sugar to their children if they knew it could cause a heart racing, leading to black out or even heart attack?*

As you read this book and the breadth of information provided, I would like you to contact us if you have further questions but I believe that you will find many helpful tips to guide you on your journey as a parent. Since I was blessed with being able to fix my own health issue, I wanted to relay this knowledge and share everything that I have learned with other parents. I have always been a believer that a doctor should be a teacher and truly help empower everyone with better information to make more informed lifestyle choices.

My experience fueled the motivation for me to write this book and put all the information into a resource guide for parents. I knew that by the time the parents took their children to see me, 95% of the symptoms could have been prevented if they knew how stress and toxins impacted the body. I knew that parents lead a busy lifestyle and often do not have the time to research all this information and as such I knew that this would be a vital resource for any parent or grandparent.

As Wayne Dyer, one of my role models states: Everybody is born and then dies; however, at our death we cannot bring with us the material collections so our true purpose in life is to give on Earth, whether it is in the form of a lesson or in the role of a doctor educating the public. This is my hopes for my contributions in this book. This book is a gift to the world in hopes that they are provided with more information than my parents had.

I was blessed with a wonderful and supportive family and as such my parents gave me the best experience and challenges along my life journey so that I would be better equipped to handle life's stressors with a healthier outlook. This is what I am forever grateful to my parents for.

My hope is that my kids will follow in my footsteps and learn to be a contributing force for society. This would give me the greatest joy as a father and a doctor to know that this book will be able to make a difference in any child's life.

Generation Hope – A Vibration of Love

Many people are beginning to question the diagnoses of their children. Are they really troubled or could they be gifted, but don't act according to the norm? These children with incredible gifts are being administered dangerous and addictive drugs such as "Ritalin and Adderall". "Ritalin" has been proven to cause irreparable damage to the brain.

On top of the potential of damage to the brain, children are taking ADHD/ADD medications with energy drinks. Are we showing our children unconditional love when we allow this to happen? Or are we letting society dictate how to raise our children?

If you are old enough, think back to the 60's. Teens in that generation seemed to be more gifted and confident. They were spiritually connected and knew what they wanted. They had a high sense of social consciousness and had good communication skills. Their right brain and left brains were connected and many experiences and learning occurred outside of the classrooms. This generation of children is launching a new revolution to bring love and peace to this world.

In the past two decades, science has opened the door to the mind of the infant. This has given parents proof that their child can have genius-like learning abilities early on in life. Research has given us much insight on the development of the brain from conception to the first three months of life.

Children of today absorb information at an incredible rate. These children are designed to continually gather information and make connections. Too often, this has been misdiagnosed with ADHD or ADD. Children are a multi-sensual being. They take in information through all five senses. They can sense light, sound, electrical currents and electromagnetic fields. They are keen to the emotions and the climate of the room. They have a great ability of assessing people and their thoughts, feelings and intentions instantaneously and with precision.

Today's children want balance and clarity. They are extra sensitive to their environment. This includes garments, furniture, house-hold materials, temperatures, food, etc. They thrive for pure food and water and organic materials. This is why we are seeing a many food allergies and sensitivities arising amongst this generation.

Children thrive in an environment of unconditional love and acceptance, in an environment free from stressors. The portrait of this child can be your child or your grand-child, dependent on your parenting style; we would recommend the Billionaire Parenting lifestyle.

As already mentioned, children absorb information like a sponge. When they are in an environment that encourages the passions of the child, these skills with be easily learned. Even when we feel it is difficult to learn particular information, a child can easily master it given the proper environment.

This is how exceptional children are. This is why it is crucial to aid our children to reach their fullest potential. Are they worth the investment of your time and energy? Do you want to make a difference in their world? How important is it to you to connect the billions of neurons in your child's mind? Do you believe they can be a billionaire in the future?

2

Prenatal Care for the Father and Mother

The Psychology of the Father

During the initial stages of pregnancy there can be a rush of fear and anticipation about the parenting approach the couple will take at the birth of their child. New parenting can elicit a state of vulnerability and poses many questions as the couple enters uncharted waters and realizes their lack of experience.

This vulnerability and these questions can trigger psychological changes to both the parents. Each future parent incorporates their emotions and childhood experiences into the ways they influence their future child's stages of life, and how they will play their roles within the pregnancy, the birth and the raising of their new child and how their lives will be impacted by this new family dynamics.

The father can be susceptible to emotional stressors during the pregnancy, and traditionally a reflection made by the father-to-be on how his father impacted his life. For instance, if his father was a positive figure within his life he will have a positive outlook on the pregnancy.

There is strong science that shows one out of ten men will have a psychogenic response to pregnancy. Essentially, this means he will gain or exhibit physical symptoms in relation to his partner's experience and attribute it to his own physical, psychological and chemical changes in the various stages of pregnancy. There is a sense of responsibility and an associated shift in life focus, exploiting the connection this father-to-be had by the way of his own father.

Data collected in a recent study conducted by Pampers Diapers uncovered a subset of males exhibiting symptoms associated with those experienced by their pregnant partner. There is such a strong tie to their partner and their "pregnancy pains" that twenty-three percent of men showed signs and symptoms essentially matching those of their pregnant partner. These symptoms include both physical pains sometimes called phantom pregnancy pains, both emotional and hormonal manifestations such as nausea, vomiting, mood swings, even random food cravings.

Traditionally, pregnancy was focused on the women and men did not actively participate in the pregnancy process. Modern-day men go to medical appointments, sonograms and child-birth education classes more regularly. By doing so the father has the opportunity to experience a bond with the baby earlier in the pregnancy. This increases the father's emotional and physical responses throughout the trimesters of the pregnancy and his child's life.

An expectant father shares the range of emotions that he experienced upon the news a baby was on the way.

During Pregnancy:
- Joy (We're pregnant!)
- Fear (What have I done?)
- Elation (I'm going to be a dad!)
- Disbelief (Holy smokes, I'm going to be a dad!?)
- Eerie calm
- Fear, of the unknown (How much will my life change once baby is here?)
- Fear, of the known (Oh, that much.)
- Happiness
- Anticipation
- Impatience (Why is the baby ignoring his/her due date?)

At Birth:
- Elation (I'm a dad!)
- Anxiety (Holy nut, I'm a dad!?)
- Pure, soaring joy
- Fatigue
- Pride (I helped create this child)
- Disorientation (Why does this child constantly cry?)
- Irritation
- Sexual frustration ("No intercourse for six weeks," the obstetrician said at the end of our hospital stay with a straight face, as if I wasn't standing right there.)
- Drop-dead fatigue
- Bafflement
- Happiness unlike any other: Love

Jenn's Insights

Males in our society are taught at a young age that being strong is to suppress emotions which cause many men to repress their feelings. It should come as no surprise when they grow up that the possibility exists that they'll have communication problems because we created this sociological issue ourselves and then wonder why. In fact, since women have a higher tolerance to physical pain, men tend to be more sensitive in general.

If you do not believe your children are here to help better this world, ask yourself this question: Are you happy with what the world has become? If you are not, do you find yourself willing to find the strength and energy to do anything about it? In truth, our world has become so accustomed to this hopeless feeling, we do not believe that we can make a difference. Most parents are willing to do anything for their children. This is why your children are here, to remind you how important it is to take care of the environment, as much as it is important to focus on what nutrients to put in your bodies.

I had a friend in junior high who told his story in one of our classes and I can still vividly recall all the details. He was born in the northern part of Vietnam and saw both of his parents and his three brothers all killed in front of his eyes. He was the only one who survived and even has the scar to prove it, a bullet scraped his ear, but he survived and his life lesson came with a hefty price. Perhaps the next time adults decide a nation should go into war they should look into the eyes of the children who will be impacted.

When you first learned to drive a car you paid careful attention to details and were fully present, right? Now when you drive, are you on autopilot, focusing on a hundred other things that seem to be preoccupying your mind while driving? Does that constitute you having ADHD/ADD?

If you truly believe that children cannot sense non-verbal communication, you have not been attentively watching for the clues. My son, even at the age of 2, is able to sense when someone is not treating me with respect or belittling me. On cue, he will throw a tantrum and start rebelling.

Our children are here to teach us lessons that we have forgotten ourselves one of respecting and being compassionate to others.

I have been programmed to be polite and not speak my mind and my son constantly reminds me how frustrated he is because what is happening to me is unacceptable. He is indirectly teaching me assertiveness. Next time your child throws a tantrum, assess what was being said around him or her and you may discover it has to do with someone who is behaving in an inappropriate manner or using negative language.

My parents are the type of people who view a cup as half full and have become very pessimistic over the years due to unresolved pain in their lives. In writing this book, I was fascinated listening to Amy Chua's interview of her book Battle Hymn of the Tiger Mom. I laughed because we experienced very similar childhoods, but my personality is more like her youngest daughter, Lulu. Amy constantly asks why her daughter does not seem to respect her, and my philosophy will most likely answer that question.

I was one of the youngest leaders in my organization but had the most respect because I believed that to gain respect, you must first give it, it's a two way street. Amy's daughter Lulu reminds her mom it is not okay for grandfather to tell her she is "trash." Her daughter is teaching her to respect herself and not allow others to talk badly about her. Self-respect is the foundation for sharing it with others.

Instead of wondering why there is so much violence and bullying in schools, we should evaluate the offending child and children's home environment and ask how the parents were treated as children. Research shows from intrauterine to age 7 your child is learning from you. The new generation of children is very astute and they can size up people's intentions very quickly. Practice what you preach to your children because if you don't, they will catch your bluff.

 Jennie's Insights

I was born in a nation filled with anger and division and I could sense the pain and the suffering of the people. My parents say I was extremely colicky and would not settle down unless I was comforted. It was very challenging to my mother because she adopted my grandmother's style of parenting and was very hands-off. She didn't know I was there to teach her a mother's role was to nurture but most importantly to be compassionate to her.

My grandfather was the one who always comforted me. As a child, I could tell when a person was open-hearted and full of light. My grandfather came to see me every day and he was my favorite person in the whole world. He made me feel safe and I knew he loved me unconditionally. When I looked into his eyes, I knew I was perfect and was a welcomed addition to the family.

When I looked into my parents eyes I knew that they were disappointed that their only child was a girl and not a boy. Baby girls are often devalued in Asian cultures and my relatives would often rub it in their faces with phrases like, "if only you had a boy." My mother used to tease me by saying she found me in a trash can and took me in. She thought it to be a harmless joke, but it was very hurtful and I interpreted it as not being good enough. I was determined to be as strong as possible and exhibit as many of the male qualities as possible so that she would not be disappointed.

My mom now wonders why I do not enjoy house chores, sewing or cooking. She often criticizes me for not doing enough in the home, but she forgets she inadvertently taught me performing chiefly female duties is meaningless and devalued. From a sociological perspective, many of the Asian cultures are indirectly imprinting this lesson to their children yet the world wonders why women are exhibiting less feminine energy.

My mom never really spent time playing with me because she was too busy trying to create the perfect household. I recall one of my older male cousins would come after school every day and always played with me, he was even the first one to discover I could walk. He was like the big brother I never had.

Suddenly he never came around and I always wondered what I had done to upset him. Not knowing the truth until much later, I felt he had abandoned me and that was my first emotions with that feeling.

What my parents forgot to tell me was that he was imprisoned. The leaders of the Northern Vietnamese Government attended a rally for peace then disguised themselves to encourage students to share their opinions. These are the same policies reenacted in the Tiananmen Square episodes. History will continue to repeat itself if humanity does not learn to change its course. The following day, law enforcement came to his house and he was deported to a reform prison. Even when we left the country, he was not allowed to be released.

When his father passed away from a broken heart, he was not allowed to attend his funeral. I did not see my cousin again until 2000. His positive outlook towards life changed due to his experience in the reformatory "school." It was sad to see another human being's hope drained away.

My parents thought I was too young to understand and did not tell me when we left the country that I would not see my grandfather for almost a decade. My core support system was yanked from me and when we came to the US, we did not have much money. For the next ten years, I lost all communications with my grandfather; I was not allowed to even hear his voice. I was too young to write to him, so I felt like I was being punished for no reason. The two people who genuinely loved me were removed from my life without any explanations. As an empath, I associated it with not getting too close with anyone because they tend to disappear once you show them love.

We escaped as refugees, but in truth we paid a hefty price to leave, approximately 12 gold bars were paid for each of us to get onto a small fishing boat with over two hundred fifty other children and adults where we were literally piled on top of each other. Numerous times my parents were scammed and they paid the price but there was no ship to take us away. My parents left everything behind, we literally left with the shirts on our backs and any jewelry we could wear.

During our voyage out, I saw the fear in everyone's eyes and I began crying hysterically which led to all the children on the boat to do the same thing. Instead of being comforted, I recalled some Vietnamese ladies snatching me from my mother's arms and threatening to throw me over board into the shark-infested ocean. How cruel and inhumane an action coming from so-called mothers, these figures was supposed to symbolize nurturing and loving qualities. Yet, this is the first time I experienced the feelings of disappointment and fear simultaneously.

My parents were so distraught they had to fight with these women then quickly stuffed many sleeping pills in my mouth to sedate me. At an early age, I learned if I opened my mouth to speak my truth which at the time were cries of fear, I could literally get myself killed or my parents hurt. So another lesson I learned was to be quiet and just blend in. It was my first association with guilt and shame, but one that left a lasting impression for decades to come.

If you believe that your children are not uploading all their surroundings, you are mistaken. Look at how many details I was able to recall from my childhood and many of these memories were buried in the subconscious level because of my coping mechanisms. But it was not truly forgotten, in writing these pages, tears are still streaming from my eyes thinking about all the emotions I experienced at such a young age.

It's not what you say but what you do that will provide your children with their lessons and role model. If you are constantly communicating by screaming, your children will interpret that as being a normal form of communications. If you are constantly abusive, you child will learn that as being acceptable for interacting with others. If you portray the silent treatment, you children will learn that as a coping mechanism and turn inwards, repressing their emotions further.

♡☮ Dr. S' Insights

It is unimaginable to see how you and your partner created such miraculous beauty. In my eyes every child is beautiful and is perfect in their own unique forms. When I stare at my own children, the beauty and love that emulates from them is overwhelming. It is truly difficult to put yourself in the mother's shoes during pregnancy and experience that wonder and joy of being able to know you are responsible for nurturing and caring for a life for 9 months. It truly takes courage but most importantly patience and love.

The stress levels have increased tremendously in our society. Our reality and our responsibilities have shifted. Nowadays there are so many two-income families that are required to sustain a living and the nurturing roles have been reversed in families and delegated often to day care providers or teachers. The stress levels are phenomenon in this nation and we have more dis-ease of the mind and body then we have had over the last century.

Technology is supposed to alleviate stress and make our lives simpler, however, we have made it so automated that we often forget roots of what it means to communicate and bond with another human being. Many of our elders are institutionalized and medicated and their wisdom cannot be transferred to the next generation. This is why we have scientists like Gregg Braden searching all over the world to restore the knowledge that has been lost.

It is more difficult to be a father when your role models had baggage from their own childhood. My father's parents were killed in a car accident when he was only 15 years old; he and his brother were the only survivors. It is hard to imagine how devastating it was for him to know a family vacation could become the worst nightmare of his life.

That emotional trauma stayed with my father and those emotions were epigenetically imprinted to me and my own children. This is why, when therapists' access fear and anxiety, the roots are beyond the superficial emotions that are presently in a child's life.

Today, I am blessed with three wonderful children and each day I am grateful for the lessons they teach me and the memories we are creating together. Our children are truly here to uplift society, if you look deeply in their eyes, there is no sadness, no grief, no pain; unfortunately it is the world that tries to instill these lessons in them.

As parents, we often fear that we are not performing the best in our roles, but in truth, if we guide by example and truly open our hearts to possibilities, we will be teaching our children the best lessons of all. As research has stated, between the birth and age 7, children upload information with all their senses, from both the right and left hand hemispheres of their brain. It's not simply what you tell them but what they indirectly observe and learn from your actions.

For instance, if you preach not to steal but you go into a store and put items into the strollers without paying for them, what lesson do you think your children are learning about integrity and honesty? If you preach about being kind and having manners, but you often blow a fuse and use profanity, what language do you think they will develop when they are older?

As I recall, it took me numerous attempts to learn to ride a bike and it took me many heartaches to find what love was about, but the moral is, to not give up. These are the indirect lessons in life that I want to teach my children about perseverance, about determination, about confidence. I truly believe these life lessons are invaluable.

It is truly difficult to step into the role of fatherhood with the title of Father without an instruction manual or role models who taught you positive experiences. But each day I challenge myself to be a better man in hopes that I am setting an example for my children that they learn to live their life without societal or cultural constraints keeping them from their fullest potential.

To me, fatherhood is not about what toys I can bring home to my children or to simply watch television with them because fatherhood is a true badge of honor. In your children's eyes, you are truly a hero and they love you unconditionally. Many parents believe they are supposed to give unconditional love to their children, when in fact our children are here to teach us unconditional love. They are practicing what we are preaching.

You could be intoxicated and one of the most abusive parents in the world, but I guarantee you your kids will want the best for you and be there to support you. However, it would sadden them because they know mommy or daddy truly deserves the best in life. This is what Anthony Robbins saw in his own mother. He knew she was hurt and angry about his father leaving, but he also knew that she was given a choice in life and that being a victim was not necessarily the best choice for her well-being.

Your kids are a reflection of you, they know if you have given up on your own potential and as such, they are here to remind you of the self-love and respect we all deserve. This is especially true of autistic kids, many do not speak but their parents are taught to understand and to communicate with them in the universal language of love. They refuse to succumb to the world of negativity and as such remain in a world filled with love and hope.

To me fatherhood represents being the constant of love for my family and providing them with security and entrusting that they can tell me anything and I will be there unconditionally to guide and honor their individuality. As a father, I value being a "doer" and being able to provide solutions or perspectives, though not necessarily resources for their well-being. This is why I spent countless hours in the office and many times miss out on all the little "Kodak moments" that my kids have each day because to me instilling work ethics and diligence are life lessons that I want to give to them.

I believe these are essential life lessons that will help them succeed with their dreams; and if one of my children follows in my footsteps into the medical profession, I hope he or she will be one of the doctors who truly cares instead of just heals. This is why I dedicate so much time and care to my patients; I want them to receive the type of care that I would want for my own children.

Some of the most memorable moments of my life were when I saw my son taking his first breath of life and delivering my own daughter in our shower. I recalled trying to ease my wife's mind by telling her that she was not delivering yet and I am grateful I could give her the experience of what birthing is truly about. It is not about fear but an unforgettable experience of how life can bring such wonders. Finally, when my second daughter's eyes met with mine and she produced her first smile, it was priceless. She knew I was her papa even though I had not been around much during that pregnancy because my wife stayed with her parents.

As the old saying goes, money cannot truly buy you happiness. Even billionaire Mark Cuban understands parenting should not be a job that is delegated. It is not the toys, but the moments that you spend with your child, being fully present to create and cherish memories together that will make a difference in the world.

Simply watching them while they play or providing them with a technological 'babysitter' such as a tablet or television will not form lasting memories of what fatherhood is about because you need to play with them and truly be in their shoes. It will be therapeutic for you and your child, your son or daughter needs that physical bond and the role model who shows what strength and courage is truly about.

Each moment I spend with my children I give them one hundred percent of my heart and soul and they have my undivided attention. This is why when I have distractions such as work and external stressors, I oftentimes ensure that I am at peak state before I put myself in their presence. They deserve the best me, not the stressed me.

For all those fathers who are reading this book please do yourself a favor, when your child is present, be fully present. When your child is in need, take the time from your busy schedule to be there. You are the first hero in their lives and the memories you provide will make all the difference in the world. The life lessons of security and trust is what they need from you.

Fatherhood is about being the glue for your child and ensuring they learn trust, integrity, compassion, honesty and courage from you. You will be their role model for when they have their own children, it's *a big job and the rewards are better than any title or power that you can achieve in your lifetime. So you should consider "DADDY" your most important job title.*

I know I have not been a perfect role model, but each day I strive to practice what I preach and I hope someday my children will corroborate that I have passed their expectations. I hope they will use the criterion that truly defines a father, one of being one hundred percent loving and open and honest with them and one hundred percent present with them. I encourage each father to be the "Example" and be the Force of Living for your children.

My father lost his father at a young age and he left my family when I was seventeen, so there was not much of a male role model for me to learn from. However, I was grateful for the time that I did get to spend with my father because he taught me an invaluable lesson, being a father is not just about being there physically, but emotionally as well. It is important for every boy to have a male role model to respect and learn from, but with loving reflection. This role model should be able to see his full potential and help guide and encourage him along the way.

Family dynamics have undergone so many changes and as such there are often many new families who could use support for this role. There is a new organization called the Fathering of the Mankind Project (http://mankindproject.org/father-new-age) whose mission is to help produce the proper role models for the next generation to follow.

It takes a community to raise a child and our children are collectively suffering from a lack of healthy fathering. As Dr. Wade Horn, of the National Fathering Initiative so eloquently put it, "Fathers should no longer be portrayed as merely economic providers only but they should be seen as nurturers, disciplinarians, role models, mentors, moral instructors and skilled coaches."

Mother's Psychological Changes in the First Trimester

There are vast numbers of changes with the onset of pregnancy. In the primary stages these are mainly hormonal and internal and aren't necessarily recognizable to those on the outside. If this is a first pregnancy these changes may be perplexing.

Everyday occurrences, activities or interactions that traditionally were commonplace and didn't evoke any emotion now may cause just the opposite. These everyday interactions may induce feelings of fear, sadness, anger, etc.... and cause physical manifestations such as crying or shivering. This is person dependent and your predisposition and ability to cope depend on the emotional experience and strength of the individual. Recognize though this is normal and all mothers during their first weeks of pregnancy traditionally experience these reactions.

The first trimester brings with it a twenty percent chance of miscarriage. With this circumstance readily discussed by your physician and published in the material you have been reading may prepare yourself for the pregnancy and evocation of fear that may accompany it. This fear for the loss of your fetus and cessation of pregnancy may also intensify if you or someone you know has experienced a miscarriage.

So this potential may become more unnerving if you have had trouble becoming pregnant in the past or are actively undergoing fertility treatment to help facilitate pregnancy.

Predisposition to life stress should strongly be taken into consideration. With external stress comes an internal chemical change to the body, cortisol and adrenaline releases during stressful events as well as continued stressful states can sustain inhibition to adrenal function. If the body is not homeostatic under stress and this could complicate pregnancy from both a hormonal and physical perspective. Susan Andrews, PhD, clinical neuropsychologist and author of the book "Stress Solutions for Pregnant Moms: How Breaking Free from Stress Can Boost Your Baby's Potential" reminds mothers that constant stress alters the body's stress management system, thus triggering an inflammatory response and causes it to overreact. Inflammation can cause problems both acutely and down the road developmentally for the baby. It can cause low birth weight or premature birth as well as predispose the baby to dis-ease processes like asthma and various allergies.

A Danish study conducted in 2008, conducted with 19,000 mothers-to-be proved that a high level of chronic psychological stress had an 80 percent greater risk for producing stillbirths. War knowingly evokes a lot of stresses, both physical and emotional on all parties involved. There is an increased likelihood of a baby having schizophrenia if they were birthed by a mother under the stress of being in a war zone.

Research from Israel found women in high stress war zones during their first trimester delivered babies that were anemic. This is of great concern because iron is a critical element to both neuronal and structural brain development in a child. In similar research, the children of mothers who were under high stress in their first trimester not only had low iron levels, but exhibited the signs and traits of irritability, anxiety and ultimately depression.

According to Janet DiPietro, a developmental psychologist at Johns Hopkins University, "Women's psychological functioning during pregnancy, their anxiety level, stress, personality ultimately affects the temperament of their babies. It has to; the baby is awash in all the chemicals produced by the mom."

Jenn's Insights

I always knew I was destined to be a mother and I would not give up that dream no matter how challenging. As a mother, you will come across many practitioners in your child's lifetime, I highly urge you to do your homework and look for the best practitioner for your prenatal and post-natal care as well as the best practitioner for your child's well-being.

The best is not necessarily defined using credentials or published success rates because these statistics can be misleading. Follow your instincts and look into the practitioner's eyes while asking this question: "What potential does this person see in me or my child?" This same rule should also relate when looking for educators for your child. The Latin root of the word doctor means to teach.

Prior to me finally being able to say I was pregnant. I went to a doctor who appeared to have all the right credentials. In fact, this doctor was an expert in the field and had even published a book. The doctor gloated about the success rate statistics. I had explained my health condition during the initial consultation, and I was reassured that there was plenty of hope for me.

In fact, as I looked around the office, there were psychological props, posters about hope and other inspirational messages. I was put through an extensive battery of tests and after everything was charged to my insurance, this doctor looked me in the face and told me, "In my expert opinion, there is nothing that I can do for you. You will never be able to sustain a pregnancy." Apparently that assessment was inaccurate, which is why a medical or healing practitioner must have your best interests at heart.

I realized this doctor had such high success rates because their statistics were skewed. Every client was carefully accepted based on the potential of being a guaranteed success so it could be included as another statistic. The doctor told me the only way I would be a mom would be to adopt and hastily moved me out of the office. This is the same doctor who had reassured me that no case was too challenging.

The information was disclosed up front there were massive amounts of medical records presented during our initial consultation. I felt so betrayed because I trusted my care to this doctor and had put my full faith in the prescribed regimens. My biological clock was ticking and I had wasted so much time. With tears streaming down my face and any hope of being a mother removed by this doctor, I felt so defeated and abandoned, but it challenged me to continue searching for the right answers and the right practitioner.

When you are selecting a practitioner, I urge you to look for someone that is truly going to listen and be your biggest supporter/coach. Unfortunately, many people are in occupations these days for the wrong reasons. The moral of this story is that the doctor was wrong and often times we believe and entrust so much care in their opinions. From that day forward, I vowed I would spend my life looking for the best resources and put them under one roof so no mother would ever have to go through what I experienced.

Going through fertility challenges, it is the psychological pain not the physical pain that is so detrimental. As a woman, you feel like a failure because the one birth right granted to you seems to not be functioning properly. What many doctors forget is that a client's will-power is the essential ingredient for healing and they can lose hope when faced with too many disappointments. This is why it is imperative to look for the right practitioners for you and your child's well-being.

We came across a client who had faced many disappointments in life she was an extreme empath. She desperately was seeking help but unfortunately ended up at the wrong practitioners. She tried the conventional route and the energy route and ended up believing that she was a mental case because of the misdiagnosis of these practitioners. Based on their recommendations, she almost committed herself to a mental hospital.

As a parent, trust your own instincts and if a practitioner is going to give up on you or your child, then find the right one! If a practitioner has not given you tools to bring out the best of your child or you, ask yourself if they have provided you with any true value from their service to help you move forward in a positive perspective. If not, it is time to fire them, and recruit someone that is in your best interest.

I once had a pediatrician rattle off the extensive amount of research and experience they had but I told the doctor, this is all reassuring, but as a mom I know my child had adverse reactions to the vaccine and is now staring in a coma state for 3 days. The doctor's response was, "This is a normal symptom." It is time for parents to oversee their child's well-being, and validate the information you are receiving as a consumer.

When I finally found the right doctor, it made a world of difference. Looking back, I still recalled how my doctor teased me for not believing I would be a mom. In truth, this doctor had hope enough for both of us because I felt so defeated from my previous experiences. There were so many emotions going on inside of me during the first trimester. I was so elated to be pregnant, but too scared to hope for the best.

Prior to this pregnancy, I had been in the same situation but at ten weeks, the baby's heart stopped and the medical professional was never able to provide an explanation. When they rolled me in for a Dilation and Curettage (D and C) to remove that little one, I was so distraught that I wanted to simply keep this baby in me forever, even if it meant being a detriment to my health. My body and my mind were not ready to give up this baby.

After having four surgeries and finally discovering I was pregnant and then without any explanation an ultrasound produced no heartbeat, I did not have any time to grieve for the loss because my support system told me I needed to be strong and to just move on. Our society has taught us to repress our emotions.

In truth until after the ten week mark, I was too scared to even dream that it would be possible to carry this new baby to term. My goal was not to tell anyone until after the first trimester just in case history repeated itself.

Besides that fear, I also felt a great deal of frustration during the majority of my first trimester. I spent about 3 years in my job position and dedicated all my time and energy towards developing the staff. I had won many leadership awards and was recognized for my abilities to promote innovation, cooperation and foster a true team environment. However, I soon realized that senior management was not interested in leadership, they were interested in compliance in carrying out their hidden agendas and those employees who participated in this scheme were repeatedly rewarded with promotions and hefty bonuses.

Apparently what was right under my nose was corruption practices cleverly masqueraded. When I was tasked with reviewing the budgets, I came across invoices for services that major contracts never delivered. I was told that there was nothing to be done to address these and they would simply be written off as undeliverable orders. However, these contracts were in the millions.

When I realized our contracting team's invoices did not match up and brought it to senior management's attention, all access to these financial records was removed from me. I was told that I was being assessed for a promotion based on my abilities to help improve the productivity of the department, so I paid more attention to the invoices than I probably should have, especially for my safety.

I was put on Special Projects to ensure that I would not be in their way. I discovered that many of the proposals did not follow the regulated guidelines and creative accounting measures were utilized in many business proposals. The variations were again in the millions. But I stayed silent because my primary focus was ensuring the safety of my unborn child.

The organization supposedly gave me an opportunity to get a promotion by going to another office. At the time, I was only worried about my financial situation and accepted the new opportunity. When I went over to the new office I did not know how detrimental it would be for my health and well-being.

I had a boss who constantly screamed and spewed profanity throughout the duration of my pregnancy. Every word out of her mouth was a criticism for things that were actually done correctly. In fact there was not a single day that I was not yelled at. She would literally throw things and slam things when she was fuming. In fact, she often would close the door and scream at all the contractors and all the people would simply tell me this is normal behavior and that you would have to grin and bear it. Irony is that all the Senior Management there participated in the same Leadership style.

I was so shocked because I had been one that had promoted the concept of human resources as being the most vital asset to a company. I honestly thought I had gotten myself into a mental institute disguised as a work place. I was so frustrated watching grown men and women sit in front of my boss and she would use so much profanity and yelling that it was horrific to sit there and watch these poor souls just take in all the verbal abuse. I was wondering how in the world everyone was just tolerating this abuse; in retrospect they all were in the so-called "post-traumatic" scenario and have become accustomed to it being a norm.

It took every ounce of strength within me to disconnect myself from the scene and not voice my opinion. I was fuming at how such abuse could occur in the workplace, but I knew if I said anything that I would be stressing myself and there was no way I was going to jeopardize my unborn child. So silent frustration and anger occurred and it kept building up.

When I attempted to report the acts to the chain of commands, I was pulled into a senior management's office and told that they can do anything to me. The exact words were, "They can put a gun to your head, as long as they don't pull the trigger."

When I attempted to report this abuse to the Human Resources (HR) department, I was told people magically disappeared or were forced to resign if they reported this information up to the chain of commands. And all these people had dismissals of mental disorders.

Ironically, it was not just my boss there were other people in the office who behaved similarly; there was a senior leader that often screamed at people every time someone went into her office. The irony was that you had to approach her because you needed her signature approval for work orders. I recalled every time I stepped foot in her office, I had to bring someone with me so that she would calm down. I was undergoing all this stress while undergoing my first trimester as a new mom.

Mother's Psychological Changes in the Second Trimester

Traditionally the second trimester can be the most overwhelming time as the fetus starts to move and give the mother an active indicator that their baby is growing, developing and the realization of parenthood becomes more real. There might also be a sense of increasing reliance on your partner as this state of change removes you from your traditional zone of comfort. Due to this increased reliance you might also invoke a state of concern or anxiety on the support both physical and emotional that your partner will provide.

There are many changes that occur to the female body during the second trimester, various regions of the body to prepare for the birth and nourishment of the baby after birth, the vagina begins to increase production of viscous lubricant and increased blood flow. The breasts start to become less sensitive and continue to increase in size, all this coupled with the diminishment of first trimester nausea the mother may notice an increase in sex drive.

These changes in addition to an enlarging belly comes the concern of whether your partner is still attracted to you, this may cause tension and concern and stress to the partner. As previously discussed with the increase in stress comes an increased release of cortisol into the mother's body. The mother should be cognizant of this stress. Studies have shown when intrauterine and exposed to high amounts of cortisol, post-birth emotional and mental problems have a high degree association. Not to mention other cognitive and motor inhibited development. Among the mental and emotional changes linked to a fetus exposed to high levels of cortisol are insomnia, ADD/ADHD, anxiety, depression, mood swings, fear disorders and the list goes on.

Traditionally in the first trimester and under high states of stress the placenta will increase the production of corticotrophin releasing hormone (CRH.) CRH adjusts the duration of pregnancy and growth rate of the fetus. To help control the maternal stress during these susceptible times of gestation for fetal development the mother must use coping mechanisms or attributes such as feeling a sense of control, optimism, expression of feelings, and happiness.

Dr. Hobel pioneered the first program to successfully reduce pre-term births in France. He prescribed nurse-midwife home visits along with mandates of bed rest by 24 weeks to alleviate the psychosocial stress symptoms that these mothers had endured throughout the duration of their pregnancy. In 1980, he implemented a similar program in Los Angeles and was able to decrease the pre-term births associated with 12,000 women, the rates went down to a staggering twenty one percent.

Jenn's Insights

At the beginning of the second trimester, I knew I had to protect this unborn child at all costs. I did not want to know the gender because I did not want to be like my parents, I wanted to truly be excited and happy to see the baby, regardless of whether it was a boy or a girl. But epigenetics is truly real, deep down, I secretly wished the baby was a boy so he would never have to go through all the feelings of unworthiness and disappointment I faced my entire life.

Can you imagine, being 4 months pregnant and constantly yelled at for no reason and told that nothing you did was good enough or correct. The stress was that it was a new position where I would have to prove myself at that level to maintain the position. The irony was that I was screamed at for making all the right judgments and for doing my job too accurately.

I have a solid background in testing applications and when I tested the so-called critical applications that were coming out; they had major flaws in them. Since I was the Project Manager, I was held accountable for approving the contractor's services. When I provided detailed documentation of why we should not pay for these services because the products delivered were inadequate, I got reprimanded and discredited in front of the Contractors and the whole Department.

I got called into the office and told I was a detriment to the projects because I had made the contractors upset. I was told in front of the contractors that I was incapable to do my job and was told to apologize for something that I did not do wrong. I was called all types of names and told how stupid and inadequate my skill sets were. It was like sitting in front of my mother and hearing all the complaints about what I had done incorrectly and how I disappointed her all my life. So for me the Tiger Mom philosophy brought more scarring than motivation.

The stress level that I endured was unimaginable. I started bleeding my second trimester and again, it brought back the fears of losing my child. I knew I could not tell my employer and I went to my doctors and pleaded for help. I felt so helpless because I knew I could not leave the job because we needed the insurance and I had dedicated ten years of my life trying to build that career. How was I going to explain away ten years of my life without any references? I also knew I could not go to a psychologist either because I had Top Secret clearance and knew the disclosure of the medical condition could be used against me.

I ended up buying two weeks of time where I was able to reduce the stress level away from that environment. And thank goodness my son was a fighter, he grew stronger and the bleeding subsided. I returned to work and my boss' first comment was, "If you had health conditions, you should never have accepted this job."

The irony is that the whole Department there should be assessed for post-traumatic stress disorder. The people that have worked there exclaimed that it is normal to endure all this verbal and mental abuse. They said that as long as they do not physically harm you, anything is fair game.

Sadly enough, I was not the only one that was treated like this, but since it became the norm, many of the victims actually became the perpetrators in the end because that was all they knew. I recalled speaking with a colleague that told me her boss that was Senior Management would close the door each day and tell her how worthless and inadequate she was and that yelling was the norm around there. Irony was that this place won many multiple awards for being the Best Workplace in its industry.

I was told that the person that I had replaced had to retire early because of a mental breakdown. Ironically, they forgot to mention that it was the Department that produced this scenario with their psychological brain-washing strategies. In fact, these episodes have occurred for the last decade and that Department has the highest turn-over rate for whichever scapegoat happens to go into that position.

My doctors knew how much I wanted to be pregnant and were so shocked when I told them that I could not disclose this at work. Thankfully, prior to my pregnancy I had to have a major surgery and it changed all my body structure. I lost so much weight that I was a size 00 before I was pregnant. That was the saving grace, because as my pregnancy continued, I prayed that no one at work would discover my secret.

It was absurd, it was in the middle of the summer at 100 degree weather, but I wore the heaviest sweaters to always cover myself up. I refused to go outside because I did not know how to explain why I still needed a sweater. I still vividly recalled when there was a fire drill and my colleague asked me why I was wearing such a heavy sweater in the middle of the summer. I told her that I was taking some medications and it made me cold all the time and that I could not be exposed to the sun for long.

That was the truth, I needed the medications to sustain the pregnancy, I had to endure many injections each evening and I told my employer that I needed to come in during the morning shift so that I could carpool home. It was the truth, towards the second and third trimester; I could no longer drive, because I was literally drained from all the stress after a day's work.

My boss made my life living hell. I was told that since I needed to come in so early, that there would be assignments that needed to be completed before she came in. Every morning there would be emergency assignments given and texted on my phone to ensure that my stress level would increase. The irony was that the rest of the team spent their whole day on the phone or on the internet surfing.

During lunch, I was so afraid to eat, my colleagues insisted on eating with me and I did not want them to know that I was pregnant. I ate so little during the day that I was afraid my unborn child would be malnourished. So every night, I tried to over-eat to make sure that there were enough nutrients. The stress level was so high that I ate away my emotions every night with ice cream. Every time I ate ice cream, I could feel my baby kick. But I was deadly afraid to gain too much weight and be noticed.

My unborn child was getting more active, and I could feel the kicks at night. Before I went to work each morning, I begged my child to reverse the sleep cycle and sleep during the day. I told my unborn child please rest in the morning so that no one would notice you. My exact words were, "Please do not make a sound, please do not kick mommy because if they notice you, we both might get killed."

Can you imagine the degree of emotions that I programmed into my son intrauterine? After doing research, I felt like I was a terrible mom for having subjected him to all this undue stress at such an early age. No wonder he gets so frustrated easily nowadays. Every time I hear someone say that he is still not talking, it breaks my heart to know the environment and messages he received from his mom while he was in my stomach. It was not his fault that his mom asked him to be silent and programmed him to believe that this world is not safe. Nowadays, when someone tells him no, my son goes frantic, who would blame him when every day that was all he heard from my boss, words such as "No, no you are so stupid."

Mother's Psychological Changes in the Third Trimester

For mothers encountering pregnancy for the first time there may be a lot of apprehensions in reference to the length and intensity of labor as well as the delivery. There are strong correlations to pending delivery time and the ambient anxiety of those around the pregnant mother. There is also a strong probability of higher states of stress for both the new mother and those around them if there were struggles to get pregnant or if the couple underwent fertility treatment.

There is also a degree of stress to new mothers on whether they will be able to recognize the onset of labor and when it comes will they be prepared. This is why so many first time parents rush to the hospital after experiencing Braxton Hicks contractions. They are on such edge and under stress to make sure they are at the hospital for the delivery due to such high levels of uncertainty and lack of experience and confidence.

These states of stress and uncertainty may invoke even more feelings of inferiority and lack of beauty. The mother to be will most certainly need reassurance and support from their partner, especially as their character changes with the progression of pregnancy. Toward the end of pregnancy and the unknown of labor nears there may be rushes of feelings on whether the adequacy of the mother as a parent will be enough.

Science has shown that as a society over the past century that we as humans are controlled by our genetic makeup. What we now know is that it isn't entirely based on the genes themselves, it is based on the expression of those genes. And over the past decade there has been a huge leap in science to show there are many ways gene expression is actually triggered. Some of these inducers of expressions include environmental signals, foods, chemicals, and emotional stressors.

It is common knowledge that the mother's DNA content is transferred to the fetus during the developmental stage; however, many mothers-to-be may not be aware that informational content, inclusive of emotions are transferred to the fetus intrauterine. Research studies have concluded that when an organism, inclusive of mothers is under duress, that these emotional toxins can actively alter the DNA composition and create differing genes to accommodate for the environmental challenges. This is part of Darwinism for the evolution of the strongest genes.

Did you know that the mother's emotions, inclusive of repressed ones such as fear, anger, love or hope can biochemically alter the genetic expression of the offspring for generations to come? The mother's perceived attitude of life, optimism versus pessimism can also be transferred to the fetus' disposition. The mother's blood-borne emotional chemicals transfer across the placenta in the same fashion that nutrient transfers are made.

Consequently, anger is often an emotion associated with the liver; as such, the same emotional chemicals will be targeted towards the fetus' cell and impact his/her liver. Most mothers-to-be may not be cognizant of how their emotions and behaviors are impacting their unborn child and with epigenetics these same stressors are chemically altering the genetic makeup of subsequent generations. One time incidences of parental anger or fear will not impact the physiology of the developing fetus; it is the chronic or repressed emotions that bombard the mothers mind and body that becomes detrimental for the fetus' cortisol levels.

If this was an unplanned or unwanted pregnancy, these emotions can leave an imprint into the unborn child's unconscious level. For mothers that may be bearing children during times of famine or war, and remain constantly concerned about their and the unborn child's well-being, this amount of stress can be problematic for the fetus.

Also women that may have experienced physical or emotional abuse during the duration of their pregnancy may be severely impacted and these adversaries may alter the genes for generations to come. These emotional stressors due to sustained and intense emotions such as fear, anger, anxiety, and grief may compromise the child's overall development from both a physiological and psychological perspective. The stressors chemically impact the fetus intrauterine and the child may acquire attitudes about life as it decodes the behavioral signals relayed through the blood-placenta neural pathways.

A study conducted by the University of Pennsylvania discovered that the first dosage of bacteria is experienced when the baby passes through the birth canal. This is one of the advantages of having a natural birthing process, the baby will be able to ingest the mother's vaginal microbe which then colonizes to gut flora and aids in shaping the baby's neurological and digestive development.

However if the mother is chronically stressed, bacterial changes may occur within her vagina and the stressors may be passed on via this medium. The bacterium in our body out-numbers our cells by about a 10 to 1 ratio. Pathology discovered that there were more types of bacteria present within the vaginal canal of stressed mothers; however, the important bacteria, Lactobacillus was significantly reduced.

The detriment of this is that science has discovered that the expression of 20 genes may be impacted by the decrease in Lactobacillus. Some of the genes being impacted related to the growth of synaptic connections within the brain and the production of neurons. Additionally, the blood diagnostics of the stressed mothers revealed that there was a lower level of essential neurotransmitters and a lower degree of the molecule that protected the brain from harmful oxidative stress.

The majority of mothers is cognizant that pregnancy is far from being a stress-free time of life and most mothers aim to provide a healthy placental environment for their unborn baby with healthy choices such as consumption of the proper food nutrients, the avoidance of medications, smoking and alcohol to ensure the most optimal environment for physical and emotional well-being; however, mothers are beginning to realize the impacts that emotions or repressed emotions may also play on the development of the fetus.

Jenn's Insights

As the seventh month came I still felt like it was unsafe for me to tell my employer. My husband and doctors wondered how long I was going to be able to hide this information from them. I had a closet full of maternity clothes but sadly enough I did not even have an opportunity to wear one. I knew that I had to hide this pregnancy for the safety of my child.

Then, it got worse. I received a phone call from the business manager and was informed there was an emergency fix needed in the critical application. I reviewed the reports sent to the accounting division for daily payoffs and realized they were inaccurate. My boss was on vacation and since the reports were critical and enhancements to the program could not be made. The business manager and I made a decision to correct the numbers manually before submitting them to the accounting division. When my boss came back and I informed her of this issue, she went ballistic and accused me of auditing violations stating that I had broken SOX compliance. My husband was an expert in SOX compliance and I asked him what this had to do with SOX and he said absolutely nothing.

Both financial applications were pulled away from my management and I was ridiculed in front of the business department stating that I had made a detrimental financial mistake and was not qualified to perform as a Project Manager anymore.

I was so upset that I decided to request for an appeal to the Senior Manager, who was also in Special Ops. I brought in the report and asked why I was receiving such a poor performance rating when the report clearly stated that the numbers did not add up correctly. The first response was "What do you want, do you want a promotion?" This is how everyone got promoted in that department; many that cooperated were guaranteed positions as Team Leads or Senior Management positions. The corruption was so rampant that there was a person that was promoted from a chauffeur position to the senior management of a division.

I soon realized then I was in BIG trouble, I went back to review the reports and noticed that on a daily basis the numbers that were submitted had a variation of 15 million dollars. I realized then that my unborn child and I were not safe. As if my stress level was not enough, things got even more intense. My computers, my cell phone, my home phone, my Emails were all monitored. It was covert and strategically carried out. Friends, family members, colleagues all acted as accomplices. Medical records were disclosed violating the HIPAA regulations.

I was under so much stress by my eighth month, my placenta starting tearing. I remember that evening I had been called in and again verbally abused and screamed at. I was told I could not go home that evening until I corrected the issue. I knew I had to take my injection shot for my child's well-being. That evening, I went to the bathroom and saw blood streaming down my legs.

My heart sank; I knew that I could not lose another baby. I called my husband and parents and immediately called my doctor. When I went into the hospital, my doctor did a scan and said there is a big tear in the placenta and that I needed to go on immediate bed-rest.

I told my doctor that I had been screamed at for the whole duration of the pregnancy. My doctor said that it was detrimental for my child's well-being if I returned to work. My doctor ordered my bed-rest and that was when my employers found out that I was pregnant for the first time!

The post-natal care was even worse than the pregnancy. Both my boss and the senior manager happened to retire suddenly and I was transferred to a new boss. Irony was that she was someone that had been a victim and now she carried out the same acts of abuse on others.

I chose to breastfeed so I needed to pump during my lunch break, I was monitored for using the restroom or even eating snacks at my desk while working because I had already used my lunch break for pumping. It was more stressful than during my pregnancy. My body was under so much stress that I lost the majority of my milk production. My son was born so malnourished that he was approximately in the 1 percentile of development.

My pediatrician was threatening me with calling the social services on me if my son did not gain weight. I was wondering, how in the world would I explain this scenario to someone without them feeling like I had lost my mind?

At work, Special Ops cleverly planned the ways to ensure I would magically resign, my department was told that I had postpartum depression and was a threat to others due to my delusional state and mental instability. They had to find viable ways to try to discredit me. Ironically, the people that were previously in my position, had a mental breakdown also and had to suddenly retire due to emotional stressors. I wonder what other mental disability will be discovered in the next victim?

I vowed that I would make it a mission of mine to never have anyone robbed of the joys of their pregnancy and that no mom should ever have to experience the amount of duress and emotional and mental abuse that I suffered through.

For those who are skeptical of emotions being transferred intrauterine, I beg of you to imagine what it must feel like to be my son. I hope that this story is able to spare at least one child from being subjected to emotions their mother may or may not have consciously been thinking. It is important not just to watch what you eat during pregnancy but also the emotions (toxins) you are transferring through the placenta.

Mother-Child Bonding Within the Womb

There is so much that a fetus receives from its mother intrauterine. It gets things from nutrition, chemical uptake to auditory stimulation such as the mother's heart beat and digestion sounds. This is so well recognized that companies even make devices for the mother to put on their belly to introduce music to the fetus in hopes that it will help neuronal development to enhance the IQ of their baby. Remember though whatever the mother takes in, essentially the fetus will as well. From caffeine to alcohol to chemicals associated with stress responses in the body. All of which can affect both the physical and emotional development of the fetus.

Every reaction, response and emotion in the body requires chemicals and energy for cells to respond and form the response to the chemical initiation. By this very nature every emotion has energy or frequency that is essentially measurable. As this energy enters and travels down the neuron pathway it triggers the release of proteins. It is these neuropeptides (NP's) or proteins that trigger the various chemical responses and changes in attitude, emotion, Etc.

There have been studies done that show certain emotions and emotion intensity can have lasting effects on the neural pathway structure. If you have a very intense emotional rush such as fear, anger, disappointment, angst, etc. They can cause a formation of "scar tissue" or lesions on the pathways. This in return inhibits the signaling in the future and can complicate and inhibit the body's flow of energy, which ultimately may lead to a dis-eased state in the body.

Did you know that the emotion of anger literally damages the liver and gall bladder? Analogously, anger toward another person is likened to ingesting poison yourself and expecting ill effects to be evidenced in the other person. Dr. David Suzuki conducted a scientific experiment and measured the condensed molecules of breath that was exhaled from a person after verbalizing expressions of words spoken to represent anger, hatred and jealousy and validated that there was enough toxins within these words to kill 80 guinea pigs within an hour's of speaking such negativity.

When you repress or stifle negative energy within your body, it can lead to an increase of anger, depression, frustration, and intensity to want to be more controlling which often results in an emotional shutdown or worse yet physical pain. Negative emotions carry a denser slower vibration that is often heavier so it is manifested into the lower parts of your body.

Often times you feel these stressors impacting your calves, legs and feet with aches and pains. This is where the majority of your trauma, resentment, jealousy and past and present emotional stressors are stored. This gives a feeling of being ungrounded because they affect those parts of the extremities more. Negative emotions are often indicative of more deep-seeded issues such as self-sabotage, self-judgment, feelings of unworthiness and possession of low self-esteem.

According to Dr. Karen Moritz, when a mother experiences extremities of stress during pregnancy, hormones are produced called glucocorticoids that cross the placenta to the baby and may impact the physiology of the baby by altering the development of its kidney and heart. Psychological symptoms that may be attributed to the fetus experiencing extreme stressors include the likelihood of developing

Attention Deficit Hyperactivity Disorder (ADHD/ADD), cognitive delays, anxiousness, depression, autistic attributes or in rare incidence schizophrenia.

Having realization of all these detrimental effects that stressors have on an unborn child, it is imperative for mothers to be equipped with stress management techniques. As a guru in the field of meditation, John Kabat-Zinn developed a stress reduction program called Mindful Birthing. Meditation has been evidenced to lower stress levels; both boosting the immune system and providing heightened positive emotions for the mothers-to-be.

A second technique is presented within the book, "Connecting with Your Unborn Child" by Mak Wai Chong. She is a certified Humanistic Neuro-linguistic practitioner, and recommends that you customize a tape that you can play to your unborn child on a daily basis. The best approach is to record your own voice and read out-loud incantations (positive statements said with loving joyful emotions) so that your unborn child can experience these feelings intrauterine.

In the background classical music should be playing such as symphonies from Bach or Beethoven. Scientist believes that stimulation of long-term growth occurs when the fetus listens to music within the womb. According to the Stress Management Institute, the following incantations should foster positive feel-good emotions for your baby.
- I am a child of the universe deserving of health, love, and respect from others
- I am a worthy and capable person
- I am handsome or beautiful, inside and out
- I am a unique individual and know that everything about me is special so no competition is needed
- I am a caring and sensitive person
- I am my own best friend, free of addictions and self-defeating behaviors
- I am balance, harmony, prosperity, creativity and peaceful
- I am strong and at the same time humble.

Incantations provide a positive foundation for your baby to steer from negative thinking or emotional patterns that may be transferred on a daily basis to him/her thru the placenta by the mother's stressors. By repeating these positive incantations each evening your baby will be provided with a new perception of reality. When you speak of positive thoughts, this way of thinking and perceiving the world will become your reality. So, intrauterine these babies are disposed to more optimism and hope. Babies normally are attuned to their mother's voice so the recording would be more effective if the mother recorded these statements rather than from another family member.

Imagination (Visualization) is a third approach to stress management. Find a sound file, device, etc., that has nature sounds. Play the natural sound of your choice in a room that is dark and otherwise quiet. Close your eyes after sitting in a comfortable chair or position and try to imagine yourself in your favorite place (mother's arms, beach, field of grass, etc.) The goal of this technique is to switch your brain into Alpha waves. These are the waves that are present during periods of deep relaxation; these waves in these states help you build your imagination, memory and concentration among others. This helps you open up and experience your subconscious.

Start the meditation by imagining a sky in your world taking the tone of your favorite color. Now take that sky and envision as clearly as possible, a very serene sky that is untouched by anything else, no clouds, no animals, nothing and the sky is blanketed with a tranquil background, similar to softly fallen snow. Now look at the sun in your sky. The sun is the biggest most bright and white sun you have ever seen. It has rays that gleam and shine down to where you are seated and you can feel its warmth. Once you feel the warm sunshine on you take 3 long breaths in an out and repeat the following words. Your breath should come from deep inside you, from your core and repeat one of the below words on the exhalation and do so with a gleaming smile on your face just like the sun in your sky.

With each breath of inhalation and exhalation, say a following word aloud:
- Love
- Compassion
- Peace
- Forgiveness
- Gratitude
- Joy
- Happiness
- Security
- Hope

 Jenn's Insights

During my emotional pregnancy, one of the saving graces was that I attended prenatal yoga. It provided me with the sanity and peace to balance my emotional state. The stress was rebalanced when I was given the opportunity to attend these classes.

In Eastern culture we are taught to look at pictures of babies that are considered healthy and intelligent. We avoid horror movies and are asked not to cry during the pregnancy. It might be an old wises' tale but my mother told me if you cry during your pregnancy, the baby will feel this sadness. So when I went home I was adamant about not crying because I did not want my unborn child to feel sadness. It is unfortunate that I did not learn that repressing the emotions would have the same effect on the baby.

Here is a technique for mothers-to-be to implement as least 3 times a week:
- *Find a comfortable spot to sit down on the ground and close your eyes for the duration of this exercise.*
- *Imagine yourself on a beach, filled with white sand and glistening blue waters. Take 3 deep breaths in and with each exhale say these words aloud: peace, love, and joy.*
- *Look up into the sky and imagine a beautiful white sun that fills the whole sky with glistening rays that shines upon your skin. There is not a single cloud in the sky.*
- *As you are sitting there getting a sun bath from the white sunshine, several birds will come and visit you and perch upon your shoulders. I want you simply to pick the first positive word that comes to your mind to share with your unborn baby for each bird that visits.*

- *The first bird to visit is a Cardinal: please tell it a positive word.*
- *The next bird to visit is a Baltimore Oriole: please tell it a positive word.*
- *The next bird to visit is a Yellow Canary: please tell it a positive word.*
- *The next bird to visit is a Green Hummingbird: please tell it a positive word.*
- *The next bird to visit is a Blue Bird: please tell it a positive word.*
- *The next bird to visit is an Indigo Bunting: please tell it a positive word.*
- *The next bird to visit is a Violet Swallow: please tell it a positive word.*
- *Take another 3 deep breaths in, and, literally smell the ocean waves with each breath.*
- *Tell yourself you will be returning there again as soon as possible this week. Take another 3 deep breaths in, and, then open your eyes.*

Fetal Programming

It is amazing when you realize that within just 270 days, the combination of two genetic make-ups form a cell that becomes trillions of diverse and specialized cells: a human being. There is a new science of fetal programming; called epigenetics which investigates how toxins and stressors can impact the fetus intrauterine. This process impacts both physiological and emotional changes that may linger into later life or has the ability to change the DNA of generations to come.

According to the Center for Pregnancy and Newborn Research in Texas, each cell has a specialized task, but it also is responsible for spurring other cells to action, as in a chain reaction effect; however, improper functioning of a particular cell can become the missing link that produces developmental issues. As in the case of brain cells, this might be even more detrimental since improper interconnections could cause disruptions or imbalances for regulating other parts of the body.

The exposure to stressors intrauterine can establish the precedence for the child's emotional resilience and susceptibility to dis-ease or illnesses by having gene suppressions or alterations occurring. The trick is to be able to assist the mother with stress management techniques because often times the stressors are beyond the mother's degree of control as in the case of a troubled marriage, financial woes during the pregnancy, or chronic anxiety associated with physical danger or emotional abuse during the duration of the pregnancy. In all these scenarios, the levels of the stress hormone cortisol will be transferred thru the placenta-blood barrier and impact the fetus' overall physiological and mental development.

The detriment is that once the fetus becomes accustomed to such a stressful environment intrauterine, the brain receptors that sense the "fight or flight" response may develop less tolerance and in the long run these children may be more susceptible to coping with stressors. Additionally, the brain possessing fewer receptors may not be able to properly regulate the influx of cortisol within the body and the tolerance/sensitivity levels become skewed.

As such, some of these infants may be infused with so much cortisol levels in their bodies that they appear to be hypersensitive to any forms of stimuli and often continue to operate in the parasympathetic nervous system on a continuous basis which produces degeneration to the body and may afflict their mental well-being. Many of these children are seen with characteristics of lashing out their frustration or withdrawing from stimuli when confronted with stress in future episodes and these children were more susceptible for developing depression as they progressed in life.

Research has proven that children born to mothers during a famine had more heart dis-ease and depression attributed to them when they became older. These fetuses had to evolve to their environments by adapting with smaller organs and fewer blood vessels that often led to the complications of higher blood pressure later in life. Infants whose mothers developed posttraumatic stress disorder after the September 11 attacks were found to be readily upset by loud noises and unfamiliar people and during school age experienced more characteristics of separation anxiety.

With every nuance, there appears to be a positive aspect of hope. There is surmounting research that a specific degree of stress may actually help bring out the best to enhance a character trait in children because certain areas of the brain may become over-stimulated and further developed than the average infant brain. The study revealed that two-year-olds whose mothers experienced moderate anxiety or a minor degree of depression during pregnancy performed better than average on reasoning and coordination tasks.

These activities involve manipulating small objects, stacking blocks or solving puzzles. It is hypothesized that the fetus was provided with a more varied intrauterine environment due to the excess of cortisol hormones that may have stimulated the speeding up of specific areas of brain development. This supports the theory of why child genius and autistic children may have similar characteristics within designated areas of the brain. Further research will be necessary to provide a more conclusive correlation.

Jenn's Insights

A positive by-product of stress is that the research supports that sometimes stress can help provide a more varied intrauterine environment with stimulants that speed up the child's brain development. I have observed my son and I noticed that this hypothesis is indeed true for him. His fine-motor coordination and manipulation of smaller objects are extremely developed.

I noticed that he performs stacking of blocks and sorting of puzzles at a much quicker pace than the norm. Often times, once he runs thru a drill, he is able to duplicate the process with precision and speed. So for those that are not able to control their environments during their pregnancy, do not despair. You are still able to find tools to counter balance the stressful environment surrounding you and escape for a moment.

Your child's sensory systems are developed intrauterine. She or he begins hearing approximately at the twentieth week. During your second trimester, it would be beneficial to read this bedtime story to your unborn child each evening. I would encourage you to customize your child's story with positive attributes that you feel your own child should possess.

Once upon a time in a land far away there lived a little baby that was waiting to visit Earth. Before the baby's visit, a magical stork granted the baby with some gifts to bring to Earth. There were twenty six gifts that came with each baby so that they would be able to share this with the world. As your mommy, I want you to know that you are gifted with the "A to Z's of perfection".

A   *is for Altruism*
B   *is for Beauty*
C   *is for Compassion*
D   *is for Dedication*
E   *is for Empathy*
F   *is for Forgiveness*
G   *is for Gratitude*
H   *is for Harmony*
I   *is for Intelligence*
J   *is for Joy*
K   *is for Kindness*
L   *is for Loving Personality*
M   *is for Magnificence*
N   *is for Nobility*
O   *is for Outstanding Character*
P   *is for Peacefulness*
Q   *is for Quick-Witted Thinking*
R   *is for Richness in the Heart*
S   *is for Sensational Accomplishments*
T   *is for Talented Gifts*
U   *is for Uniqueness*
V   *is for Very Awesome Ideas You Bring*
W   *is for Wonderful Insights*
X   *is for X-cellence in All You Do*
Y   *is for Your Inspiration and*
Z   *is for Zest for Life. You are the ABC's of hope, love and compassion!*

Forms of Communication from Mother to Child

From the moment of conception, there is a bonding between the mother and child that provides a continuous feedback loop to readily communicate thoughts and emotions by utilizing the forms of molecular communication, sensory communication and intuitive communication within the womb. During the gestational period the imaging brain of the fetus possesses its strongest characteristics.

The fetus develops sensory mechanisms early on and will be able to fully experience the energy transmission from the mother and serve as the basis for the foundations of his or her personality. The mother's emotional energy is intermixed with the genetics from the father and both sets of grandparents and the combination plays a critical role in the influence of your child's disposition.

Molecular Communication:

Your unborn fetus is as interconnected to your molecules of emotions as the umbilical cord that transfers the nutrients. These molecules of emotions consist of the mother's energetic thoughts and emotions throughout the duration of the pregnancy. This is why a fetus can sense if they are in a safe environment while intra-uterine. The stress hormones fluctuating within your pregnant body such as adrenaline, noradrenalin and neurohormones is also shared with your unborn child through the placenta and umbilical cord.

Sensory Communication:

As a mother, you can communicate with your unborn baby early on. Have you ever noticed that when you massaged, stroked or gently tapped your tummy that often times a reactive kick was returned from your stomach? Mothers and fathers both that have often talked or sung to the baby will notice movements in the belly as responses. Often times, your unborn child will communicate his/her preference to you with subtle clues. For instance, if your unborn child prefers motion, you will notice that every time you walked, your belly received a gentle kick.

Your unborn child can also communicate messages of distaste. Studies have shown that if a mother-to-be was at a loud rock concert, they reported having to leave because they felt sick in the stomach and felt strong, violent kicks received from their unborn child. Dependent on the mother's upbringing and the level of attunement to their child's energy, they will be able to communicate back and forth with messages of satisfaction and dissatisfaction coming in the formats of kicks to the belly, similar to a mommy-baby Morse code.

Intuitive Communication:

The concept of having extrasensory abilities has been demystified when you investigate the science behind the process of telepathy. As Dr. Makoto Shichida revealed telepathic communications is simply the right brain accessing the language acquisition abilities from the unconscious level.

Telepathic communication exists between humans in general but many are not cognizant of this generalization. Have you ever noticed that you think of a friend and suddenly you receive a phone call from them? For twins this is an especially dominant form of communication, twins can be half way around the globe, yet they will sense when something is not right with the other, this is because they are interconnected to a degree of sensitivity that the average human sensory may not be able to detect.

There is no deeper illustration of bonding than in the format of intuitive communication between you and your unborn child. The mother's thoughts, emotions and intentions are often conveyed to the child intrauterine, whether consciously or unconsciously. This is why having a balance check on your words and emotions during pregnancy are vital for the mental development of your child. Often times the mother may receive indirect communication from her unborn baby in the form of dreams as the baby is always communicating on a daily basis with the mother. The question is not whether this type of communication exists, but rather is the mother attuned enough to hear the subtle messages.

What Inquiring Parental Minds Need to Know

Newborns are highly sensitive to pheromones within their environment and when others around them are worried, depressed or experiencing anxiety; babies may more often cry but this is a cyclical effect because the adults than misinterpret this message with increased frustration, anxiety and depression and this condition is often known as colic.

Babies are still operating on primitive reflexes when they first arrive into the world and as such they are attuned to the facial and emotional recognition of their caregivers. They are keen on assessing the levels of stress exhibited from their caregivers and can innately distinguish whether their mother is experiencing feelings of elation (joy) or fear. They use this to assess the level of perceived security for their surrounding environment. It has been hypothesized that the psychological component with separation anxiety is due to the loss of parental cues about the safety of his or her environment and as such the child feels stressed about having to fend on his/her own.

As parents, we would like to believe that we can protect our young ones from any forms of distress and that that feelings of pain should not be a learning experience for them. However, did you know that there is surmounting evidence that from birth, the genitals of infants are hypersensitive to both pain and pleasure? As such circumcisions that occur without any anesthetic experience may form the basis for a painful learning experience that may be deemed as being traumatic for a newborn.

Studies revealed that babies that were circumcised had an accompaniment of increased blood pressure, increased heart rates, decreased oxygen level in the blood supply and an immediate surge of the cortisol stress hormone within their bodies. From a psychological perspective, recent evidence associated this experience with learning more memories of pain and fear. Ironically this is the same association that occurs during the childhood immunization process. Much of medical interventions that are performed on children do not take into account the psychological aspects that may be imprinted while enduring these procedures.

Did you know that on average, we lose one percent of our red blood cells on a daily basis as it normally retires and is being replaced with fresh ones. The dis-ease known as jaundice occurs when too many red bloods cells are simultaneously being replenished or the liver is not able to efficiently process this demand or it might be caused by this combined inadequacy of the body's functionality.

The old red blood cells that are being replaced have a yellow characteristic to them and are called bilirubin. This is why jaundice has a yellowish tone to the skin. Jaundice is a common dis-ease; however, if the conditions do not improve it can lead to kernicterus which is a severe toxicity level of bilirubin that accumulates within the brain, causing long-term impairments and neural damage.

Within the first week of life, one in 10 breastfeed infants may experience the effects of jaundice. This is normally due to a decrease of the caloric values from milk intake which causes dehydration in the baby's system. Furthermore, if there are any intestinal blockages, this may cause bilirubin to build up within the baby's system. Another common cause for jaundice is due to the incompatibility of the mother's Rh blood factor which may cause the hemolytic dis-ease because the baby is producing more bilirubin than normal to react to the antibodies of the blood incompatibilities.

Babies born in hospitals "normally" receive an injection of vitamin K after the birthing process to prevent the onset of a rare bleeding disorder that may occur to the brain. The injection is supposed to further enhance blood clotting attributes to mitigate this issue. In general, the medical profession cites this as a necessity because newborns are considered to possess vitamin K deficiencies. Normally the transfer of this nutrient across the placenta does not occur efficiently and since the liver is immaturely developed there is a decreased storage capacity to store or efficiently process vitamin K within the infant's body. This is even more pronounced in premature infants.

However, according to the International Chiropractic Pediatric Association's research of published data, they denoted that there were 1.5 extra cases of leukemia that occurred per 100,000 children that received the vitamin K injections. Even though this appears to be statistically insignificant, there are alternatives that may minimize these incidences from occurring altogether and subjecting the newborn to this risk. The same results can be achieved by having the nursing mother take vitamin K supplements daily or twice weekly for 10 weeks and providing the vitamin K nutrients via breast milk.

♡◎ Dr. S' Insights

During my training in chiropractic school, I discovered my passion was inclined towards pregnancy and children. It was a bit perplexing at the time because I did not have any children of my own but I found those subjects to be the most captivating. Somewhere deep inside I knew I was destined to help mothers. It was ironic, because often times I was the only male in those classes.

My father instilled an important lesson in me. I can still recall his words, "Son, if you want to be a doctor someday, you will need to give everything you got so that your patient truly receives the best." That was his motto and each time I was practicing or studying, I had that goal in mind.

I knew I had to empower myself with knowledge so I could share and apply this with others and bring hope into their lives. I went to pursue a doctorate degree in Chiropractic however; I still felt there was a missing link. I felt there needed to be a mind-body connection, so I went to pursue chiropractic Craniopathy.

I discovered that there was still a missing piece of the "Whole-Listic" puzzle and as my research mind went into the studies of some of the latest scientific research being revealed. I became fascinated with the work of Dr. Bruce Lipton with epigenetics and Gregg Braden with the Matrix and others. I knew there was another realm that was still preventing my patients from being their fullest potential and this is what led me to pursue my doctorate in Energy Medicine, so my patients would truly receive a "Whole-Listic" recommendation for their body's needs.

During all my years in practice I have been blessed with being able to help hundreds of women with their pregnancies with everything from pain, discomfort, nausea, vomiting, and hiatus hernia, to breech babies. I also had the fortune of providing hope to women who experienced multiple miscarriages and infertility issues and believed they had exhausted all their options. Additionally, I observed with this preventive care, their second, third or fourth babies experienced easier and quicker deliveries with less pain involved and a healthier outcome for the baby.

I am a big proponent of Chiropractic care during pregnancy because I have experienced first-hand with my wife and with all the testimonials of patients that benefitted from it. I have found that the chiropractic SOT method and chiropractic Craniopathy was able to find and restore the whole body balance because it incorporated organ therapy to help with digestion, hiatus hernia, liver toxicity, sugar handling, fat and protein digestion, anemia-type symptoms or infection, stress from the adrenal, urination and uncontrollable bladder during pregnancy. These symptoms were also rapid for patients during the prenatal stages for those that had difficulty with conception.*

One of the most memorable experiences was being able to help one of my clients. I can still recall she came to my office and wanted to have a baby but the doctors said the standard fertility treatments might not work due to her age and wanted her to use alternative methods that were more costly. She came to me for lower back pain "treatment" and within two months of treating her with my usual protocol for fertility, she became naturally pregnant.

She was ecstatic. She continued her treatment protocol with me during the entire duration of the preg-nancy and she delivered a healthy and beautiful baby. Often during the pregnancy she came to me with acne, digestive or migraine issues and it was instantaneously "relieved" before she left the office. I knew many infertility patients have symptoms due to the stressors that are kept in their body and as such I knew that being able to help alleviate their nervous system's interferences could better assist the adrenals with the body's innate abilities for reproduction.

Another memorable patient had been diagnosed with uterine fibroids. She had many surgical attempts to remove them but they appeared to continually grow back. The patient was informed by her obste-trician that there was a large fibroid that would require surgery. Since the patient had endured many prior surgeries she was looking for an alternative route. After treating this patient for about six months with Chiropractic adjustments and Craniopathy coupled with Energy Healing, the patient observed her menstrual cycles were normalizing and less painful. She then went to perform an ultrasound and they discovered that the fibroid was no longer there and could not be detected anywhere within the uterus. It was like the "tumors" automatically shrank, similar to what Gregg Braden discovered at the Huaxia Zhineng Qigong Clinic and Training Center, simply known as the Center in China, the first medicine-less hospital.

Resources

My Pregnancy Toolkit – http://mypregnancytoolkit.com
Positive Affirmations –

http://www.articlesfactory.com/articles/health/affirmations-part-iii-can-give-your-unborn-baby-a-million-dollars-without-it-costing-you-a-dime.html

Wise Parents – http://www.wiseparents.net/

Center for Prenatal and Prenatal Music – http://www.prenatalmusic.com/pages/active-music-therapy-for-childbirth.php

3

Brains "R" Us Inquiring Minds Want to Know

"Whatever the mind can conceive and believe; it can achieve."

–Napoleon Hill–

Every child brings unique gifts, talents and strengths to the world. The brain has an amazing power and the more we discover and understand it, the better we will adapt and create learning programs to facilitate its growth,

For our children's education, from birth to about the age of 8 years old it is the most critical time period. During these years, the brain is more malleable and exhibits more plasticity, meaning it can create rapid alterations and adapt quickly to changes, learning through absorption similar to sponges or the osmosis concept. This makes a child's brain more open and flexible to new learning processes and methods. No human being has ever come anywhere near to using its fullest potential regarding brain power as Professor Anokhin of Russia has remarked. This is why the next century can produce many billionaire babies that are richer in their mind than imaginable.

We believe it is extremely important for us, as parents and grandparents, to discover the unique design of our children's brains. Furthermore, it is also important to know how he or she learns best, and to recognize and intervene early when there is a problem. We also have to look at it with a positive solution that harnesses the brain's power, not to further sedate or quench its full potential. The concept of mind encompasses functions that include consciousness, cognition, language, perception, emotions, recollections, sleep and brain wave patterns and the indirect lessons that are guided by our intuition through dreams/meditation.

Fun Facts About Your Brain – Inquiring Minds Want To Know

- Your brain is composed of 60% fat. (Excessive dieting will not be conducive to learning)
- Your brain uses 20% of the total oxygen and blood in your body.
- New brain connections are created every time you form a memory (Helps promote indirect learning.)
- Your brain is made up of 75% water (dehydration = losing focus)
- Your brain consists of 100 billion neurons available to you and each neuron has somewhere between 1,000 and 10,000 synapses available for learning, hence Billionaire Baby.
- Children who learn two languages before the age of five alter the brain structure in a positive aspect.
- Oxytocin, one of the hormones responsible for triggering feelings of love in the brain, has shown some benefits to helping control repetitive behaviors in those with autism, cerebral palsy and other behavioral challenged children.
- Excessive stress has shown to "alter" brain cells, brain structure and brain function.
- Laughing is no simple task as it requires activity in five different areas of the brain. This is why laughter yoga can heal some dis-ease.
- Music lessons have shown to considerably boost brain organization and ability in both children and adults. This is why playing classical music in the background will help subliminally with learning.
- We have about 70,000 thoughts a day, whether you choose to fill your brain with positive or negative thoughts will determine your overall lifestyle. Experts estimate that in a lifetime, a human brain may retain one quadrillion separate bits of information; now, that's a super computer.
- Compared to a normal human's brain, Einstein's brain was 10% SMALLER in size except in the region that is responsible for math and spatial perception. In that region, his brain was 35% wider than average. (This illustrates why child genius may have autistic characteristics.)
- It's scientifically proven that even a small dose of power changes how a person's brain operates and diminishes empathy. (This is why it is important to read Dr. David Hawkins's book, Power vs. Force.)
- The smell of chocolate increases theta brain waves, which triggers relaxation and promotes creativity.
- Did you know that it is normal for your mind to wander? A joint study by Harvard University, Dartmouth College and the University of Aberdeen in Scotland found the parts of the brain that control "task-unrelated thought" (such as daydreaming) are almost always active when the brain is at rest.
- Did you know that the hormone oxytocin produced by your brain can play Dr. Jekyll and Mr. Hyde? Normally it plays a role in bonding (nursing infants, love hormone, and promotes trust and empathy); however, it can also amplify negative behaviors such as (envy, jealousy and suspicion.)
- The hormone dopamine produced from the brain at excessive doses makes you lose the ability to feel any kind of pleasure. Research has discovered that being addicted to fatty foods has the same effects.
- Reading aloud to children helps stimulate brain development, yet only 50% of infants and toddlers are routinely read to by their parents.
- A study showed that when mothers frequently spoke to their infants, their children learned about 300 more words by age two than did children whose mothers rarely spoke to them.

- The most creative works of art, music, and poetry, comes to the artists while they're in the alpha brain wave state. The most creative and brilliant ideas come to the scientists while their brains are in the Alpha brain wave state. Alpha waves are the bridge between the subconscious and conscious mind. This is why the meditation process begins and ends in this brain state, if not you would not remember your dreams and/or meditations.
- Did you know that when our eyes receive images, they are actually upside-down? Our brain automatically corrects them, so that we see them the right side-up!
- The reasons memories are triggered by scent seem more intense and easier to recall is because our sense of smell has a deeper emotional connection with our brain.
- The blood vessels in our brain equal a total distance of 100,000 kilometers when stretched out. That's enough to wrap around the whole Earth four times. This is why a majority of strokes may occur in the brain.
- The brain contains no pain receptors, therefore it cannot feel pain! This is the reason brain surgery is able to be performed on the patient while they are still awake.
- During the first few weeks of life, a babbling baby utters almost every sound of every known language. Later, the ability to make some sounds vanishes, which is a case of neural pruning.
- A woman's brain shrinks during pregnancy and takes up to six months to regain its full size, thus the forgetfulness syndrome.
- When a person diets or deprives himself of food, the neurons in the brain that induce hunger starts eating itself. This "cannibalism" sparks a hunger signal to prompt eating. This is why dieting is not healthy and since your brain contains the most fat the body goes for this reserve.

The Psychology of the Mind

Since this book is not intended for neuroanatomy and since Anthony Robbins states that success is 80% psychology, we will begin with how the Mind interprets things on a daily basis. We have simplified the workings of the brain and here are the seven most important things to know about your brain so you can use it to aid in producing the best life for you and your child's wealth. These concepts are designed by L. Michael Hall, PhD, who is the father of neuro-semantics.

According to Dr. Hall, a clinical psychologist, here are the seven facts you need to know about yours and your child's brain: (*All the inserts below are cited with permission by Dr. L. Michael Hall, PhD from www. neurosemantics.com.*)

#1: Brains Follow Directions

Brains follow directions. They take the directions that you give them and they follow them. Provide a little instruction and the brain goes to work representing the information on our internal mental screen. Like a movie director, brains use the information as instructions for our mental movie entitled, "Our Life."

Since, the quality of our lives is a function of the quality of the information processed by our brain. The quality of that information flows from the quality of its instructions. The most important thing you can do in life then are the instructions that you give your brain. Ask yourself this, are the instructions you have given to your brain, one that you would use to create a world-class movie? As the old saying, goes, junk-in equals junk-out and negative thoughts and limiting beliefs equate to toxic.

- What directions are you giving your brain?
- What are the default instructions that you've learned to give your brain?
- What instructions did your parents or teachers provide you about yourself, life, others?
- How useful, ecological, healthy, balanced, valuable, true, Etc. are those instructions?
- Do those instructions create empowering states for you?
- Would you want to give those instructions to your children?

Brains are also incredible instruments that never shut down. Even in sleep, we dream as brain wave activity persists. This becomes a problem if we don't give the brain lots of interesting things to process. The stimulus hunger of brains will trigger them to play the old B-rated movies or hallucinate freely.

#2: Brains Externalize Directions

Our external world will only be as exciting, vibrant, dramatic, and powerful as our internal frames of mind. So, as you decorate your internal world of mind, imagination, and memory with hopes, desires, wonders, delights, Etc., you alter the quality and content of the instructions that you give to your brain.

What kind of images, sounds, words, sensations, do you have running on the inside of your brain; this will create your external world, your reality. This is the essence of "The Secret" or the Law of Attraction.

Both failures and success are figments of the mind. Embedded in your mind frame should be "success at all times." However, success does not equate to perfectionism because it does not have any true criterion, so the measurement is subjective.

#3: Brains Run on Representations

If we picture a beautiful day with blue skies and white clouds and a green grass lawn facing the white sands of a gorgeous ocean view and imagine feeling the warm ocean breeze blowing through our hair and the smell of the salt water and the sounds of children playing and enjoy our favorite drink while getting a neck and back massage from our special loved one. Well, it doesn't take long before our body and neurology responds to those representations as if they were instructions about how to feel.

Because brains run on representations, the more expressive, vivid, dramatic, and sensory-specific, the easier it is for us to tell our brains where to go and what to feel. Then the screen play is clearer and easier to follow. Our eyes only scan a very narrow part of the electromagnetic spectrum. Our ears only receive a very narrow band of sound wave frequencies. So we have to be pretty selective, as a movie director, about what we play on our internal Cinema. Choose well, it's your brain.

#4: Brains Transition In and Out of the Present Moment

This is the foundation of all daydreaming, night dreaming, fantasizing, learning, creativity, invention, thinking, conceptualizing, mathematizing, theorizing, Etc. This is what we humans do best. We can leave our current situation and travel to distance places, times, and worlds. This is why Autistic children appear to be in their own world, yet happy.

We call this thinking. It's also hypnosis. It's also trance. It can be many things: imagination, fantasy, creativity, and hallucination. This means that we are not stuck or limited to this present moment. What freedom of mind we have! Our brains love to zone out, this why the technology media has been able to entrain a lot of minds. We mostly live in hypnotic states not sensory aware states in this present moment. This is why meditation can help alleviate a lot of anxieties because it brings the mind back to the present sensory state.

#5: Brains Induce States

Brains put us into neurological states. They affect our physiology, breathing, movement, and internal chemistry. To work up a good mad, we only have to think angry thoughts of injustice and violation. We only have to think about a dangerous threat and off we go into a fear state. And some representations of sexuality can induce our body to experience desire and lust; this is the basis of pornography. This gives us two royal roads into a mind-body state of consciousness whether it is confidence and joy and love or fear, anger, and sadness.

#6: Brains Go In Circles

Our brains are not strictly logical. To think in a straightforward way and to stay on that path for more than a few seconds is very difficult for our brains; that's why mathematics and formal logic seem so foreign to us. It's not the natural habit of our mind. We think in circles. Our brains go around in loops and spirals. We keep reprocessing the same tired old thoughts. This is what allows us to layer thought upon thought, feeling upon feeling, thought upon feeling, memory upon imagination, fear upon anger, dread upon worry, joy upon learning. This is how chunking our experiences together works, often times one scene is a reminder of an earlier trigger.

#7: Brains Frame Things

Brains deal with data overload by making generalizations. They create categories for items; they organize things into groups. This allows us to develop contextual meanings from our frames, giving us an even higher way to interpret things. This is one of the greatest powers of our brain for health and sanity but also for insanity and destructiveness, dependent on how your brain frames things.

The brain creates two levels of meaning for learning: associative and contextual. Associative meaning arises when we link up one thing with another thing. What does a cookie mean? It depends on what you have associated with a cookie. It could mean a sweet or junk food. It could mean reward or lack of nutrition. It could mean delight and fun; it could mean threat to my diet. It could mean survival, it could mean fat. Because brains link ideas, images, feelings, things easily become associated. This creates triggers. This is why if you truly want to deal with repressed emotions/feelings, you need to go back to the original trigger.

Then there is contextual or frame meaning for things. We first associate a harsh tone of voice with being spanked. Later we develop ideas and concepts that people who strain their vocal chords are mean, hurtful, and nasty. Then we develop higher frames that "criticism is bad," "confrontation always ruins things," "I'm sensitive to criticism," "I cannot handle that tone of voice," Etc. These thoughts create the higher frames of mind about an event and semantically load that event. So when someone strains the vocal chords, the meanings you experience in relation to that event put you into very non-resourceful states. All of this happens so quickly that on the inside it seems like and feels like "the criticism" (or harsh tonality) makes me upset, angry, or frustrated.

We all know people (perhaps we have been such) who experience one or more negative events in life and then (to make things worse), build their lives around that event. Center your life around a tragedy, misfortune, or injustice and you gain the proud label of "victim" and feel like life is out of your control also known as STRESS.

Food For Thought?

Did you know the brain can sense when danger is around? This is why when we eat something bad for us, we vomit! This signaling is done by the brain to protect us again garbage. But sometimes it feels like the stomach is more intelligent than the brain. Because when we feed it toxic ideas, poisonous thoughts, limiting beliefs, irrational conclusions, and inaccurate mapping, if you have other stressors that are more important to deal with, it doesn't know any better than to represent it, assume it is real, and then believe it.

Since the brain is reactive to our thoughts and emotions, it will repress certain environmental or other signals that can be potentially harmful. For example, we also have probably drunk sodas before in our life? We know that the soda is pretty harmful but our minds took over and it convinced us that the taste was what we needed to satisfy our thirst and that the sugar and caffeine would not be a detrimental factor if we consumed it just this one time, and then it became a habit.

This analogy provides you with how your brain has been censoring and persuading your thought process. Whether the information is accurate, useful, true, productive, hurtful, unintelligent, it doesn't seem to matter because your brain cannot distinguish between what is real and imagined. This is why visualization works so well towards healing and why the placebo effect works.

Consider anything that your brain produces in your body such as emotions, speech, behavior, relationships that puts you in constant conflict, that keeps repeating patterns that don't work, that creates incongruity, ineffectiveness and become barriers to resourcefulness. These negative thoughts, limiting beliefs are crippling you from achieving your mind's fullest potential.

Playing an old record of your old movies of hurt, pain, fear in the theater of your mind will only bring back these negative emotions. Wasn't it enough to live thru these painful memories once? This process is ludicrous to repeat because initially you had no choice because life presented this opportunity/challenge. Why are you going to replay it over and over again and punish yourself by reliving that incident with guilt and remorse, is that the lesson you were supposed to learn from the experience?

Brains are always learning; that's the good news. The bad news is that if you don't take charge of what they are learning, they will learn irrationality if you keep playing absurdity. As Albert Einstein, the genius behind the mind, stated, "Insanity is doing the same thing over and over again and expecting different results."

The Real Definition of Ego

"Whether you think you can, or whether you think you can't – you're right."

–Henry Ford–

Your brain reacts upon all stimulations from both the inside and outside of your body to assign a representation or a meaning. This means that all of your emotions, speech, behavior, and actions are influenced by a subjectivity factor, implying that the process is "liable to error." By restraining from our authentic self and becoming too serious (mature), we are typically undermining important human attributes such as humor, laughter, enjoyment, playfulness, silliness, and ludicrousness; and we lose our inner child.

The loss of perspective in life will be destroyed if our sense of humor and even our laughter is gone. This is the true nature of our soul and our truthfulness to be happy and joyful. If you look at babies when they are first born, they come out with a smile, not frowns, worries, anger this is the inner child that often gets hidden from the world as we mature in life.

Since the mind is controlling the brain and our body, some aspect of the human body wants to be authentic and speak our truths, but this will require courage and strength and as humans from an early age we have been conditioned to conform and assimilate. So our ego reminds us of the fear of being criticized, embarrassed or devalued for speaking and portraying the truth our authenticity.

Our ego often reminds us of past wounds that may not be fully healed and as such it gives a perception that it is sparing us from future pain by triggering the "fight" and "flight" response so that we are not further impacted. However, should you allow other people's judgments and perceptions to shape your reality; this is the ultimate question for your brain to ponder over?

You can often spot a person that is operating on ego a mile away, when their own beliefs get challenged, they explode with anger, rage, stress and fear and they begin rallying up the troops so that their beliefs will be validated. Their thoughts are how can someone challenge me or judge me; does this remind you of a two-year old throwing a tantrum? Who really controls your mind, are you empowering it or allowing it to be controlled by others' perceptions?

So many people value credentials in the form of titles and advanced degrees and believe it bestows upon them an "I know it all" entitlement. They act as if their opinions are sacred and should serve as factual. Doctors, educators, and bureaucrats often fall into this fallacy. You'll even begin to be seduced to thinking you are perfect (or should be), know it all (or should), and be everywhere and do everything (hence, indispensable); this is in truth your ego speaking.

By feeding your brain and your mind with inspiring emotions, thoughts and data you will become empowered by your beliefs and values and bring an utmost caring and supportive perspective to others; this is truly added value. Since the mind is powered by your brain, you can code and recode your destiny or your life movie to a better and exciting adventure that is filled with power and energy.

Forget "why" things went wrong and why some people are choosing ignorance; instead focus your energies and mind on resources that will make a positive impact for you and your family and model from those that have reached the state of an "outstanding" caliber in their life's accomplishment. The 2% that sets the bar for the rest of the population has learned to perform at these standards. To emulate their success it will take perseverance, accountability for your mind and actions in addition to resourcefulness to excel beyond your wildest imagination.

As Stephen Covey stated, "Live out of your imagination, not your history." You can use your imagination to create the future that you desire. As the old saying goes, "Your Wish Is Your Command." By looking out of the rear view mirror of life, you will not progress far; however, if you use your imagination to look ahead, you are destined for success.

After you practice this for a couple years, you will have habituated (formed a habit) the Movies of the Experts in your mind and embodied their emotions and characteristics. Since your brain does not know the difference between imagination and reality, you are creating your future, a more loving future. As we said, you and your baby can become Billionaires; if that is the reality you want to create. As humans you have the choice.

Latest Trends in Psychology

Media Psychology

The Media Psychology Division of the American Psychology Association (APA) investigates the human dynamics associated with technological interactions such as video games, online learning and internet resources such as Google, Yahoo and other media. Recent studies now validate the reality of a new disorder called, Internet Addiction Disorder (IAD.) IAD can cause tremors, shivers, nausea and anxiety in some addicts which may be considered analogous to substance abuse.

Attention spans are decreasing because of the exposure to excessively stimulating and fast-paced media. Research has shown that people with internet addiction have demonstrable changes in their brains. They have found that both in the connections between cells and in the brain areas that control attention, executive control, and emotional processing to be impacted. Most intriguing is the fact that some of these changes replicate what you see happening in the brains of people addicted to cocaine, heroin, special K, and other addictive substances.

American Pediatrics suggests that children shouldn't watch television until they are three. Watching 20 minutes of television will have a negative effect on problem solving and being able to pay attention. Spending too much time watching television is also linked to Alzheimer's in adults so can you imagine the effects that it can have on developing brains.

Positive Psychology

Historically, most psychologists were more interested in what constituted abnormal behaviors (weaknesses) rather than promoting the strengths of a person (intrinsic motivators.) Studies have shown that angry or critical parents can actually alter a child's happiness level until it is set around age 16. New research states that if a person sits quietly for a half-hour a day just thinking about kindness and compassion, their brain will show noticeable changes within just two weeks.

At UCLA Davis, the Shamantha Project reveals that measurable levels of happiness and empathy can be increased by simply meditating on a daily basis with compassion and love that begins from the heart. This is the most comprehensive research study to-date for the physiological and psychological benefits of meditation. Would it be beneficial to find an endless supply of happiness?

Research suggests that all individuals have this source if they can tap into the inner source of happiness, known as compassion. The study reveals that children engaging in bullying practices and people prone to depression could easily resolve their psychological issues with this inner source. The study revealed that increased levels and intensities of happiness and empathy occurred when people became more compassionate.

Across the spectrum of religions and cultures, many traditions speak of loving-kindness principles as wishing happiness onto others and compassion for relieving the suffering of others. Loving-kindness and compassion are the Dalai Lama's philosophy and mission. Wouldn't the world be a better place if one can develop a heightened sense of compassion towards our fellow human beings? Wouldn't that make us all a better person and role model for our children and grandchildren?

Psychologists Karen Reivich and Jane Gillham developed the Penn Resiliency Program. It is a school-based curriculum that teaches educators, parents, and ultimately kids the core skills of resilience and other tenets of positive psychology. They have implemented this program in schools in Australia, United Kingdom and the United States.

This program is a key resilience-building skill that teaches children how to identify the link between self-talk, what's playing on kids' "internal radios" and kids' feelings and behaviors. Negative self-talk can create self-fulfilling prophecies, leading kids to behave in ways that create new situations that only reinforce the negative thoughts they have about themselves. Say, for example, that a child does poorly on an algebra test. That may prompt her to think, "I can't do math," fueling feelings of discouragement and sadness. Because of those thoughts, she stops studying and then fails the next exam.

Psychoneuroimmunology

Dr. Candace Pert, neuroscientist was a key figure in the discovery of the endorphin molecule, the body's natural form of morphine. She is regarded as the mother of a new field of science known as psychoneuroimmunology. It is a powerful combination of the theories of psychology, neurology and immunology to investigate dis-ease.

The work of Dr. Pert and her colleagues showed a variety of proteins known as peptides (including endorphins) are among the body's key "information substances." They also have shown that each of them could affect one's mind, our emotions, our immune system, our digestion and other bodily functions simultaneously. Research of her findings was captured within a book called, "Molecules of Emotion."

Emotions have largely been ignored within the traditional confines of science and medicine. According to Dr. Candice Pert and Dr. Bruce Lipton, they are actually the key to understanding the complete picture of how body and mind affect each other. For example, it's through the emotion peptide (hormone) that an embarrassing thought can cause blood vessels to dilate and turn a face beet red.

For decades most people thought of the brain and its extension of the central nervous system as an electrical communication system which communicate between neurons firing at synapses to make connections. However, new research is discovering that this occurs approximately 2% of the time.

Dr. Pert hypothesized that the "the brain is a bag of hormones." And those hormones affect not only the brain, but every aspect of body and mind. Her book illustrates that many memories are stored throughout the body; these emotions are stored at the cellular level structure. Dr. Pert concludes that the body is the "unconscious mind" and the brain the conscious mind. This is why many alternative practitioners view dis-ease as being metaphysical because there is an emotional trigger for the physical manifestations within the body.

This further provides evidence of why the Emotional Clearings offered at the Gainesville Holistic Center was able to help remove emotional toxins even without any form of hypnosis or access to the mind. For some patients that held their emotions at the cellular/molecular level, they were able to detoxify those emotions by simply having the Etheric Weaver rebalance their energy. Other patients required the subliminal intervention using the Pulse Technique to release the unconscious emotions bottled-up in their minds.

The Biology of the Mind

"Biology gives you a brain. Life turns it into a mind."
–Jeffrey Eugenides, Middlesex–

When your brain is in balance your ability to think, learn, create and recall is remarkably enhanced. Perception expands, memory improves and you can concentrate more easily. You sleep better and are more resilient to stress. A balanced brain brings freedom from fear, worry and even addictions that have stood in the way of you experiencing more fulfillment and joy.

Why Are Primitive Reflexes So Important?

From very early on intrauterine, the primitive reflex movements literally help develop the brain. The movements lay down the patterns of neural networks and myelinization (development of growth) of pathways that allow the connection of the various areas of the brain that are so important later on for learning, behavior, communication, relationships and emotional well-being.

Primitive (brainstem-level) Reflexes are repetitive, automatic movements that are essential for development of the body's control, muscle tone, sensory integration and development. As newborns we are pretty vulnerable. Most of our brain hasn't turned on yet and, even if it had, we don't have the dataset to recognize what's safe and what's not.

To survive the first several months of life, we are endowed with *Primitive Reflexes* that tell us when to hide or be still, when to fight or run, allow us to recognize "self" versus "not-self", and help us perform other crucial acts. These primitive reflexes are normally integrated into our developing nervous system within 2 to 9 months after birth as they are replaced by recognizing "safe" from "dangerous" and by postural reflexes which allow us to crawl then walk.

If they are not absorbed or integrated, they get in the way of the postural reflexes and cognitive skills that normally follow. *Retained Primitive Reflexes* (RPR's) can cause anxiety, depression, and fearfulness, attention deficits and learning difficulties, sensory integration disorders, extreme shyness, lack of confidence, addiction, constant feelings of feeling overwhelmed, bullying, tantrums, and aggression, inability to recognize social cues, speech delays, bedwetting, fidgeting, thumb sucking, and many of the challenges seen among children and adults with learning, behavioral, and emotional issues.

Interestingly, it's not just newborns and children who show signs of RPR's. We commonly see them reappear following traumatic and hypoxic injuries and in kids and adults who have been through harsh emotional events. When I first started treating people with RPR's I tested almost everyone and found one or more of them in the vast majority of our patients. What a wonderful improvement people made when these were cleared out of their way!

Parents who are aware of RPR's have usually learned about them through the book Reflexes, Learning and Behavior written by Sally Goddard Blythe and through the work of the Institute of Neuro-Physiological Psychology in England. Her book popularized the importance of RPR's as hindrances to healthy neural and emotional development and describes them well from a lay therapist's perspective.

The best clinical therapies for RPR's have come from a group of Osteopaths and Chiropractors in Sydney, Australia including my good friend and mentor Dr. Keith Keen. Happily, more and more behavioral optometrists are also becoming aware of the role RPR play in brain performance, including several of our local optometrists.

Combining the best of INPP (Institute for Neuro-Physiological Psychology) and the Sydney group, we have been able to consistently identify and clear RPR's with completely non-invasive approaches, primarily using chiropractic Craniopathy and sacral adjusting, eye positions, acupressure points, and targeted neurotransmitter therapies. We also integrate RPR work with clinical nutrition, drug-free neurology, and chiropractic, but even done by itself the results are impressive.

Causes of Retained Primitive Reflexes

Children born via cesarean section, trauma, toxicity exposure, anesthetics, chemicals, genetics, impaired detoxification pathways Etc., are more at risk at having retained primitive reflexes which may cause the brainstem and higher centers to get overwhelmed.

Other causes may be: insufficient tummy time as an infant, lack of, or little, creeping or crawling, early walkers, head injuries, excessive falls, and chronic ear infections.

Other causes may also involve physical, neurological and biochemical which is all based upon learning and adaptation for the brain and sensory systems. But the most common trigger to the retained primitive reflexes and the sudden onset or sudden trigger in life is: emotional stressors. These emotional stressors can happen in the womb and outside the womb. Ninety percent of all physical dis-ease stems from emotional stressors.

Integration of the Primitive Reflexes Becomes Important Because

- They are the basics of our nervous system and our ability to move.
- They originate in the brain stem. This area of the brain is responsible for survival. If under stress are minds are still moving then we are not able to easily access our prefrontal cortex where we can process and readily analyze information. Instead we stay in survival and stress modes.
- As we get older our unintegrated reflexes trigger the fight or flight response even when there is no 'logical' reason for the stress. So stressed behavior becomes our pattern of responding.
- When our movements come from active primitive reflex movement patterns then there are challenges with coordination. This can lead to reading and writing difficulties, language and speech delays, disorganization, fidgeting, concentration Etc. Other challenges may be seen in poor bladder control, breathing difficulties, skin problems, and having an uncontrollable sweet tooth.
- Low muscle tones, muscle weakness, chronic body aches, poor endurance and fatigue.

Retained Primitive Reflexes may Disrupt

- Vestibular function (balance)
- Auditory perception and integration
- Visual and oculomotor function
- Gross and fine motor coordination
- Hemispheric integration
- Endocrine and neurochemical functionality
- Social cueing and individual behavior
- Learning

What Can Cause Retained Primitive Reflexes?

Unintegrated, active primitive reflexes may be caused by:

- Stress of the mother and/or baby during pregnancy; breech birth, birth trauma, caesarean birth, induced birth
- Lack of proper movement in infancy: being placed in baby walkers/rings, jumpers, being left for long periods of time in car seats/baby capsules, and being placed in front of TV in bouncers all restrict critical movements required for brain development
- Illness, trauma, injury, chronic stress
- Environmental toxins, complications with vaccinations
- Dietary imbalances or sensitivities

Reflexes that are inhibited and integrated in infancy can later reactivate because of trauma, injury, toxins and stress.

Type of Retained Primitive Reflexes

Fear Paralysis Reflex

This reflex is the first Primitive Reflex developed and, when all is well, the first integrated. If you have ever seen a deer or bunny try to hide by freezing in position, you have seen the FPR working. Normally, it's active during the first couple months of life and integrates by the age of 2 to 3 months. Beyond this, it can cause withdrawal, fear of new or different experiences, anxiety and panic attacks, hypersensitivity to sensory information, elective mutism, and even Sudden Infant Death Syndrome. Since it begins and is normally integrated first, a retained Fear Paralysis Reflex can affect integration of any other primitive reflex.

The Moro Reflex

This reflex is the "fight or flight" reflex. Where FPR creates the ultimate passive response, the Moro Reflex responds to excesses of light, sound, or touch very actively. If not integrated within the normal 3-6 months following birth, it creates automatic and uncontrollable overreactions that can range from withdrawal to immature, aggressive, even violent responses or "temper tantrums" that the person is unable to turn off. The constant drain this puts on the adrenal glands and immune system can lead to symptoms including allergies, asthma, and sugar handling problems, chronic illness, and chronic fatigue.

Asymmetric Tonic Neck Reflex

This reflex is involved with recognizing "Self" vs. "Not-Self" and developing depth perception and hand-eye coordination. It should normally be integrated by about six months. Otherwise, we see people who miss social cues and behave inappropriately to their social settings, have trouble with tasks that involve coordinating both sides of the body (e.g. catching or throwing a ball,) and struggle with organizing and expressing an idea. With kids, efforts to write are frustrated by an excessive pressure or a clenched-fist grip. In adults we see recurrent, often same-sided shoulder injuries.

Tonic Labyrinthine Reflex

This reflex is about balance. If not integrated at the right time (6-9 months) retained TLRs throw off balance, head-righting reflexes, and the visual system. There may be trouble judging space, distance, depth, and sound. People with retained TLRs are often plagued by motion sickness. They may run into things repeatedly or have trouble finding their "indoor voice." Looking up at a blackboard then down at a desk creates neurological disorganization for them, causing loss of attention and problems studying. They are often diagnosed as ADHD, but drugs rarely solve their problems.

Spinal Galant Reflex

This reflex is the wriggling reflex that helps us out of the womb. It should be integrated within the first year. Otherwise, it results in "ants in the pants" kids who cannot sit still, resulting in reduced attention and memory and frequent scolding from teachers and others. The SGR is closely connected with bladder control and since it is an automatic reflex, it can cause involuntary bedwetting despite all efforts to stop. This reflex can also affect walking and gait and contributes to spinal scoliosis.

Other Reflexes To Check

There are other reflexes, including the Juvenile Suck Reflex and the Palmar and Plantar Reflexes which can fail to integrate. These generally clear when the Big 5 listed above are integrated, but they should also be checked since they can cause problems of speech and dexterity themselves. A retained Suck Reflex can create dental problems that make learning speech difficult as well as interfering with the adult swallow reflex that pushes food down the throat. Mouthing the words as one reads or writes them or as they draw is a telltale sign of the retained Palmar/Plantar Reflex. Have your doctor check these and the "Big 5" above to assure that your child grows up to be healthy, happy, and successful.

Each Part of the Brain Learns a Subject

- The Frontal Lobe: It is the seat of emotions and judgments related to sympathy, which is the ability to feel sorrow for someone else's suffering, and empathy, which is the ability to understand another's feelings and problems.
- The Temporal Lobes: They are responsible for interpreting speech and sound. Visual and long term memory is also interpreted within this part of the brain.
- The Occipital Lobe: It is responsible for interpreting visual information, especially the ability for musicians to read sheet music.
- The Parietal Lobes: They are responsible for interpreting stimuli, sensory integration and orientation. This area is shown to have high performance in gifted and highly sensitive children. The left lobe process arithmetic. Hence, those with damage to the left lobe have difficulty with math. The left and right lobes are responsible for multiplying, subtracting and comparing numbers.
- The Hippocampus: This area converts short term in to long term memory. Gifted and highly sensitive children often have a well-developed hippocampus.
- The Amygdala: This is linked to emotional behavior most significantly fear.
- The Hypothalamus: This structure is the main controller of the autonomic system. The hypothalamus is essential to integrate the nervous system, the immune system and the endocrine system. The hormonal aspect of the hypothalamus control is partially to the digestive system and, secondly for motivational control behavior aspects and, the third aspect, involves the stress and emotional changes.

Brain Waves and Healing Effects

Our brain produce 5 frequencies (beta, alpha, theta, delta and gamma), the theta brainwave range is the one in which the body and mind's natural self-healing processes are activated and optimized. There needs to be a healthy equilibrium since all brain waves are important for the well-being of a person.

Kelly Howell has more than 30 years of experience in brainwave research. Her work led to the creation of Brain Sync to benefit medical professionals such as Harvard trained Neurosurgeon, Norman Shealy, M.D. PhD and Edward A. Taub, M.D.

She has worked with eminent scientists to develop meditation and brain optimization programs used in hospitals, biofeedback clinics and by hundreds of thousands of individuals worldwide. These meditation CDs are designed to access and rebalance all the brain waves. Brain Sync programs have been clinically tested with a record-breaking 87% success rate and are offered to patients at America's most prestigious hospitals (http://www.brainsync.com.)

- ## Theta Brain Waves

  Theta brainwave dominance is often found in highly creative individuals. Theta is also known as the dreaming waves. Theta brainwaves are more numerous in highly creative people like talented musicians, inventors, and artists. Through entraining theta brainwaves your creativity will be enhanced. Additionally, theta brainwaves are associated with your ability to feel emotions. Blocked or suppressed emotions can be experienced when theta brainwaves are stimulated. This is the essence of how Theta Healing works.

  Theta brainwaves allow your brain to retain over 300% more information than your normal daily capabilities with the sentient knowledge that is applied using the Beta Brainwaves. Theta brain waves allows for a quicker learning process, similar to osmosis. Since children from birth to around 7 years old are using more theta brainwaves, research demonstrated this reasoning for children's ability to quickly learn new concepts such as foreign language.

- ## Gamma Brain Waves

  The fastest brainwave is also known as gamma wave and it brings a higher state of focus and cognition. Most medications use the type of gamma brainwave to focus, increasing concentration and improving learning. It can help ADD/ADHD in their lack of concentration and depression and other mood changes since it will boost the mood, empathy and compassion levels. Ultimately, this brainwave will also raise your overall energy levels.

- ## Beta Brain Waves

  Beta brainwaves are active when we begin to focus a lot and it results in attentiveness. This is where children with ADD/ADHD exhibit less of these brain waves and an overabundance of Theta brainwaves. During the "fight or flight" response this brain wave will be activated which will disrupt the hippocampus during the stressed periods. This will also affect the long-term memories abilities since the hippocampus is involved in the majority of the memories that the brain utilizes.

On a daily basis, our life is filled with work and family obligations to deliver outcomes, multi-tasking of numerous priorities and daily activities that involve talking, calculating and task orientation which will primarily utilize Beta brain waves. An excess of this brain wave will generate physical distress and cause a majority of the health problems associated with stress. The EEGs of children diagnosed with ADD/ADHD have shown little to no beta brain wave activity; furthermore watching television causes beta brain waves to be suppressed; this is why many children that appear to have ADHD characteristics become calmer when watching a television or tablet.

- Alpha Brain Waves

The stress reduction wave is called the alpha state. It is also known to bring high creativity. Albert Einstein was operating in an alpha state mainly. The alpha waves act as a bridge between the subconscious mind (the theta waves) and the conscious part (beta waves.) Information, feelings, creativity, memories, which are deep down in one's mind, cannot become conscious if there is no bridge (no alpha waves,) between the two states of mind. The alpha waves slow down the heart which is conducive for those having heart problems. Alpha waves occur at the beginning and ending of the meditation phases so that you are able to consciously recall some of the visions that you saw, similar to a daydream state. A healthier form of promoting alpha brain waves would be to meditate instead of watching television. By talking less, you will increase the alpha states of the mind. Normally during the day, we are either operating on beta or alpha brain waves.

- Delta Brain Waves

Research has shown that the Delta waves help the release of the anti-aging hormone including human growth hormone (HGH), melatonin and DHEA. The HGH is stimulated by the pituitary gland. In healthy amounts, delta brainwaves can also cause a person to have an advanced state of empathy, understanding, and compassion for others. People diagnosed with ADD/ADHD already have too much delta brain waves so further promotion would not be ideal. The immune system works more efficiently when it is attuned into the delta brain waves. Cortisol levels decrease with delta brain waves stimulation.

- Binaural Beats

In 1839, physicist Heinrich Wilhem Dove discovered the concept of Binaural beats. The concept involves presenting signals of two different frequencies within each ear. The brain then notices the variation between the differing signals and tries to reconcile by creating a matching third frequency known as the binaural beat. So for example, if the first sound occurs at 220 Hz and the second sound at 210 Hz, the brain will create a binaural beat at 10 Hz. Listed below are the brainwave states and physiological conditions associated with each of the associated binaural wattages:

Visit, the following YouTube video, to receive a free healing session using Binaural Beats: (http://www.youtube.com/watch?v=kLtEbacLD8I)

12.0 Hz	Promotes mental clarity and aids with throat chakra
11.5 Hz	Increases intelligence and mental efficiency
11.0 Hz	Achieves a relaxed yet alert state of mind
10.5 Hz	Activates energy and freedom, promotes abilities to achieve, improves immunity, promotes healing in body, lowers blood pressure
10.0 Hz	Effective state for learning; good against a hangover or jet lag, increases alertness and improves memory, spelling, and reading; effectiveness for ADD/ADHD
9.5 Hz	Bridges the subconscious and conscious minds
9.0 Hz	Associated with the Sacral chakra
8.0 Hz	Effective for learning new information and self-healing
7.5 Hz	Effective for promoting creative thought of art and music and for learning math and science
7.0 Hz	Treats sleep disturbances
6.5 Hz	Activates the creative frontal lobe
6.0 Hz	Promotes long term memory stimulation, helps to reduce procrastination/laziness
5.5 Hz	Promotes intuition and reveals inner guidance
5.0 Hz	Reduces amount of sleep needed and provides creative measures for problem solving
4.5 Hz	Promotes imagination and fosters creativity
4.0 Hz	Fosters creative insight and promotes vivid mental imagery
3.5 Hz	Effective for depression and anxiety, stimulates DNA for regeneration of wholeness
3.0 Hz	Regenerates muscles and increases reaction time
2.5 Hz	Mirrors a sedative effect that provides natural pain relief
2.0 Hz	Regenerates nerves
1.5 Hz	Treats sleep disturbances and promotes overall healing
1.05 Hz	Releases Human Growth Hormone (HGH)
1.0 Hz	Fosters release of many hormones that promotes emotional wellness
0.5 Hz	Regenerates nerves, super relaxing for sleep

Are You Dreaming Your Life Away?

Researcher Calvin S. Hall collected more than 50,000 dream accounts over a period of forty years. In 1990, these reports were made public by his prodigy, William Domhoff. These reports revealed that dreams are in fact a form of revealing emotions that have been repressed. According to researcher, J.

Allan Hobson, about 95% of all dreams are quickly forgotten before awakening because the frontal lobes that activate long-term memory are not active.

Emotions such as joy, happiness, anxiety and fear were often represented in these accounts; of which anxiety was the most predominant pattern found. In general, more people appeared to express more negative emotions during their dreams than positive ones; which leads to further research opportunities of whether this is an outlet for repressed emotions to safely be represented to humans.

Fun Facts About Dreams

- Men's dreams consists of about 70% men characters; whereas, women tend to dream about both genders equally and women tend to have more déjà vu dreams.
- Frankenstein was based on a dream that Mary Shelley had, however, most people forget their dreams within 10 minutes after awakening.
- Most people over the age of 10 have anywhere between 4-6 dreams a night; during a year that equates to 2,190 dreams. We spend about 1/3 of our lives sleeping; however, the body burns more calories due to the brain's activity.
- Psychologist, Jennie Parker conducted a study that women experience more nightmares than males.

This Is Your Brain on Drugs – STRESS

Stress and Pregnancy

Did you know that during early pregnancy, approximately 250,000 neurons develop per minute within your fetus? Stress is a silent dis-ease," says Dr. Calvin Hobel, Director of maternal-fetal medicine at Cedars Sinai and a professor of obstetrics/gynecology and pediatrics at UCLA. According to him, the number one priority during pregnancy is to educate women to recognize stressors throughout the duration of their pregnancy. This is why the Whole-Listic Children's Hospatal will emphasize that all expectant mothers be enrolled in the "Angel Mom" program 6 months prior to their delivery date.

A llow your baby to flourish with the
N eeded nutrients physically and mentally. Allow him/her to
G row properly by
E nsuring no toxins impact their mental and physical health and
L et the beauty and miracle of life grow to the fullest potential.

Dr. Wadhwa stated that: "at each stage of development, the fetus uses cues from its environment to decide how best to construct itself within the parameters of its DNA genes, the basis of epigenetic." In essence, stress is an example of how a fetus responds to stimuli in the womb and adapts physiologically. Chronic or extreme maternal stress may also cause changes in the blood flow to the baby, making it difficult to carry oxygen and other important nutrients to the baby's developing organs.

Some effects from the maternal stress during pregnancy might involve pre-term birth and low birth weight, however these are more long-term effects. Pre-term babies may be susceptible to multiple complications including lung development, developmental delays, learning disorders and even mortality. Animal research studies revealed that babies who experience stress intrauterine are more likely to develop chronic health problems as adults, such as heart dis-ease, high blood pressure and diabetes.

Baby temperaments and neurobehavioral development may be affected by stress in the wombs according to animal studies. Some research also shows the link between the mother's stresses, particularly in the third trimester; it showed signs of more depression and irritability (colic) during their infant and toddler development. When the mother is stressed, there is an increased likelihood of intrauterine infection that can cross over to the placenta.

Research studied data from 1.38 million Danish births occurring between 1973 and 1995, and found out that children of women who experienced the death of a close relative during their first trimester had a 67% greater risk of developing schizophrenia and related disorders later on.

Emotional Stressors and Depression

More than 400,000 people attempts suicides in the US per year because of depression which is more common than "cancer" and diabetes. Since the signs for depression are often subtle it often goes unrecognized. A Kaiser Permanente study on adverse childhood experiences with 17,000 participants found that childhood exposure to violence, domestic abuse, family neglect or other environmental stressors can have lifelong consequences, including a higher probability of depression.

Since our body does not have resources or strategies learned during our lifetime to defend itself against emotional stressors or psychological abuse, it carries it over time and often times repress it into your subconscious levels. Your body pays a heavy physiological price for every moment that you feel anxious, tense, frustrated, and angry. Emotional stress sets off a series of reactions in your body that involve your sympathetic nervous system, it slows or even shuts down your digestive system to not waste blood, nutrients, and oxygen that could be used to run or fight; thus depression and obesity often go hand-in-hand.

Oxidative Stressors and ADD/ADHD

The oxygen we breathe creates interaction within each cell which produces cell energy. As a consequence of this activity, highly reactive molecules are produced known as free radicals which cause oxidative stress to your body. Your body's internal production of antioxidants is not enough to neutralize all the free radicals and as such foods such as tomatoes, carrots, black tea, green tea and oolong tea, citrus fruits, turmeric, glutathione and SOD (Sodium Dismutase) and Xoçai Healthy Chocolates can ensure that you obtain your daily needed dosage of antioxidants. Studies have shown a direct relationship between ADHD/ADD and oxidative stress.

Chemical Stressors and Obesity

When we reach for fattening comfort foods during stressful times, this process may be generated in order to attempt to self-medicate. "When you eat carbohydrates, it raises the body's serotonin level. Researchers have also discovered that chronic stress can cause the body to release excess cortisol, a hormone critical in managing fat storage and energy used in the human body. Cortisol is known to increase appetite and may encourage cravings for sugary or fatty foods.

Researchers linked a molecule called neuropeptide Y that is released from nerve cells during stress and encourages fat accumulation which a diet high in fat and sugar appears to further increase its release. Listed below are 13 foods that aid with alleviating stress from your body: asparagus, avocado, organic berries (blueberries, strawberries, blackberries, and raspberries), cashews, chamomile tea, healthy chocolate (Xoçai), garlic, grass fed beef, green tea, oatmeal, oranges, oysters, and walnuts.

Environmental Stressors and Autism

June 2013, Harvard school of Public Health found that American women who were exposed to high levels of air pollution (environmental stressors) while pregnant were twice as likely to have a child with autism as women who lived in areas with low pollution. Exposure to diesel particulates, lead, manganese, mercury, methylene chloride and other pollutants are known to affect brain functionality and to affect the developing baby. Two previous studies also found associations between exposure to air pollution during pregnancy and autism in children. Dr. Seuss' book, the Lorax, should serve as a reminder that we have an obligation to protect our environment for generations to come.

The Metaphysics of the Mind

"Be the change that you wish to see in the world."

–Mahatma Gandhi–

The Voices of Your Dis-ease

The body and psyche have been linked since Sigmund Freud. Our body has an innate capacity to know when something is not right. Our body wills communication by various means to let us know that dis-ease is in eminent. Sometimes we receive subtle signals and sometimes it is more drastic. Normally the process is unconscious.

In essence the body is telling us that we have a "faulty" way of thinking which causes a disharmony which will not benefit our state of balance and health. So when illness or dis-ease comes, it indicates that our change in belief systems reached its physical and psychological limits. They are warning signs to reconnect ourselves toward a holistic or balanced mind-body-spirit state of health.

Since 90% of our emotional states affect our physiology, i.e. our physical aspect, the most frequent negative emotions that are dis-ease causing agents are fear, anger, guilt, abandonment, resentment, denial, grief and shame. Those who are vulnerable to the suggestion that illness is 'contagious' will attract illness because they expect to be sick as a result of circumstances. This is how the placebo effect works and this is the premise they are using for marketing the "flu" shots.

Since love holds the highest frequency, when in dis-ease state your body just needs to be reminded that you love yourself. Through genuine self-love you allow your heart to guide you to wellness and wholeness. As the old saying, goes, "Love is the best medicine." To love yourself is to give yourself permission to live as you choose. Loving yourself allows you to be in all your humility, with fears, weaknesses, desires, beliefs and aspirations that are all facets of who you truly are.

Louise Hay of Hay House Publishing has put forward the concept that every illness is a manifestation of unresolved emotional thoughts and experiences. Our mechanism of defense buries all bad feelings and negative emotions. In return our body will suffer its effects. These unresolved emotions cause blockages and a buildup of toxins in certain areas of our body. The longer emotions remain unresolved in our bodies, the more severe the dis-ease becomes. Every negative emotion that is stored in our bodies makes us more susceptible to infection, imbalance, dis-ease and eventually death.

The most effective way to fully discharge the build-up of energy from these blockages and blocked areas is to treat the physical, mind and emotional aspects for the symptoms so that the root trigger is being addressed. This is why Whole-Listic or holistic health treats not only the symptoms but the root causes of a dis-ease.

Louise Hay has published in her book, Heal Your Body, a listing of dis-ease conditions of the body and the probable emotional causes that she felt would lead to eventual physical dysfunction. Here are a few samples from her list that may help you identify key areas of emotional buildup that may be manifesting in your child's body:

Acne	Not accepting the self. Dislike of the self.
Allergies	Denying your own power.
Asthma	Smother love. Inability to breathe for one's self. Feeling stifled. Suppressed crying.
Bedwetting	Fear of parent, usually the father.
Cerebral Palsy	A need to unite the family in an action of love.
Colic	Mental irritation, impatience, annoyance in the surroundings.
Depression	Anger you feel you do not have a right to have. Hopelessness.
Diabetes	Longing for what might have been. A great need to control. Deep sorrow. No sweetness left.
Diarrhea	Fear. Rejection. Running off.

Eczema	Breath-taking antagonism. Mental eruptions.
Epilepsy	Sense of persecution. Rejection of life. A feeling of great struggle. Self-violence.
Fat or Weight Issues	Oversensitivity. Often represents fear and shows a need for protection. Fear may be a cover for hidden anger and a resistance to forgive, running away from feelings, insecurity, self-rejection and seeking fulfillment. • Arms: Anger at being denied love. • Belly: Anger at being denied nourishment. • Hips: Lumps of stubborn anger at the parents. • Thighs: Packed childhood anger. Often rage at the father.
Fever	Anger. Burning up.
Gas	Gripping. Fear. Undigested ideas.
Influenza	Response to mass negativity and beliefs. Fear. Belief in statistics.
Mononucleosis	Anger at not receiving love and appreciation. No longer caring for the self.
Nose	Represents self-recognition. • Nose Bleeds: A need for recognition. Feeling unnoticed. Crying for love. • Runny Nose: Asking for help. Inner crying. • Stuffy Nose: Not recognizing the self-worth.
Poison Ivy	Allergy Feeling defenseless and open to attack.
Throat	Avenue of expression. Channel of creativity. • Throat Problems: The inability to speak up for one's self. • Swallowed anger. Stifled creativity. Refusal to change. • Sore throat: Holding in
Tonsillitis	Repressed emotions. Stifled creativity.
Vomiting	Violent rejection of ideas. Fear of the new.

A Look Behind the Emotions

It is imperative to understand that the depth of the unresolved emotion and the wounds determines the depth of the depression or other dis-ease related to the illness. Rejection, abandonment, humiliation, betrayal, or injustice all set the stage for tremendous mental upheaval, especially if experienced in isolation and deep-rooted within our childhood past.

As young children many may not have anyone to talk to, to hear their questions and to share their anguish. If they do not learn to trust others, they will continue to withdraw and deny their desires. The depth of these unresolved emotions steam from the capacity of the brain to learn from infants to about 7 years of age and this will impact how well your child will face their future.

If we touch on obesity, experiencing the humiliation they did as a child has caused many of them to build a protective barrier to prevent them from being taken advantage of again. They thought they could achieve their goals by being a 'nice' person. However, this often led to taking on other people's burdens. It is important for these children to learn by what means to receive instead of always simply giving.

One way we all protect ourselves is to build up walls, psychological walls can shield our emotions and add layers to the depth of our unresolved hurts. Because that hurt was in relationship with others, saying no now often becomes difficult and these anxieties stem from our fears of other people's perceptions. This has often led us to take on extra loads due to the criterion of guilt.

The perception from others, for some, dictates their life into an unsatisfactory self-love life. You may feel sandwiched between two people (normally parents); doing everything you can to satisfy both. While doing this, you're completely out of touch with your own needs and then depression may set in later in life because you feel hopeless.

As a psychological and emotional way of protection, the weight gain may be a barrier against the opposite sex who may be "harming" you emotionally. You may believe that your bulk will not be attractive to the opposite sex and you will therefore avoid being hurt, humiliated or emotionally abused by them.

Maps of Consciousness

With the help of brain imaging, scientists can watch different parts of the brain activated and functioning. This technology can ultimately help alter the brain and our consciousness with surgeries or chemicals. Scientists are also trying to figure out the relationship between conscious and unconscious experiences of the mind.

Dr. David R. Hawkins, MD, PhD developed a map of the levels of human consciousness, called the Scale of Consciousness. Dr. Hawkins believes that every word and thought, as well as every intention, creates what is called an attractor field. Dr. Hawkins also wrote the book, Power vs. Force and would be a good resource for those aspiring for Leadership roles.

Feelings such as blame, anxiety, and hate fall into negative energy attractor fields; affirmation, trust, and optimism are examples of positive attractors that are life enhancing and ultimately lead to pure consciousness. By applying principles from kinesiology and acupuncture, Dr. Hawkins explains the association between positive attractor fields and one's health, well-being and creativity.

During his work, he explains that the lower levels of consciousness, vibrating below 200, are the most painful we experience and that pain drives us in our desire for understanding an inner growth. These lower levels of consciousness often known as ego are often dominated by our life due to the animal survival instincts; they are aligned with pleasure, predation and competition. These consciousness levels determine the reasons why people behave the way they do.

Dr. Hawkins scale:

- <u>Shame (20) – Feeling Hateful</u>

  According to Hawkins, this is one step above death. At this level, the primary emotion one feels is humiliation. It's not surprising that this level, being so close to death, is where most thoughts of suicide are found. Those who suffer from sexual abuse are often found here, and without therapy they tend to remain here.

- <u>Guilt (30) – Feeling Darkness</u>

  Not too far from shame is the level of guilt. When one is stuck in this level, feelings of worthlessness and an inability to forgive oneself are common.

- <u>Apathy (50) – Feeling Hopeless</u>

  This is the level of hopelessness and despair and often is the common consciousness found among those who are homeless or living in poverty. At this level, one has resigned themselves to their current situation and feels numb to life around them.

- <u>Grief (75) – Feeling Tragic</u>

  Many of us have felt this emotion at times of tragedy in our lives. However, having this as your primary level of consciousness, you live a life of constant regret and remorse. This is the level where you feel all your opportunities have passed you by. You ultimately feel you are a failure.

- <u>Fear (100) – Feeling Frightened</u>

  People living under dictatorship rule or those involved in an abusive relationship find themselves at this level. There is a sense of paranoia here, where you think everyone is out to get you. Suspicion and defensiveness are common.

- <u>Desire (125) – Feeling Disappointed</u>

  Desire is a major motivator for much of our society. Although desire can be an impetus for change, the downside is that it leads to enslavement to one's appetites. This is the level of addiction to such things as sex, money, prestige, or power.

- <u>Anger (150) – Feeling Hostility</u>

  As one moves out of Apathy to Grief and then out of Fear, they begin to want. Desire which is not fulfilled leads to frustration which brings us to Anger. This anger can cause us to move out of this level or keep us here.

- <u>Pride (175) – Feeling Demanding</u>

  According to Hawkins, since the majority of people are below this point, this is the level that most people aspire to. It makes up a good deal of Hollywood. In comparison to Shame and Guilt, one begins to feel positive here. However, it's a false positive. It's dependent upon external conditions such as wealth, position or power. It is also the source of racism, nationalism, and religious fanaticism.

- Courage (200) – Feeling Attainable

This is the level of empowerment. It is the first level where you are not taking life energy from those around you. Courage is where you see that you don't need to be tossed to and fro by your external conditions. This empowerment leads you to the realization that you are a steward unto yourself, and that you alone are in charge of your own growth and success. This is what makes you inherently human: the realization that there is a gap between stimulus and response and that you have the potential to choose how to respond

- Neutrality (250) – Feeling Satisfactory

Neutrality is the level of flexibility. To be neutral, you are, for the most part, unattached to outcomes. At this level, you are satisfied with your current life situation and tend not to have a lot of motivations towards self-improvement or excellence in your career. You realize the possibilities but don't make the sacrifices required to reach a higher level.

- Willingness (310) – Feeling Hopeful

Those people around you that are perpetual optimists - this is their level of consciousness. Seeing life as one big possibility is the cornerstone of those operating here. No longer are you satisfied with complacency - you strive to do your best at whatever task you've undertaken. You begin to develop self-discipline and willpower and learn the importance of sticking to a task till the end.

- Acceptance (350) – Feeling Pleasant

If Courage is the realization that you are the source of your life's experiences, then it is here where you become the creator of them. Combined with the skills learned in the Willingness phase, you begin to awaken your potential through action. Here's where you begin to set and achieve goals and to actively push yourself beyond your previous limitations. Up to this point you've been generally reactive to what life throws at you. Here's where you turn that around, take control, and become proactive.

- Reason (400) – Feeling Meaningful

This is the level of science, medicine, and a desire for knowledge. Your thirst for knowledge becomes insatiable. You don't waste time in activities that do not provide educational value. You begin to categorize all of life and its experiences into proofs, postulates, and theories. The failure of this level is you cannot seem to separate the subjective from the objective, and because of that, you tend to miss the point. You fail to see the forest because you're tunneled-vision on the trees. Paradoxically, reason can become a stumbling block for further progressions of consciousness.

- Love (500) – Feeling Caring

Only if in the level of Reason you start to see yourself as a potential for the greater good of mankind, will you have enough power to enter here. Here is where you start applying what was learned in your reasoning and you let the heart take over rather than the mind - you live by intuition. This is the level of charity - a selfless love that has no desire except for the welfare of those around them. Gandhi and Mother Teresa are examples of people who were living at this level.

- Joy (540) – Feeling Whole

This is the advanced spiritual people. As love becomes more unconditional there follow a constant accompaniment of true happiness. No personal tragedy or world event could ever shake someone live at this level of consciousness. They seem to inspire and lift all those who come in contact with them. Your life is now in complete harmony with the will of Divinity and the fruits of that harmony are expressed in your joy.

- Peace (600) – Feeling Perfect

Peace is achieved after a life of complete surrender to the Universe. It is where you have transcended and have entered that place that Hawkins calls illumination. Here, a stillness and silence of mind is achieved, allowing for constant revelation.

- Enlightenment (700 - 1,000) – Feeling One's Pure Consciousness

This is the highest level of human consciousness where one has become like the Creator. These are those who have influenced all of mankind. Hawkins' Power vs. Force and his associated map of consciousness has been a groundbreaking work for those interested in human-consciousness development. In this continuum we can clearly see where we as individuals function and where we can attain to become. A view into what could be our potential is inspiring.

Like epigenetic and other fields, the level of consciousness can be affected by our surrounding, our environment. If one understands the map of Dr. Hawkins this will help us understand what drives people in making their choices and why their reactions are logical to them.

Because the scale of consciousness is logarithmic, each incremental point represents a giant leap in power. As such, one person calibrated at 600 counterbalances the negativity of 10 million people below 200. Well, this doesn't mean that because you chose to be a lower level that your peers will counteract your level of consciousness immediately.

Dr. Hawkins points out that the two greatest growth barriers seem to be at levels 200 and 500. Two hundred, the level of courage, represents a profound shift from destructive and harmful behavior to a life-promoting lifestyle.

As of 2009, approximately 78% of the world's population is below this significant level, this is why depression and obesity has become such an epidemic; the world feels hopeless and helpless. Is this the quality of life you want to keep providing to your children and grandchildren?

The second great barrier is level 500, Love. Love in this context is a way of being in the world, not an emotion, as most of us perceive it. According to Dr. Hawkins, the reason the level of love is so difficult to achieve is because our ego is so rooted in the physical domain as opposed to the spiritual domain, which emerges around 500.

The 400s represent the level of reason, guided by the linear, mechanistic world of form (our modern society that includes advancements in medicine, science, government.) Interestingly, the top echelon of intellectual genius, including Einstein, Freud, Newton, Aristotle, all calibrated around 499. The 500s represent a very difficult hurdle as only four percent of the world's population is currently calibrating in the 500s. As the infamous song goes, "What the world needs now is love sweet love."

What is Your Reality (Consciousness) – Where Are You Focusing Energy?

From the first daylight when we are born, the environment is totally new. It had no meaning and no significance until our mind began to give a meaning with your caregivers and your surroundings affecting it. As you did that, things began to have meaning because your mind was associating these situations with names and significances.

To have an experience with your surroundings, each time you reacted to a person or an object, your mind and brain created a mental picture and/or a feeling attached to it. We called this an emotional imprint. The mind constantly assigns meaning or value to reality and creates a belief system out of this judging process. What the mind thinks is good or bad is simply based on what it likes or dislikes. Thus; meanings arose in your consciousness. Reality is being formed through this process of interactions.

Why Are You Not Happy?

Happiness should be unconditional but for most of us, it doesn't really apply, or at least, temporally apply to us. So we tend to be happy when:
- I feel happy when I'm financially rich.
- I feel happy when I'm successful in my career.
- I feel happy when I have a partner who loves me.
- I feel happy when other people like and respect me.
- I feel happy when my body is healthy.

The sensation of feeling good when we get what we want has a tremendous effect in our behavior and mind. Let's face it, it just feels great to get that toy we always wanted or to get the promotion we always wanted. However, life is not giving us what we want all the time, well because it might get boring and trigger the entitlement mentality.

As Tony Robbins says that one of the human needs is the element of surprise and this consists of both good and bad surprises. Change is an inevitable factor of life. Just take a look at the daily news for example, where there are constant reports of conflicts, tragedies and economic woes. What is even worse is when these negative events happen to us personally so how can we be happy about that?

Since it is hard to break our psychological wall or barrier because this could mean more pain and more hurt each time we attempt something new, we tend to ignore that process and just remain at Status Quo or worse yet mask our desires with materialism by buying our way to happiness. Accumulation of material and wealth seems to be a brief solution to a fictive joy. It is fun and exciting at first but after a while, the level of happiness wears off and again all our uncovered and unresolved emotions will resurface, removing the facade of happiness based on status and wealth.

If you have spent any time with rich people or if you're one yourself, you would know this to be true. We recommend you watch a documentary called "I Am" by Tom Shadyac. He's a famous movie director for such films as "Ace Ventura," "Liar Liar," "The Nutty Professor," and "Bruce Almighty." In this movie he provides good examples of emotional emptiness felt inside with buying your way toward happiness instead of resolving what is holding you down or back. Most people would assume that this type of success would be fulfilling. Why doesn't it make us feel any happier?

Being financially rich doesn't get rid of your negative emotions. It is better at an early age to encourage self-esteem and body awareness with a physical activity that's noncompetitive. Fostering cooperation and compassion, instead of opposition, is a great gift to give our children. Learning competition at an early age, whether it is thru competitive sports or competitive grades, instills values for a competitive playing field in the adult world that translates to discrimination, wars and oppression.

Dr. S' Insights

I can validate the theory of Emotional stressors and its impact on the brain. As a child, when my parents decided to obtain a divorce, my siblings and I internalized the distress from the situation. Being a Highly sensitive individual, I had attributed the situation as my inability to make the right decision and as such I have led my life allowing others to over-step their boundaries at times.

My father came to me right before I turned 18 and he asked me a simple question, "If you are not happy, what would you do, stay or try to pursue happiness." From that simple question, my world was turned upside-down. So much so that I have based my decision making process based on these same contextual guidelines, but in retrospect, I realize that my parents loved us regardless of their own internal battles with happiness and that it was not the outcome of the divorce that was a stressor in itself, but rather the lack of accountability that was taken for the decision.

I was so stressed from that situation; however, it provided me with the ammunition to make a difference in my life. The point is that stress is not necessarily detrimental, but it depends on how the child is framing the situation. If my father had been truthful and shared his intent with me, I would not have felt as guilty because in reality he was not asking me for validation, but merely support. It was not so much his action or the outcome that hurt, but the fact that I felt that I had caused the separation.

I have seen so many clients that experienced this same issue as a child and sadly they are holding on to this similar mind frame and attributing their depression to their current lifestyle. In truth, these clients have been holding on to the feelings of helplessness that occurred when their family environment was altered. The moral is that emotions that are trapped in your body can wreak havoc with your physical body. This stress that I had carried over the years may have even resulted in my heart palpitations.

However, as I stated, there are always positives to every experience. From this life change, it provided me with the motivation to enroll myself into a Medical Biology Program. As a young child, all I wanted to do was follow in my father's foot-steps and become a doctor that would help others with their life and health challenges. After he left, I knew that I would be able to still succeed and continue the legacy for our family where he left out. I enrolled in the University and realized I had an innate ability to understand the information and a pure passion to learn about the brain and its workings.

I recalled a research project that I did with functional neuroanatomy, which was a fancy word for how the brain integrated with the body and its overall functionality. The project involved genetically modifying a mouse that was born blind. This meant that part of the brain dedicated for vision (Occipital Lobe) had no stimulation over the years for this animal and the goal was to see if the brain could still utilize some of the receptors in this area.

What was discovered was the concept of plasticity and neuroplasticity in the brain. The outdated model of neurology believed that you were born with a specified number of neurons and they will prune away if not in use and no new neurons would be generated. In truth, I was able to help the mouse use the same receptors to enhance its other sensory functionalities.

With the mouse experiment I discovered that each sensory modality branched off to their original pathways in the respective areas of the brain. For example audio stimulation or sound pathways branches off to the auditory area (cortex) of the brain. However, what was profound was that I discovered that the visual area in this mouse was not solely responsive only for vision, in fact there was cross-referencing to the touch, taste and all the other sensory stimuli.

This was a revelation that helped peaked my curiosity for my interest in Craniopathy. I realized that if the brain can still utilize portions of itself that was not attributed to the original functionality, then by simply stimulating and retraining the other areas of the brain, that the mouse should see substantial improvements for the other senses.

For example, have you ever noticed how a visually impaired person, has uncanny hearing abilities? This also lends itself to the Autism perspective for Child Genius. If specific areas of the brain are impaired, focused training on other areas, will provide even superior results above an average person's abilities. This is why Child Geniuses are normally excelling above others in one area of specialty. So if we focus the efforts to enhance another area in their brain of the child it will be more conducive than simply labeling them as learning deficit.

So when I went to Chiropractic College, I took this principle and applied it. During my first semester I attempted to acquire as much knowledge and to master the intricate workings of the brain and how it related to the 5 sensory senses. So as a human experiment, I tried to stimulate all 5 of my senses while learning the Chiropractic material.

I used post-it notes everywhere to stimulate the visual aspects. I used an audio recorder to stimulate the audio aspects. I used body language to stimulate the tactile sensory. I ate particular foods while I was learning that held fond memories for me so that I could stimulate the taste and smell sensory. I noticed an incredible difference in my ability to learn and grasp the information quickly.

It did not take me long to read the material once and comprehend all the information without having to perform rote memorization. In fact, I found my academics to be more manageable than most of my peers and I had enough free time to even do research projects for the Chiropractic College. I even graduated with Honors which had never occurred prior. Again, the moral is that if you give up on your child's learning ability based on a previous assessment, you might be prematurely giving up on their innate abilities to excel.

The moral of this story is that perhaps it is not the material that children do not understand, but the particular type of learning stimuli that may interfere with each unique brain's capability to learn. Some people learn better with hands-on, while others require attentive listening or visual aids to help them.

This experiment of mine demonstrated that even if your child has a supposed learning deficiency, it might just be for that particular style (area of the brain.) If learning incorporated all 5 sensory to accommodate for any areas of weaknesses in a child's brain, it should be able to provide a comprehensive ability to capture all audiences to learn.

Speaking of differing learning styles, the binaural beats were tested by Jennifer and found to be effective with focusing and attentiveness. She used this technique to help write this book since she has a tendency to exhibit more ADHD characteristics and is often performing multi-projects simultaneously.

This is very important concept and will make a huge impact for teaching learning styles with multi-factorial stimulations. Another important aspects as a parent is to focus on the proper nutrients for the brain. The brain needs DHA (hormones secreted by the adrenal) in children. The importance of proper food, alkaline water and other essentials are explained in the Nutrition chapter. But one thing I would stress is that with love and compassion, a child's education and growth will bring the best in them no matter what sub-optimal environment or genes they may have inherited. Learning can occur at any age and with the proper stimulus any brain can thrive.

4

Epigenetics: What Is Your Child or Grandchild's Legacy?

"The secret of the care of the patient is in caring for the patient."

–Dr. Francis Peabody–

"America's health care system is neither healthy, caring nor a system"

–Walter Cronkite–

"...The field of practice graduates the real doctor."

–Dr. Fred Barge–

"The doctor of the future will give no medicine, but will interest his patients in the care of the human frame, in diet, and in the cause and prevention of."

–Thomas Edison–

What do Genes and a Computer have in Common?

Let us explore the analogy of genes and computers: if our bodies were computers, the DNA would be the "hardware"; the structure which the cells are built upon. The epigenetics are the software and influence the function of the hardware, often in the operation of which programs can run.

It is common knowledge our bodies are made up of different cells, for example, brain cells, hair cells, liver cells, Etc. Inside each of those cells is the same DNA, but they become distinct from each other because of the expression of the individual genes. There are several layers of control over which part of the DNA is working at any given moment whether a process is being expressed, or has the potential to be expressed, is referred to as it being 'turned on' or 'turned off'. This is why the cells lining the veins in your nose don't try to produce mucus when you sneeze.

The way we live our lives, our diet, stress levels, habits, habitat Etc… have a demonstrable effect on how our genes are interpreted. They are relevant to our own lifetimes, but, epigenetic changes can also influence what happens one and, more often, generations later. Your genes may be an indirect expression of nutritional and emotional habits that your grandparents lived by. But doesn't need be a bad thing! You could be deriving massive benefit from your grandparents' lifestyles and environments.

What do genes "turning on" or "turning off" have to do with anything? Twins who is not identical is one example of silencing or "turning off" genes. Another important example is in the development of males because males do not have the double X-chromosome present in females.

The New Science of Health – Epigenetics

Epigenetics is an exciting new field. Each cell in a body contains a DNA molecule, except mature red blood cells. Change in our epigenetic are normal and necessary. However, they may sometimes trigger cell dysfunction, which can, in some cases, result in dis-eases. Changes in cell regulation can lead to hyper function, aberrant function or proliferation and may be the mechanism by which some "cancers," illnesses and developmental problems are triggered.

These three systems are:
- <u>DNA methylation</u>: will affect how your own genes are expressed. It is also involved in sperm and egg production. Methyl groups attach to the DNA and change which parts of the code can be 'read'.
- <u>Histone modification</u>: regardless of whether chromosomal DNA will be transcribed, winds the DNA so tightly that it slows or prevents the DNA being read by the copying molecule.
- <u>RNA silencing</u>: turn off RNA expression and other mechanisms are involved

By understanding what controls the genes' activation and deactivation, potential life changes and "treatment" can emerge. This "new" science reveals that we are in fact an extension of our environment, and includes everything from our thoughts and belief system, to toxic exposure, exercise, and everything around us. As Dr. Lipton is fond of saying, this moves you out of victimhood and into mastery over your own health.

Wouldn't it be wonderful if there were a mammal out there that could have control of their entire life? They could choose to change their life for the better. This change would increase health and decrease doctor visits, hospital stays and eventually, nursing homes. Health care costs would decrease while the standard of living would increase. These animals would work on prevention of dis-ease instead of treating the symptoms of it. Wait a minute....there is such an animal!

Epigenetic literally means, on top of genetic. Each cell in a body contains a DNA molecule. The genomic research shows DNA has about 23,688 genes, yet only a fraction of these genes are active, or expressed, at any given time.

DNA is the language which creates all the body's molecules and cells. If you consider the brain as the contractor of the body, DNA is neither the architect nor the blueprint, but the building blocks needed for the contractor to create parts and mortars.

With new technology come many advances in health care. Surgeries now are much different than they were ten years ago; however, the part of the body surgery which was performed upon will never be as good as new. Prevention of dis-ease has grown with technology as well.

Why Epigenetics are Not Just Your Average Genes

The term epigenetic refers to changes in the phenotype, or gene expression (often visible as appearance) caused by mechanisms beyond changes in the underlying DNA sequence. These changes may remain through cell divisions for the remainder of the cell's life and may also last multiple generations.

Science has shown from the nineteenth century through today that DNA materials, or blueprint, are passed from generation to generation, now, research is proving genes are not truly a fixed predetermined program simply passed from one generation to the next.

What some epigenetics research has demonstrated is that a few genes can be switched on and off by experiences, thoughts and emotions. So, environment, toxins, even fears can be subcategorized under "stressors" and which alter the expression of our DNA for generations to come. These mechanisms are recently discovered and because their effects extend over generations, the best human research is necessarily retrospective.

So environment, toxins, even fears can be subdivided under "stressors" and which alter the expression of our DNA for generations to come.

Epigenetic science focuses upon the mechanism by which environmental factors, or triggers outside the cell signal, regulate the genetic material, i.e. gene activities. These signals are proteins or molecules creating a cascade of reaction within the cell and into the nucleus.

In the whole concept of genetic regulation a signal approaches the cell and enters via specific mechanisms, reaching the nucleus, which manipulates the genes, and starts the process to create an enzyme, protein, to form the skin for example. According to epigenetics, genes are used by biology, but not in control of biology.

As Tony Robbins teaches, your blueprint is your perception of your reality based upon your system of beliefs, and values, and ultimately, your rules learned from societal and cultural norms. Because perception is the blueprint, it skews the expression and result of DNA. This essentially means your "house" would be completely different if the blueprint didn't limit you. Your "house" and your entire outlook can be more magnificent than you imagine.

Types of Epigenetic Genes

Epigenetic changes can be grouped into exogenous and endogenous, meaning from the outside of the gene and from the inside, which are gene development and the gene itself. The exogenous, or outside, factors include a wide range of physical and chemical agents and a range of other stressors such as radiation, hypoxia, or a deficiency of oxygen, nutrient restrictions, emotions and environments.

During gestation and early development, epigenetic "tags" guide development of fetal cells with appropriate genetic instructions and may indent, or set, roles for the other repressive cells. A biochemical process called signaling will continue into adulthood and can activate or deactivate a gene expression, which can produce a different mental or physiological state.

The effect of exogenous factors, positive or negative, depends on the stage of the development of a fetus. One can generalize to say that there are more windows of sensitivity earlier in the pregnancy, but specific developmental processes will have specific sensitivities at different times. Endogenous factors will interact with the exogenous factors to define the window of sensitivity.

Since the brain is the governor of all production in the body and controls each cell, it sends its information to turn on and off the production of specific molecules, but these molecules can bypass these signals and create something the brain did not intend. There are various feedback mechanisms and physiological events that all combine to turn on or off the production of molecules by the cells; in the embryo influences from neighboring cells will induce changes, some signals come from your brain and some from glands

A Pioneer of Epigenetics

Cellular biologist Bruce Lipton was awarded his PhD in developmental biology in 1971. He was a respected university professor for many years, and now writes and lectures extensively on how 'outside of the gene' signals can regulate genetic expression. There are currently three proposed signal categories that operate in the establishment of a stably heritable epigenetic state.
- The first is a signal from the environment.
- The second is a responding signal in the cell that specifies the impact of the affected chromosomal location.
- The third is a sustaining signal that perpetuates the chromatin change in subsequent generations.

The mechanisms underlie epigenetic and cell memory. They hold great importance for the fields of human development and dis-ease. In 2008, $190 million was earmarked for epigenetic research at the National Institute for Health. Epigenetics has the potential to illuminate the mechanisms of aging, human development, and the origins of "cancer," heart dis-ease, mental illness, as well as many other conditions.

"Cancer" Cells – What Triggers Them?

We all have "tumor" suppressor genes, these genes are capable of stopping "cancer" cells and are present in every cell in your body, but so are proteins called histones. Histones are proteins that make up chromosomes and act as a spool around which DNA can wind. Dr. Jean-Pierre Isa of the Anderson Cancer Center explains histones can hug DNA so tightly that it becomes 'hidden from view' to the cells.

If a "tumor" suppressor gene is hidden, it cannot be utilized. Too much histone will "turn off" "cancer" suppressors and consequently abnormal proliferation occurs, and "cancers" are able. According to Dr. Pamela Peeke, histones are influenced by every decision we make, she believes what we eat and think, as well as our actions influences histones.

Faulty signals can be present outside cells mimicking the proper signal and can access the cell and produce a bad expression of a gene which can create faulty proteins, fat, skin, Etc., which could lead to the ultimate destruction scenario, "cancer."

Foods such as broccoli, cauliflower, brussels sprouts, kale, cabbage, bok choy, garlic, and onions contain substances that act as histone blocks and can assist the "tumor" suppressing genes to activate and fight "cancer." By regularly consuming these foods, you are naturally supporting your body's ability to fight "tumors."

Dr. Nicholas Gonzalez uses a three-pronged approach to "cancer" based primarily on nutrition and detoxification, and Dr. Stanislaw Burzynski, "treats" "cancer" with a gene-targeted approach with non-toxic peptides and amino acids acting as genetic switches to turn on "tumor" suppressor genes.

In The Power of Now and A New Earth, Eckhart Tolle discusses the concept of the "painbody." The definition of which is, when the body accumulates all the psychological pain during life. If the "painbody" is ignored it can take on a life of its own, this is how "cancer" cells and other dis-eases begin.

How Does Food Impact your Child and Grandchild's Genes?

We have all heard the saying 'You are what you eat', but how many of us genuinely understand the importance of that expression? There is proof that malnutrition or excess of particular foods during childhood can cause epigenetic changes. Diabetes, obesity and early puberty are just a few of those changes. Scientists have discovered, for instance, that a group of children conceived in Netherlands during the desperate wartime famine of 1944-45 tended to have smaller-than-average offspring.

Dr. Pamela Peeke MD, MPH, FACP, mentions the reversal of genetic problems in her 2013 blog, *You* are what your *Grandparents Ate*. She discovered that a study at Duke University by Randy Jirtle PhD showed the potential reversion of genetic problems. The Agouti mouse is a genetically engineered mouse that has the obesity gene and is designed to die young of premature heart dis-ease and diabetes. Agouti mice with these genes are also yellow.

Randy Jirtle, a geneticist in the Department of Radiation Oncology at Duke University found that a specific diet was capable of reversing these genetic pre-dispositions in the following generation. After feeding leafy green vegetables, beets, onions and garlic mixture to pre-conception mice, their offspring were brown and slim. Professor Jirtle concluded nutrition was capable of having an impact on genome expression which is epigenetic in action.

A woman's diet during and before pregnancy has major impact on her baby's epigenetic tags. Improper prenatal diets have been linked to an increased risk of brain, spinal cord and respiratory defects in children. Gene expression is regulated via multiple aspects and biochemical reactions such as the aid of methylation in production of healthier off-springs. Dietary habits should include nutrients high in folic acid, methionine and choline rich foods and or supplements. Methyl donors are connected with producing several brain chemicals. These chemicals are known to enhance mood, energy and concentration. They may also fight depression, cognitive decline, and Alzheimer's.

The nutritional environment during fetal development has been demonstrated to influence growth, metabolism and brain development, and there is increasing evidence that dietary levels of methyl-donors can epigenetically alter gene expression in offspring.

Your Baby is what You Eat

Not only is eating healthy important for you, it is vital for your baby. We think we are buying the best, but please keep the following in mind when purchasing food.

Dr. Michael Greger, author and researcher of the world's nutrition, tells us the meat industry uses a substance called 'Meat Glue', used, as the name suggests, attaching smaller pieces of meat to the larger pieces. The use of this glue is found in ground steak products, salmon patties, and ground turkey, and increases the risk of E. coli in our system. The 'meat glue' contains the enzyme transglutaminase which acts like gluten in our digestive system and may have potential allergy implications for those that should be on a gluten-free diet.

According to Dr. Greger, it is not healthy to eat farmed fish because farm raised fish are fed nearly 2 dozen human antibiotics to keep them alive. Food coloring linked to retinal damage is also used to make the fish meat appear fresher.

Many people have heard of Agent Orange. This toxin was used as a defoliant in Vietnam and has since been associated with "cancer", heart dis-ease, diabetes, and other illnesses. Although the use of dioxins was banned by the Stockholm Convention in 2001, they can still occur during, for example, the burning of pesticide-treated foliage. According to the Food and Drug Administration, "over 95% [of dioxin exposure is] coming through dietary intake of animal fats" Therefore, it is important to eat large portions of vegetables high in anti-oxidants to combat the toxins in the meat. Exposure to this toxin during pregnancy can alter thyroid, brain, reproductive, and organ development.

According to Dr. Michael Gregor, when animal meat is cooked at high temperatures, "cancer" causing chemicals are created. It is suggested that a pregnant women avoid meats that are barbequed, fried or grilled.

How Does the Environment Impact your Child or Grandchild's Genes?

"Radiation safety is, without a doubt, a large concern for practicing radiologists today," said Shella Farooki, MD, author, radiologist and Director of Research for the Columbus Radiology Corporation in Columbus, OH. "However, the current focus does not account for the possibility of harm to future generations from radiation delivered today. I believe that it is equally, if not more important, to consider potential harm to the patient's offspring and their offspring's offspring."

"The effects of ionizing radiation have been demonstrated in neighboring cells, which is called non-targeted radiation and known as the bystander effect. In addition, ionizing radiation effects have been shown to affect the epigenome functionality and radiation exposure spans generations, resulting in heritable defects in mice. However, we need to bridge the gap between understanding before assuming anything," said Farooki ~ Science Daily (April 2009)

Professor Jirtle recently demonstrated that exposure of pregnant mice to bisphenol A (BPA), reduces DNA methylation. BPA is a building block of polycarbonate plastics and resins found in many consumer items ranging from water bottles to dental sealant. Exposure to BPA resulted in the birth of mice that became obese, had a higher incidence of diabetes and "cancer" as adults. The increase use of plastics in our world could be linked to the increase of obesity and "cancer" in humans.

How Does Emotions Impact Your Child's and Grandchild's Genes?

Dr. Bruce Lipton mentioned that emotion play a primary role in epigenetic modulation. Negative emotions consist of repressed or unresolved negative energy lingering in your system and creating an increase in what he terms 'emotion molecules', which was coined by Candace Pert, PhD. (see emotion molecules.)

These enter the brain and affiliate with memories to create a chain reaction which will reflect to the cells and create faulty products through normal genes. The same concept occurs in your daily thoughts. External stressors during pregnancy can alter the epigenetic tags. Animal studies have found unusually intense fear responses to loud noises or new foods, when the previous generation was negatively conditioned to those pre-conceptions.

Negative emotions

Negative emotions such as anger, anxiety, or hate, or negative thoughts such as "I hate my job," "I don't like so and so" or "Who does he think he is?" creates stress and leads to a depletion in our overall energy.

When we choose to feel negative feelings, it drains and damages our body causing mental, physical and even emotional stresses. But, by actively initiating the power of our heart, the feeling of caring, love, appreciation, the electrical output of energy creates positivity.

We can train ourselves to ward off stresses, but with the addition of positive emotions it is proven that we fortify our energy and ensure the healthy cellular level of our body.

How Do Relationships Impact your Child and Grandchild's Genes?

Research by neurobiologist Dr. Stanley Greenspan has confirmed that a baby's brain, as well as DNA is shaped by relationships. Greenspan studies reveal that this means a baby will make correlations from smiles, actions, tone of voice and the emotions expressed by its caregivers and creates from it, a body-brain relation to bridge the concept within.

Relationship bonding can be between mother and father, mother and child, father and child, grandparent and child, and so much more. This suggests that our communication, verbal, gestural, and emotional will create an influence on our baby's brain development.

The studies of rats have shown environmental enrichment reversed almost all behavioral alterations observed in the model. It has been suggested that the most important single factor in stimulating brain changes in enriched rats is the enforced interaction with the physical environment. Thus, this vital element in enriching surroundings, or environment, affects cognitive abilities. In other words, relationship with others and the complete environment are essential in the formation of epigenetic tags.

There is increasing evidence for the role of epigenetic factors in mediating the relationship between these experiences and long-term outcomes. These epigenetic modifications are associated with exposure to stress during the early stages of prenatal development and may involve dysregulation of placental gene expression.

Where it becomes very interesting, is when research demonstrates the long-term effects of the environment for the child, plasticity or flexibility can occur and change it for the better. Plasticity is the definition of an adaptation in the nervous system.

Plasticity means what was set or sculpted by the brain can now change and be remodeled. This allows us to respond in early life and later to continuous variations of environmental changes to survive.

How Does Stress Impact your Child or Grandchild's Genes?

It has been proven that children of mothers who were highly stressed while pregnant showed behavioral issues as adults. In the case of stress, the cortisol hormone is produced by the adrenals, this cortisol links to specific receptors in all our cells. These receptors relay signals from stress hormones to the cells in the brain which control behavior. The risk of having those receptors or a high level of those receptors is increased in pregnant women suffering from depression.

Dr Meyer's and Dr Elbert's study in Translational Psychiatry found women who were physically, mentally or emotionally abused during pregnancy were significantly more likely than others to have a child with these receptor genes. By contrast, abuse before or after pregnancy resulted in no such correlation.

Research shows the link from the mother's stresses on the fetus into adolescence, as decreased activity in specific receptors. It also has shown to increase risk of obesity, depression and autoimmune dis-eases. It also makes people more impulsive and aggressive.

Epigenetics of the Mother-Child Bond

The role of epigenetic modification in sustaining the effects of environmental experience has also been demonstrated in the context of postnatal mother infant interactions. Some studies show that immediate variation in maternal care during the postpartum period is associated with changes in the offspring's hypothalamus-pituitary-adrenal, or HPA activity, the neuroendocrine system involving the reproduction and hippocampal region.

Research has shown that young children who have been abused are more likely to have epigenetic changes which make coping with stress more difficult. Research of suicide victims have shown these genes have been switched off. An estimated one out of every five suicide victims suffered from childhood abuse, leading experts to consider a possible correlation between stressful upbringings and epigenetic change.

Research also demonstrated high levels of maternal care and exposure to juvenile environmental enrichment improves capacity for learning and memory association with a better long-term potential. It also suggests an improvement in the contextual fear memory formation across generations. Even proper environmental conditions have been associated with increasing histone acetylation, which inhibits the "cancer" suppressing cells and improved spatial memory.

Since billions of neurons in a brain have the same genetic coding, the differentiation is what makes them unique. Each neuron cell will have diverse function according to the demand of the brain emotionally, physically, and mentally, based upon the child's environment.

These diverse functions can be of touch, vision, hearing and behavior and epigenetic molecules will process the regulation of these genes. All experiences passed from the parents to the child affect the brain development through the sensing neurological pathway which includes sound, touch, smell, food, thoughts, drugs, injury, dis-ease and multiples of other factors.

Identical twins will have, according to the research, 20 to 30% differences in their behavior as they are growing up in the adult stages. What the mother thinks, feels, eats, and responds to in her environment can have epigenetic influence, which may be factors contributing to the development of ADHD, autism, obesity and depression.

Environmental Factors

Maternal Health
Nutrition
Placenta Function
Stress (Emotional and mental)
Lifestyle

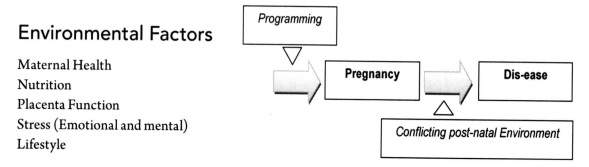

Dr. Bruce Lipton states that between the ages of one and six a child is in a hypnotic state. They absorb everything they can during that time. If what is shown or told to them is "you are stupid," it will become part of them. This learning process is imprinted into the subconscious mind. According to Dr. Lipton, this will follow them into all their life.

The real issue is that our mind is 90% unconscious and this why most traditional therapy methods do not reveal the root source of a person's dis-ease in their mind. The therapists ask the patient what is the emotion they currently feel which only accesses the conscious mind but discounts or ignores information originally stored in the unconscious portion of the mind. This is why, when properly administered, hypnosis is effective in alleviating most emotional issues.

Research shows that our ancestors' emotions are inherited, that trapped emotions can be passed from generation to generation. These emotions in the pregnant mother affect the way baby's genes are expressed.

☾ Jenn's Insights

During my pregnancy I was very health conscious from a nutritional standpoint. I would mix my own fruit smoothies as snacks and I ate a lot of vegetables. I did notice that my taste buds changed somewhat. Prior to the pregnancy I ate primarily fish and salads as my main courses; however, during the pregnancy I could not be around the smell of seafood. Just walking by the grocery store section, made me nauseous and I had to cut all fish from my diet; which with all the toxins found in fish, was probably a blessing in disguise.

My body was also craving beef and dark chocolate, but I cut red meat prior to my pregnancy, and my chocolate craving was odd because I never really enjoyed the taste of chocolate. I tried to appease the cravings by choosing healthier versions and often drank dark chocolate almond milk but once in a while I did sneak in a home-made, dark chocolate cupcake.

I was very happy to have found a practitioner who was as health conscious, so from an environmental perspective, I was also trying to minimize damage. My doctor recommended that no chemicals be put on my hair or nails. My doctor also advised against using make-up or perfume.

However, I did notice that I was literally eating my emotions during my pregnancy. I was craving gelato every single evening due to all the stress I experienced at work. In researching the section about the impacts of stress and epigenetics it brought me tears to think of how many genes were repressed due to all that unnecessary stress my son endured.

As a mother you truly want the best for your child, especially since all my life I had dreamed of being a mom and went through many challenges to become one. It really infuriates me and at the same time saddens me to know that I could have possibly increased my son's chances of being more receptive to obesity or depression or autoimmune dis-eases because I was not aware of what stress could do to his genes.

I tried my best to not engage in the stress which is why I did not say anything to my boss when she was verbally and emotionally abusing me. I wanted to rectify the disrespectful treatment by telling her what I truly felt about her lack of professionalism and leadership skills but held my tongue because I did not want my child to hear or experience those words or emotions.

The irony is that I did not know the non-verbal emotions and negative energy could be felt by the baby during my repression of those emotions. It saddens me to observe my son's reaction to dogs barking, he cries uncontrollably and it is very difficult to console him, I believe this is directly related to the stressors that he endured intrauterine that has him over-sensitive to stimuli.

Also the anxiety in my body surpassed the normal amounts that any mother should have had to tolerate. During the duration of my pregnancy I had such anxiety for myself and my unborn child's well-being due to this stressful environment. As a mother it is disheartening to know that I have not impacted his emotional state by remaining at that job, but potentially impacting also my grandkids wellbeing.

 Dr. S' Insights

Let's use an analogy to illustrate the principles of epigenetics for a pregnant mother. Let's start with the mother's body, her temple if you will, now let's conjure up a quick recipe of success for the five senses.

Let's begin with taste; the mother should look for organic, non-GMO whole foods that contain the proper balance of nutrients. It is better to consume more raw foods since cooking meats at high temperatures may cause carcinogenic effects.

Next we look at sound; mothers should avoid stressful words and emotions that may impact the unborn child. Inspirational, positive words should be spoken to the mother as well as the unborn baby.

Now we'll move on to the sense of smell; environmental toxins such as pesticides in the gardens or chemicals used in the air or around the homes need to be avoided.

And now sight: mothers should be out in nature and exercising to ensure optimal mind-body balance for herself and her baby. Finally we examine touch: mothers should avoid chemicals on their skin as well as any cleaning agents that may have toxic effects to their unborn baby.

We had our first baby in 2009. During this time, my wife was on a Standard Process whole foods nutritional protocol to provide the best for my son Sébastien. We were religious about her supplements and tried as hard as it was, to follow a proper eating habit.

However, she did "zag" here and there to satisfy some pregnancy cravings, but overall I was proud of the fact that she was able to understand the importance of watching what she consumed. Since she was breastfeeding, she followed the whole food supplementation protocol throughout the duration.

Additionally, we started to introduce whole food supplements to Sébastien as early as we could, according to his digestive tract formation. Then, my wife got pregnant with our second child, Sophie. She was born when our son was only 18 months so he suddenly had less attention.

My wife never stopped the whole food nutritional program during her second pregnancy and continued the program, even afterwards while she was nursing the two children. Sébastien weaned him self at about 3 years old and Sophie didn't particularly care for the latching aspect so we bottle fed her breast milk up to 18 months.

During all that time, my wife never stopped taking her omega-3, folic acid, B12, multi-vitamin, vitamin D and other supplements that I recommended throughout the prenatal and post-natal care. When she got pregnant with our third child, Sarah, we again followed this same regime. My wife is still taking whole food supplements because she is nursing Sarah.

Even though the nutritional component was carefully monitored during my wife's pregnancy, I still noticed that my son still experienced more illness than the other two children. We decided not to vaccinate any of our children because of personal reasons so their bodies had fewer toxins.

However, I was still puzzled by why Sébastien had the most health issues compared to our other two children and then I received my answer when I researched epigenetics. For Sébastien, my wife started her nutritional supplementations as soon as she received the first positive indicator from the home pregnancy tests. In fact, she started the supplementations earlier than any of the other pregnancies; however, I recall her first pregnancy endured the most stressful times.

She was a first-time mother and we had financial and economic challenges and were far away from a supportive network of family and friends. I noticed that even though I was away a lot during the third pregnancy, my wife lived at home and had the support of her family and friends nearby which helped alleviate a lot of her daily stressors and as such Sarah did not seem to be as impacted.

Sarah our youngest, has such a happy disposition, she was born with a smile on her face. I can still recall the moment I laid eyes on her; she just knew when she was around a loving person and would instantly connect with the person.

Sophie our second child is more independent and creative. While Sébastien is more introverted but highly intellectual with his language abilities and definitely has an inquisitive nature about him. All these children came from similar DNA genetics; however, their personalities and physiology all have varying characteristics. It's amazing how epigenetics works to shape two cells into a human life form that have unique characteristics and traits.

I noticed that since we introduced all our kids to healthy nutrients intrauterine, all the children are more prone to ask for healthier snacks and gravitate towards a more nutritional lifestyle, especially Sophie who often asks for more helpings of broccoli and asparagus.

Now can you imagine what that would feel like as a parent to hear that your child can be conditioned to enjoy healthy foods intrauterine? Further research should be done on these concepts so obesity will not continue to occur in this generation of children. It is truly a "tragedy" to see so many children prematurely taken from diabetes and heart dis-ease.

This is why the Whole-Listic Children's Hospatal will empower mothers with prenatal care that also focuses on nutrition and how their emotions can impact the gifts they are bestowing to their children and possibly their grandchildren's legacy. It's not just what you eat, but what you say or think during pregnancy that can make a world of difference.

5
Real Nutritional Fuel
for Your Body

The ABC's of Nutrition

Life's secret resides in the knowledge of what is needed to survive. The optimum recipe is to have the proper intake of alkaline water, whole foods for proper nutrients, and aerobic exercises to promote healthy oxygen levels, and proper brain and nerve functioning through chiropractic care. To promote health and be at the forefront of dis-ease it should begin on the very first day of a person's life which occurs intrauterine.

This chapter will provide a roadmap towards a more conscious eating lifestyle. Subsequent chapters will provide more in-depth nutritional information for children diagnosed with ADHD/ADD, Autism, Depression and Obesity. As parents you want to give your children the very best chance at life and provide them with the best possible nutrition and the first seven years are incredibly important to the child's development.

The pregnant mother should eat raw foods, drink properly filtered alkaline water, and eat grass fed/organic/hormonal-free/kosher meats and chemically-free wild caught fish. Following this protocol during the prenatal stages simply isn't enough because there are other toxins such as emotional stressors and environmental stressors that need to be taken into account for healthy development.

Advances in technology are increasing the chemically engineered byproducts as well as more and more toxins being introduced into our food supply. During the duration of your child's development and your post-natal care, focus needs to remain on developing a nutritious lifestyle and balancing your body's pH levels to prevent dis-eased states of mind, body and energy, this is especially critical if you are breast-feeding your baby.

You are what you eat and this is also applicable to children. If only the problem was the processing of the foods which depletes all the necessary nutrients it would be simpler, but we need to account for Genetically Modified (GMOs), pesticides, herbicides, chemicals, preservatives, coloring, added flavoring and added chemically engineered vitamins to our food.

We are losing the taste and power of the real food and what it really feels like to run on proper fuel. This chapter will reveal answers for the following: How to help rid the body of these toxins? What types of foods provide the best pH balances for our bodies? How can supplement assist with augmenting the mineral and vitamin deficiencies lacking in our food supply?

The best gift you can give your child is a perfect nutritional start. From birth to their first birthday, your child will grow exponentially and the coming years will require the most fuel because they will develop language, cognition, social and motor skills. In the first three years of life the brain will grow the quickest this is why nutrition is so important and essential during this critical period. In order for all those billion neurons to connect properly it is essential that the brain and body obtain the proper nutrients and experience true health.

If your child does not get healthy foods during this time, his or her future intelligence could be impacted. It is our role, as parents, to choose the best nutrition available for them, in restaurants, at home, and at school since research has proven that repeated exposure builds taste preferences very quickly.

Since children are uploading information from their surroundings from birth to age seven it is the parents' responsibility to direct their child towards the right track towards a healthier lifestyle. According to research, almost ninety percent of children's dis-eases can be prevented because most are caused by poor nutritional patterns and habits or emotional stressors.

Children want to be loved and will do whatever it takes to achieve this primary need and if they are deprived of attention and realize that sickness provides that attention, they learn quickly to unconsciously eat unhealthy and become sick. Sickness can be purposely acquired, as Anthony Robbins says: you can mimic any physiological state if your mind trains your body to do.

Here's what is required for a Billionaire Child's brain to thrive and to access all the available neurons:
- nutritive alive live foods (whole foods)
- breastfeeding vs. infant formulas
- primarily an alkaline diet
- avoidance of GMO (genetically modified) such as (sugar, wheat, corn, soy)
- foods free from environmental toxins (farmed fish, the dirty dozen foods)
- foods free from additives and flavorings (processed meats, juices, MSG)
- consuming alkaline water

- eating a rainbow diet
- supplementing with nutritional therapy vs. isolated or fractionated vitamins
- using homeopathy to strengthen your antibodies vs. medication to address symptoms
- foods that preserve your family legacy (nutrition and epigenetics; Chapter 4)
- detoxification

The secret to the prevention of all dis-ease in children is very "easy." Children will develop their innate or unconscious talents and gifts if their parents monitored their diets and provided them with the proper exercises for both their physical and mental bodies.

What is in the Grocery Stores?

As the food industry grows to accommodate the planet's population increases the need to mass produce has resulted in cutting the amounts of nutritive foods. Consequently, it is standardized in terms of processed production loaded with sugar or sugar substitutes, chemically engineered vitamins, additives and flavorings.

Overutilization of farmland worldwide has depleted the soil of many essential nutrients. Researchers claim for the optimal health of plants and the animals that consume them, the soil must contain at least one hundred essential nutrients. This is in stark contrast to the current trend toward hydroponic food production where plants are grown in water containing only 16 of these essential nutrients.

To complicate matters further, researchers noted that the loss of essential nutrients in the soil caused the plants to become sickly, reducing fewer yields. To combat the resulting revenue losses from a business standpoint, hybridization of food stocks became prevalent. Hybrids are simply a form of genetic modification. These genetically modified (GMO's) are specifically designed to grow in environments that utilize less soil; however, these by-products also contain less nutrition and contain more harmful side effects towards your body.

It would be helpful to have a grocery store which has everything we need but also stock the shelves with ingredients that are more optimal for our health. Whole Foods grocery store has tried to abide by these principles by maintaining a list of "unacceptable ingredients for foods." The list goes up to 78 ingredients that contains chemicals that is not recommended like aspartame, MSG, high fructose corn syrup, bleached and bromated flour, sulfite, artificial coloring and others (http://www.wholefoodsmarket.com/about-our-products/quality-standards/unacceptable-ingredients-food.) Many of these ingredients are present in processed foods, prepared, packaged foods and soft drinks that contain high fructose corn syrup and sodium benzoate.

It is "easy" to understand why we should stay away from soft drinks or other processed foods but by being able to comprehend the ingredients list properly, we are able to uncover more substance that may be detrimental to our health that have been cleverly disguised with profitability in mind. Did you know that Whole Foods has banned bottled water that is predominately sold at other grocery stores because they contain four black-listed ingredients: sucralose (leukemia,) calcium disodium EDTA (kidney and liver problems,) acesulfame potassium (tumors,) and potassium sorbate (allergies)?

Some 100% whole wheat bread in grocery stores contain high corn fructose corn syrup (risks of heart attack and type 2 diabetes), sodium stearoyl lactylate (allergies), ethoxylated diglycerides (strokes/diabetes), DATEM (diarrhea), azodicarbonamide (banned in the rest of the world), ammonium chloride (kidney dis-ease), and calcium propionate (ulcers and migraines.) Furthermore, the ingredient azodicarbonamide is banned in the United Kingdom, most European countries as well as Australia. It is used in some of the 100% whole wheat bread. And its use in Singapore has some pretty severe penalties (up to 15 years in prison and $450,000 fine.) So why are other countries banning or penalizing the use of this chemical but it is still being served to our children in North America?

Real Food, Whole Food, Fake Food

What are the Difference between Real Foods, Whole Foods and Fake Foods? As our history has shown, a lot has happened since the caveman hunting days to get food onto the table. The microwave made a huge shift in our society and contributed to a major rebellion happening with this generation including malnutrition and sensitivities (allergies.)

In the book, Real Food for Mother and Baby, the author Nina Plank described her definition of real food as being old and traditional. She further expands the definition as anything that you can hunt, fish or gather like meat, fish, fowl, insects, eggs, leaves, nuts, berries and honey being categorized as real food. In contrast, rice, wheat, beans are not real foods since they are cultivated along with other foods that may be mixed to create a new invention. Foods that are normally made in factories are considered as not being real foods since they contain added preservatives to extend their shelf life.

Nina explains that traditional foods are intact and complete and should not require any processing in factories. Real foods are something that has never been processed by any machines or humans. So technically, a Twinkie is not real food. By real food we are talking about fresh grown vegetables, fruits and other farm products, fresh raw milk from the cow and goat, fresh meat cuts and fresh sprouts from the garden. So if real foods are all the above mentioned, why do we need to further define Whole Foods? The difference between Real Foods and Whole Foods is in the semantic of the word "Whole." Whole signifies the ENTIRE nutritional value of the food.

The food can be real, meaning it came from a farm but because the soil may have become depleted or they used pesticides or other chemicals, the nutritious value of the food is depleted and may cause further harm to your body so the "wholeness" of the nutrients is lost. Whole Foods are the complete nutritious value of any real food without any processing or any chemical imbalances to the product such as inclusions of hormones, chemicals, additives and other latent factors.

Fake foods are everything in the center aisles of grocery stores. Most grocery stores have vegetables, fruits, and meats in the perimeter of the store while all the processed products will be in the focal center. These are the Fake or processed foods loaded with added chemicals and flavoring, engineered for an extended shelf life and optimal profits from a business-centric viewpoint, not for the best interest of the consumer's health.

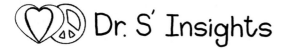 Dr. S' Insights

Since farming soil has been depleted and processed foods have replaced many home-cooked meals, there has been a constant battle to achieve optimal health. The majority of people are going to doctors because of the toxins they consume on a daily basis. The food pyramid no longer works because the ingredients do not provide the same nutrients as they used to.

It saddens me to know that many families consume this type of food because of their economic situation. I know because I have been there myself. Many times families will head to a fast food restaurant because it is more economic. With the inclusion of indoor playgrounds along with the marketing techniques used to attract younger consumers and with their daily promotions, these chains are promoting and enticing the public with poor nutritional habits. Often times, they are running so many promotions that it is easier to feed a family of 5 with $6 at these places. However, economics also consist of opportunity costs, which means what would you gain or lose if you were not consuming these products in the long run?

In July 1999 David Whipple purchased a hamburger from a fast food restaurant to illustrate to his friends the effects of enzymes on preserving food. After a decade, David found the same hamburger to be intact, without any molding issues even though it was wrapped in the original paper bag. Can you imagine how much resources the body will need to deplete to get that hamburger digested?

Promoting whole food consumption has been a passion and priority of mine. I have seen too many patients coming to my office with toxicity issues that created their dis-eased state due to eating habits and their misinformed knowledge about vitamins. Many of my patients were taking supplements that were chemically engineered and processed with gasoline byproducts.

Many of the foods they were consuming held toxicity attributes due to the radiation used to retain shelf life. I often encourage my patients to purchase from local farms or organic produce. Other venues would be to purchase from suppliers that get their products from local farms such as Relay Foods (www.relayfoods.com) or local cooperatives. However, I still encouraged the supplementation of whole food supplements because of the depletion of nutrients from the soils from the fresh produce, plus it is more economical to take the supplements.

When you are grocery shopping, please read the labels. If you are unfamiliar with label reading, consult a nutritionist to empower yourself. The general rules would be to use this protocol when selecting your foods:
- *If you cannot pronounce the ingredient: don't buy*
- *If the names are too long or sound similar to a chemical: don't buy*
- *If the term doesn't seem like food: don't buy*
- *If it a derivative of corn: don't buy it (refer to the toxicity portion to learn more)*

You Are What You Eat – Junk In Equals Junk Out

According to the Centers for Disease Control, 36 percent of U.S. adults, or 78 million, and 17 percent of youth, or 12.5 million, are obese. Another third are overweight. French fries, pizza and ice cream accounted for about 11 percent of U.S. adults' caloric intake from 2007 to 2010.

According to Dr. Gillian McKeith, author of You Are What You Eat, an estimate of half of all women and two thirds of all men in the UK are overweight or clinically obese and the estimated cost to the country is 18 million sick days and 30,000 deaths per year.

Moreover, parents in a busy society are training their children to eat whatever they want (chocolate, junk food, pizza, ice cream, Etc.) Worse yet, if they do not like the foods given to them, parents are teaching them to just add sugar or salt. This is becoming an epidemic.

If parents believe that their bodies are temples they will in turn teach this lesson to their kids. How do you treat your temple (body), are you putting in the best foods or what is deemed as Junk Food (trash) into your bodies?

Steven Witherly PhD is a food scientist and in his book, Why Humans like Junk Food, he explores some of the popular foods that adults are consuming and introducing to their children. He has done research for more than 20 years and some of his research is included below.

According to Dr. Liz Sloan, food writer and president of the consulting firm, the most preferred foods by men, women and children were: hamburgers, French fries, and pizza and by kids under 7 the foods included: pizza, chicken nuggets and French fries. Can you see the stark contrast of why we are not getting enough nutrients into our body and experience the manifestations of energy depletions that require caffeine and energy drinks to sustain our daily living. If you are not supplying your body with the best fuel (octane,) how can you expect it to run efficiently?

French Fries

One person will eat an average of seventy-five pounds of French fries annually. Women seem to favor this food over men. The reason, according to research, is the fifty percent fat content, high level of salt and high glycemic starch. Salt is the primary molecule of pleasure with this food while the actual potatoes have an intimate relationship and synergy with MSG. This chemical is known to increase the pleasure out of any food. Some fast food restaurants use wheat and dairy derivatives as flavoring agent within their oil when frying these potatoes. In fact, gliadin protein (wheat protein) is the richest source of natural glutamates (MSG) within plants. The oils used are mainly trans-fat to increase the crispiness; the oil is also reused to save money. Today trans-fats are found in forty percent of the products on your supermarket shelves. Because trans-fat is a bad fat molecule it can affect the cardiovascular system but also your digestion and insulin production leading to heart attacks, strokes and even diabetes.

Pizza

Pizza is a lucrative 30 billion dollar industry with an average of fifty slices per person a year. Over three billion pizzas were made last year in the United States. Thirty-six percent of all pizzas contain pepperoni as a topping. Salt is also used in pizza but is mainly found within the pepperoni and sausage toppings. Pepperoni has a five percent weight of salt, seventy eight percent fat which can be compared to consuming a stick of butter. Pork sausage has naturally high glutamic acid levels which can affect people with epilepsy. The crust itself is mainly made of wheat and processed wheat with additives along with the use of pasteurized dairy. This combination acts like "morphine" and adds addictive properties to the pizza.

Toxicity in Your Bodies

We are living in a world of chemically reengineer molecules and toxic waste in our food supplies. We breathe air filled with fumes from factories. We inject people with chemicals without knowing all the side effects. We take pills with side effects. We eat processed foods with chemicals made from gasoline byproducts.

Where does this accumulated trash go? In our homes we tend to have a trash can fill it and once or twice a week put it on the curb to be picked up, maintaining a healthy, clean environment.

Your body does the same thing. It accumulates toxins, processes it, puts them in "trash" bags and evacuates them by feces, urine, breathing and skin perspiration. If the body takes out its own trash why are toxins or toxicity important? Imagine living in a house filled with trash everywhere, bags and bags of trash piled up in your bedroom, living room, game room and your children's rooms.

Besides having an infestation of insects, rats and other animals, sickness will start and eventually serious illness will show up.

If the "trash" or toxicity accumulates inside your body and the clutter does not get properly flushed out, what could happen? These toxins have the potential to turn your gene switches on and off and make your genes express themselves incorrectly but it also alters the hereditary of your family's legacy for generations to come.

Our bodies are designed to "accept" only a limited amount of toxins during a day and to eliminate it with a properly functioning elimination and digestive system. These toxins are either contaminants in food or water.

All these toxins have specific and generalized effects on the nervous, endocrine, immune, cardiovascular, musculoskeletal, and lymphatic systems. They can be found in domestic products like toothpaste, deodorant, water from the faucet or shower, laundry detergent, laundry softener, and non-stick pots and pans.

Children are modeling what their parents eat. If only the problem was simply in the processing of the foods which depletes all the necessary nutrients for the child, but today we need to account for GMO, pesticides, herbicides, chemicals, preservatives, coloring, added flavoring and added chemically engineered vitamins to our children's food. We are losing the real taste and power of the real food and what it really feels like for our bodies to run on proper fuel.

This is why it is imperative to learn proper detoxification to ensure that toxins do not necessarily remain in your child's body to wreak havoc on their physical and mental developmental opportunities. By boosting your innate immunity system with proper nutrients and learning to balance the pH levels to avoid too much acidity this will ensure a healthier start for your child's well-being. To subsidize the nutritional deficiencies that are occurring from our food supply, whole food supplements will aid in ensuring that the proper minerals and vitamins are provided to boost your child's brain.

Dr. S' Insights

If the body cannot remove toxicity properly it will entrap it in fat cells. The issue with this scenario is that fat cells will secrete hormones like the "fight or flight" stressors along with estrogen hormones, which will produce more hormonal imbalances in your body. All these added hormones will disrupt the normal bodily functions.

The amount of toxicity in your body can also affect the brain, nervous system, hormonal imbalance, sleep and impact other areas of your body. Additionally, dental byproducts can contain chemicals that often introduce a hefty amount of toxicity into your body. The old amalgams that many dental fillings are made of contain high levels of mercury that could cause neurological issues.

These toxic compounds can mimic natural nutrients and trigger false responses in your body's sensory system. For example, using epigenetics, when a toxic compound enters your cell and acts as a genetic signal to start the production of a protein, it can interfere with the normal production which can create damage and, possibly, uncontrolled cell proliferation.

Here is a list from derivative corn by-products which is genetically modified (GMO) in the USA and produces toxic characteristics in your body:
(http://www.livecornfree.com/2010/04/ingredients-derived-from-corn-what-to.html)

- *Ascorbic Acid (Vitamin C)*
- *Baking Powder (corn starch)*
- *Brown Sugar: used for the look of Caramel coloring. Domino's Brown sugars no longer uses Caramel coloring*
- *Calcium Citrate: the calcium salt of citric acid. See Citrate for further information.*
- *Caramel: coloring used in soft drinks, derived from corn "or cane sugar." The "or" in Coca-Cola's explanation refers to a temporary change to make the ingredients Kosher for Passover. The rest of the year, it is from corn.*

- **Cellulose**: *Vegetable*
- **Citrate**: *can refer either to the conjugate base of citric acid, or to the esters of citric acid. An example of the former, a salt is trisodium citrate; an ester is triethyl citrate. Forms of Citrate include: Calcium Citrate, Magnesium Citrate, Potassium Citrate and Sodium Citrate*
- **Citric Acid**: *the source sugar is corn steep liquor along with hydrolyzed corn starch*
- **Corn**
  - Corn Meal: *items baked sitting on Corn Meal such as Bagels, Breads or Pizza, may not list Corn Meal as an ingredient*
  - Corn Starch: *in most over the counter medicines that come in a dry pill form. Yes, this includes Benadryl too. Watch for Corn Syrup in the liquid forms.*
  - Corn Syrup
  - Decyl Glucoside: *used in personal care products such as shampoo. It is produced by their reaction of glucose from corn starch with the fatty alcohol decanol which is derived from coconut.*
- **Dextrin, Maltodextrin**: *thickening agents found in sauces (check those frozen veggies!) salad dressings, and ice cream*
- **Dextrose** *(glucose): corn sugar is found in cookies, ice cream, and paired with glucose in hospital IVs unless specified not to! Can also be used as a carrier with anesthetic shots such as Lidocaine and Novocain. Dextrose is also injected into meat, lunch meats and deli cuts. Be wary of "honey baked" items, the sweet flavor may not be from honey.*
- **Ethanol**: *made by fermenting sugars produced from corn starch.*
- **Ferrous Gluconate**: *i.e. as found in canned olives, and comes from corn or potato acid.*
- **Flavoring** : *Artificial or "Natural Flavors"*
- **Golden Syrup**: *Sometimes recommended as an alternate to Corn Syrup, but it may contain Corn Syrup as well.*
- **Honey**: *May contain corn syrup, as High Fructose Corn Syrup is sometimes fed to bees, resulting in corn in the honey produced.*
- **Hydrolyzed Vegetable Protein (HVP)**
- **Iodized Salt**: *Morton adds Dextrose (corn) to their salt.*
- **Lactic Acid**: *Commercially, lactic acid can be made synthetically from chemicals or organically as a byproduct of corn fermentation.*
- **Lauryl Glucoside**: *is a surfactant used in cosmetics. It is a glycoside produced from glucose and lauryl alcohol.*
- **Magnesium Citrate**: *Magnesium salt of citric acid*
- **Magnesium Stearate**
- **Malic Acid**
- **Malt**
- **Malt Flavoring**
- **Maltitol** *(also known as Maltisorb and Maltisweet): Commercially, maltitol is a disaccharide produced by Corn Products Specialty Ingredients (formerly SPI Polyols), Cargill, Roquette, and Towa, among other companies. Maltitol is made by hydrogenation of maltose obtained from starch.*
- **Maltodextrin**
- **Maltose**
- **Mannitol**: *A naturally occurring alcohol that is often combined with corn derived sugars.*

- **Methyl Gluceth**: *an emollient used in cosmetics manufactured from corn sugar and corn starch.*
- **Modified Food Starch**
- **Monosodium Glutamate (MSG)**: *The (www.MSGMyth.com) site explains MSG is made from corn.*
- **Polydextrose**: *is synthesized from dextrose, and contains sorbitol and citric acid. It is a food ingredient classified as soluble fiber and is frequently used to increase the non-dietary fiber content of food, replace sugar, reduce calories and reduce fat content. Note: dextrose, sorbitol, and citric acid are all on this list of ingredients derived from corn.*
- **Polylactic Acid (PLA)**: *Plastic made from corn starch (U.S.) or sugarcane.*
- **Polysorbates** (i.e. Polysorbate 80): *Polysorbates are oily liquids derived from PEG-ylated sorbitan (a derivative of sorbitol) esterified with fatty acids.*
- **Potassium Citrate**: *See Citrate above for details.*
- **Powdered Sugar:** *contains corn starch*
- **Saccharin**: *in powder form IS Sweet'N Low and therefore contains Dextrose.*
- **Sodium Citrate**: *See Citrate above for details.*
- **Sodium Erythorbate:** *is produced from sugars derived from sources such as beets, sugar cane and corn. It is a food additive used predominantly in meats, poultry, and soft drinks.*
- **Sodium Starch Glycolate**: *is the sodium salt of a carboxymethyl ether of starch. It can be derived from any starch source (rice, corn, potatoes, Etc.)*
- **Sorbitan**: *is a mixture of chemical compounds derived from the dehydration of sorbitol.*
- **Sorbitan Monostearate**: *an ester of sorbitol and stearic acid. You will see this ingredient used in Yeast (and possibly other places as well.)*
- **Sorbitol**: *You will find Sorbitol in **Sugar Free items** such as candy, chewing gum, cosmetics, mouth wash, and toothpaste*
- **Starch**: *often this is corn starch unless it specifies something else, like potato starch*
- **Sucralose**: *Sucralose by itself may be corn free, though it is likely one best to avoid. Repackaged as the brand Splenda, it will contain dextrose and/or maltodextrin.*
- **Sweet'N Low**: *contains Dextrose, and according to Sweet'N Low, ALL sugar substitutes in powder form contain Dextrose.*
- **Vanilla Extract**: *most brands will have corn syrup, though you can find organic brands that do not, though the alcohol may be corn-derived.*
- **Vinegar, Distilled White**: *can be made from any sugar, but the most common method is to use corn that has been converted from starch into sugar.*
- **Vitamins**: *Vitamin C (Ascorbic Acid) and Vitamin E (Tocopherols.) Use caution with products that are "enriched" with added vitamins. The vitamins may be corn-derived, or corn-derivatives may be used in the binding (if solid) or suspension (if liquid) of the vitamin compound.*
- **Xanthan Gum**: *a food additive that is used as a thickening agent. It is found in sauces, spices, and **commonly in Gluten Free foods**. Xanthan Gum is most often grown on corn, or corn sugars. If an item includes Xanthan Gum and states it is corn-free, call the manufacturing company and inquire as to the source of Xanthan Gum to be sure.*
- **Xylitol**: *You will find Xylitol in **Sugar Free items** such as candy, chewing gum, cosmetics, mouth wash, and toothpaste*
- **Zein**: *used in time-release medications, derived from Maize*

Additionally, if you eat processed food with Citric Acid, Sodium Benzoate and High Fructose Corn Syrup you are increasing toxicity in your body.

A study in Environmental Health discovered mercury in citric acid, sodium benzoate and high fructose corn syrup (HFCS.) An analysis of HFCS from three different manufacturers revealed mercury levels ranging from under the detection limit of 0.005 to 0.570 micrograms of mercury per gram of high fructose corn syrup. They claim that an average person will consume about 50 grams of HCFS in America on a daily basis which is above the prescribed standards.

Inflammation in Your Body

There is good and bad inflammation. Research has shown that inflammation is the normal body's reaction against infections or the scenario of being under attack. The principle resides in the facts that most organisms, intruders, will not survive in high temperatures and under conditions of inflammation molecules surrounding them.

This is why a fever is in actuality a positive sign of the body's immune system working properly. This is a natural reaction from the body when it is trying to resolve either toxicity or an infection.

Inflammation is a problem when this mechanism of defense gets overworked which can lead to heart attacks, colon "cancer", Alzheimer's and a host of other dis-eases. According to Time Magazine's article, The Secret Killer, foods with high inflammation properties are the contributing factor for making our bodies awry with inflammation overload.

In Sayer Ji's book, The Dark Side of Wheat, he has noted that there are over two hundred adverse health effects with wheat consumption. Wheat has the highest inflammation property and according to the author, most households contain grains or wheat as a food staple.

According to Dr. Pamela Peeke, a leading expert in weight prevention, women over the age of 40 do not require dense complex carbohydrates (pasta, bread, potatoes or rice) after 5 pm. These foods are rich fuel sources and should be consumed in moderation, primarily during the day to help avoid obesity.

Additionally, Dr. David Perlmutter in his book "Grain Brain" demonstrated how gluten increases inflammation in numerous of people who either are celiac, have a gluten allergy, and/or have a gluten sensitivity that is non-celiac.

Gluten is linked to neurological and intestinal problems. Research is finding it to be implicated in increased anxiety, depression, hormonal imbalance problems, and with motion sickness issues. It can bring on multiple sclerosis-type symptoms, brain fog, epilepsy and vertigo, a spinning sensation. It can be responsible for poor coordination, bipolar disorder and memory issues.

Furthermore, wheat contains high levels of glutamic acid. The chemical is a highly addictive ingredient. It is an essential reason for the obesity epidemic. Furthermore, grains, and particularly wheat have gluten exorphins and gliadorphin in them, both are pharmacological active properties similar to prescribed drugs.

Today's generation has become dependent in eating breakfast with cereal grains. Historically that has not been the case, but due to the agriculture revolution our human race has stopped the hunter-gathering process of accumulating and searching for food. Prior to that revolution, we all existed on a non-cereal menu and were healthier.

Research has proven a minimal change in our genetics in the past 40,000 years. Meaning we most likely hold the same genes that our ancestors did but the food and our ways of eating has changed radically in the past 10,000 years and furthermore in the last century. Grains are now one of the most consumed "new" foods added in our society and lifestyle. According to Cordain, when the grain-cereals were first introduced to most of the world to replace, mainly, animal-based diets, dis-ease increased.

The changes in physiology provoked numerous changes including: increase in infant mortality, reduction in lifespan, increase incidences of infectious dis-ease, increase in iron deficiency anemia, increase incidences of osteoporosis, and other bone mineral disorders and increases in number of tooth decay and enamel defects.

The conclusion of Cordain's research confirmed that with the introduction of cereal grains there was a reduction in the quality and quantity of life. He discovered that at the same time, other parts of the world still maintained their animal-based hunter-gatherer society and did not have these same health issues. Their food intakes were primarily from wild animals, fruits, and vegetables which encompassed between 100 to 200 or more species that provided a diverse food supply.

The main concern is the loss of nutrients during the processing of cereal or grains. Grains that contain mainly omega-6 fats and contain an acidic pH may be problematic if consumed in large doses over the course of many years. Many grains also have a gliadin molecule which is the cause of gluten intolerance and can have an effect on the glycemic index which has increased the incidences of diabetes in our society.

Top 10 Foods That Cause Inflammation

1. Sugar (also refined)

2. Common cooking oils: Safflower, soy, sunflower, corn, canola and cottonseed

3. Trans fats: In fried foods, fast foods, commercially baked goods, such as peanut butter and items prepared with partially hydrogenated oil, margarine and vegetable oil.

4. Dairy: Pasteurized milk is a common allergen that can trigger inflammation, stomach problems, skin rashes, hives and even breathing difficulties.

5. Feedlot-Raised Meat: Animals who are fed with grains like soy and corn contain high inflammation due to their GMO characteristics.

6. Red and Processed Meat: Red meat contains a molecule that humans do not naturally produce called *Neu5GC* (a sugar molecule in mammals but not in humans.) Once you ingest this compound, your body develops antibodies which may trigger constant inflammatory responses.

7. Alcohol

8. Refined Grains: They have no fiber and have a high glycemic index. They are everywhere: white rice, white flour, white bread, pasta, pastries.

9. Artificial Food Additives: Aspartame and MSG are two common food additives that can trigger inflammation responses

10. The imbalance of omega-6 fatty acids vs. omega-3 fatty acids may cause inflammation.

Top 10 Foods That Help Combat Inflammation

1. Wild caught Alaskan Salmon and Tuna: They contain a high ration of anti-inflammatory omega-3.

2. Kelp: High in fiber, this brown algae extract helps control liver and lung dis-ease.

3. Extra Virgin Olive Oil: Can help lower risks of asthma and arthritis, as well as protect the heart and blood vessels.

4. Cruciferous Vegetables: Broccoli, Brussels sprouts, kale and cauliflower are all loaded with antioxidants and are naturally detoxifying.

5. Blueberries: Blueberries not only reduce inflammation, but they can protect the brain from aging and prevent dis-eases, such as "cancer" and dementia.

6. Turmeric: Contains a natural anti-inflammatory compound, curcumin, which is often found in curry blends.

7. Ginger: Helps reduce inflammation and control blood sugar.

8. Garlic: It can help reduce inflammation, regulate glucose and help your body fight infection.

9. Green Tea: This tea contains anti-inflammatory flavonoids that may help reduce the risks of certain "cancers."

10. Sweet Potato: A great source of complex carbohydrates, fiber, beta-carotene, manganese and vitamin B6 and C, helps heal inflammation in the body.

Some research has shown that the digestive system and the brain are linked together. Dr. Natasha Campbell-McBride is a formally trained Russian neurologist whose child developed autism. As a result of her own research into autism, she ended up developing the Gut and Psychology Syndrome nutritional program. The GAPS Nutritional program is vitally important for most people, as the majority of people have such poor gut health due to poor diet and toxic exposures. This program is also beneficial for people experiencing dyslexia, depression, obsessive-compulsive disorder, bipolar disorder and epilepsy.

♡☮ Dr. S' Insights

The best part about eating foods that combat inflammation is the quality nutrients you are ingesting into your body and their abilities to help combat bad epigenetic molecules. This will provide proper genetic expressions that will promote healthy genes for generations to come. In consuming these top foods to combat inflammation, it would be better to consume the organic version of the products since they will have about fifty more times of the nutritional value than their counterpart. Most inorganic fruits and vegetables have been radiated to keep their fresh look and to help sustain their perishable deadlines.

Antioxidants have multiple properties, Vitamin E, for example, has a key role in protecting the body from pro-inflammatory molecules called cytokines, and one of the best sources of this vitamin is dark green veggies, such as spinach, kale, broccoli, and collard greens. Other molecules are very effective in reducing inflammation. Capsaicin, in hot peppers, like chili and cayenne also found in topical creams, helps reduce pain and inflammation.

Lycopene, present in tomatoes, has been shown to reduce inflammation in the lungs and throughout the body. Cooked tomatoes contain even more lycopene than raw ones, so tomato sauce works, too. A 2012 study found that tomato juice consumption was also beneficial. We would suggest organic, non-herbicide and pesticide tomatoes. Also, we found that eating for blood type is a very effective guide to avoid certain foods; and tomatoes might be one if your blood type is A. Food for thought!

The antioxidant and betalain molecules in the beets or beets juice reduce inflammation related to "cancer" and heart dis-ease. They are also rich in fibers which will help constipation. Research has shown that the NF-kappa B molecule is involved in immune regulation and inflammation. Turmeric, the yellow color in curry, and ginger has a reducing and/or turn-off effect in these particular molecules.

Garlic has similar properties to Non-Steroid Anti-Inflammatory Drugs (NSAID) and shuts down inflammatory pathways in your body. Onions contain similar properties but mostly fight against free-radical who will destroy your cell if in high quantity. Free radicals are also linked to rapid aging. According to UCLA Medical School, the daily use of antioxidants can add ten healthful years to your life.

Raw and cold pressed flavonol-rich dark cocoa has multiple health benefits and helps fight free radicals. A single serving of this raw cocoa increase the cerebral blood flow (from the Journal of Cardiovascular Pharmacology,) improves insulin sensitivity which improves diabetes, reduces risk of cardiovascular dis-ease (from Dr. Eric Ding at Harvard University,) is twenty-five times more effective than a statin drug for preventing heart dis-ease (Dr. Teitebaum.) Additionally, it is a potent immune stimulator of both innate and adaptive immunity (from the Experimental Biology and Medical Journal,) improves blood pressure and cardiovascular mortality in the elderly (from the Archive of Internal Medicine Journal) and, can neutralize smoking toxins from smokers (from the Journal of American College of Cardiology.) Dr. Gordon Pederson is board certified in anti-aging medicine and Ph. D. in toxicology and has published the "cure" for malaria, endorsed these above statements and is also the formulator for Xoçai Healthy Chocolates.

Cherries have a very high anti-inflammation content which reduce the inflammation (tested in lab rats by Oregon Health and Science University,) blood vessel by up to 50%. Furthermore, the human athletes that consume this food will have performance improvement and reduce inflammation pain after rigorous activity.

You will produce about 200 billion new red blood cells every day, you will blink close to 415 million times, your skin will regenerate every month, you will get a new skeleton every 4 years, you will produce enough hair cells in a day to grow 39 inches of new hair... making the proper investment in term of nutrition will make a long-term difference.

Allergies and Inflammation (Compromising Your Immune System)

Food allergies or sensitivity, inflammation and weight problems are linked together and should not be overlooked. The allergies will trigger an inflammation process and will affect the adrenal, liver and the pancreas which in turn will increase the weight gain. This is a bad circle which will keep repeating itself until the food allergies are avoided.

When we become incompatible with our environment; we react with immunological and physiological responses. The inability to tolerate foods and environmental factors, also known as sensitivity or intolerance, induces chronic activation of the innate immune system and gives rise to the inflammatory processes. Inflammation had been identified as the common denominator in most, if not all, dis-ease processes.

According to some studies, infant and children will experience more food allergies then adults. However, food intolerance is more prevalent in the adult population. Between 1997 and 2007, food allergies increased 18% to include approximately 3 million children in the United States. In fact, allergies account for the loss of an estimated 2 million schooldays per year. By understanding allergies, we also need to look at sensitivity which often comes first and leads to the allergies when left untreated.

The symptoms associated with food sensitivities are very broad. The following are some of the major symptoms:

Bloating	Blurry vision	Constipation
Compulsive eating	Depression	Fatigue
Food and sugar cravings	Gassiness	Headaches
Heartburn	Indigestion	Joint pain
Lethargy	Mental agitation	Migraines
Mood swings	Muscle pain	Poor memory/concentration
Post drowsiness after meals	Restless sleep	Sleep disturbance
Spots in front of eyes	Stiffness	Water retention
Weight problems		

Skin problems, like eczema, can be seen in children. Some 10% to 20% of children will develop eczema worldwide. Since the body will express this stress via any means, the skin will usually signify a digestive or nervous system's irritation, or liver issues or an actual skin problem. All these tissues originate from the same place during embryology. Eczema is associated with asthma, respiratory allergies, and hay fever. The most common food triggers for eczema are eggs, milk, peanuts, soy, and wheat.

There are eight foods that account for an estimated 90 percent of allergic reactions. These eight foods are:
- pasteurized milk/dairy
- eggs
- peanuts
- tree nuts (such as almonds, walnuts)
- fish (such as bass, cod, flounder, swordfish)
- shellfish (such as crab, lobster, shrimp)
- soy
- wheat

Cow's milk allergy is the most common food allergy in young children. It is thought by some doctors that at least 50% of all school children are allergic to milk. It's partially the milk protein that causes the allergic reaction in cow's milk allergy. The process of pasteurization might also contribute to the allergy. Weston A. Price Foundation has done remarkable research regarding pasteurized milk and we would suggest reading more about it at (www.westonaprice.org.) Babies who develop cow's milk protein allergy may have one or several of the following symptoms:
- eczema or skin rash
- abdominal pain or cramps
- vomiting
- diarrhea

☽Jenn's Insights

I can still recall that every spring, I would go to my family physician and I would be prescribed allergy pills on a ritual basis. When I returned and said it did not work, the response was yet another prescription for another allergy medication because I was told my body had become immune to the effects over time.

Due to my medical conditions with uterine fibroids and endometriosis, I knew that estrogen was a major hormonal imbalance within my body so I researched and learned to stay away from foods that contained estrogen and phytoestrogen, of which soy was a primary food.

Due to my culture, I loved soy products and consumed them ritually. In fact, soy milk was my favorite drink growing up. Ironically, when my mother was pregnant, she wanted to ensure that I had fair skin and ritually drank soy during the entire pregnancy and consumed so much that I came out paler than any of the babies in the nursery.

I discovered that once I removed soy from my diet along with peanuts and wheat products that my allergies instantaneously went away. I have not had to take any allergy medications even for seasonal allergies.

My other culprit was sugar. I used to drink sodas like water in college and prior to that I often felt tired because I was hypoglycemic and my parents would give me spoons of refined sugar in my juice. If only I had been educated at a younger age with all this nutritional information, I definitely would have had to consume less allergy pills and go thru fewer surgeries. Both endometriosis and uterine fibroids are due to inflammation in the body and its surrounding organs.

My husband had shellfish allergies and I noticed that during every season, he would have to consume so many allergy medications. After being treated by Dr. Stéphane, with the Chiropractic Manipulation Reflex Technique (part of SOT Method) he was able to eat all shellfish type after three sessions. Since then, he has often consumed lobster and shrimp without any issues and I noticed a correlation with the frequency of his allergy medications. He no longer has to take the allergy pills on a seasonal basis.*

Why Avoid Having to Cook Sometimes – Raw Foods

Kristen Suzanne (http://kristensraw.com/store.php), an accomplished Raw food chef and former competitive bodybuilder states: "Nobody should take something so important as his or her diet strictly on the recommendation of one person or information source. But thanks to the tireless efforts of hundreds of researchers always pushing the envelope and questioning the Status Quo, there is now newer, better information."

She is an expert in the field of Raw Foods and has written many books with "easy" to follow recipes. The Raw diet is not a fad. It's not going anywhere because it's where our ancestors began, several hundred thousand years ago. Digestion is the #1 energy drainers for people, so if you can help that by decreasing the time your body needs to digest food, you'll automatically experience more pure, real energy without the need for caffeine or energy drinks.

Doctors Hyman and Galland say that phytonutrients (phyto means plant) help "turn-on" your body's metabolism at the cellular level and regulate hormones that help control appetite. These foods have high levels of antioxidants with health promoting properties that help prevent dis-ease in your body.

Dr. Alan Greene of Stanford's Children's Hospital neatly summarizes the argument of organics: "Eat organic produce". Your immune system won't waste energy trying to fight off the toxins that are sprayed on conventional fruits and vegetables." Because the ground is richer and less toxic, eating organics frees up your immune system and antioxidants to do their evolutionarily evolved job. It will increase their potential to fight off pathogens, "cancer", and other dis-eases originating from natural environmental sources. Your body's natural defense mechanism is capable to defend against everything from Mother Nature, but like anything else, it can only handle so much attack.

Since cooking or processing food above 130 degrees will destroy most vitamin and phytonutrient, this will impact your body's assimilation and fuel capacity of that food. In short, when you cook your food, you're destroying the nutrients. It's like eating an empty meal, no calories and no nutrients. It will take a temperature of 118 F to destroy essential nutrients like vitamins, minerals and enzymes. Enzymes are heat sensitive and destroyed at temperatures above 118 degrees. The amino acids, the building blocks of protein, begin to deteriorate at that temperature and are completely destroyed at 160 F.

According to Dr. Gabriel Cousens, she states that "enzymes can even help repair our DNA and RNA." Eating an enzyme-rich diet will increase vitality and slow the aging process. Enzymes are numerous and can be used for digestion like scissors to the food or as a catalyst (speeding) reaction to certain metabolic pathways. One of the keys for "easy" weight loss is through the action of enzymes. For example, lipase, a fat splitting enzyme, is found in Raw foods. Lipase helps your body in digestion and fat burning for energy. Proteases split up proteins into their component amino acid building blocks and help eliminate toxins.

Kristen shares a fun and important fact that many people often ask, "Where do you get your protein?" The same place elephants, bulls, and buffalos get their protein, from eating plants. See, we have been misguided and programmed to believe that the only source of protein is from meat. But in reality, plant-based foods contain plenty of extremely high quality protein that is actually easier for your body to digest and assimilate.

If you are too busy to cook, look for restaurants that now cater to Raw Foods. In the Washington metropolitan area, Khepra's Raw Food Juice Bar (http://kheprasrawfoodjuicebar.com) and Elizabeth's Gone Raw (www.elizabethsonlstreet.com) are wonderful choices. The owner, Elizabeth Petty was inspired to create this upscale dining and catering experience because this lifestyle change helped heal her from breast "cancer."

How Raw Foods Can Change Your Family's Legacy

The Pottenger-Price Cats study is a well-documented scientific research study of 900 cats conducted between 1932 and 1942 (http://ppnf.org). This research project scientifically proved the degenerative effects a diet of cooked or bioactive "dead" foods has on cats (whereas, eating a raw food diet maintains general good health. Dr. Francis Pottenger was a research scientist.

Dr. Pottenger fed his cats a diet of raw milk, cod liver oil and cooked meat scraps, which was considered the optimum diet. However, he was concerned by the cat's poor postoperative survival rates and by health issues he started noticing in the offspring. He decided to separate a group of cats and feed them the raw meat scraps instead of the cooked meat to see if it would have any effect on their health and vitality.

The cats were divided into two groups. A control group of cats was fed a raw food diet composed of raw meat, raw milk, and cod liver oil. A second group was fed a diet composed of cooked meat and processed milk plus the cod liver oil.

The control group cats fed a raw food diet remained healthy and gave birth to healthy kittens with each succeeding generation. Each generation grew up to be of uniform size and development. Their organs and nervous system functioned normally and their coordination was perfect. They were very resistant to infections. Their mental state was stable and friendly and you could play with them. There were no birth complications and nursing was normal.

The Cooked Food Diet cats gave birth to healthy appearing offspring in the first generation. However, they developed dis-eases and illnesses near the end of their lives. These dis-eased conditions developed midlife in the second generation of offspring. The third generation began manifesting unhealthy conditions in the beginning of their lives and many died before six months of age.

The following conditions were noted in these cats: Increasingly poor eyesight, nearsightedness or farsightedness, heart problems, thyroid and bladder problems, nervous system problems, meningitis and paralysis, infections of various organs, ovary and testis problems, liver problems, inflammations, uterine congestion, atrophy of various organs.

Each new generation had increasingly abnormal variations in their skeletal structure. Skin conditions including parasites, lesions, and allergies appeared worsening with each succeeding generation.

With each new generation, the cats became more unpredictable, were more irritable, were biting and scratching more, were less playful, and so on. The males became docile experiencing a drop in libido and sexual interest while the females became very aggressive.

The cats aborted about 25% of the offspring in the first generation, about 70% of the offspring in the second generation, and in all cases the delivery was difficult and sometimes the females died giving birth. The kittens that were born were about 19 grams less than the ones that were born from the cats being fed a raw food diet. There was no 4th generation of cats. Either the third generation parents were sterile or the fourth generation cats died before birth.

Another group of scientists conducted a similar study using two groups of rats. To summarize, one group was raised on organic whole wheat and another group was raised on commercial white flour. The rats raised on white flour were undersized, unable to reproduce, aggressive and hostile, and with many reports of tooth decay. The rats that were raised on whole wheat had no problems.

A similar study was done using pigs. Again, one group of pigs was given a diet of processed foods. And once again, they had health problems and deformed offspring. However, with pigs it only took one generation of healthy eating for the offspring to be born normal again.

♡☮ Dr. S' Insights

It is ironic that our ancestors who exhibited more of the hunter-gathering lifestyles had less dis-ease states than we do now. However, it makes logical sense since there were no refrigerators or microwaves, more fresh produce was consumed and people had more optimal energy levels with less stressor. Raw and living foods contain essential food enzymes that are destroyed if the food is heated to above 116 Fahrenheit.

Raw food gives you all the enzymes, cofactors, proteins, fat and natural sugars needed for your body to function at optimal levels. The more raw foods you eat, the better your body will be able to respond to the environmental and emotional stressors. You should incorporate this lifestyle into your eating habits slowly by doing a ten day challenge. During these ten days, you should eat primarily raw vegetables and fruits and limit cooking foods.

The following health benefits are highlighted by followers of a raw food diet:
- *You will have more energy*
- *Your skin will have a much better appearance*
- *Your digestion will improve*
- *You will lose weight*
- *Your risk of developing heart and cardiovascular dis-eases will significantly drop*

I challenge you to try this food habit and observe your energy levels. Incorporate alkaline water into your daily intake and drink water with lemon. You will see a whole new transformation and notice energy that you did not even know you had. It detoxifies your body of all the impurities and chemicals that may be contributing to blockages in your arteries and life force energy.

All raw vegetables and fruits contain Mega Hertz energies, this is energy it its rawest fuel form; however, this energy is reduced or destroyed by the process of cooking. Mega Hertz energy is needed to efficiently operate your organs. The liver itself requires between 60 to 90 Mega Hertz of energy to function properly and be able to detoxify your body's environment.

Some nutritionists and dietitians say the following foods should not be consumed raw (please make sure you consult your physician or nutritionist):
- *<u>Buckwheat:</u> If juiced or eaten in large amounts they can be toxic for people with fair skin. Buckwheat has 'fagopyrin' which triggers photosensitivity, as well as some other skin problems.*
- *<u>Kidney beans:</u> have a chemical called phytohaemagglutinin. Raw kidney beans may be toxic.*
- *<u>Alfalfa sprouts:</u> the toxin canavanine is present.*
- *<u>Cassava (yuca):</u> some types may be toxic, this may include cassava flour.*
- *<u>Raw eggs:</u> Avadin, which is present in raw eggs but inactive in cooked eggs, is a vitamin B7 inhibitor. The consumption of 24 egg whites may inactivate the vitamin B7. In addition, salmonella bacteria and other parasites might be present in some eggs, which can cause serious illness if they are not cooked.*
- *<u>Peas:</u> raw seeds of the genus lathyrus (Grass pea, Kesari Dhal, Khesari Dhal or Almorta) may cause a neurological weakness of the lower limb.*

- *Apricot kernels*: contain amygdalin which contains cyanide
- *Parsnips*: contain furanocoumarin, a chemical produced by plants as a defense mechanism against predators. Many furanocoumarins are toxic.
- *Meat*: when raw may contain harmful bacteria, parasites and viruses.

Eating the Rainbow Diet

Each color for a certain food has a meaning in terms of nutrition. Now, it doesn't mean you have to eat a multicolored or rainbow meal each time! It should be suggested to get a wild range of colorful foods on your plate over the course of the week. If you are going to eat your emotions, try this new recipe based on chromotherapy i.e. color therapy (from *Dr. Major B. De Jarnette 1941*):

Eating Green Foods regulates the pituitary gland, fights depression, bulimia, and other psychosomatic conditions affecting the gastric system. It is useful in calming the nervous system, fights irritability, insomnia and can be used to assist in recovery from nervous breakdowns. Some examples include: broccoli, kale, spinach, cabbage, collard greens, and artichokes.

Eating Blue/Purple Foods is calming. Stimulates the parasympathetic system, reduces blood pressure and calms both breathing and heart rate. It has anti-inflammatory and muscle relaxing effects. Fights both physical and mental tension and is used to assist in relaxation. Some examples include: blueberries, eggplants, plums, prunes, blackberries, and grapes.

Eating Red Foods is used to energize and stimulate. These foods affect the heart by increasing pulse rate, and the muscles by increasing their tension. They influence vitality and increase body temperature and can be used to develop excitement and sensuality. Some examples include: beets, cherries, red onions, strawberries, raspberries and grapefruit.

Eating Yellow/Orange Foods increases neuromuscular tone. Purifies blood, helps digestion, and has a cleansing effect. Strongly stimulates happiness, brings on a sense of security, as well as a strong feeling of well-being. Some examples include: butternut squash, carrots, lemon, sweet potatoes, peaches, and pineapples.

Eating White Foods helps with regeneration. Also, provides energy and balances the chronobiological rhythm, by stimulating the production of serotonin, a substance which regulates both sleep and the nervous system. These foods help rebalance the psychophysical and hormonal systems in people who suffer from seasonal depression. Some examples include: turnip, onions, cauliflower, garlic, and shallots.

 Jenn's Insights

There is a direct connection between what you feed your child today and what they will be feeding themselves into adulthood. Consuming nutritious food will increase their proper growth and making

sure they have all the "fuel" and building blocks to be as "perfect" as they can be and instill the lessons up front. Good nutrition also helps prevent child and teen issues such as eating disorders, obesity, dental cavities and iron-deficiency of anemia. Listed below are some resources to help make this a fun learning process for your children:

• The Rainbow Dinner Game:

The Whole Kids Foundation (www.wholekidsfoundation.org) designed the Rainbow Dinner Game. Before dinner, you draw a rainbow on a sheet of paper. Then, you bring your drawing and a pencil to the dining room table. Your family looks for foods on the table to match each color of the rainbow and write it down on your drawing. Make a list of foods to fill in the rest of the colors and add that to your weekly grocery list.

- *Today I Ate A Rainbow (http://www.todayiatearainbow.com)*
- *Eat Right With Color (http://www.youtube.com/watch?v=vYzGkoxvPX0)*
- *Food Rainbow (http://playrific.com/z/7116)*
- *Eat Like a Rainbow by Jay Mankita (http://eat-like-a-rainbow.bandcamp.com)*
- *Eat A Rainbow Everyday ([http://www.healthyschoolsms.org/ohs_main/documents/ EataRainbowTeacherActivityGuide.pdf](http://www.healthyschoolsms.org/ohs_main/documents/EataRainbowTeacherActivityGuide.pdf))*
- *Make it a Game! A face made out of vegetables. A red cheery nose reminded children red is good for the heart and blood, green helps teeth and bones, and orange helps the eyes.*

• Rainbow Fruit Sticks:

This is a simple way to make eating fruit fun. You could also do a veggie rainbow stick, makes it fun to eat! All you need is a collection of colorful fruit and some rounded sticks such as popsicle sticks or bamboo skewers. Pineapple, Green Grapes, Cantaloupe, Raspberries, Honeydew Melon and Blackberries can be used to give the skewers a nice rainbow effect and of course organic would be better. You can also freeze them to provide a different texture.

Alkaline Your Body

If we look at a battery leaking acid, the possibility of damage around the area is certain. How do our bodies become too acidic? One of the primary causes is the foods we eat; when our diet contains too acid-rich foods, our body will become acidic. Some foods are acidic and will carry that property within the body while others may not be but will create an acidic forming reaction.

What are acid forming foods? They are high protein flesh foods, high sugar and high fat, and all contribute to forming acid in your body. Dairy, flour products, most cooked grains, most cooked beans, candy, soda, coffee, tobacco, alcohol, chemical additives, preservatives, drugs, and synthetic vitamins will form acid in your body.

Acidosis, medical terminology indicating an acidic body, has been established to cause illness. The interesting fact is that acidosis will lead to a lack of acid production in the stomach, the only organ needing acid to properly function. One way to monitor your body's acidity is if your stomach does not produce enough acid, which will lead to excess burping, bloating, gas and acid coming up your throat. The toxicity of the majority of foods in a typical diet causes the body to become more acidic during digestion, and this includes most tap water.

As you recall from the battery analogy above, acidity will destroy your own cells and weaken your immune system, increasing the aging process among other dis-eases. Allergies and weight gain is also affected by this increased body acidity. It will also affect the absorption of nutrients and the inability of eliminating actual toxins and waste. In the meantime your body will try to control the level of acidity by increasing the blood level of cholesterol and will increase breathing to increase oxygen level.

Since our body requires oxygen to properly function and to fight infection, when our body is acidic this feature is either delayed or limited. When a body reaches a pH level of 7.4 (alkaline instead of acidic,) "cancers" may become dormant, and at 7.6, the majority of all "cancer" cells die rapidly, along with every type of foreign invader according to Dr. Keiichi Morishita. All alkaline components like chemicals or blood will readily absorb oxygen. Whereas pathogen and "cancer" cannot survive in an oxygen-rich and alkaline environment; this is partly why hyperbaric chamber or oxygen therapy is often used to treat these dis-eases.

In contrast, acidity or toxic chemicals including drugs and medication will lower the body's pH. This might be a reason why they have so many side effects attributed to medication. Acid decreases energy production in the cells, the ability to repair damaged cells, the ability to detoxify heavy metals, and makes the body more susceptible to fatigue and illness.

In Dr. Keiichi Morishita's book, Hidden Truth of Cancer, he quotes, "In 1965, only 1 person in 214 contracted "cancer." Today it is 1 in 3 females and 1 in 2 males. A determining factor between health and dis-ease is pH. It is not uncommon for the average American to test between 4 pH and 5 pH."

Nobel Prize in Medicine winner, Otto Warberg, discovered that low oxygen environment in the tissues was the cause of "cancer." A study published in the Journal of Biological Chemistry found that alkalosis (rising pH) causes alkaline induced cell death as a result of altering mitochondrial (cell) functioning. The mitochondria are the energy (fuel) producer for the cell.

Jenn's Insights

What children learn during this life will be various but nutrition or what she or he eats must become an important lesson to incorporate into their lives. Eating right has less meaning to our education system where math, history and science are predominant. So much time and money is geared to that education and not towards the choice of a healthy meal.

Children will find their way to explore and follow their curiosity. With that curiosity, they will try foods and might get addicted because of certain effects. Sugar is well known addictive This is why kids keep asking for more and more. Since children are mainly in a learning stage from infant to the age of seven, it is "easy" to default back to water and proper foods if they have role models to follow such as parents or grandparents.

A very fun tool is to use the ice cube tray where you can add ionized alkaline water with a slice of lemon or orange and add the frozen cube to their drink. They will love it and it will teach them a healthy habit early on.

You can also make it like a science project by getting the pH food drops and add them to some liquid like bottled water, tap water, sodas and other. Your children will learn pretty fast how bad is their surrounding just by a change of color. Teach them about acidity and its harmful effects on the body and encourage them to drink alkaline, ionized water at an earlier age.

For Adults, Shelley Young and Dr. Robert Young wrote the pH Miracle and they eloquently emphasized why it is important. The most important beauty product (or practice, rather) you can apply to your physical appearance is your diet and the way you hydrate your skin with what you eat and drink. Tony Robbins followed their protocol and it allowed him to restore optimum health to his system through pH balancing.

I had the honor to meet Kris Carr and hear about her story and it revived a lot of hopes for me because my father-in-law and many other relatives had passed away from "cancer." Kris Carr was diagnosed with a vascular "cancer" at the age of 31 years old. The lining of the blood vessels in her liver and lung was attacked. It was a 0.01% chance to have it but unfortunately she went thru the experience to empower others. Her "cancer" was at stage IV, which meant it was incurable and inoperable according to the allopathic medical doctors.

Her lifestyle had made her burn the candle at both ends with sleep deprivation, eating sugars, energy bars, fast food and drank lots of coffee. But after her diagnosis, she knew a life change was needed. So she traded her old life for a brand new one i.e. vegan diet and cucumber smoothies.

She went on a quest to explore all possibilities to heal her own self via massages, meditation, Zen monastery, and learned all about the pH and the importance of alkalizing her blood thru Shelley and Dr. Robert Young's pH Miracle Retreat. After 5 years, pathology shows her "tumors" to be in full remission.

Kris is currently developing an online community (www.crazysexylife.com) that works with top oncologists on research data to share with the world. Her website www.crazysexycancer.com provides more in-depth tips and the goal of the nonprofit organization she developed is to serve as one of the bridges between Western and alternative medicine.

Why Drink Alkaline Water?

Water is a part of the Earth and is definitely an element that is within us. The latest research states that our brain and heart is composed of about seventy-three percent water where our lungs are eighty-three percent. The Journal of Biological Chemistry, also measured the skin with content of sixty-four percent water, muscles and kidneys are seventy-nine percent, and even the bones have thirty-one percent.

Research is showing that a male would need about 3 liters a day while woman might need a little less, 2.2 liters a day of water intake. Generally, the amount of water needed is measured in ounces and is about half of our body weight. So if one weighs 100 pounds, they should hydrate with about 50 ounces daily.

Some of this water is gotten in food. Water is expelled via our breath, exercise, sweat and urine throughout the day. Alkaline water can alleviate many of the major known dis-ease to the primary organs. We understand there are some pros- and cons- to this theory, but we feel, as authors, the benefit of the alkaline water and food is important and has provided a significance in our life among our patients at Gainesville Holistic Health Center.

One organ that can help your body pH is the pancreas which should be elevated to a pH of 8.8. So if the insulin hormone is impaired by a lack of calcium ions, insulin resistance, diabetes to name a few, it will be more than likely to be less effective to help the body to reach an alkaline state. Blood vessels with excess protein buildup can also impair the pancreas function.

One of the busiest organs in term of work is the liver. It can accomplish more than 250 biochemical reactions a second. It will also regulate the acid toxins from the blood and will detoxify from poison and other substance. The liver is like our guardian angel. The liver possesses a series of alkaline enzyme to facilitate that process. In addition, all the nourishment obtained through the gastrointestinal tract enters the blood by way of the liver. The load on the liver is much heavier when acid waste products are constantly floating in the blood. If the liver becomes overworked or overloaded, it will diminish its function and many dis-ease risks can occur.

One organ who works best in an alkaline environment is the heart. Since the heart pumps the blood, it will come in a direct contact with the acidity or the alkalinity element every time it pumps blood. The heart actually pumps about 520 quarts of blood an hour which is about 13,000 quarts a day. You can see how with this amount of blood flowing through the heart how if the quality of it is impaired how it will affect the heart muscles. The heartbeat can be altered by acid wastes. These wastes rob the blood of proper oxygenation and overall degeneration of the heart follows.

Alkaline water can help prevent and heal this condition and will decrease the work load of the pancreas, liver and other organs to facilitate their work.

Why Eat Alkaline Foods?

Along with alkaline water, our food supplies can generate an alkaline body state. Some research has shown that a diet in low-acid food can prevent kidney stones, keep bones and muscles strong, improve heart health and brain function, reduce low back pain, and lowers risk for colon "cancer" and type 2 diabetes. See chart below for food guidelines:

	pH				
DRINK Ionized Water 1 Liter per 30lbs **DAILY**	**pH 10.00** 1,000x more alkaline	Raw Asparagus Raw Celery Cauliflower Cucumber Raw Kale	Red Cabbage Seaweeds Lemons/limes Rhubarb Stalk Alfalfa Grass	Dandelion Wheat Grass Black Radish Soy Sprout Chia Sprout	Barley Grass Raw Spinach Raw Broccoli Artichoke Collar Green
Consume Freely			**High Alkaline Ionized Water**		
ALKALINE pH	**pH 9.0** 100x more alkaline	Avocado Borage oil Green Tea Most Lettuce Raw Zucchini	Red Radish Red Beets Raw Tomato French Beans Parsley-Cilantro	Raw Peas Raw Eggplant Alfalfa Sprout Green Beans Beet Greens	Garlic or chives Dog/Shave Grass Straw Grass Lemon Grass Cayenne Pepper
Most foods get more acidic when cooked	**pH 8.0** 10x more alkaline	Brussels Sprout Endive Green Cabbage Cooked Spinach Cooked Broccoli Cook Asparagus	Lima Beans Soy Beans Navy Beans Cooked Peas Cook Eggplants Sour Grapefruit	Raw Almonds Wild Rice Quinoa Millet Flax Seed oil Coconut Water	Chicory Olives Bell Peppers Watercress White Radish Lamb's lettuce
NEUTRAL pH	**pH 7**	**Most Tap Water (7.3)** With Chlorine to keep it at that level **HUMAN BLOOD pH is 7.365**	Most Olive oils Pumpkin Seeds Primrose Oil Marine Lipids Sesame Seeds		Fennel Seeds Sunflower Seeds Leeks (bulb) Coconut & oil Barley

	pH					
20:1 It takes 20 parts Of Alkalinity to	**pH 6.0** 10x more acid	Fresh water fish Lentil Spelt Soy Flour Brazil Nut Coconut	Macadamias Grapes Hazelnuts Wheat Papaya	Watermelon Cantaloupe Cherries Strawberries Plums	Dates Peaches Oranges Pineapple Banana	Blueberries Raspberries Coconut Wheat Kernels Stevia / Agave

Most Bottled Water

	pH					
Neutralize 1 part of Acidity In the body	**pH 5.0** 100x more acid	Honey Cooked Beans Bread Liver Organ Meats	Cocoa Soy Milk White Rice Potatoes Cashew	Soft Cheeses Milk & Cream Cook Tomatoes Sweet Potatoes Whole Grain	Rye Bread White Bread White Biscuit Fruit Juice Cooked Corn & Corn Oil	Oyster Rice Cakes Ketchup & Mayo Figs/Prunes

ACIDIC pH

Reverse Osmosis – Distilled & Purified Water – Enhance – Flavored – Vitamin Waters & Sports

	pH				
Consume Sparingly	**pH 4.0** 1,000x more acid	Turkey Ocean Fish Chicken & Eggs Hard Cheeses Mustard	Canned Fruit Beer & Wines Cream Cheese Most Pastries Popcorn	Peanuts Pistachios Fruit Drinks Beet Sugar White Sugar	Coffee Chocolate Cranberries Buttermilk Tomato Sauce

Carbonated Water – Seltzer or Club Soda

	pH			
Or never	**pH 3.0** 10,000x more acid	Pork Veal Beef Lamp Picked	Vinegar Black Tea Hard Liquor Canned Food Processed Foods	Microwaves Food Sweetened Fruits/Juice Stress, worry, lack of sleep Artificial sweeteners Soda and carbohydrate beverage

Foods that Hinder the Brain – Environmental Toxins

On a daily basis we are exposed to environmental toxins in the food we eat, the water we drink and the air we breathe. Many adult dis-eases, including diabetes, mental disorders, Alzheimer's, and heart dis-ease can be linked to early toxin exposure that occurs even when the baby is developing in the womb. We know that toxins can cross the placental and blood-brain barrier, passing to your baby in the womb. Toxins from the mother are also passed to infants during breastfeeding.

Watching a good movie is oftentimes associated with a big bag of popcorn. Did you know the micro-wave popcorn bag can leach chemicals that are harmful, like perfluorooctanoic acid, which is linked to infertility; this toxin latches on to the popcorn and then you and remains in your body for an extended time frame.

One of the major issues with harmful chemicals, as stated by Environmental Working Group senior scientist Olga Naidenko is that they stay in your body for years and often accumulates. These chemicals have been known to cause liver, testicular, and pancreatic "cancer."

Polychlorinated biphenyls (PCBs) are one of the most commonly reported environmental contaminants. PCBs are toxic chemicals that have pervaded the soil and waters.

They are most often exposed to the environment through leaky equipment, illegal dumping, waste oils from electrical equipment, and hazardous waste.

In 1976, Congress passed the Toxic Substances Control Act (TSCA), which banned the production of PCBs because of its research link to "cancer." The most prevalent danger to PCB exposure today is through consuming farm raised salmon. These farmed salmon are fed fish feed that is designed to be high in fish oil. They are fed ground up fish, which have PCBs in their fatty tissue. Therefore, these farmed salmon ingest dangerous levels of PCBs and often make them unsafe to eat more than once in a month.

The Environmental Working Group also performed PCB tests on farmed salmon. According to their findings, 70% of the farmed salmon tested were PCB contaminated and 90% of farmed salmon failed EPA health limits for weekly consumption.

The Environmental Working Group reports on The Dirty Dozen, a list of the fruits and vegetables likely to contain the highest amounts of pesticide residue and would be better if organically consumed. For further information please visit http://www.ewg.org/foodnews/summary.php.

These foods include:

- Apples
- Celery
- Cherry tomatoes
- Cucumbers
- Grapes
- Hot peppers

- Nectarines (imported)
- Peaches
- Potatoes
- Spinach
- Strawberries
- Sweet bell peppers

Silicone (dimethylsiloxane) is one of the most highly toxic substances on earth. It is linked to allergies, brain damage, "cancer", and autoimmune disorders. Dimethylsiloxane is commonly used as a filler fluid in breast implants. It is becoming less predominant due to serious side effects. If this substance is considered to be a hazardous ingredient when it's placed inside our bodies, it makes you wonder, how consumption could be safe.

Have you ever experienced a fountain drink? Have you tasted the differences between a bottled drink and a fountain drink? Evidences have shown that the actual formula of the fountain drink are different than the bottled one, they use dimethylsiloxane. Additionally, the diet drinks often have two different artificial sweeteners from fountain to bottles.

Some chemical used in yoga mats and shoe soles are also used, according to the FDA's approved list, to bleached flour and dough conditioner. It has been found in fast food and grocery store that has one hundred percent whole wheat bread, English muffin, butter croissant, Panini bread and sesame breads.

Another harmful chemical is the hexachlorobenzene which has been banned in the United States since 1966 and globally under the Stockholm Convention since 2004. However, it is still in the environment and in our food supplies. Farmed salmon contains traces of hexachlorobenzene as well as kale imported from China.

A recent study released in Spain determined that children born to mothers with higher levels of hexachlorobenzene (HCB) in the cord blood were significantly more likely to be overweight and obese by the age of six. The scientists stated that "it is important that pregnant women are informed about the possible side effects of prenatal exposure to HCB and how it impacts the child's Body Mass Index (BMI) later in life."

Additionally, all the children measured (n=405) in the study had organochlorine contaminants in their blood. Organochlorines are compounds that contain carbon, chlorine, and hydrogen and are also found in pesticides. If we poison our world, then ultimately we poison ourselves and our children so even for those that do not consider themselves Environmentalist, the information is worth reading up on.

BPA has been a valid concern for all pregnant mothers in the last ten to fifteen years. While Duke University demonstrated expected problems such as obesity, altered reproductive functionality, and an increase risk to "cancerous" conditions in mothers who were exposed to the plastic chemical BPA during pregnancy; however, it is still present in our food supply.

In the journal "Analytical and Bioanalytical Chemistry" the study published showed that there are still products that contain BPA:

- Credit card/cash register receipts made from your purchases (thermal paper)
- The sealants dentists use to protect teeth from cavities break down into BPA when in contact with saliva (holistic dentistry would be preferred for pregnant women.) Additionally some dental sealant used for children still contains this element and holistic dentistry would be preferred for your kids.)
- Pizza boxes may contain recycled materials from thermal paper
- Soda cans contain a plastic lining made with BPA
- The canned goods container contain a plastic lining (predominant in soup, vegetable, fruit and tuna cans)
- Wines fermented in vats with plastic lining
- Microwave oven dishes

A 2005 study showed more than 287 chemicals, pollutants and pesticides were found in the umbilical cord blood of the newborn.

76 chemicals are known to cause "cancer" in humans or animals

94 chemicals are toxic to the brain and nervous system
79 chemicals causes birth defects or abnormal development in animal testing
Testing conducted on 10 subjects, revealed that all 10 umbilical cords contained Scotchgard and Teflon (non-stick cooking pans and pots)

More than 700 studies have been conducted on BPA and all scientists concluded that people are exposed to levels of BPA in excess of those that have harmed lab animals. Among the most vulnerable are infants and fetuses, which are still developing their brains.

Foods That Hinder The Brain – Flavorings and Additives

For your brain to properly function, it requires the proper fuel. Flavorings and additives do impact your brain and can cause a sluggishness effect among other consequences. Processed meats for lunch, for example, contain sodium nitrate that has been demonstrated by research to link to pancreatic "cancer", colon "cancer" and even brain "tumor." The use of fresh meats is a better choice.

So if we mentioned meat deli from the store we need to also cover the chicken nuggets. A study conducted by the National Journal of Medicine concluded that randomly sampled chicken from two national chains was mostly composed of chicken fat, bone, nerve, and connective tissue. Even worse, that chicken can now be processed in China, without Food and Drug Administration regulation of the processing plant. But the real issue about the fast food chains is not only about the quality of the meat, but rather the additives and the combination of additives in them. FDA regulates the amount of additive but not the combination which can be harmful, as stated by Food Babe at: (http://www.100daysofrealfood.com/2012/04/25/food-babe-investigates-why-chick-fil-a/)

Dr. Joseph Mercola at (www.mercola.com) have been an influencer for many years in making sure we are all aware of our choices and bringing forward the latest research. He is an influential authority in making a shift toward a healthier lifestyle. According to Dr. Mercola, a 2010 study revealed that those who ate a predominantly processed food diet at age 3 had lower IQ scores at age 8.5. Furthermore, for each measured increase in processed foods, participants had a nearly two point decrease in IQ.

If you eat Asian foods, and now pretty much all cuisine types contain this element, you may be eating monosodium glutamate or MSG. It is found in a majority of Asian foods (soy sauce) as well as many other processed snack foods that we eat. MSG is also in famous canned soups, you should always read the ingredients before making purchases as an educated consumer.

According to Dr. Mercola, becoming familiar with the hidden names of MSG can also help you determine what foods to eat. The following ingredients contain MSG: Gelatin, Hydrolyzed Vegetable Protein (HVP), Yeast Extract, Malted Barley, Rice Syrup or Brown Rice Syrup. It is also highly toxic and can lead to fatigue, hormone imbalances, as well as brain damage if consumed in high doses.

Another prevalent issue is the food coloring and dye additives added to our children's foods, more than fifteen million pounds of food dye are in use in USA per year and most of them are synthetically made with petroleum and are also approved by the FDA to enhance coloring of many snacks and food items marketed for kid's consumption.

For those who do not know what petroleum is: gasoline, diesel fuel, asphalt, and tar. They are all linked to behavioral problems such as hyperactive and inattentiveness occurring in children. The three most widely used dyes, Red 40, Yellow 5, and Yellow 6, are contaminated with known carcinogens that cause "cancer." In 1984 the FDA commissioner Mark Novitch stated that the Red 3 dye has clearly been shown to induce "cancer" and was of greatest public health concern.

Back years ago, Canada passed a law that smoking cigarettes was not healthy and all manufacturers needed to put a *DANGER* warning label on their carton stating the harm. So at least, the smoker might gage the pros and cons of their consequence. In UK, they are doing the same thing with regards to food additives and coloring. The label states that the food "may have an adverse effect on the activity and attention in children." This is why M&Ms and Nutri-Grain bars contain only natural colorings outside of the United States.

We would suggest looking at the label and watching for any dye or artificial coloring in food but also noticing these ingredients listed in your child's toothpaste, skin care, baby care, baby soap and shampoo and even in baby wipes. A reputable company for obtaining toiletries is Jessica Alba's company, called The Honest Company (www.honest.com).

Foods That Hinder The Brain – Genetically Modified (GMOs)

Science has always tried to improve our living experience by bringing innovation. Even if the intent is purely good, sometimes the original intention gets altered and the end product does more harm than good. GMOs are one of those concepts that had a noble intention of providing enough food supply for the world but the mission has been altered and now these by-products are doing more harm to our generation and for future generations.

The Institute for Responsible Technology has compiled research of GMO presence in many types of foods. They discovered ten of the most popular foods that likely contain hidden GMOs. Purchasing foods that are labeled with non-GMO Project would be a better alternative for your safety and your children's safety.

Biologist David Schubert of the Salk Institute warns that "children are the most likely to be adversely effected by toxins and other dietary problems" related to Genetically Modified (GM) foods. He says without adequate studies, the children become "the experimental animals."

GMO research has been done on rats. They have found that if fed to a female rat their offspring will die within three weeks. When males were fed, their testicular changed color and had altered sperm. The size of the offspring growth was even smaller.

Other animals like buffalo when fed GMO cottonseed had their health impacted with premature deliveries, abortions, infertility, and prolapsed uteruses. Many calves died due to this lifestyle habit. In the US, about two dozen farmers reported thousands of pigs becoming sterile after consuming certain GMO corn varieties. Some had false pregnancies; others gave birth to bags of water. Cows and bulls also became infertile when fed the same corn. This might explain why infertility rates have spiked way up in the last decades among the human population. Commercial planting of a genetically modified herbicide tolerant sugar beet began in the USA in 2008.

From the Daily Finance, by Brian Stoffel (http://www.dailyfinance.com/2013/11/21/foods-give-up-avoid-eating-gmo/) the following foods were revealed to contain GMO by-products.

Canned Soups: Tomato Soup lists high fructose corn syrup as its second biggest ingredient and nearly 88 percent of all corn planted in the United States is GMO.

Cream of Mushroom soup has listed vegetable oil as its third ingredient. It specifically says the oil comes from cottonseed, canola, and/or soybeans. The non-GMO Project says 90 percent of cottonseed, 90 percent of rapeseed (the source of canola), and 94 percent of soybeans are GMOs.

Frozen Foods: Frozen foods are often sweetened with High Fructose Corn Syrup. If not the presence of non-cane sugar is added. Sugar beets provide half of all consumable sugar in America, and 95 percent of those sugar beets are grown using GMO seeds.

Baby Formula: Both milk and soy products regularly show up in the ingredient list for baby foods. According to the non-GMO Project, 94 percent of all soy is genetically modified. Meanwhile, 8 percent of the corn fed to cows contains GMOs.

<u>Sweetened Juices</u>: To entice kids to drink more juice, many companies add High Fructose Corn Syrup or non-cane sugar to the drink.

According to the non-GMO Project, papaya grown in the USA is genetically-modified. Consequently, papaya is used as a staple food in the Eastern cultures for enhancing breast milk production.

<u>Cereals</u>: The majorities of cereals have sugar and corn starch listed as their top ingredients, both are GMOs.

<u>Vegetable and Canola Oils</u>: Some of the most popular oils are corn, soy, and cottonseed. All three of these crops, when sourced from the United States, have a greater than 88 percent chance of being GMOs. Canola Oil's parent company named rapeseed is also GMO.

<u>Tofu</u>: The main ingredient in tofu is soy milk, and the vast majority of soybeans from America, 94 percent are GMOs.

<u>Meat</u>: The main ingredient in the diet of many forms of livestock is corn feed, which usually contains GMO varieties. This also impacts the by-products from these animals such as milk. Additionally there was a GMO experiment involving pigs called EnviroPig.

<u>Sodas</u>: These drinks are pumped full of sugar and more often contain High Fructose Corn Syrup that is guaranteed to be GMO.

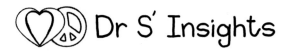 Dr S' Insights

Genetically modified (GM) foods are created based on researchers' intent to manipulate DNA for a beneficial outcome like resistance to bugs that eat them, resistance to chemicals around them or have the best genetic materials incorporated from two species. Health effects of primary concern to safety assessors are production of new allergens, increased toxicity, decreased nutrition, and antibiotic resistance.

When I initially researched on GMO foods, the standard was to only provide two or three DNA changes to the by-product; however, there were no set policies or regulations. However, with every scientific field that incorporates new technology, side effects can be produced and death or worse, deformity may occur.

Today we do not use these chemicals anymore but are playing with the core of the DNA of plants that we eat and which can affect our own DNA. If we look at our history, this parallels the medication industry. The protocols by FDA of many historic medications were discontinued due to death, permanent damage to the brain or physical parts. Some of these medications were commercialized with substances that could be harmful. For a full list see:

(http://io9.com/how-todays-illegal-drugs-were-marketed-as-medicines-510258499)

There were cocaine tooth drops for children. Did you know that in 1886, the original patent for Coca-Cola served medicinal purposes and there was five ounces of coca (cocaine) leaves in the syrup. The original formula had about nine milligrams of cocaine per glass bottle.

There are also numerous research studies that have shown "cancerous" effects with these GMO by-products. Around the world, health conscious French scientists conclude long-term study of GMO on rats; extensive research proving GMO corn causes horrific "tumors" in rats, killing 70 percent of females early, long before their average two year life expectancy. This provoked a Europe-wide ban on Monsanto GM corn and Russia also bans all GM corn imports.

We encourage you to become empowered and learn more by visiting:
http://www.naturalnews.com/037621_gmo_side_effects_cancer.html

Sugar: the Silent Killer to the Brain

The rate of conversion of food to sugar is called the glycemic index (GI.) High glycemic foods have been shown to increase appetite and are a major contributor to obesity in children. Impaired glucose control, along with obesity, and high fat diets, and sedentary lifestyle (video games and television), are influencing our next generation of health.

You Are What You Eat, by Gillian McKeith mentioned about sugar. Sugar, especially the refined white has no nutritional value. Worse, it causes your insulin levels to spike which will cause you to gain weight, and can lead to type 2 diabetes. The rate of diabetes is rising up among Americans and pre-diabetes ages are getting younger and younger.

On average, the US citizen consumes close to 756 grams of sugar every five days or 130 pounds of sugar a year. Since the evidence of sugar consumption is linked to obesity, if this rate continues forty-two percent of the US population will then be obese by 2030 and will cost close to half a trillion dollars in health spending.

When sugar is not used, it is stored in the liver or as a form of fat. But consumption of sugar has also been implicated in an increased chance of cardiovascular dis-ease, dementia, macular degeneration, renal failure, chronic kidney dis-ease and high blood pressure.

According to Michelle King Robson, founder of EmpowHER (www.empowher.com), it appears that the more sugar a person consumes the higher the risk for brain shrinkage in the memory center known as the hippocampus, which in the long-run may lead to dementia.

Food companies are cleverly disguising the sugar in their foods production by relabeling them as some of the synonym terms. Nutritional labels are required by law to list their most prominent ingredients.

By putting two or three different types of sugar in the food and calling them each a different name, they can spread out the sugar content across three ingredients:

- Agave nectar
- Brown sugar
- Cane crystals
- Cane sugar
- Corn sweetener
- Corn syrup
- Crystalline fructose
- Dextrose
- Evaporated cane juice
- Organic evaporated cane juice
- Fructose
- Fruit juice concentrates
- Glucose
- High fructose corn syrup
- Honey
- Invert sugar
- Lactose
- Maltose
- Malt syrup
- Molasses
- Raw sugar
- Sucrose
- Sugar
- Syrup

Fun Fact 1: *20 ounce soft drink equals to eating 16.5 sugar cubes*
Fun Fact 2: *3 pounds of carrots equal the sugars in one bottled soft drink.*

High fructose corn syrup is one of the most publicized which can damage memory and learning abilities. Food companies use it because it is six times cheaper and sweeter than cane sugar. It is almost in every processed food available including condiments and baby foods.

According to a study in the "American Journal of Clinical Nutrition," pregnant Danish women who consumed at least four servings of artificially sweetened carbonated soft drinks each day were at a seventy-eight percent higher risk of preterm birth.

NutraSweet is one of the most serious sugar substitute offenders. This ingredient can lead to a whole host of side effects including migraines, irritability, heart palpitations, seizures, insomnia, memory loss, joint pain, as well as fatigue and feelings of depression. Splenda is also known to explode internally and result in weakened immune function, irregular heartbeats, agitation shortness of breath, skin rash and "cancer" to name a few. The Center for Science in the Public Interest (CSPI) recommends people avoid the artificial sweeteners saccharin as found in Sweet 'N Low, aspartame as found in NutraSweet and Equal, and acesulfame potassium as found in Sunett and Sweet One.

Your brain requires about seven more times sugar to function and use as energy. Sugar (glucose) is the main fuel of your brain. However, the excess consumption might trigger causing bursts of energy followed by fidgeting, headaches, trouble concentrating, or drowsiness.

If you consume sugar with fiber, the fiber will slow the absorption of sugar and delay its rapid increase into the blood. Fruit has "good sugar" because of the presence of fibers as well as antioxidants and other nutritive factors.

Jenn's Insights

According to research from the Mayo Clinic, children between the ages of two and five are consuming on average 13 teaspoons of sugar by-products a day which equates to 280 empty calories a day. Between the ages of six and eleven they are consuming 20 teaspoons of sugar by-products which equates to 320 empty calories. And from twelve and nineteen years, they consume 24 teaspoons of sugar by-products which equates to 380 empty calories.

Some ideas for parents and caregivers:

Desserts and Sweets Limit portions of cookies, candies and other baked goods, instead try fruit-based desserts or make your own baked goods and use gluten free and/or coconut flour and healthier ingredients.

Cereals Limit sugary cereals. Look for substitutes such as oatmeal that don't have added sugar or salt and add nuts, fruit or cinnamon.

Yogurts An 8-ounce serving has about 12 grams of natural sugar. This is included in the total sugar listed on the Nutrition Facts Label. Many flavored yogurts also have a significant amount of added sugar. Avoid those and instead opt for plain yogurt and add your own sweetness by blending in frozen berries or other fruits.

Beverages Stick to water and unflavored coconut milk or almond milk. Limit juices, sports drinks and other flavored beverages.

As a parent, the importance of properly reading labels and understanding the ingredients will make a huge difference in your child's life, behavior and overall learning capacities. If you see sugar by any name near the top of list, reconsider. Is there a better option? Could you make this item yourself and eliminate or reduce the amount of sugar?

Vitamins vs. Supplements

(Contribution by Dr. Joseph F. Unger Jr. FICS)

Most medical professionals claim that it is best to obtain vitamins and minerals from the foods we eat instead of from supplementation. Unfortunately, all the essential nutrients our bodies require simply do not exist in the food supply anymore. For optimal health and optimal nutrition, supplementation, preferably with whole food supplements, is essential.

Synthetic vitamins are made from petroleum but also from GMO food derivatives. Vitamin C is mostly coming from corn and in USA, corn is 85% GMO. Vitamin C or ascorbic acid is used in multiple food processes. Vitamin E is usually derived from soy. Soy in USA is 90 to 100% chance to be GMO. Vitamin B-2 (riboflavin), vitamin B-12, and vitamin A are made from a process that involves genetically modified microorganisms. Vitamins D and K may have "carriers" that are derived from genetically modified corn, such as starch, glucose, and maltodextrin.

Standard Process Inc. formulates whole food nutritional supplements in accordance with the principles and understanding developed by Dr. Royal Lee. One of Dr. Lee's numerous innovations was to develop a line of therapeutic agents that he called "Protomorphogens" (PMGs.)

Through Dr. Lee's dedication to understanding the powers of nutritional healing, he developed the theory that specific protein chains are capable of encouraging certain healing processes in the body. Specifically, Dr. Lee extracted intact DNA from the nucleus of certain animal tissues. His first extract was that of heart tissue. The product that resulted is called Cardiotrophin PMG.

Dr. Lee had to invent the machinery capable of extracting the intact DNA chains without destroying them. This patented process is still used today and is unique to Standard Process. Dr. Lee concluded that many such compounds can already be found in nature as long as they are extracted in their intact and pure form. Therefore, when a person has a problem related to a specific organ function, ingestion of the appropriate Protomorphogens made from that particular gland or organ may be useful in facilitating that individual's self-healing and self-regenerating capacity. Dr. Stéphane believes that the PMG might be the contributing factor or support in restoring the proper epigenetics; however, more research is needed in that field.

Dr. Lee also theorized many decades ago that one of the major causes of human ailments is autoimmune dysfunction. He theorized that the same Protomorphogens used to revitalize organs and tissues could also be utilized to identify and treat autoimmune conditions. Overall, autoimmune dis-eases are common, affecting more than 23.5 million Americans.

The immune system deciphers between its own body parts and foreign invaders. If a foreign invader is identified, an immune response is enacted. If there is a sick, ailing, malnourished or stressed organ, it may not have had all the resources to reproduce perfect cellular membranes. The immune system may therefore identify the sick organ as not quite part of its own body.

The sick organ is not so different as to require a huge immune response such as a cold, flu or an infected cut, but it may warrant at least some intervention. In such circumstances, the immune system starts a response against the healthy organ to help "clean up" the debris. The result, however, is added stress to the already ailing organ or tissue. The goal with the Protomorphogens is to de-stress the organ(s.)

Medications vs. Homeopathy

Homeopathy, or homeopathic medicine, is a medical philosophy and practice based on the idea that the body has the ability to heal itself. Homeopathy was founded in the late 1700s in Germany and has been widely practiced throughout Europe and India. Homeopathic remedies have been regulated in the United States since 1938 and are considered to be safe.

Celebrities such as Paul McCartney, David Beckham, Twiggy, Caprice, Susan Hampshire, Tina Turner, Louise Jameson, Gaby Roslin, Jude Law, Sadie Frost, Nadia Sawalha, Jennifer Aniston, Jade Jagger, Roger Daltry, Annabel Croft and Meera Syal, as well as The Queen and Prince Charles, are all users of homeopathy.

Homeopathy is based on the idea that "like cures like." That is, if a substance causes a symptom in a healthy person, giving the person a very small amount of the same substance may "cure" the illness. For example, in homeopathy a medicine derived from onions can be used to alleviate watery eyes and a runny nose, which are symptoms that an onion might cause. The medicines are derived mainly from plants and minerals. The active ingredient is diluted many times, making it completely safe. Homeopathic medicines work naturally with your body without causing drowsiness or sleeplessness and can be safely given to a child, please consult your physician or homeopath.

Because homeopathic medicines are very sensitive, avoid touching them with your hands, if you are using pills, tip one into the lid of the container rather than into your hand. For babies, put one pellet in 6-8 oz of water and tap 50 times like you were tapping a bottle of ketchup and give a tea spoon as a frequency recommended for the ailment.

This concept is sometimes used in conventional medicine, for example, the stimulant Ritalin is used to treat patients with ADHD, or small doses of allergens such as pollen are sometimes used to desensitize allergic patients. However, one major difference with homeopathic medicines is that substances are used in ultra-high dilutions, which makes them non-toxic.

Here is a list of the most common homeopathy remedies for babies and toddlers which includes the following:
- Teething or ADHD/ADD: Chamomilla
- Fever: Belladonna
- Night Coughs and Nosebleeds: Ferrum Phosphoricum
- Coughing, child wants to be left alone: Bryonia
- Coughing, child is clingy and conditions worse lying down: Pulsatilla
- Coughing, child is thirsty and wants ice: Phosphorus

- Colic, child settles down on stomach: Colocynth
- Colic, child settles down when stomach is rubbed: Magnesium Phosphoricum
- Bumps and bruises: Arnica
- Rashes: Rhus Toxicodendron
- Insect Bites: Apis Mellifica

Resource:
http://www.abchomeopathy.com

Are Medications Treating the Root Condition?

"The drugging of children has gotten out of hand that America is waking up to this. This is a national catastrophe. I'm seeing children who are normal who are on five psychiatric drugs."

–Peter R. Breggin, M.D. Director–
International Center for the Study of Psychiatry and Psychology

"No one has ever been able to demonstrate that drugs such as Cylert and Ritalin improve the academic performance of the children who take them.... The pupil is drugged to make life easier for his teacher, not to make it better and more productive for the child."

–Dr. Robert Mendelson MD–

Dr. Fred Baughman, author of the ADHD Fraud: How Psychiatry Makes Patients of Normal Children shares Matthew's story in his book:

A fourteen-year old named Matthew Smith was skateboarding with his cousins and suddenly turned blue and collapsed to the floor. This occurred on March 21, 2000 and his cousins immediately called 911 but the paramedics could not revive him. He was pronounced dead from cardiac arrest, a heart attack caused by Ritalin. However, this is not an anomaly case; many others across the nation are experiencing the same side-effects.

Matthew has always been a boisterous energetic child that was very social but did not appear to be as studios and focused as his teachers would have preferred. As such, the school social worker requested a conference with his parents and prescribed the remedy of taking medications to alleviate his symptoms with ADHD.

The social worker provided them with a list of physicians and requested that they ask for the prescription from one of the designated doctors. As such the parents complied and began putting him on Ritalin at the age of six. Did you know that Ritalin is classified by the Drug Enforcement Administration as a Schedule II drug, which is the highest category for dangerous and addictive drugs?

Even though social workers are not allowed to practice medicine, the direct order came from the social worker. This process constitutes practicing medicine without a license, but it is readily being applied across school districts all across the nations and the initial recommendations are coming from teachers, administrators, counselors, school psychologists or school social workers.

The American Heart Association issued a recommendation for all children currently taking or diagnosed to begin taking prescription ADD/ADHD medication to receive a thorough cardiovascular screening. "The Drugging of Our Children" a movie by Dr. Gary Null goes in more depth about children and medications. NOTE: We strongly recommend it to any parent that currently has a child on medications.

Obesity has been an increasing epidemic in America and is accompanied with Diabetes type 2. A 2007 study in the *New* England Journal of Medicine linked Avandia, a prescription choice by the physician for diabetes type 2, to a 43 percent increased risk of heart attacks, and a 64 percent higher risk of cardiovascular deaths.

Another example is the Diabetic medication, Actos. The manufacture is being subjected to multiple lawsuits and this medication was pulled from the market in France and Germany a year ago. They have found it to cause bladder "cancer" and other "tumors." Dr. Helen Ge is stating other health related issues like heart attack, stroke suicide, schizophrenia, homicidal ideation and renal failure and she is one of the original researchers for the product.

FDA is the controlling agency for all the drugs and medications in the US but sometimes it take drastic side effects or a long time for them to pull a restricted dangerous drug, whereas the European Medicines Agency may have already pulled some of the medications off the shelf altogether.

Your Body's Own Detoxification Systems

Your body is constantly dealing with a state of balance by asking your brain to eat healthy foods and the elimination system of your body to purge the waste and toxins out. According to Dr. Oz, people may not realize that the body has its own extraordinary internal detoxification system.

Here is a brief look at three critical organs involved:
- The Liver: Your first line of defense against toxins within your blood is your liver, which acts like a filter in preventing toxic substances contained in foods from passing into your blood stream.
- The Colon: This organ has bacteria that produce both healthy and unhealthy chemicals. You want to keep your colon flowing regularly since its main role is to flush out toxic chemicals before they can do you any harm.
- The Kidneys: The kidneys are constantly filtering your blood and getting rid of toxins in the form of urine.

The lung will also play a role in breathing out some of the waste and toxins and your skin will excrete them out thru sweat. Hair also plays a major role in the process of eliminating toxins from your body.

Dr. Oz' shares some food to keep the liver, colon and kidney fully and optimally functioning. Furthermore, to be able to truly detoxify and eliminate waste products from your body:

- <u>Prunes:</u> They are high in fiber that acts like a laxative.
- <u>Juice Made of Kale, Pineapple, and Ginger:</u> Kale cleanses the kidneys, pineapple has bromelain to aid digestion and ginger to help stimulate bile flow in your gall bladder.
- <u>Smoothie Made of Blueberry and Flaxseed:</u> Blueberries are loaded with quercetin, a flavonoid that boosts immunity and is good for your liver. Ground flaxseed helps nourish the brain with omega-3 and fiber for healthy elimination.
- <u>Vegetable Broth:</u> The soup should contain fennel to help bile flow in your gallbladder, garlic to help with liver and gall bladder function and cabbage for detoxification in both the liver and kidneys. Also add shitake mushrooms to boost liver enzymes.
- <u>Sauerkraut with Sliced Apples:</u> Sauerkraut contains probiotics, the good bacteria that protect your GI tract. Apples boost both kidney and liver functionality.

♡◑◐ Dr. S' and Ungers Insights (Tips for Detoxing)

At any given time our bodies must deal with many thousands of complex organic toxins as well as inorganic toxins. In the early 1970's, a report by the American Cancer Association concluded at that time that at least 90% of "cancers" were due to environmental toxins. The Food Drug Administration currently allows thousands of man-made, toxic substances into the air we breathe, the food we eat and the water we drink. Not only is it impossible to predict the effects of the combination of all these different ingredients, but it is even more difficult to predict their effects upon a given individual.

Sherry A. Rogers, M.D. may have said it best in her book, Detoxify or Die. While Dr. Stéphane Provencher and Dr. Joseph F. Unger's research agrees with Dr. Rogers' basic premise, we have found certain methods of detoxification to be more effective in the detoxification process than those she promotes.

In her ground-breaking book, Clinical Purification, Gina L. Nick, PhD., N.D. illustrates that detoxification is a complex, multi-step venture requiring involvement at various levels. To truly cleanse the system, one must begin at the intracellular level.

If a toxic substance is trapped within cells and structures such as the nervous system, bone, liver, and it attempts to rid the body of toxins; it will be compromised until the toxic substances are extracted from those structures. The essential avenues of exit include the skin, lungs, colon, liver and kidneys.

To complicate matters further, all these various structures depend upon nutrition, nerve supply and vital energy to perform their functions optimally. For example, if one has a spinal misalignment resulting in decreased nerve energy to the kidneys, they are unable to function or detoxify properly.

If one has a cranial distortion affecting the pituitary gland, then that individual may not sweat normally and thereby be deficient in skin detoxification. Another individual may be deficient in a micro nutrient or trace mineral inhibiting liver or colon function, and the result can be improper detoxification. Ultimately, detoxification is simply one of five essential steps in the nutritional process which consist of the following. Improper function of any of the first four will result in compromised detoxification.

1. Ingestion

2. Digestion

3. Absorption

4. Assimilation

5. Elimination

General Detoxification

Most detoxification programs have a one-size-fits-all approach to detoxification. General procedures include therapies such as saunas, fasting, juice fasting, raw food diets and similar programs. Each of the above-mentioned styles can accelerate human detoxification by facilitating the natural physiological mechanisms. These are, of course, excellent things to do.

However, due to the complexity and nature of some of the toxic substances we all encounter, these measures may not yield optimal results. Some toxic substances are too chemically complex to be effectively processed by simply increasing the body's natural mechanisms.

Massage/Lymphatic Drainage

The lymphatic system is somewhat analogous to the sidewalks and back alleyways of city housing. All the trashes and garbage exit through these pathways and out into the alleyways. Since the lymph system is also intimately involved with immunity, such procedures can certainly facilitate generalized detoxification. When performing lymphatic drainage, you may want to consider using the herb Cleavers.

Liver/Gall Bladder Detoxification

Many books, practitioners and authorities in healthcare attempt to sell the benefits of liver and gallbladder detoxification or flushes. One of the more famous procedures for liver/gall bladder detoxification utilizes a variety of activities, culminating in the drinking of olive oil mixed with lemon juice. The liver has almost 500 known functions, most of which are not directly related to detoxification.

We have seen numerous people with symptoms of liver and gall bladder dysfunction experience tremendous relief by engaging in a regimen of Betacol˚ and Cholacol˚ by Standard Process Inc. If for some reason you have had your gallbladder removed, Cholacol˚ would be very good supplement to take with each meal, especially your meals containing a notable amount of fat, your essential fatty-acids and fat-soluble vitamins. Since the gallbladder holds the bile, what is needed to digest the fat, you might consider taking some sort of digestive enzymes or bile salt to mimic the role of the missing gallbladder.

Colon Cleansing

Many people experience positive effects from enemas, colonics and by adding bulk such as psyllium husk or seed to their diet. Many also achieve good results by utilizing charcoal tablets or bentonite clay to absorb toxins in the colon.

Ideally, however, the colon should be vitalized to promote its own detoxifying activities. Again, one of our favorite products is SP Cleanse', The other product that often yields tremendous positive results is called Chiro-Klenz. Chiro-Klenz is a tea (not a laxative but a colon tonic) designed to help vitalize colon function.

Chelation Therapy

In general, the body is equipped to process and eliminate organic toxins occurring as byproducts of our nutritional process or food intake. We have no physiological mechanisms in place to fully break down these inorganic toxins. This is why more aggressive detoxification protocols such as SP Cleanse' are required for optimal health in our modern world.

Some toxic molecules are actually so large or of such a makeup that they are virtually impossible to totally expel from the system. These include many heavy metals known to be severely toxic such as aluminum, mercury, lead, cadmium, Etc. Aluminum is implicated in Alzheimer's as well as other neurological conditions. Lead has a host of negative side effects, as do mercury, which has a particular affinity for the neurological system and bone. Cadmium is implicated in many "cancers."

One compound effective against heavy metal toxicity (though considered unaccepted by conventional medicine in general) is calcium disodium EDTA. This compound is routinely used for what is known as chelation therapy. EDTA can bind with some of these heavy metals to facilitate excretion from the body.

As a bonus, EDTA can also complex with fat and calcium molecules in the bloodstream and is believed to be effective in combating hardening of the arteries and well as cholesterol buildup in the bloodstream. Chelation therapy or EDTA is often observed to be effective in circulatory problems as well as cardio-vascular conditions.

The traditional method of administering EDTA is intravenously. The EDTA will also complex with minerals in the body. Therefore, mineral replacement is highly recommended. The most traditional procedure requires administration of an IV in the doctor's office one to two times weekly.

Dr. Joseph F. Unger and Dr. Stéphane Provencher have been especially impressed with the research and results achieved by utilizing a suppository form of EDTA called "Tox Detox™." Most of the studies indicate that Tox Detox™ is as effective, if not more effective, then intravenous chelation therapy.

For detoxification purposes specifically pertaining to heavy metals and other toxins, chelation agents can only extract the toxins that are already present in the bloodstream. Many heavy metal toxins tend to accumulate in nerves and bones. Therefore, it can be a long process of pulling these toxic residues out of those deeper structures.

Once you have completed a detoxification program, your body must deal with the ongoing effects of the increasing pollution of the world on a daily basis. Please note: DO NOT attempt any detox protocols during prenatal or post-natal care, especially during breastfeeding periods.

SP Green-Food®

Certain factors in nutrition are known to provide antioxidant properties which neutralize many toxic compounds that produce negative side effects. These antioxidant properties are all found in raw fruits and vegetables. They are most highly concentrated in a product by Standard Process Inc. called SP Green-Food˙. A routine dosage of 2-4 SP Green-Food˙ daily will insure adequate antioxidant properties in your bloodstream to combat free radical toxic effects.

SP Cleanse®

To compensate for the unavoidable toxicity in the environment, SP Cleanse˙ will energize your detoxification mechanisms from intracellular to excretion. For optimal maintenance, we suggest a periodic repeat of the detoxification protocol. Consult with your healthcare professional to design the optimal program to suit your individual requirements.

Billionaire Parenting Tips for Prenatal Care

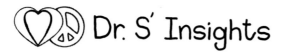 Dr. S' Insights

As a Holistic Physician, it came to my attention that suggesting folic acid as a supplement was not enough for the mother during pregnancy. Nutrition goes beyond that and we need to look at the entire physiology and hormonal changes as the pregnancy progresses.

By approaching prenatal and post-natal care with a holistic aspect it will ensure that the mother and baby are at optimal nutritional levels. Holistic care assesses the blood test within the functional range and not merely the sick range.

All blood tests have a range that allopathic, or medical doctors look to find out if we are sick or not. The problem is when blood values already reach that point you are already passed the sick point, meaning it is a red flag. What the holistic practitioners will look at is the functional range to find out if organs or systems are impacted. This is the differences between medical approach and holistic approach to the blood values and recommendations toward nutrition and wellness care.

Here's an analogy, if your body is a house, for example, when your blood values reach the sick range it means there is a fire that needs to be dealt with immediately. In a case of a fire you will call the fireman, medical doctor who will hose down the home or break thru doors and windows to save you by way of medicines or surgery. But if your house only needed an electrical repair to avoid a fire hazard, would calling the fireman be overly-dramatic?

As you read in the epigenetic section, what your grandparents ate influences your life and your child's life. Also, by eating rich methylated foods like Kale, you are able to change the expression of these bad genes and create a compelling future for your child and yourself as well. Since a lot of the chronic disease can be inflicted intrauterine it is important to have a sense of what is essential and optimal for the life you are about to bring on Earth.

Your role is to prepare the perfect environment for your fetus to grow properly, from a physical and emotional standpoint. In a nutshell, all refined foods or processed foods are to be avoided, all processed sugars and refined sugars as well. You should incorporate more raw organic vegetables and fruits and eat more of organic grass fed kosher meats or wild fish. Venison would be preferable to beef or chicken since the level of toxicity in these animals are dramatically reduced.

Unfortunately, policies "require" supermarkets to radiate their non-organic produce for better cosmetic appeal and a longer shelf life. The radiation actually kills the nutritive property of the food. Eating something that does not have a nutritious value is the same thing as buying a car with no engine!

If the produces are not organic, you risk having exposure to pesticides, hormones, herbicides, chemicals and other unknown by-products that can cause health issues and be passed to your baby. Also, organic foods have 50 times more nutritive values than their non-organic counterparts. If available you should look for non-GMO labeling. To come back to the car example, by eating organic you will increase the horse power by 50% and have more efficient usage of your energy.

The non-organic meats you purchase along with their stock such as chicken stock or beef broth are usually processed with their feces and urine due to the method they use to mass process these animals, according to Clare Druce a researcher in poultry welfare (www.mcspotlight.org/people/interviews/ druce.html.) This is what normally gives the smell and taste of these products. If you really want to taste the real taste of the meat buy kosher or halal meats.

For non-organic meats, hormones and other chemicals are usually added to their diets and sick animals (cows and chickens) are kept together with the healthy ones. This is the same concept with farmed fish. Additionally, you have the risk of eating heavy metals from their medications or GMO by-products based on their feeding. All these risks are cut by buying organic grass fed free-range meat (no grain food.) This limits all alterations to the epigenetic of the meats and to you and your child. Here are some essential supplements that will be required for a healthy baby.

Additionally, maternal obesity increases the risk of a woman developing gestational diabetes or going into preterm labor, as well as the risk of obesity and diabetes in the child. Some study also link an increased risk of asthma in the children of obese women.

In 2007 J. Katzen-Luchenta revitalized the Declaration of Olympia for the Nutritional Health journal. The Declaration of Olympia founded in 1996 is based on the health principles of Hippocrates: genetics, the age of the individual, the powers of various foods and exercise.

It was discovered that "The nutrients implicated in healthy reproduction and lifelong health included B vitamins, particularly B1, B6, folate, B12, along with 13 antioxidants. In particular vitamins C and E and minerals such as zinc, iron, magnesium, selenium, iodine, copper and essential fatty acids (DHA) were critical factors." He stated that "Today's foods are often processed beyond the cells' recognition and can result in neurological and physical morbidity and mortality"; therefore supplementation is required.

Folic Acid and Vitamin B12

Folic acid is very important because it will help your fetus build a strong and perfect nervous system. The spinal cord will take 28 to 29 days to form and the need for folic at that critical period is important. Research also showed that birth deformities are strongly linked to missing folic acid from birth. Additionally, research discovered that folic acid was able to reverse the damage of genes (epigenetics) that were exposed to the BPA environmental toxin.

The recommended dosage to take during pregnancy for folic acid is 500-1,000mg (if not using whole foods based supplements.) My recommendation would be two Folic Acid-B12 from Standard Process during the entire pregnancy (assuming your body was in the optimal range to begin with.) The Whole Foods supplement will get absorbed and utilized at 100% while the synthetic version of it will get absorbed and utilized at the maximum (rarely) at 80%.

Green leafy vegetables are also rich in Folic acid (folate) and will be recommended unless you have sensitivities, allergies or immune-compromised body reactions to these foods. Additionally, folic is found in eggs, lentils, split peas, barley, kale, cashews, sunflower seeds, avocado, oranges, and meat. Organic Kale is considered the ALL nutrients magic food and contains every essential mineral a body needs.

Folic acid is also found in the organ meats of the liver and kidney; however since these organs are normally used for filtration and detoxification of the animal's bloodstream. If the source of the meat was not free of hormones, pesticides, chemicals, these particular organs would also be contaminated because they were used for processing.

Bananas also contain folic acid however they are very high in sugar and create insulin resistance at a young age. The recommended dosage would be to eat 1/3 of a banana, but it should NEVER be eaten in the morning.

The reason is that during the night your body's system has been fasting and as such introducing that much sugar first thing in the morning will upset the pancreas, the adrenal and raise the cortisol levels to increase stress and potential emotional instability. Other symptoms would include fatigue, lack of concentration and memory. (Ironically, most children begin their days with cereals filled with sugar and often topped with fresh fruits and this is why they are having difficulty focusing and learning.)

Vitamin B12 works in conjuncture with folic acid to promote normal growth, formation of new blood vessels and healthy nerve tissues. The recommended dosage for vitamin B12 is 3mcg while pregnant and 3.5mcg during lactation. Folic Acid-B12 has both folic acid and B12 in a whole food component.

Iron

Iron is important in the transportation of the oxygen level to the mother but also to the baby. Oxygen is life and is required for a lot of biochemical reactions during the process the fetus will undergo. Proper iron intake will help against miscarriage, anemia, fatigue, forming fetal blood, promoting healthy growth rate and will help the brain, eye and bone development.

Iron is found in dark green leafy vegetables like parsley, spinach, broccoli and kale but also in carrots, pumpkin seeds, sesame seeds, sunflower seeds and dried fruits (apricots, prunes, raisins.) Iron is also in sources like red meat, fish, chicken and eggs.

The recommended dosage for a pregnant mother is between 30-60mgs and down to 12-16mgs during lactation. The best iron supplements are made from whole foods but if you decide to use synthetic, make sure you have an organic iron supplement (Chelated Iron.)

Inorganic iron supplements will deplete your Vitamin E and zinc levels which are essential for the iron to get to the rest of your body. My recommendation is Ferrofood® by Standard Process. Every pregnancy is different and might need readjustment so please consult your holistic physician.

Vitamin C

It is my experience as a chiropractic physician that vitamin C is very important but its availability in foods is so common that recommending additional supplements would render it useless. So many foods already have vitamin C inclusive of most fruits, vegetables, buckwheat, and alfalfa. During the duration of your pregnancy, you should keep consuming fresh fruits and vegetables.

Calcium

Calcium is important not only for the bone formation during your fetus' growth but also for nerve conduction, muscle contractions, and the many biochemical reactions created and metabolized during the growth of the fetus. To take 2 cells and propel it to billions of them and connect them all, you need calcium. But the real lesson is that not all calcium is the same. There's calcium carbonate, citrate, malate, lactate and many others.

The best choice is calcium lactate which does not come from the milk process. This type of calcium will serve best for you and your baby's bones, muscles, nerves and all biochemical reactions needed for a healthy pregnancy.

For those that believe in the age-old myth about milk, please read more about this at Weston A. Price Foundation (www.westonaprice.org), you will never get enough calcium from pasteurized milk. Even during regular pasteurization, milk can lose about 20 percent of its vitamin C content, with lesser damage to other nutrients like thiamine, vitamin B12, and lysine.

Magnesium

Magnesium is important for the nerve functioning and muscles and it also plays a critical role in miscarriages. Magnesium and/or calcium lactate helps with muscle cramping or restless leg. The recommended dosage is 300 mg and 340mg while lactating.

Magnesium is found in kale, legumes, citrus fruit, and cashews along with almonds, brazil nuts, sunflower seed, hazelnuts, wheat germ, figs, dandelion, seaweed, and prune. Almonds and Brazil Nuts are difficult on our digestive systems. The trick is to soak these nuts overnight in water with a splash of Bragg's Apple Cider Vinegar. This will help remove the cellular membrane that we cannot properly digest.

Vitamin K

It is my experience that supplementation of Vitamin K can be ignored if the intestinal flora in the mother is at optimal levels. The good bacteria are the ones producing mostly Vitamin K in your gut. A good probiotic is needed during pregnancy. Please make sure to read the ingredient for at least one of the two probiotic which research has proven their efficacy and benefit at the gut level: Acidophilus Lactobacillus DDS-1 and Acidophilus Lactobacillus La-5.

Vitamin K is also found in green leafy vegetables, alfalfa, nettle tea, egg yolk, kelp, chlorophyll, oatmeal, chestnut, sunflower seeds and molasses. It is also found in soya bean; however, other sources of food are preferred because soya beans have a high inflammatory property and contain the environmental toxin phthalate which promotes dis-ease.

Pork also contains Vitamin K; however, according to Weston A. Price, consuming this meat will change the configuration of the red blood cells from being a perfect round shape to an oval one, which can lead to artery blockages and other cardiac dis-ease. Additionally, a genetically modified experiment called EnviroPig may introduce GMO into your and your baby's body. I would highly recommend avoiding both soya beans and pork as the source for Vitamin K.

Vitamin E

Vitamin E protects against blood clots and other blood related issues and can help in sweet cravings, fatigue, dizziness and palpitations. Since Vitamin E is predominant in multiple foods including: almonds, nuts, sunflower seeds, sesame oil, olives, broccoli, blueberries, kiwi, olive oil, brown rice, whole grain, wheat germ, oatmeal, spinach and fish I tend not to recommend a separate nutritional supplement.

Corn also contains Vitamin E; however, I would recommend staying away from this source.

Corn is a genetically modified food in the United States which no research have been done to prove that incorporating DNA structures will not affect our biology and our bodies. Additionally, papayas also contain Vitamin E; however, the crops grown in Hawaii are all genetically modified.

Anything that tampers with Mother Nature normally does not have as much nutritive values and may cause more health issues such as microwave foods. It is better to heat your foods in toaster ovens or ovens; however, do not use aluminum foil or bleached parchment paper.

Research has revealed that obesity increases the risk of asthma, a deficiency in Vitamin E during pregnancy has evidenced to increase this chance by 5 times. Similarly, the higher the mothers' zinc levels during pregnancy the lower the chance of the baby developing eczema. The protective effects of vitamin E and zinc appeared even stronger in those children who had been breastfed.

Zinc

What on earth does stress, anxiety, low energy, and depression have to do with Zinc? The Zinc link to health expands to diets lacking in zinc. Improving your zinc status from deficiency to sufficiency can improve yours and your baby's mental functioning. Look for zinc in foods like lean meats, sesame seeds, pumpkin seeds, green peas, spinach, and mushrooms.

Current clinical trials show an undeniable correlation with the levels of zinc and depression. The lower the zinc level, the worse the severity of depression and patients who received zinc supplementation felt better after 6 weeks.

The zinc-depression link is strongly associated with brain functionality. Researchers have found that zinc acts as a neurotransmitter. The second most predominate neurotransmitter in the brain, Gamma-aminobutyric acid (GABA), regulates mood states.

Low levels of zinc can also cause irritability. Out of the 300 enzymes that require zinc for production, zinc stimulates a crucial enzyme, pyridoxal kinase, which is directly involved in the synthesis of GABA. Depleted zinc levels can disrupt healthy mental functions.

Zinc is also necessary for the synthesis of serotonin, which is just one of the many proteins that require zinc for protein synthesis. Anxiety, stress, and depression are often symptoms of dysfunction in the serotonergic system.

Recent studies have shown a connection between behavioral problems and imbalances with zinc, copper, magnesium, calcium, and manganese. The interrelationship with zinc and copper is even more compelling. Research reveals that a deficiency in zinc implies a higher level of copper in the body. Excess copper in the body is linked to depression, violence, and learning disabilities.

Good Fats

Since the nervous system is 100% fat and during the fetal development fat is needed, it is recommended to incorporate a good source of omega-3. Our food source is super rich in omega-6 and we need a body ratio of 2:1 (omega-3: 6.)

Omega-3 has two important components to it: DHA and EPA. DHA is the important structure of the omega-3 needed for fetal and children development until approximately the age of 16 years old. Then, afterwards EPA becomes the most important factor of the nervous system growth and development. The proper ratio should be a 2:1 as well. During fetal development until 14-16 years old, a DHA:EPA ration of 2:1 is recommended and for the adult will be the opposite EPA:DHA at 2:1.

Make sure to read where the omega-3 has been extracted and if it comes from fish, that a complete system of detoxification against heavy metals and other chemical components have been processed. Standard Process does this along with other reputable companies so please do your research before investing in supplemental omega by-products.

Foods To Avoid During Pregnancy

Certain foods need to be avoided along with chemicals and other toxic components. Please read the list below, all have health concerns or risk attached to their consumption:

Raw or soft egg

- *Pre-cooked chicken*
- *Processed or refined foods*
- *Fish containing high mercury: billfish (swordfish, broadbill, marlin), shark, flake, sea perch, catfish, blue-fish, ling mackerel, tile fish, oyster, clam, mussels.) If your ancestral genes did not consume a lot of fish, do not consume during pregnancy and avoid all raw fish*

- *Allergic foods (nuts, milk, dairy, soy, corn, peanut, wheat are some of the most allergen food)*
- *Trans fat oil: heated olive oil, vegetable oil, canola oil (should never be ingested),*
- *Soft drinks*
- *Tonic water*
- *Sweeteners: aspartame, Splenda, Stevia*
- *High corn fructose*
- *Caffeine*
- *Alcohol*
- *Cigarettes*
- *Prescribed or Illegal Drugs*
- *Ultrasound imaging: The World Health Organization and the USA Food and Drug Administration have also rejected routine screening because there is a distinct lack of definitive research supporting the safety of ultrasounds.*

Breastfeeding vs. Infant Formulas

The nutrients the mother ingests and in turn produces breast milk is the first nourishment a newborn should receive, as it contains all the vital nutrients that an infant's body needs, along with the added natural antibodies. The mother's body is innately designed to deplete itself of nutrients first for the survival of her newborn instead of keeping the nutrients herself.

Breast milk is the best nutrition for your baby even if your baby is premature or unwell and in hospital. It is thought that breastfeeding enhances the bonding process between baby and mother. Some evidence suggests that sudden infant death syndrome (SIDS) is less common in breastfeed babies. Also, the amino acid taurine is present in breast milk and will help proper brain physiological development as well as cognitive aspect. It is twice as much in the breast milk than cow's milk.

Some research have demonstrated that less health problems occurs later in life if the child had breast milk compared to those who had not. Some mentioned obesity, overweight, high cholesterol, high blood pressure, diabetes and asthma.

Research has concluded that the following health problems are less common in women who have breastfed one or more babies compared with those who have never breastfed: breast "cancer"; "ovarian cancer", type 2 diabetes, diabetes, and post-natal depression.

It is also recommended and evidence supports that at least six months of breastfeeding can help to limit future dis-ease and complications. Some of the benefits are lowered risk of developing high blood pressure and losing weight during breastfeeding.

In a 2004 study in Australia it was found that prolonged breastfeeding significantly protected children from asthma and allergies. In a large 2011 Dutch study researchers concluded that children who were not breastfed for at least six months were at a higher risk for developing asthma-related symptoms like wheezing, coughing, shortness of breath and persistent phlegm during their first four years.

Another study from 2011 reported at the 2nd EAACI Pediatric Allergy and Asthma Meeting (Europe) that "breastfeeding for the first 4-6 months has been shown to reduce the risk for atopic eczema and cow's milk protein allergy."

Baby Formulas

Formula can never match this perfect recipe of breast milk. The important factors for your baby's growth and protection cannot be manufactured in a factory and added to infant formula. On average, breastfeed babies have fewer infections in their early life because antibodies are passed in the breast milk from mother to baby.

Children are most at risk from MSG. The blood brain barrier, which keeps toxins in the blood from entering the brain, is not fully developed in children. MSG can also penetrate the placental barrier and affect unborn children as well. Nonetheless, most major brands of infant formula contain some processed free glutamic acid (a form of MSG.) Many people are also surprised to learn that some infant formulas use sucrose as the main carbohydrate.

According to Sayer Ji, founder of GreenMedInfo, cupric sulfate is being used in infant formulas (which is a known herbicide, fungicide and pesticide.) The Material Safety Data Sheet for Cupric Sulfate clearly states, "The substance may be toxic to kidneys, liver. Repeated or prolonged exposure to the substance can produce target organs damage." Cupric sulfate is used in most mass market infant formulas. Even Similac's "sensitive" formula contains the ingredient.

Sayer Ji also discovered that the brand Earth's Best Organic presents the same challenges (a USDA certified "Organic" infant formula.) A close look at the product label ingredients shows it contains petroleum derived dl-alpha («vitamin E») and inorganic chemicals with concerning toxicological profiles (e.g. Cupric Sulfate [kidney and liver damage], Ferrous Sulfate [liver damage], Manganese Sulfate [impairment of central nervous system and kidney], and Sodium Selenite ["cancer" and "gene mutations".])

For further research on the case studies and research done on Infant Formulas, read: http://www.greenmedinfo.com/toxic-ingredient/infant-formula for more conclusive evidence of whether you want to subject your child(ren) to infant formulas.

 Jenn's Insights

Researchers at Brown University have discovered that breastfeeding alone produces the best results for boosting a baby's brain growth. It can increase a baby's brain growth by twenty to thirty percent. A 2011 study from Oxford University found that breastfeeding improved cognitive development and allowed children to do better in school.

Enhancement of the brain development for children of age two is increased via breastfeeding compared to formula feed or fed a combination of formula and breast milk. The extra growth was most pronounced in parts of the brain associated with language, emotional function, and cognition, the research showed.

Even though I was a first-time mother, I recognized the importance of breastfeeding and its nutritional, psychological and immunological benefits. I was adamant that I was going to breastfeed my son for as long as I could. Having a caesarean birth, I was told that my body would most likely produce less milk. What my doctor did not realize was that I was going through extreme stress and the quality of the milk did not produce the ideal nutrients for my son's development.

It got so detrimental that the pediatrician mandated us to see a nutritionist. I had researched infant formulas and knew that it was not an optimum choice for my son. We had called in a lactation specialist but my son just did not want to latch properly and after the series of vaccinations it was more difficult to get him to breastfeed. So I ritually pumped the milk and tried to have enough for him on a daily basis. My husband was concerned because I literally pushed my body to the limits because I was adamant that nothing was going to deter my son from getting the best nutrients from the start.

I knew my body was slower to produce and replenish the milk supply so I tried all types of Eastern and Western remedies. I was on fenugreek and I did the papaya soup diet for the Eastern culture, but the milk production did not increase much. I was drinking so much water, I could have floated away, but my body still seemed dehydrated. I would recommend chiropractic care for improving the enhancement of breast-milk production. After my treatments, I was able to have some reserve of breast milk stored.

What I did not recognize was that stress also impacted milk production. In the back of my mind was the worried notion of, how will I return to work and face my employer who never knew about my pregnancy in the first place. I barely had enough milk to make each feeding. I recalled that my aunt was helping me babysit my son and she accidentally spilled the bottle, I was in tears because as an empath, I knew that it meant less food for my son and that I could not reproduce the next bottle until several hours later.

Then, when I returned to work, it was even worse. I was monitored constantly for how long I went into the lactation room and informed I could not use the restroom or drink water or eat snacks because I had used the duration of my lunch period already for the pumping. No mother should have to endure the ordeal I went through.

I hope mothers will recognize their emotional state will impact the quality and quantity of their milk production, so it really is not worth it to stress and that seeking chiropractic care for post-natal treatment will assist with improving the flow of your milk production.

♡☮ Dr. S' Insights

The human species has been breastfeeding for many millions of years. It is only in the last sixty years that we have begun to give babies the highly processed convenience food called formula.

Its first intention wasn't to be consumed on a large scale like today. It was conceived in the late 1800's as a means of providing necessary sustenance for foundlings and orphans who would otherwise have starved. Because no other food was available, the formula was a lifesaver.

My concern with baby formulas is how many chemicals are actually contained in them. The primary ingredient is either milk based or soy based which both have the potential to be GMO. Additionally, I have seen so many digestive complications or symptoms related to just ingesting the soy or milk-based products.

Pasteurized milk (http://www.westonaprice.org) is very allergenic and may increase sensitivity (allergies) which can produce an autoimmune reaction. First we do not know what the cow ate (whether it was non-GMO feed) and what medications the animal was under during the production of the milk.

The bacteria Salmonella and aflatoxins are potent toxins and devastating to your health; however, both have regularly been detected in commercial formulas. Additionally the toxin Enterobacter sakazaki is also evidenced in the formulas. These toxins are known to cause sepsis, an overwhelming bacterial infection in the bloodstream, meningitis, inflammation of the lining of the brain and necrotizing enterocolitis, severe infection and inflammation of the small intestine and colon in newborns.

Soy formulas are of particular concern due to the very high levels of plant-derived estrogens (phytoestrogens) and phytic acid they contain. In fact, concentrations of phytoestrogens detected in the blood of infants receiving soya formula can be 13,000 to 22,000 times greater than the concentrations of natural estrogens which equates to consuming up to 5 birth control pills per day. Estrogen in high doses, above those normally found in the body, can cause breast "cancer" in woman and infertility. Phytate can cause growth problems in children. Some studies also show soya containing a high level of aluminum which is a toxic metal for the nervous system.

Let's consider the growth hormones and how it equates to how girls are reaching puberty at earlier onsets. Cow's milk takes a baby calf to an adult size within three months and from a calf of being 300-500 pounds at birth to 1,600 to 2,500 pounds at the adult size. Could this also be a factor associated with our obesity epidemic?

Can you imagine if human breast milk mimics the same growth potentials as the cow's pattern, what giants we would all be? If the first step towards healthier eating patterns begins with breast-milk versus formula, how much time and research are you willing to invest to ensure you are making an educated consumer choice? If this represents the first step in life for your billion dollar investment, would you start him or her on the proper healthy track so that later on dis-ease is prevented and she or he is bestowed with a healthier childhood?

Nutrition to Boost your Child's Brain Power

Memories are partially created by understanding the world around us and by the interaction and the meaning of it. This process is part of our adaption to the environment and promotes growth and survival. The human brain is designed to purposely facilitate the continuous learning process, remembering and adapting to new circumstances, memories and emotions.

The neurons from birth will primarily govern and connect heart, breathing, eating and sleeping. The neurons grow at a very fast rate in response to the quick growth during the stages from infant to toddler and then from child to adolescence and finally to adulthood. The cerebral cortex of a toddler creates close to two million synapses, or communication from a neuron to another per second. By the age of three, a brain has about 1,000 trillion synapses and it has reached about 90% of its adult size.

By the time of adolescence, most of the growth and transformation of the limbic system has already occurred; this system is responsible for our emotions. Teenagers may rely on their more primitive limbic system in interpreting emotions and reacting. This is why the adolescence years appear to be so challenging for parents. The emotional aspect of their environment is the primary guiding system. Parents need to center their conversations to a nice and calm emotional state and empower the child to express healthier emotions rather than destructive or negative ones. (Refer to Chapter 8 to learn more about the Psychology of Emotions)

The brain is made of fat substance and will require fat to grow at its fullest potential. As a child develops, it needs the proper fat rich content in omega-3 to have the proper nutrient, fuel, to optimize their brain capacity. From birth to the age of 14 years old, they will need more DHA compared to EPA (type of omega-3, usually written on the bottle or supplement.) The ratio for proper nutrition is a 2:1 DHA:EPA for children under the age of fourteen to sixteen years old and a 1:2 DHA:EPA for fourteen years and up.

Fats For Your Child's Brain

Brain is made of about 60% of fat. It will take fat to replenish and feed the brain, but not fat from processed cakes and crackers, French fries and fried meats loaded with trans and saturated fats. It will build a different brain than a child who is eating broiled fish, nut butter, salad dressings made with olive oil, eggs and lean meats. An imbalance in that ratio could potentially cause stroke and other cardiovascular, immune and neurological disturbance.

According to Dr. Mercola, raw nuts and seeds, such as fresh organic flax seeds, chia seeds, sunflower seeds, sesame seeds, pumpkin seeds, and English walnuts, are also high in omega-3. Egg yolks from pasteurized hens are rich in beneficial omega-3.

Meats from animals that are free ranging and/or grass fed are higher in beneficial omega-6 for nutritional purposes. Raw milk is also a good source of omega 6's. Unfortunately, most American children are getting far too many omega-6 fats. This is because they are getting them in the form of highly processed vegetable oils that exclude most of the original nutrients.

The omega-3 consumption increase, aids children with performance at school, in reading and spelling and behavior. Since the omega-3 supports communication from neurons to neurons, it is found to be helpful with memory issues according to Fernando Gómez-Pinilla, a UCLA professor. Dr. Daniel G. Amen, a clinical neuroscientist, brain-imaging expert counts avocados as one of the top brain-healthy foods.

Dietary deficiency of omega-3 fatty acids in humans has been associated with increased risk of several mental disorders, including attention-deficit disorder, dyslexia, dementia, depression, bipolar disorder and schizophrenia.

Proteins for Your Child's Brain

Proteins are the building block of our body and the enzymes to facilitate all biochemical reactions. It helps your child's brain think clearly, concentrate and learn. Food protein provides amino acids that are used to form neurotransmitters and support structures in neurons. One example is the tryptophan, from turkey and raw milk used to produce serotonin to produce feelings of well-being.

Tyrosine, an amino acid found in almonds, avocado and meats, is used to make dopamine, associated with enthusiasm. Eating a high-nutrient protein like eggs, which have nutrients including choline, omega-3, zinc, and lutein will help kids concentrate. Making sure the eggs are coming from a free range, grain free and humane farm will also make all the differences in the quality of the eggs and the nutritional value.

Protein from animal sources is called complete, because it contains all nine of the essential amino acids. Most vegetable protein is considered incomplete because it lacks one or more of the essential amino acids or B12 vitamin. It is highly recommended to have a variety in your diets with organic, free range, grain-free meats inclusive of turkey or beef and if possibly wild game such as venison or buffalo. Additionally, consumption of vegetables should be added to each meal to ensure that amino acids and other nutrients present only within the plant based kingdom can supplement the nutritional needs.

Vitamins for Your Child's Brain

Since most vitamins are present in fruits and vegetables, it would be essential to recommend a diet with plenty of organic fresh fruits and vegetables for your children to consume on a daily basis. According to the National Health and Nutrition Survey (NHANESIII) less than fifteen percent of children are meeting this recommendation.

Green vegetables are life savers in terms of obtaining enough Vitamin B or iron nutrients. They mostly contain all essential vitamins and minerals. But the best item to incorporate on a daily basis is Kale. Along with grains, kale is rich in Vitamin B which aids in producing energy for the brain cells and helps manufacture the neurotransmitter's serotonin and GABA for concentration.

Research has also suggested that B vitamins (especially vitamin B6) promote the absorption of magnesium in the gut. A significant level of magnesium in the brain also helps with the memory process and can increase learning experiences for children. Foods high in magnesium include: spinach, quinoa, kidney beans, lentils and oatmeal.

Zinc, also involves the production of serotonin and GABA production and has a strong involvement with the learning process, the immunity functionality, growth of neurons, and aids with the repair and connections between neurons. Additionally, zinc is essential in the formation of memory, and is found abundantly in the hippocampus, the area of the brain responsible for processing short-term and long-term memory. Zinc can be found in seeds and nuts, as well as red meat.

Micronutrients, like phytonutrients found primarily in plant components help the brain undergo repairs and protects the overall structural integrity of the neurons. These nutrients act as antioxidants to eliminate free radicals and protect our memory functionality.

Jenn's Insights

I was determined from the beginning to ensure that my son established healthy eating habits. It has been a struggle because neither grandparent understood or respected my food preferences for Alex.

I knew that he had gastrointestinal issues and as such, have incorporated a gluten-free diet to alleviate more sensitivity issues. It was difficult at first because of my culture. My parents kept insisting that rice had to be a staple food, but I found other alternatives such as quinoa.

My son consumes a lot of tyrosine on a daily basis in avocados and bananas. He also appears to enjoy vegetables more than meats. He continues his daily dosage of calamari omega oils and takes his Standard Process supplements to ensure his well-being. Even though he does not appear to gain much weight, we noticed that he is very strong and has more muscle mass than someone comparable in his age group.

From an early age, my son was exposed to homeopathy instead of medications and I noticed that he has had less ear aches and illnesses than the average child. In fact, until he started more interactions with other children, he was hardly sick. I used homeopathy during his teething period and it worked like a charm and he had less symptomatic issues.

My son also consumes raw milk or coconut milk instead of pasteurized milk. In researching the nutrients for milk, I discovered that several amino acids were lost with the pasteurization process. For raw milk, the non-A1 gene of the cows (Guernsey Cows) would be preferable because of its insensitivities or intolerance characteristics. My son also enjoys snacking on organic apples and carrot sticks.

From an emotional standpoint he went through many stressors and as such, he has a strong inclination to sweet foods to balance out his internal disposition. I learned to adapt to this preference by incorporating more fruits and providing him with home-baked goods made from fresher ingredients and gluten free flour.

As I watch Alex grow every day, I am grateful and very proud to be his mom and marvel at how his energy glows and how happy he is even after all he endured. Children are resilient and their courage and optimism amazes me. The characteristic of a child is to possess an abundance of energy and it baffles me how as a society, we find it normal to squelch these innate characteristics in our children and rob them of their life energy. Does it truly make sense to reduce their energy levels through medication?

For Valentine's Day, the Whole-Listic Children's Foundation went to the Children's Center for Cancer and Blood Disorders of Northern Virginia to spread some cheer and uplift their spirits with "I Love You" balloons and hearts. It was surreal to see how much courage these children have in the midst of health adversities. These children are the real heroes. Sometimes I wonder what would happen if these children had an opportunity to work with Kris Carr or other alternative therapies, how much impact it would make if they were given hope in the form of a combination of therapeutic approaches. For those who are still trying to debate whether traditional or alternative care is better and what businesses may be impacted by revolutionizing the health care industry. I would recommend that you walk through a pediatric oncology unit like I did and stare deeply into these children's eyes; you will find the right answers for yourself.

6
Herbs and Flower Essence

Why Use Herbs?

Anyone who's, still awake after an evening coffee latte or experienced the stimulation effect of prune juice, knows that plants, and products made from them, can have a powerful impact on our bodies. When plants are used for such effects, rather than as food, they are called herbs or, more precisely, medicinal herbs (not culinary herbs.)

Herbs have been used for ages and ages within a medicinal aspect and not only by humans but also by our predecessors, chimpanzees to kill parasites. Herbal medicine may utilize a whole plant or just the bark, fruit, stem, root or seed. Herbs can be fresh, dry, in tincture (alcoholic extract of a plant), pills and capsules. Every culture utilized some form of herbal medicine. In fact, medical doctors in the United States were trained in herbal medicine up until the early 1900's.

Although about a quarter of our pharmaceutical drugs are derived from herbs, the chemicals intermixed with them produces side effects without the original medicinal benefits. Potentially, some herbs are more dangerous than the drugs derived from them. Digitalis is a good example. The active ingredient in the plant can be fatal but the actual derivative drug is a much safer dosage because it is less concentrated.

Some herbs are harmless even in the larger quantities. Others require the prescription of an herbalist. Similar or identical component(s) of a plant are often found in different plants, even when they are not closely related. For example, the flavor licorice is found in three plants. These three plants are not the only culinary herbs that are used medicinally. Other culinary plants that have medicinal effects include garlic, rosemary, sage, parsley, and thyme.

Many western herbalists use small toxic herbs to stimulate the immune system; whereas Chinese medicine and Ayurvedic medicine, usually blend the herbs together. The blending of the herbal mixture takes a skillful and precise art form, in which the ingredients augment or modulate each other.

Chinese herbs can be effective in helping children with eczema, acute bronchitis, fever, cough, wheezing and many more.

Herbs that are Beneficial for Children

- Bilberry Leaves:

This herb promotes the transportation of oxygen and restores chemical injuries caused by free radical damage. This herb is also designed specifically for brain toxicity issues.

- Echinacea:

This herb serves as a preventative measure for boosting the immune system; however, not as effective once sickness appears.

- Kava Root:

This herb promotes a general feeling of well-being by settling aggression and relieving tension.

- Lemon Balm:

This herb balances the peripheral and central nervous system's functionalities.

- Mint:

For small children, this herb combats nausea, vomiting, upset stomachs and colic.

- Nettle:

This herb balances the adrenals and clears heat and stagnation from the blood, which promotes an overall calmness.

- Rosemary:

This herb has antiseptic (for colds) and antispasmodic properties. It serves as an appetite stimulate and digestion aid.

- Tarragon:

This herb eases fatigue, stomach cramps and toothaches. It also stimulates appetite.

- Thyme:

This herb assists with diarrhea and bronchial problems. The herb's properties contain iron, potassium and zinc along with other essential vitamins and minerals.

- <u>Valerian:</u>

  This herb promotes relaxation which aids with sleeping issues.

Because safety has not been established through extensive research, allopathic Medical professionals normally do not recommend herbal remedies/supplements for pregnant woman. Unlike prescription drugs, the FDA is not responsible for regulating herbs and nutritional supplements.

It is recommended that a consultation with a naturopath, herbologist or holistic physician be contacted prior to taking any herbal supplements. This is important because the wrong combination of herbs may cause premature birth, miscarriage, uterine contractions or fetal injuries if not administered in the proper dosage.

Herbs to Avoid During Pregnancy

(It is recommended that these herbs are avoided during the duration of the pregnancy because they can be potentially harmful to both the mother and unborn child. Please consult your Naturopath, Herbalist or Physician for more information.)

- <u>Aloe Vera:</u>

  This herb may cause uterine contractions and toxins may be transferred to your baby during breastfeeding.

- <u>Black Cohosh:</u>

  This herb may induce premature labor thru uterine stimulation.

- <u>Cat's Claw:</u>

  This herb may prevent pregnancy from occurring in the first place or it may cause spontaneous abortion.

- <u>Don Quai:</u>

  This herb may cause uterine stimulations and relaxant effects and should be avoided if you are breastfeeding.

- <u>Ephedra:</u>

  This herb may promote early labor or cause sleeping problems and may exacerbate conditions such as hyper-tension, diabetes and heart attacks.

- <u>Fever Few:</u>

  This herb may cause severe bleeding that may lead to miscarriages.

- <u>Goldenseal:</u>

This herb may cause uterine contractions and the herb itself may cross the placenta in concentrated forms.

- <u>Nutmeg:</u>

This herb may cause premature labor or even miscarriages. A form of this herb is often found in desserts.

- <u>Passion Flower:</u>

This herb may cause the uterus to prematurely contract and may also impact the central nervous system.

- <u>Pau D'Arco:</u>

This herb may be capable of quickly reproducing cells which may be detrimental for the pregnancy process.

- <u>Penny-royal:</u>

This herb may induce early labor or may result in unexpected abortions. It also may cause organ failure, skin rashes and brain damage within the developing fetus.

- <u>Roman Chamomile:</u>

This herb may cause premature uterine contractions or may produce a miscarriage.

- <u>Saw Palmetto:</u>

This herb may impact hormonal imbalances and may produce developmental issues within the unborn baby.

- <u>Wormwood:</u>

This herb may impact the development of your unborn child with specific health problems and disabilities. Additionally, this herb may be toxic for your baby if transferred via breast milk.

- <u>Yarrow:</u>

This herb may cause miscarriage or it may cause the baby to be born under-weight or with gastrointestinal or breathing issues.

- <u>Yohimbe:</u>

This herb may stimulate the uterus which results in inducing a miscarriage.

Herbs for the Expectant Mother

(This list represents potentially safe herbs for consumption during pregnancy. Please consult your Naturopath, Herbalist or Holistic Physician for more information, before actual usage)

- Cranberries:

  This herb assists with Urinary Tract Infection.

- Echinacea:

  This herb works as a preventive (not as effective once sickness symptoms appear) measure to aid in boosting the immune system.

- Garlic:

  This herb assists with boosting the immune system and aids with cardiovascular and high blood pressure issues.

- Ginger Root:

  This herb assists with motion sickness and issues with nausea and vomiting.

- Licorice:

  This herb has anti-inflammatory properties and assists with upset stomachs and intestinal upsets and may serve as a laxative.

- Nettle:

  This herb aids with improving the overall energy levels during pregnancy. It also assists with preventing varicose veins and may reduce the likelihood of tearing and hemorrhaging during the birthing process. Additionally it aids with promoting milk production.

- Oats and Oat Straw:

  This herb assists with relieving irritated skin, restlessness and anxiety.

- Peppermint Leaf:

  This herb assists with the initial onset of a sore throat, relief with upset stomachs, relief of nausea, relief of "morning sickness" and relief of flatulence (gassiness.)

- Red Raspberry Leaf:

  This herb is often found as a tea format and aids with promoting the integrity of the uterus. It also aids with milk production. The herb also assists with decreasing nausea and easing the onset of labor pains.

- <u>Slippery Elm Bark:</u>

  This herb assists with relieving nausea, heartburn and vaginal irritations. It also serves as a toner for the smooth muscle organs such as the uterus, intestine and bladder.

- <u>Valerian:</u>

  This herb aids with promoting relaxation and sleep.

Bach Flower

(Cited with permission by Bach Flower Essence: <u>www.bachflower.com</u>)

While working with homeopathy, Dr. Edward Bach discovered the Bach Flower remedies. He discovered the Original Bach Flower remedies which is a system of 38 Flower Remedies that corrects emotional imbalances where negative emotions are replaced with positive. The difference is the Bach Flower remedies do not require a dilution or a specific rhythmic method.

However they are diluted, harmless, natural and gentle. Dr. Bach departed from homeopathy in believing that by correcting harmful mental attitudes you can stop the dis-ease from becoming physical or, more probably, you can treat the dis-ease when it is at an energy level rather than grossly pathological at the physiological level.

The flower remedies have a great role to play to see in the more psychosomatic (mind-body) type of illness. Dr. Bach describes the primary reason for the failure of modern medical science is that it is dealing with results (symptoms) and not causes. The Bach Flower remedies work in conjunction with herbs, homeopathy and medications and are safe for everyone, including children, pregnant women, and the elderly and even animals.

The situation is likened to an enemy strongly fortified in the hills, continually waging guerilla warfare in the country around, while the people, ignoring the fortified garrison, content themselves with repairing the damaged houses and burying the dead, which are the results of the raids of the marauders. He did not have faith in eradicating dis-ease or curing dis-ease by presenting materialistic methods for simple reason in its origin is not material.

<u>For Kids</u>

The Bach Flower remedies assists with natural stress and emotional relief including fear, daydreaming, self-esteem, worries, depression and self-acceptance.

Since their emotions are not deep-rooted, they tend to respond quicker than adults who stacked and chunked these emotions on top of the original emotions, which takes a longer duration to get to the root source. For adults, to get to the root source, it is similar to the analogy of peeling an onion, until each subsequent layer is peeled.

From Bachflower.com testimonial section:
(Cited with permission by Bach Flower Essence: www.bachflower.com)

August 2010

I became a single mother with three boys and no financial or emotional support from the father of my sons. During that time, I sank to the bottom and was not able to handle the boys growing up, who were taking advantage of divorces parents who could not work together for the well-being of their children. What a mess, you have no idea!

My mother gave me a Bach questionnaire, and she was overwhelmed by the amount that I had marked. Immediately she gave 'the rescue remedy'. After couple of hours, I felt that the enormous heaviness that I have had for a long time, you know the one located in the middle of the solar plexus (stomach area), was gone. I felt that I was able to breathe again. The few drops had lifted it up. Of course, I was done and I took a series of Bach flowers. Know that if you pick one that is not of an emotional problem that you have, it will do nothing. On the other hand, when you pick the one, you will go down before you get back up, just briefly. It is a normal process. It is cleansing, first, and then it heals. So don't be alarmed. I am SO thankful for Mr. Bach's last century discovery. Love, VD.

Bach Flower remedies for Depression

- Mustard:
  Helps you when you feel suddenly depressed without reason. It feels like a cold dark cloud has destroyed all happiness and cheerfulness. The depression can lift just as suddenly for no reason.

- Elm:
  You feel overwhelmed by your work load and matters of life and you feel depressed and exhausted.

- Sweet Chestnut:
  For those moments which happen to some people when the anguish is as great as it seems to be unbearable. When the mind or body feels as if it had been pushed to the uttermost limit of its endurance and now it must give way. When it seems there is nothing but destruction and annihilation left to face.

- Willow:
  Helps you when you have suffered adversity or misfortune and find it difficult to accept. You feel sorry for yourself and are grumbled and sulky.

- Gorse:

When you feel a great hopelessness, you have given up belief that more can be done for you. Under persuasion or to please others you may try different "treatments," at the same time assuring those around that there is so little hope of relief.

- Gentian:
  When you are easily discouraged. You may be progressing well in illness or in the affairs of their daily life, but any small delay or hindrance to progress causes doubt and soon disheartens you.

- Larch:
  When you lose self-esteem and feel depressed.

Please refer to the Depression section of this book for other remedies/suggestions and more information regarding the dis-ease.

Bach Flower remedies for ADD, ADHD, Lack of Focus, Daydreaming

ADD and ADHD, according to Dr. Bach is a result of a combination of emotions that can be rebalanced with the aid of the Bach Flower remedies. There have been parent's testimonials of how the Bach Flower remedies for children were able to alleviate the symptoms involved with focusing issues in school. After a short duration of the Bach Flower remedies' usage, teachers also commented that the children that were using this remedy appeared to be much calmer and was able to readily focus on the task at hand.

When selecting the Bach Flower remedies you should look at each negative emotion and select the Bach Flower remedies that removes it, such as but not limited to:

- Clematis:
  Helps when you daydream and have a hard time focusing on the task in front of you

- Chestnut Bud:
  Helps when you keep forgetting what you have learned, it helps you remember

- Walnut:
  Helps when you get easily distracted by noises, movements and commotion

- Gentian:
  Helps when you get easily discouraged by small setbacks

- Vervain:
  Helps when you are overly excited and hyper, from over involvement in a subject or idea.

- Impatiens:
  Helps when you easily get impatient with the slowness of others

- Elm:
  Helps when you easily get overwhelmed by homework, things you need to do and responsibilities.

- Larch:
  Helps you regain self-esteem.

Please refer to the ADD/ADHD Chapter for other remedies/suggestions and more information regarding the dis-ease.

Bach Flower remedies for Weight- Obesity

The Bach Flower remedies can help you change unhealthy eating habits and replace them with healthy options.

- Cherry Plum:
  Helps you have self-control when you are presented by unhealthy choices.

- Chestnut Bud:
  Helps you learn from past mistakes.

- Crab Apple:
  Helps you accept who you are and how you look.

- Gentian:
  Helps you not to get discouraged with small setbacks.

- Impatiens:
  Helps you have patience with yourself.

Please refer to the Obesity section of this book for other remedies/suggestions and more information regarding the dis-ease.

Bach Flower remedies for Autism

The Autism Society of Japan defines autism as analogous to "Someone who is living in some foreign country without knowing the local language, and is constantly exposed to the sense of insecurity and stresses."

- Shooting Star:
  Helps with grounding, alienation and solitude

- Scarlet Monkey Flower:

Relates to frustration that is felt when your intention is blocked. These are the types of anger and issues of power that you feel when you are pushed into extreme challenges.

- Indian Paintbrush:
Helps to integrate the body and the soul

- Clematis:
For people who seem to be bored and daydreamers that are usually not present, they tend to not have much interest in daily life or have poor memory and probably need lots of sleep. They may look spaced out.

- Impatiens:
For people who get frustrated and cannot express themselves as they would like to, great for temper tantrums

- Madia:
Helps with becoming easily distracted, inability to concentrate, dull or listless

- Violet:
Helps with Profound shyness, reserve, aloofness, fear of being submerged in groups

- Snapdragon:
Helps with verbal aggression and hostility; repressed or misdirected libido, tension around jaw

- Fushcia:
Helps when a child is agitated

- Bluebell:
Helps when a child feels afraid of being ridiculed and anxious about being noticed at all, and fearful of being punished also worried about being judged

Please refer to the Autism section of this book for other remedies/suggestions and more information regarding the dis-ease.

What is Ayurveda

Ayurvedic medicine (also called Ayurveda) is one of the world's oldest medical systems. It originated in India more than 3,000 years ago and remains one of the country's traditional health care systems. The Ayurveda "treatment" is entirely based on herbs, which have a certain medicinal value or property.

Ayurvedic medicine promotes transcendental meditation (TM). Transcendental meditation helps one experience the pure consciousness or positivity of the Universe. It focuses on positive emotions and encourages one to become attuned to the natural rhythms of your body.

Some studies have found that this alternative medicine practice lowers blood pressure and cholesterol, slows aging process and speed recovery from illness. Since they use different herbs with different properties, many "anti-aging" and anti-inflammatory benefits will then follow.

According to the 2007 National Health Interview Survey, which included a comprehensive survey on the use of complementary health practices by Americans, more than 200,000 U.S. adults had used Ayurveda in the previous year.

Dr. Deepak Chopra, an expert in the field of Ayurveda and co-founder of the Chopra Center for Wellbeing believes in the philosophy that: "The less you open your heart to others, the more your heart suffers." Dr. Chopra received his medical training in internal medicine and endocrinology; however, he has chosen to go back to the root Ayurveda to compliment his healing regime. He has authored more than 65 books that range from health to spirituality.

Our Unique Ayurvedic Blueprint

Just as everyone has a unique fingerprint, according to Ayurvedic beliefs, each person has a distinct pattern of energy. We are a specific combination of physical, mental, and emotional characteristics. It is also believed that there are three basics energy types called doshas, present in every person:

- Vata (Wind):
  Vata is formed from Air and Space elements. Within the human body, air is present in the form of oxygen, which is the basis for all energy transfer reactions. Talking about the human body, space is the considered as the vessel that receives all impressions. In the heart, it is believed that space accepts love.

  Energy that controls bodily functions associated with motion, including blood circulation, breathing, blinking, and heartbeat. When vata energy is balanced, there is creativity and vitality. Out of balance, vata produces fear, insomnia, dry skin, constipation, difficulty focusing and anxiety. Vata people tend to be thin, light, enthusiastic, energetic and changeable.

- Pitta (Fire):
  In human body, fire is present in the form of energy that binds atoms together, converts food to fat and muscle. In addition, fire creates impulses of nervous reactions and even our thought process. Pita people tend to be intense, intelligent, goal-oriented and possess a strong appetite for life.

  This energy aids with digestion and controls the body's metabolic systems. It regulates temperature and absorption of nutrients. When the pitta is in balance there is warmth, friendliness, discipline, intelligence and contentment surrounding the environment. When balanced, the person becomes a good leader and speaker. When pita is out of balance it may cause behaviors such as irritability, compulsivity, anger and ulcers may arise and a person may also experience symptoms of indigestion or inflammatory conditions.

- <u>Kapha (Earth)</u>:

Kapha is formed with Earth and Water elements. Earth symbolizes stability, permanence and rigidity. The human body consists of bones, teeth, cells and tissues, as the manifestations of the earth. About 70% of human body is made up of water, the very important liquid that is required for smooth functioning.

In addition to water, fluids including our blood and lymph move between our cells and through our vessels, thereby providing us the energy required. Kapha people tend to be easy-going, methodical and nurturing.

Energy that controls growth in the body. It supplies water to all body parts, moisturizes the skin, and maintains the immune system. In balance, kapha is expressed as love, sweetness, support-iveness, stability and forgiveness. Out of balance, kapha leads to insecurity, sluggishness, weight gain, sinus congestion and envy.

Properties of Ayurvedic Herbs

(Information about the Ayurvedic herbs presented in this Chapter is derived primarily from two sources: Medicinal Plants by Shankar Gopal Joshi (2000) and Major Herbs of Ayurveda edited by Elizabeth Williamson (2002).)

It would be helpful to know that the taste of the herb says much about the properties of the herb. Given here are the effects of each of the taste groups:

- <u>Sweet</u>:

It improves the complexion, strengthens the body, heals wounds and ulcers, and purifies the rasa and the blood.

- <u>Sour</u>:

Carminative, digestive and accumulates secretive impurities (waste material that is secreted) in the tissues to aid elimination.

- <u>Salty</u>:

Purifies tissues, digestive, relaxing, separates impurities, accumulates excretions in the system, causes the body to lose tone (relaxes it,) clears the outlets of the system, produces softness of all the structures of the body.

- <u>Pungent</u>:

Increases digestive power, purifies the body, prevents obesity, causes relaxation of the ligaments and of the system in general; diminishes formation of milk, semen, and fat.

- <u>Bitter</u>:

Separates the doshas, appetizing, digestive, and purifying, improves secretion of breast milk, and reduces the quantity of feces, urine, perspiration, fat, marrow, and pus.

- Astringent:
  Heals ulcers, checks all discharges, separates impurities from tissues, and reduces obesity and excessive moisture.

Types of Ayurvedic Herbs

(Information about the Ayurvedic herbs presented in this Chapter is derived primarily from two sources: Medicinal Plants by Shankar Gopal Joshi (2000) and Major Herbs of Ayurveda edited by Elizabeth Williamson (2002))

Herbs have been used for centuries and are known for rejuvenating, balancing, and restoring our human physiology. Many herbs are used to alter or change a long-standing condition by eliminating the metabolic toxins. Also known as 'blood cleansers', certain herbs improve the immunity of the person, thereby reducing conditions such as fever.

Internal Usage

- Some of the most common internal forms of herbal support include encapsulated herbs, fresh herbs, flower essences and essential oil dilutions.
- Certain herbs are more effective if they are ingested because their medicinal properties are intended to affect important internal organs such as the heart, liver, lungs and the kidney.
- Some other herbs used to assist with strengthening internal organs of the body may be ingested with a combination of water, honey, oil, ghee or milk. The effects of the herbs are dependent on the reactions exhibited from the person consuming them.

External Application

- The external applications of herbs are intended to treat symptoms on or near the surface of the body, such as the skin.
- Herbs taken externally are often in the form of essential oil blends, liniments, ointments, lotions, massage oils, pastes or body wraps.
- Joint problems, dizziness, muscular problems, wounds, cuts and other skin dis-eases can be effectively "cured" by the external herbal "treatment." Application of the herbs on the skin is the common way to treat such problems.
- Herbs such as ginseng, aloe, sandalwood, red clover, burdock, bayberry, black pepper, cinnamon, myrrh, and safflower are known for their alternative property, which are used to heal wounds, sores and boils as well.
- Herbs such as marshmallow root and the leaf assimilate antacid properties and may assist with neutralizing the acidity produced by the stomach. With these herbs, health proper gastric acid is promoted for gastrointestinal purposes.

- Turmeric is an herb with antibiotic properties and may be useful in reducing the growth of germs, harmful microbes and bacteria. Turmeric is often used to assists with wounds and cuts.
- To reduce fever and the production of heat caused by the condition, certain antipyretic herbs such as black pepper, sandalwood, safflower and brihati are recommended by Ayurvedic practitioners.
- An important medical property of herbs is to serve as antiseptic. Aloe, sandalwood, turmeric, chitrak and gokshura are commonly used antiseptic herbs that are high in their medicinal value.
- Certain aromatic herbs like cardamom and coriander are renowned for their appetizing qualities. Other aromatic herbs such as cloves, peppermint and turmeric add a pleasant aroma to the food, thereby increasing the taste of the meal. They serve as digestives and condiments for the food as well.
- Sandalwood and cinnamon has astringent properties and assists with helping with unexpected discharges of blood and mucus.
- Certain aromatic plants such as aloe, barberry, golden seal and chirayat are used as mild tonic. The bitter taste of such plants reduces toxins in blood. They are helpful in destroying infection as well.
- Herbs such as Chamomile, chrysanthemum, coriander, fennel, peppermint, and spearmint, ajwan, basil, calamus, cardamom, cinnamon, ginger, and turmeric are helpful in promoting good blood circulation. Therefore, they are used as cardiac stimulants.
- Certain herbs have disinfectant property, which destroys dis-ease causing germs. They also inhibit the growth of pathogenic microbes that cause communicable dis-eases. Arka, gudachi and katuka are the examples of disinfectant herbs.
- Certain cough syrup ingredients like ginger and cloves are known for their expectorant property, which promotes the thinning and ejection of mucus from the lungs, trachea and bronchi. Cardamom, eucalyptus, wild cherry and cloves are also expectorants.
- Camphor, cayenne, myrrh, guggul and gotu kola are used as stimulants.
- Guduchi, katuka, golden seal, aloe, barberry and bala can be nutritive and rejuvenative and can be used as a tonic.
- Honey, turmeric, marshmallow and licorice can effectively treat a fresh cut and wound. They are termed as vulnerary herbs.

7

You and Your Child's Chiropractic Journey

"All dis-ease results from a disruption of the flow of intelligence"

–Deepak Chopra MD–

The Defining Moment

In our journey to life, like a caterpillar, multiple transformations will take place which provides us with metamorphosis of the way we are today and will evolve into tomorrow. These transformations will change our perspective, emotion, outlook in life and the physiology of our body. Some will be tiny changes that may not be as apparent while others will be distinctive.

It is the brain and the nervous system that is responsible for controlling and coordinating the function of all tissues, organs and systems in the body. The brain is the main controller of the self-healing and self-regulating automatic system of our body. This is automatic because you don't have to think about how fast your heart needs to beat or how your lungs need to function for the air to get in. This is the beauty and complexity of our entire body.

The Intent

In the study of current medicine there is a tendency to ignore functional illness patterns in favor of pathological processes. In the study of alternative/holistic medicine, there is too often an over-simplification of clinical principles and the lack of sharp-edge diagnostic sword. The patient with functional illness too often receives a medication for a pathological process, or haphazard natural therapies applied in a hit-and-miss fashion. Both of these approaches lack insight into the nature of the patient's illness, yet, luckily, both of these approaches are effective...sometimes.

Dr. James Chesnut, a chiropractic physician and physiologist, studied the human physiology and stress responses to conclude that pathological processes are mythology. He explains that to get to that stage, a radical physiological process needs to happen in RESPONSE to stress internally.

According to him, the simple fact that the gene didn't change for more than 40,000 years and that our human stresses have increased and changed in natures i.e. we are not so concerned about a tiger running after us anymore; however, we have incorporated new stressors such as concerns about our children, bills, job, car payments, food, or scheduling conflicts.

Many health professionals overemphasize one side of health care while ignoring one or both of the other sides. The structural side is emphasized by chiropractors, massage therapist, physical therapist; the psychological side is emphasized by psychologist (traditional and energy psychologist,) psychiatrist, coaches, hypnosis and others and the chemical side is emphasized by the nutritional therapist and the allopath (today's medicine.) We must recognize that anyone or all these three factors may be involved in any given patient and we should look at all three factors from a holistic perspective.

My goal in this section is to guide you from the time you are pregnant to after birth and for your child from the moment in-uterine to when s/he is completely formed (i.e. grown up.)

Defining Sickness

In other words, the nervous system or the brain, due to chemical imbalances, emotional or physical stressors interfere with your body's natural healing abilities. Would you consider the body to be less healthy or would it then be defined as sickness?

The difference doesn't seem huge, but it is. It is the same as choosing to be bankrupt or financially independent, not being tired or vibrant and energized, not being depressed or having the most optimistic hope for the world. The choice of the word and the emotion related to it makes a big difference.

Sickness, by definition, is a lack of health. It does not exist as an independent entity. Darkness, by definition, is a lack of light; it does not exist as an independent entity. Neither dis-eases nor darkness have any physical properties. Imagine if you were in a sealed room that was well lit and outside that room was a dark hallway.

If you opened the door would darkness rush in or would light rush out? Light would rush out and illuminate the dark hallway of course. Why? Because light exists and darkness does not, if you wanted to make the room brighter could you look for darkness and remove it?

Of course not! You can't remove something that does not exist; to make the room brighter you would have to increase the amount of light. If you wanted to make someone healthier could you look for sickness or "dis-ease" and remove it?

Of course not! You can't remove something that does not exist; to make someone healthier you have to increase the amount of health, you have to increase the level of homeostatic cell function." (James Chestnut DC from his book The Wellness and Prevention Paradigm.)

If one wished to improve the world, they need to start with their own health. This is why chiropractors are one important "primary" care physician for a child, so that their nervous system will allow the natural protection mechanism and life force energy to be at optimal balanced states without any road blocks.

A Coach For You and Your Baby

One change that will be apparent and distinctive during pregnancy is you and your baby's physical body. From in-uterine, one cell will transform into multiple cells then to a whole nervous system. Out of this process structures will develop and finally organs will become the end-result. Imagine how different this journey would be if you had a coach to ensure the proper transformation into a healthy baby?

Pregnancy is quite a stressor for many women. If the mother is exhausted, according to the Hans Seyles' model of stress, the mother will steal the fetus' hormones for herself. This hormone stealing will result in her saying: "This pregnancy is wonderful, I feel energized." This will create stress to the baby's adrenal, resulting in potential health issues after the delivery like allergies and recurrent infections. This process also happens with the Thyroid hormones and others.

During pregnancy, the entire body changes to give room for this new life that is about to grow. Tissues enlarge, others lengthen and others are moved about. Some common changes are the abdominal (belly) growing and all the tissues that extend, enlarge and lengthen. The pelvic, which holds the entire baby, will have to separate to give room for the time of the delivery. Other structures will shift because the weight distribution is not at its "normalized" position and even the curvature of the spine will change. Multiple biomechanical (bones), muscles, ligaments and even organs will shift and need attention during this time frame.

Why Do I Need A Chiropractic Physician During Pregnancy

Chiropractic physicians are doctors of chiropractic. They undergo a doctorate program and study the same courses that a medical doctor will in their first three years. The only difference is; a chiropractic physician will study how the structures of the body interfere with the grand scheme of your transformation, how trauma can slow it down and the physiology of these interactions so they can break bad patterns happening at multiple levels. Chiropractic physicians study also nutrition, organ therapy, radiography and imaging and as well as how to take care of the pregnant mother and infant.

The chiropractic philosophy is determined on the simple basis that the human body is supposed to heal itself, from its own capacity, from its innate ability. It is like when you cut your finger, it's not the band-aid that heals you, but the body that makes new skin, thus, self-healing. It's also apparent that the heart beats each and every day, the lungs take in and breath out air and the body temperature is always around 98-99 degrees, thus self-regulating.

Overall, the chiropractic approach to health and dis-ease is the triad of the health model which focuses its attention to three fundamentals for well-being: physical/structural, mental/emotional and biochemical/nutritional/hormonal levels of health. This approach is consistent with the Holistic design for health awareness happening around the world. The first "treatment" was performed to a man who was deaf in one ear. His hearing was recovered with a chiropractic adjustment, removing the interferences from the mid back spine. This subluxation lesion (misalignment of two bones, vertebrae or cranial bones) created a cascade of event and contributed to his deafness on one or many levels in the triad of health.

A subluxation (or misalignment of bones or vertebrae) happens when there is interference or irritation in your nervous system that causes poor communication between your brain and body. Your brain and body are in constant contact and feedback to one and is the circle of life.

Your central nervous system (brain and spinal cord) is responsible for sending messages to every cell, tissue, organ and system in your body. This communication is made possible by your nervous system and your natural innate intelligence and is in charge of virtually every function in your body and determines whether you enjoy good health or dis-ease. The central nervous system is so important that it is the only tissue in your body that nature built as a protective armor surrounding it; this armor being your skull and spinal column.

However, even with this inborn protection, our nervous system can experience interference, injury or disturbance. We call this damage to our nervous system a subluxation. Subluxations could potentially be a very serious threat to your continued overall health and well-being. Because subluxations can have devastating effects on your overall health and well-being, our primary goal is to detect and correct the subluxations that are interfering with your child's nervous system and life flow.

This damage to your nervous system may initiate sickness and dis-ease if you become weakened. This may be caused by a number of things including lack of sleep, poor posture, stress, injuries, Etc. Our body will speak to these subluxations with organ issues, depression, muscle spasms, and "cancer", just to name a few. "Treatment" from a chiropractor is the only "treatment" that can correct these subluxations.

The concept of adjusting a pregnant mother and/or her child relates to a wellness concept or a lifestyle trend. Today, our health consciousness is moving toward wellness, prevention, maintenance, health promotion, all aspects of self-healing.

What Is The SOT® Method of Chiropractic?

One notable researcher in chiropractic was Major Bertrand De Jarnette. After having his life saved by chiropractic adjustments, he was a firm believer in the practice and principles. He dedicated his life to understanding how this mechanism functioned in the human body. His lifetime of research concluded that the most important component to the maintenance of health and healing was the dura mater (which is the "balloon surrounding your nervous system" also called meningeal.)

Another key component to the maintenance of health and healing of dis-ease was hypothesized to be the cerebral spinal fluid (CSF.) In some theories CSF is the physical manifestation of the innate energy. It is the condensation of pure innate transduced by a mechanism in the brain into CSF. This is not unlike how a condenser can produce water from moisture in the air or a light bulb converting electricity into visible light. To some, the cerebral spinal fluid is the elixir of life. An alternate view is that CSF is the medium through which the innate healing energy flows. Either way it is considered of essence to have CSF flowing properly to all parts of the body. The flow is intimately related to the proper function of the dura which has intimate structural relationship with the osseous structures of the body.

The craniosacral respiratory mechanism provides the physical mechanics for essential CSF production and distribution. According to Dr. De Jarnette, the CSF is ultimately moved by both dura and intent. Intent is the power of the mind and emotional involvement.

Since the brain produces the life force of your body, the CSF, it is imperative to make sure that the surrounding protection, the skull, is not compressing or altering this flow and interfering in the brain capacity. The CSF travels to the nerve root and to the ending of each peripheral nerve; meaning to your fingers and toes. Spinal subluxations can produce inactivity of the cerebral spinal fluid flow.

This specialized chiropractic technique allows the chiropractic physician to look at the whole body i.e. spine, cranium, extremities but also the organs and its implications to all the embryological reflexes to restore proper balance in the nervous system and ultimately into the body, with the most effective and cost effective means for the patient. While the primary function of CSF is to cushion the brain within the skull and serve as a shock absorber for the central nervous system, CSF interruption will not allow proper circulation of nutrients and chemicals filtered from the blood and the proper removal of waste products from the brain.

SOT' Method chiropractic physician will address the whole-body including the pelvic, organ and cranial. They will use orthopedic wedges and gravitational forces to rebalance your pelvic which limits all traumas to your body and your baby. This will also establish proper nutrient to your nerves, all organs and cells in your and baby's bodies.

This system allows the chiropractic physician to picture what the current stressors are and peel the onion backwards to reach the ultimate event which contributed to the body to get distorted, not in balance, not healthy or what I like to call "crooked."

The Best Gift A Mom Could Receive

The American Pregnancy Association reinforced the need for chiropractic care since the body will go under physiological, hormonal and emotional thus:

- Maintaining a healthier pregnancy
- Controlling symptoms of nausea
- Reducing the time of labor and delivery
- Relieving back, neck or joint pain
- Preventing a potential cesarean delivery

This will also affect the actual birth since the canal (depending on the pelvic alignment) might affect the baby to malposition during the pregnancy or birth process. Chiropractic care can also reduce interference to the mother's vital nerve system which controls and coordinates all of her system and functions.

The joy my wife had with our first baby was extraordinary; being a chiropractic physician herself, she recognized the importance of its benefits during the duration of the pregnancy. She felt so different and happy. Her belly grew, her skin became radiant, her face glowed and she had energy for that new life to come. Some of what will follow might explain why, my wife, had the best experience with pregnancy three times in a row. Just a thought!

When pregnancy starts, your hormones will change to let the uterus and brain know something BIG is supposed to happen. From that moment, all the key players and their teammates need to be on board. The brain, the chief orchestrator, will dictate the entire role and it will be important for the next 40 weeks or so to follow the prescribed game plan.

The chemicals surrounding the mother and fetus, whether coming from toxins from food or environmental toxins could impact the well-being of the unborn baby. The emotional distress or mental distresses play a critical role on how the set of DNA genes will evolve, also known as epigenetics. Toxic emotional patterns such as prolonged stress, anger, grief, sadness, guilt, shame are emotionally unhealthy during pregnancy and these same emotional patterns will be transferred to your unborn baby.

The role of a chiropractic physician is to assess the pelvic floor muscles and fascia (connective surrounding tissues.) The integrity of the pelvic (hip bones) and sacrum will be carefully monitored throughout the pregnancy. Without proper "treatment", malposition of any of her and the fetal structure will be apparent during the third trimester. Studies have shown that chiropractic care decreases the duration of labor itself.

The following provides more in-depth medical perspectives on what is assessed and "treated" during a pregnancy that many OBGYN do not focus on (more details into Appendix 1):

- Transverse Plane
- Diaphragm
- Hiatus Hernia
- Kidney Ptosis
- Pelvic Floor
- Psoas and Piriformis muscles

- Sacrum Involvement
- Pubic Bone
- Pelvic Instability

Should The Mom's Head Be Evaluated – Why Chiropractic Craniopathy?

Hippocrates, the father of medicine (400BC), discussed the anatomy and physiology aspect of head trauma and recommended some sort of cranial "treatment." Dr. De Jarnette developed a whole body system, chiropractic Craniopathy and SOT° Method, where the cranium relates to the body and the body relates to the cranium and to the organs and its extremities.

Eighty percent (80%) of the human nervous system is located in the cranium (skull) and therefore presents opportunity for significant therapeutic intervention. For over 75 years, chiropractic and osteopathy have recognized the value of cranial adjusting. Since the brain tells the body and all the cells to get ready for this big upcoming pregnancy, this would put a mother at an advantage for ensuring that her whole body was optimally functioning for the baby's well-being.

If the brain cannot communicate properly or, worse yet, sends too many messages to a cell, this could create chaos. The skull protects your brain because it is the most important part of your entire body. But a compression to it, can affect the cerebral spinal fluid flow and its functionality. So the skull might interfere with the brain's capacity, but how is this important during pregnancy, you ask?

Different bones in the skull have a potential to affect your physical body. For example, the occipital bone (back of head bone) can compress too severely on the brain and vision is misinterpreted. Even though symptoms are common during pregnancy, I believe it helps reassure a mom, especially a first-time mother to know that these symptoms can be alleviated by chiropractic care with a specialization in chiropractic Craniopathy. You will find all the more common bone structures in the head that may affect pregnancy symptoms in Appendix 2.

Also, research has demonstrated that the cranial bone has a link to the pelvic bone. Having your head adjusted allows the pelvic to maintain its integrity and optimally, allow a safer environment for the fetus to grow and a proper delivery.

Causes of Cranial Distortions

Intrauterine constraint

- After the seventh month of gestation any position other than vertex in an attitude of flexion (position of baby's head at birth) is considered to be a constraint of some degree
- Causes:
  1) Bony- pelvic type and biomechanical
  2) Soft tissue-uterine malformations and biomechanical

3) Placental location

4) Fetal factors (size, hydrocephaly, anencephaly, multiparus, lack of strong fetal movements)

5) Unknown etiology- 85%

Fetal presentations/positions in prenatal period

- > 95% are in the proper position at delivery
- 3% are breech
- 0.5% are transverse, oblique, face or brow presentations
- Sival et al (1983) found that infants with breech presentations had less hip extension and demonstrated an abnormally flexed ambulation pattern at 12-18 months
- Transverse positions are associated with neonatal deformities such as plagiocephaly (cranial deformation or distortion), mandibular hypoplasia (reduced growth of the jaw), Torticollis (inability to move the neck), nasal septum deviation and foot deformity.
- Misalignment of the cranial bones or fixation of their sutures can cause adverse dural tension which results in stasis of vital fluids and malfunction of the homeostatic brain and nerve centers. Disability is the end result. The child does not have 100% of his/her innate potential within its given environment.

Effects of delivery

- Prolonged labor or second stage (pushing)
- Fast labor
- Delivery in supine position
- Malpresentation: face and brow most difficult for child
- Ventouse or forceps delivery

Iatrogenic (Resulting in Medical Treatment)

- Induction: excessively strong contractions induced by oxytocin can lead to fetal head pressing against unripe cervix and cause fetal cervical spine extension thus creating undue stress on cranium and delicate cervical spine
- Stripping of the membranes to induce labor can cause cranial distress because the uterine contractions and cranial presentation into the mother's bony pelvis are not buffered with amniotic fluid.
- Forceps: 60-80 lbs of pressure often used and placed against fetal temporals, frontal and sphenoid, may lead to skull fractures and tearing of atlanto-occipital tissues
- Ventouse (vacuum): stress induced to parietals, frontal and occipital bones and may cause caput succedaneum
- Cesarean Section: lack of cranial molding and skin sensory input

Dental

Since the TMJ (jaw) connect and articulate with the temporal bone, any bite issues will be transferred to the cranium and any cranium issue can be transferred to the jaw and to the teeth. Every malocclusion can potentially affect the cranial bone and the brain activation and proper functioning.

A Mouth-Body Dentist or holistic dental who understand the cranial implications and total body implications will be a great fit.

Birth Trauma

Birth trauma is defined as any condition that affects the fetus adversely during delivery (Hughes et al, 1999.) The incidence is 3.1% of live births according to Solenen and Uusitalo. Here it was reported at 9% of live birth by Hughes.

Some of the predisposition and factors of trauma during birth include the oxytocin use, multiple gestations, malpresentation, prolonged labor, prolonged pushing or second stage of labor (optimal is 20 minutes to one hour), epidural, forceps or ventouse extraction and shoulder dystocia.

Some tissues involved during birth trauma may include bones or cartilages like the cranium (skull), face, humerus (arm) and femur (leg), vascular at the brain and surrounding the brain, nervous system including the cranial nerve, soft tissue like muscles involved at the neck and oxygen deprivation by the cord wrapped around the neck of the child or medication usages during birth.

Birth trauma may also result in abnormal irritation of the bone growth center, thus leading to asymmetrical development. In any learning disability syndrome, the visual field perception deficit can be due to the occipital lobe stress which subsequently affects the sphenoid and temporal area as well. Problems with coordination and speech are also common, as is dyslexia, the inability to properly understand that which is read. All pressure to the area of the brain affecting these modalities can irritate or limit the brain's functionality.

A breach birth may be just as traumatic as a C-section. Often the temporal bones are shoved superiorly, leading to eustachian tube drainage problem and ear infections.

If the child was delivered by C-section, the normal uterine and vaginal contraction was missing which can delay the CSF production and flow.

Getting Back To The Real You

Cranial therapy is the most amazing for opening your full potential. Misaligned skull bones change how you see your world and react to it. This was designed by Amahra Jaxen, from Vancouver, Canada (shared with permission from http://thebodybeyond.blogspot.ca/2011/03/how-does-your-brain-rate.html and www.quantumhealer.ca) and serves as a wonderful guide for you to recognize the bones that may need your immediate attention by a holistic practitioner including a chiropractic Craniopath's care:

Only check the statements that are true

1. SACRUM (spinal base)

_____ Is it difficult for you to accumulate money or materials things?

_____ Are you easily thrown off balance?

_____ Is it hard to stand your ground in an argument/confrontation?

_____ Do you feel unsafe, unstable or unsupported?

_____ Is it hard to stay in one place for very long?

_____ Are you sensitive to criticism?

_____ Do feel tense when confronted by an authority figure?

2. OCCIPITAL (skull base)

_____ Is it hard for you to accept responsibility or be a leader?

_____ Is problem solving or brainstorming difficult?

_____ Do you over react fairly easily?

_____ Do you have a problem with authority?

_____ Is it hard to feel joy or to "go with the flow" in life?

_____ Do you easily feel betrayed or "stabbed in the back"?

_____ Is it hard to be in present time?

_____ Are you often disturbed by images from your past?

3. SPHENOID (eyes)

_____ Do you have hormonal imbalances?

_____ Do you often have headaches or feel that you are "not yourself"?

_____ Do you suffer from SAD (seasonal affective disorder)?

_____ Is it hard to see your potential?

_____ Do you feel dis-connected?

_____ Do you get headaches behind your forehead?

_____ Do you feel low back pain?

_____ Do you suffer from migraines?

_____ Do you feel the desire to look to a higher power for support?

_____ Did your parents fight, shout or argue around you as a child?

4. TEMPORAL (ears)

_____ Do you have poor balance or vertigo?

_____ Do you often feel hungry, even shortly after eating?

_____ Is change and new experience difficult for you?

_____ Are you often inflexible?

_____ Do you easily over-react to situations?

_____ Do you have short-term memory lapse?

_____ Do you often feel tired and regretful?

5. FRONTAL (forehead)

_____ Are you quick to blame or judge?

_____ Do you feel a sense of longing or discontent?

_____ Do you feel disconnected from other people?

_____ Do you ever get so angry that you want to blow your stack?

_____ Do you find it difficult to hear or receive divine inspiration?

6. PARIETALS (top of skull)

_____ Are you easily overwhelmed?

_____ Is it hard to find direction in your life?

_____ Are you stubborn, obsessive?

_____ Do you often feel that you are butting your head up against a wall?

_____ Are you constantly stuck in your head?

_____ Is it hard to make long term plans and handle the details

_____ Do you get headaches when you are confused?

7. ETHMOID (nose between the eyes)

_____ Does it always seem that your life has obstacles in the way?

_____ Do you ever feel lost in a fog?

_____ Do you suffer from sinus problems or constant stuffy nose?

_____ Do you feel in despair or disturbed for no apparent reason?

8. VOMER (between palate and bridge of nose)

_____ Is it hard to put what you are thinking into spoken words?

_____ Are you always off in the future? Worrying what if?

_____ Is your mind unclear or indecisive?

_____ Do you suffer/agonize from regular sinusitis?

9. ZYGOMAE (cheekbones)

_____ Is it hard to feel proud of yourself?

_____ Is it hard to find your place of inner strength?

_____ Are you somewhat defensive?

_____ Do you have sinus problems?

_____ Do you often feel unsafe?

10. MAXILLA (upper jaw)

_____ Is it hard for you to display affection?

_____ Is it hard for you to communicate?

_____ Do you give up too easily?

_____ Are you unable to sing or write poetry?

_____ Is it hard for you to do nice things for yourself?

_____ Are you afraid to tell the truth?

_____ Do you easily feel resentful?

_____ Do you feel awkward or ungraceful?

11. PALATINES (soft palate support)

_____ Are there often times when you feel you've "had it up to here"

_____ Do you find some circumstances hard to swallow?

_____ Do you find it hard to cry?

12. MANDIBLE (lower jaw)

_____ Do you have a fear of speaking up?

_____ Do you hold in unexpressed aggression?

_____ Is your determination level low?

_____ Is it hard to see who you are, what your identity is?

_____ Is self-expression difficult for you?

_____ Is it hard to express or get in touch with your sexuality?

Tally up your score and become empowered by helping your chiropractic Craniopath understand your most critical needs.

_____ Sacrum (base of spine)

_____ Occiput (base of skull)

_____ Sphenoid (behind the eyes)

_____ Temporal (ears)

_____ Frontal (forehead)

_____ Parietals (top of skull)

_____ Ethmoid (upper nose bridge)

_____ Vomer (under nose)

_____ Cheekbones

_____ Maxilla (upper jaw)

_____ Mandible (lower jaw)

_____ Palatines

What Does Chiropractic Care Provide the Mom?

Since the spine protects the nervous system and all the circuits from the brain and gives orders to all the other cells in your body, if a subluxation is present in the spine, this means the nerve flow and potential muscles, ligaments, organs might not be optimal and thus the fetal development is impacted. What is important during pregnancy is to:

1. Have a proper brain-body connection so you can respond to the demand your baby needs without conflicts nor interferences, remember stress can be transferred via the placenta.

2. Have a proper nest for your baby, a perfect pelvic alignment where all the muscles, fascia (tissue) and ligaments are not too tight and the baby will have room to turn and "play" inside.

3. Breathe properly to let the oxygen flow since it will help your baby grow.

4. Have an optimal digestion system since 1/3 of what you will eat goes directly to the baby. You need to be able to naturally break down proteins, carbohydrates, and fats into progressively smaller components so that they may be absorbed and sent to your baby on a consistent basis. All these processes are orchestrated by organs, nerves and the brain, so the connection must work properly.

5. Have an optimal elimination system to ensure that the toxicity will be evacuated instead of stored and given to the baby, which these systems are also orchestrated via the nervous system, organs and from eating proper nutrients.

Fun Facts Before Your Delivery Date

Your chiropractic physician will be able to provide in-depth information regarding the best delivery option for your family's needs. The most important thing is to make an educated consumer choice with all the relevant information. Did you know the following facts?

More and more parents are seeking chiropractic care for their children and are aware of how it is important to take care of their children's spine and skull at an early age. Also, by having the mother receive chiropractic care and allowing her nerve system to flow without interference will allow for better development and growth for your baby's needs.

Chiropractic will help to allow the baby the room to develop without restrictions to its forming skull, spine and other skeletal structure. It also offers the baby the room to move into the best possible position for birth. With proper fetal positioning, there is a significant decrease in dystocia (failure to progress during labor) and a reduce chance of having birth trauma and/or complication.

Your Baby's Brain

The most dramatic increase in brain volume occurs in the last three months of gestation and in the first two years of life. Head circumference increases strikingly before and after term birth from 23 cm at 28 gestational weeks to 35 cm at term and 45 cm by 8 months postnatal.

Head growth of the fetus and infant is largely determined by brain growth. The brain reaches 90% of adult size by 1 year of age; it is 95% of its ultimate adult size by 6 years of age and growth is complete by age 7. Skull anomalies may originate prenatally or may develop postnatal during the first 2 years of life.

During the birth presentation the cranial bones must overlap to allow the skull to pass through the pelvic outlet. Following this process, the cranial bones must adjust to normal position and expand to normal size, something like a blossoming flower opening to the world.

Your Baby's Position Matters

After the seventh month any position other than the head first towards the vaginal canal is considered warranting of an intrauterine constraint. Sometimes if there is excess Cerebral Spinal Fluid (CSF) in the brain, swelling that occurs which causes hydrocephaly and the correct fetal position is not achieved. Often times it is due to the location of the placental itself or the size of the fetus.

Rarer occasions are when a fetus has a birth defect where they are born with parts of the brain and the skull known as anencephaly. Having twins or larger number of fetus in the uterine may also cause the positioning of the fetus to be incorrect. Additionally, if the fetus has lacked strong movement throughout the pregnancy, this may impact the fetus' readiness for the proper positioning.

Your fetus' position can also have long-term effects on their health. In general over 95% of babies are properly positioned before delivery. Sival et al (1983) found that infants with breech presentations had less hip extension and demonstrated an abnormal walking pattern at 12-18 months.

Transverse positions (lying sideways) in the stomach are associated with neonatal physical deformities such as plagiocephaly (cranial deformation or distortion flat head syndrome), mandibular hypoplasia (reduced growth of the jaw), Torticollis (inability to move the neck), nasal septum deviation (deformity of the nose) and foot deformities.

The Delivery Method Matters

The chosen method of delivery, unless it is an emergency situation may have an impact on the learning abilities of your child at a later date. Issues may occur if the labor is prolonged and extensive pushing is required for an extended period or if the delivery occurs too quickly. Delivering on your back is not the best method; ideally delivery should be performed sitting up-right. If the fetus is delivered face up, this may present health challenges later in life.

If the delivery was performed using induction by producing excessively strong contractions induced by oxytocin, this can lead to the fetus' head pressing against the unripe cervix. This causes undue stress on the baby's cranium and cervical spine, the first subluxation.

If breaking the water was involved to induce labor it can cause cranial distress because the uterine contractions and the baby's cranium into the mother's bony pelvis may not be buffered with enough amniotic fluid.

If the delivery method consists of forceps, imagine 60-80 pounds of pressure placed against the baby's temporal, frontal and sphenoid bones. This often leads to skull fractures and tearing of the atlanto-occipital tissues that causes birth defects. When your frontal bone is misaligned some physical symptoms can develop later in life such as migraines, immune system issues, anxiety, ADD/ADHD, inability to focus, frequent frustration, seizure and autism.

When the temporal bone is misaligned it can lead to jaw issues later in life. Other issues involved are vertigo, short-term memory lapse, tinnitus (ringing in the ear), anxiety, noise sensitivity, hypertension, irritable bowel syndrome, gastrointestinal disorders, bi-polar disorder, and PMS. It also relates to the vagus nerve in the stomach that relates to the sensation of hunger (precursor for obesity.) With the sphenoid bone, the pituitary gland can be impacted.

If the baby is delivered using the vacuum method, stress is induced to the parietals, frontal and occipital bones. When the occipital bone is affected the visual processing may be disrupted. Some of the visual disturbances that could occur are visual field defects, impacted discrimination of movement and color, and hallucinations. Based on its location, the frontal bone can have an influence on your body's energy and emotions, as well as your sinuses and vision.

If the baby is born with the Cesarean Section, there may be a lack of cranial molding (asymmetric head shape) and skin sensory input. The skin sensory input may be a precursor to Autistic characteristics that involve the deficiencies in the touch sensory. Much research has shown the impact of cranial asymmetry at birth and found that it affected many issues such as: the positional preference during sleep or breast-feeding, head pain, sinus issues, allergies and personality disorder, headache, poor cervical biomechanics, chronic head and facial pain, or tilting of the head while swallowing.

What Is The Webster Technique?

The Webster Technique is a clinically proven method that allows chiropractors to balance the mother's pelvis which in turn reduces stress on the fetus. Balancing and aligning the mother's body is another reason to seek chiropractic care during pregnancy. The pelvic misalignment reduces the room for the baby and can provide a uterine strain for fetus and affect the development of the baby. This restriction is called intrauterine constraint.

Having a properly aligned pelvis is crucial for the baby to be in the best position for birth. If this does not occur, a more traumatic birthing process may take place (use of forceps, Breech, c-section.) It is not uncommon for babies to be in the breech position. A vast majority of babies are successfully turned when the Webster Technique is used. It is best performed during the 8th month of pregnancy if the baby is breech.

Your Child's Second Coach –
The Chiropractor/Pediatrician Relationship

Chiropractic care for infant and children has happened since the beginning of the industry. Daniel David Palmer published the first adjustment to a child in 1910. Hippocrates was another huge supporter of chiropractic care. In fact, in one of his published articles he says, "Get knowledge of the spine, for this is the requisite for many dis-eases."

An article in the January 2007 issue of Pediatrics described chiropractic as the most common complementary and alternative medicine practice used by children, who made an estimated 30 million visits to US chiropractors in 1997. Research showed that it takes 2 weeks for a subluxation to be engraved within the nervous system as a bad pattern. This is why it is recommended to get at least your child evaluated by your chiropractic physician every two weeks in the first 3 to 7 years of their life.

It is very important that a child have both a pediatrician and a pediatric chiropractor. A pediatric chiropractic physician is not there to replace the role of the pediatrician. The pediatrician provides medications when necessary and delivers care in times of serious illness and injury. A pediatric chiropractic physician is there for preventative wellness care and maintenance of the child's structure. The two are very complementary.

The chiropractic philosophy is determined on the simple basis that the human body is supposed to heal itself, from its own capacity, forming its innate abilities. Again, it is like when you cut your finger, it's not the band-age that heals you, but the body that makes new skin, thus, self-healing.

Since doctors of chiropractic do not treat dis-ease or illness like medical doctors or even "cure" them, many common childhood disorders and dis-eases may be the result of the nervous system's interference by the spine, skull or extremities. Numerous researches have shown that chiropractic "treatment" resolves or helps many dis-eases while restoring proper nervous functionality.

Children Symptomatology for the Chiropractic Care

Spontaneous

Spontaneous symptoms are such that the children are presented with symptoms of being cranky or generally ill-natured, a child that doesn't exert any trauma, muscle rigidity or fever. Parents would describe this type of child as being generally happy. The child may or may not be able to tell that pain exists or comprehend what pain is due to his/her development. So it is possible that the child has a headache, but cannot communicate it effectively.

Autonomic

This category ranges from the fight or flight (sympathetic) and parasympathetic (digestion) symptoms. These symptoms are mainly: colic, constipation and diarrhea, bed wetting, skin disorder, childhood dis-ease (fever, measles, chicken pox, Etc.), bronchial and lung issues to name a few.

Traumatic

This category involves trauma, accident, fall including rolling off the bed, fall down the stairs, sliding. This category needs to assess the gravity since fracture and internal damage might be serious. This category is most likely handled with caution and with the possibility of referring to the emergency room or for an x-ray. Your doctor of chiropractic is well trained and will do the best for your child at any moment.

When Should Your Child Have His/Her First Visit?

Like we mentioned above, even in the womb, space might be constrained and pressure applied to some areas of the fetus. The birthing process, natural or not, might potentially be traumatic. During the pushing phase of the labor, the neck and spine might be forced out of alignment or injured as the baby is compressed and pushed down the birth canal. During c-section for example, normal uterine and vaginal contraction is absent, therefore, it might delay neurological functioning and cerebral spinal fluid production and flow.

When their spine gets out of proper alignment during delivery, it may cause the nerve to become stretched or twisted which may disrupt proper vital communication systems. Subluxation occurs frequently during natural birth. If medical interventions are involved during the birthing process (C-section, vacuum, forceps, epidural, Pitocin, fetal heart monitor), there is a stronger likelihood of trauma to the baby's spine and nervous system and a subluxation occurring.

Since the misalignment of these subluxations affects the baby's neurology, it could create complications if left uncorrected. Among them, respiratory depression and SIDS could occur. In most cases, you will find immediate symptoms because of its direct implication to the nerve and structures affected but it can happen that these symptoms are delayed. The child's ability to fight against dis-ease, for example, may be lowered. Cold, ear infection, colic and other illnesses may also be of results.

Organ functions could be sped-up or diminished because of a subluxation. This might result in an inability to produce proper enzymes or chemicals responsible for raising or lowering body temperature as needed or regulating the immune system in response to an infection. Studies have shown the improvement of white blood cell activities after a chiropractic adjustment. It can also affect the surroundings of the organ which is responsible to hold them in proper place and create a series of minor complications which, left unresolved, can lead to hiatus hernia, dropped organs or even a flipped uterus in some cases.

To be efficient and recognize when to bring your child to a chiropractic physician look for: difficulty in nursing, poor sleep, waking up due to a nightmare, colic, fussiness, seems always uncomfortable, delayed in response and delayed development. Subluxations that have not been corrected by chiropractic adjustments become embedded with scar tissues in the muscles, soft tissues and bones. Within 7-14 days, that layer of scar tissue becomes permanent and another layer forms.

Who Wants To Be A Billionaire?
Would The Stars Do This For Their Kids?

If you begin chiropractic care before any permanent scar tissue is laid down or any neurological set definitive path, and continue wellness chiropractic care so all future bumps, bruises, emotional upsets,

Etc. don't become embedded in the spine and nervous system, you are providing your child with the best gift in life. That is what a Billionaire Parent would do.

These famous people all have the ability to choose any health care in the world, but they have all chosen chiropractic for its health and life enhancing capabilities. Listed below are just a sample of celebrities, there are many more that have included this care into their family's lifestyle.

Celebrities and Pro Athletes Using Chiropractic

This is how I found out the best way of going, is to use chiropractors, not only after injuries, but also before injury." - **Arnold Schwarzenegger**

*"I've been going to chiropractors for as long as I can remember. It's as important to my training as practicing my swing." -***Tiger Woods**

Candice Michelle*- WWE wrestler, model, chiropractic patient, wife of a chiropractor*

"Chiropractic makes me feel a few inches taller each time I come out." - **Christie Brinkley**

"I've always been a proponent of chiropractic care. The problem doesn't get fixed until I go to a doctor of chiropractic." - **Derek Parra,** 2002 Olympic Gold Medalist and World Record Holder, men's 1500 meters

"I have to have an adjustment before I go into the ring. I do believe in chiropractic. I found that going to a chiropractic physician three times a week helps my performance. The majority of boxers go to get that edge." - **Evander Holyfield**

"I probably wouldn't even be here now if it weren't for chiropractic. - **Merle Haggard**-country singer

"I use chiropractic as my main source of healthcare." - **Gerald Wilkins**

"Chiropractic is a wonderful means of natural healing!" - **Bob Hope**

Lance said that he could not have won without his chiropractor's help. "I am just coming into my best years. - **Lance Armstrong**

"I've found that it's a great stress reliever to get adjusted. It takes away a lot of the tightness in the muscles" - **Jose Canseco**

"I got a chiropractic physician to come along to the [Patriot] shoot, because they can actually stick you back together within 15 minutes. He spent a week and worked on the entire crew." - **Mel Gibson**

"By getting adjusted once a week, I feel I can sustain my career a lot longer. I'm happy we have chiro services at the park, I don't think we would ever go without it!" - **Barry Bonds**

Demi Moore	Cher	Clint Eastwood
James Earl Jones	Kim Basinger	Richard Gere
Whoopie Goldberg	Sylvester Stallone	Robin Williams
Denzel Washington	Alec Baldwin	Christie Brinkley
Macaulay Culkin	Jerry Seinfeld	Ted Danson

Authors:

"Chiropractic works in harmony with the basic healing forces of the body, whereas the allopathic, western medical establishment doesn't have nearly as holistic a vision." - **John Robbins**, Author of Pulitzer prize-nominated international best seller, "Diet For A New America"

Dr. Norman Vincent Peale	Candice Pert	Anthony Robbins
Mark Victor Hansen	Kim Basinger	Richard Gere

Musicians

Van Halen	Air Supply's Graham Russell	Madonna
Connie Smith	Travis Tritt	Kenny Loggins
Victoria Williams	Members of Grateful Dead	Members of Extreme
Members of Bon Jovi	Ohio	The Eagles
Peter Frampton	Fred Schneider and Kate Pierson - B2's	
Rosanne Cash	Members of Dwight Yoakam's Band	

What May Happen to Your Child if You Ignore the Subluxations

In a growing child, it is imperative to prevent subluxation since it can handicap how they perceive the world, making sense of it, adapting, responding appropriately, feeling connected, and succeeding in life. An uneven leg length due to a subluxation at the top of the neck, or in the hips will make crawling difficult, as an example. Frustration will settle in and the baby might compensate by scooting on the rear instead.

It can also prevent balance and coordination of left and right side of the body. This will affect the proper formation for the left and right brain. This improper or delayed connection can make the child more prone to dyslexia or other learning disorders including poor social skills. It is so important for your child especially during the critical period where they will be attempting their first steps, to have proper feedback to and from their brain to help coordination and proper feet placement and if not s/he might have greater difficulty with balance, agility, speed, endurance, and may appear clumsy.

Other factors during imbalance is the weight placed on only one side of the body will be much increased, this will generate more injury prone and more stress applied to that side. It will take more nerve energy, muscle energy and brain energy to get the same activities done. Subsequently it will leave less energy for concentrating, anticipating consequences, strength, endurance, creativity growth, healing and learning.

Our children will be affected by the physical handicap or diminished performance and they will tell themselves how inadequate they are. Their thinking will than shift toward a more self-lowering state and they will start to believe they might be defective or non-athletic or slow. Also, the host of possible direct consequences of the spine and cranial subluxation on the brain, neck, head, connected organs, hormones and immune system is not worth putting your own child thru.

It is in the know that the power of action resides. If the misalignment is left uncorrected and can affect your child's body and even their mental and emotional state, would it also concern the adults? Depending on how old the subluxation is, and how much degeneration and decay is present. In some adults, it may never regain a perfect spine in their lifetime. It is like a tooth cavity, if left untreated with improper care; your dentist might need to pull it out. Chiropractic care improves the spinal alignment and restores proper nerve flow for the best possible functioning and healing of the body.

Chiropractic offers hope to leave behind mediocrity, frustration, compensations and handicaps and instead give you an opportunity to thrive, excel and feel truly alive. What is your choice?

How Would Subluxations Impact Learning Abilities

The child's brain is like a raw piece of clay, just waiting to be molded into something wonderful. There are trillions of neurons just waiting to learn. With infinite possibilities, the child's brain begins to develop as they experience life. The experiences and impressions on that child's nervous system will determine if they become brilliant or slow, enthusiastic or dull. Harry Chugani of Wayne State University states these experiences "can completely change the way a person turns out."

More importantly there are periods of time in the child's life when certain learning experiences are critical to the full development of the child. Sharon Begley writes in her article, Your Child's Brain, "once wired (the brain), there are limits to the brain's ability to create itself. Time limits. Called 'critical periods,' they are like windows of opportunities that nature flings open, starting before birth, and then slams shut, one by one, with every additional candle on the child's birthday cake."

These specific "learning windows" in the brain must be nurtured and if the child receives good stimulus while they are open, magical things can happen. There are "learning windows" for math and logic (birth to 4 years), language skills (birth to 10 years), music (3 to 10 years) and emotions just to name a few. These are the periods of time in a child's life that their brain is ripe for development. If the "learning window" is missed, it snaps shut forever.

In a child, the right and left brain hemispheres are somewhat independent of each other until the crawling stage commences at around six or eight months. The crawling mechanism is important in building symmetry and strength of the spine, and reflex activity between the two hemispheres. Neurological development may be hampered if the child has crawling dysfunction or is made to stand before the child is ready.

A reading disability results if a brain hemispherical integration is abnormal. Some children read backwards better than forwards. Cranial manipulations can assist the progress and usually solve the integration portion. Chiropractic adjustment in children differ from adults, the pressure and the hand contact are different leaving no possibility to the well trained chiropractic physician to harm a child. It is important to note that 65% of the child neurological development occurs in your child's first year.

It seems that many children and individuals have hyper reactionary neurological systems. This may be the result of numerous possible causes. Any disturbances in the craniosacral mechanism, including spinal and pelvic dysfunctions, can also disturb the cranial mechanism.

By alleviating these distortions and the subluxations, the central nervous system can be affected in a calming fashion. Children and adults with ADHD, autism, fibromyalgia, chronic fatigue, sensitivity disorders and sucking problems, ticks, Tourette and many other dysfunctions can be linked to this concept of hyper reactivity.

Cranial strain or cranial torques is the description of what a chiropractic Craniopath would use to determine the level of compression and how it is done. Dr. Stephen Williams, in his book *Pregnancy and Pediatric- A Chiropractic Approach,* provides different strain patterns and corrections to the well trained chiropractor.

He quotes a study by Miller RL who studied the developmental outcome of children with cranial strain at preschool and he found that they compromised a high-risk group for developmental difficulties. But what if there is interference to the nervous system during these critical times? The child has no chance of developing to their fullest potential, even with the best stimulus and experiences. We know from research that over 80% of children suffer subluxations and nerve interference from the birthing process. What do you think the impact of subluxations would have on the child's development? Your child only has one opportunity in life; don't wait until it is too late to have their nervous system checked for interference.

Children's Symptoms Relieved by Chiropractic Care

Chiropractic adjustment can make the life of every mother so much simpler. When your child cries in the middle of the night before the age of 1 year old, this is usually not because he has nightmares but because he has a cranial-neck compression.

If your child wets his/her bed, this is usually because of simple misalignments of the sacrum and other vertebrae. If your child stutters or has dyslexia, it could be because his skull is irritating the brain and cannot interpret the signal properly, chiropractic Craniopathy can help. Sucking dysfunctions can be caused by a TMJ (jaw issue) not set in the joint properly or a temporal bone rotated which may cause the TMJ not to sit properly in the joint.

If your child has ear infections after ear infections, usually the first cervical and the occiput bones are big contributors. Colic can be due to formula but also a vagus (stomach) nerve compression relieved by cranial manipulation or some other vertebra (C1 and/or T5 most commonly.)

This section will provide more in-depth medical terms than normal. The goal is to allow you as a parent to become educated so that you are empowered with seeking the proper health care provider. By understanding the general concepts, you will be able to help your practitioner pin-point to the specific regions that are impacted.

Research is showing the interaction of the mechanism of interference of the nervous system and its role in dis-eases. Additionally, research shows promising results and life changes involving "treatment" in common health challenges in children's conditions such as:

Colic	Ear infection
Bloating	Bed wetting
Sucking difficulties	Learning disabilities
Torticollis (Twisted Neck)	Cerebral Palsy
Autism	Down Syndrome
Birth trauma	Structural issues like shoulder dislocation at birth

Colic

Infantile colic is characterized by pain at the abdominal cavity and extreme crying that no soothing seems to resolve. It is one of the worse feelings for a parent because they feel helpless. The proper explanation is a stomach upset. The infant does not have any way of communicating or a way to move their body to relieve the pain, but they are very good at getting attention so it comes out in the form of crying.

Infant colic is a very common problem between the ages of 3 months old to 2-3 years old. It is one of the most prominent cases in chiropractic care. Before mentioning about how chiropractic can help, one thing you need to look into is the ingredients used in the baby formula. If you are not using baby formula and strictly breastfeeding then you need to look into the supplements or diet that you are practicing.

The excess iron as ferrous sulphate in formula will bring colic symptoms since this type of iron is not easily digested. Also, calcium carbonate is similar to a rock, making it hard to break it down. Just imagine eating gravel rock and hope your stomach will be happy! The gut walls will tighten after 1 year old or so and it will make more sense to give the child "harder" food or supplements. So, yes the nutrition and food given will affect colic but also the stimulation to the organs from the spine and the cranium.

To fully understand why the stomach is upset we need to look at the entire picture. Cranium hosts the brain and project nerves to the stomach. These nerves go from the skull to the organs i.e. vagus (stomach) nerves. Also, other nerves go through the spine to certain levels of the thoracic spine to send messages to the stomach. All these nerves travelling can be corrected by chiropractic if bones are subluxated.

Also, the stomach might be malpositioned i.e. hiatus hernia or stressed at the stomach itself from the inside of the abdominal cavity. A diaphragm release would need to be assessed. CMRT, mentioned above, would be the best approach to clear and restore the organ itself.

A six-step CMRT gut correction for aiding mobility developed by Buddhing (1990) which will take care of the stomach, pancreas, small intestine, colon and gallbladder mobility and functions. Certain reflexes could also be implicated like neurolymphatic and neurovascular reflexes which specialized chiropractors like Applied Kinesiology and SOT' Method would know. Since the neurological aspect of the lymph drainage or vascular flow might be disturbed at these specific organs, these additions will help.

Failure to Suckle

Failure to suckle is an inability to latch on the breast or the bottle. This presentation could be multifactorial for example tongue tied might be a strong possibility but other area needs to be investigated. Sucking involves the tongue, the TMJ or Jaw and other muscles also stimulation to these structures from the brain, cranial nerve and cervical nerves.

Sucking is observed in-uterus from 18 weeks and the ability to coordinate and have an effective sucking happens around 32-36 week in-uterus. The anatomy of the jaw and the front part of the neck is essential to correct the structural issue related to the sucking reflex. Also, the temporal bones host the articulation of the TMJ which is a quick check and correction might be needed.

Since the muscles on the front part of the neck attaching to the jaw also attach to the clavicle and shoulder, your chiropractic physician needs to assess these structures as well. In other words, skull, TMJ, throat, cervical vertebra and the front neck muscles and shoulder including the clavicle need to be assessed and corrected.

Bed Wetting

Bed wetting, is a more complex problem. It can involve a psychological aspect and a mental aspect but also an infection aspect and a structural aspect. It seems chiropractic care has the most response in correcting the issues according to research. But if your child has an infection, please seek medical attention if severe or holistic care (homeopathy, nutrition, chiropractic, acupuncture.)

Your chiropractor, who understands stimulations of the bladder and kidney, will need to assess the vertebra level correspondent but also the sacrum, the pelvic and go use the Chiropractic Manipulation Reflex Technique (CMRT) that involves the bladder and kidney reflexes. The pubic bone and femur head misplacement distortion can also trigger bed wetting symptoms.

Ear Infections

Ear infections have been published by the journal of Pediatrics to NOT give antibiotic to children due to their ineffectiveness. Some implications of this issue are skull distortion or strain pattern, cervical vertebra subluxation, TMJ misalignment or caused by food sensitivity or allergies.

The most common food allergies that can cause repetitive ear infections are wheat, soy, corn, milk, peanut and refined sugar. Pay attention to the formula given to your child, it might contain highly allergenic substances such as milk and soy.

Asthma

Asthma is a reversible obstruction to the airway and could be caused by a hyper response of the immune system. The most common area for a chiropractic physician to look and treat is the cervical and thoracic spine, cranium, ribs and shoulder, diaphragm and lung reflexes.

Vagus nerve involvement might be implicated at the first cervical but also at the level of the cranium, seek SOT° chiropractic Craniopath for proper "treatment." Dr. De Jarnette also describes a CO2 technique to SOT° Method certified which help during an attack:

> Put 5 lbs of constant pressure on the right side of Thoracic (chest) 5 (transverse process)
> Put 5 lbs of constant pressure on both side of Thoracic (chest) 10 (transverse process)
> Put 5 lbs of constant pressure on both side of Lumbar (lower spine) 2
> The pressure needs to be for 20 seconds, and repeated three times.

Please do not disregard the diet and allergic/sensitive food that can be implicated in the asthma attack.

Cerebral Palsy/Autism

Cerebral palsy (CP) is usually caused by abnormal central nervous system (brain) development and as well as injuries. Autism also implicates the central nervous system. Autism will be discussed later but the chiropractic approach is similar for both.

All transverse fascia (tissue) planes need to be assessed and treated including the cranial (tentorium), subclavicular (below collarbone) or thoracic (chest) outlet and diaphragm (lungs), Psoas (muscles that run from spine to groin) and pelvic floor muscles.

Some studies show an involvement with the femur (thigh) head and acetabulum (hip joint) and these needs to be assessed and treated by your chiropractor. Muscles stretching of the muscles might be indicated, as well as all extremities assessed and corrected.

As far as the cranium, the common fixated structure would be the occiput, temporal and parietal bones. But your chiropractic physician should not limit his findings to those listed above. An array of recommendations in terms of supplements could be given, but every child is an individual and might require something else. What I would recommend is to investigate in omega-3, some detoxification process, antioxidants and green vegetables like kale would be a good start.

ADD/ADHD

ADD/ADHD is also a complex dis-ease since it can involve multiple structures and reflexes like the primitive reflex i.e. Moro reflex still activated in young children and teenager (even adult.) A section on primitive reflex is added in the book.

Since the adrenal are the fight or flight organ, proper CMRT to the adrenal might be needed to reduce the stress and increase proper function. Some area of the spine that has shown results in the research is the occiput-C1-2 and T8-9 area which will reduce the interferences to the entire body and the adrenals.

Cranial distortion at the sphenoid, occiput, parietal and temporal bone can cause a brain irritation provoking an ADD/ADHD-like symptom. Diet is also not to be neglected, all refined sugar and stimulants, as well as allergic and sensitivity foods need to be removed from the child's diet.

Dyslexia/Dyspraxia

The most common "treatment" for dyslexia and dyspraxia are the correction of the retained primitive reflexes like: Moro Reflex, Palmar Grasp Reflex, Asymmetrical Tonic Neck Reflex, Tonic Labyrinthine Reflex and Symmetrical Tonic Neck Reflex. Proper omega-3 is needed also and some detoxification needs to be assessed.

Depression

While medical science has not determined the exact cause of altered serotonin levels that are suspected to produce depression, recent research has pointed towards a likely trauma-induced origin for certain cases of mood disorders.

Evidence supports that trauma (in particular mild concussive injury to the head, neck or upper back) increases the risk of onset of depression. Following the trauma, mood disorders can be triggered immediately or can take months or years to develop. Chiropractic care may reverse the trauma-induced injury; thereby reducing irritation to the injured nerves in the central nervous system (brain and spinal cord.)

While serotonin has stolen many of the headlines about depression, in neurology depression is defined as "decreased firing of the frontal lobe of the brain." This means the nerve cells in the brain are not as active in a person suffering from depression. The next obvious questions are, "Why aren't these cells active, what do they need to be active, and what could be blocking them from doing their job?"

One of the major inputs these cells need to be active is messages from the cerebellum and input from the body. This is where a chiropractic physician can help! Numerous research studies have documented improvement in depression and related symptoms as a result of chiropractic adjustments which reduce pressure on the brain stem and spinal cord caused by misaligned vertebrae.

Common Tips to Follow

Stay active and do not avoid activities that cause pain simply because they cause pain. The amount and type of activity should be directed by your doctor, so that activities that might actually cause more harm are avoided.

Relaxation training, hypnosis, biofeedback, and guided imagery, can help you cope with chronic pain. Cognitive therapy can also help patients recognize destructive patterns of emotion and behavior and help them modify or replace such behaviors and thoughts with more reasonable or supportive ones.

Distraction (redirecting your attention away from chronic pain), imagery (going to your "happy place"), and dissociation (detaching yourself from the chronic pain) can be useful. Involving your family with your recovery may be quite helpful, according to recent scientific evidence. It provides you with a support system so you do not feel as isolated.

Obesity

Where the chiropractic physician might help for obesity is in numerous factors:

1. The proper brain to body communication to tell the body to restore the proper metabolism, endocrine function and fat metabolism process needed,

2. Reducing the pain in every joint prone position for painless exercises

3. Help detoxification and get proper mobility and functionality via CMRT and other specialized reflexes. In no instance am I saying that a chiropractic adjustment will make you lose weight, but it will influence the neurology and help normalize proper function and in turn, might help with losing the extra weight.

The Chiropractic Children's First-Aid Kit

During the first years of her/his life, your child will develop from helpless infant into fearless explorer (or, what I call my son, monkey.) Falls, bumps, and boo boos naturally occur with their desire to learn, be curious and explore the world around them. These bumps, falls and boo boos might create a trauma to their spine, skull and other part of their body.

When a vertebra or a bone loses their normal position (misalignment or subluxation), it will limit the current movement of that joint and can restrain the ability during the child stage of growth, to obtain its full potential. Some authors, like Dr. Claudia Anrig, suggest possible permanent deformities can occur if these misalignments are left uncorrected. First aid kits are necessary so that you can treat ailments and injuries that happen at home. This First Aid Kit will include items on how to treat certain specific symptoms for a particular ailment.

The neurological reflex first aid guide has been compiled in case an emergency strikes where care to a holistic physician or chiropractic physician is not available. This book is design so that a parent with limited formal chiropractic training can understand the basics. The book was authored by Major De Jarnette (Founder of SOT' Method) and re-written by Dr. Joseph F. Unger.

The procedures herein are not meant to replace proper chiropractic and/or medical intervention when required. We understand that without the proper medical background, it might be difficult to understand all the terminology but it is used a reference so that when you do receive "treatment" for your child's services, you can monitor whether it has been accurately diagnosed and/or treated.

The complete guide is available at www.atriumhealthservices.com and www.sorsi.com only. This book provides a useful reference guide as well as greater understanding of the neurology behind reflex first aid. We will list some of the more children's and pregnancy's techniques. This is not to replace the book since it has valuable emergency information for about 99 dis-eases or pain scenarios. See Appendix 3 for full details of the list below:

Asthma
Chills
Cold (with sore throat)
Cold (with nasal congestion)
Cold (with headache)
Cold (upset Gastro Intestinal – Stomach Flu)
Cold (with sinus)
Colic
Constipation
Cough
Croup
Diarrhea
Earache
Ear Wax
Fever
Hay Fever
Headache (front or back)
Hiccup
Jaundice
Tonsillitis

We suggest buying the book for common conditions to help alleviate the symptoms for:

Aching	Amenorrhea (absence of menses)	Aneurysm (swelling of arteries)
Angina pectoris (chest pain)	Apoplexy (inability to feel or move)	Appendicitis
Arthritis	Bronchitis	Buzzing ears (ringing in ears)
Cerebral (brain) congestion	Cerebral (brain) induced paralysis	Choking
Chordee (curvature of penis)	Colic involving the kidney	Coma
Convulsion	Muscular cramps	Cystitis (inflammation of bladder)
Diabetes mellitus (diabetes)	Eczema	Emesis (vomiting)
Epilepsy	Epistaxis (nose bleed)	Erysipelas (skin infection)
Facial paralysis	Fascial spasm (tic)	Flatulence (gas)
Floating kidney (kidney drops)	Frequent urination	Goiter (swelling of neck)
Migraine	Heart attack	Hernia
Hoarseness	Hypertension	Indigestion
Iritis (inflammation of eye)	Knee injuries	Low back pain (lumbago)
Menopause	Nausea	Nephritis (inflammation of kidney)
Palsy (paralysis)	Pharyngitis (throat inflammation)	Pile (hemorrhoids),
Pleurisy (lung inflammation)	Pneumonia	Priaprism (erect penis)
Proctitis (anus inflammation)	Pyelitis (pelvic inflammation)	Rheumatic fever
Sciatica	Skin dis-ease	Stomach issues
Strabismus (cross-eye)	Strain/sprain	Tachycardia (abnormal heart rate)
Sore throat	Ulcers (gastric and legs)	Urination issues (pain and retention)
Pain (direct type, arm and hand, leg and foot, female, male, spinal, reflex type, vagus/stomach)		
Hemorrhage (bronchial, gastric, uterine)		
Hysteria-neurasthenia (nervous disorder)		

Jenn's Insights

For my pregnancy, it would have been ideal to have experienced chiropractic in conjunction with my OB/GYN visits. Unfortunately that was not my destiny, even though it was a very traumatic time for me that could have alleviated a lot of stressor toxins that were transferred to my unborn baby. If I had known about the impacts of chiropractic care during pregnancy, I would have invested in this time and care.

My first encounter with chiropractic care came about because of my sons' colic condition. The day that he was born, he was colicky and I still vividly recall bringing him back from the hospital after a Caesarean delivery.

He was so fussy that I barely had sleep. He would not let anyone else comfort him and I spent hours in the late evening and up to the mornings just walking him in my arms. I had trained him to sleep during the day in my uterus so that he would not be noticed. So I did not blame him for being so stressed and fussy. The exhaustion did not bother me except that I knew that I had a shortage of breast milk already and that my body needed the rest.

I spoke with my pediatrician numerous times and the response was that, "Unfortunately you are one of the unlucky ones that had a colicky one and they will grow out of it by 2." The colic got worse though. At first it occurred only at the evening hours, but then after the first series of vaccinations, he started becoming colicky all day.

Again, when I attempted to address this with my pediatrician, there was no known solution for me except to bear it out. I was so exhausted and trying to do my best as a first-time mom. I was blessed to receive a phone call from my best friend that recommended that I take him to Dr. Stéphane.

When he first introduced himself as a Licensed Chiropractor, I was wondering if my best friend had lost her mind. I had said colic not car accident. In my limited knowledge, I had always equated Chiropractors to whiplash or back injuries only.

I was extremely impressed during my initial visit. My son received several adjustments and immediately when we took him home the colic was much better. He was able to also latch better with breastfeeding. I had used a Lactation Consultant but it was still not helpful.

As I sat in the waiting room and spoke with some of the mothers, I was fascinated with all the reasons why they had brought their children to him. There were moms that dragged their kids in with severe flu and viruses. While others were being treated for teething and even learning issues which helped enhance their memory and refocus with chiropractic Craniopathy "treatments."

It was so fascinating to hear these mothers' stories of why they were supplementing their wellness visits with pediatrics. A mother so eloquently put it, "Besides vaccinations, I normally didn't see the pediatrician unless my kids were sick, but wouldn't it be better to prevent the sickness."

I saw mothers themselves that were pregnant visit the office and I began to ask them about their experiences and I was intrigued enough to research the effectiveness of chiropractic care during pregnancy what this might mean from a prenatal perspective of producing an even healthier kid next time.

Another experience that I personally could have used chiropractic care for was Tonsillitis. As you recalled I had an extremely weakened immune system because I took so many antibiotics when I was a child. I had two episodes of the Chicken Pox and one was within the refugee camps where there was limited access to medications. At an early age, I took adult antibiotics at its maximum dosage because there was no access to anything else and no doctors available at the refugee camps.

So you can imagine how quickly I developed immunity and had to increase my dosages of medications. It got so bad that I had to take codeine in my cough syrup by the time I was 5 to suppress the symptoms. My parents could not afford a pediatrician when I was younger, so my primary care physician was the only guidance I had.

At the age of 4, he had recommended that I remove my tonsils and said that this was the only way that I would not be sick. I was constantly sick as a child and would develop multiple colds throughout the year. My parents could not afford to take sick leave so they were dependent on the doctor's judgment.

I am glad that I had more common sense than the doctor and refused to go to the surgery. I told him that I was deathly afraid of hospitals, which was true at the time. The moral is that I never had my tonsils removed and eventually my immune system got stronger and all the colds subsided. In fact nowadays, they are reversing the decision to recommend tonsil removal realizing that it serves its purpose for fighting off bacteria.

I can also attest that chiropractic care was extremely helpful for increasing my breast milk supply. Due to the extreme stresses I had to endure during both my prenatal and postnatal time-frame, I had a limited supply of milk for my son and the quality and quantity was less than desirable. Even after working with a lactation specialist and consuming fenugreek, the milk supplied was not adequate, until I began receiving weekly chiropractic treatments. After the treatments, I had enough to even store away some of the milk supply.

As a parent, I highly encourage you to obtain second opinions from different healing modalities. This way you can compare all information and make an educated consumer choice. Nobody truly knows your child better than you. As seen in this book, there are many alternative choices for promoting a healthier lifestyle for your child. Techniques such as CMRT (bloodless surgery) can fix organs without any surgical intervention.

Having experienced so many surgeries in my life, I can tell you that it does take about 7-10 years for your body to fully recover. The scarring may go away in a month or two, but there are so many layers and so many intricacies to your body that gets in-balanced when you are operated on. Not to also mention the anesthetics that impacts brain cells.

Bloodless Surgery For Your Children and You

Chiropractic Manipulative Reflex Technique (CMRT) is also known as bloodless surgery. The discipline of chiropractic maintains that there is a working relationship between organ function and the stimulations of the organ from the spinal nerve roots. It is proposed that the "treatment" of spinal dysfunction in the form of a chiropractic subluxation can influence the function and health of an organ system.

During our early development in the embryo, a vertebra, muscles and organ all originate from the same source, called the somite. As a result, they all share common neurology pathway and reflexes. Stimulation at any point in any of the related organs and tissues can potentially affect all other related organs and tissues.

In turn, this subluxation results in a loss of vital neurological function of the organ. Organic dysfunction is also likely. CMRT is utilized to normalize the organ function and may include the necessary exercise, dietary or nutritional indications depending upon the patient, as well as the laboratory work, Etc... involved, and any other procedures indicated by whatever diagnostic measures are undertaken.

This will include the diversified adjustment of the involved segment. This specific technique among SOT Method is useful to treat, accelerate or slow down any organ implicated like kidney ptosis (dropping), hiatus hernia, digestive issues, diarrhea, constipation, bloating, gallbladder sluggishness, liver detoxification, pancreas function, increasing digestive enzymes and Hydrochloric Acid (HCL) production, relieve the lung coughing or irritation.

During the CMRT procedure, the chiropractic physician will be able to associate the proper vertebra link to the organs in dis-stress. The organ or vertebra can be associated with emotions or unresolved emotions or unbeneficial emotions. In the Appendix 4 you will find a sample list (from the book *Art and Practice of Chiropractic* by ML Rees and Chiropractic Manipulative Reflex Technique by Major B. De Jarnette.)

Essential Oils in Assisting Organ Therapy

The information following comes from Reference Guide for Essential Oils by Connie and Alan Higley, cited with permission and are fully listed in Appendix 5.

Adrenals
Endocrine system
Digestive
Kidney
Liver
Lymphatic
Pancreas
Spleen
Stomach
Sympathetic / Parasympathetic

Jenn's Insights

I can personally attest that the CMRT technique does wonders for a lot of emotional and physiological symptoms. If you or your child has characteristics of being extremely sensitive and possess a lot of empathy, it would be beneficial to receive chiropractic care for the stressor toxins that are accumulated in your body.

I noticed that I was constantly constipated on a daily basis and thought it was a symptom of having a perfectionist attitude (being anal and controlling.) But I realized when I developed endometriosis at its most severe stage and fibroids that I had issues with my Lumbar vertebra 1. With proper adjustments I noticed that my ultrasounds did not show any issues of the endometriosis coming back or the fibroid issues that constantly had been there all my life. Once a surgery was performed the fibroids appeared to grow back, so I knew it was only a temporary fix.

I never understood why I was easily fatigued and always had anemia even outside of the pregnancy. After following chiropractic care for my T7 vertebra that often became misaligned I noticed the increase in my energy levels and my blood tests revealed that the anemia significantly improved.

8

A Whole New World: How Much "Sense" Can You Make Out of It?

"Children's talent to endure stems from their ignorance of alternatives...
When you know better, you do better."

–Maya Angelou–

Children are instinctive learners and their cognitive mind is developed using all five of their senses: sights, sounds, taste and thru exposure to tactile experiences. However, there are some cases of people that possess unique variations of sensitivities in their central nervous system which make them hyper-sensitive to smell, light, taste, sound and touch.

Learn how to impact the billion neurons available to your child and allow him/her to become a Billionaire Baby! We will be exploring alternative care options that help enhance all 5 of your child's senses. Children truly resemble blank canvases when they are born and each year of life will resemble more colors and elements for them to add to their masterpiece. The younger the child, the more responsive they will be to energy medicine since they do not have as many tainted colors (emotions) on the canvas.

The brain processes differing kinds of information with the various sensory experiences that your child receives on a daily basis. Information that is carried from the sensory organs to the brain is known as sensory neurons. As the brain sorts thru information on a daily basis and builds new connections, the process of learning occurs. When a baby is born, many of the neurons in the brain are not fully connected; however, the neurons will relay messages amongst each other, which further promotes learning and neuron connections taking place.

A catalyze to healthcare reform is on the horizon as powerful forces are converging with a blend of Western medical science and alternative medicine. Consumers are becoming aware that by reverting back to simplification and reduction, that better control of their health is produced. Many people are seeking alternative care approaches towards healing to bring back the roots of the traditional science.

Alternative care is being utilized by over 50% of the population in industrialized nations such as Europe and North America. In India where traditional healing forms of Ayurveda originated, over 70% of the population are turning to alternative care healing. As we approach the next millennium, we have an ideal opportunity to create a better world for ourselves and our children. The world comes nearer to health as each person takes on the personal challenge of healing.

The first major "alternative movement" that impacted the modern Health Care industry occurred in the 1960s with Humanistic Psychology. During the 1980s, the term Holistic Medicine was coined. Soon afterwards, many other alternatives have been designated under the terminology of Complementary, Quantum, Integral, Integrative, and Alternative Medicine. In fact these became synonyms for anything that did not fit the model of allopathic medicine.

How Does Energy Impact Your Child?

If we can recall our grade school science lessons, we are reminded that every form of matter has a vibrational state. In fact, every atom has a specific vibratory or periodic motion with a particular quantifiable measurement. Each periodic motion corresponds to a frequency, which is equivalent to the number of oscillations per second and is measured in Hertz. This applies with every element within the Periodic Table and any solid, liquid or gas form.

In his book, the Body Electric, Dr. Robert O. Becker states that the human body has an electrical frequency and that a person's health corresponds directly to the frequency level. In the 1920's, after graduating from Johns Hopkins University, Dr. Royal Raymond Rife developed a high-powered microscope that was capable of magnifying an object almost 1,500 times beyond the norm. With this microscope, Dr. Rife was able to see toxins, parasites, bacteria, viruses within the blood. As such, he concluded that every dis-ease was attributable to a particular frequency range. His research findings concluded that specific frequencies could prevent the development of dis-ease, while other frequencies merely neutralized the symptoms of the dis-ease.

From this research, he developed a "frequency generator" which allowed the generation of electrical frequencies to impact a dis-eased part of the body. For over a hundred years, medical science has shown that by passing electrical currents into a wound or broken bone that an acceleration of healing occurred.

Your Child's Body In Energetic Terms

Dr. Rife discovered that every cell, tissue and organ contained is own vibrational resonance. The human body in a health state will vibrate between the optimum range of 62 and 68 MHz. Tainio and colleagues discovered that when a person's frequency drops below the optimum range, the body's immune system becomes compromised.

In Tainio's research, they discovered that every organ and tissue within the body has an optimal frequency measurement that represents its healthy state:
- The normal brain (head) frequency between the hours of 6:00 am to 6:00 pm is 70-78 MHz
- The healthy body (neck down) frequency between the hours of 6:00 am to 6:00 pm is 62-68 MHz
- The Brain frequency at 80-82 MHz, indicates a genius level
- The Thyroid and Parathyroid glands are 62-68 MHz
- The Thymus Gland is 65-68 MHz
- The Heart is 67-70 MHz
- The Lungs are 58-65 MHz
- The Liver is 55-60 MHz
- The Pancreas is 60-80 MHz
- The Stomach is 58-65 MHz
- The Ascending Colon is 58-60 MHz
- The Descending Colon is 58-63 MHz

Tainio's research also discovered frequency information for the following:
- Human cells start to mutate (change) when their frequency drops below 62 MHz
- Thoughts and feelings can also be measured from a frequency (vibration) perspective. Did you know that a negative mental attitude can lower a person's frequency by 10-12 MHz While a positive mental attitude such as meditation or prayer can raise it up by 10-15 MHz
- When your body has a cold or flu, your body drops to 58 MHz
- When there is Candida present within your body, your body drops to 55 MHz
- When your body is infected with the Epstein-Barr virus, your body drops to 52 MHz
- When your body drops to 42 MHz it is more susceptible to "cancerous" cells
- When death occurs in your body, the frequency drops to 20 MHz

Another concept to consider was proposed by Nikola Tesla regarding certain outside frequencies that often bombard our bodies' energetic levels on a daily basis. He hypothesized that technology and external stimuli were exposing our bodies to a greater potential for dis-ease.

In the early 1980s in Stockholm Sweden, Bjorn Nordenstrom, a radiologist wrote a book entitled "Biologically Closed Circuits" that showed that "cancerous tumors" could be dissolved or further growth prevented by simply putting an electrical current through a "cancerous tumor." He discovered that this theory was made possible because the human body has both electropositive and electronegative energy fields and this discovery serves as the foundation for Energy Medicine.

What Can Disrupt Your Child's Energy?

Since everything in our environment is also made of frequencies, an important factor to consider is how they may be impacting our personal frequency levels. For instance, electrical devices such as lamps, televisions, radio, microwaves and phones all emit electromagnetic frequencies that are both chaotic and confusing to our own energetic bodies. The two biggest environmental disruptors are geopathic stressors and electro-magnetic stressors.

Geopathic Stressors

According to Dr. Mercola there is a form of natural radiation that arises from the Earth's core and through distortion transforms itself into electro-magnetic fields when it reaches the surface. These electro-magnetic frequency disruptors are known as geopathic stresses. It is formed naturally by subterranean running water, fault lines, certain mineral concentrations and underground cavities that may be situated near your office, school or home.

Since geopathic stressors are comprised of electro-magnetic frequencies, they may be weakening your body's frequencies without your prior knowledge. Subterranean running water can consist of underground streams, whereas fault lines automatically occur when two Teutonic plates meet and the by-product may become an Earthquake.

There is a field of science known as Geomancy and its purpose is to diagnose the Earth's magnetic energies and then help neutralize these magnetic fields before it arises to the core service and becomes problematic for the inhabitants of homes, offices or schools.

Health issues that may be unexplained over the years due to your surrounding environment has seen potential benefits from a Geomancy treatment. This type of service has been used to assist with health issues such as infertility, miscarriages, "cancer", insomnia, headaches, frequent colds and flu, hyperactivity and children with learning difficulties once the environment has been energetically balanced.

Even though there are natural elements that may be emitting harmful energetic fields; there is often a balance that occurs naturally. As such, there are natural geographic areas that emanate healing qualities for your body and spirit. Sacred sites that have been formed, such as natural wonders inclusive of the Grand Canyon, Sedona, the Matterhorn, Ayers Rock and countless other places around the globe possess these natural healing properties. By simply being at these places, your body is provided with subtle higher levels of vibration that uplifts your emotions and spirit.

In 1950, Dr. Ernst Hartmann, a German medical doctor discovered that the Earth contained natural electro-magnetic grids and he coined the concept the Hartmann knot. If you recall from school, the globe is often represented with grid-lines going in both directions.

Dr. Hartmann discovered that there are electro-magnetic lines run both vertically from north to south, which are spaced approximately every 8 feet and 2 inches apart. Additionally, these natural grid lines also run horizontally from east to west, appearing approximately every 6 feet 6 inches. The height of these lines can range from 60-600 feet. He discovered that where the lines intersect both vertically and horizontally is what he coined as the Hartmann knot. According to Dr. Hartmann, this is the worst geographic place that a person can sleep, work or attend school because it impacts their natural body's frequency levels.

The range of geopathic zones may influence animal and human bodies between 2 to 200 feet wide and may reach a height of 600 to 30,000 feet. Since there are natural electro pathological energy arising from these geopathic zones, modern technology has decided to utilize its benefits and often built telecommunications towers, electricity pylons, transformers, and radio towers on top of these zones to intensify its natural resource.

Have you ever noticed a building that often appears to cause ill health or non-wellness in people without any explained medical issues. This can range from hyperactivity amongst hypersensitive children due to frequency disturbances. If possible, home, office, or school environments should not be built on these premises due to the frequency disruptions it causes in animal and human bodies.

It is particularly disruptive to have homes built upon these geographic areas since we spend about one third of our lives in bed. If your home is situated on top geopathic zone, it can be particularly harmful to your body since your brain is not able to fully rest, thus allowing it to innately repair and regenerate cells within your body. To maintain optimal health, it is important to avoid being within the vicinity of geopathic stressors as much as possible.

Electro-Magnetic Stressors

On a daily basis, our bodies and minds are often bombarded with electric and magnetic fields surrounding our environment. Some are naturally produced while others have been formed by technology such as radio waves and television broadcasts. At the higher end of the technological spectrum, are x-rays and gamma rays that are found in chemotherapy usage that all interfere with our body's natural frequency pattern.

Some studies have suggested a link between exposure to 60 hertz of electromagnetic frequencies and specific types of "cancer", primarily the predominance of leukemia and brain "cancer." However, according to a study performed by the Environmental Protection Agency entitled, "EMF In Your Environment", there are not current regulations/standards being implemented in the United States for limiting exposure to less than 60 hertz.

Household appliances emit both an electrical and magnetic energy frequencies. If a household appliance is plugged into an electrical outlet, then an electric field is present even if the appliance is turned off. However, to produce the magnetic field for that appliance it must also be operating and electrical current flowing into it. The most common household by-products that emit both electrical and magnetic frequency disruptions are microwaves and cellular phones.

Recent research discovered that when a mobile phone is turned on and in use, there is between 30-70% electro-magnetic frequencies (EMFs) going into the head dependent on the type of phone used. This could impact hypersensitive people's frequency by producing headaches and migraines. However, studies have shown that if the phone is carried around your trousers it could impact the stomach area and liver. For those that are choosing to carry their mobile phone in the breast pocket of the jacket it may impact the heart and chest area. In men, research has shown that increased cellular phone usage could have an impact on the heart and prostate.

Since children are more attuned to the frequencies in their environment, it is recommended for parents to minimize the source of EMFs in their bedrooms. This is important because children are continuously growing physically also cognitively in the primary developmental years and they need a proper sleeping environment so that cell repair and growth hormones can be maximized. EMFs are emitted from baby monitors, ceiling fans, televisions, digital clocks, portable heaters, window AC units, fluorescent lights and computer monitors that may be placed within a child's room. Worse yet, if your child has a metal frame bed, it serves as a conductor for generating electro-magnetic fields around the bed while your child is attempting to sleep. If you do have any of these items in your child's room, it is best to unplug as many from the electrical outlets before bedtime.

NASA has discovered that specific plants such as the spider plant, weeping fig, dwarf banana plant and the peace lily help absorb EMFs naturally; therefore, it would be ideal to place them not only for decorative purposes but also to help improve health and healing in your home. Also, natural crystals that are placed within your homes can help to reduce the EMFs that are emitted from your computer, TV and phones. The most effective of the crystals include the clear quartz, rose quartz and the amethyst. For girls or women, it might be conducive to wear one of these jewelry pieces to have a natural protection against EMFs bombarding your body.

Microwaves

In theory, there are very small amounts of radiation leakage occurring from the viewing glass of microwaves; however, the FDA designated that these levels are well below the standards known to be harmful and thus have classified microwaves to be insignificant contributors of radiation. An organization called Powerwatch recommends that microwave ovens be checked at least annually since radiation emissions can change with normal wear and tear. To be more cautious, it might be better to purchase a $20 testing device to check the levels of radiation that are emitted from your appliances, especially for microwaves.

However a recent studied revealed dramatic change in both the heart rate and its variability caused by approved devices that generated "micro-waves." This is the first study of its kind to document that the effects of 2.4 GHz of radiation may cause impact to the heart. Wi-Fi routers and microwave ovens operate at this frequency. Therefore, if you are experiencing rapid or irregular heartbeat, pressure or pain in your chest, you might want to test out the theory yourself and avoid microwave usage. There is also growing evidence that 2.4 GHz of radiation may cause blood sugars to spike in susceptible individuals and may be one of the contributing factors for one type of diabetes.

The Russians were the first to research microwave ovens during WWII and conducted thorough research on its biological effects to humans. Alarmed by what they discovered, the Russians banned microwave ovens in 1976; however this ban was later lifted during Perestroika's governance. There is twenty years of surmounting Russian research along with German dated from 1942 in Berlin that makes a strong argument against the safety of microwave cooking.

These findings led the Russian government to issue an international warning about possible environmental and biological damage associated with the use of microwave ovens and other similar frequency devices such as mobile phones. Did you know that the microwaving of grains and milk products convert some of their amino acids into carcinogenic ("cancer") substances. Additionally, microwaving prepared meats has caused the formation of many "cancer-causing" agents such as d-nitrosodienthanolamines to form.

Additionally, by thawing frozen fruits by microwave, it is converting the glucoside (glucose) and galactoside (enzymes) into carcinogenic substances. Additionally the microwave usage of raw, cooked or frozen vegetables have converted the plant alkaloids into carcinogens. Research discovered that carcinogenic free radicals were formed especially in microwaved root vegetables. Research showed that there was structural degradation in the foods tested, with a decrease value of 60-90% of nutritional value. In the foods tested, there was a significant decrease in the bioavailability for vitamin C and E, the B complex vitamins, essential minerals and lipotropic (substances that prevent abnormal accumulation of fat.)

How Can Your Child's Energy Be Diagnosed?

The use of diagnosis for energy medicine is based upon the physiological aspect in the body has an electrical charge. Early 1900, physiologic research has demonstrated the production of electrical disturbance in embryo, in organs and in every physical states. Today, we are able to monitor and measure the heart and brain by electrical aspects. Measurements such as EEG, XRAY, MRI, and HRV are technology using energy medicine.

Some illness shows a pattern in energy field while others are more scattered. The capacity to monitor and be as accurate in today's day in age is more advanced than years ago via our current technology.

Muscle-Testing (Kinesiology)

Dr. George Joseph Goodheart, Jr., founder of Applied Kinesiology and former SOT® Method student, developed a testing involving muscles testing. His concept works on the neurology and brain activation of weak vs. a strong muscle to command a process. Today, many people utilize muscle testing as a means to test our own self for supplements/food intakes and many holistic practitioners still use this format for diagnostic assessments.

One caveat is that since muscles testing involve the emotional and mental capacity and adaptability of the tester and the patient. To maintain objectivity, both the tester and you, the patient, must be in neutral emotional and mental states while testing is conducted, otherwise false positives can occur. Both parties must not have emotional involvement during the testing for the most reliable findings. Therefore, at Gainesville Holistic Health Center to minimize these risks, we chose to implement technological testing methods instead.

Intuitive Body Scanning

A technique called intuitive body scanning can help determine health blockages within people and is even safe to use on animals. Traditional medical procedures can be augmented with medical intuitive professionals to help locate body parts that contain energy blockages or that may be experiencing turmoil within previous medical symptoms.

With the dual roles for diagnostics it helps improve accuracy and expedites the healing process because it gets to the root source of the issue. There are many variations of the scanning technique based on the practitioners' preferences, but they all have some basic commonalities that are followed in principle.

Scanning the body to gain medical details is the basis of the x-ray machine; however, the difference is that the intuitive scan provides an energetic portrait using the human practitioner instead of the technology. Since the human body possesses an energy blueprint, a trained medical intuitive will be able to scan the body and look for energy blockages and areas of stress that has diminished the body's functionality. In essence, the medical intuitive serves like a "human" x-ray machine.

This concept has been revolutionized by some of the more prominent practitioners that are practicing in this field. For example, a Harvard neurosurgeon and researcher named Norman Shealy was introduced to a young woman with the gift of seeing illness in other people guided by her intuition. Today, the medical intuitive, Caroline Myss is designated as a guru in the field of intuition and energy healing. Being skeptical at first, Dr. Shealy conducted extensive testing of her diagnosis and discovered that even from remote distances; she produced a 93% accuracy rate of the client's condition. Another medical intuitive is Dr. Lichuan Chen. Dr. Chen has been tested against X-rays, MRI and other equipment and was found more accurate.

Another prominent medical intuitive is Dr. Yam Yuen, a 35th generation Shaolin priest that draws upon his expertise from knowledge of ancient Chinese energetic, chiropractic, quantum physics, and structural engineering. He also incorporated the martial arts format of Qigong and Tai Chi along with feng shui into his exclusive healing technique. Dr. Yuen's unique technique identifies the root causes of illnesses and corrects these issues so that the body may return to its optimal state of health.

The Yuen Energetic method is analogous to the body being a bio-computer, where the body's state is either weak or strong, and on or off at any given time. The premise of the technique is that by correcting the weaknesses, the normal flow of all connections will occur and the body will be restored (reset) to its optimal state of health. Often times, clients experience instantaneous results. At worst all symptoms from dis-ease can be minimized and at best the dis-ease is eliminated altogether using Dr. Yuan's technique. Deepak Chopra references Dr. Yuen in one of his books, describing him as the man who can "cure" illnesses simply with a wave of his hand.

Why Study the Five Senses?

To bridge both our outer and inner worlds, our senses become instrumental. The interaction of these two worlds allows the combination of the psychological processes with the nervous system and the immune systems of the human body. This is the concept that is related to as Healing Through the Senses.

A new scientific field known as psychoneuroimmunology (PNI) is an inter-disciplinary approach towards healing and combines the fields of endocrinology, rheumatology, psychology, immunology, neuroscience, pharmacology, psychiatry, physiology, behavioral medicine, and infectious dis-eases. The primary focus of PNI is to investigate the interaction between the nervous system and the immune system.

Each of our cells pulsates with vital energy and our senses are the portals into them. By stimulating all five of our sensory mechanisms on a daily basis, it helps us harmonize and gain a peaceful and calm experience, which dissolves any unnecessary stress from our lives. Even though the world may be changing and viruses and pathogens mutating, as Darwin stated, the human species is resilient and is more than capable of adapting. We are built with innate healing abilities to boost our immune systems. We have seen this evidenced time and time again, even with the most chronic of dis-eases such as in the cases of Anita Moorjani and Kris Carr with "cancer" cells.

The Sense of Touch

The Sense of Touch

On a daily basis, you should give yourself a healing benefit of touch with a self-massage. When your skin is stimulated by a massage or even a loving touch, your body releases many healing chemicals that enhances immune functionality, improves circulation and promotes restful sleep. This is fundamental for health and well-being.

To gain a more intense healing experience incorporate massage oils with essential oils. If you are feeling excess stress levels and feel ungrounded, then use heavy, warm oils such as almond or sesame. If you have been feeling overheated or irritable lately, try cooling oils such as sunflower, olive or coconut. If your body has been feeling sluggish or lethargic, try using massage oils such as sunflower, safflower, or mustard to gain an invigorating sense.

Acupuncture

One of the world's oldest medical systems is the Traditional Chinese Medicine (TCM) and should be considered the forefather of "holistic medicine." This system believes that it is imperative to balance a person's vital energy, also known as the life force energy or Qi. TCM maintains the belief that health is achieved when there is proper flow and balance of a person's life force energy.

The energy itself is thought to flow through meridians that are channeled along the body and the meridian points are the stimulation points that are utilized in acupuncture and acupressure (needleless) treatments. The principles of Traditional Chinese medicine is based on five basic elements: air, fire, water, space and earth. This healing modality has been found to effective as a complement to the allopathic medicine or it may even serve as an alternative healing treatment by itself to further prevent more invasive medical treatments or procedures.

A list of over fifty dis-eases successfully treated with acupuncture was published by The World Health Organization. Acupuncture has been recognized by the World Health Organization as effective for treating a wide range of medical problems, which include:

- Respiratory disorders: asthma, sinusitis, bronchitis, sore throat and recurrent chest infections.
- Muscular and neurological disorders: sciatica, frozen shoulder, rib neuritis, tennis elbow, various forms of tendinitis, low back pain, osteoarthritis, neck pain, facial tics and headaches.
- Digestive disorders: diarrhea, constipation, hyperacidity, spastic colon, and gastritis
- Menstrual, reproductive and urinary problems.

Acupuncture in Prenatal Care

There are many health benefits of receiving acupuncture treatments during pregnancy. A recent study has shown that morning sickness is effectively relieved by acupuncture. Surprisingly, a more dangerous condition known as hyperemesis gravidarum (severe vomiting during pregnancy) has also been effectively treated using acupuncture.

An Australian study published in the journal, "Birth" reported that out of the 593 pregnant women that was in their first trimester for those that received acupuncture treatments there was less frequency of nausea and the duration was reduced when symptoms occurred. These patients noticed the improvements immediately with the treatment and noted that the effects endured over the 4 week period. During the first trimester, acupuncture can also help relieve migraines, bleeding and fatigue.

During the second trimester, acupuncture can assist with alleviating hemorrhoids, heartburn and stress and helps with maintaining balance. Acupuncture is also effective with treating elevated blood pressure, edema or excessive weight gains. During the third-trimester acupuncture treatments can help relieve backache, sciatica, public and joint pain and even carpal tunnel syndrome. By 32 to 34 weeks, the acupuncturist should pay particular attention to the positioning of the baby and can help stimulate a head-down position.

Research findings reported in the November 1998 issue of the Journal of the American Medical Association concluded that a form of Traditional Chinese Medicine called moxibustion assists with breech positioning. This initial study was conducted on 130 pregnant women and it resulting in an increase of head-first births. China has been using this technique for over centuries. This technique should only be used in healthy pregnancies during the 32 to 36 week mark. The technique utilizes a long stick of the herb moxa which produces smoldering heat and smoke that stimulates the acupuncture point in the little toe, providing an overall impact to the positioning of the breeched fetus.

Both acupuncture and acupressure treatments are generally safe during pregnancy; however both services may cause muscle contractions and the uterus itself is a muscle. It is important to select an acupuncturist that is nationally certified as a diplomat of acupuncture and has extensive experience dealing with pregnant women.

It is important to limit your acupressure massages within an hour timeframe and the therapist should not focus on anyone part of the body for more than 15 minutes at a time; otherwise the pressure may release way too much energy, which often results in headache or nausea symptoms. Caution should be used with some of the acupressure points located on the feet because overstimulation can induce premature labor; unless this is the goal of you and your therapist to induce labor without the use of drugs. During the acupressure massage, you should not feel any unusual contractions or any effects after the session. If you do, it is imperative that you contact your prenatal care provider immediately. Acupuncture is also useful during the labor itself to provide a boost of energy and to facilitate pain relief.

Acupuncture in Post-Natal Care

During the first weeks of the postpartum period, acupuncturist can often offset years of a sub-optimal lifestyle that was impacted with stressors. Preventive care from a Chinese medical practitioner can also rectify abnormalities in lochia (discharge of blood) flow and correct years of menstrual irregularities.

The postpartum timeframe is one of the most critical times for intervention and regular preventive care from a Chinese medical practitioner.

Theoretically, postpartum depression may be a normal recuperative cycle for a woman that just gave birth along with all the hormonal changes that occurred within the mother's body 9 months prior, acupuncture can restore a mother's energy levels after the stress of giving birth. Acupuncture can be used postpartum to alleviate depression and anxiety, to relieve backache, perineal or other kinds of physical pain. In fact, researchers from Stanford University found that 63% of women that received just 8 weeks of acupuncture therapy for post natal depression held a better disposition.

Auriculotherapy

(Copied with permission by Terry Oleson PhD from http://www.auriculotherapy.com)

Auriculotherapy is a health care procedure in which stimulation of the auricle of the external ear is utilized to alleviate health conditions in other parts of the body. While originally based upon the ancient Chinese practices of acupuncture, the somatotopic correspondence of specific parts of the body to specific parts of the ear was first developed in France. It is this integrated system of Chinese and Western practices of auricular acupuncture which is presented.

Auriculotherapy is considered one form of alternative medicine, which also includes acupuncture, chiropractic manipulation, homeopathy, and biofeedback. All these techniques are also referred to as Complementary Medicine, in that they are not only an alternative to conventional Western medical treatments, they can serve as an additional procedure which complements the practice conventional medicine. Auriculotherapy can reduce the tension, stress, and pain not fully relieved by other medical procedures, but works best when implemented as part of a multidisciplinary complement of multiple treatment approaches. While ear acupuncture is often used in conjunction with body acupuncture, auriculotherapy can also effectively relieve pain, stress and tension when used by itself.

Contraindication

As with other forms of acupuncture, there are few contraindications for the use of auriculotherapy. It is important not to treat any pain needed to diagnose an underlying problem, not to treat any pain needed to limit range of movement of an injured area of the body, not to treat women who are pregnant, and not to electrically stimulate the ear points of patients with a cardiac pace maker.

Reiki

A famous Japanese technique that promotes healing and relaxation while reducing stress is known as Reiki and treats the whole person from a mind, body, emotions and spirit perspective. There are many beneficial effects of this healing modality which includes feelings of peace, relaxation, security and overall well-being.

Emotional or health problems tend to manifest in our bodies when there is a disruption of weakened or blocked "Life Force Energy" flowing from the body. When emotions are repressed or not expressed in a healthy matter this can cause stagnant energy flow and blockages to our bodies. Imbalance of energy can be caused by differing circumstances occurring in our lives such as: physical or emotional trauma, injury, negative thoughts and feeling that run the gamut from fear, anger, anxiety, worry, doubt or negative self-talk. Living a destructive lifestyle and toxic relationships along with consumption of environmental and nutritional toxicity may contribute to this phenomenon.

Reiki healing is safe for everyone inclusive of babies, toddlers, children, adults and even the elderly. Reiki Energy is designed to enhance the bodies healing system and improve the overall immune function's capabilities. Reiki Energy provides a means to balance the human energy fields (Auras) and energy centers (Chakras) within a person and helps facilitate healing on all levels. Negative thoughts and feelings that are stopping the flow of your life force energy can be transformed with the touch of a Reiki practitioner. A skilled practitioner is able to break up and wash away the negativity patterns from your energetic body, allowing you to improve both mental and physical aspects you're your health.

The founder of the Reiki system of natural healing, Mikao Usui recommends that everyone practices the simple ideals of promoting peace and harmony, which appear to be universal across all cultures and religions. Did you know that Reiki is currently being supplemented to assist the traumatized veterans from an emotional perspective but also from a physical perspective to treat wounds? Additionally it is being augmented with "cancer" patient treatments to help facilitate relaxation and recovery. Reiki is being used to decrease anxiety and treat pain in nursing homes, hospices, emergency rooms, operating rooms, organ transplantation care units, pediatric, neonatal and OB/GYN units.

Reiki and Pregnancy

In this day and age, many pregnant women are juggling both the demands associated with a home life and a career. During the pregnancy, changes in their physical body along with changes in their relationships with their partners and expectations from the family may intensify fatigue and mood swings. With Reiki treatments, expectant mothers can reduce stress, remain more emotionally grounded, feel a sense of serenity and peace and help alleviate her fears related to the overall delivery.

In general, a Reiki treatment during pregnancy can help promote overall relaxation for the expectant mother; it also greatly reduces fatigue, anxiety and sleep deprivation. It is an effective healing modality for relieving physical discomforts and provides relief from hip, back or ligament pain that may occur as the pregnancy progresses. Gastric issues are often problematic during pregnancy due to the increases of hormones, but with an energy healing treatment during pregnancy it will help relax the gastrointestinal walls, helping to alleviate the symptoms of nausea.

Did you know that Reiki treatment given during the time of labor helps reduce pain associated with the back and pelvic area. In fact, studies have shown that pregnant women who practice Reiki during the duration of their pregnancy are less likely to require having a Cesarean surgery even if they had undergone this process in earlier deliveries. The use of this healing energy helps to reduce or eliminate the need for pharmaceutical pain relief or an epidural.

Reiki and Children

In general children are better at learning and practicing Reiki energy because they are very pure and are a perfect medium for directing this healing energy. Since children have not fully awakened their concept of self and ego, they are more able to be fully present in their Reiki healing moments. In fact, Reiki can be learned and practiced by children of all ages. Due to their short duration on Earth, children do not carry a lifetime of "emotional baggage" that is often present in adult healers. The emotional (unresolved grief, anger, sadness, hurt) baggage lowers one's vibrational state which impacts the quality of the healing session.

Reiki is ultimately the connection to the Universal Life force, which is also known as universal love. This Universal Love is the key to achieving a bright future on our planet. By having your child learn Reiki you are enhancing and instilling in your child indirect lessons such as a greater sense of intuition, generosity, quietness, compassion, growth, joy, sacred-energy, happiness, creativity, self-love, loving-kindness, harmony, imagination, truth, goodness, beauty, equanimity, inspiration, understanding, attachment to nature, integrity, peace and wisdom.

Children who practice Reiki are more aware of their special place and purpose on this Earth by learning to tap into their own inner powers. These children exhibit more selflessness and become more devoted to the interests and welfare of others as well as their own well-being by helping them gain confidence and self-esteem. Reiki helps the children get rid of fear, worry, relax and alleviate symptoms such as lack of interest which seems to be effective with Autism, Asperger's, ADD/ADHD and other developmental syndrome labels that children may be diagnosed with.

By providing your gifts will the gift of Reiki at a young age, it promotes a healthier way of making better choices in life and to promote balance within their daily environment when faced with stressors, this allows them to cope with change and stressors better than adults. Some of the evidenced benefits for receiving or teaching Reiki for children and adolescence include:
- Helps with asthma symptoms
- Helps improve concentration and focus which leads to improvement in test scores
- Helps enhance relaxation and sleep
- Help enhance self-esteem and self-awareness
- Helps promote calmness and balance into their life
- Helps alleviate symptoms of overstimulation (excitability) or under-stimulation (depression)

Reflexology

Reflexology is a healing art that has been around for centuries but is not regaining wide acceptance amongst the people. This technique is based on the principle that the whole body is reflected within the feet, hands, cranium and ears and specific reflex points/zones, meridian lines and nerve pathways may be stimulated to promote healing aspects versus the acupressure of manipulating the energy flow.

Reflexology serves as a preventive measure for tuning up the body's immune system, to promote stress relief and overall sense of relaxation and general well-being. The designated reflex points connected via the foot correspond to body parts that stimulate extra oxygen, blood flow and energy to the designated organs and nerves, thus allowing energy balance and enhancing the promotion of the body's innate healing abilities. The most common forms performed for this healing art is to apply the reflexology through the hands and feet.

The healing process generates a signal throughout the peripheral nervous system which corresponds directly to the central nervous system and coordinates signals to the various parts of the brain. These signals are then sent to the associated organs within the body and encourage adjustments in oxygen levels to aid in proper circulation. This process also sends a response to the body's gross and fine motor systems to carry out their specified task. Proper circulation is imperative in the body in order for every organ to function optimally and for the proper nutrients to be transported within the blood stream (anabolic substances,) for the maintenance of optimal oxygen levels, for the regulation of hormones and antibodies and for the overall removal of toxins from the blood stream (catabolic substances.)

Chronic and acute conditions inclusive of asthma, hypertension, headaches and colds can also be alleviated with regular treatments. This healing process can stimulate the endocrine system and boost the immune system. It is evidenced to relief symptoms of allergies and sinusitis, lung congestion; and promotes enhancements of the lymph and blood flow, and digestive and elimination discomforts.

Reflexology and Pregnancy

As with any form of alternative therapy, you should consult your practitioner before beginning any reflexology treatments and some reflexologist prefer to wait until after the first trimester to perform these services. As with any practitioner, you should ensure that your reflexologist has been properly trained and has extensive experience working with pregnant women.

Both the National Center for Complimentary and Alternative Medicine (NCCAM) and Suzanne Ezner, the author of the Maternity Reflexology Manual promotes the utilization of maternity reflexology as effective treatments for the following common ailments faced by mothers during the progression of their pregnancy:

- Backache
- Cramps
- Incontinence (inability to control bladder functionality)
- Pain and discomfort
- Morning sickness
- Lack of energy and fatigue
- Swollen extremities
- Heartburn/indigestion

- Sore swollen breasts
- Digestive disorders
- Induction of labor
- Aiding in subsequent fertility issues

The Association of Reflexologist in London, England conducted a study that revealed that continual reflexology treatments during pregnancy aided in the reduction of 50 percent of the symptoms that were associated with heartburn, irritable uterus symptoms, hypertension, and edema (swelling.) The initial purpose of the study was to provide an alternative means for the labor-stimulating drugs. Many women undergo reflexology treatments to encourage labors that are overdue.

Reflexology and Children

A research study was conducted by Dr. Jesus Manzanores of Spain with a group of children diagnosed with ADHD and underwent 20 weekly reflexology sessions. The results provided evidence that there was an average improvement of 19% on reading speed and improvement of 21% for mathematical calculations.

It is also evidenced that reflexology may help to relieve many of the symptoms associated with the conditions of Autism and Asperger's Syndrome. Research reveals that by reflexing the pituitary and pineal glands, there is a release of the following hormones to enhance the body and mind's functionality.

- ACTH: Reduces stress and anxiety since this is a cortisone related hormone
- Oxytocin: Improves interpretations of emotions by the brain while decreasing repetitive behaviors
- Melatonin: When melatonin levels drop, one may experience insomnia and depression since this hormone is needed to regulate body rhythms.

Reflexology has also been found to be effective for relieving symptoms of depression thru the stimulation of specific acupressure points and nerve endings within the hands and feet, which further helps enhance the body's abilities to:
- Eliminate toxins built-up in the body;
- Stimulate the lymphatic system and drainage;
- Activate the optimal functionality for the endocrine system;
- Decongest energy pathways so that the Qi may flow properly and the nervous system functions at its optimal level
- Reduce the body's stress response by encouraging the release of the natural feel-good hormone, endorphins
- Restore harmony to both the sympathetic and parasympathetic nervous system which induces a state of relaxation
- Cause increase oxygen and blood flow to be delivered to the organs

By stimulating specific acupressure points within the body, a reflexologist may alleviate symptoms of depression by investigating the following trigger points that may:

- Correspond to the lungs, heart, solar plexus, upper limbs and chest.
- Correspond to the glands that regulate the release of neurotransmitters and hormones in the body, which when imbalanced may cause the symptoms of a depression. Some of the glands that are impacted include the thymus, parathyroid, pituitary, pineal and thyroid glands whose corresponding acupressure points are located on the inside of the foot, the ball the foot, under the big toe and on the big toe itself.
- Promote the release of the natural feel-good chemical known as endorphins to help reduce stress levels.

Polarity Therapy with Magnets

Approximately 3000 year old Chinese manuscripts reveal how life force is generated by the earth's magnetic field. Dr. Paracelsus, a Swiss-German alchemist and physician that founded the concept of toxicology demonstrated the power of healing of magnet. Dr. David Daniel Palmer DC, the founder of chiropractic, also used magnetic healing prior to founding the first chiropractic college.

Polarity therapy was developed by Randolph Stone DC, DO, ND., who was deeply interested in the electromagnetic energy currents of the human body. He based his work on the Eastern concept that illness originates from blockages in energy flow.

Polarity is mainly hands-on technique including manipulation of pressure points and joints, massage, breathing technique, hydrotherapy, exercise, reflexology and even simply holding pressure points on the body. It results in positive changes in physical, emotion and mental levels and may incorporate the use of magnets.

Based on the research in 1930 by Davis and Rawls and more currently by Dr. William Phipott, the following results are discovered in magnets.

Magnetic North (Negative) Pole

- Relieves Pain
- Reduces Swelling
- Promotes Tissue Alkalization
- Promotes Sound Restful Sleep
- Calms Central Nervous System
- Assists Relief of Addictive Tendencies

Magnetic South (Positive) Pole

- Accelerates Growth Indiscriminately
- Increases Swelling
- Promotes Tissue Acidity

- Decreases Tissue Oxygenation
- Disturbs Sleep
- Promotes Anxiety

In 1990, the Journal of the National Medical Association published a study stating: "cancer" cells in petri dishes were placed at either the bio-magnetic north or South Pole ends of an MRI facility for 3 weeks. They discovered that North Pole cells exhibited dramatic decreases in size but South Pole cells had a measurable increase in growth. This lends opportunities for further research in this field.

In modern research, Tufts University School of Medicine discovered that Fibromyalgia patients experienced pain relief on magnetic mattress as opposed to ordinary ones. Additionally, the New York Medical College of Valhalla discovered that Diabetic Neuropathy magnetic foot pads relieved numbness, tingling and pain. Evidence suggests that roughly 80% of chronic pain sufferers could benefit from magnetic therapy. 1997, the Journal of Rheumatology confirm the effectiveness in relieving arthritis pain with magnetic healing.

The Sense of Sight

The Sense of Sight

Did you know that by watching violent movies or television shows that it triggers your body's stress response and creates jittery cells that will suppress your immune system's abilities to perform? The visual impressions you take in have a surprisingly profound impact on your mind, body and emotions, this is the real meaning behind subliminal messaging.

Did you know that surrounding yourself with images that uplift your spirit is as important for your emotional and mental health as nutritious food is for your body? When your brain interprets peaceful or beautiful imagery, it creates a cascade of soothing neurochemicals within your body. This is why spending time in nature and seeing the natural forms of beauty can replenish your mind, body and spirits.

Hypnosis and Adults

The Autonomic Nervous System controls our entire body through the subconscious mind that governs our memories, our perceptions, our cultural and societal beliefs and our overall emotions and feelings that we experience on a daily basis. A single thought triggers millions of neurochemicals within your brain to be triggered which impacts how you will feel. These chemicals directly influence what happens within our physical body and guides our emotional well-being by shaping the perception of our lives.

There have been many marketing spins on the effectiveness and usage of hypnosis that have left many people skeptical. In truth, the purpose of hypnosis is to normalize the reactions of your autonomic nervous system, which allows for the creation of both positive and powerful innate healing becoming stimulated within your bodies by removing the toxic energy blockages from deep seeded emotions that have been repressed over the years.

This results in an overall reduction of stress and anxiety and promotes overall well-being and generalized health. Hypnosis, also known as guided imagery helps you tap into your creative abilities to develop (imagine) positive thinking and feeling so that undesirable habits and behaviors can become transformed into healthier alternatives.

The medical arena has now proven that many illnesses are psychosomatic, which literally means that the body has been made ill by the workings of the mind. This is why labeling can be detrimental for a person's potential and well-being, it provides them with the belief that this is all their body and mind is capable of achieving and set-worth. Since this applies to many illnesses, both acute and chronic, it is important to examine the emotions behind that mind that may have inadvertently affected adverse health.

Hypnotherapy works as an aid to finding your own answers that are part of your innate guidance system. Nobody truly knows you better than yourself, it is through oppression and doubt that has often made one untrusting of our own judgments and perceptions. Hypnosis will provide access to your sub-conscious mind, where all the memories, emotions, feelings that you experienced since intrauterine are all stored.

Once access is retrieved from the subconscious, the client can evaluate the information and learn from it and assess what perspective can be learned from this newly acquired knowledge. After pondering over the thoughts, one can then learn their lessons from it and change their behavior accordingly. Once a person does a deep introspection of what originally triggered the distress that made them bury these thoughts and emotions, they can free up the space that these toxic thoughts had occupied which results in a freeing up of energy, and the illness can rapidly dissipate and permanently be resolved.

During the 1970's, research investigations in America lead to studies that measured the electrical changes that occurred within the brain during hypnosis. The research founded from these studies concluded that the brain wave patterns along with the neurochemicals from the nervous system displayed varying positive results. Most hypnotherapists would agree that any hypnosis is self-hypnosis and is rather more of a state of cooperation with the Practitioner; therefore, in truth no one can be hypnotized against their will by using this mode unless other mind-altering substances are added.

If in the past you have not been able to be hypnotized by a particular practitioner, this normally implies as with any medical profession that there is a rapport issue with the practitioner. The basic foundation of the suggestive will-power involves the presence of trust. Therefore, if you have not had success with hypnotherapy, you should seek another's assistance that you may feel more comfortable with or has your best interest at heart.

A majority of people have some form of emotional distress that was repressed and serves as the root source of their weight problems. Often times the stressors represent one of the following aspects: stress at work, a history of emotional or physical abuse, unhappy relationships, economic problems, chronic tension, sleep disturbances, or just boredom and wanting to seek pleasure in food as a coping tool.

In general, these repressed emotions have been buried beneath the surface of the unconscious mind and the most effective method of retrieving this information is to unlock it with hypnosis. This is the most appropriate means for identifying the root trigger and for reframing the event or situation so that your belief system will be permanently altered about yourself and your relationship to food as a coping mechanism.

Hypnosis and Children

In 1975, Crasilneck and Hall conducted a study on dyslexia and it showed that over 75% of dyslexic showed improvements to their condition with the assistance of hypnosis. The research proved that hypnotherapy provided suggestions for improving performance and pronunciation, allowing the recipient to recognize the words more rapidly and automatically.

Hypnosis is shown to alleviate some symptoms involved with the following:

Bed Wetting	Conduct at Home	Conduct at School
Don't Start Smoking	Enjoying Life	Fears and Phobias
Improved Grades	Improved Writing	Nail Biting
Nightmares	Pain Control	School Illness
School Illness	Stress	Sugars
Surviving a Divorce	Test Anxieties	Weight Reduction

At a young age, children have learned the art of self-hypnosis without realizing it when they play imaginary games. Hypnosis is a natural mental state. Athletes and actors often use it to improve upon their performance abilities when they are taught to visualize the winning moment or the perfect scene on stage. With this suggestive state, your mind is open to learning to change and adapt your feelings, thoughts, behavior and attitudes.

Hypnotherapy for children often resembles lessons in daydreaming and fantasizing. This allows the child to enter into the altered mental state, also known as hypnosis. By teaching a child these skills they are learning the art of self-hypnosis which they can use to their advantage to control bad habits, physical symptoms and other undesirable conditions that they may be consciously or unconsciously exhibiting.

If you analogous the child's mind as a computer, then hypnosis helps reboot the old software that has been operating in the mind and replacing it with more up-to-date perceptions. Once the child reaches this relaxed state, the brain wave patterns are altered so that the therapist can readily make suggestions that are aimed at producing the desired changes in the anxiety level, actual behavior or the intensity of the symptom that is experienced. This may range from having the child that is in chronic pain recall feelings of happiness and wellness and seeing it vividly in their minds.

Small studies have discovered that hypnotherapy can be used to manage chronic pain that children may be experiencing with "cancer" and larger studies are underway. Additionally, research revealed that children that had complimentary treatments with hypnotherapy in conjunction to pre-and post-chemotherapy experienced less nausea and vomiting.

Revolutionizing the Field of Medicine (Energy Medicine)

(Contribution by Dr. Joseph F. Unger Jr. FICS)

Many cultures share similarities with their understanding of the energy center that are present in our bodies. Historically the Egyptians, the East Indians, the Chinese, the Greeks and indigenous societies like the Native Americans understood these principles and effectively applied them for healing purposes. The foundation for the study of energy healing began in the Greek era with the Hippocratic school of thought.

The ancient Mayan and Aztec civilizations were also pioneers of spiritual energy healing and formed a well-developed system of healing elements for today's modern civilizations to follow. Ancient healers long ago discovered that energy (often called prana, Qi dependent on the culture) could be directed and manipulated for healing purposes so that those with a deficiency or blockage could benefit from a rejuvenated boost of energy.

The old thought that between a nucleus of an atom and the electron resided empty space (void) is now obsolete. Research has shown that there is the existence of frequencies that vibrate in between these two structures and by changing its vibration, it can create physical changes. It shows that 99.99999% of an atom is energy where 0.00001% is actually physical substance. With his discovery of homeopathy, Samuel Hahnemann of Germany outlined many of the major principles of energetic healing in 1790.

Fritz Albert Popp, PhD, from Mainz University of Germany was the first to demonstrate that people actually emit radiation, including visible light. He and others uncovered the mechanisms by which animals can communicate energetically for such observed events as a school of fish or flock of birds shifting directions in perfect synchrony.

Herbert Frohlich at the university of Liverpool was first to introduce the concept that some sort of collective vibration was responsible for detecting proteins to cooperate with each other and carry out instructions of DNA and cellular proteins. He found that once energy reaches a certain threshold, molecules begin to vibrate in unison, until they reach a high level of coherence.

It appears that all living beings including humans have such an energetic communication system at work, and it is essential for maintaining optimal health and physiological function. Each cell, organ and system in the human body emanates certain frequencies of energetic radiation. These are essential for coordination of physiological function throughout the entire body.

A sick organ, cell or system cannot adequately produce a spectrum of essential frequencies and thus contributes to dis-ease in the person. If one can restore the proper resonant frequencies by adding them to the individual's energetic system, then often the organ or system can be healed. Frohlich found that in "cancer" patient, the periodic photon emissions of energy are incoherent. Further he proved that "stress" alters and increases the biophoton emissions in a body.

In 1989, the International Society for the Study of Subtle Energies and Energy Medicine (ISSSEEM) was founded by Dr. Elmer Green and colleagues and the term "Energy Medicine" as coined. Later, Congress mandated that the National Institutes of Health Office of Alternative Medicine (NCCAM) Unit recognize Energy Therapies as a sub-field within the complementary and alternative medicines unit.

Energy medicine is safe and natural. Some energy use hands, solar and/or warmth energy. Others's usages of energy medicine are in form of electromagnetic and imaging technologies that are mainly present in hospitals.

What Is Energy Medicine?

Energy is everywhere and our hands can innately produce it. When your hands warm up when you touch somebody it is part of energy medicine and you do it without realizing it. The same thing occurs when your child hurts themselves, you rub on the "boo boo" and it makes the pain disappear. Well neurologically there is another explanation for this, but energy is also used to heal that "boo boo." When you hug them, the tears disappear; when you kiss them the hurt is gone. Your child knows your energy is healing. This is partially why they come to you for comfort in times of pain or fear.

When your child changes their attitude in front of a stranger or a sibling, or even changes their demeanor in front of guest, or dispositions change when their diapers are wet vs. dry; parents are in fact witnessing all the subtleties of energy. The change in emotion, temper, facial changes, body language or the reactionary moments when there is parental conflict are all part of these energetic patterns that children display and comprehend on a daily basis.

It is "easy" for parents to recognize positive energies, a smile and a laugh are very distinctive. Have you ever noticed how some children will gravitate towards some people and not others? They are particularly keen with the subtleties of a person's energy and they can see thru the facade that most adults hide beneath. Children are genuine with expressions of their emotions/feelings and as such are wonderful truth detectors for the authenticity in adults.

A person doesn't usually associate energy medicine with children. However, consider when a child gets hurt. What is the first thing they do? They run to the parent and look for what they think is consolation, but it is really your healing energy. You rub or kiss the sore spot and hug them until they feel better. That is why you are the first healer they seek; similar to telepathy and intuition, everyone has these gifts innately but many have dismissed their abilities away due to their internalized hurt and pain and as such are not accessing the inner strengths for healing.

Parents get glimpses of energy at work in their children under certain conditions. This usually happens when all is well in their world. They are in a calm environment, they are not hungry and their diaper doesn't need to be changed. It is "easy" to see when the child has positive energy flowing. They usually smile and laugh. It is also "easy" to see when the energy of the child is going down-hill. This happens when they are tired, their tummy is upset, teething episodes or during an unhappy exchange of ideas or words with other children or adults.

Energy medicine is neither mystical nor mythical. "Energy healing often works at levels beyond the physical dimension, areas inaccessible to more traditional forms of medicine," says Brian Dailey, M.D. Not only does Dr. Dailey practice and teach Western medicine, but he is also trained in the field of energy medicine as a Reiki master. Dr. Dailey is convinced that combining traditional medicine with energy medicine is often the best complement for health, and children can be the best recipients.

Some calming and security sensation can be transfer to the in-uterus baby during energy healing, like Reiki, coupled with pregnancy massages. Stress isn't the only condition under which energy work can be used intrauterine. In circumstances of trauma, fatigue, and emotional upheaval on the expectant mother, energy therapy can create peaceful change. Energy healing is very beneficial for the unborn child as well as the pregnant mother. This coupled with pregnancy massages can make the mother feel calmer and a sense of security that will transfer to the baby and help decrease the cortisol levels within the mother-to-be. However, caution is to select reputable practitioners especially during pregnancy, as with many industries, there are some people that are doing it for the wrong intentions.

Pioneers of Energy Medicine

One, of our infamous mentors, often reminds us, "Who do you listen to?" The advice was to listen to someone that you strive to become, as Tony stated, if you want to become the best, learn from the best or someone that has experienced the pain and can relate to you on a human perspective.

Donna Eden was diagnosed at the tender age of a 16 with Multiple Sclerosis symptoms and she was fully diagnosed at the age of 20. Then at 27 she had a heart attack, suffered from asthma and hypoglycemia. By the age of 30, she could hardly walk and was destined to be in a wheelchair according to her doctors for the rest of her life.

Then she went to Fiji and was bitten by an insect and went into a coma. The only person that was willing to help her was a Shaman and she recovered in Fiji and learned from him. Then she came back to the United States and saw her first sign of her destined career at the airport; a girl had a T-shirt called Touch for Health. She inquired about it and she went to learn all about that healing modality and built her career upon that. Her doctors gave up on her and it was the best thing ever because she learned to heal herself and to teach this science and art form to others.

Touch for Health was created by a chiropractor, John F. Thie, DC. The first Manual was published in 1973 and launched a worldwide movement in a holistic approach to health. It teaches the restoring of our natural energies. He uses acupressure, touch and massage to improve postural balance and reduce physical and mental pain and tension and is the principles of Eden Energy Medicine.

Energy medicine, explained by Donna Eden, is the art and science of fostering physical, psychological and spiritual health and well-being. She promotes that by focusing on your body as a living system of energy you begin to realize that powerful energy resources are already inherent in your hands and in your body and you simply have to ignite the passion to release its abilities.

Mietek Wirkus, a Polish bioenergy practitioner has been practicing energy medicine for 60 years. As Tony Robbins' states, if you want to learn from the best, seek out the best talent out there and we found some local gurus. While in Poland, Mr. Wirkus was one of the first professional bioenergy practitioners employed by a medical center to complement the work of physicians and on average worked with 400 people a week.

Mr. Wirkus has conducted workshops and professional groups throughout the United States including the Menninger Foundation of Kansas, the Institute of Noetic Sciences in San Francisco, the A.R.E. Clinic of Phoenix, Arizona, and the International Society for the Study of Subtle Energies and Energy

Medicine of Boulder, Colorado for physicians, nurses, medical technicians and body work therapists. The Wirkus Bioenergy Foundation was established to further research efforts. In June 1992 the Foundation created a VHS video cassette entitled: "Bioenergy: A Healing Art." Mietek lives in Bethesda, Maryland.

Seane Malone, owner of Inn on Thistle Hill, grew up in India, Indonesia, and the Orient where she developed her healing abilities at the age of 7. She was trained in both eastern and western philosophies, yoga, meditation, music and dance and in the Energy Balancing techniques which she has refined. Seane studied with many highly respected people in the field including Dr. D. Gary Young, Founder Young Living Essential Oils and Carolyn Myss.

Seane Malone is an authentic energy visionary and she has worked with and developed this particular technique of Energy Balancing over the past 35 years. She actually coined the phrase "Energy Balancing" over 35 years ago. The Inn on Thistle Hill is a bed and breakfast where you can enjoy fabulous organic food, sip on alkaline water and relax, rejuvenate and re-energize with energy healing that combines these various healing modalities.

Some of the more reputable mentors she has worked with include: Rev. Eleanor Button, Ram Dass (Dr. Richard Alpert), Healer Olga Worrell, Hypnotherapist Dr. Winkler, Dr. James Judd, Sant Keshevedas, Sadhu Singh (3HO Foundation), Pir Vilayat Inayat Kahn (Sufism), Red Eagle (Shaman), Peter and Eileen Caddy of Findhorn, Scotland and Seth.

Jenn's Insights

When I was first introduced to the prospects of learning Energy Medicine, I wanted to learn from the best, but my definition had multiple criteria. I wanted to truly learn from someone that experienced both allopathic and alternative healing mechanisms. What was important to me was the person's intent for practicing energy medicine; I knew that if someone was truly passionate about something that the love of their work will be reflected in their services.

I was first introduced to Eden Energy Medicine from my son's godmother. She is a registered nurse that has incorporated Energy Healing into her practices and seen phenomena results. She has worked with some of the best healing modalities inclusive of Carolyn Myss and Jo Dunning's Pulse Technique to help with her own personal healing journey and to share her gift of healing with others. Her heart is one of the most beautiful attributes about her and she has endured plenty without having closed that heart to others, something her son had taught her.

Before, I decided to invest my time and energy, I wanted to learn more about Donna Eden and what made her passionate about this work. Donna's story really moved me. When Donna's grandmother was 4 years old, her mother passed away and then her father left them, she then lived with the grandmother.

But the grandmother was tragically murdered in front of her eyes at the age of 6 and she was sent to live in an orphanage.

When Donna herself turned 4, history almost repeated itself when her mother caught Tuberculosis and was sent to a terminal ward. At the tender age of 4, a little girl's wish was answered, she stared at her mom on her death bed and exclaimed in a prayer, "Mommy is too important for this world, I just got here; I wish I was the one that had TB instead. I just got here so I can easily go home and return later." That was when Donna developed TB and her mom recovered. Talk about a heart filled with empathy!

Donna recalls the most valuable lesson that set the stage for her career. She saw her mom refusing all medications even though she had only one working lung that had been severely damaged. The doctors had told her mom that she should be on medication for the rest of her life, but her mom refused all medication and trusted her body's wisdom to innately heal and made a full recovery. Those indirect lessons that her mom taught her, has made a world of difference for that little girl and humanity through Donna and her families services to others.

As the Universe has it, Donna hardly came to the Northern Virginia area, but she and her husband, David Feinstein held a training seminar and I was fortunate enough to learn from both of them and that served as the foundation to ignite my passion for healing.

Both of her daughters are also associated with the energy business. Titanya and Donna wrote the book Energy Medicine for Kids... and Their Parents, Too! Titanya is also a certified Waldorf Education teacher (K-12) and has years of experience teaching children's dance and movement. Titanya's techniques will be incorporated into the Whole-Listic Gifted Academy for all the children to experience. Innersource is a service organization run by the family and has been a pioneering force in Energy Medicine, Energy Psychology, and consciousness studies.

Personally, I have benefited from Energy Healing from both a physiological and emotional perspectives. I had fallen rolled down a flight of stairs and could hardly move and even Chiropractic care was not enough; however, after two intense sessions of Energy Medicine, all the bruising and inflammation went away and all the bruises and aches disappeared. The healing was in record-time and I did not have to endure any side-effects from medications or interference with my energy levels from x-rays

Energy Medicine and Children

As we mature, adults find ways of unconsciously blocking pain. We put on armor and set up barriers and go about our daily living as if we were truly free and passionate about life. This makes it harder and more time consuming for the practitioner to access our energy to allow healing to occur. When adults receive energy healing treatments, it's analogous to peeling the layers of an onion before you can eventually get to the root source of the hurt/pain/grief/guilt.

From a sociological perspective, it would make so much more sense to apply energy medicine as a means of preventive care so that 20 years down the road, there will not be as much need for substance abuse centers or detention centers and the resources can truly be allocated to the advancement of humanity and the well-being of the generations to come. Many of the mental illnesses that are being treated during the adolescence and adults years could have been prevented if early intervention was available to address these psychosomatic issues up front.

It is much easier to treat from the unborn child to the teenager. Energy healing has been proven to help colicky babies, emotional issues, bonding problems, weight issues and fussy, sleepless babies. It helps teens with feelings of social inadequacies (remember your high school years!)

Emotional repression begins early on in life. When children feel ignored or rejected they begin to shut down their feelings. This also happens when they don't feel supported to express their emotions freely and in a positive manner. This will cause stress within the child. Repressed emotions may manifest as asthma or poor body postures that can lead to a number of physical ailments or may remain in the body and literally cause autoimmune illnesses later in life due to energy blockages.

From an energy practitioner's perspective all negative experiences in life (self-esteem, compulsive behaviors, addictions, Etc) are identified as energy blockages. When a healer is able to open or clear these blocks, they are relieving the problems in all areas (physical, mental, emotional and spiritual) of the patient's life. When a child does not feel safe and cared for, they will start to build armor around themselves and the chakras may begin to shut down.

Our society today tends to suppress the expression of deep emotions. People need to distinguish between expression of deep emotions and destructive behavior. Unfortunately sometimes when we try to stop destructive behavior, the child's emotions is scorned and once again blocks are put up. It is a fine balance to discipline and guide while still providing a sense of autonomy for them to learn from their experiences and to thrive from both an emotional and mental perspective.

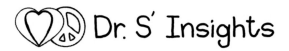 Dr. S' Insights

Repressed emotions can manifest in blocks to the child's breathing (asthma/bronchitis) and body posture and can lead to various physical ailments. This is why we believe that the "Time-Out" techniques for parenting are not the most ideal for Highly Sensitive children and children with extreme empathy skills. Jennifer is a prime example of this concept, she grew up repressing her emotions and as both an empath and a highly sensitive child she chronically had bouts of bronchitis even into her adulthood.

Forty years of pediatric experience have taught Dr. Parnell Donahue that the unique perspective of teens is an invaluable resource for parents who want their children to become men and women of character and his book, "Messengers with Denim" helps parents that are distraught about how their adolescents are expressing their individuality in a world that often misunderstands them; however, adolescents are here to teach the parents lessons just as they did when they were first born.

As, Dr. Donahue eloquently put it, "Kids respect their parents, they love their parents, and they become their parents", what lessons are you truly teaching your children directly or indirectly? Kids at a young age want to be like mommy and daddy, are you truly being the best role model you can as a Billionaire Parent? Another helpful book resource is Tools for Effective Parenting. In his latest book, Dr. Donahue explains how peer pressure can be utilized as a parenting tool. Another innovative tool includes having a pet and one of the easiest tricks that most parents in a stressed out lifestyle forget to utilize is to simply listen to your kids. Foremost they need to feel like they are understood and will be unconditionally loved.

When children misbehave it is often a sign of other issues. This could be from thirst, hunger, being over tired or over stimulated. The consumption of process and sugary food could be the cause of this as well. Over stimulation may occur from all the media technology; often times children are in front of computer screens or tablets more often than being outdoors. If a child misbehaves frequently, it is suggested to cut out sweet foods.

Many people have heard of the bio-energy field that surrounds the body called the Aura. The healthier the person, the larger and brighter the energy field is. Sick and stressed people typically have smaller and darker energy fields. Our surplus energy is stored in the Aura. It is like a saving account that we can withdraw from when needed.

Allowing negative thoughts (fear, anger, resentment and frustration) can deplete the Aura. Feelings of love, joy and appreciation will replenish and restore the frequencies of the body and the Aura.

Based on the magnet theory, the Aura Exploration patches were able to create frequencies based patch to put on your bed that creates 300 Gauss electromagnetic fields without the magnet side effects. Please visit: http://www.auraexplorationpatches.com to learn more about these alternative products that can increase your frequency levels.

Many health care professionals are recommending that women stop wearing underwire (plastic and metal) bras. Many are recommending wireless ones. When it comes to energy medicine, it is felt that the wire does not allow the proper flow of energy. As a result, harm is being done to the lymph tissue in the breast. This can create pain and future health problems, including breast "cancer."

Energy medicine has definitely been able to assist with ailments that many allopathic treatments have not been able to find resolutions for. Tony Robbins explains how his wife, Sage, was helped by Energy Medicine when the allopathic means did not alleviate the issue. Tony exclaimed that when Sage was born, her vestibular system, which controls balance and eye movement, was damaged, and the result was severe motion sickness. With him constantly traveling, she was throwing up on every flight and drastically losing weight.

For nine years they went to doctors, nutritionists, natural healers, even experts at NASA and the U.S. Navy's Top Gun school, but nothing worked. Tony admitted that it was a natural hands-on healer on *the eastern coast of South India who ultimately helped Sage. He helped Sage learn a form of self-meditation that calms the parietal lobe of the brain and she was able to tolerate motion after that.*

Revolutionizing the World of Thoughts – (The Real "Secret")

Bernard Grad, at the University in Montréal, discovered that a healer could reduce the growth of "cancerous tumors" in laboratory animal. He demonstrated that our state can influence yeast, fungi and even isolated "cancer" cells. Russian researchers confirmed these findings when they discovered that hydrogen-oxygen bonds in water molecules undergo distortions in the crystalline microstructure during healing.

In another study, experienced mediators used intention to affect the molecular structure of water samples they were holding throughout the meditation. When the water was later examined by infrared spectral photometry many of its essential qualities, particularly its absorbance characteristics, had been significantly altered.

Schwartz and Connor also demonstrated that directed intention manifests itself in measurable electro-static and magnetic energies. While Carroll Nash from St. Joseph's University in Philadelphia found that people could influence the growth rate of bacteria just by willing it so. Can we someday "shrink malignant and benign tumors" in 2 minutes and half without any surgical intervention? The answer is yes, according to Gregg Braden.

Through the 1990's, Dr. Masaru Emoto performed a series of experiments observing the physical effect of words, prayers, music and environment on the crystalline structure of water. Emoto hired photographers to take pictures of water after being exposed to the different variables and subsequently frozen so that they would form crystalline structures. The results were nothing short of remarkable.

The two water bottles that held the negative words were, "You make me sick, and I will kill you" and "Adolph Hitler." The two water bottles that held the positive words were "Thank you" and "Love and Appreciation" The positive words formed aesthetically and symmetrically figured shapes. Now let's imagine if the words and effects that comes out of our mouths or indirectly thought about from our minds has this effect on water crystals, what it would have on a person.

Did you know the average adult human body is 57-60% water? The percentage of water in infants is much higher, typically around 75-78% water. Have you thought about what words you have been saying around your kids lately, are they positive or negative?

The World's Largest Medicine-Less Hospital (Healing with Energy)

Gregg Braden spent over two decades visiting remote villages and monasteries and forgotten books to uncover their secrets. He is among the first to share about the Center. The Center is known for healing "cancerous tumors" in less than three minutes.

Braden had a strong technical and scientific background. He knew science was important, but he felt there was more to helping the world. He decided to see what needed to be done to connect science and spirituality to explain everyday miracles.

The Huaxia Zhineng Qigong Clinic and Training Center in China (aka the Center), had about 4 thousand staff and patients living there. It was first built in 1988 in Zigachong and was moved to Qinhuangdao in 1992. In 1995 it expanded to Fengrun.

The Center focuses on exercise, love, life energy and healthy foods. There are no pharmaceutical medicines. It is the largest hospital known of its kind in the world. The Center has 95% successfully treated almost two hundred different dis-eases. People have been "cured" of "cancer", arthritis, paralysis, and diabetes (just to name a few.) Since no medication is involved, each person seeking treatment is a student instead of a patient. This is because the student is held accountable for their own healing.

The Director of the center Dr. Pang Ming is a guru in the art of Chi-Lel and has written almost a dozen books about this method. Chi-Lel is an ancient form of Qigong that combines modern medical practices, known as Medical Qigong. Frank and Luke Chan brought the Chi-Lel movement to the United States.

Frank was one of the first Chi-Lel Masters to be certified outside of China. He has written four books detailing the science and the art of this healing technique. The books are entitled, "101 Lessons of Tao, Secrets of the Tai Chi Circle, Journey to Enlightenment, and 101 Miracles of Natural Healing. The Chi-Lel technique for wellness consists of four essential healing processes:

- <u>Strong belief (Shan Shin)</u>: a belief that chi or life energy can heal all ailments, including one's own. Students build belief by listening to testimonials of recovered patients and learning about chi and its healing effects.
- <u>Group Healing (Chu Chong)</u>: before a group of students begins Chi-Lel, the teacher verbally synchronizes the thinking of the group to obtain chi from the universe and bring it down into a healing energy field, shrouding everyone including the teacher himself or herself. The healing effect is enhanced because the group is acting as one (collective consciousness.)
- <u>Chi Healing (Fa Chi)</u>: Facilitating chi healing by teachers brings healing energy from the universe to each individual to facilitate healing (similar to Reiki.)
- <u>Practice (Lan Gong)</u>: Students learn easy-to-follow Chi-Lel movements and practice them over and over again (continuous self-healing on a daily basis)

Since true healing requires taking accountability for your emotional and physical well-being, all the candidates that are admitted are deemed as "students" rather than patients. Once they enter the premise, initial consultation with a doctor consists of the benchmark diagnosis. Then, the student is assigned to a class of 50 people and the duration of the treatment protocol is a 24 day intensive. The student focuses on healing the majority of the day and practice Chi-Lel at least 8 hours a day.

There are no telephones allowed or televisions or newspapers that can influence the mind or lower any vibrational states with external stimuli. The students that are mobile will practice their exercises standing up; for those that are confined to wheel-chairs they will practice their exercises sitting and those that are ambulatory will practice their exercises within their beds. The goal is for them to invest as much time within a day towards healing one's mind, body and spirit and practicing the art of healing.

The video that Gregg Braden witnessed was of a "cancer" patient being treated by four Chi-Lel teachers while the patient's bladder "cancer" was viewed on a screen via an ultrasound machine, and monitored by two doctors. The "cancer tumor" literally disappears within less than two and half minutes as the teachers emitted chi into the patient, dissolving the "tumor." After it was reviewed ten days later, the "tumor" was still in remission (http://www.youtube.com/watch?v=VLPahLakP_Q.)

Consequently, due to political reasons, the Center was closed in 2001; all forms of Qigong where more than 50 people congregated were officially banned. However, Chi-Lel teacher's still exists and this form of healing is needed for humanity.

The History of Energy Psychology

For more than thirty years, Dr. John Diamond has been a pioneer in the field of holistic healing. He discovered the link between the acupuncture meridians and the emotions, which became the foundation for Energy Psychology.

Life Energy is the name Dr. Diamond gives the innate healing power of the body. He discovered that underneath the symptoms of any illness you will always find an emotion that is draining the Life Energy. Normally these emotions are referred to as negative emotions such as grief, hurt, anger, shame, guilt.)

Dr. Diamond discovered that there is indeed a Healing Power within us, an innate restorative power of our own body, and the only true healing comes by raising the Life Energy. This is also the principles of Acupuncture, Homeopathy and Chiropractic. He believes a practitioner's role is to help raise your Life Energy and that is why the Chi-Lel Qigong is able to help with "tumors."

Energy psychology utilizes imagination (visualization) coupled with other guided meditation formats such as trances (hypnosis) to reduce hyper-arousal conscious thinking and allows one to access the subconscious mind. Normally, the treatment focuses on acupressure points to help release the blocked energy. It is an integration of physical, mental and cognitive procedures that will shift the emotion, mental and behavioral state of the client/person.

Energy psychology is a derivative of energy medicine that postulates that mental disorders and other health conditions are related to the energy disturbances of the body and its field around it. Dr. David Feinstein is one of the leaders in energy psychology and has published many studies that proved that it is a more effective and efficient technique than traditional therapy. Energy psychology can involve about 12 specialized techniques and some of the more popular ones are Thought Field Therapy and Emotional Freedom Technique.

The basis of energy psychology is to uncover all the buried unresolved hurt that happened throughout the client/person's life and the removal of all mechanisms of defense (walls) that our body and mind has built up for our own protection against the heart. Research revealed that every traumatic event or negative memory triggers an emotional imprint into our subconscious brain (in the form of Megahertz) but it also impacts our physical body until we choose to let go of this memory. This is why forgiveness is an important aspect of healing; it ultimately releases that energetic imprint from your body.

Furthermore, our body and brain tends to stack these emotional triggers and events and clumps them together. Have you ever noticed that when you are upset or angry, it is normally because it reminds you of a past betrayal or hurt? For example, if multiple times in your life a man was the trigger associated with hurt. Your brain, especially your subconscious will equate that with being problematic, even if the scenarios occurred in different timeframes. Your subconscious brain will associate MAN = HURT and eventually you will create a set of rules that says: Men will hurt me so I should stay away from them from a physical perspective.

Energy psychology is able to remove the energy imprints of a situation and use suggestive tools to allow your subconscious to feel safe of letting go of your trapped (repressed) emotions. Then those memories are replaced with an updated perspective that promotes learning from that "bad" experience. The difference with Energy Psychology is that it goes to the root source of the issue, which normally occurred during childhood. This way it is not treating just the symptoms of the present day distress.

Traditional therapy is similar to allopathic medicine; it treats the symptoms but does not get to the root source as readily. Also, since traditional therapy is based on diagnosis, practitioners are observing symptoms and attempting to correlate them with a particular mental dis-ease. However, no two human beings are truly alike and as such; their perceptions of what is deemed as hurtful may differ. This is especially true when you are dealing with people that were highly sensitive or empath as a child.

Epigenetics has shown that you can also turn your genes off and on with your emotions and that it can become hereditary to two subsequent generations. Many, if not most people carry emotional scars; traumas that can adversely affect health to them and their off-springs. Using techniques like energy psychology can truly free yourself and correct the trauma. It also provides incentives to allow the fullest genetic expression for your children and grandchildren. According to David Feinstein, Energy psychology has been proven to be effective even for Post- Traumatic Stress Disorders (PTSD) and severe trauma.

Some techniques utilized in energy psychology are from acupressure, yoga, Qi gong, meditation. Energy medicine can also teach people simple steps for initiating changes in their inner lives. Some works on stimulating energy points on the surface of the skin which, when combined with specific psychological procedures, can shift the brain's electrochemistry to help overcome negative emotions, habits, beliefs, and behaviors. There are many techniques within the Energy Psychology arena; however, the one that we have found to be most beneficial and produced the quickest results was the Pulse Technique.

One caveat of Energy Psychology is that it may not work for those that are not ready to become accountable for their own healing aspects. These are normally the ones that find comfort with the identity of the "victim" mentality. Traditional therapy allows them to obtain validation that they are indeed experiencing "abnormal" thoughts and as such deserve a special labeling. It is normally easier to blame others for all your mishaps and it is less risk-averse to avoid another probable perspective for incorporating change into one's life.

Energy Psychology forces one to truly meditate and find the answers within themselves, but the true question is: Is the person ready to become accountable for making changes in their life? It takes courage and energy to look introspect-fully at you. Sometimes, in adults, they are not ready to let go of this emotional baggage because of the identity that it has provided them throughout. Children have less emotional baggage and are more receptive to this technique of healing.

Pulse Technique

The Pulse Technique, founded by Jo Dunning is one of the most effective means for resolving repressed emotions. It utilizes a reverse psychology approach along with meditative processes. During a Pulse session you will spend 2-3 minutes focusing on anything in your life that is getting in your way or that you would like to change. These are items or situations that are limiting your fullest potential or you just don't like experiencing.

While you focus on what you don't like or want in your life the energy follows your focus and clears whatever is the cause of the unwanted experience or symptom. By focusing on something you don't like the energy will automatically clear it, leaving more room for the things you do want. Repressed or stagnant energy is cleared out and pushed to flow again. It brings the subconscious memory to the conscience level so that it may be cleared out.

The powerful clearing Energy used in the Pulse processes has intelligence that goes to the core of the problem. It shifts and clears the original experience that created the present situation as well as the many layers of experiences from over the years that have added to the original, core issue. The most effective practitioners to perform this technique are the ones that are combining it with Positive Psychology as a guided meditation.

Jenn's Insights

When I studied Psychology, I was more intrigued with Developmental Psychology, Abnormal Psychology and Industrial Organizational Psychology. I wanted a broad perspective to have comparison opportunities. I knew that no matter what business industry I was going to pursue a career in that it would have to deal with people.

So I wanted to learn what were the intrinsic values that motivated people because I knew I was meant to be a Leader and I wanted to know the stages of mental development because I suspected that the chronological and mental ages of people did not often match. To me bullying is an example, these people exhibit more of temper tantrums until they get their ways.

I also suspected that many people were being assessed with surface level diagnosis because I had experienced it myself from counselors and knew that they were not getting to the root of the issue so I wanted to understand what impacted so-called "abnormal" behaviors. As my studies progressed, I felt that there was still a missing component, so I decided to pursue another degree in Sociology so that I would gain the macro view of the cultural/societal norms that had constricted people's choices.

Psychiatry never appealed to me because I did not believe that medicating people was the solution to finding out what their true discomfort was. I suspected that beneath every emotion there was an underlying trigger that invoked the changes in a person. For example, a person that is angry normally has a lot of hurt that has not been resolved and under that layer, grief or shame for not having the expected outcomes.

During my duration at Gainesville Holistic Health Center, I observed how "Emotional Clearings" performed with Energy Medicine and the Pulse technique had assisted many clients with their healing at much quicker rates. We noticed that many clients that had come to the Center with physiological issues such as back pain or bodily aches were able to resolve this within 1-2 visits, a lot quicker than the normal chiropractic regime.

With diagnostics tools we were able to observe all the trapped emotions within a person's body and this provided the client with an objective assessment of how emotions were actually the root trigger of the pain. I had observed a client that had evidenced her sister's gruesome murder, and as such her energetic field was filled with a lot of energy blockages. The most prominent was in her throat chakra. Her singing career ended when she needed surgery in her throat and her doctors told her she would never be able to sing again; however, after one Emotional Clearing and after 12 years of not using those vocal cords to sing, she heard herself singing for the first time again.

Another client I observed came to the Center for extreme back pain and she had used various forms of massage therapy and Chiropractic treatments to alleviate the pain from her sciatic. It was so bad that it was difficult for her to function properly in an office setting; however, after two Emotional Clearings, all of her pain instantaneously disappeared. The root issue was the grief from her grandfather's passing.

Another observation occurred when a Client came in that was experiencing anxiety attacks after her delivery. The doctors had diagnosed it as postpartum depression. After an Emotional Clearing session and a Hypnosis session with the hypnotherapist, all anxiety disappeared and she was able to properly attend to the newborn's needs. The root trigger was that during her adolescent years she was bullied by a group and physically threatened and as such when she started a family again, she was in constant fear for her and her family members' safety.

Another observation occurred when a Client came in that was diagnosed with Depression and had many physical ailments that were impacting her body. After an Emotional Clearing, it was discovered that she had held onto the emotion of guilt from childhood. She blamed herself for her parent's divorce all these years and as such felt hopeless during the duration of her life. So much so that she has lost confidence in her own abilities to succeed and felt scared to pursue her own dreams because she felt that was not good enough.

It saddens me to see how much emotional baggage many people are holding onto in their bodies, which manifests into dis-ease of the mind-body connection. These people are not "abnormal", it is normal to feel emotions, both good and bad ones, but our society has tabooed it at an early age. We have seen so many clients come in that were using alcohol and smoking as coping mechanisms because there were no other outlets to help them relieve their stress or pent-up emotions. The majority of the issues when traced back all stem to childhood hurts and grief.

If society invested in these children at an earlier age, we would probably see less pain and grief within society. From a sociological perspective, if we alleviated the stress levels of children and adults, we could see a decrease of dis-ease as well as mental disorders. Post-traumatic disorders still have the root issues buried within the person until those images and memories can be successfully coped with and medications will not be able to alleviate this issue because the original source of the trauma occurred first to the mind rather than the body.

The Energy of Emotions

It is not necessary to have a PhD or to have studied functional neuroanatomy to understand the role and importance emotions play in our daily lives. We live our life based upon our emotions, finding techniques to bring pleasure and happiness while steering away from pain (i.e. fear, anger, frustration, ruthless, grief, sadness.) Emotions provide a neurological pattern that involves multiple aspects of the brain linking together various systems in the body such as immunology, neurology and digestive systems, forming an intricate network that when balanced provides optimal wellness for the mind-body-spirit.

During the past 30 years, neurologist Antonio R. Damasio and Hanna Damasio have strived to show that feelings are what arise as the brain interprets emotions in our decision-making processes and in our self-image. He has shown how certain feelings are cornerstones of our survival.

Using imaging techniques such as magnetic resonance imaging (MRI) and positron emission tomography (PET) to study patients with brain lesions as well as normal subjects, we have begun to make some inroads into understanding the areas of the brain involved in different types of emotion.

If you were to ask a neuroscience scientist, they would probably go in the explanation of how the emotions are based upon stimuli. When we are afraid of something, our hearts begin to race, our mouths become dry, and our skin turns pale and our muscles contract. This emotional reaction occurs automatically and unconsciously. Feelings occur after we become aware in our brain of such physical changes; only then do we experience the feeling of fear.

But not all emotions are from external stimuli or from the brain itself. For example, when we feel sympathy for a sick person, we recreate that person's pain to a certain degree internally. Also, extreme stressors or extreme fear and even physical pain can be dismissed; the brain ignores the physical signals that are transmitting the pain stimulus.

To properly understand the emotional realm, we must differentiate emotion from feeling.

When we experience any of the primary emotions, sadness, grief, happiness, anger, fear, anxiety, surprise, disgust, our experiences are expressed in a physical form. Feelings, by contrast, are our conscious perception of all those changes happening in the body, and of very subtle changes that are happening in the way our cognitive apparatus functions.

> *This is why Energy Psychology utilizing the Pulse Technique works better than the traditional means. With the Pulse Technique you are accessing the emotions that were subconsciously imprinted when you had that undesirable experience. With traditional psychology you are asked to consciously recall the actual feeling; however, as John Gray mentioned in his book, You Can Heal What you Feel; however, our society has programmed us to become numb to pain and hurt.*

Our cognitive capacity allows us to assign emotional value to a stimulus, and to change this value that was previously assigned to a stimulus requires neuro-linguistic programming (NLP) coupled with positive psychology. For example, a child may be initially fearful of dogs, but through positive experiences the child may eventually enjoy and approach them. As another example, imagine the emotions associated with a new relationship. Initially, seeing the person may evoke positive emotions of desire and happiness. However, after a nasty breakup, the same person could easily elicit emotions of anxiety, tension, and anger. This is the basis of how neuro-linguistic programming can assist a client with their perceptions of experiences they had attained in life.

The "Emotional" Brain

The limbic system in the brain is the center of all emotions. The Amygdala has an important role in evaluating the emotional valence of stimuli. Emotions are modulated by a myriad of chemical neurotransmitters. These include the serotonin, norepinephrin, and dopamine systems.

The Amygdala may also be involved in what is termed "emotional memory." It means that we will be able to better bring forward all memories to experience that were strongly negative rather than the positive ones. So many people still today can recall events or tragedy because they triggered a memory and a strong emotional imprint in their nervous system.

Emotions of Fear and Anxiety

Many people have heard of the fight or flight response. This is when our emotions are threatened and we are alerted to potential danger. Our bodies either engage in defensive (fight) or protective act (flight) so we can survive. Sometimes we even freeze instead of withdrawing from a situation or fight (paralysis or numbing with unhealthy coping mechanisms: drinking, promiscuity, smoking, and drug usage.)

Some developmental studies suggest that some infants will differ in the way they exhibit fear. For example, some infants become extremely agitated when confronted with unfamiliar stimuli such as a stranger. These infants display high levels of crying and motor activity, e.g., flexing and extending the arms and legs.

In childhood, they often appear socially repressed. In an unfamiliar context, these children are characterized as very shy, timid, and cautious. In adolescence and young adulthood, suppressed individuals may begin to develop problems dealing with anxiety. They may have nightmares and develop phobias.

Emotions of Sadness and Grief

In a lost of an important social relationship (death of a spouse for example) or object (loss of a home by a fire), the negative emotion of grief and sadness might predominate. Sadness is the barometer for the need of seeking supportive social relationship. It usually is need for affiliation and functions to motivation.

If the emotion is present at birth, the child will then express early signs for a caregiver to meet its attention demands. If the maternal-infant bond is disrupted for prolonged periods it could impact the child towards subsequent sadness behavior. Also, isolation from early age is link to a sequestration and not wanting to deal with people at later age. These people would not play nor fight nor show any sexual interest when they were older. This can lead to depression which is a mood by thoughts of self-worthlessness and excessive guilt. This can affect physical issues like insomnia, altered appetite, pleasure and fatigue.

Emotions of Anger

Since love cannot be appreciated without anger, we all feel this emotion time to time. The degree where anger is felt or expressed can be different. Anger can be brought up by hearing a criticism; not getting what you want; or experiencing unjust treatments is but a few of the potential triggers.

It can range from mild irritation, to frustration, to all the way up to seething rage. Boredom is a mild version of anger. It is seen as a form of dissatisfaction with what is happening. Boredom can generate anger or irritation because there can be a subtle sense of loss or fear associated with the experience of not engaging in something stimulating or productive.

Anger can also create positive action or feeling. Taking a stand against unfairness or injustice can be driven with anger. But it is like an internal alarm telling us that something is wrong either emotionally, mentally, physically or surrounding us. Regrettably, however, the anger humans feel is being triggered by far less consequential factors than serious wrongdoing and create actions and behaviors that are neither productive nor positive.

Usually anger is not the primary emotion involved. Fear and /or sadness are found to underneath the anger and trigger the series of events that occur when we go towards anger. Anxiety, worry, sadness comes from experience of loss, disappointment or discouragement and are all part of fear.

These feeling make us feel uncomfortable and vulnerable often times not in control. This is one of the reason people tend to avoid these feelings as much as they can by switching subconsciously to anger. Since anger can create a surge of energy instead of vulnerability and helplessness, it brings us a sense of power and energy in face of disappointment or discouragement. By working with the fear, sadness, or both, you will develop more skillful ways of relating to your anger.

Emotions of Disgust

It is when we feel disgust that our connection to morality is disempowered. A sense of expression for a feeling of moral outrage is present. Fear and disgust goes together and feed off each other. The power of self-exploration is very useful especially when the emotion of disgust comes about. This reflects on the type and amount of nurturing in our life we had. It reflects also on our moral standards or judgment. This tool is powerful because it reveals how this emotion may be cleverly manipulated based on societal political view points and cultural perspectives that were infused upon us.

By suppressive disgust, the feeling of disgusting things or feelings more negative over people is more predominant. It is like looking at the world with an evil eye and always thinking evil is there to get you. This is because they cannot get rid of their feelings by expressing themselves. This is why people that are brought up in very controlling parental environments often are very critical of themselves and others as they become adults.

Emotions of Pleasure

All our human reactions and actions are geared towards two simple principles: to either seek pleasure or run away from pain. There is an important difference between pleasure and joy. Pleasure can be perceived as a temporary feeling where it may be a one-time instance that generates a good feeling, but the good feeling wears off when the dosage expires; whereas, joy is achieved from within, and is therefore sustainable. That's not to say that it's permanent or automatic. Nurturing joy and pleasure is essential which is difficult to do constantly with our level of stress these days.

Dr. Barbara Fredrickson, author of Positivity, has spent more than 20 years investigating the relatively new field of positive emotions. She says that positive emotions can make us healthier and happier if we take time to cultivate their growth into our lives. Below a certain threshold for positive emotions, Fredrickson says, people get pulled into downward spirals, their behavior becomes rigid and predictable, and they begin to feel burdened and lifeless.

She also states that when people who increase their daily diets of positive emotions; they find more meaning and purpose in life. Dr. Fredrickson also found that increasing their social support is proportionally linked to the increase of positive emotion. She explains that perhaps they just notice it more, because they're more attuned to the give-and-take synergy because human interactions.

Living in a positive state of mindful-awareness increases positive relations with others. These people tend to feel more effective at what they do, possess an optimistic outlook for life in life. Sleep is also improved by living a more positive life. These people also report experiencing fewer aches and pains, headaches, and other physical symptoms.

Our emotional states are mainly in reaction to the current circumstances. They aren't a permanent state; they're feelings that come and go. That's true of all emotions, but positive emotions tend to be more fleeting. However, these emotions are a catalyst for a healthier and happier lifestyle where one finds internal comfort and happiness without revealing your true identity (See Chapter 16 for further details.)

How can we increase positivity? One way is to be aware of the present moment, because most moments are positive. We miss many opportunities to experience positive emotions now by thinking too much about the past or worrying about the future, rather than being open to what is.

Unlocking the feeling of gratitude will unleash the human kindness in you. To be grateful for you and others brings a self-peace inside and can change somebody's day. Sometimes it start by just paying attention when you are kind and this will reverberate toward a more positive feeling. This is why gratitude, similar to forgiveness is not just for others but more so for ourselves.

The Loving Kindness Meditation

The Dalai Lama said: "This is my simple religion. There is no need for temples; no need for complicated philosophy. Our own brain, our own heart is our temple; the philosophy is kindness."

The Loving-Kindness Meditation (LKM) is the practice of wishing oneself and others to be happy, content and at ease. The medication self-explore difficult feelings or emotions and invite love and kindness to reside and send well wished to oneself as well as others.

The benefits are numerous and the effect of opening your heart can impact the way to see yourself. Stress reduction is another benefit since the meditation changed several brain regions linked to empathy, attuning the emotional center for better and positive feelings.

Mirror Reflections of Our Emotions

It usually takes somebody who can push our limits or whose personality or actions push our button that turn out to be our greatest teachers. They usually serve as a mirror and teach us what needs to be revealed about ourselves. If you see what you do, will you change it if you experience pain instead of pleasure? Seeing what we don't like in others help us look deeper inside ourselves for similar traits and challenges that need healing, balancing, or changing.

It will always be easier to see all the flaws in others instead of us. Come on, who would like to have their problems, pointed out to them on a daily basis. However, the Universe is clever and will force us to assess things that we have not been able to cope with.

Without knowing it, the people surrounding us will feed on our energy and mirror us, and this will create an emotional change which will make us go into introspection. It will help us to be able to see our short comings more clearly. Mirroring is often magnified to enhance getting our attention. What we see is enhanced to look larger than life so we won't overlook the message, making sure we get the "Big Picture" loud and clear.

The mirroring effect will repeat itself until we change our behavior and emotional state. How many times have you experienced the same type of scenario over and over again with different people? Maybe it is time to self-analyze yourself on your repressed feelings to help bring them to the surface for balancing/ healing. So if you have internalized anger within yourself that may manifest into dis-eases in your body such as endometriosis or "cancer", then you will most likely encounter situations and people that have intense characteristics of anger that openly express them.

This is to remind you to allow your subconscious to free up the emotions that have been trapped within your body. Many cultures have taught people it is normal to repress their emotions and feelings and as such they grow up as adults with internalized emotions. We also serve as mirrors for others without consciously realizing it. We are both students and teachers in this life.

Mirroring is the ability to recognizing ourselves in other people. Everything and everyone as the potential to act as a mirror. When the understanding of what it truly means to see you reflected back and then there is no room for blame, there is no room for judgment and there is no room to feel like a victim of another person's actions or words. People are place on your cross paths for a particular reason. For example, for those that have been victims of bullying, the Universe will continue to bring about people and scenarios that often are intensified which each subsequent lesson, until we learn from the experience and become assertive.

The Sense of Hearing

The Sense of Hearing

Sound is all around us, but it is chaotic for the most part. A car, a truck, an ambulance passing by with somebody yelling or the TV to load are bombarding our nervous system on a daily basis and can increase your body and mind stress. But if optimally directed and isolated, every sound has a physiological effect. When you listen to a beautiful piece of music or inspirational words, a cascade of pleasure-producing chemicals courses through your body and it promotes mind-body wellness.

Music Therapy

Music has been present for many decades and sometime for only pleasure while it appears in the writings of the Greek philosophers Pythagoras, Aristotle, and Plato. Native Americans and other indigenous groups have used music to enhance traditional healing practices for centuries.

We link music to a mood. For example, we will play dance music to dance because it makes us want to move and be happy. Songs generate a series of emotions like happiness, sadness, being energized, or relaxed. Because music can affect a person's mood and emotional state, many holistic practitioners have now used this tool to help many health conditions.

A lot of health benefits are generated from a variety of music. Different types of music differ in the neurological response and stimulation. For example, classical music will have a more soothing, relaxing and comforting response. Many disorders respond very well to music like the autistic spectrum disorder for example. Applying music in a teaching scenario helps teach verbal and nonverbal communication skills. This in turn will help promote normal developmental processes. In depressed adult women, music therapy may reduce their heart rate, respiratory rate, blood pressure, and depressive mood.

Take an agitated baby for example, they respond very well to soothing music to calm them and make them feel secured and loved. Pre-term newborns exposed to music may have increased feeding rates, reduced days to discharge, increased weight gain, and increased tolerance of stimulation. They may also have reduced heart rates and a deeper sleep after therapy.

Jonathan Goldman, sound healer for over 30 years, and Gregg Braden has discovered a series of sound which can bring harmony and heal ourselves and the planet. Their CD is called Divine Name. They have found that the right music can serve as a vehicle for accessing our deepest emotions, bypassing the thinking mind and resonating directly with the heart.

Sound Therapy

It is interesting to experience all the different modality to be used to obtain a change in the brain and have a positive healing experience at all levels of our being. Since all modality intercommunicates with each other at one point, Sound Therapy is a unique listening system that utilizes new technology to help balance the brain waves.

Some are using special recorded program of high filter fractal sounds for rehabilitation of the ear and to stimulate the brain. Others use it to reach a deep meditational state which activates specific sections of the brain to experience happiness. Other uses instruments like tuning forks to emit harmonics and frequencies to work at an atomic and molecular level to restore balance. Some use computer programs with sound emission to record and reprogram the brain frequencies.

The brain will be activated at different areas and stages dependent on the frequencies generated or listened to. High frequencies for example can increase blood flow which increases the electrical activity of the brain. The brain functionality is also improved in presence of high frequencies. The sound "shh, shh" whispered in the ear of a crying baby has that effect. It will increase blood flow and sooths the baby. More benefits have been observed like increased energy, reduced fatigue with improved focus and creativity, a reduction in the need for sleep, and an almost permanent state of peace and relaxation.

Dr. Tomatis offers Sound Therapy Mini MX2 which is a headphone required to listen to specific frequencies or music (www.soundtherapyinternational.com/). Others in the field also use music like Monroe Institutes and the Hemi-Sync CDs (www.monroeinstitute.org) and Brain Sync brainwaves technology (www.brainsync.com).

Chakras and Tuning Forks

It is just like tuning a guitar or a piano, to achieve optimal balance. Tuning forks hold a single harmonic and frequency that can affect the biochemistry and the nervous system, muscles, organ to its harmonic balance. These harmonics cannot all be produced by instruments or in a single song or tape without the tuning fork. Since sound frequencies travels through the walls and body, it will affect any part of our body, helping to recalibrate and rebalance your body. (Dr. Stéphane uses: www.beatpeace.net/forks.htm)

<u>Why are so Many People Using Tuning Forks?</u>

- Provides instantaneous, deep state of relaxation
- Enhances immune system
- Improves mental clarity and brain functioning
- Integrates left and right brain patterns
- Increases your level of physical energy and mental concentration
- Removes emotional blockages
- Relieves stress by drawing your body into a centered space
- Increases healthy blood flow
- Develops and refines your sonic abilities
- Brings your nervous system into balance
- Clears and balances the chakras
- Enhances massage, acupressure, dream work and meditation

Sounds can have multiple effects and release emotional entrapment. They will affect the conscious and unconscious level. According to many practitioners, it will balance the physical and emotional responses.

It has also energetic properties when tired or helps one relax when wired-up. You probably had experienced it with your favorite music and just dancing on it for no known reason. It also has an ability to lift our spirits in times of sadness or depression and grief.

Each cell and atom of our body works on a frequency and a vibrational level to maintain its correct anatomical position. This is required to achieve optimal health. As soon as stresses appear within your energy or frequencies or it goes distorted, your health because imbalanced. The harmonics of sound carry the frequency to allow the body to self-correct. Vibrational therapy has long been used by NASA to increase bone density in astronauts to counteract osteoporosis in gravity-free outer space.

Chakras

According to the Energy Medicine principles, we have 7 spirals of energies that take the universal energy, energies surrounding us, into our body to utilize it and heal. These energy centers have been documented for thousands of years. These wheels of energy portal are called Chakras.

The chakra's healing potential and functionality can influence the state of our physiology and our emotions. When blockage arrives into our chakra systems, usually negative sensations or emotions are manifested into our physical body. It will depend on the chakra influenced. Chakras are extremely susceptible to how we think and feel.

Since the chakra systems are in place to deal with the surrounding energies and it may be too open or closed, this will affect our daily life. When these changes in our chakra system occur during childhood and are not fully resolved, it may force us to be something we are not. When we repress emotions and we do not acknowledge them, it gets stuffed and will affect negatively our chakra system. Understanding the relationships between our chakras and our physical bodies can help us to lead balanced, happier and more harmonious lives.

Deepak Chopra MD explained that each chakra has a specific vibration or primordial sound that we can repeat to heal any energy that may be congested in that region. It is like the sound of Reiki energy. The following is a list of the energy centers and their corresponding vibrational sounds that can promote self-healing when repeated as daily exercises:

- (1st) Base of Spine: LAM
- (2nd) Reproductive Area: VAM
- (3rd) Solar Plexus: RAM
- (4th) Heart: YAM
- (5th) Throat: HAM
- (6th) Forehead: SHAM
- (7th) Crown: AUM

When chakra healing is done, it is best to start with the first chakra and heal your way up to seven. When you master this healing process, you will be attuning to your body and do the appropriate exercise depending on the chakra involved. Make sure to focus your attention to the area of the chakra and making the sound mentioned above the LAM/VAM/RAM/YAM/HAM/SHAM/AUM at least seven times. It is important to feel the sound vibrating at the area of the chakra so you need to sustain the sound for several second and allow the vibrations to be felt.

Then, afterwards, complete another variation of sound therapy by repeating the following vowel sounds using Jonathan's Goldman's Divine Name technique that brings healing to you and the planet. Jonathan has 30 years of experience in the field of sound therapy. Continue the exercises below using visualization while making these vowel sounds.

First Chakra:
It is situated at the base of the spine and comes through in the front of the body as a spiral or a wheel.

The intention of the visualization during the chakra meditation clearing is to visualize the sound resonating at the base of the spine. Now speak the word "UH" (as in the word huh), seven times.

Second Chakra:
It is situated 2 inches below the belly button (navel.)

The intention of the visualization during the chakra meditation clearing is to visualize the sound resonating at that area. Now speak the word "OOO" (as in the word you), seven times.

Third Chakra:
It is located seven inches above the belly button.

The intention of the visualization during the chakra meditation clearing is to visualize the sound resonating at that area. Now speak the word "OH" (as in the word go), seven times.

Fourth Chakra:
It is situated at the center of the chest.

The intention of the visualization during the chakra meditation clearing is to visualize the sound resonating at that area. Now speak the word "AH" (as in the word ma), seven times.

Fifth Chakra:
It is situated at the throat.

The intention of the visualization during the chakra meditation clearing is to visualize the sound resonating at that area. Now speak the word "EYE" (as in the word my), seven times.

Sixth Chakra:
It is situated on the forehead between the eye and slightly above them.

The intention of the visualization during the chakra meditation clearing is to visualize the sound resonating at that area. Now speak the word "AYE" (as in the word may), seven times.

Seventh Chakra:

It is situated on top of head.

The intention of the visualization during the chakra meditation clearing is to visualize the sound resonating at that area. Now speak the word "EEE" (as in the word me), seven times.

The Sense of Taste

The Sense of Taste

Since Chinese Herbs and Ayurveda are covered in-depth in separate chapters, this section will focus on the taste receptors that promote healing for these two modalities. Each of the tastes has a unique effect on our mind-body physiology and provides the flavor that makes eating a pleasure. If you include the six tastes in a meal, you will get the nutrients you need and will feel completely satisfied and energized. If one or more of the tastes are missing from a meal, however, you may feel full but unsatisfied.

Ayurveda

According to Dr. Deepak Chopra taste is the second to water in terms of importance. Rasa is the immediate taste on the tongue, the one we remember, and the immediate experience of how that particular taste influences the body. Ayurveda categorizes food into six tastes: sweet, sour, salty, pungent, bitter, and astringent.

The 3 Dosha Types

Doshas are the energies that make up every individual, which perform different physiological functions in the body. Each person has all three Doshas, but usually one or two dominate:

- Vata Dosha: Energy that controls bodily functions associated with motion, including blood circulation, breathing, blinking, and your heartbeat.
  - Sweet berries, fruits, small beans, rice, and all nuts and dairy products are good choices for Vata types.
  In balance: There is creativity and vitality.
  Out of balance: Can produce fear and anxiety.

- Pitta Dosha: Energy that controls the body's metabolic systems, including digestion, absorption, nutrition, and your body's temperature.
  - Choose fresh vegetables and fruits that are watery and sweet, especially cherries, mangoes, cucumbers, water melon, and avocado. Have lots of salads with dark greens such as arugula, dandelions, and kale. Avoid spicy and fried foods.
  In balance: Leads to contentment and intelligence.
  Out of balance: Can cause ulcers and anger.

- Kapha Dosha: Energy that controls growth in the body. It supplies water to all body parts, moisturizes the skin, and maintains the immune system.
  - Tea with dried ginger and lemon is a great pick-me-up for Kaphas. Avoid heavy oily and processed sugars, which are detrimental to Kaphas. Use lots of spices such as black pepper, ginger, cumin, chili and lots of bitter dark greens.
  In balance: Expressed as love and forgiveness.
  Out of balance: Can lead to insecurity and envy.

The Six Rasas

- <u>Sweet tastes decreases vata and pitta, increases kapha</u>

  Of all the six tastes, sweet is the most grounding and nourishing.

  Foods: wheat, rice, maple syrup, brown rice syrup, agave nectar, dates, licorice root, and slippery elm bark.

- <u>Salty tastes decreases vata, increases pitta and kapha</u>

  Salt stimulates digestion, helps maintain proper electrolyte balance, softens tissues, and has a mildly laxative effect when taken in moderation.

  Foods: Sea vegetables, salt, tamari, black olives, and processed foods

- <u>Sour tastes decreases vata, increases pitta and kapha</u>

  Sour improves appetite, digestion, and elimination

  Foods: Lemons, ume plum, amla berry (sour Indian gooseberry), vinegars, pickled and fermented foods.

- <u>Pungent tastes increases vata and pitta, decreases kapha</u>

  Pungent taste improves appetite, clears sinuses, stimulates blood circulation, and motivates the senses.

  Foods: Fresh ginger, hot peppers, onions, garlic, mustard, and hot spices

- <u>Bitter tastes increases vata, decreases pitta and kapha</u>

  Of the six tastes, bitter is the coolest and lightest.
  Over intake of bitterness can lead to increase in coldness and depression

  Foods: Dandelion root, turmeric, and fenugreek

- <u>Astringent tastes increases vata, decreases pitta and kapha</u>

  Many beans and legumes are astringent in nature thus aggravate the vata dosha.

  Foods: Green grapes, unripe bananas, cranberries, pomegranates, alfalfa sprouts, green beans, and okra

Chinese Herbal

Herb and foods are categorizing in traditional Chinese medicine according to the five tastes i.e. flavors: spicy, salty, bitter, sour and sweet. These tastes also represent the five Chinese medicine elements: Metal, fire, water, wood, earth. Taste is an important consideration when choosing the right medicinal herb to treat a given condition, because the taste of an herb plays an important role in its therapeutic action.

The Spicy Taste

The spicy taste, also referred to as pungent or acrid, corresponds to the metal element. It deals with the lungs and large intestine. It is energetically warm or hot, has a dispersing action. It stimulates digestion, and promotes the circulation of blood and Qi (vital energy.) Spicy herbs are warming to the body, open the pores, stimulate sweating and help to clear congestion. Warming diaphoretics are a class of herbs that are often spicy or pungent, and are used to induce sweating at the onset of colds and flu. Some examples of spicy herbs are black pepper, cayenne, ginger, garlic and prickly ash.

The Salty Taste

The salty taste corresponds to the water element. It deals with the kidneys, adrenal glands and urinary bladder. The salty taste is energetically cold and has a moistening and softening action. Salty herbs or foods may be used to treat conditions including swollen lymph nodes, cysts and lumps, and constipation. It also helps adrenal fatigue and adrenal stress. Excess of salt in the diet can cause fluid imbalances, water retention and elevated blood pressure. All types of seaweed are salty, and some herbs with a high mineral content, such as nettles and plantain, are considered to be salty.

The Sour Taste

The sour taste corresponds to the wood element. It deals with the liver and gall bladder. Energetically, sour is cool and dry, and has an astringent action, which dries and tightens tissues. Sour herbs may be used to prevent excessive fluid loss through perspiration, frequent urination or diarrhea. Some examples of sour herbs include blackberries, raspberries, orange peel, lemons, and schisandra berries.

The Bitter Taste

The bitter taste corresponds to the fire element. It deals with the heart and small intestine. The bitter taste has a dry and cool energy, and descending, detoxifying and anti-inflammatory actions. Goldenseal and Oregon grape root are bitter. The production of bile is stimulated via this taste. Eating bitters before a meal aids digestion. Since they have a drying action, bitter herbs can be used to treat conditions of excess dampness such as diarrhea and boils or abscesses of the skin. More examples of bitter herbs include dandelion root, gentian, and artichoke leaf.

The Sweet Taste

The sweet taste corresponds to the earth element. It deals with the digesting organs of the stomach and spleen (spleen is part of the digestive system according to Chinese Medicine.) Sweet taste is categorized as empty or full. Empty sweets are composed of simple sugars and have no nutritional value. They cause the blood sugar to rise rapidly and then drop. Full sweets, on the other hand, consist of complex carbohydrates that have a strengthening and nourishing action, and help to build and tonify the stomach and spleen. Nourishing sweet herbs include cinnamon, jujube dates, ginseng, licorice and marshmallow.

The Sense of Smell

The Sense of Smell

Smell is one of the most primitive of the five senses. It connects with our memories, emotions and instincts. The smell molecule goes through our nervous system. Smell is known to be one of the biggest influences of the brain. The molecules go to the hypothalamus which is the master controller of our hormones and is linked to our emotions. This is one of the reasons why so often something that we smell will trigger a memory or remind us of something or someone.

Here are six scents that aid boosting your digestive productivity and moods. Apply under your feet, smell or apply on your heart for the emotion, on your neck for your mental stress and on your belly for digestive issue:

- Lemon

  Lemon scent promotes concentration. It has calming and clarifying properties that are helpful when feelings of anger, anxiety or run down are predominant. Lemon also has antiviral and antibacterial properties and can help fight sore throats and colds by boosting the body's immune system and improving circulation.

- Lavender

  Lavender has calming properties that help control emotional stress. Lavender has a soothing effect on nerves and can relieve nervous tension and depression as well as treat headaches and migraines.

- Jasmine

  Jasmine is also used to calm nerves, but this oil is also commonly used as an antidepressant because of its uplifting capabilities that produce a feeling of confidence, optimism and revitalized energy.

- Rosemary

  In addition to improving memory retention, rosemary has stimulating properties that fight physical exhaustion, headaches and mental fatigue. Rosemary can also be used topically to relieve muscular aches and pains.

- Cinnamon

  The stimulating properties in cinnamon can help fight mental fatigue and improve concentration and focus.

- Peppermint

  Try peppermint when you brainstorm. An energy booster, this scent invigorates the mind, promotes concentration and stimulates clear thinking.

Additionally, here are the average frequencies of some of the therapeutic grade essential oils that have been measured by Bruce Tainio:

- Rose   320 MHz
- Lavender   118 MHz
- Myrrh   105 MHz
- Blue Chamomile   105 MHz
- Juniper   98 MHz
- Aloes/Sandalwood   96 MHz
- Angelica   85 MHz
- Peppermint   78 MHz
- Galbanum   56 MHz
- Basil   52 MHz

It's Not the Smell but the Breathe of Life (Chi-Lel Qigong)

Everyone is born with their chi potential. Everyone has the potential to use chi for many purposes. Once a person is trained how to use their chi energy, he or she then can use chi for martial arts, dancing, weight lifting and of course, medical, self-healing.

Chi-Lel Qigong was developed by Dr. Pang Ming and is based on the 5,000 years old concept of Qigong and integrated modern medical knowledge, known as medical Qigong. Chi-Lel consists of four principles:

Strong Belief (affirmation):
"A belief that all ailments, including one's own, can be healed." Healing comes from within. We have to regain trust in our innate ability to heal.

Relaxation:
Chi-Lel Qigong not only emphasizes relaxing the physical body but also relaxing the mind. Letting go not only the stress, but also what holds us back.

Group dynamic:
The teacher verbally synchronizes the thinking of the group to enhance the healing effects.

Practice:
Students learn easy-to-follow Chi-Lel Qigong movements and practice them over and over again.

Evidence demonstrates that Qigong may be an effective adjunct in the treatment of many illnesses and some effects are:
- When the mind is at peace, the whole universe seems at peace. It will ease the decision making
- Deeper, more restorative sleep.
- Increased energy, including sexual vitality and fertility. People who practice Qigong have more energy; it can reverse energy and restore youthfulness.

- Circulation improves, and the body generates more internal warmth when it is cold especially for people with cold hands and feet.
- According to Chinese medicine, as your Qigong improves, your body eliminates toxins, and the skin becomes clear.
- Practicing moderate Qigong exercises creates an optimistic and joyous disposition. Creating a happier life.
- Improves digestion and metabolism and hair and nails grow more quickly.
- Normalize physiological function, for example, breathing rate, heart rate, blood pressure, hormone levels, and states of chronic inflammation or depletion.
- The eyes also appear bright because the spirit and soul are luminous and the heart is open.
- Intuition and creativity generate each other and come from the same source, a body-mind balanced

9

Stress-Less: Living

The Big Picture of Stress

If one goes back in time we would be amazed at how technology has made our lives more efficient as in the cases of our transportation system or the delivery of mail with today's instantaneous formats in Emails. However, one must question, is technology truly easing our lives or complicating our stresses? Our ancestors did not have any gadgets or technology to help them with their daily life, yet, they must have lived a more peaceful and relaxed lifestyle, free of all the multitasking and appear to have less stressors in life.

Humans from generation to generation have felt stress and this is not a new concept. As we advance into the new millennium, stress appears to have grown exponentially. Some people are even terming it as the new dis-ease of this century. In 2012, the Journal of Applied Psychology said that stress has gone up around 20% over the last 25 years. A lot is due to the modern life and the increase scheduled hassles, deadline frustrations and demands our world has become familiarized to.

Just in 2010, the US healthcare has spent more than $1.95 trillion for chronic illnesses that are known to be preventable by changing the stress level from our daily lifestyle. This expensed amount was 75% of the total healthcare budget. According to Bloomberg's, Most-Stressed Out Countries ratings, some of the top nations made the list: India ranked 14, Russia ranked 25, China ranked 29, South Korea ranked 37, United States ranked 54, United Kingdom ranked 56, and Japan ranked 60. Ironically, the majority of the high-tech jobs have migrated to India but the staggering statistics reveal it to the one of the highest stressed out nations.

Many people consider anxiety and stress to be synonyms. However, there is a difference. Often times anger and frustration go hand in hand with stress; while, worry and uneasiness are linked to anxiety. Stimulants like caffeine and cigarettes create the physical sense of stress artificially by constricting blood vessels and raising the heartbeat. The need of sleep aides like alcohol or medication are also signals that one is stressed out.

Sufferers may also have a high incidence of depression and physical ailments, including migraines, high blood pressure, heart dis-ease, digestive disorders and chronic pain. People who feel they are under a lot of stresses have a tendency of neglecting to take care of themselves which creates unhealthy lifestyle habits. In contrary, if one has too little stress it might cause withdrawal and lack of ambition. This can also lead to depression.

The National Institute of Mental Health estimated that stress disorders affect about 40 million American adults, which equates to about 18% of the population per year. Consequently, it is estimated that only one third seek treatment for it while the other two-thirds are not even aware of this debilitating condition. When we allow stress to totally consume us, it can change our DNA. In other words, the way we are made up (our biology) changes and may impact the genetics of future generations. (See Epigenetic chapter for further details.) For the purpose of this chapter, we will use the word "stress" as the general catch-all phrase to incorporate all types of stressors, inclusive of symptomatic anxiety.

Defining Stress

Stress is a normal physical response to events that make you feel threatened or upset your balance in life. When you sense danger, whether it is real or imagined, the body's defenses kick into high gear in a rapid, automatic process known as the "fight or flight or freeze" reaction, or we will call it the stress response.

The stress response is the body's way of protecting you and helps you to stay focused, energetic, and alert. In emergency situations, stress can give the extra strength to defend you and meet challenges. However, the worst case scenario is when stress sneaks up on us and we get so use to it that it becomes a part of our daily lifestyle, or worst yet our cortisol levels have become so tolerant that we are immune to them and supplement our lifestyle with even more stressful habits. That is when it creates damage and affects us. It takes a heavy toll on your body until you receive big signals to slow down your pace, such as any dis-ease and/or "cancer" cells invading your body.

When you perceive a threat, your nervous system responds by releasing a flood of stress hormones, including adrenaline and cortisol. Your heart pounds faster, muscles tighten, blood pressure rises, breath quickens, and some or all of your senses become sharper. These physical changes increase your strength and stamina and unfortunately some people thrive on this "feel-good" feeling and turn to artificial stimulants such as drugs to obtain similar side effects. Stress overload will present itself with pretty much anything and affect the intellect, body and behavior.

Everyone experiences stress differently. When ignored, overwhelming stress will cause numerous health concerns. Your quality of life, moods, productivity and relationships may all decline. A recent study, conducted by Dr. Robert Sapolsky compared animals in their natural environment (wild) versus moving them to a structured setting (captivity.) He noted that animals in the wild are able to ward off dis-eases like the flu and anthrax with their innate immunity; however, these same animals left in the captivity environment often became ill or worse yet had premature deaths from far simpler dis-eases due to the stressors of being in captivity.

The author paraphrases: "Social isolation can be as deadly as smoking, obesity, hypertension, or lack of exercise. And regardless of gender, age, or ethnicity, poverty is the most determinant of human dis-ease." Illness is not just from pathogens, but is also from harmful social surroundings. A toxic environment can lead to negative emotions that can suppress the immune system and release repressed emotional toxins in the body.

Stress-Tolerance Measurement

We all react to situations differently and are created differently with tolerance levels. Our genes and experiences are what made who we are today. These factors affect our ability to handle stress. Some people are able to let stress roll off their back like water on a duck, while some people fly off the handle at the littlest sign that something negative is going to happen. Some people thrive in high-stress situations while it completely wears another person out.

Your stress level may be influenced by:

- Your Support Network

  If you don't have a great support system of friends and family, you may have a higher chance of suffering from more stress. It is important to have people in your life that you can trust to "dump" on when you need to.

- Your Sense of Control

  The more self-esteem and self-confidence you have, the better you will be able to weather the hard times in life. If you let things feel like they are spinning out of control, you will have a lower tolerance for stress.

- Your Attitude and Outlook

  Are you a pessimist or an optimist? People who look for the positives in life are often better able to handle stress. They know that change is inevitable, look forward to a challenge and often have a sense of humor.

- Your Ability to Deal with your Emotions

  It is important to keep your emotions in checks. Do you often have a feeling of rage or anger? If you are not able to calm yourself down, you will be more susceptible to stress. Being able to balance your emotions can be learned at an early age and is a lifelong skill.

- <u>Your Knowledge and Preparation</u>

  If you know that a stressful situation is about to occur, then it is very important to be as prepared as possible. The more knowledge you have about it, the easier it will be to deal with it. For example, if you know you have to have surgery, be prepared for what you will be facing after the operation. This will make recovery less traumatic.

Technology and Stress

It has been proven that the lights from televisions, computer screens, and many other electronic devices are changing melatonin production. This means that we are not getting the quality of sleep that our bodies need. This may eventually lead to increase stress levels or depression.

Today, it is very "easy" to get caught up with electronic devices. We often find ourselves saying, "I will get off the computer/tablet after I lose my next life on this game," or "I will only check 5 more emails." How much time is really spent from our daily lives on instant messaging, text messaging or glance thru social media profiles? These habits take our attention away from where it is truly needed, but would a stroll in nature or empowerment of your mind in a good book be a better means of decompressing. Yes, we need a break every once in a while, but how often do we take more time than necessary? Then we are stressed for time to meet our deadlines or to accommodate to others' request and it often creates mental overload.

Research has found that those people who are constantly on their computer, tablet or phone are at a higher risk for developing stress and depression. Some people feel they always have to be "on call" to respond to the text messages and answer phone calls. They often feel like they are never free and have a hard time separating work life from home life. The inability to relax and get away from stress can lead to mental health issues later in life and a higher level of dissatisfaction overall.

Do you still watch the news? There doesn't seem to be many positive stories broadcasted anymore. Today we see stories on violence, "terrorism" and natural disasters. Not only can these stories cause us stress, but they often cause stress to our children. Children are not able to separate what happened on the other side of the world from their current environment. They project these awful events onto their family and friends and become anxious on a daily basis for their loved one's safety. They are fearful that something bad will happen to someone close in their life, especially highly sensitive or empathetic children. These fears are not only based on the news, but can also be coming from movies, books and video games.

Why Do Negative Feelings Bring About Stress?

If you experience negative emotions (stress, worry, frustration, depression, shame, guilt, Etc.) it can manifest itself into physical illness. Sometimes it is hard enough to deal with our own emotions. It is also hard at times helping our children deal with their negative emotions; however, if left suppressed in the body for a lengthy duration, it becomes blockages that drain our life force energy.

Parents often try to protect our children from negative experiences in life. However, children need to learn how to deal with stress and other people. Emotional intelligence is defined as the ability to understand, and manage our emotions and behavior. Studies have shown that kids need to build their emotional intelligence to successfully manage stress.

Some common sources of how children learn to suppress their emotions include:

- Parents often try the "fix-it" approach. They don't want to see their child in pain, so they try to fix-it themselves. This is harmful to the child because it is teaching an unhealthy coping behavior. It is teaching that if you are unhappy, simply reward yourself with something else to avoid facing the real issue.
- Parents often tell the child to "just get over it" instead of teaching them how to properly deal with negative emotions. As children grow, this "just get over it" mentality may cause children to see negative feelings as being weak or unacceptable. The more they use this habit the more they will bury their true feelings. They may get to a point that they see negative emotions as a normal part of life.
- Parents often compare situations with other people. They tell the children other people have worse scenarios than they do. This will lead to an association that their feelings are not as important in the bigger scheme of life. In some situations, it is important to put others before us, but not all the time. Parents must not belittle children's emotions and make them feel ungrateful.
- The other side of not being able to properly empathize with your child is the feeling of "my problems are bigger than yours." Children are often made to feel insignificant when this is communicated. Children who continuously feel this way will learn to internalize negative emotions.

Work Place Stressors

A study by the American Psychological Association in 2009 showed that 69% of employees feel that work creates the majority of their stress and 41% say they feel stressed out during the day. Job related stress costs the U.S. about $300 billion a year in indirect costs which are associated with: sick days, hiring new employees, and slower productivity. Seventy-five percent of people report their jobs as being stressful. Interestingly enough, people in developing countries report having less stress at work than in developed countries. According to research, the most stressful workplace is amongst British employers.

Robert Ostermann reported that factory workers face stress in dealing with dangerous, heavy equipment. Office workers tend to feel more stressed dealing with people (rumors and office politics.) The lack of supervision and tension between co-workers are also causes of major stressors. Many times the demands at work carry over to our home life. This may cause stress to be brought into the home life. The U.S. Department of Labor conducted a recent survey. It reported that 10% of workers who were married or had children under the age of 18 in their households experienced work-family conflict. Part of this conflict may be the fact that people work more hours a week today than they did 25 years ago.

When we graduated from high school, we probably thought our days of being traumatized/terrorized were over. How wrong we were! More than a million people report that they are victims of bullying at the work place. Talk about stress! Violence in the workplace contributes to $55 million in missed time across the US nation. Assertiveness is a crucial skill to have. Once one uses assertiveness and enhances their communication skills, stress may decrease exponentially. Speaking your needs in positive ways in the work place is crucial and may be the only venue to gain respect from bullies.

Listen to your body! It will let you know when you are stressed! Studies from around the world have shown that work related stress may lead to hypertension and high blood pressure. Heart dis-ease and sometimes "tumors" can be linked back to the job or its overall stressful environment.

Spiritual (Soul) Stressors aka Mid-Life Crisis

Spiritual stressors make a person face change. They can improve a person's character, change how one observes things in life and in general will guide a person to become a nicer person for themselves and to others. Often this happens to associate with age which gives it the connotation of being "mid-life"; however, it is most attributable to gaining enough stressors in life where the tolerance level reaches its maximum overload, but it happens to occur in conjunction with one's mid-point in life. However, in truth it has nothing to do with the chronological age and can occur during any duration of the lifespan.

If a person is constantly living in stress, it can deteriorate the spirit and reduce motivation. One may seem to be more compulsive or more fearful. They may fall into procrastination, and utilize drugs or alcohol as coping mechanisms. Although we know that many things in our life are unpredictable, we should still try to create our own reality with a positive outlook.

Stress causes us to think about the consequences of our behavior instead of what we desire out of life. The law of attraction truly works if you apply the principles correctly. If you read the Secret, by attracting what you think about most of the time with the right intentions, it often manifest into your daily life. The caveat is that your mind does not distinguish between positives and negatives. This means that whatever you say "no" to, you are also attracting into your lifestyle and whatever you say "yes" to, you are attracting into your experience. And whatever you focus on will come to be in the physical dimension even if it is a negative focus because your mind thought about it.

Our current society tells us that it is often better to repress some emotions rather than express them. Unexpressed emotions can affect us negatively. It is important that we express our emotions even if it means that we have to punch a pillow, write down our emotions in a journal, paint, draw, walk, or cry ourselves to sleep. At least the emotion does not remain trapped in your body.

Many of us think that it is selfish to say "no" when we are asked to do something, even though we know that it will cause stress in our life. This means that we have our priorities backwards! Too many people have too much authority over our decision making process and influence. In other words our self-love is based on our reactions by others. Saying "yes" to everything that is asked of us causes people way too much stress and is not a realistic outlook for life. This produces more anxiety because we feel helpless and a lack of controlling.

Instead of demanding so much of yourself on a daily basis, you need to laugh more at life's challenges. Laughter is the best medicine. Have you ever noticed that laughter is infectious? Have you ever noticed that you felt closer to people after you have laughed with them? A sense of humor makes you feel like you have more hope. It lowers stress and increases the immune system. Smile more and see how much more you laugh.

School Stressors

Have you ever heard the saying that too much work and too little play can make you a dull person? It is actually proven to be true, especially in students. Many colleges are discovering that students are more depressed, and are more anxious. The demands of students are causing them to be more anxious and feel a need for attaining perfection. In other words, today's college students are feeling more stressed than those students ten years ago.

Stressors for Preschoolers

Remember that each person responds to stress differently. However there is a growing trend that students feel stressed at younger ages these days. Think about a preschooler that has been home with a parent their entire life. They may be feeling separation anxiety when they start school for the first time. They can handle stress better when they have a balanced diet and adequate time for play, sleep and relaxation. A predicable schedule is also vital, especially with highly sensitive and empathetic children.

Children can start to learn how to de-stress at a young age. It is important to teach them stress-reducing exercises. Children learn best by watching and by doing. Complete the following exercises together. Pretend that you are blowing up balloons inside your stomach and blow the air back out of your mouth. Blow bubbles to teach deep breathing. This technique is often used in hospitals during treatments to ensure that the proper oxygen level circulates throughout the body.

Touching children is also another way to help children cope with stress. Children know that they have someone that can help them with their problems when they know their relationship is secure. Being able to play during unstructured time is also extremely important. This play time helps children release stress. It is suggested that children ages 1-5 should experience at least two hours of unstructured daily playtime. Play time in the bathtub is particularly soothing to children with hyper-sensitivities.

Allowing children to feel like they are in control is also helpful. A very small choice, such as what color shirt to wear, can go a long way. Little choices such as that help them to have a sense of control in life. Later on, they will be able to make have healthier options when faced with stressful situations.

Common Sources of Preschool Stressors

- being hurried in the morning
- difficulties with friends

- disagreements with siblings
- frequent changes of caregivers
- have to deal with new situations without preparation
- new experiences (new babysitter or beginning school)
- separation from loved ones
- the absence of a security from the home environment (parental role models)
- too many demands
- transitions from place to place or activity to activity

When a child feels stress, it will show in their behavior. Have you ever experienced a child having a temper tantrum? The tantrum is in response to stress. The stress could be as simple as being tired, hungry, bored or frustrated. Other signs of stress could be seen thru the symptoms of:

- becoming withdrawn or listless
- going back to less mature behavior
- increased behavior problems, such as biting, kicking, poor listening, acting out, impulsiveness
- increased dependency or clinginess
- increased whining, crying, fighting
- inflicting pain
- intensification of nail biting, hair twisting, thumb sucking
- overreacting to minor problems, e.g., yelling, crying, melt-down
- sadness, panic, anger, anxiety
- trouble eating and relaxing
- unusual sleep patterns or nightmares
- unusually low energy, or, very high levels of energy or restlessness

Stressors for Older Children

It is healthy for children to experience a normal dose of emotions so they learn how to deal with stress. It is proven that when people talk about their feelings, the urge of acting out is decreased. When you take the time to talk to a child, he/she feels that you care about them and a deeper association is made.

When you notice that your child is not acting like (s)he usually does, but does not want to talk, go do something together. Going for a walk, playing a game, baking or watching a movie together will strengthen your bond. It will also show them ways to cheer themselves up.

Within the USA, the government thought they were doing a great thing when they wrote the "No Child Left Behind" policy. However, these tests created more stress for the children and teachers. Many students do not perform well on these standardized tests because they are afraid of making mistakes and allocation of many resources have been reduced or ceased altogether to ensure that rote memorization occurs in learning rather than the experiential experience of developing both hemispheres of the brain.

Do you feel that your child is jumping from one activity to another? Everybody needs to have a little quiet time here and there. This constant running from activities creates a lot of stresses, even though it may be enjoyable. The pressure to fit in to these activities or cliques may lead to stress in children as well.

Unhealthy Coping Mechanisms for School Stressors

- When children try to escape stress through means of alcohol, drugs, promiscuity, frequent illnesses, sleep, overeating, or starving themselves; a permanent withdrawal can occur.
- Gifted students link being successful with achievement. When failure occurs, their self-esteem is threatened. Often times when children set their goals too high and fail; their self-esteem can be crushed and it leads to a lack of motivations to attempt things in the future or take risks.
- Aiming too low is another issue. This reduces stress by eliminating intense pressure or possible feelings of failure. Selecting less rigorous courses, or dropping out of school rather than bringing home poor grades allows students to avoid feelings of failure in the short run.
- Children are often expected to go from activity to activity on a daily basis. Once they are done with school, it's off to practice, extra lessons or church activities. While these can be important, it is crucial that students and parents understand that they need time to just "chill" (decompress) as well.

Adolescents and Stress

Each year, it seems that there is more and more things expected of our teens, which increases the level of stress. An average of 31% of teens say they felt stress has increased in the past year and 34% are predicting it will continue to rise again within the next year. This stress is from the pressure to perform well in school, standardized testing, sports, peer pressures and other activities.

Sometimes students, who are beginning to feel stressed out, don't say anything. They simply allow the stress to just build and build. If this goes untreated for a long period, the teen may develop anxiety in the future. This anxiety can present itself in depression, substance abuse, promiscuity, decrease in overall interests, as well as missed opportunities in career and relationships. It doesn't just stop there. Psychiatric disorders can also stem from untreated stress. Oppositional defiant disorder, ADHD/ADD, and irritability are some of the issues related to being over stressed.

Home Stressors

Major changes may be challenging for some adolescence as well. Planning and preparing can help ease some of these changes, while others happen so abruptly, that they often times do not have time to react. Some of these situations include moving, death of a loved one, divorce or the birth of a new sibling. Some of these changes can turn a child's world upside down. They may lose their sense of security, feel anxious, stressed or feel that their home life is chaotic and helpless.

Children watch their parents to see how they react to situations. If parents deal with stress in healthy ways, then the child will most likely react that way as well. However, if the parent chooses unhealthy ways, those poor behaviors are also passed down. It may start very minor with the child acting out (especially if the parent(s) are loud and angry), but the behavior may escalate from there into abusive relationships if they believe this communication style is appropriate.

We are in a monkey see, monkey do situation. It is important, as parents that we behave in a positive way when confronted with stress. We need to schedule time for ourselves so we are better able to handle stress. If we have our fears, our children will. If we are positive, our child will be. Ask your children to describe your characteristics. Optimistically they will use words like calm, caring, willing to listen and fun to be around. If they do, hurray for you!!! However if they use words like busy, tense and stressed out, it may be time to look in the mirror and reassess your lifestyle. Is that how you want your children to live and learn to turn into?

When is the last time you have been at the park and saw a child fall? What is the first thing that child does? S/he looks at their mom or dad to see how they will react. If the parent is calm, the child will mirror that. However if the parent over reacts, then the children will get more worked up and will cry or feel anxious. Be a great example for your child. Take the time to sit and listen (yes that means putting electronics away) to them.

Too often children sink to a world of their own when they are confronted by stress. They will seek time alone in their rooms, drift off, or get sucked into video games. These actions are signs of stress related "depression." It is crucial to talk to your child to see what is going on in their life that is causing them to want to be alone.

Stress level can be increased by not only what is occurring within their life but also what the parents are saying, doing and what is happening in their lives. Parents should watch how they discuss stressful issues or conflict when their kids are near because children will pick up on their parents' anxieties and start to worry themselves.

Many military children experience relationship distress with friends, at school, with teacher and with their community. This is mainly due to their frequent moves from city to city or country to countries. This is also true of the scenario of when the parent returns home after being gone for a period of time. Some children also experience the trauma especially if the parent went to combat injury or illness, or of facing a parent's death. Recent research reveals an increase in military child maltreatment and neglect since the start of combat operations and deployments to Afghanistan and Iraq.

Perspectives of Dis-ease Due to Stress

How can we balance the good stress which energizes us or help us, described prior, and the stress that paralyzes us and makes us ill? Back in 1908, a Harvard psychologist found that moderate stress to the state of arousal will enhance performance in athletes, but only to a point. Sports athletes and coaches understand the benefit of relaxation prior to an event.

Small dosage of stress might provide you with the adrenaline and get things done quickly and easily. It might inspire you, under pressure, to do your best. The issue is the burnout or exhaustion when the flight-or-fight response is chronically impacting your mind and the body.

Psychologist Connie Lillas uses a driving analogy to describe the three most common ways people respond when they are overwhelmed by stress:

- <u>Foot on the Gas</u>: An angry, agitated, or "fight" stress response. You're heated, keyed up, overly emotional, and unable to sit still. **Also known as ADD/ADHD.**
- <u>Foot on the Brake</u>: A withdrawn, depressed, or "flight" stress response. You shut down, pull away, space out, and show very little energy or emotion. **Also known as Autism and Depression.**
- <u>Foot on Both</u>: A tense or "freeze" stress response. You become frozen under pressure and can't do anything. You look paralyzed, but under the surface you're extremely agitated. **Also known as Obesity** on one end and bulimia on the other end of the eating spectrum.

Stress and Depression (Empath and Hope)

Empathetic people already know where you are coming from by using their capacity to energetically merge with someone and feel everything they are feeling. Because most of them do not realize they are empathetic or possess this capacity. They often merge their own feelings with others (positive and negative) and get lost in that ocean of feelings, without realizing that it was attributable to someone else's pain.

If one has emotional scars and absorbs more negative emotion, their health might suffer and leave them hopeless, also known as depression. Others can block the absorption process and not take the other people's feelings within themselves. The majority of empathy is absorbed like a sponge. They will become stressed without noticing or realizing it. This will lead to depressing states since their innate positive emotions will be overridden. Interestingly enough these children may appear to be introverted because the over stimulation amongst crowds is too draining for them since the majority of people are at vibrational states that are below 200 (negative energies.)

For an empath, the energy of being around crowds might affect you; therefore, you should eat a high-protein diet or vegetables from the ground (to ground you) and try to not be at the focal center of groups that are negative which will limit the proximity of energy drainage. Being at the focal point can be an easy target for people who are emotional vampires, meaning who drains somebody of their energy. They tend to take the positive out of empaths and gives them fear and anger in return. Everybody experiences a person like this in their life who just "sucks out" the energy from you and you are left feeling lethargic or extremely depleted and unmotivated.

The absorption of these negative energies can also trigger panic attacks, depression, food cravings, sex and drug binges and a plethora of physical symptoms. According to Dr. Judith Orloff, empaths are notoriously misdiagnosed. Patient after patient has come to her labeled as "agoraphobic" or with "panic disorder," having received only minor effects from traditional treatments such as valium and behavior therapy. It is easier to stay happy by surrounding the empaths with love, compassion, happy and peaceful people. You will feel alive and rejuvenated when surrounded by positive like-minded people.

According to the journal of patient education and counseling, physician's empathy helps manage stress and pain for their patients. Another study by Michigan State University discovered truth and empathy are associated with a positive physician-patient relationship that changes the brain stressors and pain level. This study was one of the first to study physician and patients' relationship from a neurobiological point of view. It was concluded that the psycho-socio-behavior factors during a physician interaction will improve the overall patient symptoms and ultimately, affect their health.

Stress and ADD/ADHD (Gifted and Talented)

It is perceived that when a child is gifted s/he will accept more tasks and responsibilities like leadership in school activities, clubs or sports. The increase of activities will create a physical and emotional demand that often times increases the overall stress level. These gifted children have strong emotions to create positive meanings to their life experiences. It is imperative for these children to acknowledge their feelings and emotions up front to avoid any internalization/repression that may lead to stressors further manifesting into their physical bodies.

Because gifted children will have high expectations for achievement and put pressures on themselves to excel, it can lead to a very stressful life. The majority of them carry internalized fears of being mediocre. This is why they need intellectual stimulation. If it is too boring or monotonous, work or school becomes stressful or they focus their energy elsewhere which often results in them being misdiagnosed as having attention deficits. These children's minds are always operating at simultaneous processing speeds and as such they will look for more stimulating activities to help them feel alive and challenged.

For these children, to be bored might result in anger, resentment, or, in some cases, setting personal goals for achievement and success that significantly exceeds those of parents or the school standards. However, if this environment is not available for them, they simply shut down and assimilate into operating below sub-par standards.

This is especially detrimental when these children are inadvertently put in learning disabled classrooms, often times they simply lose the motivation to even perform. This often is why these children are misdiagnosed. School personnel may mislabel these children as "class clowns", "problematic" or worse "mediocre" children. Another side effect of these gifted children is that since they value independence and leadership, they can become lonely or rejected from their peers. It might be difficult to find a group who will not judge them nor reject them for their over achievement standards.

Gifted student will challenge themselves at all times to excel if given the proper environment to thrive. They utilize in-depth thinking processes to derive answers for challenges that are poised to them. This however might complicate the decision making process and lead many of these children to become paralyzed with indecision.

Furthermore, not every problem has one obviously correct answer. Thus, decision making may be a very stressful process for these children. It becomes more difficult when the expectations are unclear or unrealistic. Since gifted children have a pressure to excel, they may auto-sabotage themselves via self-doubt. This is also known as the imposter syndrome.

Then, there's the overly optimistic people with the so-called "ADHD/ADD" disorder that often has an insufficient sense of urgency to get things done. The best way to guide these people's thought processes is to stress the negative future consequences of not finishing and explaining that once the task is through, they will feel calmer and a sense of relief and accomplishment. These people often need to know there is a purpose for their focused energy and efforts.

There is another group of people who cannot get anything done without some level of stress. These are the individuals who subconsciously set life up to give them a thrill, by always being late, nearly missing a deadline, spending more than they should monetarily. These people intrauterine most likely were submerged in an environment full of cortisol, so their tolerance level and threshold for stress is above the norm so they are always looking to raise the bar.

Stress and Obesity (The Highly Sensitive Ones)

Highly sensitive children will feel stressed in an amplified fashion and react to it differently than your average person. They tend to absorb more environmental information than others. This process can be tiring. It is largely unconscious. This means these children are not aware of this process until their body gets the residual effects of the stress.

They not only absorb information but also feel people's energetic states (both the positive and negative dispositions.) These children often feel overwhelmed by all the stimulation and the over-sensory attributes that wear these people down on a daily basis. With the constant absorption, the person will be impacted. What the mind won't deal with, however, the body will. Engaging in relationships with negative people or situations can literally make highly sensitive souls sick or feeling depressed.

Highly sensitive children are often very creative which will provide a healthy release for all their feelings absorbed. As a parent, it is important to put an accent on a creative outlet to express all daily stressors into an activity like drawing, singing, dancing, and playing an instrument for example. They also need more rest and more quiet time in the forms of meditation. This time is to allow them to recharge their own energy and to relax both their mind and body.

Because highly sensitive children absorb all energy and feelings in from their surroundings, they are prone to multiple colds and flu or unusual physical reactions such as hives or rashes. As a subconscious defense, highly sensitive people may gain weight as a buffer. When thin, they are more vulnerable to negativity. Dr. Judith Orloff's book, Positive Energy explains the concept of obesity and how it relates to a padded protection for these children.

Stress and Autism (Child Genius)

The similarities between gifted and autistic children seem remarkable. A new study published in Intelligence conducted by Yale and Ohio University, discovered that both special skills have been associated with both types of children. The child geniuses (ranging from math to art prodigies) were given the Autism-Spectrum Quotient assessment and they had elevated scores of autistic traits. Additionally, half the child genius had a family member or close relative diagnosed with autism spectrum disorder.

One of the hallmarks in autistic children is the attention to detail. The gifted genius scored higher in this category. Additionally, working memory is the area of the brain that enables people to contain various pieces of information in their mind for a short time in an effort to perform a task and both autistic and child geniuses held comparable scores. The researchers believe it is why some autistic children are observed as having bursts of brilliant intelligence along with keen memory skills. Autistic characteristics appear to be the foundation for the child genius; however, if their brains are not further challenged, the critical period of development is stifled.

As an example of similarity, Kristine Barnett's book, The Spark: A Mother's Story of Nurturing Genius supports what the study had discovered. This was the case of Jacob Barnett, diagnosed with severe autism as a child and told he will never be able to read; Barnett is now 15 and one of the world's most promising physicists. His mom broke a bunch of rules: she didn't listen to therapists, took her son out of special education, and let him simply think about the world with his own perspective. She explains her journey and how it made a big impact in her son's life instead of following the cookie cutter diagnostic recommendations.

Mothers with autistic children spend extra time to calm their child during stressful events. They spend on average an extra two hours more each day. Two studies published in the Journal of Autism and Developmental Disorders found that a hormone associated with stress amongst autistic children was extremely low and was consistent with people that had experienced chronic stressors such as soldiers in combat (post-traumatic stress disorder.)

Additionally, mothers with autistic children had the most pronounced cases of chronic stress. The survey also showed that mothers were more often disrupted at work every four days and had less time to focus on their own needs, which often led to a lack of attentiveness and patience towards their children. If the mothers did not have adequate time to help foster these children's innate talents, the genius capabilities might become under developed.

How to Help Your Children Creatively Handle Stress

In her book, The Power of Your Child's Imagination: How to Transform Stress and Anxiety into Joy and Success (Perigee/Penguin, 2009), child educational psychologist and UCLA associate clinical professor emeritus Charlotte Reznick, PhD (www.ImageryForKids.com), shares creative tools that help kids access their inner world so they can better navigate the trials and tribulations of growing up. Here's a brief look at Dr, Reznick's valuable tools for providing a positive venue for releasing the stress within your child.

<u>Deep Breathing</u>: Have your child imagine that they have a balloon in their belly, about two inches below their navel. They need to breathe slowly in and out pretending they are blowing up the balloon.

<u>Find a Quiet Place</u>: This is great place for children to find where s/he can escape the pressures of life. They can relax, regroup or just "chill." This place could be a tree house, in a garden, or just a special place in their room, wherever they feel loved and protected. It's one of Dr. Reznick's "foundation tools" a place to tap their inner wisdom.

<u>Magical and Wise Friends</u>: Some people have reported that their child feels better when they have an imaginary animal or wizard. These creatures may act as mentors or guides. They can help the child feel safe when they face an obstacle or offer "gifts" of possible solutions. These gifts can be in the form of thoughts or objects that the child needs to solve their problem.

<u>Focusing on the Heart and Stomach</u>: When the children is able to focus on having a quiet place within, they can learn to connect with the wisdom of their own heart. Just asking for a message that can help "right now" is a fast, "easy" way to teach them how to develop their intuition. If the heart or belly doesn't feel right about something happening in their life, then it should be an indicator as a "red flag" or as a suggestion for further exploration.

This can also be done with Other Body Parts. Kids benefit from knowing where different emotions live in their body. Once this is mastered, their stress can go down. One child reported that "calmness" lived in his arms, and when he felt overwhelmed, if he breathed in that feeling of calmness, his stress was reduced. That helped him relax and have more fun in life.

<u>Color Healing</u>: Just like the body, different colors are associated with different feelings. For example, for one child courage was purple, that he breathed into calm his orange fear. Afterwards, drawing the experience helps make it more real and concrete.

Playing with dolls or puppets is another great way for children to release fears or frustrations. They may not be able to verbalize these emotions to you, but they can release them in form of play

Why Focus on Stress for Health?

If we breakdown all illness and dis-ease except for a small percentage (maybe 3% is what Bruce Lipton PhD suggests), a common denominator was found: stress. The stressors either caused the illness or aggravated it and, if not treated, may make it worse.

There are five major categories of stress:
- <u>Physical Stress</u>: such as overwork, lack of sleep, over-trained, demanding more from your body than what it is capable.
- <u>Chemical Stress</u>: such as toxins from the environment, diet/food, water, from refined and processed foods, added hormones or antibiotics given to the animals/foods we eat; pesticides and herbicides on the fruits/vegetables.

- <u>Thermal Stress</u>: overheating or over chilling of the body.
- <u>Emotional Stress</u>: feeling a negative emotion and holding it inside your body and/or repressing it into your subconscious- calling it "depression" or "post-traumatic stress-disorder."
- <u>Mental Stress</u>: such as thinking of yourself as being stupid or as procrastinator or not worthy.

The Physiology of Stress to Your Body

Part of what happens when our minds are stressed is that there is a mind-body correlation and it results in physiological changes to other areas besides the adrenals. Adrenaline increases your heart rate, elevates your blood pressure and boosts energy supplies. Additionally, some imbalances of hormones and mis-alignments of organs may further exacerbate stress into your physiological body. Some areas impacted in your body which may trigger dis-ease include:

<u>HPA</u>
The Hypothalamus-Pituitary-Adrenal axis can be implicated. This hormonal team will control all hormonal balance in your body. If this system is implicated under stressed; breathing, hormones release, heartbeat, detoxification processes, and elimination processes will be altered.

<u>Hypothalamus</u>
The hypothalamus is the general of the army of glands and controls the entire autonomic nervous system. If the hypothalamus gets stressed; blood pressure, blood sugar, immune activity and its strength, body temperature, all hormones, blood volume, fat metabolism will be altered. And these can have side effects like dizziness and weakness to name a few.

When the hypothalamus does not function properly the water in the body will be depleted; dehydration have been linked to so many dis-ease including Fibromyalgia, chronic fatigue, depression, excess body weight, high blood pressure, fatigue, low back pain, and neck pain and headaches. Dehydration will also deplete the tryptophan neurotransmitters which can lead to insomnia, increase pain and depression.

<u>Human Growth Hormone</u>
Because the human growth hormone (HGH) is produced by the hypothalamus, when its function is diminished by stress, the functionality will be impacted. HGH helps increase energy; repairs damaged muscles, stimulate immune functionality, reduce body fat, improve sleep, and enhance short-term memory.

<u>DHEA</u>
DHEA is a hormone produced by the adrenal which is used to make estrogen and testosterone which impacts the energy levels and maintains the feelings of well-being and helps balance the sexual drive.

<u>Cortisol Levels</u>
Cortisol is also a hormone produced by the adrenal in response to increased stress levels. During high levels of stress, cortisol will cause immune dysfunction, increased inflammation, hypoglycemia (low blood sugar), suppresses the digestive system/reproductive system/growth process, and hypotension

(low blood pressure.) Cortisol increases sugars (glucose) in the bloodstream, enhances your brain's use of glucose and decreases the availability of this substance to repair tissues.

Ovarian and Testis Functionality
Low levels of regulated hormones can contribute to decreased blood flow to specific areas of the brain, creating brain fog and impact immune dysfunction.

Thyroid
The thyroid is the master metabolism organ in the body. Having a low thyroid function can produce low body temperature, cold hands and feet, tingling in the extremities, fatigue, and depressed mental activity.

Gut Link and Allergies
Since the digestive systems primary role is to digest, if the integrity of the intestinal tract used for absorption is impacted by stress in your body, your fuel will be depleted. One of the most prominent by-products is the growth of infection inside your gut such as: parasites, bacteria, fungus, prion and viruses. These "bugs" usually lives in symbiotic (balance) with us. The only way bacteria or "bugs" grow and create damage to their surrounding is if your body's immune defenses were lowered by stress.

The immune system is a very intricate system that has a simple role: to protect us for any invaders and to create and maintain a useful balance between all cells (self or non-self) in our body. It requires seven (7) times more energy to run this system than anything else in your body. However, if your body is stressed, citrus fruits or kiwi will give the amount of energy required for the immune system to recreate that required balance, refer to the nutrition portion of this book for more details.

The other common intestinal possibility is food allergens or chemical sensitivity or toxicity. The chemicals will block the absorption and even compete with certain nutrients for their absorption. Food allergies or allergens will create a fight inside the gut from the immune system and require so much energy to settle that after a while, your gut will "give up" and this may create gut dis-ease like leaky gut syndrome, Crohn and ulcerative colitis. The only issue with prolonged immune reactions inside any organ is that the cells will attack each other, causing an autoimmune dis-ease.

Obviously, the integrity of the intestinal tract can also be impacted from the main controllers, the brain and the nervous system. If the nerve carrying the electricity or power to the organ has interference, the function will be impacted. Multiple researches have shown the benefit of chiropractic in resolving organ (visceral) conditions.

Liver and Detoxification
The liver does about 250 bio-chemical reactions a second to cleanse the blood and the gut and produce bile and store sugar. This organ is the "multitasker" of your body. It also serves as the primary detoxicator of our body. Parts of these toxins are chemicals, solvent, pesticides, microbes, food and many more. All these may have an influence on the health and genetic expression to the offspring so it is best if the system is working at optimal levels.

Parasites

According to public health expert in USA, 60% of Americans will encounter a parasite infection in their lifetime. If these parasites enter and habitat your intestinal tract they will be eating your nutrients and create also damage to the structure of the intestine and their by-product will increase the toxicity in your body. Our science is still finding new parasites that were not discovered 10 years ago. We can only imagine what "friends" we have inside us.

Fungus

The most common fungus infection is Candida. It lives in the intestinal tract but can also go elsewhere in your body. Candida feeds off of sugar and your body will be signaled by desiring sugar cravings. Candida can cause skin and digestive tract problems and cause eczema to your unborn child if contracted while pregnant.

Inflammation

Any physical trauma will increase internal stresses at the muscles, ligaments, vertebra, nervous system but also the sympathetic/parasympathetic autonomic nervous system and natural chemical involvement. Inflammation will increase in your body. Chiropractic and chiropractic Craniopathy can release the structural, nervous system and organ stressors.

Infections (Bacteria, Virus, Prion)

All infections in the body will increase stress and deplete our level of energy by a factor of 7. Helicobacter Pylori and Lyme bacteria (and other forms) are known to be resilient in the body and hard to remove. However, Dr. Stéphane has found homeopathy with herbs is effective to support this issue.

Hormonal Imbalance

Lack of sleep will create internal and external stress in your life. It will bring all hormonal levels down except the stress hormones like cortisol and affect the pancreas and the sugar level in the blood and the entire system gets off balance.

Psychological Symptoms of Stress to Your Brain

Many studies have confirmed that both working memory and long-term memory are inhibited by stress. Research has shown that chronically high cortisol levels released during stress can lead to the death of neurons cells in the hippocampus (located in the limbic system), which is critical to forming long term memories.

Frequent symptoms of stress such as low impulse control, difficulty concentrating and irritating behaviors often match the definition of Attention Deficit Disorder (A.D.D) or Attention Deficit Hyperactivity Disorder (ADHD.)

Research on traumatized (stressed) children found a greater concentration of brain cell growth in the mid-brain (emotions, survival) at the expense of the prefrontal cortex area (higher level thinking.) There is an underdeveloped capacity for empathy (also regulated by the prefrontal cortex.) There was a tendency for traumatized children to be overly sensitive to cues of perceived threat as a result; these children have a predisposition to impulsive, aggressive behaviors or withdrawal and "depression."

Psychological stress has been shown to increase activation of the sympathetic nervous system and the hypothalamic pituitary adrenal axis. This increased activation releases too much adrenaline, noradrenalin, and cortisol which leads to faster heart rates, increased cardiac output, and narrower arteries. Changes, in turn, create increased blood pressure. Activation of these systems also accelerates the progress of atherosclerosis (dis-ease of the arteries) and can lead to acute plaque rupture, which results in ischemia of the heart (blockage of the heart arteries) and coronary heart dis-ease and stroke.

Chronic stress lowers serotonin (a calming neurotransmitter) levels. Low levels of serotonin are linked to aggression, obsessive compulsive behavior and depression. Low serotonin leaves a person overwhelmed with life until ultimately the system shuts down with depression or causes a person to explode with aggression.

Dopamine is a neurotransmitter that acts as a stimulant and sensitizes brain cells to look for patterns. Strong dopamine levels are reflected in sharper thinking and focused behavior. However, stress can cause an overproduction of dopamine resulting in anxious, hyper vigilant and/or perfectionist behavior.

Stress can also cause an underproduction of dopamine if the person's defensive behavior (coping mechanism) is to tune out and retreat. Low levels of dopamine are associated with inattentive, unmotivated behavior. High levels of stress hormones, including cortisol, can suppress the body's immune response. This can leave an individual vulnerable to a variety of infections and chronic health problems.

The hypothalamic-pituitary-adrenal (HPA) system releases certain neurotransmitters (chemical messengers) called catecholamines, particularly those known as dopamine, norepinephrine, and epinephrine (also called adrenaline.) During the stressful event, catecholamines also suppress activity in areas at the front of the brain concerned with short-term memory, concentration, inhibition, and rational thought. It also interferes with the ability to handle difficult social or intellectual tasks and behaviors during that time.

The Secret Ingredient to Empower the "Stress-O-Holic" – The Spa

(Cited with permission by Jeremy McCarthy's book, The Psychology of Spas and Wellbeing, (http://psychologyofwellbeing.com/about/about)

Jeremy McCarthy's book The Psychology of Spas and Wellbeing compiled research on the many components of the spa industry, explaining the physical, psychological, and spiritual benefits of those practices for stress reduction and why these facilities are no longer a luxury pampering item but a must have preventative health measure. The secret ingredient for health is stress reduction. Spas can also help their clients to handle stress through recommendations on healthful eating and food preparation.

Spas also encourage social interaction in a way that supports behavior change. Most spas today offer couples' experiences as well as being an outlet for small groups of friends (usually women) to come together and share in an enjoyable, healthy experience. The social aspect of spas is important to how a spa lifestyle is learned since "feelings of relatedness or connectedness" within a social support structure can aid in changing lifestyle behavior. Spas have the potential to help their clients navigate the aging process, not only by helping alleviate the physical aches and pains of aging but also by helping people find psychological wellbeing.

The ancient Greeks and Romans went to certain natural hot springs resorts to "take the waters", because these waters had special healing properties. In European countries like Romania, in which many of the old Greek and Roman spas are still functioning, balneotherapy, or medicinal bathing, is a recognized subspecialty of medicine. This is the essence of the modern-day "spa" concept. Research reveals that 71% of people would be more likely to visit spas if they learned that scientific studies demonstrated treatments delivering measurable health benefits.

According to McCarthy, medical studies related to spa/wellness approaches are growing: from those proving lifestyle changes can prevent 90% plus of all heart dis-ease to those revealing proper nutrition, exercise, and stress reduction does a better job of preventing and even reversing heart dis-ease than most drugs and surgical procedures. Massage has been shown to increase naturally calming and pain-killing hormones, such as encephalin and endorphins, while simultaneously decreasing the levels of stress hormones like cortisol in the body.

He also cited many research studies that supported the benefits of spa/wellness services inclusive of:
- The use of aromatherapy at an Irish hospital has been found to significantly improve patients' sleep patterns and reduce the amount of night sedation required.
- A Louisiana State University study on the effect of deep tissue massage therapy on blood pressure and heart rate found that 45- and 60-minute deep tissue massages led to an average systolic pressure reduction of 10.4 mm - a diastolic pressure reduction of 5.3 mm – a mean arterial pressure reduction of 7.0 mm - and an average heart rate reduction of 10.8 beats per minute
- A University of Virginia review of 25 clinical trials concludes that yoga improves risk indices for patients with type 2 diabetes, including: glucose tolerance, insulin sensitivity, lipid profiles, blood pressure, oxidative stress, coagulation profiles and pulmonary function - and has promise for preventing cardiovascular complications in this population.
- A Kagoshima University (Japan) study found that 3 weeks of sauna therapy combined with underwater exercise significantly improved the pain, symptoms and quality of life of female fibromyalgia patients.
- A clinical trial (120 women) that had surgery for breast "cancer" that involved dissection of lymph nodes demonstrated that early physiotherapy, including manual lymph drainage, massage of scar tissue and shoulder exercises, was significantly effective in preventing secondary lymph edema.

Studies have shown to determine that massage therapy improved the classroom behavior of preschooler autistic children by showing:
- less touch sensitivity

- less distracted by sounds
- more attentive in class
- relating more with their teachers
- receiving better scores on the autism behavior checklist
- receiving better scores on the early social communications scales.

Psychologist Robert Epstein said that 25% of our happiness is determined by our ability to manage stress. And spa goers cite "reduction in stress" as the number one reason they go to spas. Unlike other healing institutions (doctor's offices, hospitals) in modern society, spas are places that people look forward to visiting and enjoy their time while they are there.

This is why the Whole-Listic Children's Hospital is designed with a Spa component to ensure that the anxieties that children and their parents normally feel in a hospital setting are alleviated. This is the power of the spa environment, creating healing experiences that people actually enjoy. Although children's specialty hospitals represent less than 5.0% of all hospitals in the United States, they are the backbone of the pediatric healthcare infrastructure; and as such, we would like the Whole-Listic Children's Hospital to be the leading example for the world's healthcare reform.

In the meanwhile, the best prescription for removing stress from your lifestyle and approaching your health from a preventative mentality is to find a reputable Spa in your area. If you are in the Washington Metropolitan area, there are two facilities that might cater to your interest. One consists of a bed and breakfast environment and the other end of the spectrum is a 5-star Spa Resort.

Some Current Examples:

The Inn on Thistle Hill Bed and Breakfast and Wellness Center Spa is found in the foothills of the Blue Ridge Mountains. Rejuvenate and pamper yourself with a Raindrop Technique aromatherapy session and/or Aqua-Chi foot soak in the Wellness Center Spa. Indulge and learn about some of the world's finest supplements and essential oils and which is right for you.

One of the specialties of the Inn Owner is to clear out the effects of past events that may have traumatized/agonized you. The Energy Balancing technique that has been developed and honed by her for over 35 years will leave your mind and body rejuvenated. The food served is all organic, natural and local foods No MSG, additives or preservatives and alkalinized water is used at the facility. The ambience consists of cottage rooms filled with top-of-the-line linens, candle-lit dinners and personalized hand-painted champagne glasses. (www.theinnonthistlehill.com)

For those that prefer a modernized retreat, the Salamander Resort and Spa located in Middleburg, VA features 168 luxurious rooms and suites, a luxury spa, and full-service equestrian center. The owner Sheila Johnson is the owner of the Washington Capitals, Wizards and Mystics and co-founder of the Black Entertainment Television. This resort is in a class of its own; at the Salamander Resort and Spa guests will enjoy transportation in luxury and style inside an innovative and meticulously crafted Audi vehicle.

Sheila is not new to the hospitality industry and brings extensive experience and expertise to this facility. She is the CEO of Salamander Hospitality that manages resorts in Florida, South Carolina and Virginia. The Spa Director, Penny Kriel brings expertise from her experience at the exclusive Mandarin Oriental hotel. Sheila is a firm believer of health and is providing Executive Physicals on site from Inova VIP Health 360 along with other nutritional and health empowerment workshops. Resort guest can empower themselves with weight loss and nutrition workshops. (www.salamanderresort.com)

Stress-Less Living Expo

In North America, only a small amount of economic resources are allocated to preventative care. Ironically, focusing on wellbeing in a positive direction could actually be our best defense against illness and dis-ease. As a preliminary introduction to the "Billionaire Parenting" lifestyle, an expo was designed to empower the community with information and resources regarding the importance of reducing stress. We realized from clinical observations and research that this was the root of a majority of the dis-ease and illnesses that were prevalent. Research studies found that 90% of all physicians' visits are due to some symptoms of stress.

In 2013, Dr. Stéphane Provencher, Gainesville Holistic Health Center and the Whole-Listic Children's Foundation founded the Stress-Less Living Expo in Northern Virginia. This Expo was presented to the community to provide them with resources for reducing stress. A total of 41 vendors participated in this two-day event and helped empower the community with their products and services. The theme song was "Return to Innocence" by Enigma.

There were 3 types of coaches available for the participants: Mind Coach, Body Coach and Spirit Coaches and they all focused on differing stressors. Each of the participating vendors was classified amongst one of these three categories so that the participants could receive a Whole-Listic (well-rounded) perspective for their health needs.

Jessica Haney is the leader of the localized Holistic Mom's network chapter. She also is an avid journalist for the Washington Times. Additionally she contributes to several blogs inclusive of the DC Moms and Crunchy Chewy Mama. She attended the first annual Stress-Less Living Expo and you can read more about her review at (http://crunchychewymama.com/index.php/taking-steps-toward-wellness.) If you are located in the Washington metropolitan area, Jessica is creating a new venture entitled Mindful Healthy Life (http://www.mindfulhealthylife.com/) and her goal is to unite holistic-minded businesses to this community so that parents have a wealth of resources available to them.

Services were provided on-the-spot for participants to experience as well as sampling of healthy fare such as gluten-free and organic products. Xoçai Healthy Chocolates that is gluten and vegan free and diabetic friendly was formulated by a toxicologist as a healthier alternative for the everyday consumption of chocolates for children and adults.

The company also has a healthier version of energy drinks. These products have anti-inflammatory properties that helped Naomi Howison who was in a severe car accident that left her almost paralyzed from waist down to fully recover. She had the same results with the Xoçai products as she did with the 4 pain medications. To learn more, please visit http://www.youtube.com/watch?v=KAkUzcDSh1o. Health seminars were presented by the hour to further inform the public with health tips. For more information on the next scheduled event, please visit: www.billionaireparenting.com

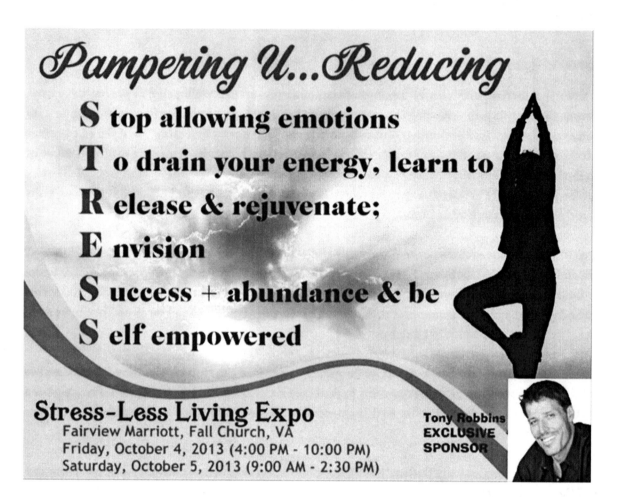

BODY STRESSORS		
Low Energy	Insomnia	Headaches
Chest pain and rapid heart rate	Cold or sweaty hands and feet	Aches, pains and tense muscles
Loss of sexual desire and/or ability		
Upset stomach, including diarrhea or constipation		
Nervousness and shaking or grinding teeth		

MIND STRESSORS		
Constant worrying	Racing thoughts	Inability to focus
Poor judgment	Avoiding others	Changes in appetite
Forgetfulness and disorganization	Having difficulty relaxing and quieting your mind	
Becoming easily agitated, frustrated, and moody	Increased use of alcohol, drugs, or cigarettes	
Procrastinating and avoiding responsibilities		
Feeling overwhelmed, like you are losing control or need to take control		
Feeling bad about yourself (low self-esteem), lonely, worthless and depressed		

SPIRIT STRESSORS		
Have a morbid fear of death	You are unforgiving: martyr	Feel your life has been wasted
Doubt your ability to succeed	Constantly need to prove yourself	
Experience a sense of inner emptiness	See very few positive things in life or cynical	
Feel little obligation to others; apathetic	Have self-doubts about your work/future	

A sampling of some of the vendors from each of the categories is included below:

BODY COACHES	
Blanchard's Coffee (www.blanchardscoffee.com)	Brian Cooper's Healing Hands (www.bchhmt.com)
Golden Valley Farms (www.goldenvalleyguernseys.com)	Marble Arch Gardens (www.marblearchgardens.com)
MTO Kombucha (www.mtokombucha.com)	Relay Foods (www.relayfoods.com/Home)
Simply Pure Products (www.simplypureproducts.com)	Thrive Food (www.relyonus2013.thrivelife.com/relyonus2013)
Weston A. Price Foundation (www.westonaprice.org)	Xоçai Healthy Chocolates (http://mxi.myvoffice.com/unitedwestandmin)
MIND COACHES	
All Eco Design Center (http://allecocenter.com)	Creative Healing Trends (www.creativehealingtrends.com)
Paws for Holistic Pet Care (www.drverna.com)	Suppose LLC (www.supposellc.com)
VIP Integrative Medicine Center (http://vipimed.com/)	Vista View Publishing (www.vistaviewpublications.com)
Whole Health Dental Center (www.wholehealthdentalcenter.com)	
SPIRIT COACHES	
DoTerra Essential Oils and Reiki (Beth MacMonigle) (www.mydoterra.com/lovingaromaoils)	
Money Wisdom Empowerment (Money Healing) (http://moneywisdomempowerment.com)	
Young Living Essential Oils and Aromatherapies (Cathy Bower) (http://www.abundanceandwisdom.com/cathybower/)	

 Jenn's Insights

For the past two years, I should have changed my middle name to "Stress." Having stage IV of endometriosis and numerous fibroids, I can validate the research findings. Studies state that: in women with fibroids and endometriosis, stress may negatively affect hormonal balance and muscle tone. It can also upset the estrogen and progesterone balance and trigger excessive output of adrenal stress hormones. This can increase scarring and inflammation caused by the endometrial implants. Stress can also contribute to growth in the size of fibroid "tumors."

All mothers know that stress during pregnancy can be detrimental; however, in cases of chronic exposures to stress it can have physical and emotional impacts to your unborn child. Even in the womb a child picks up the mother's stress-stress chemicals such as adrenalin and cortisol cross the placenta and I have first-hand knowledge of how this impacts their abilities to cope with stress later in life.

I was not provided the luxury to reduce my stress level with prenatal massages during my pregnancy; however, in researching for this book, here is the medical evidence for why the maternity ward at the Whole-Listic Children's Hospital will have spa services for the family and will be prescribed for the mother's care.

Massage therapy addresses different needs through varying techniques which relax muscle tension and improve lymphatic and blood circulation. Mild pressure is applied to the muscle groups of the body. Swedish massage, is one example, and is recommended as prenatal massage method during pregnancy because it addresses many common discomforts associated with the skeletal and circulatory changes brought on by hormone shifts during pregnancy.

<u>Other Potential Benefits of Prenatal Massage</u>:
- Reduced back pain and nerve pain
- Reduced joint pain
- Improved circulation
- Reduced edema
- Reduced muscle tension and headaches
- Reduced stress, anxiety and better sleep
- Improved oxygenation of soft tissues and muscles

10

ADHD/ADD Children's Gifts to the World: Gratitude and Compassion

The Current Label of ADHD/ADD

Americans spent $31.6 billion on ADHD and ADD in 2000 and is a common behavioral disorder that affects an estimated 8% to 10% of school-age children. Boys are about three times more likely than girls to be diagnosed with it. It is estimated that one-third of children have ADHD/ADD.

Kids with ADHD are diagnosed as acting without thinking, are hyperactive, and have trouble focusing. They may understand what's expected of them but have trouble following through because they can't sit still, pay attention, or focus on details. ADHD is diagnosed using a 14 symptom checklist. A child is diagnosed with ADHD if they consistently exhibit 8 of the 14 symptoms. The diagnosis is often made by people unqualified to make the call. People who are diagnosed with ADHD/ADD can typically have three main behavior patterns. These signs are:

Inattention

- losing or forgetting things
- failing to pay attention to details and making careless mistakes
- rarely following instructions completely
- avoiding tasks that require focusing for long periods of time
- easily distracted

Hyperactivity and Impulsivity

- leaving a chair when sitting is expected (like in a classroom)
- feeling restless, fidgeting, or squirming
- yelling out answers before the question is finished or before being called on
- feeling as if motor driven (needs to always be on the go)

To be diagnosed with ADHD or ADD, the person must fit certain criteria. The behaviors listed above must be present from an early age (before 7) and be consistent for six months. The behaviors must also be existent in more than one area of life. For example, they must be present at both the home and the school environments, or both at home and at work. Some children outgrow ADHD/ADD, or least they know how to control their symptoms. In the brain of a person who is not diagnosed with ADHD/ADD, several neurotransmitters function normally. However, in the brain of a person with ADHD/ADD, there is a 50% reduction in the function of these neurotransmitters.

According to the current research, nobody has clues about what causes it, no one knows for sure. Some causes have been identified including genetic, prenatal exposure to heavy metals and chemicals, pesticides, nutrition, omega-3, allergies and blood sugar. All we do know is that Ritalin, the chief medical treatment for Ritalin, is a multi-billion dollar a year business. Some of the side effects of Ritalin include death, suicidal tendencies, insomnia, Tourette's syndrome, psychosis, addiction (similar to cocaine,) and growth problems as Ritalin interferes with growth hormone.

ADHD can wear out the affected child and their family. Parents must learn how to deal with the child's attention issues and help him/her to restrain impulsivity. Parents must also accept the fact that the child may not be welcomed in other homes. The attention given to the affected child is taken away from other siblings. Marriages may also suffer due to the constant stress of dealing with ADHD.

The Better Label for ADHD/ADD – "GIFTED and TALENTED CHILDREN"

Many gifted and talented children are often misdiagnosed by health care professionals. They are often diagnosed with ADHD/ADD when it is truly the intensity gifted children have. Gifted and talented children tend to be extremely intense. This intensity can be in what they are pursuing, rivalry, power struggles or emotional responses. These children also tend to be impatient with themselves and others.

Not only can gifted children be intense, but they tend to be sensitive. These sensitivities can range from emotions, touch, and taste. They tend to cry at the littlest thing, have a keen sense of hearing and smells. They also insist on having tags removed from clothes, or only wearing certain fabrics. They are also very tactile, they must touch everything.

These children are driven by questioning things to try to understand better. They like consistency and tend to think outside the box. Children also have the intense sense of idealism, and moral issues. Parents need to be on the look for signals of anxiety, depression due to this intensity. Adults tend to value the above mentioned characteristics of gifted children as long as they don't occur in a structured classroom or important business meeting. Gifted people tend to challenge traditions and the Status Quo.

Gifted children tend to be bored in a regular classroom. Once they are done with their work, they often have to wait until others are caught up. This extra time on their hands may make them have high expectations of themselves. They want to be accepted by others, but are often not because they are different. This may lead to the child to portray a depressed state.

There are very successful gifted people who learned how to deal with ADHD. Paul Orfalea, the founder of Kinko's knew at a young age that ADHD would trouble him from menial tasks. His skills helped him to hire the right personnel for his stores. Since sitting still was an issue for him, he often visited his stores and applied his strengths in this area. While he was there, he had many discussions with his employees on how to improve his company. Kinko's became so successful and was well known for being an innovative work place. It was such a successful model that FedEx bought the company and today it is worth $2.4 billion. A company that Orfalea started in 1970 with an investment of $5,000 has become one of the booming industry leaders.

David Neeleman, the founder and CEO of JetBlue, also says his success is because of his ADHD. Although he couldn't pay his bills on time, he was able to create a business model for a fleet of planes in a troubled airline industry and revolutionize the concept of translating efficiency and value for its consumers.

Personality and Characteristics of ADHD/ADD Children

A Polish psychologist and psychiatrist named Kazimierz Dabrowski developed one more theory on the traits of gifted children. They all exhibit "positive disintegration" and the theory of "over excitabilities," better known as the "ADD" and "ADHD" phenomenon.

Dabrowski stated that gifted children tend to have peaks of high energy. This strikes when the child is passionate about something. The child is naturally curious, asking a lot of questions about the topic. They have a strong fantasy life and have strong connections with other people. Dependent on what limelight they are observed it can make the difference, because it is common these children excel in the area they are passionate about, but are weak in other areas.

For instance a middle school child can solve math problems on a high school level, but spells on an elementary level. Since the child can compensate up to a certain point, the discrepancy in weaker subject are (spelling for example) may grow and grow until there may be a perceived learning disability.

Characteristics of Gifted Children

- Gifted students learn more quickly, deeply, and broadly than their peers.
- They have a higher degree of depression and anxiety.
- They usually have learned to read early and have larger vocabularies than their age-peers.
- The culture is tough on gifted kids, and many of them self-isolate to avoid stigma. Many more try to avoid being stigmatized as gifted by hiding their abilities and underachieving to win social approval.
- They tend to have outstanding memories and have a larger knowledge base than most students.
- They tend to be loners or to hang out with older children or adults.
- They are very curious and ask a lot of questions.
- They tend to have many interests, hobbies and collections.
- On the downside, they tend to be physically behind their peers, emotionally oversensitive, perfectionist, and challenging or rebellious of authority, including the teacher's authority.
- Are fluent at generating ideas and much better at elaborating.
- They don't need much practice, but can master new concepts or skills almost immediately.
- May be nonconformist in clothing, hairdo, thoughts, and practices.
- They are often called "intense" with strong concentration powers, and either can't stand the slightest noise or distraction, or could read a book in the midst of a hurricane without blinking an eye.
- They tend to operate at the same level as normal children who are significantly older, oftentimes many grade levels older, thinking in the abstract many years before their age-mates.
- They demonstrate high reasoning ability, creativity, curiosity and excellent memories.
- They can get cranky about not wanting to do things that "bore" them.
- Tend to prefer to work alone than to work in a cooperative learning group.
- May "blurt out" without worrying about inappropriateness of timing.
- Tend to be "the class clown."
- Know things about current events and global issues that most kids the same age have never even heard of.
- The things they do at school or home produce a "wow!" from parents and teachers.
- Standardized test scores may be off the charts but classroom grades not that hot or vice versa.
- Some tend to be sloppy, careless and lazy.
- They tend to be bossy in group situations.

The Psychology of ADHD/ADD

According to Shelley Carson, a Harvard psychologist, creative, gifted individuals can qualify for an ADHD diagnosis. Studies have found that a surprising number of individuals with ADHD scored above average on divergent thinking tests. Highly creative individuals and those with ADHD/ADD tend to be disruptive. They do not stay on tasks, they interrupt, and they appear moody or demanding and impede the flow of things.

Both of these individuals are distracted easily, appear to be inattentive, are novelty and sensation seekers, and could appear to be underachievers. They do not conform to the norm. People with ADHD/ADD and creative people grow in a creativity-stimulating setting. It is essential that parents provide a rich environment to children at an early age. They need to encourage creativity, and explore curiosities that sustain the child's interest.

It is unfortunate when a creative child is misdiagnosed with ADHD/ADD. Often creative children use deviations classified as ADHD/ADD (easily distracted) as a way to think creatively. Where Frank Lloyd Wright and Thomas Edison are considered geniuses, however, they had the same symptoms for ADHD/ADD as well.

Dr. Bonnie Cramer of the University of Georgia conducted a scientific study on people considered creative and those diagnosed with ADHD. Her study revealed that both types of people have many things in common. The brain structure, temperament and moods are all about the same. They don't care for tasks that demand repetition but may be over stimulated with too much spontaneity. These people do not thrive well in strictly structured environments. They do not like to be conformed by rules. They have their own way of organizing ideas and how things should work. They are great with innovation and original thinking.

Many people are put into situations when they have to work with someone with ADHD/ADD. It is important to remember that these people are great at multitasking. They are not single task oriented and often get bored if constrained within this type of environment. Many great entrepreneurs and project managers are those with ADHD/ADD.

Many parents remember the stage their child went through of "Why? Why? Why? Why?" We didn't want to hear that word for a while. Now imagine your child never outgrowing that stage. The child seems to question everything! It is important that we try not to get frustrated, but encourage our children to find their own answers in books or other available resources.

Gifted children may have difficult time with peer relationships compared to typical children. They create coping behaviors to try to fit in by often trying to hide or deny their giftedness. They try to conform to the expectations of their peers to try to gain popularity and simply fit in or assimilate into the crowd.

Behavior Difference of ADHD/ADD and the Gifted Child

The symptoms of gifted children and those with ADHD/ADD are similar. Deciphering between the two can often present a challenge. Medical doctors don't allow enough time per patients. Parents and teachers are often asked to fill out a survey with symptoms of ADHD/ADD. This speedy diagnosis usually ends with the prescription of such drugs as Ritalin or Adderall. If gifted children are evaluated at all, they usually get a psychiatric label where a more challenging class is all that is needed.

In one case, a parent felt forced by the school district to have their child take a stimulant drug. Please keep in mind schools cannot diagnose your child, not coerce you into making your child take medications. This child became very violent. At one point in time he took a steak knife and started to stab his stuffed animals due to the side-effects of the medications. The parent decided it would be best to take his some off the drug since he was a danger to himself and others in the family. However, the principal pressured the parents to put him back on the medicine. The matter is now in the hands of the court.

Another parent refused to give her child the medicine. She decided the best thing would be to home school her son. To her it didn't make sense to have a child that was on the Honor Roll to be labeled as "learning disabled."

Behaviors Associated with ADD/ADHD

- More active and restless than normal children
- Impulsivity, poor ability to delay gratification
- Poorly sustained attention in almost all situations
- Diminished persistence on tasks not having immediate consequences
- Difficulty adhering to rules and regulations
- Impaired adherence to commands to regulate or inhibit behavior in social contexts

Behaviors Associated with Gifted Children

- Low tolerance for persistence on tasks that seem irrelevant
- High activity level, may need less sleep
- Poor attention, boredom, daydreaming in specific situations
- Judgment lags behind intellect
- Questions rules, customs, and traditions
- Intensity may lead to power struggles with authorities

Foods That Impact ADHD/ADD

It is important to monitor your child's diet carefully. Food sensitivity or nutritional deficiencies could be the cause of hyperactivity. Foods with artificial coloring and flavoring need to be avoided. Look for whole foods that have not been processed.

In the mid-1970s, Benjamin Feingold, a California allergist, generated a huge controversy. He stated that artificial colorings and flavorings and certain natural chemicals (salicylates in foods) could trigger ADHD/ADD. Salicylates are chemicals that occur naturally in many plants. They are like a plant's built in pesticide.

Salicylates are found in foods from plants, herbs, spices, tea, and flavor additives. Salicylates are also found in medications, fragrances, industrial chemicals, plastics and some pesticides, and can cause adverse effects when inhaled as well as eaten. Children naturally eat more food containing salicylates than adults. This is because they eat more candies, sodas, and other foods that are artificially colored, flavored or sweetened.

Food additives such as dyes and colorings have been implicated in ADHD. In 16 out of 23 studies on food additives and ADHD, it was found that these food additives exacerbated the symptoms of ADHD in some children. Research published in 2007 for the UK's Food Standards Agency (FSA) suggests that certain artificial colors, when paired with sodium benzoate may be linked to hyperactive behavior

Many people, even health care professionals, believe that sugar triggers hyperactivity. This generalization is difficult to prove because there are so many types of sugars out there. Foods that contain sucrose, corn syrup, glucose and high fructose corn syrup all contain the same characteristics as sugar.

Milk is one of the most common food allergens in children. Studies show a prevalence of milk allergies in around 2% to 5% of children in several countries around the world. Some estimates are much higher, as the researchers in this study propose. Cow's milk contains at least 20 protein components that may cause allergic responses. The milk protein casein and whey are the main problems. In a study of twenty-three children with ADHD researchers found abnormal levels of peptides in their urine. The children followed a strict casein-free (milk-protein) diet a year, and 22 of the 23 children showed "clear improvements" in their behavior and attention span.

It is also important to monitor the amount of aspartame children are consuming. The aspartic acid is an essential part of the body. It facilitates the transfer of information from neuron to neuron. If there is too much aspartic acid (eating too much aspartame) in the body, these neurons will be damaged or killed. Many symptoms of children diagnosed with ADD/ADHD have improved when foods with MSG and aspartame were removed from their diet. Pregnant women should also avoid eating MSG. The baby may have difficulties with complex learning as an effect of this chemical.

Other foods that cause hyperactivity are:
- chemical sensitivities
- deficiencies with essential fatty acids (omegas)
- deficiencies of zinc
- deficiencies with vitamin B group
- deficiencies with magnesium
- candidiasis (yeast infection)
- toxic effects of chromium
- food intolerances or allergies, and sensitivity to sugar

Studies have shown that children's behavior and artificial food additives can lead to hyperactivity. The research has taken a look at children who consumed no food additives and those that consume food additives and found astonishing results leading researches to conclude that consumption of artificially chemically engineered by-products, lead to a change in children's behavior.

Billionaire Parenting Tips for ADHD/ADD

Creative Children

It makes complete sense that everybody has an easier time focusing when they are working on what they love to do. When this happens with children, their out-of-the-box thinking usually goes into overdrive. However, teachers tend to not explore these ideas because they think the ideas are too advanced or not articulated well enough for others to understand.

During the 1950s, E. Paul Torrance took a special interest in the creativity of children. His eyes really began to open while he worked at a military academy. Many of the boys sent there were deemed as trouble makers. However, it turns out that these boys had a lot of energies and their ideas where not the exact ones the school expected.

This prompted Torrance to conduct some research. He discovered that teachers preferred highly intelligent students over highly creative ones. They stated that the highly creative students were harder to control. The teachers also didn't understand a lot of their answers. Torrance was determined to prove that being creative is just as important as being smart. Torrance developed a creativity test that is used when screening for gifted and talented classes. This test is used around the world.

Others have come up variations of this testing format that are used as well. James Catterall's test was used on elementary and high school students. Surprisingly, the younger students out-performed the older ones in their scores of creativity. A person has to question if schools are extinguishing creativity in our students.

Common practices in schools and homes that may be killing creativity include:
- Praise - The excessive use of prizes deprives a child of the intrinsic pleasure of the creative activity itself.
- Hovering over kids - making them feel that they are constantly being watched while they are working. When kids are under constant observation, the risk-taking, creative urge goes underground and hides.
- Numerous evaluations - When we constantly make kids worry about how they are doing, they ignore internal satisfaction with their accomplishments, which further impacts self-esteem.
- Competition - Putting kids in a win-lose situation, where there is only one winner negates the process children progress at their own rates and so many give up before they even begin.
- Pressure - Establishing high expectations for a child's performance often ends up instilling aversion for a subject or activity. Unreasonably high expectations often pressure children to perform and conform within strictly prescribed guidelines, and deter experimentation, exploration, and innovation.
- Over-bearing - Constantly telling a kid how to do things often leaves children feeling like their originality is a mistake and any exploration a waste of time.
- Restricting choices - Telling children which activities they should engage in instead of letting them follow where their curiosity and passion leads may be detrimental. This further restricts active exploration and experimentation that might lead to creative discovery and production.

- Strong emotions can also be powerful forces to motivate our creativity, or not. When some people feel very strongly about something, they are inspired to act. Rage, anger, loss and grief are just a few emotions and can stir our creativity if guided correctly. One great organization created by anger, loss and grief is MADD (Mothers Against Drunk Driving.)

Super Brain Yoga

Everyone is familiar with yoga. Grand Master Choa Kok Sui became very interested in the study of yoga. He focused primarily on the body's energy that impacted the brain. He discovered that the activity of the Alpha waves increased after performing just one minute of Super Brain Yoga. Not only that, but our left and right hemispheres were synchronized from this activity, which further promoted learning speeds. The more often a person participates in this kind of Yoga, the longer the two halves of the brain will be synchronized.

People are the most creative while they are in the Alpha state. This is when artists, writers and musicians produce their most creative and brilliant pieces. Not only does Yoga give your brain a work out, it also makes you healthier, more emotionally stable, and clears your mind. Yoga is not just for the young and fit. Anyone, regardless of age or health or physical abilities will reap the benefits of this practice.

Creative Dance

It is also common knowledge about the importance of exercise. Did you know that while you are trying to get a healthier body, you are also growing new brain cells? So walk that extra mile! These extra cells may increase learning.

How exercise increases learning:

1. improves alertness and attention
2. cells bind together which increases the rate of information retained

Babies and infants learn by exploring their environments and moving around the new world. This is part of normal growth and development. This is why creative movement should be an integral part of early learning programs. Creative movements encourage children to learn how to control their bodies and learn about personal space. Once they learn how to control the body, their mind can focus on following directions and respecting other children's space. Not only is creative dance a great physical activity, it also helps the children to express themselves.

Kinesthetic learning (using movement) is easily incorporated into education. Many children have a hard time expressing themselves on paper. There is a block from the brain to the hand to the paper. Instead of causing frustration in the child, s/he should be allowed to express themselves with movements.

When children grow up and enter the workforce, they face a whole new world of problems. They need to be taught critical thinking skills, to look at problems in new ways and to work as teams today so they will be prepared in the future. Movement helps the child with all these skills.

The Energy of ADHD/ADD (Energy Medicine)

The energy associated with ADHD is often described as being fast and frantic. Energy healers found that if the energy is focused or channeled it can be very creative and stimulating. Kids with ADHD are affected by the environment and people's energy surrounding them. It is important to monitor the surrounding energy and find ways to rebalance their own energy on a daily basis with tools such as meditation.

When a substance is brought into the electromagnetic field of a person, an attraction or repulsion takes place between the energy of the person and the substance. If attraction, the person can benefit from association with the substance. If repulsion, the person can experience the repulsion of his or her energy from the other as a pain or discomfort in the body. This is especially critical in the cases of ADHD children where they tend to be over-sensitive to energy.

According to Oriental medical theory, allergies and allergy-based disorders are the results of long-term energy disturbances in the energy pathways. In this case, the brain chemicals are not produced or distributed correctly such as in ADHD patients. If given a chance, appropriate stimulation to the spinal nerves, the brain and nervous system can produce substances within the body and distribute them appropriately. The brain has the ability to create appropriate remedial secretions that release targeted tissues and organs to assist with healing infections, allergies, imbalances, and immune deficiency dis-eases.

Energy medicine can unblock the blockages in the energy pathways and restart normal energy circulation through the once blocked energy channels. This enhances the supply of right nutrients to the brain. When the brain receives the right nutrients it can function normally and coordinate with the rest of the body to operate at its optimal level.

Many children have a very active imagination. The problem is that they want to replay everything in the real life. Too often they don't think before acting or speaking. "Treatment" for this hyperactivity will come in handy. The type of "treatment" will depend on the severity of the issues with the child. The first step is to find a Reiki practitioner. You and the practitioner can sit down and determine the best "treatment" for your child. Reiki "treatments" have been found to be very beneficial for hyperactive or ADHD children. The easiest way to start this "treatment" is to play a meditation CD while the children are falling asleep. This may help to calm the brain activity of the child and provide them with a more restful sleep.

The Mind-Body Connection of ADHD/ADD
(Cranial and Chiropractic Care for ADHD/ADD)

ADD/ADHD is one of the most commonly diagnosed disorders of childhood, found eight times more often in males than females. This condition has been medically described since 1902. Before 1940 children with learning difficulties or concentration issues were considered mentally retarded, and culturally disadvantaged.

Following research during the 1940's children who were impulsive, hyperactive, and easily distracted were said to have Hyperkinetic Disorder of Childhood. In 1980 it was renamed Attention Deficit Disorder and in 1987 it was changed to Attention Deficit Hyperactivity Disorder to reflect the commonality of hyperactivity/impulsivity that accompanied this disorder.

Children with attention deficit disorder lack the ability to concentrate and focus, complete school work, and are often in trouble with teachers and parents. Symptoms are of gradual onset appearing over many months and if not managed correctly can lead to low self-esteem and behavioral problems for many years.

There is no specific test for this condition/disorder. Diagnosis is made based upon judgment of degrees of behavior and is complicated by the fact that ADD/ADHD commonly is present with several other disorders including lead poisoning, fetal alcohol syndrome, Tourette's syndrome. Additionally substance abuse, personality and anxiety disorders, depression and manic depressive illness share common symptoms with ADD/ADHD.

This complex situation is most successfully managed by a multifocal approach including parents, teachers, classmates, siblings, physicians, counselors, and chiropractors. The conventional "treatment" that we are most familiar with is the pharmacopeia, Ritalin, Adderall, Concerta, and Stratera. In fact, Ritalin use has gone up 700 percent since 1990.

It is the most abused prescription drug with a street value of approximately $15/pill with enticing names such as Kibbles and Bits, Kiddy-cocaine, R-Ball, Skippy and Vitamin R to name a few. Long term side effects of these drugs are unknown. Current short term side effects include but are not limited to psychotic episodes, drug dependent syndrome, palpitations, cardiac arrhythmia, insomnia and headaches.

The preceding list should be enough to raise questions about alternative options such as nutrition, homeopathy, and balancing biomechanics and neurophysiology. This is where your local chiropractors can be utilized. It is not a secret that physiology and behavior are intricately linked. How many of us know people in chronic pain that have become depressed due to the presence of that pain? What about people whose grumpiness is relieved with a balanced meal?

The effects of chiropractic care on learning and behavior display dramatic results with improvements noticed such as: improved grades, increased IQ, enhanced athletic performance and improved behavior. Chiropractors are well suited to identify and correct neurologic imbalances or impairments.

Many combined holistic approaches which include nutrition, therapeutic movement, spinal soft tissue and cranial corrections allow those treated to experience enhanced vitality, diminished expression of symptoms, more regulated sleeping patterns, greater ability to concentrate, and tolerance for managing the stress of everyday living.

Other Strategies include:

- <u>Gluten-free diet</u>: ADHD children placed on gluten-free diets have shown remarkable improvements in their concentration and behavior.
- <u>Eliminate grains, sugar, and fructose</u>: Both grains and sugars can trigger allergies in sensitive children. It is best to remove them to see if their behavior improves.
- <u>Replace soft drinks</u>: Replace with water that is non-fluoridated.
- <u>Increase omega-3 fats</u>: Studies have shown that increased omega-3 in the diets were more effective than Ritalin, with no side effects.
- <u>Avoid all processed foods</u>: Processed foods contain many food additives, chemicals and often food colorings.

Jenn's Insights

For those that still believe that the ADHD/ADD diagnosis is valid for your child, let's first ask, who was the first person to recommend this diagnosis? The majority of diagnoses are coming from school counselors and social workers within a school setting. When have we formally legalized educators to make medical decisions? So, let me share my stories with you about my experiences with these two groups of professional.

During my junior year in high school, I was in a traditional high school and I can still recall my High School Counselor's exact words. "Jennifer I will not be able to write you a recommendation to go to a University because I do not believe that you are meant for that track. You are better off selecting a vocational school and learning a craft such as cosmetology. (That was stereotypical because I was a cheerleader.) Your grades in pre-calculus clearly revealed that you are not fit for furthering your academics and it would be a waste of your time."

I walked out of her office furious and her ignorance was the best thing in the world for me. It gave me the motivation to come out of my comfort zone and stop pretending to be what others wanted. I was determined that no one was going to dictate my life anymore. My parents were always the type that remained in Status Quo and did not want to cause scenes, but they felt this was unjustified. At the most critical time where entrance into colleges were a year away, the High School Counselor felt qualified enough to make recommendations based on her assessment and experiences.

This all began because I had complained to the High School Counselor that my pre-calculus teacher did not allow me to make-up a test and was being biased. I had been in a car accident and had legal medical documentation. The Counselor stated that since my grades in that class were not good anyway, it really did not matter if I took the exam or not. I explained to her that the teacher was not qualified to teach and could not answer questions if someone did not understand something.

My mother escalated the case to the Counseling Director and then to the Principal regarding the Counselor's action. Their response was to remove me from all my Gifted and Talented classes because my grades did not reflect one of aptitude. In truth, I felt like I was in prison in that school, there was not an inch of opportunity to be creative in that school. With one year prior to entrance into University, I decided to take matters into my own hands. As Tony Robbins' says, "It is never about resources, it's about resourcefulness."

I knew it was almost next to impossible to get back into the Magnet School because they hardly accepted candidates unless someone had resigned and to accept a student during senior year was almost unheard of. I decided to request for a meeting with the Assistant Principal and she remembered that I had started my education with them. As the Universe would have it, a student just moved away from the area and I transferred back to the Magnet School where I had originally started my junior high education.

I passed Calculus with all A's that year and had A's in the rest of my classes. The Magnet School had so much freedom that all my creativity was able to return and all my abilities flourished again. Fast forward several years and I graduated Suma Cum Laude from a MBA Program and Magna Cum Laude from a Masters in Information Technology Program. So was my High School Counselors assessment accurate? Thank goodness she did not recommend that I be put on Ritalin because I am sure I must have portrayed enough characteristics for that diagnosis too, especially in an environment that felt like prison.

Often times, Gifted and Talented Children are often misdiagnosed as learning disabled because they may focus on one area of interest versus another. If they happen to encounter a teacher that sees their weakness as their overall capabilities than they might become labeled as being "class clowns" or "problematic kids" or "kids that should go on a vocational track." This is very detrimental to the child's potential.

A rare incidence of misdiagnosis you may say, let's explore how I was encouraged to leave the Magnet School in the first place. Again another recommendation made by a Guidance Counselor and a Psychologist. Growing up I was always involved in gymnastics so my coach had us on much regimented diets and everything we ate was scrutinized. I love the sport but the control mechanism took the passion out of the sport for me. I recall that our weight was always announced in front of all the other gymnasts and we were publicly ridiculed if we could not meet our target weight.

So when I went to the Magnet School, I was able to have so much freedom to explore that my buddy and I began to have an addiction for pizza. In truth, it was also a time when we were blossoming and discovering boys. My friend and I discovered that pizza was one of the favorite foods of the guys that we had a crush on. They were older so we figured the best way to get their attention was to give them some pizza, so we ordered pizza on a daily basis.

My High School Counselor decided that she was going to psycho-analyze the situation and had us both committed to the on-site Psychologist. As soon as I stepped foot in that Psychologist office, I already knew the assessment that she was going to portray. She kept asking questions on why we spent money each day and where the money was coming from. In truth it was about $4 a day, a little over your normal lunch costs.

Bottom line is that she came out with a diagnosis that both my friend and I were problematic kids and probably obtaining funds for drugs. The exact words were, if we are not utilizing the funding for drugs, that we were exhibiting patterns that might lead to this lifestyle. Another misdiagnosis that wrongly shaped a child's life, I left that school and ended up in the traditional high school because I just did not want to be targeted and on that teacher's radar anymore.

The irony was that this same High School Counselor continued to target several students each year and many of them left the Magnet School because they felt that they were being labeled as problematic instead of gifted. Could you imagine how much progress these students could have made and the experiences they could have gained if they continued at the Magnet School full-term; if only there was not a person that had misdiagnosed them in the first place.

Often times, Gifted and Talented Children, learn at a pace above the average norm and as such they get bored and restless because they are waiting for their peers. I recall as a child, the assignments were so "easy" to me and I often times could read a book once and recalled all the content. Growing up I had all A's in my report card until Grade 6.

School was just not challenging enough so I had to fill my time with other activities that challenged me mentally and physically. I had an abundance of energy as a child. This often drove my mother who was a "Tiger Mom" crazy and she often asked if I could just sit still. I found sitting still to be a waste of time and resources and wanted to try everything and explore on my own.

As a parent, I would highly encourage you to truly take time to get to the root of your child's issues before entrusting in the decisions of a professional because no one knows your child better than you. And if you do not know your own child, then it is time to assess where your energies and focus are being put.

As I mentioned before Grade 6, all of my report cards were A's except for oral communication. So let's further explain why it is important to get to the root of your child's issues. Gifted and Talented children exhibit more depth than an average person can relate to. For oral communications, it was not that I did not know how to speak English or my subject matter. I was just fearful because at an early age, I learned that if I cried or spoke up, I could have my life taken away by being thrown overboard into shark-infested waters.

Let's explore another story that grades do not often tell. During the summer before 6th grade, I went to Patrol Camp and prior to that I was just a trainee, not any Officer. The rule was that the two highest scores from Patrol Camp would become the Captains. Many of my friends were already officers (Sergeants and Lieutenants) before the camp. I went there for fun only but when I took the test, I came back with the highest score. My score was even higher than the co-captain who had always been a Lieutenant.

When that announcement was made in the beginning of sixth grade, all the Officers that had dreamed of being promoted, was so upset with me and everyone saw me as a threat. I lost so many friends because of that one promotion. Subconsciously I must have equated having good grades and scoring the best to being more problematic. From that day on, I learned to dummy down my abilities and just blend in.

I vowed that I was not going to be noticed for my abilities because it would bring more disappointment to everyone and it would promote anti-social behaviors towards me and amongst the people, I had always valued unity. I did not see the achievement of getting the Captain status as an honor, but more than a curse. So much that I had to make up a story and was caught in the lie and kicked off the squad so that everyone again felt that I was no longer a threat.

My mother blamed the fact that my grades went south because I was spending time with the wrong crowd; in the truth the Patrol Camp was the primary trigger. If my mother had only taken the time to truly understand the emotion of why I did not want to excel and be smart, I could have probably gotten back on the right path a lot sooner. It was too painful and lonely to excel, too ostracizing, so I learned it was better to be average. Not until I got to the Magnet School did I feel comfortable again with portraying my abilities.

The same thing occurred in the workplaces. I indirectly learned that being proactive and creative would be a hindrance instead. This is probably why Tony Hsieh felt like he could only work in a corporation for 6 months. So I learned to dummy down my capabilities, so much so that my infamous answer to everything was, "I don't know." Perhaps the question for parents to ask is, why is my child trying to hide their talent, what is truly going on in their thought processes? And what is the best environment to help foster their talents?

Why is it important to possess creativity and proactive attitudes you may ask? Let's think about Bill Gates, Michael Dell, Tony Hsieh, Anthony Robbins, if they simply conformed to the norms and stayed within the lines of their coloring books, where would the products or services that they are offering be today? Tony Hsieh's innovation is going to make a sociological impact for business leadership. By removing titles, his company will allow people to truly excel in their talent and curb abuse of power and authority.

The labeled ADHD/ADD children are here to teach the lessons of gratitude and compassion. Research studies have shown that the majority of these kids come from ancestry that valued perfectionism and achievement, where control was an indirect lesson they observed from their parents or grandparents. These children are teaching their parents to have self-compassion for all their grandness in life.

As Oprah Winfrey so eloquently said, "Be thankful for what you have; you'll end up having more. If you concentrate on what you don't have, you will never, ever have enough." Often times we get so busy with chasing after the things we want, after the things that are somewhere out there, which we forget to enjoy the present moment.

From a psychological perspective, if you trace the ancestry of the parents or grandparents of those that are deemed as having "ADD/ADHD" you will see a pattern that many have self-mandated many stressors in their life. These people normally go on to planning the next thing and the next thing and forget to enjoy the things they achieved so far, these are the indirect lessons their children picked up. A lesson of gratitude will help alleviate a lot of their stress.

Let's examine this issue from a sociological perspective. Does it truly make sense to put these children into a learning disabled environment? If these kids pick up things quickly and easily get bored, does it make sense to further decrease the speed of their learning? Here's something more for you to ponder over?

Based on my experiences the best mode of learning for grade improvements for the gifted students' weaker topics is to recruit a private tutor versus putting them in a learning disabled class because it is not their inability to learn but more their inability to remain focused. These children often times are inquisitive and quick learners, with the proper tutoring they can excel in the subject. With a one-on-one tutor they are learning at their desired pace.

I had private tutoring for both English when they put me in ESOL and calculus when they tried to tell me I could never comprehend the subject matter. The only issue was I had questions that the teachers did not take the time to answer or could not readily answer. Private tutoring often is a short duration because these children have tendencies to be quick learners. These children adapt better in private institutions or smaller classrooms because there is more attention provided from the teacher.

This comes from an excerpt that was presented to the U.S. House of Representatives Subcommittee:

The legislation which is now the Individuals with Disabilities Education Act (IDEA) was originally the Education for all Handicapped Children Act of 1975. The legislation which is now the Individuals with Disabilities Education Act (IDEA) was originally the Education for all Handicapped Children Act of 1975. In 1998, 51.1 percent of special education children were in the category of "specific learning disabilities."

At that time, the IDEA legislation provided schools with an additional $400 per year for each child in special education. There followed a dramatic spike in the amount of methylphenidate (Ritalin) consumed in the US. According to the DEA, the production and use of methylphenidate increased almost 6 fold between 1990 and 1995.

The so-called learning disorders have, sadly, become a way for financially strapped schools to make ends meet. In many states, schools have become authorized Medicaid providers and funds can be collected in behalf of a child labeled with one of the learning or behavior disorders.

In a letter dated October 8, 1996, the Illinois State Board of Education strongly encouraged the superintendent of one of its districts to participate in Medicaid incentives. The letter stated that Illinois had received $72,500,000 in federal Medicaid money in 1996 and those Medicaid dollars have been used for a variety of non-medical purposes and that "the potential for the dollars is limitless."

♡☮ Dr. S' Insights

Dr. Unger and I created an ADD/ADHD presentation for my patients in St. Louis which outlined extensive chiropractic, nutritional, neurological, vaccination research and "treatment" protocols that helped enhance these patients lifestyle. These recommendations were based on proven clinical success with helping children improve their well-being and lifestyles with these particular diagnoses.

Children today are growing up in a fast-paced environment and the trick was to help these children learn to complete tasks in a timely fashion that accommodated to this face-paced world. These children were often classified as not being able to complete task because of their attention span limitations so one of the primary goals was to help them improve focus and attention.

These patients were the most challenging because the parents had so much reservation and disbelief in our "treatments" at first. These mothers often wondered if it was a myth that their children could truly be helped. These cases provided me with more motivation to excel and disprove their own theories of what is possible within their kids. Many at times, these mothers looked at me with doubt and would simply state that "Nobody else was able to address this condition and help my son or daughter, what makes you different?"

What they did not realize was that I had differing healing modalities to work with. As a chiropractic Craniopathy I was able to put my hands on the child's head and instantaneously the mother saw these hyperactive children relax and melt into a calmer state.

What these mothers were not cognizant of was the brain-body connection that triggered many of these issues. If the brain is irritated it will try to shake it off by ramping up the stimulation. But with chiropractic Craniopathy it will aid in decompressing and removing the irritation quickly and restore balance to the child's brain. Simultaneously the "treatments" have improved their grades as well as their overall behaviors in both the home and academic settings.

I have experienced so many successful cases within this arena, but the most rewarding aspect of working with these children is when the parent or the teachers calls my office and sings praises on how the child is listening better and being more socially inclined in school (participating in projects and initiating or volunteering on their own.)

Here are some of my professional insights regarding ADD/ADHD:
The first thing I look for is any cranial distortion or strain pattern, which is explained in the Chiropractic chapter. If the brain cannot communicate properly with the body we can expect a deficiency to occur. So just imagine your brain not being able to tell the legs to move, how could walking be possible then?

Another metaphor is you telling your child to go clean their room and they just ignore you, what would be your next instinct: to shout right? The brain will do the same thing and increase its communication until action and expectations are actually met. The issue is that by increasing the intensity of the communication from the brain, it makes the ADD/ADHD child vamp up with even more energy and intensity.

The brain not only increases the communication to a single part of the body, but shouts this command across the whole body that can cause overstimulation. This is kind of like the mother that screamed at her child for not cleaning the room. Not only did the child receive the message but everybody else in the house and perhaps even some neighbors heard the message loud and clear.

Another issue is that parts of the cranial distortion are caused from the retention of the primitive reflexes which are corrected at the cranial using eye movements. Even though this rectification to removing the retained primitive reflex has good results, the child and its body might need time to adjust to this new pattern of thinking/learning. Therefore, the cranial adjustment might take 1-3 visits before it is permanently resolved.

The primitive reflex, explained in the brain section, can trigger an old pattern of neurology and limit the advancement of the child. These patterns can come back even as adults when stressors occur in our life. To metaphorically illustrate what it will be like to live by the old pattern, imagine trying to live your life today but using the same lifestyle and standards as back in the 70's, how productive or effective would it be for your daily living habits. This is why it is important to have primitive reflexes fixed early in life and to reduce stress levels that might retrigger them.

Correlation with the first cervical and the occiput bone also have shown a relaxation process and an increase in focus for these children. But every child is unique and if trauma created the initial problem, please allow time for their body to accept the change and stabilize the changes toward a more permanent lifestyle within their body's balance.

Another memorable client that had primitive reflex issues and exhibited hyperactive behavior was also pleased with the medical interventions that I performed. This young child was probably 6 years old. She had a host of emotions and crisis since she was born. She also wasn't able to wear long pants at all and wearing shoes was not possible due to her sensory sensitivity.

She was categorized as having hypersensitive sensory disorder and was told that nothing could be done to help alleviate this issue or improve her lifestyle and that she was destined to live this particular mode of life for the remainder of her adulthood.

However, after I treated her twice, her behavior changed so much that her mother wondered what happened and who this new girl in front of her was, it was a total transformation that made her mother extremely grateful. After 1 year the girl was able to wear pants, shoes and socks. She also listened and did not scream anymore to communicate. She was given back a normalized lifestyle and could experience many things that were not deemed possible with her condition.

Resources

The Joyfully Parenting Mastery Program - http://joyfullyparenting.com/
Colour Your Way to Creative Consciousness - www.createspace.com/4243850
Tweedle Wink Right Brain Kids - www.rightbrainkids.com/ new/home.php

Stress Free Kids - www.stressfreekids.com/
Mercury Learning Systems - www.acceleratedlearningmethods.com/index.html
Kids Psych - www.kidspsych.org/parents.html
Imagination Stage - www.imaginationstage.org/about/about-imagination-stage
Centers for Research on Creativity - www.croc-lab.org
Creative Kids Magazine - www.ckmagazine.org
The Gift of ADHD and the Gift of Adult ADD by Dr. Lara Honos-Webb - http://www.visionarysoul.com/
Brain Sync - High Focus - http://www.brainsync.com/high-focus.html
Brain Power - http://www.brainsync.com/brain-power-16049.html

11

Autistic Children's Gift to the World: Unconditional Love

The Current Label of Autism

Imagine if you will that feeling you had when you found out you were bringing the most precious gift into the world. The way your heart may have fluttered, the sudden feelings of panic infused with an unexplainable joy, that rollercoaster of an emotional journey that took you through curves, turns, flipping upside down, some of which you already knew were coming so you threw your arms up with your head back smiling as the adrenaline rushed through your body. While some of the other twists and turns were such a surprise you quickly pulled your arms down, grabbing the bar across your lap for safety as your heart nearly bursts through your chest with instantaneous shots of fear.

That also has been the emotional rollercoaster for nearly 1 in 50 parents in the United States as they find out that the perfect bundle of joy they have been preparing for over the last 9 months is diagnosed with autism. Although the most prevalent and undesired childhood developmental disorder, they are still no less than perfect as that parent looks at their tiny little hands and feet, precious little face, and those beautiful eyes that look up without a care in the world.

This is happening almost every 20 minutes to parents across the world, and even with the joy and love they have as they look at their new son or daughter, it is accompanied by worry, "will I be able to supply all of his/her needs," fear, "I don't want him/her to have to go through ridicule or mistreatment as they grow up," guilt that they may have caused it, and the strain of "what could I/we have done to prevent this?" Between 1997 and 2008, the number of children with autism rose from 8.2 million to roughly 10 million, or more than 15% of all kids between the ages of 3 and 17, the researchers at the Centers for Disease Control found.

According to data from the Autism Society, the annual cost to society from the illness is $137 billion. The Autism Society cites estimates of $3.2 million for the lifetime costs of such care. Behavioral therapies for children can cost $40,000 to $50,000 per year. Caring for an adult with autism in a supported residential setting can cost $50,000 to $100,000 per year.

It is not a 'new concept' that the world is in desperate need of change, change in health, wealth, education, compassion, empathy, and understanding just to state the least bit; With the growing number of children and adults being diagnosed daily it is a clear indication that the change needs to happen yesterday. The chemicals that are so freely used in our everyday existence need to cease to exist as these delicate human beings require more natural living conditions as it is essential to their quality of life.

Energy and blood circulation (for individuals diagnosed with autism) are blocked at the surface of the body so that the skin and senses don't feel normally, and the deep energy sources cannot be nourished by the outside world. This usually causes the delay in cognitive development, socialization skills, and physical growth.

Autism symptoms are represented in one of three areas: social interaction, social communication, and imaginative play. All the symptoms on this list are possible in an autistic child; however, the diagnosis is made when a child exhibits:
- 2 impairments of social interaction
- 1 impairment in communication
- 1 repetitive and stereotypic patterns of behavior, interest, or activity
- 1 delay or abnormality prior to age 3 in the area of social interaction, communication, and symbolic or imaginative play

It has been said that boys are much more likely to be gifted or autistic. Research shows that at least 6 times as many boys are diagnosed autistic as girls. Recent research also indicates that left brain is slower to develop in boys than girls. But girls with autism are often more severely affected than boys and score lower on intelligence tests. So what does that really mean on a global level?

There is no exact count of number of babies born as there are a wide range of factors involved, however, statistical mathematical calculations that are done show the average number of births a day is about 353,015 according to the World Almanac and Book of Facts 2014.

With that being said, if approximately 1 in 50 babies born will be diagnosed with autism, there are roughly 2.5 million children per year with this disorder. At growing rates like that we need to be proactively and diligently transforming the current state of our societal habitat, instead of reactively and lethargically as it has been thus far. Not only for the current need of our existing millions of people that have it, but for the millions more to come, but even more than that-for the millions we may be able to prevent by changing and educating.

The Better Label for Autism – "CHILD GENIUS"

Gifted children can have an intense focus on certain subjects, poor cooperation skills in a group setting, and may have difficulties in social situations. Surprisingly yet interestingly, these same traits are also common among students with Autism Spectrum Disorder (ASD.)Giftedness and ASD can sometimes mask one another so that a child is only recognized as having one, but the two can also coexist.

Gifted children can be intensely focused on certain subjects, have poor cooperation skills in a group setting, and may have difficulties in social situations. Take a moment and think back to your school days or visualize your workplace. As this thought/visual begins to come to focus think of some of the smartest, most intellectual people you encounter/ed. Now that you can see them, what kind of personality did they have? Were they outgoing and social, or timid and introverted? Interestingly, these same traits are also common among students with Autism Spectrum Disorder (ASD.)

Recent studies of gifted and talented children indicate that gifted children typically also have disabilities in language related or social skills. Interestingly 1 in 10 children within the autism spectrum exhibit gifted abilities. All child geniuses had an absolutely amazing memory for detail and scored above 99% of the world at attention to detail which are similar characteristics of autistic children.

This could also mean that of the 10 million children that have already been diagnosed, if 1 in 10 of them shows gifted abilities there are close to 1 million children that may have otherwise been recognized as gifted which would have ultimately impaired them in the future because a lot of their emotional and psychological needs would not have been assessed or met.

This type of oversight could deem catastrophic going forward like a growing wildfire. Think of that small stack of dry leaves or pile of sticks that catch fire. People start to walk past if because it seems contained and harmless. What they didn't pay attention to were the other elements around it, which later caught the shards of fire sparks that also began to burn and soon spread to the next area and so forth with no attention until once it has gotten so big that it is uncontrollable, and is now the center of all attention.

Dr. Ruthsatz has studied child prodigies for over 15 years and recently has focused on Jacob Barnett.

As a child, doctors told Jacob Barnett's parents that their autistic son would probably never know how to tie his shoes or be able to read. Not only did he teach himself all of high school math in just two weeks, when he was just 10 years old, Indiana University accepted him as a student. He has an IQ score of 170 in math which is the highest possible score. Some experts have been on record as saying the 14-year-old prodigy has an IQ higher than Einstein's and is headed toward a Nobel Prize.

His parents provided him with all the typical autistic therapies; however, by third grade they realized that their son needed more than the average special education program and as fate had it he started attending college classes with his mother due to time constraints on her part. At the end of the semester, at eight years old Jacob aced the astronomy final exam.

Iris Grace Halmshaw, a 3-year old British toddler loves water, trees, wind, dancing on tiptoes and holding things in her left hand. Although she can't talk yet due to her autism, amazingly she is able to express herself through beautiful paintings that have been sold to collectors for hundreds of dollars. Alexis Wineman, Miss Montana 2012, is the first-ever Miss America contestant who lives with autism.

In fact some of our greatest minds in history might have been labeled "Autistic" if they'd had such diagnosis at the time. It just takes time to see these hidden treasures, and unfortunately, many people don't want to take that time to unlock the potential these kids have. Children with Autism are like the pot of gold at the end of a rainbow, or the buried pirate's treasure. If you dive deep enough, and look with open eyes, you'll find all the riches they have to offer, priceless.

In the movie Rain Man, Raymond has autism, and one of the manifestations of his condition is his photographic memory usually with little understanding of the subject matter. He is also a mental calculator with the ability to instantly count hundreds of objects at once, far beyond the normal range of human abilities. With all of this, he is not affectionate, yet loveable and delicate.

Research reveals that music can be a powerful therapeutic tool for building language and language rehabilitation within the brain. Some people, who have difficulty with stuttering, will not stutter when they sing their words. People sing what they want to say, and some show improvement in their fluency of speech. This implies that there is a great opportunity to use music as a bridge to language to train the musical area of the brain to take on the ability to comprehend and process language.

Take for instance the piano. The ability to 'tickle the ivory' with two hands increases bilateral coordination, as well as auditory processing to hear what is being played and memory of those sounds and sequences to replicate it. Having practiced over and over, balancing that hand-eye coordination has refined fine motor skills which also leads to better handwriting.

Singing is also another great form of communication, which can be said for more than just in the capacity of those diagnosed, but people in general. Music touches the soul, it caters to the human need to feel, whether it be to feel love, power, excitement, joy, motivation, expression, anger, hurt, sorrow, or celebration. Through the lyrics, structure, patterns and repetition language is built.

The Brain's Anatomy of Autism

Approximately one-third of children with autism are macro cephalic, that is, they have an exceptionally large head and brain resulting from an excess growth of brain tissue. This excess of brain tissue is believed to alter neural networks, not to be mistaken for Down syndrome. Autistic children without abnormally large heads may have altered synaptic channels. Both environment and genetics seem to be implicated in autism. New research studies from the "Annals of Neurology" shows a troubling correlation between a woman's thyroid function and her child's risk for autism

A little known fact is the vestibule, which is part of the inner ear, controls balance, coordination, and muscle tone. In fact, there is not one single muscle of the body, including the muscles of the eyes, that is not under the control of the vestibular system. It also impacts speech: this is demonstrated by the fact that children, who do not talk, often start to make sounds when their vestibule is stimulated. A proper functioning of the vestibule is therefore of prime importance.

The vestibule also plays a key role in processing sensory input. When it runs smoothly, sensory-integration is optimal and no problems arise. If this is not the case, the child feels bombarded by thousands of pieces of information all at once and tries to protect himself/herself by cutting off his/her environment. This can only reinforce the child's sense of isolation. The ear-brain-larynx link is essential in producing language.

Earlier the point was made around energy and blood circulation and how they affect the body in a way that abnormally utilizes the senses which can cause delays in cognitive development, socialization skills, and physical growth. This is apparent when an autistic person, albeit a child or adult throws a fit/tantrum when they hear loud or unsettling sounds, covering their ears or making other noises to block out the unwanted sound.

In the world of what's considered 'normal' (as opposed to having any type of disorder, special circumstance, or dis-ease) we tend to protest these behaviors when there is an unwanted stressor. Prime example would be when the wife walks around the house nagging about the trash and the toilet seat as the husband is trying to decompress and watch CNN or ESPN after a long work week. He may not put his hands over his ears like he would've in kindergarten, while yelling "blah, blah, blah, blah, blah" as loud as he can to block her voice, whilst sticking his tongue out and marching around in circles. But in his head he is.

Same as when your boss comes to talk to you about things that you couldn't care less about so in your head you start to hum or sing your favorite song not only to block him/her out, but because it just soothes you and makes you feel better. The difference for someone with autism is that it isn't just that easy. That unpleasing sound or noise is not just effecting the auditory system, but their other senses, their whole body, causing not only discomfort in the ears, but the whole body as they cannot screen/filter that 'stressor' to one compartment.

To make things worse, sensory channels are often not isolated from each other: autistic children can experience light as sound or vice versa which is an example of how the senses are also responding to this onslaught of stimulations. Tactile defensiveness is, in some cases, another way to attempt to protect oneself. Lack of eye contact might be another strategy to avoid to "taking in" what is perceived as overwhelming.

This can only lead to the feeling that the world is a terrifying and chaotic place, which is an understatement in reality for the non-autistic population so imagine the amplification of that for someone that doesn't have the ability to phase part of it out, or adapt to the environment. It is thus clear that reducing hypersensitivity, regulating sensory-integration are key steps in reconnecting the autistic person to the environment.

As long as problems of this kind persist, the autistic child will not be willing to come out of his/her shell, deeming the world as unsafe and harsh. This almost seems like a gift, the ability to avoid experiencing the unpleasant reality of what is an unsafe and harsh world. But when it is not by choice, and potentially debilitating, it would be the 'holiday fruitcake' or 'ugly sweater' of gifts, the one that you hide, burn or throw away.

Autistic children's nature is to be the "voice" of love so they tune all harshness of the world out. This thing that seems like an unfair disadvantage that holds them back from potentially experiencing all that life in this chaotic world has to offer is the very thing that gives them the power to bypass the negative and embrace the positive.

The Theory of Mind Deficit

This theory has been successful in suggesting a cause of the core social and communicative impairments in ASDs. Theory of Mind refers to the everyday ability to attribute mental states (beliefs, desires) to understand and predict behavior.

People with ASDs appear to be specifically impaired in this ability, as reflected in tests of mental state attribution. The ability to 'know what someone is thinking' as assessed in these tests, is related to everyday social and communicative competence. Non-verbal communication is the foundation of verbal communication. Without good non-verbal skills, verbal skills will not develop.

The Executive Function Theory

This theory postulates deficits in those abilities thought to depend on the frontal lobes that allow flexible behavior.

'Executive function' is a term covering a range of high-level abilities such as planning future action, modifying behavior according to feedback, shifting between different behaviors, resisting habitual but no longer adaptive behaviors. People with ASDs have been shown to perform poorly on tests of many of these functions

The Central Coherence Theory

This theory and one of its variants, the theory of enhanced perceptual discrimination, attempt to explain the uneven profile of abilities and difficulties in ASDs. Central coherence refers to the everyday tendency to put information together to extract higher-level meaning, to remember, for example, the gist of a story rather than its details or exact words. People with ASDs seem to show a bias, instead, for part over wholes and often excel at noticing and recalling detailed information.

Perception and processing of features is believed to be superior, possibly at the expense of processing global information, disentangling weak coherence and executive dysfunction and drawing in autism and attention deficit/ hyperactivity disorder. In the case of Autism/Asperger's research believe the underactive and suppressed hemisphere is, primarily the right hemisphere.

This fact can be used to explain the other two primary theories, lack of central coherence and theory of mind. In this theory, involving the lack of central coherence, autistic individuals seems to be stuck in a local processing mode focused on detail not able to place themselves in the context of the big picture. It is well established that the left hemisphere is primarily responsible for local processing and right hemisphere is involved in global processing.

Also, in theory of mind it is believed that autistic individuals primarily lack mind reading capacities or the ability to non-verbally communicate with other individuals. They cannot read body posture or facial expressions that non-verbally and subconsciously relay information especially about emotional natures to other individuals.

They seem to be very literal in the receptive and expressive communication abilities and they lack permeability in speech. They also seem to be unable to auditory hear changes in tone and absorbency related especially to emotion. All these abilities are well recognized to be right hemisphere abilities.

Foods That Impact Autism

Autistic children frequently have digestive disorders. Around half of all autistic children have gastrointestinal (GI) symptoms, such as diarrhea and constipation, and the prevalence increases as the children get older.

Being the parent or guardian caring for a child with autism means much more than being able to help protect them from the environmental triggers; It is also from the things that can/will eventually cause internal discomfort with their immune system. This can be inflammation (immature digestive system) and enzyme deficiencies also known as detoxification. Because of this, vaccinations are more dangerous than they are preventative since they have a more difficult time breaking down and eliminating toxins; it instead remains in their system longer. This concept is known as toxic overload.

The lighter side to dealing with toxic over load is that parents/guardians have two ways to decrease the latency of toxic load. Oddly enough they are the same two ways all living beings/organisms deal with the need to change, through diet and home environment. Some children will display a positive change when the diet is altered and some may not respond at all. The same could be said for changing the environment as well. It will be a process that can only be proven by test, you won't know which will be more helpful until you put it to the test and actually try it.

There are over 20 studies of vitamin B6 with Magnesium for autism. Vitamin B6 is required for over 100 enzymatic reactions, including but not limited to the production of major neurotransmitters (serotonin, dopamine, and others) and glutathione (needed for detoxification.) Magnesium is used to prevent the possibility of hyperactivity, which can occur if the vitamin B6 is taken by itself

Many children and adults with autism have both

1. A decreased ability to convert vitamin B6 to its active form

2. Defective enzymes for making key neurotransmitters that require an unusually high amount of the active form of vitamin B6.

There is a newly identified milk protein in formulas, casomorphin, and it has been shown to be a possible cause of ADHD and autism. High concentrations of casomorphin are found in the blood and urine of children with autism and schizophrenia. This research was done by a physiologist at the University of Florida Dr. J. Robert Cade. Preliminary findings from that study showed 95 percent of 81 autistic and schizophrenic children studied have 100 times the normal levels of the milk protein in their blood and urine.

Some children with autism have low levels of beneficial bacterial and high levels of harmful bacteria and yeast. The harmful bacteria and yeast produce toxins that can severely affect mental functioning and behavior. Although vaccines are in place to help, in the case of autism they cause gastrointestinal damage which causes malabsorption of nutrients necessary for proper brain function. Also, many children with autism had increased use of oral antibiotics in infancy, which alter gut flora and thereby almost completely stop the body's ability to excrete mercury

In recent studies of behavioral patterns in preschoolers, processed foods, particularly containing red dye (in addition to other artificial coloring) result in more negative behavior problems. If you are looking for a good starting point, or 'baby step' eliminating artificial coloring would be a good place to start. By simply taking a few extra minutes to read the labels you could be decreasing the opportunity for your child to ingest petroleum, lead, mercury, arsenic, and other byproducts.

Lead usually targets the oxygen-carrying protein in red blood cells first, eventually attacking your nervous system. The primary effects of mercury on infants and children may result in damage to neurological development. Different levels of arsenic can cause several kinds of "cancer," as well as headaches and confusion. While it is true that colorings don't have large amounts of any of these contaminants, there is no good reason to consume them, they offer no nutritional value. The connection between the Yellow Dye #5 and asthma was the reason the Food and Drug Administration (FDA) first required it to be listed by name on ingredient labels

Research has shown that some children with autism improve on the gluten-free/dairy-free diet. This can also be said for children (and adults) with other health issues such as weight, and eczema. Positive changes include more awareness of the environment, more eye contact, decreased self-injurious behaviors, decreased aggression, better bowel function and eating a wider variety of foods.

We use many chemical products in the home ranging from cosmetics and hair products, air fresheners, fabric softeners, bleaches and cleaning solvents, to garden chemicals that contain additives that are harmful to children and the environment. Children are exposed to these both by inhaling them, and touching them, and they contribute to toxic load

Is it possible to live without these modern day advancements in the products that we use? Would it be reasonable to ask of such a thing on a much larger scale to cause a 'movement' and not just small 'ripple' in this ocean sized issue? It absolutely is possible, sixty plus years ago these products didn't even exist yet the world was still turning and the people were still flourishing. It is far beyond reasonable as well, look around you and begin to notice how many other natural or healthier alternatives are more visible and easier to find.

Take for instance five years ago, Whole Foods and Farmer's Markets were far and few in most all places, not to mention considerably more expensive making it more difficult for the vast majority of people to start making healthier decisions. Now fast forward back to now, now there are starting to be as many Whole Foods stores as large chain grocers. Even if you don't have one close to you, the chain grocery stores now have larger fresh produce and vegetable isles, and actually offer more organic/all natural options. There are even some grocery stores that have a whole section of the store just for organic/gluten free/ all natural products. It is no longer a scavenger hunt to find the things necessary to create a healthy living lifestyle for anyone.

Not only in the market place are these changes happening but also in the food business. In years past the best alternative for a sweet treat for kids (and adults) were Dairy Queen, Baskin Robins, and a few others dependent on what part of the country you lived? Now there are more frozen yogurt places than ever from Sweet Frog to Five Spot and others between that also give a large selection of fruit toppings with the candy toppings. In the new shopping centers that are being built there are more all-natural salons and restaurants available making it easier to choose versus having to settle for something less desirable because of proximity?

The choice is yours; however the challenge is leverage. What is more important is its indulgence in the things that may seem quick and "easy", or putting yourself in a position to notice the alternative options that are equally as available? With more people choosing to give up the chemical and processed products this paradigm shift will be more than a 'movement' it will be a driving 'force' in the way we live, anywhere from health care to our sustainability as living and breathing organisms. Recreating the natural habitat that once existed will not allow better care for anyone with pre-existing disorders, dis-ease, or ailments but begin to prevent more people from being born with them later.

Billionaire Parenting Tips for Autism

Vaccinations

It wasn't until the early 1940's that the first case of autism was recorded, ironically that was a few years after a preservative called Thimerosal was introduced in vaccines. Thimerosal is made with 49.6% mercury and has been credited with the massive growth in cases of autism, attention deficit disorder, speech delay and other disorders over past decades. Ines Ligron the Director of the Miss Universe pageant faced autism with her youngest child Luca. Luca at 18 months showed signs of autism due to mercury poisoning from his second shot of DTP followed by a flu vaccine. Her son went into shock and did not begin talking again until after 5 years old.

Exactly five years ago, the federal government disclosed that most American children were being exposed to levels of mercury in vaccines above federal safety limits. Since then, officials moved to phase out mercury from childhood vaccines. Thimerosal has been removed from most routine vaccinations given to American children. But it is still found in the majority of flu shots, which the US government now recommends for pregnant women and children between 6 and 23 months of age.

Mercury is also found in tetanus, diphtheria-tetanus, pertussis and meningitis vaccines, which are sometimes, though not routinely given to children. It is also still used in many over-the-counter products, including nasal sprays, ear and eye drops, anabolic steroids, and even a hemorrhoid "treatment."

The United States federal court has presided over landmark cases for the autism community, filing official court decisions that have linked vaccinations as an environmental trigger of autism. The U.S. government created this specific court in 1986 to protect pharmaceutical companies from the direct lawsuits arising due to the preponderance of illnesses and injuries that were stemming from the companies' vaccination products.

In that same article it used the case of the Bailey Banks Family in 2000 as an example. The Court ruled that the MMR vaccine at issue actually caused the conditions from which Bailey suffered and continues to suffer from the spectrum of autistic disorders.

It wasn't until Bailey's fifteenth month check-up, he received the MMR vaccination. Bailey then experienced a seizure 16 days later during which Bailey's mother witnessed his eyes rolling back and him choking, and he was taken to the Emergency Room.

Dr. Ivan Lopez, board certified Psychiatrist with a subspecialty in Child Neurology said that Bailey's neurological deficit was the result of a vaccine he received. Bailey was found to have a high fever and irritable and to have vomited three times. MRI, EEG, and full neurological exams were performed on Bailey. Dr. Lopez explained to the Court that ADEM (Acute Disseminated Encephalomyelitis) is a rare inflammatory dis-ease of the central nervous system. ADEM occurs when a person has been exposed to a foreign protein, in this case (the "vaccine",) which causes the body to produce antibodies (specifically T-cells,) such that the body's antibodies turn against and destroy foreign objects.

Rhythmic Movement Training

Rhythmic Movement Training (RMT) developed 25 years ago by a Swedish psychiatrist by the name of Dr. Harald Blomberg, has been successfully used to treat people with learning and developmental disabilities in Europe. RMT is based on infants and the movements they develop during what is considered the fastest stage of brain development which is in their first year.

You have probably observed a baby in a crib doing little rocking, rhythmic movements. Those movements are hard-wired into the baby's brain (primitive reflexes) and are essential for healthy brain development. By using similar movements at a later age, kids and adults can build new neural pathways (nerve nets) in their brains, increasing the speed and efficacy of their brain.

All babies are born with primitive reflexes. Primitive reflexes are what makes infants begin to raise its head, roll over, put things in its mouth, rock on its hands and knees, crawl, and eventually walk. If one of these developmental milestones is skipped it may cause problems later in life. When the primitive reflexes remain active or are retriggered by "fight-flight" responses, then many difficulties can appear.

If the Primitive Reflexes are retained past the first year of life they can interfere with:
- Vestibular function (balance)
- Auditory perception and integration (listening and hearing)
- Visual and oculomotor function (movement of the eyes, visual, eye tracking)
- Gross and fine motor coordination (sports or drawing are examples)
- Hemispheric integration (Left and Right brain connection; artist versus math)
- Endocrine and neurochemical functions (hormones, stress)
- Social cueing and individual behavior (interaction with people and peers)
- Learning

Primitive Reflexes are repetitive, automatic movements that are essential for development of head control, muscle tone, sensory integration and development. They form the basis of our postural, lifelong reflexes. These primitive reflexes surface intrauterine and in infancy and become inhibited as the movements do their job and movements become more practiced and controlled.

These necessary reflexes can react negatively for children born via cesarean section, trauma, toxicity exposure, anesthetics, chemical, genetics, impaired detoxification pathways which may cause the brainstem and higher centers to get overwhelmed.

According to the Environmental Working Group, American researchers have found an average of 200 industrial compounds, pollutants, and other chemicals in the umbilical cord blood of newborns, including seven dangerous pesticides that were supposedly banned in the US more than 30 years ago.

Emotional Stressors (in life) have been credited as being the most common sudden onset or trigger to the retained primitive reflexes. These stressors may be occurring pre/post pregnancy as well as in and outside of the womb. Medical peer-reviewed research has said that 90% of all physical dis-ease is linked to emotional stressors.

Contributing causes of ADD/ADHD, autism, learning challenges, sensory integration disorders (including challenges with vision and hearing,) and developmental delay are linked to incomplete integration of primitive reflexes. It doesn't stop there, it is also a contributor to other behavioral identifiers such as addiction, extreme shyness, lack of confidence, and constantly feeling overwhelmed. Rhythmic Movements assist both children and adults in the completion of those primitive reflex patterns and make the transformation of what was challenging before they became integrated.

There are many primitive reflexes. The major retained reflexes that should be evaluated include the following:

- Moro Reflex

The Moro Reflex, sometimes called the infant startle reflex, is an automatic response to a sudden change in sensory stimuli. A sudden change of any kind (bright light, change in body position, temperature, loud noise, intense touch, Etc.) can trigger the Moro Reflex.

- Tonic Labyrinthine Reflex (TLR)

TLR provides the baby with a means of learning about gravity and mastering neck and head control outside the womb. This reflex is important for giving the baby the opportunity to practice balance, increase muscle tone; and develop the proprioceptive and balance senses.

The TLR interacts with other reflexes to help the infant to start developing coordination, posture and correct head alignment.

- Asymmetrical Tonic Neck Reflex (ATNR)

The ATNR is important for developing one-sided movements. When the infant turns his head to one side, the arm and leg of that side automatically extend. Intrauterine the ATNR provides the necessary stimulation for developing muscle tone and the vestibular system.

It assists with the birth process, providing one of the means for the baby to "corkscrew" down the birth passage. ATNR also provides training in hand-eye coordination. By six months of age, this reflex should evolve into more complex movement patterns. If the ATNR remains active it plays a significant contribution to academic problems at school.

- The Symmetrical Tonic Neck Reflex (STNR)

This is not a primitive reflex; however, it is transitional. It is an important developmental stage that transitions the baby from lying on the floor up to being able to crawl. At this stage in development, movement of the head is automatically linked to movement of the arms and legs.

If the STNR remains active, it is another main cause of inability to function in school. This is because up and down head movements remain linked to arm and leg movements, making school work effortful and difficult.

- <u>Spinal Galant Reflexes</u>

The Spinal Galant Reflexes works in conjunction with the Asymmetrical Tonic Neck Reflex (ATNR) to help the baby's journey down the birth canal. It is also thought to help babies balance and coordinate the body for belly crawling and creeping. It is thought to be connected to bladder function because a high percentage of children who are bedwetting past age 5 have an active Spinal Galant reflex.

- <u>Fear Paralysis Reflex (FPR)</u>

The FPR is a withdrawal reflex that emerges in the embryonic stage. It is a total body withdrawal away from stimulus that is normal intrauterine. The baby intrauterine reacts to this stimulus by withdrawing inward and freezing. As the fetus' tactile awareness develops, withdrawal upon contact gradually lessens.

Fear can be a lifelong challenge for some people, and often it is the result of FRP not being fully integrated at birth. Moro reflex, which is thought to be the first step in learning to cope with stress but when merged with FRP, becomes inactive before birth. Signs of FRP active in people may come off as more drawn to negativity and may often appear to be very anxious. Now just because someone is an unpleasant person doesn't mean they have FRP active, so don't go diagnosing your family member, or that annoying manager or co-worker, or that neighbor that always seems to have a grunt. But in all seriousness, it may be what has prevented someone from being able to achieve forward movement to a meaningful, interactive life.

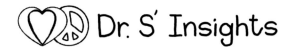 Dr. S' Insights

According to Dr. Stéphane, the most effective way to resolve the retained primitive reflexes is the combination of chiropractic Craniopathy and ocular reflexes. The late Dr. James Blumenthal was the pioneer who put together this unique way to integrate these reflexes. Some chiropractors utilize this technique.

Conscious Discipline

The developer of the Conscious Discipline program, Dr. Becky A. Bailey is not only a recognized expert in childhood education and developmental psychologist, but is an award-winning author as well. Two books we highly recommend are: "I Love You Rituals" and "Easy to Love, Difficult to Discipline."

The frame work for understanding the internal brain-body has been set up by the Conscious Discipline Brain State Model. It creates an awareness that the internal workings of the brain-body are most likely to produce certain behaviors in children and ourselves which can lead to a better understanding of how we can begin to consciously manage our own thoughts and emotions and model that behavior for children to mirror the same.

Life experience, when cognoscente, is a key indicator of how our internal emotional states dictate behavior. As an adult, you start to hear yourself and sometimes laugh at the thought that you "sound just like your parents". This could be something with your own children or in a social environment with many age group types when you notice what "undesirable" behavior to you is manifested.

Although there are some disciplinary behaviors that are necessary in order for children to differentiate right from wrong and positive versus negative reinforcement; some can be harsh, brash, or hurtful. Being able to identify these patterns in behavior from a parental or adult role model in ourselves will deem more effective by modeling the positive behaviors and reinforcing them, rather just going with the old mantra "do as I say, not as I do."

There are 7 goals of Dr. Becky A. Bailey's model:
- Take responsibility for our own upset and, in turn, teach children to be responsible for their own behavior.
- To perceive compassionately, and offer compassion to others and to ourselves.
- To create images of expected behavior in a child's brain.
- Learning to connect and guide instead of force and coerce.
- To learn to respond to what life offers instead of attempting to make the world go our way.
- Seeing the best in others keeps us in the higher centers of our brain so we can consciously respond instead of unconsciously react to life events.
- To teach a new skill rather than punishing others for lacking skills we think they should possess by now.

Healthy families have at their core commitment, trust, communication, and managing conflict. As we become more conscious of our reactions to conflict, we can choose a different response. The seven skills teach you to respond to conflict in a way that helps children move from the resistant, lower centers of their brain to the more cooperative, higher centers. The seven skill sets that will be taught to your children and you will be:
- Composure helps with: Anger management, gratification delay
- Encouragement helps with: Prosocial skills (kindness, caring, helpfulness)
- Assertiveness helps with: Bully prevention, healthy boundaries
- Choices helps with: Impulse control, goal achievement
- Empathy helps with: Emotional regulation, perspective taking
- Positive Intent helps with: Cooperation, problem-solving
- Consequences helps with: Learn from your mistakes

Positive Parenting

There are five key steps to the Triple P-Positive Parenting Program, founded by an Australian Professor of Clinical Psychology by the name of Matt Sanders. This five step program has been noted to have helped nearly 6 million children and their families. Now translated into 17 languages and being used in 20 countries, the most important, yet seemingly simple concept of positive parenting is that cooperation begins with trust.

The tips you will get in your Triple P sessions are based on these five steps. They are:

1. Create a safe, interesting environment

2. Have a positive learning environment

3. Use assertive discipline

4. Have realistic expectations

5. Take care of yourself as a parent

Pro Social Activities to Increase Empathy

Pets in the home have been known to help with social development for children. Learning the responsibilities of caring for the pet as it pertains to the walking, feeding, attention, and affection will be beneficial as the child grows and enters society and begins to play, work, interacting with others while they themselves are getting to understand who they are.

Be the catalyst in the journey with your child early on when it comes to taking responsibility, and acknowledging mistakes, especially in your actions not just theirs. This goes back to the modeling piece. When they see you take ownership of a mistake and move forward, they to feel as if it is ok to make mistakes and they will be able to replicate the process of owning up to it and being able to go forward.

Show compassion to them when you may have hurt their feelings, let them hear you say "I apologize" or "Please forgive me," this way they know how it feels to be on the giving and receiving ends of the situation. On one hand being the person that was affected by someone else's mistake or wrong doing, also to be the one that made the mistake to someone else and how it should be reconciled.

The study, published in Psychological Science, examined the link between prosocial media and levels of empathy and helpfulness in children from seven countries: Australia, China, Croatia, Germany, Japan, Romania, and the United States. Media has a strong influence on children at a time when they are still developing and learning social norms.

Video games are not just for entertainment, and are not another way for children to become introverted and secluded. They are actually very engaging. The stimulation to the brain they cause by neuroimaging is awarding to the brain. The association is between the brain's basis of learning and attention. The enhancement of a range of cognitive functions while engaging in action games can be affective teachers of response whether it is empathetic learning via prosocial gaming or violent gaming which renders aggressive tendencies.

Some examples of prosocial gaming include:

- Zoo Vet: Where you care about the condition of the animals and help them when they are ill or injured.
- Animal Crossing: Where you help other characters in your town by running errands for them

- Super Mario Sunshine: Where you clean off graffiti around the city, although there are some levels with aggression in this game.

Energy Medicine

Based on Chinese doctrine, human Chinese medicine, human beings are made with matter and energy. There are three energy sources that generate growth: head (upper Dan Tian) for mental growth, chest (middle Dan Tian) for social and emotional growth, and belly (lower Dan Tian) for physical growth. Think of the Dan Tian as a place of inner strength, it is often used in martial arts, Tai Chi and Qigong (the predecessor of acupuncture.)

In the situation where a child does not feel pain, he/she seldom has empathy for others; they can hurt themselves without realizing it, like a stubbed toe or a cut. Because they don't identify with pain or the unwanted and unpleasant sensation, they aren't aware of the emotional aftermaths that are attached and because when circulation gets really bad, there is no pain at all to them.

Reversely, sometimes even most gentle touch can cause pain, if there is some pressure in the chest, the child may refuse to be hugged. For instance, when there is blockage of energy and circulation in the chest, the child's fingers may not get adequate circulation in which case a gentle touch may hurt their fingers. That same blockage in the belly may cause constipation or diarrhea. In the instance that a child takes a long time to calm down and it seems for them to settle there is likely blockage in the head.

Qigong massage has been used in China for thousands of years to treat a variety of children's ailments. There is now a way to perform this technique from the comfort of your home. It was developed for autistic children that can reduce the symptoms of autism. Parents who have participated and given feedback have reported that after giving their children this simple, daily, fifteen minutes massage report that within a few months, tantrums and difficult behavior decreases, and language and social skills improves.

Another very effective method of energy medicine is sound therapy. Sound therapy utilizes specific harmony or sound to connect the voice-ear-brain connection. Research claims that by manipulating the body energy field with sound therapy the body's cellular physiology is restored and balanced.

Transcranial magnetic stimulation (TMS) may also be used for autistic children. It involves placement of an electromagnetic coil on the scalp with the production of low level electrical currents in the cortex secondary to rapid magnetic pulses; however, this technology is still in the research phases.

The Tomatis Method

(Cited with permission by Pierre Sollier PhD (http://articles.mercola.com/sites/articles/archive/2008/01/02/ tomastis-method-and-autism.aspx) and Grégoire Tomatis)

The Tomatis Method was created by Dr. Alfred TOMATIS, a French doctor who specialized in oto-rhino-laryngology (nose-throat-ear.) He devoted a significant part of his professional life to studying the relation between the ear and the voice, and by extension, between listening and communication.

According to Dr. Mercola, the Tomatis Method has shown encouraging results in the "treatment" of autism. About 60 % of autistic children seem to respond positively to it. The aim of the Tomatis Method is to develop or reestablish communication when it has been lost or impaired. The ear and its various functions, Tomatis points out, plays a key role in this respect.

Tomatis points out that although the ears were made for both hearing and listening, there are actually two different processes. Listening is more active, creating the desire to make use of the ears; while hearing is more passive.

A common example of this would be when we tune out, absorbed totally in the world of our thoughts, we do not hear the music on the radio. This small "autistic" experience is generalized in autistic children. It is not the "tuning out" that is exceptional but the "tuning in." Restoring the desire to "tune in", to listen, is therefore the key to restoring communication with the external world and with oneself.

The Tomatis Method desensitizes children who are hypersensitive to sounds. It takes time for the nervous system to integrate, reorganize and digest the "treatment", and to implement cognitive and behavior changes. During this period, the child may express more emotionally.

S/he may be more demanding for a while. It is his/her way of expressing feelings as s/he comes out of the shell. S/he may also spontaneously show more affection, accepting to be held and cuddled. At this stage, it is important not to try to elicit such expressions of affection because the child is only able to express those sporadically at first; affectionate behavior will increase as the child becomes more tuned in to the surrounding people.

Autistic children are also known to be afraid of transitions and to stick to a very rigid set of rules and behaviors. Parents' observations indicate that they start to show progressively more flexibility and that new behaviors appear. Hand flapping, repetitive body movements and self-destructive behaviors decrease also. Usually a rift in their usual routine can ruin an entire day (at the least.)

Why Chlorine Free Diapers Are Better?

Making decisions as a parent range from large issues such as how to give birth (natural or caesarian) to what may seem like a small choice as to what diapers or formula to use. That seemingly small choice around food and diapers is actually just as big of a decision as regardless of whether to let them stick their fingers in electrical sockets. Millie Holiday, RN has done extensive work with Autistic Children, children with ADHD and those with neurological disorders and concluded that environmental toxins truly impact their behaviors. Such toxins can surprisingly be found in ordinary disposable diapers.

According to the Columbia University School of Public Health 95% of all "cancer" is caused by chemical toxins of one sort or another. These chemicals also affect the immune system making children more likely to get viral infections. Millie Holiday observed that autistic children have such a high level of inflammation affecting all the systems of their bodies that they are far more sensitive to added chemical toxic exposures.

There are 7,700 chemicals in production in north America 3,000 of these is added to our food supply so food contains many chemicals. Most American children have 400 to 800 chemicals stored in their bodies before even 2 years of age.

Kimberly Synder is a New York Times bestselling author, and nutritionist for many of the top celebrities inclusive of Drew Barrymore, Fergie, Hilary Duff, LeAnn Rimes, Ben Stiller, Justin Long, Reese Witherspoon and many others. She is a holistic nutritionist and provided the following information regarding chlorine-free diapers.

Most babies wear diapers nearly 24 hours a day, and those diapers are in constant contact with both skin and mucus membranes. This means that any chemicals in diapers are likely to wind up in your baby's system if he or she wears disposable diapers.

Many baby diapers are bleached with chlorine, resulting in remaining traces of dioxins. According to the World Health Organization, dioxins are "persistent environmental pollutants" that can cause an array of health problems including developmental delays, damaged immunity, hormone interference, and certain "cancers."

Many disposable diapers release Volatile Organic Compounds (VOCs) such as ethylbenzene, toluene, and xylene. According to the Environmental Protection Agency, some VOCs are "carcinogens." Others can cause neurological problems, eye irritation, and decreased immunity.

The absorbent center in disposable diapers is made from Sodium Polyacrylate (SAP.) Once used in tampons, SAP was responsible for the cases of Toxic Shock Syndrome associated with the products. SAP also irritates skin, can cause staph infections, and may be related to other health problems, as well.

Diapers can contain "cancer causing" dioxin when the paper used to make them is bleached. They can also contain polyurethane, adhesives, inks used to create the cartoon images found on many disposable diapers. Polyurethane is made from petroleum and other chemicals and often is an issue for eczema. Listed below are some resources for reputable diapers, there may be others out there; we encourage you to do your own research:
- Honest Company - www.honest.com
- Diaper Pin - www.diaperpin.com

Why Drink Alkaline Water?

Highly acidic bodies and dehydration are two of the most common physical symptoms of Autism and Asperger's Syndrome. Harsh chemicals which can be found in tap water such as chlorine, pesticides, herbicides, lead, and mercury are now known to stimulate symptoms of ADHD in small children. For children who live in older homes and inner cities, the amount of lead poisoning increases in the drinking water from older pipes that were installed long before the adverse health effects were known, so many children to this day are still suffering from "neurotoxins" that cause this neurological condition. Water filtration can assist in the process of taking care of your home, but make sure you choose ones that are highly rated.

Most public water supplies are loaded with hazardous contaminants, such as disinfection byproducts, fluoride, and pharmaceutical drugs. The Environmental Working Group tested drinking water and thirty-eight low-level contaminants turned up in the water, with each brand containing an average of eight chemicals. Disinfection products, caffeine, Tylenol, nitrate, industrial chemicals, arsenic and bacteria were all detected, which have been linked to "cancers" and miscarriages.

Arsenic, another common contaminant in drinking water, has been linked to an increased risk of "cancer" of your bladder, lungs, liver and other organs. Arsenic can also damage the chromosomes which house the genetic material inside the cells of your body and potentially lead to reduced intelligence in children.

Why Use Holistic Dentistry?

Mercury is the second most toxic element known to man after Plutonium. The World Health Organization believes that there is no safe level of Mercury and that the body's predominant source of mercury exposure is from silver fillings. The Federal Environmental Protection Agency (EPA) considers mercury in teeth to be so toxic that when a tooth containing mercury is extracted it must be handled as hazardous waste. This is something everyone should get a taste of (pun intended with factiousness)

Putting the amount of mercury present in an average filling into perspective, a four foot fluorescent bulb, which should be disposed of as hazardous waste, has approximately 22 milligrams of mercury. The average dental amalgam filling contains about 1,000 milligrams of mercury. So you become the judge of what you want to put in your mouth?

Mercury exposure from amalgams crosses the placenta and into the fetus and breast milk. With the rising rates of infertility a lifestyle change might help resolve the majority of the issues. The vapor from mercury fillings easily passes to all the tissues and organs, including those of reproduction. With regards to the male reproductive system, mercury has an affinity for sperm. Mercury and other heavy metals are found in male ejaculate and seminal fluid, with the heaviest amount in the sperm.

A German study conducted in 1994 found that mercury in Sudden Infant Death Syndrome (SIDS) babies' brains was directly proportional to the number of fillings in the mother's mouth, providing further compelling evidence that mercury travels to the developing fetus and may be a factor in SIDS9. Patients with Alzheimer's dis-ease have higher than average levels of mercury in the tissues of the brain, as discovered by Dr. Haley, establishing a correlation between the two (Alzheimer's/ mercury amalgam fillings.)

Many dentists are rapidly discovering that their patients are recovering from a broad range of illnesses when their silver and/or other harmful amalgam fillings are replaced with less toxic materials. People who were barely functioning have regained "all or most" of their abilities.

Whole Health Kids (WHKs) is a proactive program that combines sound nutrition, healthier lifestyle, and head-jaw-spine alignment and full dental-facial development to help avoid extraction orthodontics whenever possible. Since cranial (skull) bones are connected to jaw bones, and since humans develop from the head down, children with full dental-facial development grow into «winners» whose mind-body works well together, and whose teeth and jaws have optimal form and function as Nature intended. Dr. Felix Liao is now teaching oral appliance Therapy and Oral-Systemic connections to dentists and health professionals about the importance of holistic mouths for children since he has "evidenced improvements for Autism and ADHD."

The Toxic Sandbox

The author of the Toxic Sandbox, Libby McDonald began to immerse herself in research after her young son had elevated lead count. She interviewed the top experts in every field from medicine, to education, and even anthropology to name a few; visited families who suspected their children had been harmed as a result of environmental contaminants; mailed off samples of cosmetics, soil, hair, and paint chips to be tested for toxicity. She unearthed the key toxins that threatened the well-being of our children.

Lead
Lead is a neurotoxin. The Center for Disease Control (CDC) has stated that anything below 10 micrograms of lead per deciliter of blood is safe. However, from lead experts and updated research, McDonald discovered that anything above a lead level of 2 can be dangerous. Research has discovered the following to be associated with an overload of "lead" toxicity:
- Associated with: loss of IQ points, anemia, reading problems, failure to grow, hearing loss, speech deficits, attention deficits, antisocial behavior, aggressive behavior, delinquency and criminal behavior
- Probable exposure: swallowing or inhaling (nearly impossible to absorb through skin)
- Lead paint in homes built before the 1978 ban, especially chipped/peeling paint
- Home renovations, which may release lead dust from old paint into the air
- Soil near roads (contaminated by old leaded gasoline)
- Soil near old fences/homes (contaminated by lead paint)
- Lead pipes that still transport drinking water into many homes in the U.S.
- Lead may be used to seal imported canned food
- Dishes painted with lead paint or from old pewter made from an amalgam of metals, including lead
- Some imported traditional medicines (many from southern Asia)
- Toy jewelery, lunch boxes, fishing rods, hair dyes, and even calcium supplement tablets may be threats

Research has discovered that half of the lead we ingested/inhaled when we were girls gets stored in our bones for up to 30 years. Then during pregnancy and lactation, when our bodies require additional calcium, the lead from our bones activates and enters our bloodstream. Lead is a calcium look-alike, and may accelerate the uptake of lead in unborn babies and young children.

Plastic: Toss the bad plastics

Two primary issues with today's plastic:
1. Phthalates (makes PVC plastic soft)

2. Industrial chemical bisphenol A (BPA), used to make polycarbonate, a hard shiny plastic.

These chemicals are endocrine disruptors, meaning they interfere with the normal functioning of hormones, including estrogen and thyroid. Exposure to these hormone-mimicking chemicals during critical periods in a child's development, both intrauterine, and in infancy, can result in lifelong injury. They are now banned in many countries, though not yet in the United States.

Research has shown that about 25 percent of US women have levels of phthalates high enough to "affect" the genital development of baby boys in the womb. The FDA issued a public health warning in 2002, recommending that prepuberty boys, baby boys, and pregnant women carrying boy babies avoid medical devices that contain DEHP. Some hospitals may not be aware of this warning.
- Phthalates are associated with: liver "cancer," damaged kidneys, slightly smaller scrotums, undescended testicles, smaller penises, reduced sperm count, reduced testosterone, and testicular "cancer."
- Probable exposure to Phthalates:
    - DEHP (diethyl phthalate):
      vinyl products, floor tiles, upholstery, shower curtains, cables, garden hoses, rainwear, car parts and interiors, packaging film, sheathing for wire and cables, some food containers, toys and soft baby books, and medical devices
    - DBP (dibutyl phthalate):
      nail polish, cosmetics, and insecticides
    - BBP (benzylbutyl phthalate):
      adhesives, paints, sealants, car-care products, vinyl flooring, and some personal-care products including hair products and lotions

A study conducted by the American Academy of Pediatrics concluded that many young infants are frequently exposed to phthalates in common baby lotions, powders, and shampoos thereby making them more vulnerable to the developmental and reproductive adverse effects of these chemicals.

The Center for Disease Control reports that children are exposed to phthalates by:
- Breathing air contaminated with phthalates that have migrated out of phthalate containing products in our homes.
- Mouthing soft plastic toys that contain phthalates
- Applying personal-care products that contain phthalates, especially to highly absorbent areas of the body like armpits, the palms of the hands, or the scalp.

- Eating food that has come into contact with packaging that contains phthalates and BPA
- Receiving a medical treatment like a blood transfusion or IV feeding tube that uses medical tubing that contains phthalates (including babies in intensive care units.)
- Household dust

BPA is associated with: early onset of puberty, obesity, larger than normal prostate, smaller sperm-carrying ducts, reduced sperm count, breast changes that represent early stages of "breast cancer," altered immune function, attention deficits, hyperactivity, poor learning skills, and learning disabilities. The greatest exposure comes when food/liquid come into contact and soak up the chemicals.

Probable exposure to BPA:
- Clear plastic baby bottles
- Toddler sippy cups
- Dental sealants
- The interior of some food cans
- Heating food/liquid containers containing BPA. Never use cling wrap especially in the microwave.
- Avoid plastics with a number 3, 6, or 7 in the triangle on the bottom. Instead, choose products in containers with 1, 2, 4, or 5.

A Must Have Toy - Brachiation Ladder

An important part of growing up is the brain's ability to process left then right in an alternating pattern. A childhood activity most of us have tried creates this pattern, swinging on monkey bars. It is actually therapeutic. Australian playgrounds now have brightly colored, twisted versions of the once simple monkey bars. These have rungs that are too fat for a child's hand to swing from. The Institutes for The Achievement of Human Potential describes swinging from the monkey bars as "brachiation." For any child, brachiation is beneficial but for a child labeled as Autistic it can have extraordinary benefits. Brachiating and hanging not only helps to open up the lungs hence allowing more oxygen into the brain, it helps in improving manual competence, convergence of the eyes, balancing and most importantly, speech.

Jenn's Insights

Autism is often defined as an escape from reality into a fantasy like dimension. Imagine this for a minute, a little girl inside her mother's uterus, gifted with life and then hearing that because she was weak and bleeding that she was not perfect enough for her mother. That she might not be able to come out and see the world? How would you feel?

Imagine waking up one morning and your home disappears, your friends disappear, your favorite person in the world disappears, your grandfather. Your favorite playmate disappears. All your toys disappear and no one tells you anything and puts you in a new place where there is no food, no medicine and no water? How would you feel?

Imagine some ladies snatching you out of your mom's arms and threatening to throw you over board to shark infested waters because you were crying because you were scared to be in such a small boat with 250 strangers? Imagine not eating for days, and watching families hoard all the food and not sharing with a little girl that had been starving and very sick? Imagine seeing your own father beaten up by security guards for trying to get you water while you are running a high fever? Imagine your mother having to sell the last piece of jewelry off her neck to get some antibiotics to stop your fever? How would you feel?

Imagine going to class and being embarrassed because you did not have more than 4 outfits to change into because you lost all your clothes in your homeland? Imagine your teacher accusing you of not showering because you kept wearing the same outfit? Imagine you not being able to get the last chocolate milk because you could not speak the language? How would it make you feel?

Imagine being in a car accident with all the back and side panels shattered and all the glass pieces going straight into your little arms and legs. Imagine then having to sit there while your mother took a needle to scrap each piece off because your parents could not afford to take you to the doctors? Imagine the person that hit your parent's cart, outright lie and sue for so much that they are denied car insurance from that company for life, imagine how you would feel because you couldn't speak English and defend your parents?

Within all those passages, did you feel a sense of Anger coming from that little girl? Unfortunately, she was born in a culture where emotions, especially negatives ones were condoned. When you see so much inhumanity at an early age, you have a choice to voice your anger or stay quiet and hopefully dream of a better world.

Now, is this truly a disorder, or a coping mechanism from the mind? You be the judge. I learned that if I remained silent that at least no one would notice or hurt me anymore. So you must ask are these children really disordered or is this world so disordered that they are coping with their best defenses, to stay in their own little world, filled with love and hope.

The spectrum of Autism is so broad that often times I can reassure you that we all can identify some degree of a symptom within ourselves. Due to the extreme amount of stress that was endured by my son intrauterine, I believe one of his primary coping mechanisms was to retain the Fear Paralysis Reflex. This reflex often contributes to his frustration levels and gets mistaken for resembling Autistic behavior.

If the Fear Paralysis Reflex (FPR) does not follow the intended route of development, the child's (or adults) system is left locked in a fear state that permeates all waking and sleep activity. If Fear Paralysis is still active all situations are seen through a filter of fear or what psychologists like to deem as anxiety.

I noticed that with my son he has exhibited some of these symptoms. A superficial diagnose of him would deem him as having OCD traits, especially with his tendency with patterning all his toys. He also detests controlling environments. Often times it is challenging to watch my mother with him. She expects him to conform and be respectfully obedient, characteristics of most Eastern cultures.

Additionally, if you tell my son no, he begins hitting his own head out of frustration. It brings tears to me because I feel like I transferred those emotions to him. During my pregnancy I wanted so badly to voice the injustice that I was enduring. I was verbally and mentally abused on a daily basis.

The threats and the anxiety were all transferred to my son. I felt so much emotional stress that when I went home, I had to slap my own face to take away the emotional pain that was bottled up inside of me. I knew no human being; especially a mother should have endured that type of treatment. Unfortunately, this is the lesson I transferred to my own son and every time he gets frustrated he hits his own head.

Then as a mother, I subjected him to more pain by having him go thru vaccinations that literally left him a comatose state for days and having the pediatrician tell me it was a normal side effect. I firmly believe that children can have autistic symptoms if they endure severe stressful situations intrauterine and during their childhood.

Through my love for my child, I'm learning to accept myself and understand problems I struggled with as a kid and younger adult—blending in at school because I knew they wanted conformers instead of thinkers and developing a phobia of public speaking because I learned that people did not want to hear the truth, just the illusions that everything was perfect.

Autistic kids are here to teach the world authenticity and to give unconditional love back to this world for all the inhumane acts that are being displayed across the globe. They are not a liability to society; they are actually leading by example and a gift of unconditional love.

Autistic children value authenticity and genuineness in a person and often times if they are near people that are missing this element, the feelings of anxiety will be present. The anxiety is actually not coming from the autistic child but they are picking up on the emotions of the people surrounding them. It is often a projection of that person's fears (shadows) because light has shown on their unresolved issue.

For educational purposes, more in-depth analysis should be used to evaluate children as being Learning Disabled. Due to the traumatic experiences of immigrating here, I did not speak in class for over two years. They put me in ESOL (English as a Second Language Classes) but knew that I did not belong after two weeks.

I was able to express everything with written communications. I did not feel safe enough to speak yet from the incident of nearly being thrown overboard on a ship. If your child is Autistic, I would encourage you to use creative means of communication to determine your child's strength and the source of the self-inflicted anger.

Our voices were designed for inspiration and encouragement and not to strategize for destruction and defeat of a person's spirit with judgmental words. If you trace back the family legacy of an autistic child, there most likely is a family member that used the "silent treatment" as the coping mechanism of control and passed on this preference to their lineage.

Research has proven that Autistic children have a stronger inclination within one region of the brain so that they exhibit more Child Genius qualities if encouraged and supported correctly towards their passion. Many of these children do not have to be trained for a long period; they innately can pick up a particular topic of interest. It is time to bring out their strengths instead of pointing out their hindrances.

♡◯ Dr. S' Insights

As I mentioned in the insight section about ADD/ADHD, I was involved in putting together a lecture, CD and set of tools for parents and doctors with regards to autistic children back in 2009. Research showed a lot of areas of "cause" for autism and today they all contradict themselves depending on who you read.

The best treatment case I had was when parents had brought their two autistic children to me and had heard that I would bring hope for improving her sons' quality of life. These children had been through so much abuse by the school system, specialists and doctors. The mother explained the process she went through with them. She was disappointed because they didn't understand and treat them with any sensitivity.

During their first appointment, I did my examination and found an area where the nervous system had interferences and needed to be corrected. Among them were retained primitive reflexes, cranial distortions and some vertebra misalignment. I also saw that the relationship between the sacrum (and hip) and the cranial bones were not in sync.

Her children were 7 and 9 years old at the time and the oldest had moderate autistic symptoms while the younger was categorized as a milder case. She lost her first severe autistic child years ago and this gave her more motivation to ensure that these two children would deserve the utmost care. Nonetheless, they had their routine involving a lot of teaching, one to one time and the parents were involved in everything they were doing.

They had no TV, no computer, and no electronics at home for the distraction of both parents and the child. Both boys' vocabularies were limited to simple words and displayed the "typical" autistic behavior aspect of their inner world, with child-like hope and dreams.

After 3 or 5 adjustments the mother came to my office without her child and asked for a private consultation. She was so emotional that I almost cried during our conversation. She said that her foremost dream was to give as much love to her children as possible during their lifetime. For her, love was the most healing and important emotion to give and receive in the world.

Even though she was angry at the abuse, misdiagnosis and incompetence from multiple people, she valued love for her children which surpassed everything else in the world. She told me the story of that special morning. Like all mornings, both boys had a routine and rituals so they tried not to deviate from what their children knew best so that it wouldn't increase unnecessary stressors in their life.

But that morning, she was cooking and her oldest son was around, like usual. He turned around and said: "Mommy," she said: "huh huh!", "I love you" and he went into his normal routine and continues his day. It was the first time her child said to her the words: I LOVE YOU. Without repeating it or being asked... by himself he said these words.

She was in bliss! For the first time in 9 years, her son was able to tell her what she always knew deep down in her heart and verbalized it to seal the gap, she said. The moral is that there is always hope for any condition as long as you as a parent do not give up believing in your children. They learn thru your examples. You are their biggest fan and they need your full support to see their potential(s).

Resources

Autism Movement Therapy - www.autismmovementtherapy.org
Age of Autism - www.ageofautism.com
Generation Rescue - www.generationrescue.org
Brain Fitness Strategies – www.brainfitnessstrategies.com
Positive Parenting - www.triplep-parenting.net/glo-en/home or www.triplep.net/glo-en/home/
Peaceful Parenting – http://www.drmomma.org/
Qigong Sensory Training Institute - www.qsti.org/QST_parents.html
Information on Synthetic Dyes Preservatives in your Children's Food - www.feingold.org
Autism Network for Dietary Intervention - www.autismndi.com
Generation Rescue - www.generationrescue.org
Tomatis Method - www.tomatis.com
Moms Against Mercury - www.momsagainstmercury.org
EWG's Skin Deep Cosmetics - http://www.ewg.org/skindeep/
The Green Guide for Everyday Living - http://www.thegreenguide.com/
National Vaccine Information Center - http://www.nvic.org/
Nourishing Hope - http://nourishinghope.com/
Brachiation Ladder - http://naturallybetterkids.com/resources/equipment/brachiation-ladder
Awesomism Programs - http://www.suzymiller.com/
Sports and Performance Psychology - http://www.peaksports.com/the-composed-sports-kids-cd
Thomas M. Caffrey - http://tomcaffrey.com/2014/02/13/aldo-exercise/
Conscious Discipline - http://consciousdiscipline.com/

12

Children with Depression Gifts to the World: Empathy and Hope

The Current Label of Depression

In 1990 the (economic) cost of depression was an estimated $43.7 billion in the United States alone. Depression is likely to occur in as many as 1 in every 33 children and up to 1 in 8 adolescents. Consequently, twenty years later in the United States, the second leading cause of death among those 10 to 24 years old was suicide.

Depression may arise as the result of a traumatic event or everyday worries and/stress. Its symptoms include listlessness (lack of energy,) insomnia, and intense feelings of despair and lack of overall self-confidence. Children and teens who are under stress, who have felt grief from a significant loss, or who have attention, learning, or conduct disorders are at greater risk for developing clinical depression.

A major area of research is the impact maternal depression has on very young children. Both mother and child suffer when depression is unaddressed. Depression raises stress hormones to toxic levels in both mother and child and can affect the mothers' capacity to nurture and meet their children's basic care needs.

Postpartum depression after child birth has even grown increasingly more volatile over the years, resulting in catastrophic events. Babies of depressed mothers are more than three times as likely to be born ahead of time, and four times as likely to be born at low birth weight or with birth complications. This, in most cases causes long-term effects on the child's physiological and emotional well-being.

This condition may have lifelong consequences for the child's relationships with his or her parents and others in their lives. If not addressed, children of depressed parents are more likely to fall behind their peers across an array of developmental areas, including cognition, physical and mental health. Social-emotional health is largely impacted as well. They are at higher risk for needing special education in school, being involved in juvenile justice in adolescence and developing mental health and health problems in adulthood.

The mother's heightened cortisol levels can affect the development of the baby's stress response and immune system. After birth, they may continue to have high cortisol levels with lifelong effects, including higher rates of chronic dis-eases into adulthood as a result of damage to multiple organs and systems from these elevated stress hormones. The effects are not only damaging but can also be disabling, a handicap in the dream of the quality of life because their overall perception is often one of hopelessness.

Growing up with a depressed parent for some children, means a childhood of negative and unpredictable parental behaviors, irritability, and inconsistent discipline, frequently accompanied by heightened marital struggles. As a result of the mothers lack of support when the baby is learning and attempting to communicate, the infant may be less likely to develop the confidence necessary to explore and learn through his or her environment and are "unable to cope" and become passive and withdrawn.

This type of environment has the potential to reflect in poorer mental, motor, and language skills during school years, along with lower concentration, and more difficulties behaviorally. They are more likely to exhibit attention and hyperactivity disorders during grade school and their pattern of interacting negatively with others may escalate. Additionally, they may frequently exhibit aggressive behavior that are prone for bullying episodes, and have higher rates of asthma, and tobacco, alcohol and substance use. Chronic maternal depression even predicts cardiovascular problems in adulthood for the child.

The Better Label for Depression – "EMPATHS"

Has there ever been a time you caught yourself reading someone's body language? It's like you're listening to what's *not* said. Now think of a time when you were in a conversation or interaction with someone and you began to mirror their mood or emotion, were you trying to do it or did it "just happen"?

Well what you experienced was how neuroscience is demonstrated in the pathways. They help us to read other people's feelings and actions, and may be the foundations of empathy. The conversation you were having that you felt how they felt, or did what they did is how the mirror neuron system is stimulated by each other. Felt the emotions beneath words are sadness or jubilance then similar facial muscles will move and the same areas of the brain will turn on.

We resonate with other people, leave impressions on them, and for some people whose central nervous systems are more sensitive than others, will feel a much deeper emotional gravitational pull causing them towards over-identifying with other's emotional pain. This can be so drawn in for empaths that they are driven to lessen suffering, pain, and illness (Etc.) to support or quickly help the perceived victim.

Empathy is the ability to understand the feelings, the thoughts, and the intentions of one or another. We call these persons "empaths." New research indicates that people who are most empathic were found to have a variation of an oxytocin (love) receptor gene within their brains. Empaths genuinely care and want to connect with others to help. Empathy, by definition of Webster's Dictionary is "the capacity for participation in another person's feelings. Empathy is what makes other people matter to us and reminds us to acknowledge the people around us as we understand and share their feelings. It further promotes the interconnectedness philosophy.

Consequently, the intensity of their desire to help often leaves empaths feeling depressed, unmotivated, emotionally distressed or developing stress disorders because they do not recognize boundaries. They begin to absorb all the negative feelings from the other person to relieve the other person of such emotional distraction. Some people are so sensitive to environmental stimuli (electromagnetic frequencies or geophysical stress) and the emotional energy of others that it causes disturbances in their overall health and the predisposition of their spirit.

The condition known as fibromyalgia is a result of sensory overload or negative energy being stored in the muscles. Dr. John Lowe-Houston correlated fibromyalgia with an underactive thyroid problem, which leaves the associated empath tired and overwhelmed. Anytime there is a crowd of people, there is abundant energy, both positive and negative.

Many empaths feel depleted in these social situations, overwhelmed, nervous, depressed, or angry much of the time and often have a difficult time finding peace or concentration (meditation is a must but a challenge for many empaths.) As you may recall, the majority of the population is vibrating at levels below 200, which represents extremities of negative energy encompassing the streets.

An empath is sensitive to what is obvious (body language, gestures, or tone of voice), as well as unseen things such as the thoughts, emotions, and illnesses they sense in another person. Empaths may get hunches, see mental pictures (right brain), hear internal guidance or have a gut feeling that supplies hidden information about people and situations, primarily their motives and their intents. This is also known as emotional intelligence.

They may also get a physical sensation in their body that lets them know where another person is afflicted or suffering. It goes further than the normal human intuition, because they cannot ignore the signs, and it takes over all their senses to the point of being hypersensitive. However, if the person utilizes this trait to their advantages, it can further promote emotional intelligence which is a much demanded skill set within the business arena.

Empathy, also known as the sixth sense, allows us to access mental and emotional information that has not been verbally communicated. Empathy is the ability to show concern for people; it allows us to pick up information and process it through sight, sound, touch, smell, and taste. Untrained empaths can go too far in trying to lessen the burdens of others by carrying their emotion or pain for them, again showing no boundaries. It is not uncommon for empaths to desire to lessen a person's pain that they actually manifest the symptoms into their own bodies. This is similar to the psychosomatic symptoms that many fathers-to-be experience during their wife's pregnancy. The majority of these fathers are empaths, whether they consciously or unconsciously realize this skill.

The more we embrace the fact that we are spiritually, mentally, and emotionally connected to one another, the more responsible we must become in managing our personal energy and our electromagnetic field. Once we fully embrace this concept, you will see a difference in the surrounding relationships, how you respond and how others respond to you; effective communications on a whole new platform, will promote peace and harmony in our society. Everything we think, say, or do affects all of humanity and ultimately our planet.

For some this concept seems "bizarre and impossible," but for others, the proof is in the pudding. As Anita Moorjani stated, she saw the big picture during her near-death experience with her battle with "cancer" and eloquently described the bigger scheme of humanity. We are all interwoven and interconnected similar to a thread in a tapestry. We all play an integral role for promoting or destroying humanity and both our conscious and unconscious thoughts will impact the well-being of generations to come. New science such as epigenetics is validating this theory on a daily basis.

The Psychology of Empaths

Empathetic children are generally labeled as "crybabies." Dr. Elaine N. Aron states that 10-15% of the populations are empaths. As children we have the natural ability to be more attuned with our environment and capable of absorbing concrete and abstract things, without the ability to express thoughts, feelings and emotions verbally we rely on the environmental cues, the energy that others exude.

This is when we use our instinct most often, where we train it to be safe, or get what we want. Babies cannot talk so they cry when they are hungry, wet, or need attention. When they start to cry someone appears to take care of them, so when they need help again, they will cry knowing that someone will come. This is why many say that our children are smarter than us because they innately master the law of cause and effect and the mechanisms for controlling or negotiating their circumstances.

Consequently, adults provide the best role models to demonstrate how to hide our true feelings (diplomacy.) Depending on a wide range of contributors throughout life, the way in which we express our thoughts, feelings, and emotions change as we grow. If the conditions are not conducive to fostering the genuine displays of open emotion we then retract and bottle them up letting only the one's out that we see as "okay" to use. In some cases it can be acceptable to show anger but not affection or vice versa. As children age, they learn to live with "bottled-up" pain rather than live authentically because of their role models.

Like a foreign pathogen (bug), you can potentially "catch" them from people without realizing it. Empaths are like surrogates for carrying the burdens of others. Through quantum physics, it has been scientifically proven that everything, even items that seem to be solid, when viewed at an atom or subatomic level is energy manifested in different forms, states and frequencies. Emotions such as fear, anger, and frustration are energies and as such Albert Einstein already proved the law of energy. Energy cannot be created nor destroyed, it can only be transferred.

As discovered in 1944 by Max Planck, we are submersed in a matrix or field of energy. We are affected not only by this ever-changing field of energy, but also by our DNA, thoughts, feelings, and beliefs which can rearrange the field as we interact with one another. We are much more powerful than we realize which also makes empaths unable to identify or separate their own energy from that of another person. For example, have you ever walked into a nursing home or a hospital and feel drained or a sudden feeling of sadness or despair? Have you watched a movie and could literally relate to the actor or actresses' emotions that tears come streaming down your eyes? These are all subtle acts of empathy.

Empaths are not the only people that can feel others' emotions, we are all born with that ability; the ability to feel another's emotions, thoughts, and physical sensations. We are all also born with the gift of intuition, to be able to feel that we cannot trust someone or if someone is hiding something or indirectly lying. Being able to recognize these thoughts and feelings is a way of protecting ourselves.

It is an innate characteristic similar to the parasympathetic nervous system that triggers the fight or flight stress response. The primary reason why many haves hidden these talents is because they have allowed hurt, grief, disappointments to rebrand their identity. And as such they are masking their own abilities and replacing these gifts with a facade to hide their inner feelings so they tend to perceive the world with the cup being half full syndrome.

For these people there is a fog or cloud that hides their truest identities and they have become so risk-adverse that they are not willing to be vulnerable so they cannot truly feel genuine love for themselves nor feel the love of others. It becomes a recurring cycle so they feel solitude of loneliness and despair.

Empaths are healers, they come with a mission to serve, heal and protect. As a result, many of them have taken on so much external energy that they spend a lot of their time trying to clear that unwanted energy. You will encounter them in professions or volunteering in a position of servitude to and for other people, hospice, caregivers, and medical professions (Etc..)

Empaths want to heal others and make everyone happy. They tend to absorb negative energies such as fear, depression, or rage instead of empowering people with tools to resolve these issues themselves. They may feel responsible for other people's happiness and try to provide solutions to things that are wrong in other people's relationships, physical bodies, and even the world. Because of this they are particularly easy targets for what we will call 'emotional vampires' those who don't want to take responsibility for their own choices and seek someone to do everything for them or someone to blame for their discontent, also known as the victim mentality.

Since empaths are often absorbing surrounding stressful emotions on a daily basis and chronically subject themselves to these types of environments. They may unconsciously or unwillingly, take on the burden of others and their negative energies to such a degree that it physically impacts their overall well-being. Many empaths experiences panic attacks, depression as well as food, sex, and drug binges.

Sometimes they may have tendencies to be overweight as result of overeating to cope with the emotional stress or use their body weight as a shield or buffer for the perceived security that is required. Empaths emit such an unconditional understanding and compassion that those who are ill, suffering, or those with weak boundaries are drawn to them without even being aware of it. It's like they are a magnet to suffering on Earth.

John Gottman, PhD, who works with children to master emotional intelligence to increase their self-confidence, enhance greater physical health, promote better performance in school, and healthier social dynamic relationships. He believes it is a more vital life skill than intellectual skills alone. This is one of the strongest skill sets for an empath and an important coping mechanism for them to possess to counteract their sensitivities.

Behaving irrationally as an empath may be a result of picking up someone else's emotions that is surrounding you, suddenly feeling angry for no reason or complaining about something you care nothing about are indicative of this trait. This type of irritable behavior is more prevalent when one is exhausted or stressed out and is a known as a type of "mirroring" of the other person's internalized feelings or emotions.

When an empath is around someone that possesses repressed negative emotions more than often the empath becomes mislabeled by others as being angry or dark; when in fact that empath is projecting the feelings and emotions of the other person onto themselves and mirroring it back to the person so that they may have a better sign of what is being hidden or repressed within themselves.

This is often the case of why empaths cross paths with people that appear to be so different in characteristics then themselves. Therefore, next times you feel irritated by a person or feel compelled to judge a person; it might be conducive to reflect introspectively of why that emotion has not healed within your body. As the Universe states, we are all interconnected and no soul is better than another.

Overuse of alcohol and drugs (including prescriptions) can lower your empathy levels. Could this be a contributing factor to the increase of prescriptions of antidepressants and Ritalin that is readily prescribed for our children? Another commonality of empaths is to be cold or uninvolved to turn off their sensitivity to others' emotions. The consequence to that, however, is "dis-ease" of the body because it is "going against the grain" of an empath to treat people unkindly or shut them out of their hearts. This is why forgiveness is not for the other person but in the case of empaths truly for your own well-being.

Empaths tend to feel emotionally distressed in places like funeral homes, prisons and crime scenes. If you enter a place and suddenly feel tense, uneasy, gloomy, or even frightened, or if you get physical sensations such as chills, goose bumps, headaches, or dizziness, you are likely picking up energies from what may have occurred on-site The thoughts and emotions of all who have ever been inside the place is encompassed and kept there and is the premise for how feng shui operates.

Consequently, most people are so numb to their own feelings and so unfamiliar with how they themselves feel because they have repressed (internalized) so many emotions that they cannot differentiate their own energy from the energy of others. This is an important element of mindfulness meditation or being present on a daily basis.

Empaths need a place each day where they can be alone to replenish their positive energy; this is why meditation is critical for empaths. On the contrary, animals and young children normally will calm an empath down because they present themselves honestly and are pure beings at all time, without a facade. This is why many empaths are drawn to working in occupations involving these demographics.

Emotional Intelligence

Emotional Intelligence (EQ) may actually be more important than IQ as suggested by author Daniel Goleman in his 1996 book Emotional Intelligence. Standardized measures of intelligence (as represented by IQ tests) are too narrow being that they only base it on standardized testing and do not encompass the full range of human intelligence as believed by some psychologists. Emotional intelligence instead suggest the ability to understand and express emotions which can play an equal if not even more important role in how people fare in life.

IQ is represented by a number on a standardized test as previously stated. Scores are calculated by dividing the person's mental age by his/her chronological age and then multiplying that number by 100. For example, a child with a mental age of 15 and a chronological age of 10 would have an IQ of 150 on the original IQ tests. Today, it is mostly calculated by comparing the test taker's score to the scores of other people in the same age group.

EQ, on the other hand, is a measure of a person's level of emotional intelligence. This refers to a person's ability to perceive, control, evaluate, and express emotions. This is where the empaths will score fairly significantly better if they are able to tap into their core strengths. Surprisingly, this is one the most valued attributes in the new business arena, especially within the field of International Business.

Research has found that individuals with strong leadership potential also tend to be more emotionally intelligent, suggesting that a high EQ is an important quality for business leaders and managers to possess. With that being said many companies now mandate emotional intelligence training and utilize EQ test in their hiring process which seemingly has a strong impact in the business world.

In conclusion, again we go back to "modeling" the behaviors. The greatest impact you can have on a child or any person is to lead by example. If you can show me through your actions I am more likely to "mirror" or replicate the same behaviors. For some, it will be difficult not to dismiss others' emotions, especially youngsters'. To respond to a child that is sad, or angry, or even in a frustrated tantrum with "grow up" or "get over it" is disapproving and later causes the behavior or the repression or internalizing of thoughts, feelings and emotions. Thus making it harder to bond or connect with other people in a more open communicative way.

The Psychology of Depression

A little known fact about the uniqueness of a person's personality is that it is determined at the moment of conception, when the egg and sperm join. This also is the determining factor of the difference in requirements with regards to educational experience.

In our culture, however, these differences are not recognized, and most students are lumped into an educational system that caters to the needs of left brain dominant learning styles. Our society severely neglects the limbic system and the right cerebral hemisphere of the brain with their education methods.

This is very damaging to the development of mindfulness. The exclusion from proper stimulation of the limbic system makes people become dull and lifeless. Connections to thoughts and emotions are completely ignored and people given the message to stop feeling. This is why people are disassociating themselves with others and our world has become such a competitive versus a collaborate environment.

The simple resolution some find in coping with the harshness of society is by not showing emotions altogether. As this forms into a habit, the denial of emotions becomes the standard that the person abides by for their daily living. Apathy, anger, and abandonment of the sense of self are the consequences of control from authoritarian leadership, emotional and physical abuse, or forced busyness that is often imposed upon a child. Over time, these feelings become so painful that the brain severs neural connections between the limbic system and awareness. To adapt to the pain, the person unconsciously loses touch with his/her emotions.

This is analogous to an animal having its foot caught in a trap. The animal will chew its own leg off to survive. Similarly, the brain dismembers itself to preserve its more basic functionality. This enormous loss is dealt with through denial or repressing the emotions to the subconscious level where they can skillfully be buried. This process also affects the ability to feel large amounts of happiness. By protecting ourselves from pain, we also inhibit ourselves from experiencing heightened degrees of happiness. The loss of such emotions is every bit as severe as the loss of an arm or a leg.

Studies have conceptualized depression as arising from a lack of self-acceptance and of emotional understanding from parents, triggering ambivalence, low self-esteem and guilt/shame in the child. Self-directed anger is an inevitable byproduct of this process. Anger directed toward the self will result in depression, the occurrence of which has reached epidemic proportions in our culture.

Anger at the parent becomes directed at the self to protect the parent's ego. Children became more empathic when discipline included calling attention to the distress their misbehavior caused for others. Our children are truly here to guide us back on path towards a more humane and meaningful lifestyle, they are our teachers in a sense and not vice versa. These are what Dr. Doreen Virtue deemed as the

Indigo, Crystal and Rainbow generation of children. They are at this juncture to serve a bigger purpose for preserving the kindness and gifts of humanity.

The Brain's Chemistry of Depression

For over 30 years, scientists believed what is commonly referred to as "chemical imbalance" mono-amines, mood-related chemicals such as serotonin, norepinephrine and dopamine, are low in the brain during major depressive episodes. Dr. Jeffrey Meyer investigated whether brain monoamine oxidase A (MAO-A), an enzyme that breaks down chemicals like serotonin, norepinephrine and dopamine, was higher in those with untreated depression. On average, MAO-A was 34% higher.

Of the approximately 40 million brain cells, most are influenced either directly or indirectly by serotonin. Although serotonin is manufactured in the brain, where it performs its primary functions, some 90% of our serotonin supply is found in the digestive tract and in blood platelets. This includes brain cells related to mood, sexual desire and function, appetite, sleep, memory and learning, temperature regulation, and may account for some social behavior.

Regarding the theory on chemical imbalances noted researcher Richard Davidson states, "the idea that there is a global derangement of the serotonin or norepinephrine system is not sustainable in the light of recent brain imaging data. What distinguish depressed from non-depressed individuals are patterns of regional brain function, differences in specific circuits." (Psychology Today April, 1999; Davidson et al., 1999)

Depression may occur when there is a suppression of new brain cells and that stress is the most important precipitator of depression, according to Barry Jacobs, a Princeton neuroscientist. Jacobs also states that common antidepressant medications such as Celexa, Lexapro, Prozac, Paxil and Zoloft, which are designed to boost serotonin levels, help kick off the production of new brain cells, which in turn allows the depression to lift only temporarily.

The effects of reduction in serotonin are hugely different in men and women and their reactions to such as shown in a study published in September 2007 in the journal Biological Psychiatry. By reducing serotonin levels in the brain by using a technique called "tryptophan depletion," researchers found that men became impulsive but not necessarily depressed. Women, on the other hand, experienced a marked drop in mood and became more cautious, an emotional response commonly associated with depression. This is why it is not uncommon for therapists to diagnose depression with anxiety symptoms.

Dopamine is important for motivation and a sense of readiness to meet life's challenges. As a brain neurotransmitter, dopamine influences well-being, alertness, learning, creativity, attention and concentration and allows humans to experience feelings of passion and pleasure.

Dopamine is not released only during pleasurable experiences, but also in the presence of high amounts of stress. This is why when people are stress they tend to eat more. Too much dopamine may create paranoia or a suspicious personality (this is where the anxiety portion is often diagnosed with depression), although more of this hormone in the frontal area of the brain relieves pain and boosts feelings of pleasure.

One of the most vulnerable key neurotransmitters, dopamine levels is depleted by stress or poor sleep. Alcohol, caffeine, and sugar all seem to diminish dopamine activity in the brain. It's also easily oxidized, therefore eat plenty of fruits and vegetables whose antioxidants help protect dopamine using neurons from free radical damage. Attention deficits are also connected to dopamine deficiencies.

Norepinephrine, also called noradrenalin, is the primary excitatory neurotransmitter needed for motivation, alertness, and concentration. Your brain requires norepinephrine to form new memories and to transfer them to long-term storage. Neurons manufacture norepinephrine and dopamine, two neurotransmitters that promote alertness and activity which is caused by raising tyrosine levels in the blood and brain which is apparent when one becomes energized (natural high) for hours.

Even more powerful than serotonin, oxytocin is another "feel-good" hormone often called the "cuddle hormone." Oxytocin is released when we feel love, trust and comfort. If you need a lift, remember the power of simply spending time with your significant other or family members and friends or even your pet.

The Energy of Depression (Energy Medicine)

If you are experiencing depression, realize that it is a state of mind to which you retreat to escape the feeling of pressures, especially emotional pressures; therefore, you may be creating an emotional blockage. It is opinion based on observation that determined that most depressive people carry unresolved issues with opposite sex parents.

This may be a plausible explanation why it is common to attribute the blame to their spouses for their depression. The resulting torment the spouse goes through was meant for the parent. By refusing to get help, you continue to feed the monstrous frame of mind a steady diet of bitterness and hatred that builds and increases the weight of the depression. This cloud of accumulated destructive thoughts and emotions becomes heavier and heavier.

Wounds of rejection, abandonment, humiliation, betrayal, or injustice set the stage for tremendous mental upheaval, especially if experienced in isolation and the depth of such emotional wounding determines the depth of depression. As young children, depressives felt they had no one to talk to, to hear their questions and to share their anguish, which may be because of the lack of open empathetic practice in the home or environment. If they do not learn to trust others, they will continue to withdraw and deny their desires.

Since on the outside a depressive person seems to not want to be helped, it's usually the people close to them that want to help. They may just have that mental blockage, If you are one of these people and have someone close to you who is depressive, it is suggested you be quite firm with them. Tell them they are the only one capable of digging themselves out of the pit they dug for themselves and, thereafter stop trying to solve their problem. They are the only one that can make a sustainable release of chain to the problem, as they are the ones that consciously or subconsciously created it.

The most important thing for the depressive person to realize is that the depression is a result of tremendous emotional wounding, when young, on the deepest level, the level of BEING. You refuse who you are. You reject yourself and believe you are unlovable and unworthy because of the profound rejection of someone you loved and trusted.

It is a necessary human need to want nurturing and need to trust someone completely. If those needs are violated through rejection or abandonment, we will naturally be bitter, as we feel intensely alone and afraid. If you can understand that the parent or loved one that you feel rejected by was inadvertently subjecting this form of punishment on your because they themselves were coming from their own pain and rejection.

Therefore it is a cyclical cycle and if you can learn to see them as fellow human beings and have compassion for them, you will have taken the first step toward your own recovery. It wasn't a lack of loves that caused them to reject you; it was their own wounded inner child that made them unable to express their love. That can also be said about how you yourself can better deal with the situation and be the leading example for others to follow, especially the initial perpetrator of the hurt.

It is important in this step not to blame the other person for their "inner hurt from childhood" or even from another era, but to take responsibility from where your actions and behaviors are coming from and how the two affected each other. Also, speak openly (to the person involved) and let them know how their actions (be specific) have made you feel. By identifying your issues as your issues, you are showing ownership of your thoughts, feelings, and emotions that may have created the same negative feeling in that person about either you or themselves.

By doing this you may see the other person begin to "mirror" your behavior and want to express the same type of forgiveness, or build a more effective communicative relationship going forward. Not in all cases, sometimes people need more help, or just have to be ready to and want to change on their own. If this is the situation you should now be in a mind frame where you can forgive and love unconditionally through your own healing process.

Once you have expressed your feelings, reconnect with your own self-worth. If you are not sure what that is, or if this is difficult for you, ask others close to you to show you your positive attributes. It may seem superficial at first, but you will slowly begin to feel validated. If you have been having suicidal thoughts, there is just a part of you that you want to die, not your whole *being,* to make room for a healthier, more vital part of you—your true self. You are simply confusing the part of you that wants to die with yourself.

Foods/Others That Impact Depression

Dr. Russell Blaylock, a neurosurgeon states that aspartame is a poison that affects protein synthesis; affects how the synapses operate in the brain, and affects DNA, and it can affect numerous other organs. Therefore it should be removed from your diet. Serotonin can come from the foods you eat; however, there are many people who cannot produce enough of it from the foods consumed which makes them more susceptible to depression. Consequently, aspartame found in the majority of diet sodas causes a blockage of the formation of serotonin in the brain, further depleting it from your body's reservoir.

Adequate levels of folic acid are essential for brain functionality which can be found in various foods, including spinach, orange juice and yeast. Folate deficiency can lead to neurological disorders such as depression.

Studies have shown that children with depression almost always have a deficiency of one or more of these nutrients. Chronic depression has been linked to deficiencies of:
- vitamin B complex,
- calcium,
- magnesium,
- copper,
- iron,
- potassium,
- folic acid, and/or
- essential fatty acids (omegas)

Women have signs of depression before their menstrual period which may be caused by a vitamin B6 deficiency, and post natal depression may be caused by a deficiency of vitamin B12 and folic acid. Vitamin C helped to ease the symptoms of depression by consuming at least 1 gram daily, and also you should have plenty of Vitamins B6, B12, and folic acid in your diet or supplement it with vitamin B complex.

There are foods and some nutrients that can increase levels of tryptophan, the amino acid from which serotonin is made. Tryptophan works best when consumed in conjunction with a small bit of carbohydrate, such as a scoop of brown rice, a handful of nuts, or a few tablespoons of legumes. These complex carbohydrates are essential to helping your brain properly process the tryptophan in protein. It is found in higher amounts within these foods:
- eggs (organic, free-range),
- turkey (organic),
- avocado,
- bananas

Many smokers eat more when they are trying to quit because both food and nicotine share similar dopamine reward pathways in the brain. Alcohol, cocaine, nicotine, amphetamines and even sugar can also mess with our dopamine balance. Tyrosine is an amino acid that is crucial to the production of norepinephrine. Eating more of nutrients high in tyrosine may help boost your brain power and naturally elevate your mood. Foods highest in tyrosine include:
- fava beans,
- duck,
- chicken (organic),
- ricotta cheese,
- oatmeal,
- mustard greens,

- edamame beans,
- dark chocolate (cold-pressed),
- seaweed,
- wheat germ

Omega-3 fat DHA are associated with reduced levels of DHA in brain tissue. Supporting the brain's electrical signals is just one way DHA boosts dopamine.

Foods highest in tyrosine include:
- beets (supplies the amino acid betaine to regulate dopamine),
- artichokes,
- avocados,
- tahini (paste from sesame seeds),
- almond butter,
- herbal teas (fenugreek, peppermint, ginseng, milk thistle and red clover)

Billionaire Parenting Tips for Depression

From birth, babies have the ability to respond to the emotions of others. As you were likely told by your OB/GYN during your pregnancy, even before birth they are sensitive to the mother's feelings, whether positive, neutral, or negative. You probably noticed how they imitate your facial expressions, smiling in response to your smile. They also may cry if they hear another baby cry. This is the initial step in the development of empathy and the ability to share the feelings of another person.

Dr. Kyle Pruett has stated that children's brains develop empathy from birth to age eight years. Babies absorb the mental and emotional energy of the surrounding people. They do not filter anything; they simply receive it. It is also found that female brains have variations, which correlate with higher empathy levels than a male brain. This research supports the correlation for the higher depression incidences in females.

Your Subconscious Knows the Answer – Hypnosis

The Latin word for emotion is *emovere* which means movement. Suppressing an emotion prevents the natural movement of the vital energy. Feelings buried alive never die, this is why hypnosis (subconscious level) is wonderful for getting repressed emotions back to the surface (conscience level) so that they can be dealt with once and for all.

According to Dr. Bruce Eimer of the Hypnosis Help Center, in a sense, when you are depressed, you fall into a state of Negative Self Hypnosis. Negative self-suggestions repeated over and over again become imprinted in your subconscious mind. Negative thinking becomes a habit that must be changed in order for you to recover from your depression. Hypnosis is used to uncover and reprocess past experiences and memories that have sensitized you to continued depressive reactions in the present.

Truthfully, we are all born with empathetic abilities; however, most of us shut that ability down at some point because of the internal discomfort. As a result, we live inside of our heads, our thoughts become out of touch with our bodies and our own emotions. When this is done as a child it creates inward feelings and emotions that become a continuous pull downward for years to come, resulting in depression.

The power of the subconscious mind is much greater than that of the conscious mind. Approximately 90% of our processing brain power comes from the subconscious mind (this includes bodily functions like digesting and breathing.) Your subconscious is not trying to undermine you; on the contrary it's looking out for you. It's like an overprotective guardian and thinks they know what's best for you, regardless of your opinion. It's trying to protect you from pain, failure or heartbreak, but with such control (perfectionist) there is no passion to live. This is why people feel unhappy because they feel stifled.

In other words, programs we learned as children were imbedded in our subconscious mind and are still in control. I'm sure we can all remember a time we lost our temper or were impatient. Sometimes people even avoid certain food for no (conscious) reasons. If so maybe you are reacting from a program that was imbedded in your subconscious mind years ago as a child. Hypnosis can help remove these walls.

Gratitude Meditation

It is important to show gratitude for the things and people in your life. Not only will it nurture those relationships, it has been shown that people who show more gratitude are often more happy and content.

In any situation you can take the opportunity to meditate. It is easier when there are no distractions, however, many people are able to block out distractions. To do so, close your eyes and be very still. Breathing slowly in and out, beginning to take deep breaths in and then exhaling the deep breaths out to figuratively dispel any tensions out of your mind and body.

In those breaths begin to think of the things in your life that you are grateful for, people, your home, your job, and even things you want to happen. Spend time in those thoughts saying "thank you" and thinking about how lucky or blessed you are. Even little things that you are thankful for like a working car, clean house, or most importantly good health.

Now, continue to breath and feel a warm feeling of gratitude surround you like a blanket, think about your friends and people that you laugh and play with. Feel yourself smiling inside as you think about your friends and how lucky you are to have special friends. Spend a few moments thinking about all the special adventures and experiences that you have had no matter how long ago or recent they were. What did you do that made you feel happy inside? As you sit there really quietly, appreciate how lucky and blessed you are to have been able to have any of those experiences, feeling a sense of calmness engulfing your mind and body.

Flower Essence Remedies, Essential Oils and Supplements

Edward Bach was a medical doctor and one of the earliest homeopaths at the beginning of the twentieth century. Here's a list of flower essences that have aided with depressive symptoms:

- Elm

  When you are feeling overwhelmed, anxious, or depressed because you are overworked or have too many responsibilities, Elm is the remedy of choice.

- Gentian

  When you feel pessimistic, discouraged, or have lost faith. It is used for depression when a person knows the reason for his or her sadness.

- Gorse

  When you feel hopeless, that there is nothing that can be done for you, or resigned to your less-than-ideal fate, gorse may be helpful.

- Mustard

  Mustard is used for sadness or depression that has no apparent cause. It feels like a dark cloud has blocked out happiness and joy.

- Sweet Chestnut

  Selected for feelings of hopelessness, Sweet Chestnut reflects a long, courageous battle that feels lost. It is particularly suited when it feels like an inner transformation is occurring and a "dying off" of a person's old self is taking place.

- Willow

  Willow is best suited for negativity and a tendency to blame others for the problems in life. Alternatively, if your sadness is linked to a grudge that you're holding onto but would like to let go of, Willow is a good choice.

Essential oils can be used for easing emotional upsets and calming sensitivities associated with being an empath. There are different oils for each emotional upset. Fill a bathtub with warm water and add one handful of (Himalaya) sea salt and add the essential oils (sage, cedarwood and purification) in the water. Soak in the bath and be sure to be submerged. This will help draw out toxins in the body and remove contaminants from your energetic fields.

- Frankincense

  Frankincense essential oil may be helpful in alleviating symptoms of depression and is an excellent oil to use for anxiety when you have a lot of things going on and you do not know where to begin. A single breath in and your mind is cleared and focused for the most important task at hand.

- <u>Valor</u>

  Valor is a Young Living essential oil blend that has similar qualities to frankincense simply because frankincense is one of its ingredients. It also contains spruce which is grounding and helps create positive memory. It uplifts the spirit, restores confidence, and can bring motivation. Other oils that can be used include: lavender, frankincense, harmony and joy.

- <u>Lemon</u>

  The essential oil lemon uplifts the mind and increases joy, while supporting the solar plexus chakra. The solar plexus chakra is the center of self-esteem, confidence, responsibility, and protection.

St. John's Wort has many effects on both the brain and the body and is noted as the most used herb for treating depression. It is known to help balance the neurotransmitters GABA, norepinephrine, serotonin and dopamine. St. John's Wort can affect the effectiveness of other medications. Two studies show it can help the drug Plavix (heart problems) work well in people for whom it did not initially work. Other studies show using St. John's Wort can lower the effects of birth control pills and immune suppressants.

In research studies, saffron has been compared to both Prozac and Imipramine, and found to work at least as well, or better, with fewer side effects. Saffron is a well-known Persian spice used for its ability to help the digestive system heal. Because most neurotransmitters are made in the digestive tract, this might be the reason saffron has been shown in studies to elevate low mood.

A recent study published in Phytotherapy Research discovered that curcumin, found in the yellow Indian spice turmeric, has amazing health benefits, including elevating mood and combating depressive symptoms as effectively as the prescription drug Prozac. This is primarily found in curry powder. Curcumin, which has a powerful antioxidant and anti-inflammatory properties, is the most active constituent of turmeric.

Emotional Clearings for Empaths – Detoxing

It does not matter what the form your anger takes (sarcasm, criticism, judgment, apathy, depression) when carrying around a burden of anger, fear, sadness or vengeance, you are asking for the same people to appear within your life. This is what is known as the "Secret – The Law of Attraction." Energy in any form attracts energy similar to itself.

When you are angry with another person, you continue to send negative energy to them, remember whatever you send out comes back to you, magnified. Most of us do not accept sadness, fear, and anger as a normal part of our human experience, then again there is a lot that do. We tend to repress these emotions by being busy with work (work-a-holics), watching TV, playing video games, eating, drinking alcohol, smoking, or doing drugs. Some of these activities can actually make you more susceptible and vulnerable to those feelings.

Even after you stuff an emotion deeply enough that you no longer feel it, it is still alive and actively destroying your aura and chakras as well as causing dis-ease and damage to your physical body.

Let's look at this in a more tangible way, if someone were trying to break into your home you would do something to protect yourself whether it is by force, weapon, or even calling the police. It's highly unlikely you would just stand there and not do anything. Yet, we allow intruders (energy vampires) in our personal space often, taking advantage of our minds, emotions, and physical body, without so much as an attempt to block them or their negative energy. You are not doing yourself or the other person a favor by your almost saintly acts. These people are analogous to the grown-up versions of bullies, they are disrespectful and do not believe in being self-less so they tend to control and manipulate people and circumstances around them to portray and illusion of perfectionism.

Earning degrees in traditional Chinese medicine, acupuncture, herbology, and shiatsu, Luis Angel Diaz, is arguably one of the world's foremost authorities on emotional healing. He has been a holistic health practitioner since his early 20s and acquired certifications in homeopathy, hypnotherapy, Touch for Health, specialized kinesiology, Neuro-Linguistic Programming (NLP), Emotional Freedom Technique (EFT) and reflexology.

Cellular Memory Release (CMR) is an effective, practical synthesis of tools for accessing and freeing the trapped, stagnant life force held inside the cells of your body. The Cellular Memory predisposes or, "programs" you to perceive and behave a certain way as thoughts and feelings are manifested within your consciousness.

Cellular Memory by nature contains both Positive Emotional Charge (PEC) and Negative Emotional Charge (NEC) that is constantly flowing and influencing our state of mind and body health. The PEC can be described as an energy field of life force that is free flowing, expanding, peaceful, non-fearful, whole and alive beyond words.

The former Chief of the Clinical Neuroscience Branch at the National Institute of Mental Health, Dr. Candace Pert studies health influences at the neurochemical level and stated recently that "repressing emotions can only be causative of dis-ease in the body." These kinds of neuropeptides available to cells are constantly changing, reflecting variations in your emotions throughout the day. The probability of staying well or getting sick is influenced by the kind and number of emotion-linked neuropeptides available at receptor sites of cells. The brain contains about 60 different neuropeptides, including endorphins. Individual cells, including brain cells, immune cells, and other body cells, have receptor sites that receive neuropeptides.

It is extremely important to pay more attention to emotions with respect to our health. They are the root triggers for health vs. dis-ease. Viruses use the same receptors to enter a cell and depending on how much of the natural peptide for that receptor is available, the virus may have an easier or harder time getting into the cell. The chemicals that are running thru the body and brain are the ones connected to emotion.

When you work on the development of listening and accessing your internal information that is stored in your body, you then have the power to let go of what's holding you back from living up to your true potential and fullest life possible.

Energy Medicine – Reiki Energy

Even though it has long been known that activities of cells and tissues generate electrical fields that can be detected on the skin surface the laws of physics demand that any electrical current generates a corresponding magnetic field in the surrounding space.

David Cohen of MIT confirmed the biomagnetic field projected from the measurements of the human heart by using a SQUID magnetometer in 1970. Two years later in 1972 he had made improvements to his instrument that enabled him to measure magnetic fields around the head produced by brain activities.

Subsequently, it has been discovered that all tissues and organs produce specific magnetic frequencies, which have come to be known as biomagnetic fields. The traditional electrical recordings, such as the electrocardiogram (EKG) and electroencephalogram (EEG) are now being complemented by biomagnetic recordings, called magneto cardiograms (MCG) and magneto encephalograms (MEG.) These technologies are becoming as common as the x-ray technology, which operated with the principles of energy.

E=MC is the Quantum Physics' equation discovered by Albert Einstein, which revealed that mass (M) and energy (E) are interchangeable. . The most important concept of this is that Mass is nothing but a form of Energy. So everything is a form of Energy, objects at rest have stored Energy. Quantum science recognizes matter in its most elemental form to be energy. This is why humans are in essence a form of energetic being.

As we are likely already aware of, energy is all around us, everywhere in all different wavelengths and frequencies. Energy can exist as either solid matter or as non-solid matter, such as radio waves, infrared waves; microwaves and x-rays are all forms of non-solid Energy. Everything, in its fundamental level of being, is energy from your voice when you speak (sound waves) and your brain when you think. As energy, all is one and inseparable. As energy, all is changeable, and the possibilities are truly limitless.

Aquamarine is known to be a powerful healing crystal, known for its ability to improve mental clarity and promote peace. Crystals and gemstones respond to the electricity that is coursing through our body, and if the energy is sluggish, the constant electrical vibrations of the stones will help to harmonize, balance, and stimulate these energies.

The theory of using crystals was discovered in 1880 by Pierre and Jacques Curie. This principle was called the piezoelectric (pressure electricity) effect. These same quartz crystals were used within the probe of the earlier version of the ultrasound machine and were safe enough for usage on the mother and baby.

The Etheric Weaver is the more modern day version of this instrument. When an electric current is applied to these crystals, they change shape rapidly. The rapid shape changes, or vibrations, of the crystals produce sound waves that travel outward. Contrarily, when sound or pressure waves hit the crystals, they emit electrical currents that help rebalance energy. For empaths, wearing an Etheric Weaver pendant aids with protecting you from other people's draining energies. For those interested, we will have a selection of these crystals for purchase at the Billionaire Parenting website (www.billionaireparenting.com)

Introduced to the United States in the 1960's, Reiki, discovered about 100 years ago by Dr. Mikao Usui, incorporates elements of other alternative healing practices such as aromatherapy (essential oils), crystals, chakra balancing, homeopathy, meditation and naturopathic medicine.

Treating depression and anxiety with Reiki is becoming a more and more sought after alternative to taking drugs. As anxiety and depression often accompany one another Reiki deals with depression and anxiety as a negative energy. Negative energies manifest as imbalance in the Chakras or energy centers.

Researchers used certain drugs to manipulate the behavior of stressed animals, and then concluded (erroneously) that the drugs would be "good antidepressants" but antidepressant drugs were not originally developed for depression. Further research shows that chronic stress doesn't cause the same molecular changes that depression does, making the assumption invalid. Antidepressants were designed to treat stress, rather than depression, furthering the reason they are so ineffective for many.

Many hospitals around the world are recommending Reiki as a parallel system of "treatment." Treating depression with Reiki is becoming a recognized practice within renowned hospitals within the United States such as Johns Hopkins, Columbia University Medical Center, Yale-New Haven Hospital, and Harvard University. Reiki is safe during pregnancy and in childbirth and while breastfeeding infants. It has also been useful in treating infertility and miscarriages. Reiki has also been useful in cases of endometriosis, ovarian cysts, and polycystic breasts.

Receiving Reiki during pregnancy will allow you and your baby to evolve and synchronize on many levels and the blending of energies will help to unite you both. It can also assist with successful deliveries, with contributions from reducing stress and relaxing the body. Don't be surprised by an increase in movement during a Reiki session, baby's sense and love Reiki energy, feeling energized.

Finding the right practitioner will be the key. The practitioner must truly be balance within their own heart chakra to maximize the full healing potential since Reiki energy heals from the heart. This is where it becomes challenging because many people are in occupations for the wrong reason.

Tuning Fork (Sound Therapy) for your Chakras (Energy Flow)

Energy Patterns can be stored in us from previous events that may have happened as earlier than yesterday or even further back than we consciously remember. Some of which will contain different memories of things that may have happened to us, some pleasant and some unpleasant. These memories are sometimes hidden deep into recess in our Chakras and in our Auras (Energy fields around us,) and we try to forget about them, but they never truly go away. The result of this unbalanced Energy is dis-ease. To balance the Energy, healing is necessary.

The Energy used in Healing is equally real, with the human body as the measuring device. We all have Chakras, which are storage centers in our bodies that store Energy and Energy patterns. The individual may feel listless, tired, out of sorts, or depressed if the chakras are not balanced, or if the energies are blocked.

There are a total of seven chakras within the body where energy (repressed emotions) may be trapped. These energy centers also just happen to be where the nerve centers are found along the spine that sends impulses to the different organs, so by energizing these areas, you stimulate the organs into greater health promoting their innate abilities to perform. *(With permission from Kellie JO Conn, GG, she shares all the chakra wisdom from her excerpt at Avalon Crystals (www.avaloncrystals.com))*

- Chakra (Root Chakra)

  The root chakra is located at the base of the spine at the tailbone in the back, and the pubic bone in front. This center holds the basic needs for survival, security and safety. This is also the center of manifestation. When you are trying to make things happen in the material world, business or material possessions, the energy to succeed will come from the first chakra. This is one of the essential ingredients from the Law of Attraction, "The Secret." An individual may feel fearful, anxious, insecure and frustrated if the first chakra is blocked. Problems like obesity, anorexia nervosa, and knee troubles can occur.

- Chakra (Belly/Sacral Chakra)

  It is located two inches below the navel and is rooted into the spine. This center holds the basic needs for sexuality, creativity, intuition, and self-worth. This chakra is also about friendliness, creativity, and emotions. It governs people's sense of self-worth, their confidence in their own creativity, and their ability to relate to others in an open and friendly way. It is influenced by how emotions were expressed or repressed in the family during childhood.

- Third Chakra (Solar Plexus Chakra)

  It is located two inches below the breastbone in the center behind the stomach. The third chakra is the center of personal power, the place of ego, of passions, impulses, anger and strength. A lack of confidence, confusion, worry about what others think, feel that others are controlling your life and depression will be present when the third Chakra is out of balance.

  Physical problems may include digestive difficulties, liver problems, diabetes, nervous exhaustion, and food allergies. Being balanced creates feelings of cheerfulness, being more outgoing, having self-respect, expressiveness, enjoying taking on new challenges, and having a strong sense of personal power.

- Fourth Chakra (Heart)

  It is located behind the breast bone in front and on the spine between the shoulder blades in back. This is the center for love, compassion and spirituality. This center directs one's ability to love themselves and others, to give and to receive love. Almost everyone today has a hard, hurt, or broken heart, and it is no accident that heart dis-ease is the number one killer in America today. This is why love is truly the best medicine.

Feeling sorry for yourself, paranoid, indecisive, afraid of letting go, afraid of getting hurt, or unworthy of love when this chakra is out of balance. Physical illnesses include heart attack, high blood pressure, insomnia, and difficulty in breathing. When this chakra is balanced you may feel compassionate, friendly, empathetic, desire to nurture others and see the good in everyone.

- Fifth Chakra (Throat)

It is located in the V of the collarbone at the lower neck and is the center of communication, sound, and expression of creativity via thoughts, speech, and writing. When this chakra is out of balance you may want to hold back, feel timid, be quiet, feel weak, or can't express your thoughts. This is because this is where possibility lies. The possibility for change, transformation and healing are located here while the throat is a storage place for anger and allows for the emotions to be freed from this place as well.

Physical illnesses or ailments include, hyperthyroid, skin irritations, ear infections, sore throat, inflammations, and back pain. When this chakra is balanced you may feel balanced, centered, musically or artistically inspired, and may be an outstanding speaker.

- Sixth Chakra (Third Eye)

It is located above the physical eyes on the center of the forehead. It also assists in the purification of negative tendencies and in the elimination of selfish attitudes. Physical symptoms may include headaches, blurred vision, blindness, and eyestrain when this chakra in not balanced. Emotions involve with this chakra includes feelings of non-assertiveness, fear of success, or opposite of it and become egotistical. When this chakra is open you do not fear death because you have faith.

- Seventh Chakra (Crown)

It is located just behind the top of the skull. It is the center of spirituality, enlightenment, dynamic thought and energy. It allows for the inward flow of wisdom, and brings the gift of Universal consciousness.

When this chakra is unbalanced there may be a constant sense of frustration, no spark of joy, and destructive feelings. Illnesses may include migraine headaches and depression. Balanced energy in this chakra may include the ability to open up total access to the unconscious and subconscious.

Sound Therapy through Tuning Forks help rebalance the energy levels within the chakras. Like adjusting a guitar, your body can be tuned to achieve optimal physical balance. Tapping two tuning forks will instantaneously alter your body's biochemistry and bring your nervous system, muscle tone and organs into harmonic balance.

Energy Psychology

The fact is there been many techniques within the Energy Psychology and Emotional Freedom Technique which requires tapping on specified acupressure points to release the energy flow (memory of the emotion), however, the Pulse Technique, founded by Jo Dunnings is the most effective means for resolving repressed emotions (in our opinion) because it utilizes a reverse psychology approach along with meditative processes.

A Quick Pulse session will include you spending 2-3 minutes focusing on anything in your life that is hindering the changes you would like to make. These are the situations or objects that limit you or you just don't like experiencing and have simply repressed or buried within your subconscious thoughts. Repressed or stagnant energy is cleared out and pushed to flow again utilizing this method.

It brings the subconscious memory to the conscience level so that it may be cleared out. While you focus on what you don't like or want in your life the energy follows your focus and clears whatever is the cause of the unwanted experience or symptom. By focusing on something you don't like the energy will automatically clear it, leaving more room for the things you do want

The most effective practitioners to perform this technique are the ones that are combining it with Positive Psychology as a guided meditation because it shifts and clears the original unpleasant experience that manifested the present situation as well as the many layers of experiences that have been a result of it. The powerful clearing Energy used in the Pulse processes has intelligence that goes to the core of the problem

Positive Parenting

1. Positive parenting starts by creating a good relationship with your child, so that s/he responds to gentle guidance as opposed to threats and punishment. Having a close bond with your child is the most effective disciplinary strategy.

    Kids who feel connected to their parents naturally want to please them. Evaluate all teaching based on whether it strengthens or weakens your relationship with your child. Think Loving Guidance, not punishment.

    Negative punishment is destructive to your relationship with your child and ultimately creates more misbehavior. Discipline is necessary but through loving guidance you set the limits and reinforce expectations as necessary, but in an empathic way that helps the child focus on improving his/her behavior rather than on being angry at you.

2. Start all correction by reaffirming the connection. Remember that children misbehave when they feel bad about themselves and disconnected from us. Sometimes it may simply be because there were unrealistic expectations or boundaries set, not to mention they mirror what they see.

3. Stoop down to his/her level and look him/her in the eye: "You are mad but no biting!" Pick him/her up: "I know you want to stay up longer but it's time for bed."

4. Don't hesitate to set limits as necessary but set them with empathy. Of course you need to enforce your rules. But you can also acknowledge your child's perspective. When kids feel understood, they are more able to accept our limits. You wish you could play longer, but its bedtime. I know that makes you sad." If you are not assertive however, this may not be affective as they grow older.

5. Defiance is always a relationship problem. If your child does not accept your direction ("I don't care what you say, you can't make me!"), it's always an indication that the relationship is not strong enough to support the teaching. This happens to all of us from time to time.

   At that point, stop and think about how to strengthen the relationship, not how to make the child "mine" with control mechanisms. Turning the situation into a power struggle will just deepen the rift between you.

   Again, setting boundaries is important and the obligation of the parent is to be just that, the parent. We want to be friends with our children but we have to be sure to define the character of parenthood and child so that it is not forced into a stressful situation for either when it is time to discipline and the "I am the boss of you" speech doesn't have to be made.

6. Avoid Timeouts. They create more misbehavior. Timeouts, while infinitely better than hitting, are just another version of punishment by banishment and humiliation. They leave kids alone to manage their tangled-up emotions, so they undermine emotional intelligence. That being said, there are times when it is necessary for a "break" or "space." This will allow both parent and child to decide how they are feeling without it being in the heat of the moment. The time-out strategy often erodes, rather than strengthening, your relationship with your child. They set up a power struggle. This strategy is in essence a more humane form of bullying than physical discipline because as an authoritarian figure you can deem to remove or punish as you see fit based on your status.

7. What you think and feel is more important than what you say in how your child responds. Kids will do almost anything we request if we make the request with a loving heart.

8. How you treat your child is how s/he will learn to treat herself/himself. If you are harsh with him/her, he or she will be harsh with himself/herself. If you are loving with him/her while firm about setting appropriate limits, s/he develops the ability to set firm but loving limits on his/her own behavior.

Volunteer – Altruism Takes the Focus Off You

Contribution is one of the 6 basic human needs. It is the need to help others, servitude, volunteering, making some sort of positive difference. The act of altruism can act as a form as stress relief. There are studies that show the act of giving as being an activator for the area of the brain associated with the positive feelings, lifting your spirits, and making you feel better as you give more. Altruism can lead to a more sustainable emotional well-being, more positive perspective and effect on others, and a better social standing.

A key risk factor for depression is social isolation. Volunteering gives you the opportunity to practice and develop your social skills, and can provide a healthy boost to your self-confidence, self-esteem, and satisfaction in life since you are meeting regularly with a group of people with common interests. Once you have momentum, it's easier to branch out and make more friends and contacts, defining your sense of pride and identity which will also give you a more positive view of yourself and future goals.

The findings of researchers at the London School of Economics examined the relationship between volunteering and measures of happiness in a large group of American adults, was that the more people volunteered, the happier they were, according to a study in Social Science and Medicine.

Volunteering is a fun and "easy" way to explore your interests and passions or to find what those passions are. Doing volunteer work you find meaningful and interesting can be a relaxing, energizing escape from your day-to-day routine of work, school, or family commitments. Volunteering also provides you with motivation, and vision that can carry over into your personal and professional life.

Incantations (Affirmations) – Positive Psychology

Optimism is active positive thinking. It's not avoidance or ignoring, just the choice to see things for how you choose, not giving the 'unwanted' more attention than it needs. Most times the bad doesn't need any help to be seen because that is what the majority of people are looking for, the good, however, sometimes needs a little help to be seen through the shadows of the dimness that is cast by the overwhelming scene of chaos and dismay. It doesn't really matter how you see "the glass," it is neither half full nor half empty, and you have already acknowledged that there is at least something in it.

Positive psychology is primarily concerned with using the psychological theory, research and intervention techniques to understand the positive, adaptive, creative and emotionally fulfilling aspects of human behavior which was discovered in 1998 by Dr. Martin Seligman and Mihaly Csikszentmihalyi.

Research has found that positive thinking can aid in stress management and even play an important role in your overall health and well-being. Positive psychologists seek "to find and nurture genius and talent" and "to make normal life more fulfilling", rather than merely treating mental illness.

Positive thinking actually means approaching life's challenges with a positive outlook. It does not necessarily mean avoiding or ignoring the bad things; instead, it involves making the most of potentially bad situations, trying to see the best in other people, and viewing yourself and your abilities in a positive light.

Incantations are used to plant the seeds of positivity in your subconscious mind. The unconscious mind cannot tell the difference in what it takes in through the sensors and what is imagined. Spend more time concentrating on the visions that you want to see, manifesting them as if they already were. What you truly believe in your heart and soul will become real so it is important to focus on what you want to attract into your reality (aka The Secret.)

Say each incantation slightly different each time with slightly different emphasis by varying your tone. Say each incantation at least 3 times over and over to store it in your unconscious mind and to activate the mind-body connection, go for a walk or dance or anything that engages your body (physiology) while saying these positive statements.

"***I am*** the master of my success."

"I am the ***master*** of my success."

"*I am the master of **my success**.*"

Charles F. Haanel's Master Key System is the basis for the original version of the Law of Attraction combined with incantations and positive thinking. Incantations have been utilized by infamous psychologist such as Carl Jung. For thousands of years yoga masters of India have used affirmations. Here are some effective ones:

- I am now creating safe ways and places to express my anger.
- I am forgiving myself completely and will give myself the care and attention I need.
- I am given choices. I can choose new responses to old situations. I can learn to recognize my true needs and choose positive ways of satisfying them.
- I am able to do all I am meant to do because I have all the guidance, energy, ideas, creativity, and power I need.
- I am responsible for changing what I do not like about myself and all things are possible in life given they are performed one-step at a time.
- I am going to face and feel my fears so that I can become empowered.
- I am loved and I am lovable and very blessed.
- I am confident and will achieve all the goals I set for myself regardless of my environment and resources.

Psychologist Martin Seligman often frames positive thinking in terms of explanatory style. Your explanatory style is how you explain why events happened. People with an optimistic explanatory style tend to give themselves credit when good things happen, but the caveat to that is they typically blame outside forces for bad outcomes. They also tend to see negative events as temporary and atypical.

On the other hand, individuals with a pessimistic explanatory style often blame themselves when bad things happen, but fail to give themselves adequate credit for successful outcomes. They also have a tendency to view negative events as expected (always expecting bad to happen, anticipating it) and lasting. Blaming yourself for events outside of your control or viewing these unfortunate events as a persistent part of your life can have a detrimental impact on your state of mind as you could imagine, or even have experienced.

Transcendental Meditation

Meditation is a source of comfort, calm, creativity, and relaxation for people of all ages and even more importantly with kids so that they learn early how to cope with stress, anxiety and depression. It is a natural technique that increases happiness and self-esteem.

Parents that include it in their children's activities have said that it helps their children to better understand themselves, as a result of which they are able to deal with their emotions and get along more harmoniously with their family, friends, siblings and teachers. It provides children with the capability to manage stress and stressful situations without negative behaviors such as eating, or cutting, or fighting.

In 1958 when Yogi Maharishi first introduced the Transcendental Meditation technique, he emphasized that individual peace is the basic unit of world peace. He used the analogy that *"just as there cannot be a green forest without green trees, there cannot be a peaceful world without peaceful individuals"* and thus Transcendental Meditation was born for the world.

Stress is a major contributor to many illnesses and suffering and transcendental Meditation is the best natural approach to reverse the effects of stress. According to the American Heart Association, the Transcendental Meditation technique is the only meditation practice that has been shown to lower blood pressure.

According to the American Heart Association, the Transcendental Meditation technique is the only meditation practice that has been shown to lower blood pressure. Neuroscientist Fred Travis performed electroencephalogram (EEG) tests to measure and record the electrical activity of students' brains as they performed a demanding task.

The study showed improvements in brain functioning, increased brain processing, and improved language-based skills among students practicing the Transcendental meditation technique. Plasma cortisol is a stress hormone. The study shows that plasma cortisol (stress hormone) decreased during Transcendental Meditation.

It is a unique experience of "restful alertness" in mind and body, an experience associated with higher metabolic activity in the frontal and parietal parts of the brain, indicating alertness, along with decreased metabolic motion in the thalamus, which is involved in regulating arousal, and hyperactivity. Or in laments terms, it is a vacation from you, within yourself, no movement.

More than 5 million people worldwide of all ages, cultures, and religions have learned this simple, natural technique and over 350 research studies have been conducted at more than 250 universities and medical schools (including Harvard, UCLA, and Stanford.)

When you are overtired or under intense mental or physical stress, the brain bypasses its "higher," more evolved, rational frontal executive circuits, it starts using more primitive stimulus/response pathways. Damage to the neutral connections between the brain's prefrontal cortex and the rest of the brain are/can be caused by stress, pressure, fatigue, poor diet, alcohol, and drugs.

Consequently, you respond to daily demands without thinking; you make impulsive, short-sighted decisions. Again, your unconscious mind makes more decisions than your conscious. When you utilize your primitive response," strong emotions, such as fear and anger, take over, adversely coloring your view of the world as being hopeless and depressed.

Transcendental Meditation is taught in hundreds of schools worldwide, one of which is Maharishi School in Iowa which has been adding a few minutes of Transcendental Meditation for pupils and teachers at the beginning and end of the school day since 1986. It has increased creativity and intelligence and it has been proven in the examination results. It only made sense that a technique that can reduce a child's level of stress should also improve his or her cognitive functioning since stress significantly compromises attention and all the key executive functions such as inhibition, working memory, organization, and mental flexibility.

It is said that when meditation is practiced as a child, teenage years are easier, and these children become more balanced as adults. Transcendental Meditation has been used and found to be very effective in assisting with ADHD/ADD within inner city schools in the US and South Africa with dramatic results in reducing violence and improving pupil behavior.

Sound Therapy (Music) – Using Analog

> *"Music is your own experience, your own thoughts, your wisdom. If you don't live it, it won't come out of your horn. They teach you there's a boundary line to music. But, man, there's no boundary line to art."*

> –Charlie Parker–

There is a great deal of evidence showing that music is a powerful therapy for everything from the heart, depression, stroke and ADHD. Australian holistic healer Dr. John Diamond has studied this very notion. He is a trained psychiatrist who uses music as a focal of his therapy and was inspired himself by George Goodheart D.C., the founder of applied kinesiology.

Dr. Diamond, after testing thousands of his patients over the years has, concluded that the most life-enhancing music is anything by Beethoven and Brahms, traditional jazz, pop songs from the 1920s and 1930s like Ain't She Sweet, and, I'm happy to say, anything written by the Beatles. He's also found that his patients test weak on hearing digital music of any variety; possibly the reason all your analogue televisions had to be replaced by digital televisions, to keep the vibrational states of the mass below 200 so they live in constant anxiety, fear and hopelessness (depression.)

Once when shopping for a CD player years ago Dr. Diamond went to specialist music equipment shop and the salesman played the same piece of Art Pepper jazz, first as a CD and then as analogue vinyl on a high quality turntable. Sitting still, clinically listening to it when the CD played. But as soon as the analogue version was played, suddenly, the music had come alive and indeed he had come alive. This explains why digital televisions and music does not produce the same "feel-good" endorphin effects.

The very popular game scrabble plays psychology at its finest with subliminal messages. What pattern do you see between the words "entrainment" and "entertainment" what's truly missing? Who would've thought it was about more than just being able to spell. You not only have to spell, but concentrate on the letters to form a word, the more letters in the right point spaces, the more points, which means the opportunity to win if you can truly decipher the subliminal messages.

What is entrainment? Entrainment is something all of us have experienced. It's being in an energy field (essence of astrology,) and having that energy field go through you and you feel the field just as everyone around feels the field and is either positive or negative depending on where the field coming from, what part of you is it vibrating and what's the intention of the person or the group which is at the center of the field. Have you noticed how some types of music promote more peace and calming effects? For some it may be classical, gospel for some, Celtic for others, but all in all music being the common denominator.

One of the obvious places we all get entrained is through entertainment. Entertainment is necessary for certain types of growth through music, through TV, through the media. Every time we participate we have an energy flowing through us. The energy is either high or low, or restrictive or expansion, dependent on what the intent of the music or the subliminal messages behind the television shows or movies. This is often times why your children's brains do not develop well when they are exposed to media junkies; they become put into a temporary "zone" state.

Music, because of its very nature, can stimulate a wide spectrum of energies and stimulate a whole range of frequencies and emotions inside you. Some music is designed to stimulate lower levels, lower chakras, while others are designed to uplift. So music is a super valuable tool for keeping your moods. The right kind of music can make any situation, can exude whatever energy you are looking for, and create or change any atmosphere.

Jenn's Insights

Often times, there is a correlation between obesity and ADHD/ADD and depression. It's the age-old saga of which came first, the chicken or the egg? Research has shown that children with ADHD/ADD symptoms may also have higher incidences of depression because these "gifted and talented" children are often perceived as being beyond the norm and often feel like an outcast. The same scenario occurs with children impacted by obesity, because the emotional scars often lead to a feeling of hopelessness. There are varying emotions that are internalized that lead to depression such as deep grief, sadness and shame/guilt.

What You Feel You Can Heal was John Gray's first book to give real insight into understanding human emotion and interpersonal dynamics. The main premise of the book is that your repressed emotions block the flow of love into your life. Everybody needs love, it is what brings happiness and happiness is not a characteristic of depression. The idea of broken dreams, hearts and relationships all ending will result in depression are common as human psychology and often makes us feel emotionally alone, both helpless and hopeless.

One of the most touching stories I had the fortune of hearing was the story of Anita Moorjani. When I heard her story I was moved to tears. Anita was born in Singapore but her parents are of Indian descent. In April 2002 she was diagnosed with "cancer" and her book, Dying to Be Me explains how emotions are truly the deep rooted seeds behind 95% of the dis-ease states (both acute and chronic) in your body.

Unable to move as a result of the Hodgkin's Lymphoma "cancer" that had ravaged her body for over three years, on February 2006, doctors at the hospital had given Anita just hours to live when she arrived at the hospital that morning. She was in a coma and all of her organs were shutting down, her body was filled with swollen lymph nodes and "tumors" the size of lemons, from the base of her skull all the way to her lower abdomen. Her story is one of courage, not just to live, but the courage to truly face her emotions and become free of the dis-ease in her mind and body.

Anita describes how she was returned on Earth after being in an intense coma because she realized that "heaven" was a state and not a place. She felt an overwhelming amount of love that was able to detoxify all the shame/guilt/anger that she had been carrying for years in her body and as such all her "cancer" cells went into remission and she realized that life was indeed a gift and if she chose to live and embrace that gift that should would indeed fully heal.

That is where the real "Secret" comes; where your focus goes your energy will flow to, especially if the focus is on something that promotes a bigger purpose than just your immediate needs. She realized she was a powerful being that can manifest love and peace but most importantly in her own body first so that she could be the shining example for others.

Her "cancer" went into full remission within days and her tests and radiology scans came back clear for any "cancer" cells. Anita then understood, as most people do that when people have medical "treatments" for illnesses, it rids the illness only from their body. What is not understood most times is that although it is true for the body but not as true for their energy so the illness ultimately returns. Realizing that love is truly the best medicine, she found that if she loved herself instead of rejecting her self-identity for all those years that her body would be able to function properly because her energy would shift towards a positive healing realm.

By doing this, eventually the physical body would catch up to the energetic conditions very quickly and permanently and her dis-ease state would miraculously disappear. Knowing that this would apply to both physical and psychological conditions because we are truly not here on Earth to be suffering or enslaved by our thoughts/emotions she then understood how illnesses start on an energetic level before they can become manifested on a physical plane. By-product of all the emotions that have been ignored over the years is a product of the feeling or seeing dis-ease in our body.

Emotions are a form of energy and for Anita's story; those emotions were the seeds that brought her to the state of "cancer." Earlier in life, given her culture, she had walked away from an engagement and brought shame and disgrace to her family based on cultural/societal norms. Anita is a strong empath and took on the responsibilities for her parent's societal disgrace and from these seeds her body was being destroyed by her emotions of shame and guilt that eventually took over her body into physical dis-ease of "cancer" cells.

Anita came from a culture that highly regarded reputation and face/image that is predominant in many Asian cultures. The shame/guilt that was instilled upon her and her family brought her to a dis-ease state of mind and body that held an unforgettable lesson. When Anita finally chose self-respect and forgiveness of herself her body instantly healed and was able to let go of all the toxicity that had been burdening her mind and body for years.

The courageousness of our brave men and women in the military is not necessarily in the feat of battle, or the deserts of harm, but in the war of depression within them that they face while serving and worse when they come home. Retired Navy Seal Lt. Mark L. Donald was a combat medic who wrote the book "Battle Ready" in which he provides the public with a raw perspective for what our military personnel sacrifice for us on a daily basis and this on an emotional level. He received the Navy Cross, Silver Star, Bronze Star, and Purple Heart awards, but the most important recognition should be the one that he receives for battling post-traumatic stress disorder. Coming back from serving a changed man, so much so that he nearly lost the will to live not only for himself, but also for his family provides a firsthand experience in the battle for self through depression. Fundamentally, this is where and how he established his roots, if you will, in the arena of depression. Lt. Donald's book gives you a clear lens into the feelings of hopelessness faced by military men and women regarding the inhumane acts they've encountered.

I recently had the honor to meet Dr. Mario Garcia. He served as the Captain in the Army during his military career and has degrees in Sports Psychology, Neuro Psychology, Theology and is a licensed Attorney. As accomplished a human as he is, he shared the story of how even the strongest of warriors can be defeated by a powerful emotion called "hopelessness." He shared how his grief of his father and his grandchild almost disabled him to provide the care to others because he felt hopeless and was trapped in the energy of the depressive state.

The reason I am sharing these Military stories are in hopes that you relay these to your children that may be suffering from depression. They need to realize that even the strongest of heroes face their own battles with depression and that they are not alone in having this feeling of hopelessness but that true heroes will survive and be able to share this lesson with others.

Jennie's Insights

I myself have many personal struggles with the issue of "hopelessness" and not depression itself. The reason I say this is that I believe that depression is a label that often leaves a person in a victim mentality. By possessing strong empathy skills, it made the current world very challenging at times. After enduring losing a 10 year career due to injustice, I felt very hopeless and did not have the strength to believe that there was something better for me around the corner.

When my parents left their country and sacrificed everything that they had worked so hard for, I vowed that someday I would make them proud and repay them for all their sacrifices. This is what motivated me to excel in my education. I knew they came here and gave up everything because of the opportunity for me to have a better education and true freedom. I vowed that I would make them proud so that they would never have any more regrets or remorse in life.

My mother was given a choice to leave Vietnam on the helicopters during the end of the War, but she stayed and risked her life and suffered through all those memories because of me and as such, when they took away my career, it was more devastating than ever because I had promised myself that I would climb the Corporate Ladder and go far in life. It wasn't for me, but the gratitude that I had for all my parents' sacrifices. And when this dream was stripped away from me on March 2012, I felt like my world had again been taken away. I worked so hard to get a 6 figure job so that I could afford to help my parents again. But this was not the first time that something or someone was taken away from me.

The first time this happened, in a blink of an eye, I was waking up a new country, without the abilities to speak the language, all my friends, some of my family and all my home and belongings were gone. My security blanket, my grandfather, the one person that truly showed me unconditional love, was nowhere to be found, left in my homeland. I vowed to work hard and to rebuild everything that was taken away from my family but thru ethical means and hard work. That was my first broken heart.

I grew up as an empath, I recall when we first came here and my parents hardly had any food to eat. My father was so skinny he barely ate because we could not afford any groceries. I recall we used to count the pieces of food on each person's plate so that it would be divided evenly and my father would always give me more to ensure that I had the proper nutrients to grow.

As an empath, I knew he was going to save all the food for me. So I would clumsily drop food on the floor because I knew that once it was dropped, he would eat it because I could then tell him that it was dirty and I didn't eat from the floor. That was my way of sharing with others and knowing and feeling their pain, without hurting their pride. I repeatedly saw my father coming back from work defeated and knew that he had been professionally bullied (yelled at and reprimanded) and I felt so helpless but knew that someday hopefully I could repay for all his sacrifices. Again, more memories of feeling hopeless came to me.

My earliest hero was my Grandfather. I woke up one day and was not told that we would be immigrating to a new world. I lost touch with him for 10 years without being able to even hear his voice. When he did have the opportunity to come out he lived with my uncle in Canada. I can still remember my first episode with "depression." My grandfather had promised me that he would visit that summer and I knew he was the type that never broke promises. My parent had bought their first home and was finally living the American Dream and my grandfather was going to spend the summer with me.

A week before we moved into the home, I received a phone call; my grandfather had passed away unexpectedly from a heart attack. What made it more difficult was that my aunt had refused to take him to the doctors in a cab and he had endured the long walks to the bus station. I was so furious when I found out years later that my aunt had a chunk of money to remodel her whole house, but she couldn't afford a cab ride that cost my grandfather his life.

His passing devastated me and changed my whole personality. I felt the one person that unconditionally loved me was gone and that I had to fend for myself in this world. I stopped showing emotions and did not care much about anything in life; subconsciously I felt grades and doing well were no longer important. The moral of the story is that if your child feels hopeless (depressed) you need to find out what is the root trigger, by providing medications to numb the symptoms it does not help alleviate the emotional or physical pain they are experiencing.

I have experienced so many disappointments, betrayals, hurt, and grief in my life, but the hope never subsided. Thanks to Louise Hay, I was in tears when I met Congressman Ryan. Even after everything that occurred to me from my last employer, I knew there was still hope. There was a politician right in front my eyes that believed in humanity and was willing to provide tools to empower the next generation with tools such as meditation in schools. It was like receiving oxygen for the breath of air that I had been holding in for so long, a pure sign of hope.

I personally can attest that hope can alleviate the majority of depression symptoms. When my grandmother was in the hospital, the doctors told us that she probably would not make it past the night. Her vitals were weak and she went into a coma state. Psychology is truly one of the most powerful sciences out there. I saw my grandmother lying there in bed with barely any life force in her and recalled how I was not able to save my grandfather, so I vowed I was going to try everything possible and disprove the doctor's diagnosis.

I asked for my cousin who had grown up with her to help save her life. I asked her to conjure up a small lie and the whole family played along. My cousin sat next to grandmother and told her that her boyfriend just proposed to her and that she wanted my grandmother to be there at the wedding. Within a couple hours my grandmother woke up from her coma and within a day she was fully up and running, not an ounce of sickness left in her body.

The doctors were amazed at the turnover, but I knew secretly that hope is what fosters life and the lack of it is what slowly kills a person. People diagnosed with depression, need role models and a sign of hope for their full recovery because the majority of them are empaths and taking on the pain of the world in their bodies and minds.

A recommendation to empaths is to try to minimize your time in environment that may deplete your energy (mood) levels. For me, being at nursing homes and hospitals is difficult because I can literally feel their pain and the hopeless feelings in those environments. So you might wonder why having empathy would be something that this world needs and strength for humans?

Can you imagine what it would be like to make strategic decisions about nuclear wars and other psychological and physical forms of violence if we could truly empathize with what the children and civilians would feel if their homeland was destroyed? Of if feel the emotional repercussions of such animosity for years to come? Do you think our world would still be in the same state?

♡◐◑ Dr. S' Insights

It always baffled me when parents would bring their children with a diagnosis of depression to my office. How could a 6 year or 8 or 12 year old be depressed, I was wondering how practitioners could accurately assess this?

One of the youngest clients I had was a 12 year old boy. He was home-schooled and appeared to be well adjusted in life. He had friends, played sports and had great grades. The mother was diagnosed as having depression and since she was concerned about the son's state of mind, she took him to the psychologist that also presented the same diagnosis.

As an empathy myself, I knew that some further investigation needed to occur. After speaking with the son, I knew that his issue was multi-factor. Indeed, he did have some trauma that occurred to his head that caused subluxations and imbalances to the brain-body connection.

He also experienced some emotional trauma during his life. He seemed to feel anxious when he was around his friend too much and was not able to do any sleep over's with him. I soon realized that he was an empath and was picking up the anxiety from his friend as well as his mother.

I performed SOT Method along with chiropractic Craniopathy on his structural body and after about 4 to 6 visits we revised the anxiety levels and his mother admitted that he was better adjusted to his friend and was able to even participate in social gatherings.

His mother felt that he was able to regain trust in life and seemed to enjoy activities a lot more. I only saw him for 2-4 months at very sporadic intervals; however, a year later, he told me that he was no longer experiencing any depression or anxiety and that the "treatments" had helped his outlook and perceptions improve dramatically.

I personally observed many clients with high empathy levels alleviate their depressive states with energy medicine. I had a mother bring in a teenage daughter that had been diagnosed by the Psychologist as being depressed and wanted to administer Zoloft for the girl.

The girl attempted to cut her wrist and appeared to be very distant. The mother was concerned because the girl had always been very attentive of others needs and very caring (empathy) but one day after the breakup of her relationship she turned this way.

After treating the girl for less than two weeks, she fully went back to her sunny disposition and no longer had the depressive state. She was carrying the burden of others energetically, especially the emotional baggage of her ex-boyfriend.

I had another client that was experiencing many odd physiological symptoms such as release of colostrums when she was not even pregnant. She suffered so much anxiety that she was not able to function in her role as a nursing student and felt a panic attack and a depressive state every time she was in a hospital. Her conditions worsened and expanded to every medical clinic that she stepped foot in.

I later learned that this particular patient has extreme sensitivity for others and needs to be in uplifting environments to excel. For her to perform well, she has to see that there is hope given to patients as the outcome. When she was in the hospital and saw severe depressive states of patients and the pain they were enduring it was too much sensory overload for her to remain optimistic and function properly and to give the world her gift of healing others.

It is very intriguing to me how compressions of the brain via the cranium (skull) might increase the hyperactivity in one child; whereas, in another child, it makes them more depressed. Further research should be explored in this field. But one thing that is evident to me is that hope and love is one of the best medicines in the world to treat this condition.

Resources

Wings Helping Kids Soar - www.wingsforkids.org
Heartfelt Affirmations to Release the Past –
http://store.vitalaffirmations.com/product/heartfelt-affirmations-release-past-cd/#.UvbKNdGYYdU
Relax Kids - http://www.relaxkids.com
Positively Kids - http://www.positivelykids.com
American Music Therapy Association - http://www.musictherapy.org
Transcendental Meditation - http://www.t-m.org.uk/meditation-children-and-teenagers.shtml
David Lynch Foundation - http://www.davidlynchfoundation.org
Flourish - http://www.emiliya.com
Change Your Energy - http://www.changeyourenergy.com
Gainesville Holistic Health Center – www.drstephane.com
Robbins Madanes Center for Strategic Intervention – http://www.robbinsmadanes.com/about.html
Mojo Life Masters – www.mojolifecoaches.com
Creative Healing Trends - www.thetahealingmaryland.com
Rebounding - http://www.reboundoz.com.au/rebounder-kids.htm
Integrative Medical and Wellness Programs - http://vipimed.com
Dr. John Demartini - https://drdemartini.com/
Insight Meditation Community of Washington - https://imcw.org

13

Children That Are Obese Gift to the World: Forgiveness

The Current Label of Obesity

In 2008 the economic cost of obesity was estimated at $147 billion in the United States and that was representative of only the medical costs, without taking into the associated indirect costs such as absenteeism, insurance premiums and overall wages. Did you know that people designated with the label of obesity pay higher life insurance premiums, had lower household incomes and employers had to pay more worker compensation claims to this sub-category of workers? Additionally obesity-related conditions accounted for an 8.5 percent of Medicare spending and 11.8 percent of Medicaid spending.

Obesity is likely to occur in as many as 1 in every 5 children and this number is continuing to rise. This is more than 23 million children and teenagers in America. According to the American Journal of Clinical Nutrition, there were six common obesity-related conditions that produced indirect costs associated with this epidemic such as: type 2 diabetes, high blood pressure, cardiovascular dis-ease, gallbladder dis-ease, colon "cancer", and postmenopausal breast "cancer." The overall indirect costs attributable to obesity based on these obesity-related conditions were: $11.3 billion for non-Insulin Dependent Diabetes Mellitus (NIDDM), $22.2 billion for cardiovascular dis-ease, $2.4 billion for gall bladder dis-ease, $1.5 billion for hypertension, and $1.9 billion for breast and colon "cancer."

Obesity may arise as the result of "energy imbalance," emotional disturbance, hormonal issues, epigenetics, actual physical/brain dysfunction, and/or taking in more calories than a person expends.

Overweight adolescents between the ages of 12-17 years old consume on average 700-1,000 more calories per day than what is needed to support their growth and physical needs.

Obesity is defined as a child and adolescent who has a body mass index (BMI) at or above the 95th percentile for their gender and age, while "overweight" describes those with a BMI at or above the 85th but below the 95th percentile; therefore if this trend continues there will be many that exceeds the threshold for being overweight and the obesity numbers will exponentially increase.

Even though obesity is defined as dis-ease, it does not have any symptoms per se besides fatigue, lack of vitality, overall pain, inability to move, or an overall lack of motivation to exert energy. However, being overweight and obese has a direct correlation to other ailments; there is a 52-60% increased risk, respectively, for new diagnoses of asthma among children.

Obese children and teens have been found to have risk factors for cardiovascular dis-ease, including high cholesterol levels, high blood pressure and abnormal glucose tolerance. The prevalence in Diabetes type-2 in the next 25 years is expected to increase by 36% in the United States and 75.5% in China and 134% in India all attributed to the growing epidemic of obesity.

There appears to be a long-term impact or consequence for spending six hours per day watching television and playing video games or using the internet. To further exacerbate the issue, schools are cutting down the amount of time spent in physical education or for recess which is inclusive of physical activities in America where only 2.1% of high schools, 7.9% of middle schools and 3.8% of elementary schools provide daily physical education or its equivalent.

Growing up addicted to media and television, children also are susceptible to infomercials and publicity which promotes at least 13 food commercials on a daily basis, which equates to 4,700 messages a year; and teens see more than 16 per day, or 5,900 messages that consequently provide them with inaccurate perceptions of healthy lifestyle choices.

More than 98% of the television food ads seen by children and 89% of those seen by adolescents are for products high in fat, sugar, and/or sodium. In comparison, children see about one ad per week for healthy foods such as fruits and vegetables, and bottled water. Increased time spent in front of the television can result in a net gain of 350 calories per day that over a week would result in a 0.7 pound gain in body weight per week, which equates to 36.4 pounds per year simply by performing the "couch potato" activity. In fact, for each hour of television viewing per day, children, on average, consume an additional 167 calories. Studies also revealed that an increase in food intake and being overweight are linked to higher video game usage.

Gut-brain research has shown that our immune system is primarily supported by our digestive system and its capacity to properly regulate and fight against bacteria, virus, parasite, and fungus is imperative for maintaining health. Approximately 80% of our immune system is located within our guts. However, by creating an environment that have inflammation properties due to the improper food intake like fast foods or snacks loaded in sugar or high fat content we are consequently overloading the digestive organs with toxicity. This can increase your child's risk for sickness which further promotes illnesses such as asthma, eczema, allergies and food allergies, autoimmune dis-ease and all types of infections.

The Better Label for Obesity – "Highly Sensitive Children"

Has there ever been a time where you caught yourself being highly sensitive towards a comment or a situation? It's likely someone touched upon a sensitive cord inside of you. According to Dr, Elaine Aron, who coined the term highly sensitive people, she states that there are approximately 15 to 20% of today's children that fit within this category. These children are born with a more sensitive nervous system which will react faster and interpret their surroundings in a highly sensitive matter? The stereotype is that females are more sensitive than males when in fact this does not elicit a true statement and that there is no true gender bias.

Some of the other characteristics of a highly sensitive child might present themselves as possessing a fairly difficult temperament, extremely active, emotionally intense, demanding and often persistent. Thirty percent of highly sensitive children are actually extraverted while the majority is often calm, turned inward not prone for group settings and tends to withdraw from large crowds. Parents tend to categorize them as being "too sensitive" or "too shy" or "too intense." This is not helping a highly sensitive child which will take it personally and resolve this emotional insecurity via a means of coping with food to decompress.

However, this coping mechanism has two ends of the spectrums, where bulimia/anorexia lies on end and obesity on the other end. In either instance, food is seen as a shield against the harshness from life. If the child deems that protection is required in their life, they will revert to padding on more pounds with the obesity condition. Whereas for those that believe that they have disappointed their parents and are imperfect, they will utilize a subvert control mechanism to rectify their perceived flaws by reverting to bulimia/anorexia.

Consequently, these children are easily overwhelmed by high levels of stimulation, sudden changes, and the emotional distress of others. It also means they are more easily overwhelmed when they are out in a highly stimulating environment for too long where they are bombarded by sights and sounds until they feel exhausted. They will tend to demand more depth in their relationships to be satisfied.

A sensitive person's ability to pick up subtle cues and ambivalence in the unconscious processes of the other party can affect communication in relationships including intimate interactions with family and friends. They also tend to see more in depth into another person's flaws or behaviors and this intolerance adds to the stress levels. This further promotes them to wanting to be alone. Many obese children are dealing with internalized anger, fear and frustration because they are misunderstood and/or not loved enough according to their core beliefs.

Many of these children may have been subjected to being bullied. Bullying is one of the greatest challenges facing schools today. Consequently, the children most likely to be the target of bullying are the highly sensitive children. This is why physically they have taken on the form of needing extra protection, within their fat layers. For those highly sensitive children that have a thinner body structure, they are also impacted by absorbing higher degrees of negativity from the surrounding environment because these children also have a high degree of empathy.

Inside the mind of a highly sensitive child is colored with creativity, intuition, surprising wisdom and empathy for others. These children have a tremendous amount of talent to offer the world. Their level of contribution could be more if they were given the proper degree of attention. These individuals need to learn to focus on themselves instead of or before focusing on others and to learn to get their own needs met fist; needs they typically are not aware of themselves or that were not satisfactorily nurtured as a child.

All the world truly needs is love and highly sensitive people are meant to bring much of that happiness to light. If only parents would be cognizant that highly sensitive children truly want to be recognized within their parent's hearts. If these children could look into their parents' eyes and see a reflection of unconditional love, this would make a bigger impact for helping them resolve the psychological pain that is repressed within. Excess weight, metaphysically, is a way of putting distance between ourselves and others and a way of emphasizing our separation and isolation from others.

Physically, they need time and space to process the amount of sensory input they absorb and to further analyze it. This is why many cases of obesity and depression go hand-in-hand. These children tend to need more down time and can be needy because they are constantly craving attention, which can cause loved ones to misunderstand their needs.

They find different things enjoyable compared to others and as such are often mislabeled as anti-social because of their introverted characteristics. Low tolerance to noise and any sensory stimulus that is too heightened when it comes to sensations is a hallmark of the highly sensitive person. They also seem to have more body awareness and can feel when their body is not comfortable in an environment. It is like having a highly developed sixth-sense. This is why obesity is hindering them from expressing their true gifts; it is a layer that is blocking out their innate talents.

These highly sensitive children also have to connect to nature and do regular exercising, relaxation techniques, meditation and any other activities to calm down and recharge themselves after the over stimulations. They have to allow themselves to be vulnerable, face problems rather than running away from them, relate positively to life, learn from their experiences and find love and peace within in themselves to thrive in their natural elements.

It is more difficult for these children to adapt into the western culture because the values of toughness, resilience, higher productivity and expedience are predominantly the norm which counters the culture that highly sensitive children would thrive in. These children need to learn the art of assertiveness and to establish clear boundaries with people as be comfortable declining to assist people in every situation because they have an inclination to be too altruistic. These children tend to put others' needs before their own and as such have unconsciously neglected themselves, so they need to carve out "me" time to help bring balance back into their lives. They have to learn to receive as well as just give and recognize that self-sacrifice or being a martyr does not lead to emotional well-being.

While many parents' intentions to toughen up their highly sensitive child may be well regarded, the contrary will benefit them. Furthermore, providing more nurturance will promote less anxiety and fussiness, clinginess and help them cope more with age appropriate stress management strategies. Parents need to convey that self-sacrifice that leads to emotional deprivation is not a healthy coping mechanism for stressors. These children have to learn that vulnerability is acceptable and learn to face problems rather than running away from them. These children need to learn to relate positively to life, and learn from their past experiences so they are no longer bullied or victimized. Parents need to help foster their temperaments and bring out the innate gifts that are hidden behind all the protection mechanism and layers that these children have developed.

More of these children need to start coming out of their shells in order for their gifts and talents to be shared with society. Many writers, investors, creators, imaginaries, discoverers who contributed their products and services to the world, were all classified as being highly sensitive souls. In fact we need more of these people in this world to help make the world a better place for all. They have an innermost desire to help others be happy and if their gifts are used in creative fashions they are capable of bringing out the best in others as well as themselves. There are approximately 1.4 billion people on Earth designated with this label and their gifts need to be recognized in society not shunned or ridiculed.

The Psychology of Obesity

Creating a demeaning message portraying obesity as a dis-ease or illness undermines healthy behaviors and beliefs among the obese, according to the Psychology Science journal. By having this type of message portrayed in society, these children will not focus on health-related behavior and diet which in turn predicates more unhealthy food choice beliefs because they endure the victim mentality.

Food has always been a means to fuel our body and a way to survive. Since multiple technologies have modified our food habits and ease of access to it, it became easier to eat for the purposes of producing a "feel-good" epidemic rather than for nutrition. It is like defying evolution. The brain needs to adapt to not requiring as much energy and believing that the food is the primary stimulate for enhancing our emotions, otherwise it becomes an emotional roller-coaster. In today's high-stress society, many of us, adults and children, eat high fat or high sugary content foods to soothe our emotions or temporarily relieve our stress, anxiety and the high demands we have imposed on ourselves.

Obesity has a negative connotation from our society that impacts our self-esteem and can lead to depression. Depressive children also can bring about obesity so it becomes cyclical in nature. If the child lacks energy to exercise or is immobilized it could be due to stress. Dr. Kiecolt-Glaser proposes that inflammation in our body (even the fat tissues) is directly affected by our behavior, such as eating habits, emotions, and stress. By discovering the underlying causes of the discomfort, the stress eating habit which results to food addictions, are often a result of internalized stressors and repressed emotions such as loneliness, deep grief/hurt, sadness and depression. Food addiction can be physical but often it has an even stronger emotional component to it.

One way an obese child protects themselves from the distress encountered by their emotions is to build up walls, psychological walls can shield our emotions; however, these children are also manifesting it into physiological forms. They use the physical barriers of the fat cells to double up their protection. Experiencing the humiliation as a child has caused s/he to build a protective barrier to prevent them from being further taken advantage of and experiencing more hurts and pain in their lives; it is merely a coping mechanism for these children. The harsh perceptions and critical nature of interactions from others are too much to "stomach" for these high sensitive children.

Some of these children may feel sandwiched between two people (normally parents); doing everything they can to satisfy both. While doing this, they become completely out of touch with their own needs. Professionals estimate that 75% of overeating that is done is caused by emotions. It is a way to soothe and self-medicate. After all, food brings short-term comfort.

The Brain's Chemistry of Obesity

As a reaction to internal and external stressors, the brain will dictate to the specific organs and glands to produce the appropriate levels of chemical hormones; however, often times when our mind-body connection is imbalanced, there will be deficiencies or a surplus of the hormones that impact stress. If the endocrine system, which is influenced by the immune system and nervous system, produces hormonal imbalances, it ultimately can produce superfluous weight gain.

The center which controls the hormonal aspect of our body is known as HPA axis and consists of the hypothalamus-pituitary in the brain and the adrenal. These three portions of the brain work together maintaining the glands chemical equilibriums. However, when the body is under stress, the HPA axis often releases extra cortisol, the so-called "stress hormone" and the body gets imbalanced. It plays a critical role in energy metabolism as well as other functionality.

The cortisol hormone triggers a series of mechanisms that prompt the body to deposit fat around the belly. Fat has the highest amount of energy and serves as a good source of reserves under stressful periods. This strategy was helpful during prehistoric times when we depended on this reserve for fueling activities such as hunting and escaping from harm; however, since we are still operating with the same genetic makeup today we are still utilizing this innate response to handle the modern day stressors in our lives, and as such the fuel levels do not get expended yet the cortisol levels continue to increase, thus translating into extra pounds.

According to the journal, Neurology, obesity in and of itself increases the speed of mental decline over time. Food intake is regulated by several neurotransmitters, but of particular Dopamine is of interest because it seems to regulate food intake by monitoring the "reward" circuitry of the brain. Scientist found that obese individuals had fewer dopamine receptors than normal-weight subjects. Additionally, the pituitary gland in our brain produces growth hormones. Growth hormones also affects metabolism (the rate at which we burn kilojoules for energy.) Researchers have found that growth hormone levels in people who are obese are lower than in people of normal weight.

Insulin, a hormone produced by the pancreas, is important for metabolism of fat. Insulin stimulates glucose (sugar) uptake from the blood in tissues such as muscles, the liver and fat. In a person who is obese, cortisol hormones shut down the insulin signals and therefore the tissues are no longer able to control glucose levels. This can lead to the development of type II diabetes and other metabolic syndromes.

The hormone leptin is produced by fat cells and is secreted into our bloodstream which controls how the body manages its storage of body fat. Because leptin is produced by fat, leptin levels tend to be higher in people who are obese than in people of normal weight. However, despite having higher levels of this appetite-reducing hormone (leptin), people who are obese are not as sensitive to the effects of leptin and as a result, tend not to feel full during and after a meal. Ongoing research is looking at why leptin messages are not being decoding correctly within the brains of people with obesity factors.

Foods That Impact Obesity

Diet soda, according to Dr. Charles Livingston, is the first of the major offenders that most dieters take in far too often. Dr. Livingston is a leading expert with weight loss and has several publications including "Fat Loss Factor" and co-authored with Jack Canfield the book titled, Dare to Succeed: The World's Leading Experts Reveal Their Secrets to Success in Business and in Life - and Dare You to Succeed!

Dr. Livingston explains that diet sodas are riddled with artificial sweeteners that will not only cause side effects such as headaches and severe stomach pains in some people, but it also leeches away the calcium levels from your teeth and bones. When studies are done on diet soda drinkers, there is a diminished activation of an area in the brain associated with the food motivation and reward system. Decreased activation of this brain region has been linked with elevated risk of obesity.

Diet sodas are rich in artificial sweeteners and can promote obesity and become toxic. Some forms of these sweeteners by-products convert to formaldehyde and can cause other serious health issues (aspartame is an example.) On average people in the United States consume approximately one gallon of diet soda per week. The amount of sugar in a can of soda is astronomical which also will influence the metabolism rates and can eventually lead to obesity or diabetes.

If you are not staying away from bread because of the high level of flour, you should stay away because of the additives and high fructose corn syrup content. Many bread varieties contain this ingredient and high fructose corn syrup has been linked to obesity, brain damage, and even lowered IQ levels.

All white and refined flour based foods such as white bread, breakfast cereals, pasta, pastries, should be limited or altogether removed from your diet plan. The issue with these is that they are carcinogenic (molecule who can create "cancer") due to the fact that they are bleached and bromated during the production process. This process strips them from the natural nutrients they would otherwise contain. This is in addition to the fact that they will cause your blood glucose levels to skyrocket, really encouraging you to start packing on body fat rapidly.

The Brain often seeks micronutrients and empty calorie foods like white bread, pasta, cakes, and cookies; however, they don't provide much nutritional value. Empty foods are also associated with foods that have been radiated or process. They lack nutrients and enzymes or cofactors for your body to absorb or utilize it.

One of the issues of eating empty caloric foods is that your body will deplete from your reservoir of nutrients (take you own building blocks/nutrients) to digest what you just ate. Since the food was empty (no viable nutrient) you then send to waste your own proteins/enzymes/vitamins/minerals that your body could have expended elsewhere to produce more optimal results.

Dr. Frederick vom Saal said that the cans themselves from canned goods contain bisphenol-A, or BPA. BPA has been linked to heart dis-ease, diabetes, and obesity. In fact, you can get 50 micrograms of BPA per liter out of a simple can of tomato. Canned food are also made in aluminum (and don't forget our lovely aluminum pans and cooking foil) which are now known to attribute to strokes and vascular (blood circulation) problems.

This mechanism was explained in mice by which the aluminum helped in the autodigestion of the genes and brain, decreasing the protein expressions and elevating blood-brain barrier permeability, which left the brain vulnerable to multiple toxins and infections. Some research also linked aluminum in the process of neurotoxicity especially Alzheimer's dis-ease. BPA also mimics estrogen and as such is one of the prime reasons why obesity rates in both males and females are increasing in our nation. In fact, BPA has the ability to bind and alter the functionality of the estrogen, testosterone and the thyroid hormone receptors and cause many hormonal imbalances for a body.

Since dopamine levels are lower in children with obesity, the right amount of amino acids and antioxidants can help further escalate these levels by consuming foods that have higher values of these nutrients.

- <u>Protein Foods</u>

  High in amino acids, eating proteins will help trigger dopamine production and stimulate your metabolism. Eggs, fish, poultry and red meat are all rich in protein. Wild caught fish has the added benefit of being high in omega 3 fats, which contributes to brain function. Try to buy organic versions that are free from antibiotics, hormones and pesticides.

- <u>Folate Rich Foods</u>

  Folate also helps produce dopamine. Leafy greens, broccoli and cauliflower are all vegetables high in folate. Eating raw vegetables gives you adequate amounts of nutrients. Lentils, chickpeas and black beans also contain folate.

- <u>Fruits High in Amino Acids</u>

  Blueberries, strawberries and prunes all contain an amino acid called tyrosine. Tyrosine prompts dopamine production in your brain.

- Red Beets

  Red beets are rich in the amino acid, betaine. Because it works as a kind of antidepressant, betaine not only helps dopamine production but also gives your morale an added boost.

- Apples

  High in the antioxidant quercetin, apples can prevent neurodegenerative dis-eases as well as stimulate dopamine production. The organic version should be eaten because apples topped the list of being the most pesticide contaminated produce.

- Watermelon Juice

  A great source of Vitamin B-6, watermelon juice also helps produce dopamine.

Multigenerational studies speculate that soaring obesity and autism rates could be due to our grandparents' exposure to "the chemical revolution of the 1940s," including the introduction of new plastics, fertilizers, detergents, and pesticides. Please read the epigenetic chapter for more information about how your grandparents' consumption of foods and environmental toxins could affect the expression of your obesity genes. This is why it is of utmost importance to focus on this epidemic now so that further legacies will not be impacted by gene mutations.

Billionaire Parenting Tips for Obesity

There are many factors that contribute to children becoming overweight. Usually it can be contributed to genetics, lack of physical activity, repressed emotional blockages, eating unhealthy foods, or a combination of these. Overweight children tend to be more likely to be the victims and instigators of bullying.

Empowering Kids with Healthier Choices

Children need to be empowered with healthier lifestyle choices beginning at a young age. These lessons should include self-control, self-discipline and respect for their bodies. Preschool and elementary schools need to incorporate these lessons into their curriculums. Unfortunately many of these programs that may be available are being cut from the curriculum due to budget cuts and state testing demands on the teacher from the No Child Left Behind policy. However, nutritional information can easily fit into the curriculum. Cooking requires reading and math skills that can be incorporated into the school and healthy ingredients can be incorporated into these lessons, it just takes a bit of creativity.

These lessons should also begin within the home. Your young child can quickly learn basic math skills by using a sugar counting system. They would be allowed a certain amount of sugar dollars each day. They can learn to subtract the money every time they eat food that contains sugar. Once they get the idea of what foods have sugar and which ones don't, they usually will choose the healthier food choices. This system is treated like a game. Some parents allow children to trade their unused sugar dollars for real money at the end of the week which provides them incentive to truly watch what they are consuming on a daily basis.

Below are recommendations to help with incorporating healthy eating lessons into your child's educational curriculum. Many materials are free, some require payment for the resources.

- The Power of Choice

  It was developed by the Food and Drug Administration and the United States Department of Agriculture (USDA) and contains materials for children and families.
  (www.fns.usda.gov/tn)

- Action for Healthy Kids

  It designed the program ReCharge for students in grades 2-6 to learn about and practice good nutrition and physical activity habits.
  (http://www.actionforhealthykids.org/resources)

- California Project Lean

  It offers information on promoting healthy eating and physical activity and on strategies to create a healthier environment.
  (www.californiaprojectlean.org)

- Exploring the Food Pyramid with Professor Popcorn

  This is a curriculum with lessons for individuals in grades 1-6. The lessons include visuals, handouts, recipes, and evaluation forms.
  (http://extension.missouri.edu/fnep/standards/profpopcorn.htm)

- SuperKids

  Offers fun ways to teach students about the importance of fruits and vegetables. It is tailored to grades 3-4.
  (http://www.dole.com/SuperKids)

- FoodPlay

  This is a nutritional media company that offers free materials and links to other resources. It offers hundreds of activities for all age groups on nutrition, fitness, and body image.
  (www.foodplay.com)

- Cooking with Kids

  Uses nutritional education activities for grades K-6, which allows students to explore, prepare and enjoy fresh affordable foods from around the world.
  (http://cookingwithkids.net)

- The California Adolescent Nutrition and Fitness (CANFit) Program

  This program provides resources on improving the nutrition and physical activity status in low-income communities and communities of color for youth ages 10-14. (www.canfit.org)

- The Washington State Dairy Council

  This site offers nutrition education resources including Fuel up to Play, Five Food Group Sticker Activity, coloring books and several other activities. (www.eatsmart.org)

- Songs to Teach Nutrition in Preschool Classrooms

  Songs, chants, and finger plays can be incorporated into nutritional educational activities to reinforce and introduce basic nutrition concepts. (http://www.healthypreschoolers.com/Websites/healthypreschoolers/images/Song_List_Final.pdf)

- Food Songs and Nutrition Songs

  These food and nutrition songs are for teaching about fruits, vegetables, food groups, junk food, and healthy snack choices. (http://www.songsforteaching.com/foodnutrition.htm)

- Child Fun

  Where Play and Learning Go Hand in Hand (http://www.childfun.com/index.php/activity-themes/food/219-nutrition-activity-theme.pdf)

Building Self-Respect in Kids

Some people think that self-respect and self-esteem are synonyms. Although both are very important in life, they are different. When a person lacks self-respect, they feel insecure. They try to be someone they are not. When a person develops their self-respect, their self-confidence is cultivated at the same time. This will allow them to deal with issues that life throws at them a little easier.

A person with self-respect simply likes him or herself. Self-respect is not based on success and failures. It also means that we don't compare ourselves to others. We simply like ourselves for who we are not because of our abilities. Here are some further tips for cultivating this skill set:

1. Be True to Yourself

   Each of us has our own path we need to follow. We should not make decisions based on what other people think. It is important that you make your own decisions based on your values, even if you feel others won't respect that decision. People from the Eastern culture often have a difficult time with this due to the shame and guilt control mechanisms that their parents used on them as a child.

2. <u>Learn to Handle Criticism</u>

   Nobody likes to be criticized. Criticism tends to make us feel bad about ourselves. When we know we will be criticized, it is important to look at it from a detached perspective, DO NOT take it personally. Sometimes the criticism can be helpful to develop our character.

3. <u>Look After Your Appearance Without Being a Slave</u>

   Dressing for success is important; however don't become a slave to fashion. How we appear is very important. It can help build our confidence, or it can make us feel awkward. Dress in an appropriate way that makes you feel comfortable while enhancing your confidence levels, the goal is not to please others with your style.

4. <u>Avoid Comparisons</u>

   It is a very difficult thing to do because at an early age we are often taught to be competitive in school and with sports activities, but we need to stop comparing ourselves to others. When we compare ourselves to others, our own self-respect begins to change. You will not be able to keep your self-respect high when you are striving to impress others. Each of us has our own successes and comparing them will diminish our self-worth.

5. <u>Forgive and Never Hate Yourself</u>

   If we live in the past over hurtful feelings, we will live a guilty and unworthy life. It is important to forgive ourselves and others that have done us wrong. Spending our time with people of good qualities will help us to remember the good qualities within us. If you look for good qualities in people, it is easier to remember goodness within ourselves.

Building Self-Esteem

Many factors play in to a child's self-esteem. When a child is physically punished, or feels unloved by their parents, then s/he will have low self-esteem. Prolonged separation from the parents, neglect and abuse will also lower the child self-esteem.

These children may develop coping mechanisms such as bullying, quitting and cheating. They may also be shy and have difficulty having fun and being silly because they have adopted their parent's demeanor. They easily succumb to peer-pressures which leads them to become more susceptible for substance abuse. They are afraid of failing, so they don't try new things, and often give up easily or become so risk adverse as adults that it produces emotional paralysis in their lives. As children get older, their self-esteem often declines.

Children can pick up when their parents have self-esteem issues themselves and since children often model after their parents so they indirectly learn at an early age the levels of acceptability in this arena. Consequently, parents often times extend their feelings of inadequacy to their children and project their fears upon them. This can lead to parental rejection, neglect or hostility. Parents who are critical of themselves also tend to be critical of their children. They are setting a negative example for their children because these children grow up with less tolerance for others' imperfections.

When we overhear our children making negative comments about themselves, we often wonder where they are getting these negative thoughts from. Although we may have never called our children fat or stupid, how many times have you called yourself that in front of them? Remember, children are sensory learners, they learn and model your actions.

Parents who have had low self-esteem for an extended period of time feel as if they are a victim in this world. They don't feel they can express themselves freely. As such they feel helpless about changing themselves and miss out on experiences and opportunities because of their risk aversion factor. Many times these frustrations are inadvertently taken out on their children because they have not developed healthier coping mechanisms for their stress levels.

Some parents often verbally attack their children. They say things like "Why can't you do anything right? Why are you so lazy? Why don't you have any friends? Why can't you do better in school?" These attacks will develop a critical inner voice in our children. They will begin to think they are fat, are lazy, are stupid, are a failure, aren't good enough. These children begin to feel vulnerable. Their physical bodies respond by building layers of protection or fat cells.

As parents we want to empower our children. We want them to believe in themselves, and to take on new challenges. Parents can take simple, small steps to build the child's self confidence. They can begin by providing experiences that will allow for self-master thru repeated practicing of their skills. Kids need to make mistakes so they learn to keep on persevering even after the disappointments.

To lead a healthy life, people must get to the root cause of their confidence issues. If one continues to live in a low self-esteem life style, they will attract someone that feels the same way about them. This will lead to a negative cycle in which you will be unable to get the approval and acceptance in yourself and from your loved one.

Mary Anderson, HEALS™ Facilitator, founded CORE Value, Inc. in March of 2006 and Self Esteem Boot Camp in May of 2007. The basics from this program provide the following empowerment tools:
- Balance self-compassion with compassion for others
- Live with less stress and anxiety
- Think clearly even during emotional times
- Act in your short and long term best interests
- Control emotional outbursts caused by anger and defensiveness,
- Give to others without losing yourself.
- Heal from or end abusive relationships
- Stop road rage
- Maintain healthy self esteem
- Have stronger and healthier life relationships and success

Kids Yoga

Yoga can be very beneficial for everybody, including children battling obesity. Yoga combines breathing, exercise and meditation techniques. It helps to further exacerbate the condition of obesity and rectifies energy imbalances in the body and teaches the importance of promoting a healthier lifestyle.

The meditation aspect of yoga will help the child with stressful situations and to feel less anxious. It will help increase will power and concentration levels. They become aware of their diet, posture and daily activities further promoting health along with binge eating and boredom reduction in frequencies. Participants of yoga practice stretching and bending using all the muscles of the body. They learn how to breathe using full lung capacity as a result posture and self-confidence increase. At the end of the yoga sessions, people feel positive and refreshed.

Forgiveness Meditation

It is imperative for children to learn how to forgive themselves and others. This is an important process in healing. Forgiving others is often difficult to do when we are hurting. However, the first step of forgiveness is to identify the experience that caused the pain. Children need to understand how the incident made them feel before they can begin forgiving. In John Gray's book, "What You Feel, You Can Heal" provides the rationale for this step; it is imperative that this serves as a precursor because repressed emotions block the flow of love into your child's life.

People often don't forgive because they think they are saying the other person's actions were justified. People also think that if we forgive we have to forget. In reality, we all know it is impossible to forget. When we forgive, we are expressing the idea that their actions or words were not appreciated, but by choosing not to hold onto the hurtful feelings they caused or by repressing these emotions, it will avoid further damage to your physical body.

Anger is a vicious cycle. People need love and compassion to heal. Parents need to teach children techniques to let go of harbored feelings. One way is by using an invisible balloon. The child needs to pretend they are holding a balloon in their hands. Whatever negative feelings they have need to be blown into the blown. When they are ready, they need to allow the balloon to sail off high into the sky. The small void of these negative emotions can now be filled with love and compassion.

Older kids can write letters. Writing will help them express what caused them to be upset and help them get their feelings out. Your child can then write another letter of compassion and forgiveness and describe the lesson they learned from this experience. Lessons learned do not become repeated in our lives since everything on Earth is granted to us based on our wish to experience a variety of emotions. This letter can be to the offender or to him/herself. If they feel led to do so, they can mail the letter to the offender. Some can also tear up the letter signifying the release of forgiveness.

Attachment Parenting

It is common knowledge that bonding with the infant is crucial for their development. It has been proven that newborns are "hardwired" with needs to be nurtured and remain physically close to the parents, usually the mother, through the toddler years. The emotional, physical and neurology developments are increased when these basic needs are consistently met.

A recent report showed that British children ages 3-8 showed lower levels of the stress hormone cortisol when they slept in their parent's rooms. Co-sleeping has been shown to be advantageous also in Dutch infants, who showed signs of being able to better handle stressful situations due to lower spikes of cortisol.

If you choose not to do the co-sleeping technique, there are plenty of other ways to build trust, teach empathy and respond attentively to the needs of your child. As the parent, you need to have good communication and rational explanations of rules for your disciplinary lessons.

You Are What You Eat – (The Frankenstein of Foods)

Frankenstein was a science experiment that went horrifically wrong. Well, today scientists are conducting experiments with the foods we eat. "What a scary thought!" They are inventing new foods by combining foods and chemicals to taste like real foods. Have you ever seen "artificial flavoring" in the ingredients on the label? Some scientists working on the experiments have gotten sick by handling the compounds and chemicals that are being put into these foods. For more information on these foods, look for a magazine called Food Scientist.

The food industry's number one goal is to be profitable, even at the expense of health. They know that people are trying to eat healthier, so they market their food as such. Many times, it is the packaging and labeling that is being altered, not the food. As consumers, we need to shop very carefully making sure our food is giving us all the nutritional value we expect it to have.

Look carefully at the labels. Although cookie and cakes may be labeled allergy-free," "gluten-free," "heart-healthy" or "whole-grain," they are still cakes and cookies and often times the substituted ingredients contain higher fat content. If it says "produced without antibiotics that impact antibiotic resistance in humans," antibiotics were actually used, but not ones that caused issues in humans. These companies are using semantics to deter consumers' purchase power.

There are more people with celiac dis-ease and gluten-related issues today than ten or twenty years ago. Numerous of people with these issues have not been diagnosed. Here are better eating options:

1. Whole real foods such as vegetables, fruits, beans, nuts, seeds, whole grains, and lean animal proteins like small wild fish and poultry, and whole omega-3 eggs.

2. Small amounts of grass fed, antibiotic and hormone-free beef or lamb. Venison or buffalo would be a better choice.

Eating Wheat-Free (Gluten Free Lifestyle)

Wheat is one of those foods that scientists have experimented with. Japan and Korea have stopped purchasing wheat from the U.S. because it is a GMO product. Researchers from Australia have also reported health issues in people who have consumed GMO wheat.

This new, improved wheat is engineered to be tolerant to salt. This means that farmers with high levels of salt in their soil can still grow it. The molecular structure has been designed to match the humans of genes. When humans consume GMO wheat, our own genes may be altered because of this scenario.

Reactions to wheat can include asthma, eczema, migraines arthritis and irritable bowel syndrome. Some people have had difficulties digesting pasta, bread and other wheat based foods. This is because these foods absorb the water content causing more discomfort in the body (flour + water = glue.)

If you look back in history, chronic dis-ease and obesity have been on the rise as wheat has been changed. Grocery stores have aisles and aisles of wheat disguised food. It is estimated that Americans eat 55 pounds of wheat flour each year.

The GMO wheat may look like wheat, but it is very different from the wheat of 100 years ago.

1. It contains a Super Starch, Amylopectin A, which is super fattening.

2. It contains a form of Super Gluten that is super inflammatory.

3. It contains properties that resemble a Super Drug that is super addictive and makes you crave and eat more.

Do you eat a sandwich for lunch every day? Those 2 slices of bread raise your blood sugar with over two tablespoons of sugar. The extra sugar in foods causes people to have extra belly fat, causing inflammation, and inducing diabetes.

Original wheat contains fourteen chromosomes that contain a few of gluten proteins. The new wheat has twice that many chromosomes and produces large gluten proteins. These larger proteins include the one causing inflammation, celiac dis-ease, obesity and diabetes.

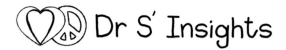 Dr S' Insights

Remember your first days in elementary school where it was fun to experiment and discover things? How many of you took flour and water and learned it actually made glue? Now, let's imagine that as a child you were curious and wanted to know what it tastes like, so you put it in your mouth? Fast forward a couple years, do you remember this texture in your mouth but with more tasteful ingredients? What are the main ingredients that cookies, bread and pasta are made out of: flour and water?

This is why so many children have difficulties with digestion issues that range from the gamut of allergies, eczema to ADHD, Obesity issues. It takes about 2-20 hours for these ingredients to properly digest within your stomach. And this all depends on the amount and types of ingredients used. Processed flour instead of whole grain flour will be worse. Furthermore, if it is coupled with excessive sugar than you have an even slower digestion because your pancreas will be overloaded and consume some of the energy.

The key is to consume things in moderation and if you want to treat yourself in life, learn how to counterattack these processes with digestive enzymes. If your kids have cookies every day or bread every day as a staple, how much energy do you think is being utilized in digestion instead of fueling your kids minds? Could this be what is consuming your energy and making you or your kids tired?

Eating a gluten free diet is not just for the celiac, it is about selecting the best foods for your children to maintain their highest energy levels so they can explore through their surroundings and learn each day? Time is of the essence, the most critical years for learning are from birth to 7 years old.

Eating Non-GMO (Genetically Modified Organisms) Foods

GMOs are plants or animals that have been genetically engineered with DNA from bacteria, viruses or other plants and animals. The premise of the GMOs is to make them resistant to what can kill the plant or add attributes to increase nutritive values. In more than 60 countries around the world, including Australia, Japan, and all the countries in the European Union, there are significant restrictions or outright bans on the production and sale of GMOs. Whereas US still approves the usage of GMOs products.

According to the Massachusetts Institute of Technology (MIT), a study published cited GMOs crops as the cause of majority of chronic disorders. A weed killer sprayed on 80 percent of genetically modified foods including corn, soybeans, sugar beets (by-product of sugar,) and cottonseed was linked to obesity, digestive dis-eases, and other chronic disorders including diabetes, Alzheimer, and even "cancer."

The Environmental Protection Agency set a new rule in April 2013 limiting the amount of Roundup residue allowed in various foods mainly from cereal grains to carrots, oil seeds, and sugar cane, beef byproducts used for hot dogs and school lunches, and potatoes.

Glyphosate is known to have antibiotic effects and destroy good bacteria in our gut, which contains 70 percent of the cells that comprise the immune system. Additionally, there's a disruption in production of three essential amino acids, including tryptophan, the precursor to serotonin, a brain chemical that helps regulate appetite, satiety, and insulin levels. This substance is present in the weed killer and transferred into our GMOs food that we eat.

Because of the prevalence of soy and corn in processed foods, about 30,000 genetically modified food products sit on US grocery store shelves. New labels are coming out on foods that represent the non-GMO Projects approval of reputable products. The goal is not to become fearful but to become educated consumers and demand the best products for your children. Economy is about supply and demand. It is time that consumers demand more from the companies that are serving their children.

Here are 9 Genetically Modified (GMO) Ingredients to Watch for

- SOY, genetically modified since 1996

  94 percent of the US soybean crop was genetically modified in 2011, according to the USDA.

  Soybeans show up in many traditional (not organic) soy products, such as tofu, soy milk, soy sauce, miso, and tempeh, as well as any product containing the emulsifier lecithin (often derived from soybean oil), such as in ice cream and candy. If we are eating foods that we have sensitivities to such as gluten or soy it can also trigger a toxic reaction and contribute to acne.

- COTTON SEED, genetically modified since 1996.

  90 percent of the US cotton crop was genetically modified in 2011, according to the USDA.

  The cotton plant, genetically modified to be pest resistant, produces not only fibers for fabric (organic cotton is a better alternative,) but also cottonseed oil, available on US shelves as a standalone product, and also commonly used as an ingredient in margarine, in salad dressings, and as a frying oil for potato chips and other snacks.

- CORN, genetically modified since 1996

  88 percent of the US corn crop was genetically modified in 2011, according to the USDA.

  GMO corn can make its way into hundreds of products: breakfast cereals, corn-flour products (tortillas, chips), corn oil products (mayonnaise, shortening, Etc.), and literally anything sweetened with high fructose corn syrup, which covers sweetened fruit drinks, processed cookies and other snacks, yogurts, soups, condiments, and many other products.

- CANOLA OIL, genetically modified since 1996

  90 percent of the US canola crop was genetically modified in 2010, according to the New York Times.

  This popular cooking oil, originally derived from rapeseed oil by breeders in Canada (the name is a contraction for "Canadian oil, low acid") comes from a genetically modified plant that is no longer simply cultivated, but grows wild across the Dakotas, Minnesota, and Canada. According to the biodiesel fan, this is the best oil usage for their trucks.

- U.S. PAPAYA, genetically modified since 1998

  80 percent of the US papaya crop was genetically modified in 2010, according to the New York Times.

  Hawaiian papaya was genetically engineered to withstand the ring spot virus in the late 1990s, with the GMOs version rapidly taking over the industry. In 2009, the USDA rescinded regulations prohibiting GMOs papaya on the US mainland; they have since been introduced to Florida plantations.

- <u>ALFALFA, genetically modified since 2005</u>

  The USDA deregulated GM alfalfa, though cultivation was later halted in 2007, following law-suits from the Center for Food Safety and others who demanded a full evaluation of the threats to conventional alfalfa plants, and the emergence of herbicide resistant weeds.

  It is grown primarily as feed for dairy and sometimes beef cattle. This is why organic meats are safer. It is difficult to tell from a meat or dairy product whether it is from cows fed GMO alfalfa. Look for organic dairy products and organic or 100 percent grass fed meat.

- <u>SUGAR BEETS, genetically modified since 2005</u>

  95 percent of the US sugar-beet crop was genetically modified in 2009, according to the USDA. Around half of the sugar produced in the US comes from sugar beets. This is why "sugar" is so detrimental for your kid's well-being.

  What to watch for: If it is a non-organic bag of sugar or a product containing conventional sugar and the ingredient does not specify "pure cane sugar," the sugar is likely a combination of cane sugar and GMOs sugar beets.

- <u>MILK, genetically modified since 1994</u>

  Recombinant bovine growth hormone (rBGH) is a GMOs synthetic hormone injected into dairy cows to boost milk production. 17 percent of US cows were injected with rBGH in 2007.

  Milk from rBGH treated cows contains elevated levels of Insulin Growth Factor-1, a hormone linked to increase risks for certain "cancers." No label is required for milk from rBGH treated cows, though many brands of non-treated milk label their containers as such. If you are going to drink milk, raw milk is the best alternative. There are other alternatives such as coconut or almond milk.

Laughter Yoga

Laughter Yoga is a unique workout regime that oxygenates the blood and other organs, leaving them full of energy and brings physical fitness. Laughter gets the heart beating faster and boosts blood flow. The chest rises and falls and abdominal muscles get a good workout.

Furthermore, laughter relieves stress and stimulates both hemispheres of the brain to enhance learning. It helps ease psychological stress and eases muscle tension which helps the brain remain alert and to facilitate more retention of the material. Laughter also improves our memory and stimulates creativity.

Laughter aides with improving feelings of insecurity and loneliness that is often prevalent in early child-hood. Right from the beginning of our lives we often have heard that rhetoric that, "Laughter is the best medicine" but as we grow the laughter appears to be fading out from our life. Laughter also promotes better concentration power, increases the learning ability and helps to enhance academic performance.

As children begin to laugh unconditionally, they become adept at handling pressures as laughter builds self-confidence and the ability to handle stress. Their immune system will be boosted along with increased good feeling endorphins to help reduce the stress levels.

Dance Therapy

As Anthony Robbins says Emotion is created by motion. Movement is not of pleasure for the child who is set in a sedentary lifestyle. Dance and movement therapy will set the stage for a healthier healing modality by combining physical activity, social support, creativity and emotional expression. The goal is to have individuals reconnect with their body by experiencing and expressing feelings, and discovering the sensory connection between what they become aware of and metaphorically how they move throughout life.

There are numerous forms of dance which may appeal to children and which could help in the battle against childhood obesity: Hip Hop and Capoeira are two dance forms which children may find appealing along with cardio salsa and Masala Bhangra. Capoeira is a Brazilian hybrid dance and martial art.

Cardio Salsa is a low-impact but high intensity workout combining precise, fast-paced Latin choreography. Masala Bhangra, is a challenging workout, based on the traditional folk dance of India. It involves a choreographed series of hops, foot stomping and hip gyrations accompanied by hip-hop influenced Bhangra music and live drumming.

Ho'oponopono Meditation

Ho'oponopono is a very ancient Hawaiian art of problem solving. The main purpose of this process is to discover the peace within oneself by allowing one to learn to ask that in each moment, our errors in thoughts, words, deeds or actions is cleansed and be uplifting for our own morale and to inspire others.

Self-Identity through Ho'oponopono uses techniques to create a working partnership within the mind and allows us to reclaim our personal inner connection with love, our Creator, resulting in peace, harmony and freedom.

Taking 100% responsibility for everything in your life, and repeating the four phrases to cleanse as explained by Joe Vitale in his book "Zero Limits" Often times in life we do not hear these words said enough to us from perpetrators of injustice and unkindness.

The four phrases:
- I Apologize
- Please forgive me
- Thank you
- I love you

Charan has written a children's book that comes in electronic format called, Heba the Ho'Oponoponoist, which incorporates the meditation into a children's format. This book is a fun and effective tool for opening up communication with your child and teaching them the power of kindness and love. When we have situations in our life that upset the flow of energy in our body, and we experience emotions, these emotions can become trapped in our energy field. This is an important book that will help children to learn how changing their thinking can heal their lives.

☾ Jenn's Insights

As the saying goes, some people often eat their emotions. If you tend to enjoy fried foods or foods with rich fat content such as "cheesecake", your food is trying to tell you something about your emotional needs. Your body is screaming that it needs protection and feels it needs to be safer with a fat layer. For the majority of my life, my favorite dessert was cheesecake and it became a ritual to treat myself to that to cope with life's stressors. I was fortunate that I did not gain a lot of weights because I participated in a lot of activities to balance off the calories.

This also occurs with emotional toxins. Many obese children are highly sensitive children and as such they tend to feel the intensities of emotional scarring deeper than a physical scar. I was always told I was too sensitive for my own good, but for me sticks and stones could break my bones but words would hurt me more. Perhaps growing up with a "Tiger Mom" that always had words of critique rather than praise, made me realize how much I detested people's verbal and mental abuse and found them to be more damaging to a psyche.

One of the sociological issues involved with obesity is the victim and perpetrator mentality. This is one of the most disturbing issues that many children face. Consequently if it is not dealt with properly there are more repercussions that occur into adulthood. For instance, if a child was bullied as a kid, when they grow up they can attribute fear to other areas of their life or worse yet they can reverse roles and become the perpetrators themselves.

The first story consists of me experiencing bullying characteristics myself. During my freshmen year in college, I had a roommate that exhibited bullying using the passive-aggressive style. In truth she had a lot of insecurities in herself, but she decided to compensate for it by surrounding herself with tons of friends or should we call it by its proper term, allies. She chose to strategically manipulate situations to her advantage by falsifying information and getting people to empathize with her. She often times would turn on the crying routine and accused me of ill behavior towards her when she was the one that actually carried out the abuse. I realize that she was a compulsive liar and was a wonderful actress in manipulating people's perceptions and often times was overdramatic so that they would empathize with her.

She cleverly got all my friends to take her side and they stopped talking to me. I was not the type that would readily defend and being highly sensitive I knew that raging a counterattack would only bring more ill feelings and besides I felt if someone was truly a friend they would not judge me based on allegations. She turned everyone against me and she made sure I did not feel welcomed even in our own dormitory room.

I tried to tell our Hall Monitor to switch me out of the room, but she said they could not do anything. In truth my roommate was very emotionally instable and often would yell at me and accuse me of things that I did not even commit. Her passion was to spread gossip in general and her idea of unity was to rally up the troops in support of her opinions. It was one of the most horrible experiences I had because I had always had more of a Miss Congeniality reputation and could not fathom how someone could be so manipulative for their own selfish reasons.

It got so bad that her parents would show up on weekends and participated with the abuse and she got her friends to tag team on me. I was afraid to go back to my room. My grades suffered so much during my freshmen year because of this incident, but I was too afraid to tell my parents because they would blame me for picking the wrong roommate.

I was such a sensitive person that I could sense the anger and resentment coming out of my roommates' nonverbal cues and I could not stand to be in the same room with her. I used to study in the library but would be so upset that someone could treat another human being this way that my grades suffered and along with it my dreams of becoming a pediatrician.

Fast forward several years and during my graduation, the friends that she "convinced" that I "had been" a trouble maker realized that I had been telling the truth all along. They even admitted that she was mentally instable and took the aggression out on others in a competitive stance. The moral of this story is that as parents, sometimes there are circumstances that your children just do not know how to express to you. If your children's grades are suffering or if they are gaining too much weight drastically, it could be a sign of some emotional abuse that is occurring in their life.

Ironically lessons not properly handled in life appear to come back into your life. Professionally I had the same incident occur where the bullies were perpetrating the same techniques, rallying up the troops with emotional tactics such as crying and defamation of my character and even staging dramatic scenes during business functions. These people cleverly strategized and manipulated to ensure that they looked like the victims.

These bullies will go to great extents to reverse the role and gain empathy by providing falsified information to others so that they may justify their improper actions without any conscience remorse. They are great at interrogating others to try to gain a sense of support for their viewpoints and their justifications for their intimidation tactics.

The second story involves another person serving as a bully. I was leading a team that had some very challenging personnel. In particular there was a woman that appeared to be very disrespectful and I *recalled she would have shouting matches with other employees and verbally use profanity and physically tried to beat up other employees.*

As you can imagine, my physical stature was half her size so I recognized that this person had padded herself with protection based on deep hurts. So I attempted to fully comprehend the source of her pain which had taught her to exhibit this violent expression of behaviors. I knew it was an episode of an "adult" temper tantrum. In truth, that is what bullies do, if they do not get their way, they conjure up stories to justify why their physical, verbal or mental abuse is valid on another human being. In truth, these people need to seriously cope with their past emotional scars instead of projecting their pain onto others.

After taking the time to discover her true pain, I found out that this particular employee had seen her father murder her mother in cold-blood in front of her eyes. This child grew up with so much emotional trauma and became the perpetrator because she had internalized that being the victim would be painful. After extensive management sessions mixed with a psychological spin I was able to gain this person's respect and convinced her to forgive herself and to respect herself again.

I asked her a simple question, if your child saw how you behave on a daily basis in this office and decided to model your behavior as a role model, how would you feel? Yes, reverse psychology, but it worked, these people are like the autistic ones that cannot sense empathy in others when they are in their zone so you have to get them to truly understand the hurt and pain they are afflicting to others.

This also occurred from my last employer. One of my bosses was victimized repeatedly for a year and it was so inhumane that legal actions were enacted on the Employer and the person threatened to sue the Organization for all the acts of abuse. In response to the threats, she was promoted to the Management Team. This is how dysfunctional the place was. When she became a Manager, she perpetrated the same acts onto me but at a higher intensity.

As a Sensitive Person, what hurt the most was that I knew this person had been a victim and truly understood the pain that was being inflicted upon me as a first time mother. What was more astonishing to me was the overall integrity of the person's characteristics.

The person spent the whole day voicing religious acts of kindness and claiming how altruism was in the core of their beliefs, yet they could still consciously carry out all these inhumane acts to another innocent human being. Victims of bullying acts can become so disassociated with the pain that they attain a level of being delusional with their justifications of why it is valid to treat another human with such disrespect and abuse.

My third example consists of a client that I worked with. The client had severe anxiety attacks after giving birth to her child. The family attributed it to postpartum depression; however, after further investigation, I discovered that the person had been physically and verbally abused by a group of teenagers as a child. But the person had blocked the memories and had never shared it with her mother.

When her child was born, it triggered a panic of what would happen if these same people were out there to hurt her or her child again. This is a common effect of unresolved emotions that are buried deep down. This is also the basis of the post-traumatic stress disorder and how triggers can remind someone of the initial painful experience.

After working with her to address the initial memory of those teenagers that had bullied her all of her anxiety disappeared. This particular client is a very sensitive person and as such often times feels others' distresses but attributes it to her issue. In truth, there is nothing wrong with her; it is the people's dispositions around her that is causing her stress.

Since she is gentle person, all this conflicting energy is causing her to feel anxious. This is what happens to many sensitive people. Sensitive people tend to feel the injustice and pain deeper than the average person. As such, forgiveness is often an issue they must work on within themselves and others so that they do not continue to carry these emotional pains with them.

♡☮ Dr. S' Insights

I have treated some overweight children in my past experience but nothing where chiropractic services were performed to help them shed the pounds. It was a compilation of empowering them to adjust their mental attitude, providing alternative perspectives, encouraging the benefits of exercising, educating them on eating habits and adjusting them with chiropractic Craniopathy to aid improvements with their brain-body communication receptors that helped many of these types.

What was helpful was to utilize the Chiropractic Manipulation Reflex Technique to alleviate some of the stressors on particular organs. There was a pattern with these clients in their liver and gall blabber being imbalanced. These organs are associated with anger, frustration, and stress. When these emotions are internalized (repressed) inside of us, it creates an organ imbalance. So, these two organs are normally treated in overweight or obese children to alleviate many of the physiological issues.

The colon and intestines are also important components to ensure the proper functioning. If there are indicators that the intestinal tract shows that organ therapy is needed, this also means that the child has historically had repeated issues with eliminating anger, frustration, stress and other negative emotions from their physical body and emotional mind frame.

I discovered with my clinical experiences that if we looked at what emotions are involved in the obese child and if they are still repressed inside, that this pattern could be fixed by treating the organ that was impacted by these emotions. However, this would only be a temporary fix, it was imperative that we got down to the root source which often times indicated that the child had a failure or challenge to eliminate stressor/emotions and did not have healthy coping mechanisms to deal with life's ups and downs. As such they used food as an alternative mode of expressing their pain and frustration.

Furthermore, it was necessary to see if the emotions had impacted other organs such as their intestines. Since all organ reflexes are in the frontal lobe of the brain, located towards the anterior forehead section. It was important to make sure that pressure from the skull was not the interference for why these organs were not functioning properly.

We have found at our practice at GHHC, that emotions are the foremost cause of the majority of our physical issues, including obesity. By clearing the emotions, 90% of our physical pains and compensatory systems are rewired for more optimal healing and a healthier lifestyle.

We utilized a technique that removed the energy imprints of the negative emotions along with the picture imprint of the actual negative experience and allowed the client to directly face this issue head-on. We realize that societal/cultural norms have taught many children to repress their emotions, especially negative ones and as such they stay trapped in the body until another one comes along that reminds them of the initial pain but all subsequent issues intensify the pain further.

For example at an early age, when we throw a tantrum because we felt upset, we are further punished so we learn to stuff in the emotions and not be able to properly communicate the emotions that caused the distress. So we learn that vocalizing or abusing was more acceptable formats and thus the breeding ground for bullying behaviors occur.

From a nutritional perspective, obesity can be rectified with the proper eating habits and knowledge of client's nutritional needs. It is important also to find the allergenic foods that might be adding inflammation to the body. Unfortunately many people are prone to eating allergenic foods like wheat, sugar, corn, and soy in their diets. Just cutting these allergic (inflammatory) processes out of your diet will help remove some of the extra pounds.

Personally I had experience with this issue. I was obese when I was young. Granted I was not eating the best foods and my parents were such unconditionally loving people that they accepted me the way I was and I was not belittled or shamed into making any changes.

During my high school years I noticed that there were some dysfunctions that became apparent in my family life and as such, I was using food and the extra pounds to help protect me from reality. It was my protection layer from facing the inevitable issues in life.

I noticed that when I faced the fear directly and left my family and headed for Paris that my weight started shedding immediately and I lost close to 60lbs in 6 months and I maintained it until Chiropractic College.

During my chiropractic studies, I ate the healthiest I had in years; however, I still gained 55 lbs. It was pure stress and the emotional sensitivity in me that created that extra weight. My brain was telling my body that I needed the extra protection to cope with all the emotional stressors in my life.

When I moved to Virginia, I again surrendered to the endless possibilities of life and I lost all the 55 lbs and didn't gain it back since. For me, being a hypersensitive child and person, everything was getting to me and bombarding me with sensory overload. I took everyone's hurt and pain along with my own inside, like an empath. I am super caring as a person and a doctor and I have learned to set my boundaries to keep my mind and my body healthy.

Resources

Move With Me (Yoga for Kids) – www.move-with-me.com

ABCS of Yoga for Kids - www.abcyogaforkids.com

Stress Free Kids - http://www.stressfreekids.com

Songs for a Healthier America – www.ahealthieramerica.org/songs

Upside Down Yoga Games – www.upsidedowngames.us

Coordinated Approach to Child Health (CATCH) - http://catchusa.org/

Self Esteem Boot Camp - www.selfesteembootcamp.com

Laughter Yoga University - www.laughteryoga.org

Zumba Kids Jr. - www.zumba.com/en-US/party/classes/class-kids-jr

Sports Psychology for Parents, Teachers, Coaches - www.peaksports.com

Psych-K Centre International - https://www.psych-k.com/

Nourish Interactive - http://www.nourishinteractive.com

Heba the Ho'Oponoponoist –
http://www.amazon.com/Heba-Hooponoponoist-CharanSurdhar/dp/0956485103/ref=sr_1_1?ie=UTF8andqid=1321310637andsr=8-1SOS Mentor Shaping Our Students - http://www.sosmentor.org/our-mission.html

14
Project Hope Whole-Listic Children's Hospatal

How to Give Hope to the Next Generation (Whole-Listic Children's Hospatal)

> *"You must not lose faith in humanity. Humanity is an ocean; if a few drops of the ocean are dirty, the ocean does not become dirty."*
>
> –Mahatma Gandhi–

We face serious challenges in this country, economic and personal, large-scale and intimate. The more hope we cultivate today, the better equipped we will be to survive and thrive in the months and years ahead. The choice of hope over fear is vital for all of us.

And yet we must face the fact that we live in a society where our children have a fearful existence. Many do not feel safe in school or at home. The opposite of hope is fear or hopelessness (depression.) The choice is vital. Hope and fear are not mere words or facial gestures. They are deeply felt neurochemical stances which will filter our perceptions of what is around us and what is to come. They alter our outlook, actions, and influence the unwinding paths of our lives.

Hope literally opens us up. It removes the blinkers of doubt and despair and extends our peripheral vision to the glittering big picture. We become creative, propelling our dreams into the future. Deep within the core of hope is the belief that things can change. No matter how awful or uncertain they are at the moment, things can turn out for the better.

In Dr. Lissa Rankin's book, Mind Over Medicine, she describes the story of a little girl who was diagnosed with terminal "cancer". The little girl's greatest desire (hope) was to have a little sister. When she heard that her mom was pregnant with a girl she found the will to bring her body into full remission and was there to welcome that sister to the world. Hope is the medicine of the Mind, it is the placebo effect and there are countless stories of the miracles it can bring into bloom.

The authors passion is to change the world through empowering people, to create a haven where healing on all levels (mind + body + spirit) is respected and brought to your child with smiles. The mission of the Whole-Listic Children's Hospatal is to steer the healthcare industry toward empowerment and positive life changes. We are also empowering the next generation with Emotional Intelligence and helping them to access the billions of neurons available for their intelligence within our Gifted Academy.

We are changing the way the world sees dis-ease, and restoring faith (hope) through our work in the realms of medicine and education and ultimately humanity. We are focused on healthy living through Mind, Body, and Spirit; starting from prematernity through adolescence.

We will provide this by giving children HOPE and acknowledging that their dreams and fairytales do come true; thus creating a new generation of mentally and physically sound members of society capable of standing before the world as it is now and meeting challenges ahead. Each of them will be equipped to make a difference. This movement will prove that Dreams, Love and Peace are all possible as we are Committed and Passionate about making a Difference in Total Healing and Empowerment. You are also part of it.

We have already spent $359.3 BILLION to help "fix" children that are deemed to have health challenges (Obesity, Depression, ADD/ADHD, and Autism); can you imagine what could be done for these children if that funding were used to bring out their talents?

We invite you to empower your children with HOPE for the next Generation and leave them with a legacy which brings their inner strengths to the forefront, embodies love and spreads the light of inspiration. Truly, it takes a community to raise a child and we need your help to fund this dream of HOPE.

By joining the Billionaire Parenting Family, you help provide hope for children and increase awareness. Children will find hope in the future, and life is no longer meaningless to them.

Help build a community for your children and grandchildren. All proceeds of this book will be donated to the Whole-Listic Children's Foundation (www.billionaireparenting.com).

Whole-Listic Children's Hospatal – A One-of-a-Kind Concept

The "Whole-Listic Children's Hospatal" will be located within the nation's capital. From there it will create a wave of revitalizing hope that will spread out across the nation for the next generation. It will serve as the prototype for the education and health care reform in the next century. We expect it to be the first of an international network of Whole-Listic institutions.

The Billionaire Parenting movement has several projects which then connect all the communities it comes into contact with. This is supported by three centers of excellence which constitute the main pillars of our organization: the children's hospital (HO) + children's spa Eight 7 (SPA) + children's gifted academy focusing on prenatal and post-natal education (TAL.) Together they constitute the Whole-Listic Children's Hospatal.

Dr. Stéphane's focus will be on Health and Healing, K. Raichelle's focus will be on de-stressing and confidence building and Jennifer's focus will be on empowering and educating the next generation. Jennifer will bring an educational psychology perspective to ensure that the full range of the children's potential is being nourished by a creative and fully rounded curriculum. As Tony Robbins stated, "Across all industries, success is 80% psychology and 20% skill set." Let's equip the next generation with the most powerful technology ever known their brains!

The Spa Eight 7 will be one of the first state-of-the art facilities with entertainment that truly stimulates the mind of these children and builds the self-esteem and confidence within them. It will be the first Children's gym membership to fully exercise both the mind and body.

Children will spend their hours within this facility being pampered and treated like royalty while finding a venue for expending their natural abundance of energy on activities that will stimulate their minds and tone their physical bodies, preventing obesity. As you can see the root trigger for both the educational and healthcare issues stems from constant and chronic stress. As Congressman Ryan so eloquently put it, a "Mindful Nation" is one that will help keep us bring out the best in humanity.

Education will be provided up front to the Maternity clients so that they will be able to make more informed consumer choices regarding breastfeeding versus infant formulas. The goal is to return the miraculous events of childbirth back to a celebration of life and not one that is attached with fear or pain.

The goal of the maternity ward is for all patients to become an "Angel Mom" since education begins within the womb. Each mom will be treated like a Star and truly pampered. They will learn that the Angels that they are bringing into this world are perfect and each unique personality helps make the world a better place.

A llow your baby to flourish with the
N eeded nutrients physically and mentally. Allow him/her to
G row properly by
E nsuring no toxins impact their mental and physical health and
L et the beauty and miracle of life grow to the fullest potential.

Each birth will be celebrated in style and all accommodations will resemble a 5-star treatment. It is time to truly celebrate life and be grateful for the essence of being human. We are truly a unique species that has so much to offer and teach.

Additionally, the Whole-Listic Children's Foundation will serve as the basis for providing education outside of the classroom. The foundation will be the nonprofit entity of the business and will focus on the humanitarian aspects for the whole community regardless of their socio-economic status. The mission of the Foundation is for philanthropic projects.

This will provide an avenue for the children to learn empathy, compassion and altruism that are extended beyond the classrooms. Jennifer is the President of the Whole-Listic Children's Foundation and Dr. Stéphane and K. Raichelle serve as Vice Presidents.

The foundation is already reaching out to the Washington metropolitan community with projects running throughout the year. We would love to have more parents participate in this endeavor: www.billionaireparenting.com.

The foundation depends on the generosity and the support of the community thru volunteer efforts. This is the true definition of leaving a family legacy for this world, sharing these moments with your kids.

This facility will empower the family with nutrition, alternative care, education and de-stressing opportunities. It will be the world's first playground where children can truly be themselves and appreciated for what they bring to the world. The environment will be conducive to the thriving minds of children, an area of play and enjoyment for learning and healing. The vision is to "Spread A Smile A Day, Melting Troubles Away" (de-stressing the Next Generation.)

Whole-Listic will be unique from all the holistic practices in the industry that focuses on the mind+body+spirit concept. We firmly believe that the key to freeing humans from dis-ease of the mind-body connection is to embrace and be empowered by our emotions. Research has proven that 90% of dis-ease and primary physician visits are due to "stress" induced symptoms. A commonality of both educational and health care issues stem from the source of "stress."

Within our facility, Whole-Listic means the ability to stimulate both the "Left + Right" Brains = Whole Child. Then we incorporate all the Alternative Care Services (Holistic) to derive at the word "WHOLE-LISTIC." Traditional holistic services focus on the mind but they have not successfully tapped into the full potential of both hemispheres of the brain.

Infants, toddlers, and young children learn through exploring with their whole bodies, including all their senses. This will be the first "playground" in the nation that will allow them to use all their sensory from both the left and right hemispheres of the brain. Research has proven that when the synergy of the right and left hand hemisphere is balanced, a unique concept is produced "Geniuses." Historically, Einstein, Beethoven and others have proven this theory.

Our emotions are what make us "human" and the essence of humanity. The heart was the first organ to sustain a person's life and it is also the biggest contributor of dis-ease (cardiovascular) within the nation. It's time to open up everyone's hearts and our children will pave the way. As stated, they are here for us and to teach us the lessons to bring us back to humanity's path.

The lessons many have blocked from their hearts due to hurt. The lessons of forgiveness, unconditional love, gratitude, compassion, empathy and most importantly hope is being delivered by your kids. It is time to remember the lessons we were taught as kids ourselves and to truly learn to enjoy and appreciate how we can live peacefully beside each other in love and support on Earth. What distinguishes us from animals is the "humane" portion of the word humanity.

The first phase of clientele will consist of: a 5-star maternity ward, Gifted Academy and the Spa services. The culture that we strive to foster at the facility will be similar to the innovation and leadership shown at Zappos headquarters. We firmly believe that if our employees are not truly passionate about their roles, it will indirectly transfer to the care of our clients. As such we will be investing in the biggest resource in the company its people.

As Zappos' CEO, Tony Hsieh's motto is "Delivering Happiness" with their products. Ours will be "Delivering Love" to the next generation. Forgiveness is love, and love allows you to hope. This is the missing element that is needed in this world.

We will be tapping into the potential and gifts of these children and truly help release their gifts for humanity. Regardless of any former labels, we will turn any child into the essence of who they are meant to become because we know they are the biggest assets to society and an investment worth beyond a billion dollars.

The Hospatal Known for 3D Printing Health Solutions

There are a vast number of physical deformities that affect children and can have a particularly significant effect on their self-esteem and social interactions in life. Since, the Whole-Listic Children's Hospatal's mission is to "Bring Love" which comes with hope; some physical extremities may be fixed with technology. This is why 3D Printing Solutions will provide some hope back to children that may have experienced a limited life due to physical impairments.

3D printing is revolutionizing the way that healthcare will be delivered in the next decade. Also known as 'additive manufacturing', it works by laying down successive films of plastics, ceramics, metals and other materials until the object is rendered whole. Printable objects can be created in computer-aided design programs. A printing application then analyzes how to slice it so that it can be printed most efficiently. The printer heads layer the construction materials one on top of another and sliver by sliver it is created. No waste or cut-offs and no dangerous machinery. It is a revolution in the means of production.

There are many ways in which this technology is being mined for its medical applications. There are obvious benefits for the construction of prosthetics, but there are also opportunities for training applications.

At the Children's National Medical Center in Washington they use a $250,000 machine to print life-sized models of their patients' hearts. Doctors practice on the models, which are exactly the same as the heart they will eventually cut open. Several different types of plastic may be used simultaneously, just as different colored inks create a color picture, so the different textures of the flesh can be brought to life. The model heart is not only anatomically accurate, but mimics the way the patient's organ will feel under the surgeon's knife.

At Boston Children's Hospital researchers use MRI scan data to print brain models and are testing a neurosurgical robot. Doctors at Phoenix Children's Hospital have used about 100 printed heart models to help them operate on children with congenital heart defects. These were printed by an outside company.

Every 4.5 minutes a baby is born with a birth defect. About 150,000 babies each year in the United States according to the March of Dimes is born with birth defect. That is a global total of 8 million. Birth defects are labeled 'major' when they cause structural changes in one or more parts of the body. They can pose a serious, adverse effect on health, development and functional ability namely that child's freedom.

In the United States the birth defects of one in every 33 babies have accounted for over 139,000 hospital stays during a single year, resulting in $2.6 billion in hospital costs. They account for more than 1 of every 5 infant deaths. Affected babies also have a greater chance of illness and long term disability.

While progress has been made in the detection and treatment of birth defects, they remain the leading cause of death in the first year of life. Parents of children with birth defects experience shock, denial, grief and even anger. Acknowledge your feelings and give yourself permission to mourn the loss of the healthy child you thought you would have.

Remember to let yourself enjoy your child the same way any parent would — by cuddling or playing, watching for developmental milestones (even if they're different from those in children without a birth defect), and sharing your joy with family members and friends.

3D Printing for Cleft Lips

When you think of 3D printing solutions for surgical problems one condition immediately presents itself. The Centers for Disease Control and Prevention (CDC) recently estimated that each year 2,651 babies in the United States are born with a cleft palate and 4,437 of those have a cleft lip, making one of the most common birth defects observed. Luckily it is also treatable.

During embryonic development the jaw and facial structures grow towards each other, from the top and bottom and sides of the head, to meet in the middle. Cleft lip and cleft palate arise when there is incomplete or partial union of these structures. These "orofacial clefts" occur during the first 6-8 weeks of pregnancy. They remain common in the developed world because they are sensitive to environmental factors such as toxins and maternal diet. Unsurprisingly, smoking and diabetes are implicated.

A team from the Shriners Hospital for Children in Springfield, Massachusetts has applied 3D printing technology to revolutionize the outcomes for these children. Using Geomagic 3D software the team and data from CT scans are utilized and the team creates customized orthoses on a Mor-Tech SLS 3D printer. The orthotic gently pulls the separated tissues towards each other, mimicking intrauterine growth. This reduction in the width of the cleft prior to surgery improves results and creates an almost seamless join. Years later the children still look healthy and happy.

Clefts are a major problem in the countries where millions of children will never receive surgical repair. Most cannot eat or speak properly, aren't allowed to attend school or even hold a job. The situation is particularly bad for female children and many girls and boys are left to die when they are born with this issue. Every year more than 170,000 children are born with cleft lip or palate. There is plenty of hope for these children. (http://www.smiletrain.org/our-model/)

Prosthetics for Children

A major problem in the field of prosthetics is mass production and the economy of costs. Since each device must fit perfectly in order for the prosthetic to be comfortable and functional, it is difficult to match the cost of providing prosthetics with the huge demand for them worldwide. As such, 3D printing technology is an immediate game-changer set to revolutionize the quality and availability of these essential medical devices.

In the US you are looking at a range of $25,000-$50,000 for a child's prosthetic and most insurance companies won't pay for them because they are quickly outgrown. But that's why they're so important. Growth is a process of responding to the environment, and a child who grows up without a prosthetic may not have the same level of functionality or learning opportunities as their counterparts. They are also more likely to suffer from a greater level of arthritic pain due to the way that the body has had to adapt around the missing limb.

Easton LaChappelle has invented a brain controlled wireless driven arm. That means a child or adult who has lost an arm doesn't wear a block of plastic to put strangers at ease, but can have a replacement limb which they are actually able to use. It is controlled by thoughts, facial expressions and blinking patterns. But it's better than that: they can control it from ten feet away! He presented this invention to President Obama.

Easton plans to make his invention affordable for the masses with a nominal fee of $1,000 each. The goal is to enhance human functionality by making the arm capable of lifting 200 pounds and rotating 360 degrees. The story is one of those amazing marriages of science and science fiction.

LaChappelle used a modified 1980s-era Nintendo Power Glove to convert real hand movements into robotic motion. Mental activity generates faint electrical signals which will change depending on what sort of brain activity is occurring. They can be read to provide data on seizures, comas, sleep and brain activity in general. They are better known as 'brainwaves'. You can consciously alter them by imagining, for example, playing tennis, or listening to music. Mindflex headsets read them for a board game, so

LaChappelle "hacked" one to create a brain-based-Wi-Fi-robo-hand-controller. Using the power of the mind he can open and close the 'robo-hand'.

Some Trends in the industry include:
- Note Impossible Lab (Technology for the Sake of Humanity) - http://www.notimpossiblelabs.com/#!about/cl5vq
- Center for Technology and Innovation and Innovation in Pediatrics –
- http://www.scctip.com/projects/
- National Pediatric Innovation + Awards Summit - http://bostonchildrensinnovationsummit.org/overview/

It is not hard to imagine that soon everyone will want a robo-hand. However, that is the least of this technology's applications.

Emma Levelle was born with a condition called arthrogryposis. It affects muscle tissue making it tough and inflexible. Joints are stiff and the muscles around them prevent their proper movement. Emma's legs were folded up by her ears, her shoulders turned in, her fingers skewed and she had rocker-bottom feet. Using a 3D Printer, the researchers at the Alfred I. DuPont Hospital for Children created a custom designed, light-weight robotic exoskeleton for Emma. Once Emma was in the exoskeleton she almost immediately regained power over her limbs. She reached for a toy. She put food in her own mouth. Thinking about that moment: her excitement and her parents' joy, is almost unbearably moving.

Thanks to innovative and creative minds involved in all the strands of this research, children who thought they would watch their lives from wheelchairs will now have access to some autonomy. But more than that, just hearing this story is a message of hope for everyone.

Jennifer's cousin also has the same condition and she has had to see her live a life in a wheelchair from birth. It will be so rewarding to see her be able to use her own arms and legs in the future to feed herself thanks to innovative and creative minds bringing hope for humanity.

A Second Chance (Heart) for Children

Nearly 1% of babies born each year in the United States have congenital heart defects. They are the most common birth defect and their severity ranges from a tiny hole between two of the four chambers of the heart to the absence of entire chambers. The doctors at Phoenix Children's Hospital who practice on printed hearts get them from David Frakes' company Heart In Your Hand.

By possessing this technology at the Whole-Listic Children's Hospatal this will be aligned with the localized industry trend. Currently, Children's National Medical Center is the only one equipped with this technology within the area.

The Hospatal Known for Customized Fun Solutions

As a parent, it can be heartbreaking to watch your child becoming distressed and worrying about being separated from you when they have to stay overnight at a hospital. The goal at the Whole-Listic Children's Hospatal is to make the environment as conducive for play as possible so their worries and minds are focused elsewhere and your children's visits are made as enjoyable as possible.

During their stay, the children should leave with a lasting memory that is conducive for their well-being. They will have an option of activities to preoccupy their time during their stay at the Whole-Listic Hospatal which will allow them to tap into their own creativity and imagination.

By tapping into this part of the brain, it will help release endorphins and help reduce the stress level of the children being admitted into the hospital while providing them with loving and lasting memories of hope instead of fear for any future associations.

Softie Showcase

Child's Own Studio is a place where your child and a craft artist, together, can create a keepsake to be cherished for a lifetime. (http://www.childsown.com/softiemaker-showcase/) And it's "easy!" Many companies will turn children's' drawings into printed or soft toys. These incredible expressions of childhood can be cherished for a lifetime. For the children, seeing their raw ideas turned into something so tangible is a fantastic lesson in the possible and this will serve as a souvenir for their stay at the facility.

Crayon Creatures

Parents can have their child's art on a pedestal by having it 3D printed through a new service called Crayon Creatures. (http://crayoncreatures.com) Barcelona dad, Bernat Curi, has a business which grows emerging 3D printing applications. His daughter asked him to make her drawing into a toy one morning and this serious-minded businessman was soon creating a variety of fantastical creatures! He takes the outline of the picture and uses computer aided design to 'inflate it like a balloon before exporting it for 3D printing. The amazing thing about this story is not just that it makes it clear that the technology is well on its way, not just that a child saw a new application for it, but that it demonstrates the utter versatility of the printers and how they can bring entertainment to a facility that often is associated with fear and pain. It also provides children with the opportunity to realize anything is possible with imagination.

Leo the Maker Prince (3-D Story Books)

Author Carla Diana used 3D printers in her consulting work. Impatient to see where this amazing technology was going to go next and understanding that a generation 'born' into it would have the freshest ideas, she created a story book around the technology. *Leo the Maker Prince* introduces preschool children to the creative principle of 3D printing and comes with animals and objects that can be printed on the domestic version of the technology: 3D printers will become common household items. Each of the objects featured in the story also serve to advance the plot but also expand the core creative concepts for the children. There are musical instruments, a chess set, action figures and even a functional habitat for a hamster.

Technology is all about helping people. Technologists love to solve problems; it's what they do best. We need to provide new models for how to accomplish great things with technology. We are at a critical intersection in the evolution of technology and social enterprise. Working together, the technology, philanthropic and user communities can ensure far-reaching success.

We can demonstrate the power of collaborative successes on the global stage, using these exciting projects to catalyze the creation of technological innovations to help humanity around the world and to create new stories that will bring about hope and love for generations to come.

"An individual has not started living until he can rise above the narrow confines of his individualistic concerns to the broader concerns of all humanity."

–Martin Luther King, Jr.–

15

Education: the Whole-Listic Gifted Academy

Introduction

In this chapter we will look at the stages of brain development to see how to best support the child's biology. We also take a child's eye view of the early years via Jenn's and K. Raichelle's honest recollections. We will also review the humanistic (reasonably and logically) movement of the psychologists, neurologists and doctors who founded the compassionate early years' education model.

Learning from the best work of their successors we will consider the social and philosophical context in which education occurs. Having evaluated best practices by educators from around the world, we will show why specific programs were selected for the Gifted Academy and set out how these programs will be implemented at our outstanding school! This chapter encompasses our opinion of the best of the best experts in the field with the simplified version for parents to read and understand why they would want to enroll their children into this type of academic setting.

The Genesis of Genius

A common feature of nearly all gifted children is that they were brought up in richly varied surroundings with plenty of opportunities to directly or indirectly learn from their environments. Numerous studies on geniuses and gifted children suggest that their mental abilities are not genetically inherited in the same way as physical attributes, such as hair color. Mental aptitude is greatly influenced by the quality of the prenatal environment and what happens around the child during its first seven years of life.

MIT researcher Deb Roy turned his home into a laboratory where the linguistic progress of his son was followed for the first three years of his life. There were cameras and microphones in every room. The results showed that some words were very location specific: for example, 'fridge' was almost exclusively used in the kitchen. The more unique the location/frequency profile of a word was, the shorter the delay between first hearing and first speaking it.

Interestingly there was a feedback loop between the child and his cares that none of them had been aware of: as each new word emerged, the adults simplified the way they used it. It was placed in shorter, less complicated sentences. Once the word had been acquired the adult use of it became more complex again. We evolved as a migratory species so it is no great surprise that we learn new words more quickly in new places. A screen can fascinate a child, but it cannot begin to provide the high-level feedback loops that humans are not even aware of. The most important ingredient, as ever, is people.

Mozart had instruments around him throughout his infancy and by five was playing and composing for the violin. He wrote his first symphony at eight. In New York, in 1952, Aaron Stern, a survivor from a Nazi concentration camp, did everything he could to make the world around his daughter Edith as interesting as possible. The radio was turned to classical music all day. He talked to her often, though baby talk was forbidden, and showed her flash cards with numbers and animals on them. At one year she spoke simple sentences; at two she knew the alphabet and was reading complex adult books by the time she was four. Her IQ score was a consistent 200, on a scale where 150 represented genius.

A teenage mother who could not afford a television listened to a sophisticated radio station all day with her child. Ten years later that child won a scholarship at an academy for the linguistically gifted. One example cited by Steve Biddulph in The Secret of Happy Children, the parents of two exceptionally high functioning girls were asked how they had nurtured this intellectual development. They said that they had not done anything more complicated than talk to their children about the world around them. For example, when hovering (with the baby strapped to their back,) they explained how the vacuum cleaner worked, with a motor to create suction, Etc. By making the world a rational place and taking the time to explain things means that children grow up in a world that is filled with things that are possible to understand. Curiosity did the rest.

But there is more to it all than simply interacting with your child. We often use the phrase 'a rich environment', but what exactly do we mean by that? Toys? Space? Gizmos? No. Mostly it's just ideas. The idea that you can play with cardboard boxes; the idea that we think about what and how we do what we do; the idea that we can play with children of any age; the idea that grown-ups have to try not to be naughty all the time as well and that we're all in this together. Yes, pens, paper and books are essential basics, and paints and glue and pasta shells also help, and yes, gardens, chickens and ponies would be wonderful, but actually, a scrunched up page of a newspaper can be used as a ball for indoor play.

"The irony is that by thinking more like a child and seeing the potential in everything, we can create a rich environment for a child almost anywhere."

However, we still impose handicaps on the young child trying to learn language. At the time when his/her brain is soaking up language, we use baby language built around cutesy abbreviations, such as 'woof woof' and then, 'doggy' and don't construct proper sentences. The same is true of the plague of strollers. This is particularly bad in cities where parents trundle around with children strapped in and wearing passive expressions long after they have learned to walk. Many working parents simply do not have time to walk at a child's pace. It is a great loss for the parents as well as the children.

We can also learn a great deal by looking at examples from other cultures. The International Association for the evaluation of educational achievement found that children from more economically successful countries did better at reading tests despite those from Scandinavian countries starting school as late as six or seven. While financial security may be the most significant factor, starting school earlier is also advantageous.

Balancing Creativity and Analytical Thinking

Several studies in Europe and the US have shown that the arts and the sciences are mutually beneficial. In Connecticut, children at the Mead School in Bryam, spend fifty percent of their time in art classes of one form or another and the other half in "regular" subjects. As a result their performance in mathematics, science, and other subjects actually increased. Tragically cutbacks in the public funding of education usually target the arts first. This may seem a good short-term saving, but in the long run it is a grave loss to society.

Other schools in both Europe and America that have tried similar projects have found the same: The extra time spent on developing the faculties for creativity (previously known as right brain only theory) also helps those associated with analytical (previously known as left brain only theory.) This is because the two do not work in isolation, each supports and complements the activity of the other; however, there is still dominance if both muscles (brain hemispheres) are not fully utilized.

If we look at the great minds throughout history, we find that, time and again, those people who maximize the faculties of both the left and the right hemisphere of the brain are most creative in their thinking; whether they are artists or scientists, have the most powerful ideas. Albert Einstein is a classic example. He was a great scientist and mathematician; but his initial ideas often came to him in the form of images.

In 1975, Dr. Bernard Glueck found that the electroencephalogram (EEG) patterns of subjects practicing the Transcendental Meditation technique showed an increased synchrony between the left and right sides of the brain. The corpus callosum connects the left and right hemispheres, and will be more active when the subject is in a state of relaxed concentration. Learning abilities, memory, problem solving and creativity also improved with transcendental meditation.

Goldberg's theory gives us a different way of looking at how the brain learns. It suggests that upon encountering a novel situation for which the individual has no coping strategy, the right hemisphere is primarily involved and attempts to deal with the initial situation. While in "learned" situations, both hemispheres will be mostly activated but research is still trying to understand all the specifics of neurological pathways.

For the purpose of this book we will focus on the distinction of the various hemispheres; however, we recognize that both hemispheres are attributable for the whole learning process and the ideal is to have synergy between both. However, the field of brain studies is as widely divided amongst the two ends of the spectrums supporting their own viewpoints. The goal is not to disprove which theory is better but to take the best from all these theories and combining it into a unique concept to help stimulate the billions of neurons.

Jenn's Insights

In my opinion, Goldberg's theory supports why learning for adults is more difficult. Since learning anything new requires access of the right brain according to Goldberg and since most Eastern cultures and the United States predominately values left brain thinking, learning becomes slower and change becomes even scarier.

According to some theories, before the age of 3, most children operate on the right hemisphere of the brain; however, many children are then exposed to a regime of traditional learning methods such as rote memorization. As such, they quickly alter the frequency of usage from the right hemisphere of their brains. This is why learning a foreign language at a younger age is easier for children; it is because they are still primarily right brain dominance with their learning style.

As Maya Angelou so eloquently puts it, "We are all creative, but by the time we are three or four years old, someone has knocked the creativity out of us. Some people shut up the kids who start to tell stories. Kids dance in their cribs, but someone will insist they sit still".

I believe my saving grace was that even though I was raised with a Tiger Mom (Amy Chua's concept), from an early age, I knew that my parent's truly sacrificed their lifestyle and came to this country for me and as such I was grateful and was going to make the best out of every opportunity. For every left hand experience my mom gave me she inadvertently balanced it with right hand activities (music/dance) that provided balance.

I tried to make everything fun in life because innately I knew that to truly learn, it had to be something I enjoyed doing. This is why those that are truly passionate about what they do excel beyond belief because they are applying what they are learning. As you recall in the Brain Chapter, the right hemisphere is actually the one that has more long-term memory instead of short-term memory.

For me I had always believed that the best way to learn was by making things into games and making it fun. This is what got me the Leadership Awards during my professional career. I knew that to influence and be effective in instilling change, I needed to bring the lessons in a format that would not be seen as another mundane task to do. I wanted my team to believe that they wanted to learn and tackle the projects on their own.

At the age of practical application:

My son is two, I am teaching my son to count, but not in the form of using books. I observed that he truly enjoys playing with (cars and trains) and we often take each car and start counting while we are passing them back and forth. He is learning motor skills, creativity and his numbers all in a simple activity. Even though my son is not talking yet, I know that this will be beneficial for his learning because when he is able to vocalize it, the numbers will simply be repetition.

# Jennie's Insights

As the research stated, "A common feature of nearly all gifted children is that they were brought up in a richly varied environment with plenty of opportunities to learn." As Tony Robbins says, "It is never about the resources, but the lack of resourcefulness that stops a person from achieving their goals." Our family was very poor but I probably led as rich an environment as a kid that could afford preschool.

For every issue, there is always a positive outlook and the negative outlook. For instance, if your child was born under a very stressful environment, like a War zone, which I was, research proved that intrauterine stress does provide a very varied environment and as such you learn with Darwinism, survival with adaptation.

When I was in my mother's womb, the message I received, was that since the fetus is weak, that it is better to just let it go. So the lesson I internalized was to be very strong and never give up to the last breathe because it could cost you your life. This is probably where I get my label of being stubborn. But the positive word would be perseverance.

By the time my family immigrated to the United States, it was a whole different experience; the variety of my upbringing from my own country versus the USA provided a lot of varieties. My parents were very grateful to have been given the opportunity to come here. As such they had always had strong work ethics and values instilled in them that one should not be too greedy.

Our family never used public assistance and when we were taken to the church to get clothes, they told us we each could get 4 outfits and that was the exact number my parents took, nothing more. They were grateful for the help already. When we came to the United States, times were so tough that we barely had enough to eat and I literally had 4 changes of clothes to wear the entire year. This was in stark contrast from my homeland where all my outfits had been custom tailored. So at a young age, I had inadvertently been given variety in my learning environment.

My parents were the type that were selfless, and that was something I truly respected about them and one of the primary reasons that I was self-motivated. My parents could not afford to send me to preschool so what they did was to go to the teacher-supply stores and take books that were donated from the County and brought them home to me. Fortunately my mom worked as a secretary for one of the administrators in charge of the County's public education and we were given a lot of free books.

My parents could not afford an official babysitter so for the longest time I was a latch key child, way before the legalized age. I was left alone a lot and as such I learned to become self-motivated. Every day, my mother would leave me a bunch of books to read and assignments to perform and told me that when she got back she was going to check all the work. Before every grade, I was doing workbooks for the next grade. So when I went to school, I was often times bored out of my mind and not very challenged, school was a breeze for me because what I was learning was repetition.

I did this all the way to 4th grade where I met friends that my mom still blames to this day on being the stumbling blocks to my ultimate success. The friends that I met in 4th grade used to tease me saying that my mom was brain washing. My mom was an extreme "Tiger Mom" but she was providing me with experiences based on what she knew best.

To occupy my time, I would repeatedly do my homework but at that age, I did not think it was brain-washing. As an only child, I was very lonely so I used my imagination a lot to keep me preoccupied. I imagined all the home work my mom assigned, as playing school. So I would literally pretend that I was in school and was doing my homework. At the age of 3, my mother had already left multiplication tables for me to memorize. I did not even understand multiplication nor could speak English, but I memorized them and made it into a song in my own native tongue.

I remember we could not afford toys, so I turned my pillow into a stuffed animal and gave it eyes and ears and it was my student. I pretended to play school and every day all the assigned homework was done. I remember for Christmas my mom's boss provided us with a tape deck and all the donated tapes of books. I would listen to it every day and that was how I learned my English. My homework assignment was to memorize it and recite it when they came home. It was fortunate that my mom had worked for the US Embassy in her homeland so she did know some English.

I used a lot of imagination to keep me preoccupied, and it's ironic how the formalized definition of Schizophrenia and Autism states that these children are in fantasy worlds. In truth, this is a normal mechanism for children that may have had a lot of trauma in their life or felt extremely alone so they retreated into their world as a safety coping mechanism. I recall when I was sick my parents worked in jobs that did not have sick days. My mother would take me to the doctor and then bring me back home and left the medications and food for me to fend on my own, so from that I learned to improvise and become self-sufficient.

Brain Based Approach to Learning and Teaching

Though all human brains have the same systems for running our bodies, our senses, and our emotions, each individual's systems are integrated in different ways. When something is learned it actually changes the structure of the brain itself. Variety and choices within lessons will facilitate learning based individual interests.

The brain processes many functions simultaneously. It integrates huge quantities of data about the world around us, only a fraction of which we are aware of as sensations; it carries the swell of emotions, thoughts, imagination, and our own individual predispositions with the development of knowledge. Teachers need the ability to orchestrate an array of strategies which will address many dimensions of brain capability.

Just as breathing, it is possible for learning to also be either inhibited or facilitated. Experiences are stimulated by neuron growth, nourishment, and synaptic interaction. There are both positive and negative stimulus' which may cause different responses; stress or boredom may cause a shut down while motivation or challenge may encourage learning.

When one is embarrassed, scared, or feeling threatened, learning ability is decreased. An unthreatening environment enables the neocortex (part of the brain) to operate most efficiently. Academic learning can only take place in an environment that is free of threat, provides content that is meaningful to the student in an enriched environment, and allows time, choice, and feedback for the learner. In addition, they need the freedom to be led by their passions and curiosities.

Emotions are central to organizing information, and facilitating memory. Classrooms that combine a supportive climate of mutual respect, and student-teacher reflection on schoolwork create a positive cycle that leads to more and better learning. Although repetition creates memorization, continuous focus on memorization by itself may discourage understanding ultimately interfering with effective functioning of the brain.

Classrooms built on brain-based learning theory strive for the following elements:
- Relaxed alertness: A classroom that combines a supportive environment with significant challenge. The learning environment needs to provide stability and familiarity; at the same time, provision must be made to satisfy students' curiosity and hunger for novelty, discovery, and challenge.
- Immersion: The curriculum and the life of the school are merged into real life experiences that allow students to make sense of what they are learning in the context of their lives.
- Active processing: Encourages learners to take ownership of their learning in a way that is personally meaningful.
- Create Patterns: Learners are patterning, or perceiving and creating meanings, all the time in one way or another. Ideally, teaching should present information in a way that allows brains to extract patterns, rather than attempt to impose them.
- Holistic Learning: Good teaching orchestrates the learner's experience so that all aspects of brain operation are addressed (emotions, imagination, analytical thinking.)

Children should learn the art of speed reading at a young age. What we see in our left visual field is transmitted to the right side of the brain. Conversely, the right visual field of each eye is transmitted to the left side of the brain.

According to Peter Russell, when we read, we can take in about five chunks at a time. The more meaningful the material, the easier it is to understand how to chunk the information. Also, children should learn to slide their fingers across the page to help facilitate using the periphery of their visual field while reading. This single action can increase reading speed by up to 500 words per minute.

The mind unconsciously organizes new material into groups or patterns that will be easier for recollection later. Having an interest in whatever the new information is will dictate whether it is stored in long-term or short-term memory banks. Being able to adequately recall any information later will be reliant upon taking breaks periodically while learning or studying.

One reason that the potential of human memory has been underestimated is that verbal memory is usually researched; however it is less acute than visual memory. If there is an immediate need to memorize something in large portions, it will be more beneficial to organize the information into smaller groups as the mind usually can remember about 7 items in a sequence or pattern whether it be numbers, shapes, colors, or random objects. Research has shown that out of ten thousand pictures, people can recognize 99.6% correctly.

Many children are capable of eidetic imagery: they can maintain a strong full color visual image of a detailed scene. When children give meaning to what they see, they learn and retain more. Mnemonics is a great way for children to learn while making strong associative links with the thing to be remembered. Given all the literature about methods and challenges of teaching it is "easy" to forget that we evolved to learn our brains are designed for it.

Nevertheless, the variety of different mnemonic methods helps with what has been called 'artificial memory' which is the things that we must make an effort to remember. It is different from the 'natural memory' which enables us to recall our friends' faces. This allows an increase in stimulation and activity of the right brain hemisphere which will maximize the entire brain function for learning and memories for example.

According to Russell, it is better not to teach the individual letters of the alphabet but instead words and their associated sounds and meanings. The "a" is for "apple." In the 'Look-Say Method' from the 1950s the child is given pictures of a familiar object, such as a cup, with 'cup' written underneath it in large letters. Numbers are learned using rhymes and rhythms such as 'One Bun, Two Shoe'. It is no accident that chants, songs and rhymes have been used to help children learn for thousands of years: they work.

Revisiting the information learned will be essential in the long-term programming of it. Looking back at the end of the day, but also in spaced out increments throughout the day be it 15 minutes after initial learning, and then maybe an hour after that. Eventually you will review it more sparingly, like in a few weeks, or month and so forth and so on. This will be most valuable in trying to make sure the information was retained.

When Does Education Begin?

The embryonic brain develops exponentially; however, there are two particularly active phases: Eight weeks after conception, the number of neurons explodes, increasing by many millions per hour. The completion of the proliferation of cells is the first stage of brain development; at which time during this stage the fetus has most of its' lifelong nerve cells. During the second phase of its development, these billions of isolated nerve cells begin making connections with each other. At the time of birth, a typical nerve cell may communicate directly with several thousand other cells.

Further proliferation of these connections takes place in the newborn and infant. That said, proliferation and connection are not everything, and once these connections are established the crucial factor in neurological development is the pruning of these connections. It is thought that babies are fully synesthetic.

Their sensory inputs or sensorium has not organized itself into discrete senses, so they will, for example, feel color, hear, touch, and see sounds. In rare cases the latter will persist into adulthood. Despite the extensive pruning and organization necessary for functional development, by the time a child is six years old the brain is 70% of the way to maturity.

By the age of 10, it is almost 90%. Making corrections or changes later on does not come as naturally as it did before, as any teenager will tell you! The learning processes of infancy and childhood have been linked to building a house. For the rest of your life you can fill that house with furniture and ornaments, but it's almost impossible to create new rooms. Nevertheless, the average adult will have nerve cells making direct connections with as many as a quarter of a million other cells.

Nearly 100 years ago the famous Italian educator, Maria Montessori said that education should begin "nine months before birth." It is now known that babies receive things other than nutrients from the mother while in the womb, things like physical impressions due to the mother's physical and/or emotional responses. What happens during pregnancy effects the baby's development, directly or indirectly!

What Are The Teaching Tools?

From the moment of conception (and for some believe it happens even before that) every person is assigned a unique personality that will determine how they learn and the contribution they will make to society. This kind of "freestyle" development is in place usually until school-aged, when they get into a formal institution of learning where a teacher then tells them that "they will learn what is taught and do what is asked and if not, there are consequences.

Eventually the pressures of meeting certain demands and expectations create a stressor in children/ students over a constant period of time that the brain kicks into "emergency mode", where the brain will then make it its primary mode of function, later creating a more uncontrollable hyperactive state.

Thomas Edison, though he never went to school, was one of the most creative and productive people that the world has ever known. Children master language and a multitude of other things before the age of five as part of their natural development and many of them never set foot in a traditional classroom.

Most people, even as infants, detest being controlled. Many of today's schools constitute an attempt at sustained mind control. Children can be rough and cruel: verbal and physical abuse is extremely common in any group of children, particularly among younger boys and older girls. Every school will have its bullies and scapegoats. Teachers often have their favorites and "problematic" kids.

The tragedy here is that many children either become conditioned to passivity or will not react to protect themselves or their peers, or they may be brutalized, whereby anything challenging is met with a violent rejection. For the rest, "busywork" shuts down mindfulness. Many students spend 70 hours or more per week on assignments. In this kind of environment, the brain has no opportunity to integrate or question the complex array of data that it encounters.

In this environment, meditation is and would be extremely beneficial. The essence of meditation is to sit quietly in a place where there is no distraction. Many people simply cannot do this. Coming face-to-face with their own, the conflict and disorganization is too uncomfortable. Many people prefer to be detained by flurries of avoidant activity than stick it out.

Children want to learn things that will help them make sense out of the world. Often, when they graduate, they feel lost and bewildered. The real world is very different from all the theories that were taught to them in college. Yet they may go on to make a valuable contribution to society. It is terribly important to support them during times of transition so that they don't lose hope.

Most times the most interesting things or things we may see as useful are the things we remember. When it comes to children, they to want things to be useful, something that will aid them in figuring out all the, "why's" behind the "what's" they see. I mean let's be real, the world is confusing even to us adults, now imagine that confusion for a child that has not yet had any experiences but is still trying to adapt. They too, even at a young age, want to make valuable deposits into the world and will not need to be forced into doing so. There are and will be a multitude of motivators, some positive and negative.

Jenn's Insights

I am constantly struggling with my mom with the parenting style for my son. My mother raised me with her "Tiger Mom" style and as such she is often telling me that I have to teach my son to model more of

the same behavior. I totally disagree because I know males in particular do not like to be controlled; in fact most human beings do not like to be controlled. They like to be persuaded and understand why something needs to be done.

I recalled when I had a Hypnosis section with an amateur, I was hastily misdiagnosed. The comment I received was that I had issues with authority figures. The truth is I have issues with authority figures that are abusive of their power. As you recall at an early age, I learned that male values earned more respect and love in my family, so I adopted that mentality and for me to listen to you; I operated on respect, which meant it was a two-way street.

My mother was such a controlling element and her rationale for listening to her was "because it was an order," a "mandate." In truth most people use control as a coping mechanism for fear. With control they feel more secure because they perceive that they can control the environment and all its surroundings. This is an illusion!

I will give you a prime example of abuse of power within the education system. Unfortunately some teachers do have their favorite students. I recall being in a traditional high school that felt like prison. I was in all the Gifted and Talented classes but the teacher's personality and mine just did not mesh. In my opinion, the teacher had no creativity in her and taught the classes thru pure rote memorization. The irony was that it was an English class, which should allow more open-ended creative answers.

I remember dedicating a lot of time to my essays and when they came back with C's, I was wondering what the real issue was. I was a cheerleader at the time and I felt that this particular teacher had some emotional healing of her own to do and had stereotypical notions of what a good student persona was. I was not a problematic child but I was probably more an out-of-the box thinker than her preference.

I then asked a friend of mine to help me test a theory. There was an assignment to write an essay about Huckleberry Finn. I wrote the paper and then I asked my friend to switch papers with me. I turned in her paper with my name and she turned in my paper with her name. When the grades came back, it confirmed my theory. She received an A+ for the paper that I had written but I received a C for the paper that she wrote and she had always received A's.

What baffled me was that if the teacher was not biased (not abusing authority), then it should have been clear that the writing style was not even consistent all along. It was apparent to me that she did not truly dedicate the time to read the papers and was randomly assigning the grades based on her preferences of students. This made me much unmotivated and made me consider why bother to try? The moral of this story is that the traditional means of education may be losing a lot of gifted potential with their learning styles. It is truly important that parents start monitoring the education that their children are receiving.

Personally, I know my son's personality and as such I know that he will thrive more on a balanced-brain curriculum and this is one of the reasons why I have decided to dedicate my career developing a Gifted

Program that will truly enhance both the right and left hand hemispheres of learning and simultaneously share this gift with the world.

Jennie's Insights

Looking back the parts of my schooling that I enjoyed most were when I was in elementary school and also the Magnet school. When I was given a lot of freedoms to be creative, my learning and my grades flourished. My home environment was so controlling and stifling that it was reassuring to be able to go to school and feel freedom. When I went to a traditional high school for a couple years, I felt like I was literally in prison.

But my outlook has always been to make the best of your experience. Even during those years, I learned to develop leadership skills with opportunities to be class officers; I learned to develop influence and motivational skills by participating as a cheerleader. In my opinion there are not really any right or wrong extracurricular activities it just depends on the intent of why a child is being put in those activities that will determine if they will get the maximum potential out of them.

At a young age, I was often developing and enhancing the learning opportunities for both brains. Even though I was memorizing and drilling mathematics and exercises on a daily basis. The free-time that I spent was used on maintaining the development of my right brain.

I hardly watched television. I would prefer instead to read a book and get lost in imagination and pretend I was one of the characters. This was my way of traveling all around the world and visiting my imaginary friends and escaping from the harshness of reality. I played with dolls a lot and I would talk and come up with all types of pretend-scenarios, this is where I learned my communications skills.

My parents sacrificed and gave me ballet and gymnastics lessons at a young age. In elementary I volunteered for every activity they had. Learning the lessons was "easy" for me so I had to find things to occupy my time. I played the Recorder and then the violin because we could not afford a piano at home. I joined chorus and was in the Special Arts group. I did all this while maintaining a report card of A's. I even had enough time to explore Leadership at a young age by being in the Girl Scout Troops and the 4-H Groups.

These activities were important to me because it was my only opportunity to see other friends and indirectly learn from different cultures. My parents did not believe in sleepovers, the only person that was allowed to go to my home was my Korean-American friend. Her mom was also a Tiger Mom. But she was put in the same activities as me and we both spent our childhood just trying out everything possible. Her mom was very competitive and as such, it allowed her to help guide both of our up-bringing.

I knew that her family was better-off but she had more of a diverse background, her father was Caucasian and he would often read stories to us and that was how I learned a lot of my English skills, simply by listening and observing. As Tony Robbins' said "it is about proximity," by hanging around her, I was given a lot more opportunities that my family could not afford. In turn her mom had selected me as her best friend because (yes that was how controlling her mom was too) I had the highest grade and would help her daughter excel. She interviewed my parents and physically came to visit our home before she allowed her daughter to have a designated playmate.

Her mom would take us to plays, the movie theater and the swimming pool. My friend had private lessons for everything but by being around her, I inadvertently learned and was given more breadth than just what all the kids around the apartment complexes were doing, playing out in the playground with the same group of kids based on their comfort zone, their own ethnicity. I knew my goal early on was to learn English well and be so fluent in it that you would not be able to tell that I was not a native. I knew it did not serve me justice to hang around people that hardly could speak English so I chose to immerse myself with friends that were often more Westerners.

♡♡ K. Raichelle's Insights

Although my childhood was the polar opposite of Jenn's upbringing there are similarities. My mother was a single parent with two small daughters. Though she herself was not fully raised by her parents she was still cared for by a relative, her fraternal grandmother. My mother was born in a time when it was not acceptable for interracial couples and in some places illegal. Her mother Caucasian, and her father African-American and Indian, was not the 'ideal portrait' in society or in her mothers' family's perspectives.

The eldest of 4 (at the time,) she had two brothers both of which shared the same father, and a younger step-sister that had a Caucasian father. My maternal grandmother, not the more responsible one, would leave for days at a time leaving my mother in charge of the kids even though she was as young as 9 years old herself. This was where I would say she learned her "survival of the fittest" mentality.

At some point a neighbor realized there had been no adult in the home for some time and decided to reach out to any relatives they could find. They got in touch with her mother's family who were in close proximity and they came to get the kids. The stipulation to the "mixed" children going home with her was that they had to stay outside in a trailer, while the youngest fully Caucasian sister stayed in the house. The children's fraternal grandparents were later contacted and came to get the 3 eldest (my mother and her 2 brothers.)

They then grew up in a household that was run with a yard stick. My great-grandmother was a very Christian woman that ran her house with rules so strict that it caused the opposite of her intent, rebellion. Perhaps she too would be called a Tiger Mom to Jenn's description. Each of the children, though raised in the same house, all ended up doing totally different things in life.

My mom though within the first seven years of her life was not raised with love or compassion; however, was able to raise my sibling and me with a lot of love and compassion. She knew, however, that there were things she was not able to teach us personally so she provided us with proximity to people that could. One of which was my great-grandmother, the other was her son (my uncle) who was a pastor.

By doing this, she did for us what she ran away from because she never adhered to these principles. However, I believe she wanted to provide us with the opportunity to have a strong religious foundation. In retrospect, I understood now her well-intentions, even though often times I felt upset and abandoned.

In retrospect, I am grateful, for the things I learned from my great-grandmother. I learned to develop my own personality and emotional well-being through praying, singing, dancing, memorization of scriptures infused into my life. To this day, these life skills have helped me with my interrelationship skills and my parenting. Some may not believe in religion, and have their own ways of communicating with their 'source of higher power'; however, I believe the commonality in all religions is peace, love, understanding and goodwill.

In school I was very smart, creative, imaginative, and very, very talkative (as described by my teachers, especially during conferences and letters home to my parents.) This did not in any case land me in the Gifted and Talented program in school. Instead of it being seen as an attribute, it was punished. As I looked at the kids that were in the "Gifted" programs I often wondered what made them better or smarter than I, what "gifts" did they possess? This often brings children to more thoughts of inadequacies or promotes more competitive natures.

I was often very bored at school because I was taught a lot of things before I was in kindergarten. My aunt had a daycare and they would teach us letters, numbers, reading, math, all the essentials before you were school-aged, not to mention being in an environment with a lot of older cousins and relatives. Once I would finish my assignments (which was usually before anyone else in class) I would talk to them. This of course was a distraction so I was put in the corner or moved away from the group. Later I became very shy because I indirectly learned that talking could get me in more trouble.

Still a very quick learner, I was not as socially adaptable as I was before. Making friends was in some ways beginning to exhibit more challenges dependent on the circumstances. I was always one of the top students in class and always made very good grades. All of this was without the supplementation of my parents helping me at home. There was no study time or homework time with either of them.

My latter school years were when I found 'myself' again. By junior high I was breaking the shell that was put around me to limit my talking and socializing. This was a time when I realized no one knew who they were, but astonishing enough, I did. This was when I decided I could be smart and popular and it was okay. Without the influence of my parents I joined the Math Club, Spelling Bee, and the

National Academic League. I also had a teacher that recognized how gifted I was in math and practically begged me to take his advanced math class as an elective (which I did.)

Like Jenn, being involved in different activities allowed me the opportunity to relate beyond what was at home. It gave the freedom to learn in ways I wanted to learn, and achieve my goal of being "different" than everyone else. I was raised in the inner-city with limited resources for affordable upper-class education such as private school or tutors. However, the resourcefulness of the people around me educated me on the things I could not learn in school, how to survive in society.

My mother really didn't involve herself in our school life. We were good kids and always made good grades. I guess it was an "if it ain't broke don't fix it" way of thinking. Education was important but the meaning of such importance was different in our community. The meaning was to be better than your parents were, to go further than they had, and to accomplish what they didn't or couldn't.

Being scholarly was a choice, we were given the choice to perform academically and we chose to go for it. She didn't implement many rules, but instead allowed us to make our own judgments. The best example I can give would be around curfew. In high school we never had a curfew, not even on school nights. She would just say, "Be in at a reasonable hour." Huh? My friends were so dumbfounded at that that they would be envious. My sister and I on the other hand would be stuck trying to figure out how not to test her. So we just decided to stick to what our friends' parents said as far as time. We never got in trouble!

The purpose behind sharing this story was to show a different side of how parenting was done, and how the environment was different; however, here we are, Jenn and myself; together, with the same vision, dream, and contribution. We represent two different cultures working side-by-side to empower the next generation with the same dreams of instilling hope and peace.

Although as parents there are some things that may not be conducive to the personal or education growth of our children, the personality was placed in them and us before we saw the light of day. There may be both positive and negative contributors, but nonetheless all a part of the path that will ultimately give more definition to the character that was designed just for them.

Being able to give a child tools before birth however, is a gift. My daughter, now 11 years old, has a wonderful personality. It is all her own and I promote her finding what makes her happy. She will sometimes tell me, "I have this joy on the inside that I can't seem to keep to myself, it's so awesome." However, when I was pregnant I was stressed, unhappy more times than not, and worried. Because of that, she sometimes worries about things she shouldn't, has spells of unhappiness with no apparent cause, and has physical dis-ease like asthma, really bad allergies, and very severe case of eczema which may have been manifestations of all the emotions that I endured during my pregnancy.

Is My Child's Personality Free to Emerge?

When you stop to consider the changes in the demands on time in the last two generations, the difference is phenomenal. For children growing up in the 1970s television was the big time-thief. Aside from that most people's childhoods were characterized by long stretches of aimless daydreaming, boredom or wandering around the neighborhood. In the days when people could afford not to be working mothers many 'day-care activities' involved a parent or caregiver trying to cook, clean, tidy and stop you from having an accident. In the 1980s came the first of the computer games and it hasn't stopped accelerating from there. It is very important to assess who or what is controlling a child's time and attention.

Of the 168 hours in each week, children sleep approximately 56 hours; go to school for 30 hours; do an average of 7 hours of homework and spend an average of 8 hours getting ready for and going to and from school per week. Mealtimes take up approximately 3 hours and, of course, there is the greatest rival for their attention: TV.

According to the recent reports, the average American child watches between 18 and an astounding 55 hours of television per week. Some children watch TV after school and all weekend. However, this doesn't even factor in time spent looking at screens and phones while in transit or during school breaks. It leaves roughly 9 hours for your child to be HIM or HERSELF and explore the world.

A study of infants between the ages of 15 months and 4-years old found that those who began watching television before 12 months of age, and who watched more than 2 hours each day, had six times the likelihood of language delay than children who started watching television when they were older than those who watched less overall. Additionally, those who watched television alone were over eight times more likely to have a language delay than children who watched with a parent or caregiver.

It might seem like something which is difficult to really study but by measuring when a child speaks, how long they speak and how many times the ball crosses the net in conversational tennis, it is possible to draw solid conclusions. All the measures listed above were reduced in two to four year-old children for every single hour of television watched.

A significantly larger study of over 1000 children found that those with attention problems at 7 years of age were more likely to have had early television exposure. Similarly violent programs seen by 2-4 year olds significantly increased the risk of antisocial behavior at 7-9 years, among boys in particular. There are also links between childhood aggression and violence in adolescence.

In an ideal world, time in the home environment would be shared with parents, grandparents and siblings. Together the generations can develop and hone thinking and reasoning skills. If you don't think that the children can challenge your reasoning skills, then you need to spend more time with a child in the 'why?' stage. No one asks tough questions about the world like a child of four! And when that's enough socializing, people can go and rest or explore by themselves. If only the above were the rule and not the exception! One family bans screens from all social situations. It takes new guests by surprise, but they often find that they've enjoyed it and had more fun and focused interaction as a consequence. Yes that means you too can do the same.

While the internet can be an incredible tool for supporting children with a hunger to learn, it also feeds that hunger with distraction and misdirection. That is even before we stop to consider mobile phones, (complete with games, apps, texts and web access), television, films, computer games, extra classes, competitive sports, socializing and school. Today's children are *busy*. Even very small children hanker after their parents' screens and there are 'baby apps', ostensibly for learning, but effectively conditioning their relationships to screens.

Cartoons, a seemingly harmless past-time for children, may actually have the ability to negatively impact a child's problem solving skills, attention, and ability to delay gratification in only a time span of 20 minutes of watching a fast-paced cartoon.

New information helps us to better understand the relationship between natures (genes) and nurture (experience.) Brain development is the exquisite interplay between genes and experience. Talking and singing to your child triggers his/her brain to start building the connections that s/he requires for proper development of language skills. Babies who are severely neglected and deprived of stimulating experiences have been found to have brains 20-30% smaller than others their age group. They do not have enough active neurological pathways to enable them to reach their full potential.

One example of this is feral children who, growing up devoid of contact with other humans can sometimes learn to communicate, but will never master certain parts of speech. Violence and abuse in the early years can severely alter brain development and skew perception such that any sign of perceived danger can trigger a cascade of stress hormones. Aggressive behavior may seem to come out of nowhere but probably has some logic rooted in that child's terrible experiences.

Another coping mechanism for these kinds of stress may prompt children to withdraw or fade, becoming unnoticed into the background. The former is more typical of boys, but neither response is definitively male or female. These are not things that children can simply grow out of and addressing those takes work. Changes in the brain's neurochemical balance and connections have been linked to mental health problems, family violence, aggressive behavior, criminal offending and ultimately even suicide. Intervention is not optional. The modeling of our reflex responses does not only occur in extreme cases but with all of us to a greater or lesser extent.

New neuroimaging techniques provide biological evidence of the addictive properties of some screen media (tablets, hand-held video games.) The brain releases dopamine, a neurotransmitter associated with pleasure, reward and alertness, during fast-moving video games. A similar effect is seen after the consumption of some addictive drugs, including sugar.

Newer technologies may also interfere with parent-child conversations. The so-called interactive electronic books in which screen images respond to touch with sound effects or words or simple movements, are less likely to induce the kind of adult-child interactions that promote literacy than traditional books do. Certainly, part of the fun of reading with a child is making the noises and doing the actions yourself.

Gaming companies have warned that children under the age of six may damage their eyes when playing with 3D consoles. In the UK, one manufacturer highlighted the potential dangers their 3D technology posed to people with certain medical conditions as well as the elderly, pregnant women, and children.

While no special glasses were required, there was a risk of triggering epileptic fits, convulsions, disturbed vision, nausea, dizziness, and muscle problems including cramps, spasms or twitches. They further advised people who were under the effects of alcohol or sleep deprived should avoid watching a 3D television.

Because advances in neuroscience have increased our awareness of the remarkable plasticity of a child's brain during the first few years of life, we have a better understanding of the mechanisms by which environment affects development. Over 90% of children in the US begin watching TV regularly before the age of two. The average amount of television watched by the children less than 3 yr ranges from 1 to 3 hours per day. Given infant sleep schedules, this may equate to around 30% of their waking lives.

Dr. Dimitri Christakis, a researcher at Children's Hospital and Regional Medical Center in Seattle, makes the case that the speed at which the images change on TV causes a child's brain to respond quickly causing those children's brains to be "rewired" after prolonged exposure. He found that children who watch a great deal of TV are more likely to be diagnosed with attention disorders.

When we watch television our normally active eyes focus on a single area. For a young child the necessary practice in moving, coordinating, and focusing is considerably reduced. To succeed in reading, rhythmic and well-controlled eye movements are essential. Children with learning problems often have impaired visual development. Taking into consideration the fact that children between the ages of 6-7 years old are still under-going the maturation of their eye muscles, an image on a TV screen with lines and dots that rapidly reappear over 25 times per second.

Television addresses only a limited area of cerebral functioning. Brain waves produced during TV viewing are primarily Alpha waves normally associated with sleep. In this trance-like state the brain receives information without any conscious analysis or selective association. Children who are slow to read may be further impeded by time spent in front of a TV due to this dream state as well as poor eye coordination and a reduced capacity for concentration. This undermines the left and right hemispheric connection, i.e. entire maximized brain cooperation and utilization.

Many skills necessary for reading, analysis, auditory association, phonics, symbol recognition and handwriting, are predominantly left hemisphere action centre. Children who are slow to read are frequently one-side predominant in their development and TV viewing can increase this imbalance and had six times the likelihood of language delay than children who watched less television and began watching it when they were older.

Since play is vital to a child's development, specifically their motor skills, creativity, social skills, concentration and reasoning, the potential cumulative impact of many hours of television is a concern. Research has shown that the combination of these effects on children's play and the decrease in parent-child interactions made background television "an environmental risk factor in children's development."

But how? What is this powerful mechanism? The truth is that television exploits an inbuilt reflex to be fascinated by things that move. The features of the medium itself are inherently hypnotic; (music, bright lights, moving colors) and the fast pace of the action where visual and auditory changes occur roughly every 6 seconds trigger a child's 'orienting reflex', literally compelling them to watch the screen.

One child-minder reported that when a group of children were playing together while a television was on in the background, they ignored the programs but would be automatically interrupted in their play when the advertisements came on. Additionally, ramped-up drama and suspense change the emotional tone, creating a world where histrionics are the norm.

Real life seems less interesting by comparison. The theory of displacement proposes that the (in some cases vast) amount of time spent watching TV results in less time spent on more developmentally enhancing activities, such as interacting with parents, reading, games, pretend play and actual study.

One suggested mechanism for the link between a poor attention span and exposure to television is that it may be a learned response: since the television program continues regardless of the child's attention to it, they may actually be learning that they do not need to pay attention. The American Academy of Pediatrics strongly discourages television viewing for children ages two years old or younger, preferring interactive play.

Jenn's Insights

In writing this book, I had to share a lot of my son's time with this project. As such, my husband took on a lot of the responsibilities of watching over him and resorted to the "technology babysitter." I also noticed that I had used the tablet as a form of "easier parenting" on my part due to timing constraints. It really made me realize what I was doing to my son one day when I truly observed him. This is a true-life example of what prolonged electronic media exposure could do to your child.

My husband is all into the latest electronic gadgets and as such at an early stage, we had disagreements on why having a television in his room or a tablet for him was not the appropriate route for his well-being. To entertain him, due to the lack of time, we ended up putting the tablet in front of him at restaurants so that he would not be bored.

But the more he watched the more he became addicted even at age 2. He would demand the tablet even at home. What was worse was that sometimes my husband would put two tablets out at a time so that when he got bored with one movie the other was in the background.

To occupy his energy and time, we would put the tablet in front of him so that other house chores could be completed on time. I knew that we had a tight deadline to meet with the publisher and as such I was already exhausted with 4 hours of sleep on a daily basis and it was just easier to keep him occupied with the tablet.

Prior to that we never allowed any television and we still do not. The tablet consisted of the baby Einstein series and the incorporation of the Cars and Planes. However, in doing the research for this book, I realized how many limits I was imposing on my son from a neurological perspective by even allowing prolonged exposure to this type of entertainment.

I held myself accountable and realized that I was using the tablet as a babysitter replacement thereby making it easier on me as a parent. My husband would put the tablet in the car everywhere we went to help calm him down. I pointed out to my husband the impacts of this.

My son used to look out the window and point to things and start making sounds, but now he was zoned to the tablet in the car. He did not even notice that we were there. I noticed he was less affectionate and stopped giving hugs and kisses and did not want to receive affection either. In fact he did not want to do much; he did not want to play with his toys. He did not want to go outside for activities. Irony was that he was not even watching the screen at times, it was just background noise, but it was enough to put him into a zombie like state.

As a compromise, we have instituted movie nights instead, where my son looks forward to family time and sees the movies as a treat rather than an entitlement.

 # Jennie's Insights

As a child, I did not watch much television. It was mindless to me and I found it to be a waste of time since it did not really allow me to use my own imagination. I did watch television on weekends as a treat, but I had so many activities and things that I occupied myself with that I never really had down-time.

I used to turn on the television more so as a friend. When I was left alone a lot, I would turn it on in the evenings so that I felt like someone was home with me, but I never really watched it. I found it to be more of a distraction and a tool that was trying to mesmerize my mind with junk.

I remember when my parents could afford a babysitter they put me in one of those home environment ones. It was not even a daycare because the babysitter would simply turn on the television all day and plopped us in front of it and then ignored us the rest of the day.

I was so upset which probably agitated the babysitter a lot. I kept trying to help and wanted to learn. The more I did that, the more I annoyed the babysitter. In retrospect, children require a lot of patience and most adults these days are so stressed out that they do not have enough time or energy. I truly advise you to carefully consider (or reconsider) your daycare options for your children.

When I was growing up, my parents' decision was based on the price so I went to a babysitter that took me in because she had to watch her own kids. She used to scream at us all the time when we did not sit in front of the television or were in her way. When we tried to play amongst each other, it agitated her and she literally locked us in closets as the Eastern form of punishment.

She even threatened to put us in the attic if we continued to misbehave. To this day, I do not like going to the attics or basements of homes. These are the lessons that often are indirectly given to your children if you as a parent are not careful with monitoring the types of services provided by caregivers.

The Brain Dominance Learners

Research identifies the left brain as the Academic Brain because educators generally emphasize its processes in the traditional classroom. Left brain stimulated-dominant people tend to be more logical and analytical in their thinking and usually excel at mathematics and word skills.

The Stimulated-Dominance Left Brain Learner

- Likes structure and closure
- Mathematical (easily learns math facts)
- Analytical (requires the majority of the information to come to a conclusion)
- Auditory (oral repetition of math facts and spellings words greatly helps in retention of material)
- Sees details more easily (likes phonics and step-by-step processes required in math formulas
- Learns easily with black and white
- Right eye dominance slightly more common
- Learns better with book and workbooks. This person is an auditory learner
- The left brain accesses the short-term memory

The Stimulated-Dominance Right Brain Learner

For a long time the right brain was labeled to be the only controller of creativity, also known as the Artistic brain. With new research, they have found that it is still its dominant feature but the left hemisphere will also help out. Stimulated-dominance creativity is neglected in our traditional education system leaving half of a student's brain potentially undereducated.

According to Dr. Shichida's research, he believes that when children are born they are mainly right brain activated dominant. He also suggests with disuse atrophy occurs or become recessed. This theory still needs further investigation. He points out that from birth to age 3 is the best time to maximize the development of the right brain. This is because it is the age where the brain naturally begins its shift of left or right brain dominance. If developed between birth-7 years of age, the right brain abilities will remain with the child throughout life.

The Right-Left Brain Dominance

No recorded human being has ever come close to using the brain to its fullest potential. With the emergence of technology and computers I bet less than half of the world is aware that the human brain, with all its power and versatility, by far surpasses that of any computer. The human brain is what comes up with the very idea of the computers and such, making it still the most complex and involved system on the planet. This only means that we tend to be either more creative or more intellectual without quieting the other part of the brain, though it still remains (less) active.

Knowing an individual's brain dominance can help you understand his/her ways of thinking, behaving, speaking, and functioning. Also, it can help parents and educators tailor activities to a child's natural learning preferences. Being identified as either a "left" or "right" brained thinker only identifies their natural way of taking in information and processing it. Having knowledge of someone's brain dominance can help parents and educators understand the way in which they behave, think, or learn; Thus creating a better opportunity to tailor activities to the child's preferential learning type. There is no optimum learning style because everyone is unique.

The brain, which works on the "use it or lose it principle," has often been linked to a muscle — the more you use it, the better it gets. If we understood what left brained or right brained dominance truly represented it would make it easier to help promote any perceived differences within the hemispheres. But if you are using an area of the brain more than your peers during one task for longer periods of time and you stop, it doesn't mean you will lose that capability. It simply means your brain will learn to accommodate with the other hemisphere.

In 1935 psychologist John Stroop came up with a test where the names of colors are written in ink of different shades. For example, the word 'Yellow' may be written in yellow or green. The difference in the ease with which colors and/or words are spoken has been refined into a standardized psychometric test. It measures: selective attention, cognitive flexibility, processing speed and executive function. This means that it plays a part in deciding which part of the brain will tackle a particular problem.

Dr. Shichida postulates that there are two distinct types of hemispheric brain functions which result in two different types of memory and mental operation. One type of brain operates at the Beta wave frequency (14-30 hertz cycles per second.) This is the brain wave pattern most frequently in use in our awaken cycles. He suggests that the other part of the brain image works at Alpha wave frequency (8 to 13 hertz cycles per second.) This is the frequency of the brain associated with a relaxed alert state of mind such as in meditation, just before getting out of bed or while listening to music.

We are aware that even though it is a little less-effortless, it is still possible to be trained as an adult. It is possible to use meditation and breathing methods as pathways into the right brain as taught by Dr. Shichida. Although challenging to some, being able to visualize images is key to maximizing right brain skills. Everything being done with speed is how peripheral vision is developed according to Dr. Shichida.

This is in the form of speed listening, speaking, and watching to develop image memory. In testing, the kids have about a second to say what they see on a picture, later this will scroll through a child's mind like a movie once s/he is highly skilled at this type of learning. The shift from Alpha to Beta wave states are easier for children with less transition time needed. The left brain is very different from the right as it usually has to have time to practice information and conscious learning, while the right brain can use a single image to store information.

As previously stated, dominance is present at birth. That said, the establishment of such dominance may not be available until they are around 5 years old because their brain preference continues to develop until puberty. The nurture theory suggests that genetics have a major influence on brain preference with regards to an infants' preference and their parents' in which some relationship exists.

The following chart reflects additional differences between left and right brain dominance.

Left Brain Dominance	Right Brain Dominance
Classical music	Popular music
Being on time	A good time
Careful planning	To visualize the outcome
To consider alternatives	To go with the first idea
Being thoughtful	Being active
Monopoly, scrabble, or chess	Athletics, art, or music

Jenn's Insights

To me brain dominance illustrates the age-long debate of nurture vs. nature. As I mentioned, my mom was a "Tiger Mom" everything had to have a perfect facade. For instance, I remember I had a project at school to create an art piece using apple seeds and drawing pictures of an apple orchard. My mother in reviewing the work did not think it was an adequate presentation, but I thought it was a masterpiece.

I quickly learned that everything had to look perfect and within specified "guidelines." This was her belief system. So the next art project I learned, I decided to gain approval up front. I took carbon paper and traced all the art work instead, this way it was a perfect image and beautiful, something that my mother would approve; however, if you evaluate this further it probably quenched some of my creative abilities.

I was attempting to figure out whether I was left brain or right brain dominant and due to the varied environments I was subjected to, I felt that it depended on the circumstances. For instance, I was given a full scholarship to pursue accounting which is definitely a left brain dominant career; however, before I even set foot into the university, I turned down the scholarship because I felt I need to do more humanitarian work. However, I ended up graduating summa cum laude in the MBA Program.

I believe that the qualities instilled in me by my mother warranted more left brain dominance. However, I see the same issue in my mother. She is highly regimented and pursued an accounting career in her homeland but when she is not under stress, I noticed that she is one of the most creative individuals I have seen. Her cooking exemplified this. She was often mixing different ingredients and probably could have been one of the forefathers for discovering fusion food.

Balancing the Brain – Synergy of Both Hemispheres

According to Dr. Shichida, there are five important functions located exclusively in the right brain. Nevertheless they will connect up with other parts of the brain; without these connections they would be useless. Due to the high levels of connectivity where something is in the brain can tell us about the evolutionary timescale of its refinement, however, it does not have greater significance, any more so than whether you live on the right or left side of a street influences what your job is.

Yes, your commute and the routes you take to work will have some bearing on who you meet and how you travel, but they do not determine whether you're an artist or a banker. What matters is function what we can surmise from a region's electrical activity, blood supply and main connections. This kind of in-depth brain study is in its infancy and our understanding of it is far from complete. These five important functions are explained fully below…

Evolution places things where they are safest: the veins are always closer to the surface than the arteries, and when they are vulnerable they're nestled in the crook of your elbow, or hip, safe behind reflexes which also protect the eyes and genitals. It goes against evolutionary pressure to have so many vital brain functions entirely dependent on cells located only on one side of the brain.

A healthy brain means a healthy body and vice versa based on an expert in neuropsychology and neuro-behavioral disorders by the name of Dr. Robert Melillo. Also as a renowned author, he identifies proper digestion and immune system functioning and increased intellects are the result of a balanced brain. When imbalanced, the child may show signs of learning disabilities, issues with motor skills, hormonal problems, and issue with their digestive system.

Traditionally, kindergarten teachers who use music, dance, storytelling, drama, or numerous other creative and kinetic (movement) activities as part of their routine teaching strategy not only help their students become more competent in other spheres, but increase the speed at which that learning is accomplished. After third grade when the use of these aids typically diminishes, learning rates drop significantly as well. Although this may coincide with changes in the natural rate at which new information is absorbed, studies show that continuing to link some information with movement and music does help.

In the 1960's and early 1970's, two scientists, Roger Sperry and Robert Ornstein, discovered that certain brain functions are lateralized to one side of the brain or the other. This is not to suggest the other side of the brain switches off or is not working just that the part of the brain dealing with that specific activity is there like living in the north or the south of a city. Some examples of lateralization include certain parts of language or fact retrieval.

Basically, the discovery of left brain being more logical in thinking and the right more intuitive can be accredited to Sperry and Ornstein. We have been under the assumption that "right brained thinkers" are the creative people until more recent studies have tested such theory and concluded that creative people indeed are more likely "whole brain thinkers" utilizing the ability to somehow effectively use both sides of their brain for multi-thinking.

Here's a list of creative geniuses.

- <u>Picasso</u>

  While he was an artist, Picasso made many margin notes about the specific compilation of colors. What's more, his Cubist paintings introduced a mathematical (left brain) concept to his work.

- <u>Einstein</u>

  A scientist: an activity you would normally associate with left brain. Einstein was nearly thrown out of school for daydreaming. His theory of relativity was born out of daydreaming about riding sunbeams through space.

- <u>Lewis Carol</u>

  As well as writing Alice in Wonderland and nonsense poems such as "Jabberwocky" (right brain), Lewis Carol was an expert mathematician, a deacon in holy orders and a university lecturer.

- <u>Leonardo da Vinci</u>

  Leonardo da Vinci is possibly the greatest example of a whole brain thinker. He was an artist (he painted the Mona Lisa), and sculptor, as well as being a scientist, inventor, architect and mechanic. He designed a flying machine that resembled the modern helicopter more than 400 years before it became a reality.

In the West, educationally we focus more on logical reasoning/thinking. Tests both standardized and not will have structured essays to write or math. In doing this there is devaluing of artistic activities. Could you possibly be creating the barrier that stands in the way of your child becoming a next generation billionaire by not exposing them to alternate styles of learning? Dr. Howard Gardner would likely say yes as he highlights that there are many types of learning styles to enhance development throughout a child's early years.

Jennie's Insights

Growing up I looked forward to attending school, especially during the elementary years. Since my mother was drilling all the information in me at home, when I went to school, I was hoping to learn something new with the teachers. In retrospect, the teachers I admired the most were the ones that made learning enjoyable and fun.

I can still recall my American history teacher he was truly a stellar performer. What I most admired about him was that he took the time to make the information fun and inclusive for everyone. Even the so-called class-clowns and the ones with the average grades, all excelled in his class. Before every exam, he had us play Jeopardy as a review in teams.

Everyone paid attention in that class. I knew that I was going to score well because I would read, but even the ones that were not into their academics became "A" performers. He would post out all the achievements of people that excelled on their test, not by the 1st, 2nd places, but all the best improved. I truly admired his teaching style and felt that I learned something from this teacher. It was not about American history; I could have read the book myself and learned the same things.

What I learned from him that was more important was how to be a Leader and how to motivate people. Many teachers are forgetting that the most important lesson may be the indirect ones that they are sending to their students.

I recalled in 4th grade, I used to love the Math Bees because it was so much fun and everyone learned their multiplication and was excited about learning. For me it was "easy" since I had been memorizing my multiplication table since I was three. But it was so much more fun to see the numbers being applied in a real-setting and it helped boost my self-esteem because everyone wanted to be on my team which was not the case when it came to sports.

The Magnet school I went to deserve kudos for their learning style. For instance, during my senior year instead of learning about The Great Gatsby and stuff that I could have read on my own, our English teacher actually divided each quarter into a topic of choice. I recalled the first one was about the Holocaust. We read many books; watched videos and later classes even went down to the museum itself.

After reading a book, we actually had book discussions in a group where we learned to communicate better and facilitate discussions, learning more life skills. To improve our writing and creativity styles, we were told to pretend that we were someone like Anne Franke and after reading all the assigned novels, we were to pretend we were a character and write our own diaries.

The assignments covered the subject matter but brought about so much creativity. I still recall when I learned about Beowulf. I wrote my own Rap song and it was presented into a talent showcase so that others could see the innovation around.

The school had smaller graduating classes but it was similar to the Montessori style where we got to interact with high school kids even when we were in 6th grade. I remember as a senior I was able to take some time to tutor 6th graders in mathematics and I was able to develop the curriculum using creativity skills. The theory behind that school is ingenious and definitely applies the concepts of educational psychology.

The irony was that there was so much freedom in that school and the students and teachers had more of a peer relationship and as such more respect was given to the teachers than the majority of the high schools. I was fortunate that I had the experience to attend this school as well as a traditional high school and the contrast was stark.

At the Magnet school, I wanted to wake up and take classes and even took elective classes before school started. In the traditional school, I never really wanted to go to school. Many times I would find excuses to be sick or simply skipped classes because it was like going to prison and having someone reciting back something that you could have read on your own. So for parents, I would challenge you to truly assess whether your child is problematic or whether the school environment is problematic for their learning styles?

Defining Education in America

"If you think education is expensive, try ignorance!"

–Derek Bok, former president of Harvard.–

Education Matters campaign scholarship finalist, Yash P, spoke on learning for the human existence and so eloquently said: "It is what we do during our time on this earth that distinguishes us for who we are. From crying infants to mischievous children to rebellious teenagers to mature adults to wise elders, we grow day after day, taking in the world and attempting to recognize it for what it is. Lifelong education is the one goal that keeps us on the track of humanity and civility, guiding us towards the shining light of wisdom. This beacon of education is what helps us maintain our direction through life's various ups and downs."

Learning is far beyond cognitive or intellectual processes. "Done well it becomes an attitude, a way of and approach to life, done effectively it creates greater opportunity and knowledge of responsibility", which is K. Raichelle's outlook. The freedom to take risks and make mistakes creates a platform where the uniqueness of an individual's strengths can be found and nurtured to be able to see them as gifts.

Suffrage ranges from emotional, physical, and verbal abuse and neglect. Children need to be able to see and feel love, to know that even when they misbehave or act out, are still loved, included, and listened to. We (adults) no matter what our role in a child's life need to accept that we play a critical part in the process of a child's development at any stage. Showing compassion, gentleness, or forgiveness even from afar can leave a lasting impression on a child. It may give them the glimpse of hope that there are good people, or that just because in my home it doesn't happen doesn't mean it doesn't exist.

Children desperately need to be listened to, included and loved and it is the moment when a child is least lovable that they need that love the most. This covers the complete spectrum from damaged and neglected individuals who are lashing out in fear, to privileged children from loving homes learning the limits. What drives a damaged child to provoke? It seems to make no sense, and yet, they too are testing themselves against the world, sometimes terrified of their own power and the trouble they can cause. They are aware that if we fail them a loveless void awaits. Forgiveness is love, and love will give them hope.

Because the school system utilize stimulus that are primarily left brain dominant and other activities of creativity are mainly right brain and limbic system stimulated, the student seldom has the opportunity to use them together. To them, work and play can never be integrated as they are seen as two different worlds.

Surprisingly, young children are fascinated by boundaries. It is evident when they know the rules yet they test the parents or teachers just to see how far they can go or how much they can get away with before one loses patience. The challenging aspect for them is when it involves new environments with new people with different personalities, new rules, or altered routines especially for an only child that is not accustomed to sharing (things or attention.)

> *"Without genuine pride, all they have left is the fake sense of entitlement learned from advertisers. (You're worth it!) When they have to stand on their own two feet they will face a bleak economic climate."*

Children's lives have become increasingly polarized. The huge differences between what is expected of a student in the school environment and what they experience in front of screens must be profoundly confusing. Without genuine pride, all they have left is the fake sense of entitlement learned from advertisers. *(You're worth it!)* When they have to stand on their own two feet they will face a bleak economic climate.

Their life experience has taught them that work and play are diametrically opposed. In the brief moments when they face up to their 'professional' futures they need to remember someone, somewhere, who showed them that work is one of life's greatest pleasures.

Simultaneously involving logic, creativity, emotional engagement and movement, education is something that is not only learned, but known with our bodies in addition to our analytical brains. If this is done in a manner of the student's choosing and is not orientated around the need to please someone else, work and play would become one.

However, in the presence of fear, indifference and powerlessness, work and play can never be united. We evolved to avoid discomfort and threat, forgetting this literally turns a student away from learning.

Tests and grades are tools both of control and fear of failure. This further promotes competitiveness and often times a lowered self-esteem.

For many children school is not a safe place, but the tragedy is that for some children it is the least dangerous one. It is not simply a question of improved teaching methodologies; the micro societies within schools must also be tackled. Maya Angelou wrote, "We are all creative, but by the time we are three or four years old, someone has knocked the creativity out of us. Some people shut up the kids who start to tell stories. Kids dance in their cribs, but someone will insist they sit still. By the time the creative people are ten or twelve, they want to be like everyone else." We also have to ensure that those doing the menacing and shushing are not the other children.

Educational Reform – Freedom to Learn

Children may learn the information required for passing standardized tests, but unless it has some relevance to their daily lives, they won't remember or apply it. According to Peter Gray, PhD., author of the book Free to Learn (Basic Books) and contributor to the popular magazine Psychology, children need time on their own. Children seem to learn more when there is no one facilitating how they must do things.

Through play kids learn how to explore, yet also will get bored with the same things so they eventually find new things to learn or as to not do the things that no longer interest them. This gives them the freedom of self-exploration and using their own skills, ideals, and more to grow. Montessori concepts are ideal for this type of enriching environment, as well as a variety of age groups as they all learn something from each other, some being nurture while others may be skill.

Children come into the world 'designed' to survive by learning the rules of the physical, social, and cultural world around them. Survival, when you're as vulnerable as a human baby, also means being lovable. And there's more to being lovable than just having great big eyes and one itty bitty tooth! Infants become so skilled in psychology that they can manipulate adults to a shocking degree! They use charm, noise torture, threat and punishment! And even when we parents are not doing what the child wants, we're probably doing what the child needs instead. It is no myth that your baby will teach you how to look after it because that's exactly what they do.

Infants learn the greater part of what they will know in their whole lives during their first four or five years. There are very many things that we simply cannot prevent them from learning however hard we try. That includes gravity and other painful parts of Newtonian physics; falling over, breaking things, fitting one shape into another stuff that may seem dull to us, but enables a child to become adept at tackling the physical world.

They can operate incredibly complex machines: children used to run in and out of looms weaving massive swathes of cloth during the industrial revolution. Three and four year olds were put to work doing complex and physically demanding tasks. They also master language first body language and how to read non-verbal clues, and then up to four languages simultaneously if they live in a multilingual environment. In cases where some of the above is not possible due to actual brain damage or injury, the body and brain will construct amazing alternative strategies to maximize function.

The aim of the Whole-Listic Gifted Academy is not to follow any single established educational practice, but to constantly assess all the methods available and apply anything which achieves good results. As such we expect to include elements of the Montessori and Waldorf educational systems as well as aspects of traditional educational practice. We will look at schools all over the world to model and build on their successes.

Those gifted and inspiring teachers, who understand how to lead a class to learning and show them how to drink deep, will be made offers they can't refuse! Imagine a Centre which combines top-rated techniques to provide a true place where young minds are motivated and inspired from an International Perspective. Today's world is one of global connections: from international business and finance, to multiculturalism in society and the arts and digital communications, to the collaboration going on in academia, the sciences and technology.

This shift has occurred only in the last 50 years, and education has to change with it. The United Nations' Global Education First Initiative benefits from some of the world's foremost educational pioneers. They are paving the way for educational reform within their countries. For example members of the Youth Advocacy Group have revolutionized the delivery of the '360 Youth Development Education Initiative' in China.

The United Nations of Education – America (Dr. Howard Gardner)

Dr. Gardner was inspired by French developmental psychologists Jean Piaget and studied neuropsychology and psycholinguistics. His theory of discrete multiple intelligences received a great deal of acclaim when it was first proposed, though it turned out that these smarts are not so independent of each other after all. However they remain a useful way of thinking about human competences and can help to identify an individual's strengths.

1. Naturalist Intelligence ("Nature Smart")

Discrimination of all living things, as a human ability, along with sensitivity to actual natural features of the world (clouds, mountains.) This showed value not only in our ancestry with hunters and gatherers but even now with chefs or botanists. The exploitation of naturalist intelligences by society is sometimes apparent in the material things we show preference over.

2. Musical Intelligence ("Musical Smart")

Individuals strong in musical intelligence often sing or drum to themselves. They are also much more tuned in to the 'soundscape' finding melodies in the creaking of a door and noticing noises where others do not. They can discern one note from another, may have perfect pitch, and are blessed with a good sense of rhythm. Really talented musicians will be able to create, recognize and remember complex musical scores. There is a strong link with mathematical skills and the two skills share many thinking processes. This link is one of the things which works against the theory of multiple intelligences and more recent research suggests that being good in one of these spheres is an indicator that you will be good in all them.

3. Logical-Mathematical Intelligence ("Number/Reasoning Smart")

People with this kind of strength are generally interested in patterns, categories and problems. They may enjoy doing experiments and be drawn to strategy games and arithmetic. They will be able to perceive relationships between ideas and things which are not immediately obvious. They also use abstract and symbolic thought as well as sequential reasoning skills. They are good at both deductive reasoning: working out a fact from other facts, and inductive reasoning; drawing a probable conclusion based on a synthesis of incomplete information and (this is the best bit) acknowledging that this conclusion may be wrong. Unsurprisingly, they are detectives! Also doctors, scientists and mathematicians are in this category.

4. Existential Intelligence

This was one of the categories that Gardner added later on and can be described as the capacity to tackle deep questions about human existence, such as the meaning of life, why do we die, and how did we get here. They are also sensitive to these themes where others may miss the metaphorical relevance in, for example, the melting snowman. These people are thinkers, dreamers, philosophers, poets, gurus and priests. Most four year olds are here, but their big questions can take us by surprise.

5. Interpersonal Intelligence ("People Smart")

Interpersonal intelligence is not only the ability to understand others by being able to decipher someone's mood, but also interact by using effective verbal and non-verbal forms of communication.

People successful in careers such as teachers, social workers, actors, and politicians will display interpersonal intelligence. Young adults will demonstrate it by being leaders amongst their peers and show an understanding of people and their thoughts and emotion.

6. Bodily-Kinesthetic Intelligence ("Body Smart")

Bodily kinesthetic intelligence is the capacity to manipulate objects and use a variety of physical skills. These skills are physically shown in athletes, dancers, and surgeons to name a few. This intelligence also involves a sense of timing and the perfection of skills through mind-body union

7. Linguistic Intelligence ("Word Smart")

Linguistic intelligence is the one that brings us all together. It is safe to say that humans are good talkers! People who love language: just the sound and taste of it in their mouths as well as the way that language can take huge ideas and simplify them until they are communicable. People who think in words and appreciate the nuance of meaning that comes from sentence construction and rhythm are frequently fascinated by the idea of language as a tool. You may find them reading, playing word-games or telling stories. They are writers, particularly poets and PR people, journalists, good public speakers and spies!

8. Intrapersonal Intelligence ("Self Smart")

This is the 'know thyself' smart. Surprisingly our sense of ourselves is based on islands of memory rather than what we do on a day to day basis, which means that we are generally poor judges of our own characters unless our self-smarts are top dollar. Self smarter are in tune with their own thoughts and feelings and apply that information to set reasonable goals. They are good at planning their lives; they are good at making the most of their gifts. To do this they not only have an honest and constructive view of themselves but also the human condition they are compassionate with themselves. Such people may well be introverts, particularly when younger, but often go on to become psychologists, spiritual leaders, philosophers and entrepreneurs; they are good in business because they are self-motivated. Actually that means they're good at getting things done in general.

9. Spatial Intelligence ("Picture Smart")

Young people who are fascinated with mazes and puzzles, which draw a lot and simply spend time day-dreaming probably, have "spatial intelligence." The internal cinema of their imaginations is sharply in focus and they think well in three dimensions. They also have graphic and artistic skills and do well as architects, painters, sculptors, sailors and pilots.

The United Nations of Education – America (John Dewey)

"Education is not preparation for life: Education is life itself."

–John Dewey 1859 -1952–

When Dewey was a school child he sat, like the other children, quietly and obediently. The children received the wisdom of their teachers in a state of almost complete passivity. They were expected to learn and remember, at least, in theory. It was probably as chaotic as most classrooms, perhaps more so with bright and energetic Dewey passing notes in the back row.

You can't force a child to passively absorb things: it goes against his or her very nature, especially Dewey's. When he grew up he went on to become one of the greatest educational reformers of his day, but it still involved being completely passive. Quiet obedient children in classrooms memorizing random facts were the environment(s) Dewy grew up in. Believing that interests, activities, and natural instincts were how education should originate, Dewy had to be less that pleased.

The Laboratory School at the University Chicago was founded by Dewey in 1896. The Lab School came to be reckoned with in American education. Dewey was inspired by the curriculums of early European educators Johann Pestalozzi and Fredrich Froebel. They recognized the importance of learning by doing and play in facilitating children's development.

The European school felt that it was a mistake to treat children as miniature adults. They gave voice to the idea that childhood is a phase during which the child should be free to enjoy life on its own terms, as a prelude to adult responsibility. The theory was that by interfering with the idyll of childhood, later development risked becoming twisted.

That said, Dewey was not in any way anti-education; he just believed that socially desirable qualities would not result from pouring a ready-made curriculum into the child as if he or she were a passive vessel. He emphasized that it was easier for everyone when the normal motor activities and irrepressible inquisitiveness (Note, it is normal for a child to have outgoing energies and they should be encouraged, the concept of ADHD and ADD is an oxymoron for this concept.) of the child were allowed to drive the child's interests.

Dewey believed that whenever possible, children should be encouraged to go out into their communities. Being outdoors was vastly preferable to being cooped up in a classroom. This allowed the child to explore his capacities, only in an unobstructed environment limits instead of those of his parents and teachers.

The view romanticizes the child to some extent and needs to be given some historical context; cars were rare. Children still worked in mines, fields and factories in parts of the US until the 1920s when compulsory education came in across the board. The idea of unaccompanied children was not at all revolutionary, though the idea that they might entertain themselves through play was!

Dewey proposed that the primary stage of education should revolve around games. It's the spontaneous use of recently acquired information that causes children to remember what they have learned. But that spontaneity can only occur when there is something fascinating to trigger it. Being drilled in prefabricated material is not the most efficient way to teach. Allowing the children to experiment and change something with a specific purpose in mind is how they learn.

While children do benefit from aimless free time they also benefit hugely from working in groups. Together the group chooses a task, plans, works out and experiments with it. They help each other, learn and conspire. They experience self-reliance, helpfulness, cooperative habits, critical intelligence and initiative, all validated by being involved in their immediate community.

Learning must be more than assimilating; the next generation will need to be equipped with attitudes, habits, skills and flexibility that will enable them to cope with these changes. Dewey aimed to integrate the school with society. He wanted to connect the processes of learning with the actual problems of life through an application of the principles and practices of democracy. It is necessary for teachers and parents to cooperate so there is fusion and cohesiveness in all aspects of the child's needs. The imposition or formation of ideals or habits are not the role of the teacher, however, assist in the selection of influences and how to respond to such.

"Plays, games, and constructive occupations," were all incorporated into an ideal curriculum, and the artificial division between school and 'real life' is bridged. Dewey set out the following principles:

1. When kids use their natural impulses, school is better.

2. Learning is by-product of work and play.

3. Making ready-made models does not help judgment and perception, the creative and constructive attitude is more important.

4. Raw (unformatted) materials help kids gain a more genuine knowledge.

5. Kids should learn how to use tools as they use them.

6. Subject matter belongs to life, not just the classroom, and it has social ends.

7. Educational situations should present new but familiar

8. Thinking occurs when things are uncertain

Interestingly, Dewey's greatest sphere of influence was in China, where he spent two years lecturing and consulting on education in the 1920s. His ideas have had enduring influence on the reform of curriculum, textbooks and teaching methods in China ever since.

Jenn's Insights

There are some preschools that have designated playground teachers. When I initially toured these schools they highlighted this feature; however, not until researching more about Dewey's educational theories did I connect the ultimate importance.

They had explained that many lessons such as natural science was better taught outdoors and the playground teacher had planned activities on a daily basis to introduce the various sensations (sight, touch, smell, and hearing) within an outdoor context.

Every preschool should extend the classroom into the playground. In fact, children with right brain dominance would value the learning curriculum more when they are in a less structured and confined environment. When children can equate learning to a fun environment, there is more synergy between both hemispheres of the brain.

So if we are equipping our children with the same resources/preparation as China, and since their principles are founded on Dewey's theories. What is the variant? Could it be that our focus in America is not fully harnessing the potential in our kids and that the educational system's focus does not truly apply the principles in the best limelight.

It's ironic that in 1896, Dewey had already discovered that the principle of learning from sitting there assimilating the textbooks or the rote memorization was not ideal. Now in the new millennial, we are repeating the same cycle but this time due to lack of resources and patience, we have adults that believe children should be medicated because they are disruptive to the classroom. This is amazing that we have not learned from history yet!

Would innovation within our educational system help the next generation emerge back into the global market, if we take accountability as parents/grandparents and invest in the nation's biggest assets the children? In the professional scene, we are taught that innovation/creativity is what distinguishes business apart from each other. However, as our children are being equipped to go out into this world, we are contradicting what we are preaching.

Did you know that the most successful Japanese companies like Toyota or Honda use tactics to prepare their leadership team in unconventional methods? If you are not a strong presenter in the group, they will not provide you with a book or have your watch a video from a leading expert. They make you face your fears; they will put you in front of their public train station and have you sing children's songs at the top of your lungs.

Once you conquer that fear, you will not have any more issues with public speaking. As Tony Robbins says, "80% of success is about psychology, not the skill set." Anything can be learned, is the mind frame that needs to be trained. Ask yourself this, are your children truly being equipped properly to make a contribution in the professional arena? If so, why did we develop Emotional Intelligence and value it over IQ in the workplace?

The United Nations of Education – America (Dr. Glen Doman)

Glenn Doman of The Institutes for the Achievement of Human Potential discovered that young children can be taught anything and everything given the right environment and techniques. He dedicated his life to researching human performance and has instructed thousands of families on the practical ways we can all affect brain growth. Much of his work was with children whose neurological impairments were so extensive that society has discounted their potential contributions.

His works applied the connection between mobility and brain development. Starting from birth children should be given every opportunity to acquire mobility. Doman's book, *How to Teach Your Baby to Be Physically Superb*, is something every parent should have. It explains how a child's physical condition is the foundation for brain development and learning capabilities.

Physical activity stimulates brain growth in much the same way that physical exercise causes muscles to develop. It stimulates nerve cells and the proliferation of neurological pathways. The crawling and creeping stages are as vital for stimulating healthy brain growth as they are for stimulating healthy physical development. They are correlated with how well that child can see and hear and how well they will be able to speak and read.

Patterning is a series of exercises designed to improve the "neurological organization" of a child's impairments. The child's body is helped to recreate movements that mimic the prenatal and postnatal movements of non-impaired children.

Parents or assistants may be required to manipulate the children's head and extremities for many hours each day. This accesses the 'developmental cascade' whereby each stage of development flows from the next. There are developmental 'windows' as certain parts of the nervous system mature at different times; patterning can open them or mimic their openness. Neurological regeneration was considered impossible or minimal until the early 1960s. It was the astoundingly successful work with brain-injured children that led to the discovery of neuroplasticity.

The United Nations of Education – America (David Weikert) – High Scope Model

The High Scope Early Childhood Education curriculum is based on the research of Jean Piaget and John Dewey.

Since children are "active learners" who benefit most from activities and have planned for themselves, the teacher's role is simply to ensure that all the children are involved. Children are also encouraged to organize their own "work." Consistent daily routines are an essential part of the High Scope method, so 'planning time' is a key component.

Children describe what they intend to do during the day to the other members of the group and, guided by the adult, the group will suggest ways to enhance their plans. Tasks have a variety of expected durations which allow for variations in age, ability and concentration spans. They have the added bonus of flexibility for children who are having an "off" day. The adult's function is to help focus the child's interests and learn to build on their own strengths rather than focusing on what they cannot do. This also ensures that the material is adapted to their current level of functioning: the adult matches learning activities to a child's skills.

High Scope stresses that free play is more beneficial than formal lessons or structured therapy. Selected projects will demand varying times that a child will need to participate in the activity which will also call for a variation of skill levels.

> "The underlying goal of early childhood education should be to provide
> the same ladder, but allow children to be on different rungs"
>
> –L.L. Dunlap — Pearson Allyn Bacon Prentice Hall–

Keeping in mind that our children do not have the same representation of time is crucial. This is especially important for children of two to four years old. As any parent will tell you, children need advanced warning of a change. "OK, time to stop playing and put on your coat in ten minutes", is much more effective than "Put your coat on now!" A number of people have an egg-timer whose ticking reminds children that they need to break away from what they're doing. As they get older they can look at it and know how much time they have left.

The High Scope method is designed to:

1. Help children with decision-making by offering them choices;

2. Help children develop purpose and discipline by seeing their plans through;

3. Help them develop negotiation and other social skills through cooperation with others;

4. Conscious application of skills and knowledge: not 'paint a picture', but 'the picture is paint, painting skill and ideas';

5. Encourage self-expression in a variety of ways and remove preconceptions about what that means;

6. Help children with listening through an understanding of verbal and nonverbal communications;

7. Develop their ability to respond to problems with positive, solution orientated reasoning;

8. Foster children's creativity, initiative, and openness to learning.

The United Nations of Education – Germany (Friedrich Froebel)

"Play is the highest expression of human development in childhood, for it alone is the free expression of what is in a child's soul."

–Friedrich Froebel–

Froebel opened his first Kindergarten in the German town of Blankenburg. In 1840's Germany there was no formal education available for children under seven years of age. It was not even recognized that infants were capable of learning, let alone acquiring the social and intellectual skills which would serve them their whole lives.

He believed that humans are, in essence, creative beings and observed that play was a necessary developmental phase in educating the 'whole' child. He saw that when absorbed in what they are doing, children are expressing the power of their imagination while physically expressive and at ease.

He developed the use of blocks in his kindergarten movement of the early 1800's, which soon became alphabet blocks. So next time you get one in the tender arch of your unsuspecting foot, you can shout "Froeballs!" with perfect accuracy. As far as Froebel was concerned the wooden cubes represented the building blocks of the universe: the symmetry of the soul is manifested as a child builds and separate units are brought together to form a whole.

Architects would agree. Drag and drop doesn't quite have the same metaphysical punch. The fine motor skills employed to balance and stabilize teetering towers are not also lacking from techno-toys, nor can they be used to tackle and attack a child's fears. Play can be quite rough you see the child experiment with surges of violence as well as tenderness. You hear; "Green Dog fell off the table and the truck fell on top of her and then I made her better with scissors like when the baby came out of your tummy." And you know that you wouldn't want to be Green Dog right now! A child can't work through those experiences with a screen.

Froebel's philosophy was built on four basic components:

- a) free self-activity,
- b) creativity,
- c) social participation, and
- d) motor expression.

During free play a child satisfies his own images and educational interests; when absorbed in creative self-activity the child should be given complete emancipation from the prescribed system of activities around him. That said, the materials around which the children constructed their play were highly structured. There are ten 'gifts' and 'occupations' which create a hands-on curricular system. This system, as well as his understanding of how rich and important play is still informs the best of today's teaching.

They introduce children to the physical forms and relationships found in nature as well as the mathematical and natural logic underlying which underpins those forms and relationships. The first ten, the gifts, are simply tools for discovery. His system moves deliberately from the simple to the complex: from solid, to plane, to line, to point, and then reverses to arrive back again at three dimensional activities in 'peas-work' and modeling clay. The gifts were not only brilliant inventions but fit the cognitive and developmental needs of children.

The first gift was a collection of six soft woolen balls, each one on a string. The three balls are of the primary colors: red, blue, and yellow, while the others are violet, orange, and green; secondary colors resulting from the combination of two primaries. Froebel chose the ball, a perfectly round shape or sphere, because it was an idealized form, equally proportioned on all sides without and without end or beginning.

From a practical point of view, the first gift was used to introduce children to basic concepts in the world around them as it was: grasped, dropped, rolled, swung, hidden, found or held. The children learn prepositions, orienting themselves in space with up, down, here, there, behind, larger and smaller. The balls can be arranged in mathematical groups such as two times three or three times two, they can socialize or be solitary. They can visit and be a favorite or get lent out.

The second gift consisted of a wooden sphere approximately three inches in diameter, a wooden cube, and a wooden cylinder. In the case of the sphere, all sides of the object are round. In the case of the cube, all sides are rectilinear or square. But the cylinder is the living algebra of flat and round, a synthesis of the two. However, it is much more metaphysical than that; he drilled holes through the center of each piece of wood from plane to plane. Pushing a long dowel through the holes turned each into spinning tops. Spun, the cylinder rapidly became the image of a sphere.

The next four gifts were sets of blocks, something we take for granted today. He asked children not to imitate the world around them, but to use the blocks as elements to create their own structures. They made simple pieces of furniture, complex patterned designs, or fantastic architectural structures. With his seventh gift Parquetry, comes a further transition to the abstract. The brightly colored wooden or cardboard pieces were square, equilateral and isosceles triangle, circle and semicircle.

From these, as well as later occupations (13th-cutting, 14th-weaving, 18th-folding), come a familiarity with the symmetry and the neatness of form and endless combination and recombination the satisfaction of fitting things together. They are deliberately fanciful and move into both abstract creativity and higher understanding but grounded in the skilled manipulation of real objects for dexterity and concentration.

In selecting items of different sizes and shapes and comparing surface volumes and areas, or any other feature, they are unwittingly using classification and serialization. Cleaning up involves math too: sorting identical and dissimilar shapes, and organizing by size. It may not be immediately apparent that this kind of play improves a child's ability to form mental images. The child measures with their eyes and imagines fitting things together.

The remaining Froebelian gifts dealt with different aspects of line, pattern, color, and structure and activities such as drawing, printing, sewing, folding, and cutting. Among the most important of the later gifts was Peas Work (nineteenth gift), which was a primitive Tinker toy system using peas or cork balls and small lengths of wood.

Its purpose was to take point and line and project them into volumetric forms that could also support structures and objects the children created. This is what gave us Lego, Stickle bricks, Mecano and other variants. Frank Lloyd Wright, the infamous architect, was introduced to and inspired by the Froebelian materials by his mom. He recalled that it was through the paper-cutting exercises that he became aware of the use of color. Wright also credits the peas as having introduced him to the concept of the skeletal structure of objects. He said that Froebelian toys awakened "the child-mind to rhythmic structure in Nature giving the child a sense of innate cause-and-effect otherwise far beyond child-comprehension."

The twentieth and final gift, involved children doing free-form modeling using clay or bee's wax; thus allowing children to work with a totally flexible form with the ability to impose on it whatever shape they imagined.

Froebel and his gifts ground our abstract theories of play by creating tangible and engaging learning tools. The gifts are not only worthy of being reintroduced into the classroom but can provide the means to bring abstract and philosophical ideas to light for teachers and children alike. And although easily dismissible for yet another form of "child's play", the gifts were concrete learning using reinforcement through hands-on implementation, Jean Piaget's work, which has proven to be his significant contribution to education.

Researching an "All-Around" Education – The Best of the Best

Instead of investing in high-tech teaching aids, the Academy will bring back the fundamentals of child's play into this world, namely; movement, dexterity, independence and cooperation. Lego, Tinker Toys, Lincoln Logs, Erector Sets, Bridge Street Toys, Puzzles and Blocks will be the primary focus in each of the infant classrooms where they will be mindfully used to promote cognitive development as a whole. Skill at given curricular tasks is a natural consequence of this. The technology that will be incorporated will be ones that help maximize left and right brain hemispheres.

Math, architecture, engineering and even design can be discovered through block play. Problem solving by figuring what goes together and what doesn't, also a part of construction is the main objective of blocks. These skills are naturally attained from simply putting things together and taking things apart, putting like pieces in groups, or those that work together in separate groups.

Imagination is integral to this kind of play. Children learn to create, bouncing ideas off one another and thinking for themselves, thus fulfilling the ultimate goal of education. Each child is unique, and personalities are free to emerge in such groups but are actively inhibited by the passivity of the screen. A shy or insecure child may create a safe haven in his building. The diffident child may gain confidence, because there is no right or wrong way to play. A frustrated child may find release in knocking down towers.

Did you realize you learned geometry and algebra likely before you were school-aged? Well if you played with blocks you did. Having to measure by eye helped in the development process of being able to create relationships between length, and widths.

In her book *The Art of Block Building,* Harriet Johnson has categorized the evolution of block play as follows:

- Stage 1: Children under two years of age will carry blocks around. They are not yet used for construction.
- Stage 2: At two or three building begins. Children make horizontal rows or stack vertically.
- Stage 3: Bridging: two blocks with a space between them, connected by a third block.
- Stage 4: Enclosures: four blocks placed to enclose a space.
- Stage 5: Age three to four. When facility with blocks is acquired, patterns and symmetry can be observed.
- Stage 6: At four or five children will name their structures; usually in relation to their function.
- Stage 7: Beginning at age five, buildings often represent actual structures children know from real life or stories use them as 'sets' for dramatic play.

The United Nations of Education – Switzerland (Johann Pestalozzi)

Johann Pestalozzi valued the inner dignity of each individual, young and old alike. To him, personality was the manifestation of this inner dignity, and as such, it was sacred. He proposed that education in self-control should be gradual and careful because play is the natural gift, propensity, and inclination of children.

He saw pressure to learn beyond the child's natural pace as harmful. Trial and error are the best teachers and, to his mind, preventing opportunities for failing not only inhibits the development of learning, but more importantly, character. In Pestalozzi's How Gertrude Teaches Her Children (1801) he rejected painful punishments, rote memorization, and bookishness, and proposed home-like schools where teachers engaged students in learning through sensory and motor experiences.

Such schools were to educate with hands, heart and head in balance such that a well-rounded individual emerged with physical and moral competence, as well as intellectual. It was his belief that without love, neither the physical nor the intellectual powers would develop naturally; a belief that has since been proved by countless experiments. Kindness ruled in Pestalozzi's schools, much to the amazement of outsiders who thought that corporal punishment was an essential ingredient of education.

He placed a special emphasis on spontaneity and self-activity because they were expressions of human nature, while directed assignments go against it. He thought that children should not be given ready-made answers but find solutions themselves using their own powers of seeing, judging and reasoning.

For all students he included physical exercises in the schools, including time for outdoor activities was essential for the promotion of cheerfulness, 'comradely spirit', frankness, courage and perseverance. The objective of education was not perfection in the accomplishments *of the school*, but to equip the child with a fitness for life; not the acquisition of blind obedience or prescribed diligence, but initiative.

After coming across Pestalozzi's ideas as a student at Yale, Henry Barnard brought them to America, and later the United Kingdom, where he established a teacher training school. The principles were summarized as a head for thinking good thoughts, a heart for being kind and hands for helping poor people with skills learned.

Barnard created and implemented a new model for the common school system that distinguished between primary and secondary school education. Intended for children under the age of eight, the main emphasis of primary schools was moral education. Secondary schools were aimed at children between the ages of 8 and 12, where further moral education and fine manners were cultivated. High schools consisted of two departments: a classical one devoted to traditional subjects and one focused on preparing students to pursue work in commerce, trade, manufacturing and another for the mechanical arts.

The United Nations of Education – Japanese (Dr. Makoto Shichida)

Dr. Shichida is an influential figure in an educational revolution which is changing the way we understand children, their brain capabilities and their learning styles. For the past forty years he has investigated techniques which stimulate early development of creative education that begins in the womb and continues to adulthood. He feels very strongly that habits of the heart should precede other education.

Love between the parent/teacher and child must be present before any didactic education can be effective. It is that love which neurologically opens the child to learning. Dr. Shichida reminds us there are no "bad" children and that all children, regardless of their disabilities, need to feel unconditional love in order for their education to be successful. Loved children feel safe, comfortable and calm and will make almost any home or school the best learning environment.

It is always difficult to find the balance between love and discipline. On the one hand children will actively seek boundaries to test, and are often more secure in their presence, and on the other hand maintaining those boundaries basically involves being mean to them. One mother says she often explains to her child that grown-ups have to try not to be naughty too, and that being good is something we struggle with every day of our lives.

Dr. Shichida's methods are very popular in Japan, not only for "normal" children but also for children with Down's Syndrome and other disabilities. He stresses the importance of family dynamics, particularly when expressed through body language such as good eye contact and caring communication. Rather than a parenting style that is concerned with scholastic scores, Dr. Shichida believes in promoting compassionate, empathic understanding.

It's said that human beings die having used only three to four percent of the ability they possess during their lifetime. The people who are capable of using the remaining ability as extra potential are called geniuses or said to have extrasensory perception. Perhaps they have simply found a way to engage the parts of the brain that others haven't reach.

> *"It's said that human beings die having used only three to four percent of the ability they possess during their lifetime."*

Such intelligence appears only here and there in the world. And yet, as it stands our current population of living people is a larger number than all those who have ever lived before. Human capital has literally never been greater. Coupled with an age of unprecedented connectivity, it is no wonder science and technology has exploded in the last thirty years.

If, instead of distraction, disempowerment and dissociation, we can harness these skills for worldwide action, empowerment and community, then perhaps we could have a compassionate revolution just when we need it the most. Children with a range of abilities, uninhibited creativity and the power to observe and make the most of every available resource should be the goal of child rearing. This is what we patented as the "Billionaire Parenting" style.

The brain is a super high performance computer. It has more connections than there are stars in the sky. It calculates at lightning-speed, utilizes an image visualization function to record the environment, intuition, visualization capacities, perfect pitch, creative imagination and linguistic vigor. Who knows where these skills can take us? Telepathy? Clairvoyance? When we've helped these individuals reach their full potential, we hope they'll spread hope through their communities and even save the world!

There is archeological evidence that the Mediterranean and the Black Sea were once valleys full of people. There are many flood myths in central Europe. They run west to east, just as the water did when the Atlantic came pouring in. In these stories there is always a Noah. He always felt compelled to build an arc. In the face of the coming changes, our educational program is such an arc.

In the fetus the brain develops all the time, with two periods of hyperproliferation. The right hemisphere is highly active while the left hemisphere is relatively dormant according to Dr. (Mrs.) Reeta Sonawat. In this manner, the cells act as ESP receptors which allow the child's soul to act with extrasensory perception to filter through the fetus to enhance right brain dominance within every cell it contains in its body.

The capacity to absorb huge amounts of data at extremely high speed is the key to activating exceptional mental ability. Comprehension and conscious memorization are of secondary importance. Image training, memory play, foreign language training and exposure to music are just a few of the techniques which can be used to promote integrated brain function of the highest level. At this point learning becomes an automatic and simultaneous process whereby large amounts of information are understood without the need to be broken down into individual processes.

Does that strike you as being too good to be true? Well, it's actually normal brain function. It happens all the time. Watch a child painfully lean to stand, then walk now think of them running and doing cartwheels. If they thought about the individual movements they might even fall over! When you read you don't sound out each word letter by letter. If someone is absorbed in a good book, they are barely present, seeing instead what the words in the book describe almost as if dreaming or watching a film on some inner screen.

Learning to create your own Mandala, the space where inner and outer worlds meet and also holds and manifests the energy of intention/creation, is very empowering and essential practice for focusing your mind. This is why memory work is important in the program. Using different types of cards, some with picture or patterns, three are chosen to begin. As you proceed more are added to the reel. Mandalas can be used to indicate a shift needed to occur to attract the intended "goal."

Dr. Shichida theorizes that the unconscious mind stores the images and then brings these images deliberately to the conscious mind when needed. Because visualization is the key to right brain development, image training is used for speed reading, memorization, creative composition, and most other right brain functionality.

He thought that a baby's thoughts are images gained through telepathy from the right brain and clairvoyant abilities made possible by information from the skin; Dr. Shichida has found that learning can take place in the womb. He also says that the knowledge of love or desire for them (the baby) is also received while in the womb via its skin receptors. This is how they initially communicate with the parents.

Due to the high levels of interconnectivity, where something is in the brain can tell us about the evolutionary timescale of its refinement, however, it does not have greater significance, any more than whether you live on the right or left side of a street influences what your job is. What is important is function: what we can surmise from their activity and connections and from what occurs when there is damage. This kind of in-depth brain study is in its infancy and our understanding is far from complete.

According to Dr. Shichida, there are five important functions located in the right brain. They connect up with other parts of the brain; without these connections they would be useless, but they are most active in specific locations of the right hemisphere. These five important functions are explained fully below but can be summarized as:
- Resonance function (basic function)
- The ability to build and examine complex mental images
- High speed mass memory
- High speed Automatic processing function
- Empathy, Social instinct, Predictive capacity

Resonance Function

This function is based on the notion that all things in the world exist as subatomic particles that vibrate at an ultrahigh frequency. Every thought, feeling, or object in our environment invades the physical body constantly. In this case the right brain acts as a type of tuning fork in that it receives then processes the frequencies which are not always at a conscious state. Dr. Shichida has speculations regarding the ultra-high frequency signal and how the brain unconsciously understands them. To rebalance calibrations in the body, tuning forks are used for enhancement.

Image, Visualization Function

Image visualization function is the brain's ability to capture and hold an image in the mind exactly as it is in the environment. A person being able to perfectly visualize an object in your mind, and modify the image as desired, would have likely perfected this function. The development of imagination early on would be a great asset as it is essential for this type of skill.

High Speed Mass Memorization Function

This kind of memory works with multiple pieces of information simultaneously and can absorb and memorize masses of information at high speed. What is commonly called photographic memory, the ability to memorize something at one glance by looking at picture instead of using their imagination.

High Speed Automatic Processing Function

The brain processes massive amounts of information automatically. Language acquisition for children is not a conscious process; language that is heard from birth is somehow stored and then suddenly, as if by magic, about the age of one a child will begin to speak. This is why if you begin speaking and reading to your child intrauterine, they will develop this skill set at an earlier chronological age.

As the child develops they learn to speak with increased fluency and accuracy. Dr. Shichida postulates this occurs as a result of the high speed automatic processing function. He believes this automatic processing function is the reason why children can master foreign languages so effortlessly, as well as their open minds: children will not dismiss any sound as possibly constituting language until the age of about eight. It is thought that adults with a gift for languages retain this capacity. The adult is attempting to learn as an act of willful cognition, while a child assimilates language automatically.

Dr Schichida recommends that from birth parents play a 20 minute tape of one (or more) foreign language conversations to the infant once a day. It needn't be the focus of the child's activity, having it on in the background while they play is enough. After 6 months to a year of listening the children are bilingual. By age 3, 4 or 5, they develop the ability to write stories in the second language. Likewise he has shown that children exposed to music at an early age will develop perfect pitch. Although received wisdom has it that after the age of 6 it is not possible to acquire perfect pitch, he has found that children who trained specific kinds of memory and learning are still able to do so.

One of his exercises teaches infants to recognize the number of dots on cards at a glance. They are accurate to 100! Eventually they can learn the answers to complex arithmetic problems before they acquire any conscious understanding of mathematics. Ability for calculus and algebra is increasingly understood as pre-verbal.

ESP Functions (Extrasensory Perceptions)

A development by Dr. Shichida uses the concept that for all the five natural senses (sight, touch, smell, taste, and hearing,) there are 5 corresponding right brain senses that also get information to the body's cells. This is based on the above mentioned resonance function.

Tactility (guessing by touching,) precognition (predicting events,) clairvoyance (seeing the hidden,) telepathy (mental communication,) and telekinesis (moving objects in space) are all considered aspects of ESP. Being able to receive information in the womb is one of the abilities resulting from the ESP function of the right brain.

Foreign Language Instruction

Dr Shichida offers the following program for language instruction: language tapes of stories are played over and over until the child has memorized them. Thousands of word and picture cards introduce vocabulary and these are matched to words from the story tapes. When the vocabulary reaches 3000 to

4000 words, small books are added alongside the language tapes. Children read and follow the tape and then children begin to write stories themselves

What follows next is a more systematic kind of learning whereby vocabulary is broken down into 10 basic language concepts: names of the colors; names of the shapes; words for size; words for numbers; words for quantity; prepositions of location (up, down); words for comparisons and sequence (1st, 2nd) words for concepts about time; and finally, words for money. The children become fluent.

Jenn's Insights

As a parent that went thru many fertility challenges, I was a bit nervous throughout my pregnancy and I can recall that when I could not feel a kick during the later months even after drinking something cold (which I was told would stir up movement), I would simply ask my son to give me a sign and sure enough there was a movement shortly afterward in my belly. In my opinion, it is indeed true that children and parent communications and bonding occur intrauterine.

An example of the foreign language instruction was evident in my experience with learning English and then learning Chinese. When I first learned English, my parents had me listen to many audio tapes but it came with the book so when the person read the book aloud, I was able to look at the words and indirectly learn what the words meant. But sometimes, we are taught a foreign language by simply memorizing and reading the book.

This was my experience learning Mandarin. To this day, I can still memorize the book, but did not know what the characters or words looked like or mean. I was too focused on the left hemisphere of training and focused specifically on rote memorization.

If you still believe in the phenomenon of ADHD/ADD and other learning disabilities as a blockage towards full learning potential, then I would truly ask you to investigate this question. Did Dr. Shichida, Dr. Glen Doman, and Dr. Maria Montessori all develop their learning principles originally for children that were deemed as learning disabled and unable to contribute fully to society?

Since the answer is yes, how come today, ironically we are utilizing these same principles and developing Gifted Institutes out of them. The Montessori experience is supposedly one of the best in preschools but it was developed originally to cater towards learning disabled kids. Think about that for a moment... Still believe your child should be labeled as having learning deficiencies?

The United Nations of Education –
Italy (Dr. Maria Montessori) – Montessori School

Dr. Maria Montessori was appointed the director of a school for children with learning disabilities in 1898. She had worked with special needs children at the University of Rome's psychiatric clinic. The children were considered impossible to educate and yet, by 1901, a mere two years later, many of them took and passed a school examination along with regular students.

Her methods evolved from the observation that children concentrated most effectively when they were interested in the activity; when they are intrinsically motivated to learn. She understood that children prefer order in their lives and strive to maintain it. She found that when presented in an enjoyable way, they prefer real, purposeful work over playing with conventional toys. When children play, it often takes the form of work. They might play "house" or build things, or cook or change nappies, fantasizing that these activities are real.

"Never help a child with a task at which he feels he can succeed."

–Maria Montessori–

The aim of Montessori education is to give the child the independence of being able to do things for themselves. Given opportunities to move, to dress themselves, to choose what they want to do, and to help the adults with tasks, children are often delighted and diligent. When the children are able to do things for themselves there is an increase in their self-belief, self-confidence and esteem that they may carry throughout their lives.

This observation is considered to be a 2-way event; it is by observing the child that the adults can learn about its needs. For example, a child who bangs objects *needs that* gross motor activity, so give them a drum. If children are pushing things around the room as they totter towards being able to walk, give them a wagon to push. Thus, child and caregiver are in harmony.

Children make mistakes but must never be afraid to do so. A child who fears punishment and error will never try something new. Giving children freedom and choice, supporting them in their choice by making sure they are safe, feeding their inquiring minds in a way that they can understand, and observing their needs and fulfilling these can be the key to helping your children develop their full identity.

Children of three and under do not need lessons: they simply absorb everything in around them, so it is important to make sure that they are in a stimulating and constructive environment. This includes what you say. Express your anxieties and a threatening world is created. Using swear words, you can expect your child to use them too. 'Stop!' is always preferable to 'no' for this reason.

A child who learns a good, firm 'no' from you will not hesitate to use it. 'Wait!' is also useful, because it is uncritical and does not necessarily mean the end of what they are doing only a modification of it. Unless you are prepared to take your child to the park naked, avoid 'Would you like to get dressed now?' It is literally asking for trouble! Your child could reasonably respond with that lovely 'No'. After all, you did ask! 'You need to get dressed in five minutes.' And 'Please get dressed now,' are not rude, but you have avoided the issue.

Mixed age groups are a hallmark of the Montessori Method: younger children learn from older children, who in turn reinforce their knowledge and confidence by teaching. Younger children feel supported but also see that they too will grow into the skills. A mix also gives the classroom a unique heritage where specific games and jokes are passed down.

Children often make the best teachers of other children. In many schools 'paired-learning' is encouraged; it promotes teamwork and a natural, morale-building function that is one of life's great skills. Several Montessori schools also allow children to judge their own work and that of their peers. The adult in the classroom is there to listen, and provide help when asked to do so.

In an environment where cooperation and a sense of community are emphasized, individual differences are more likely appreciated. This fostering of children's' individuality creates a family atmosphere but also mimics the real world where different age ranges mix all the time. By embracing the individual they are better able to come to terms with their difficulties and celebrate their strengths. Everyone is then responsible for the functioning and maintenance of the environment.

Maria Montessori was another developmental psychologist who believed that moving and learning were inseparable. The child must involve his/her entire body and use all his/her senses in the process of learning: looking, listening, smelling, touching, tasting, and being. We can all remember some older children who seemed impossibly gymnastic and strong.

The older children provide role-models for the younger children, but that also means learning how to lead them. The mixed group is also particularly fertile ground for the formation of a variety of safe, lasting and meaningful friendships. Small village schools have the same set-up, and the children have a sense that they will share that village forever; it changes how they behave. For city children the anonymity of school needs to be tackled.

The best predictor of future success is a sense of self-esteem in childhood. Research has also shown that, among other things, self-worth comes from helping others. The self-directed, non-competitive approach of Montessori schools has made them successful the world over: they cultivate an attitude that response to challenges with confidence and faces change with optimism.

 Jennie's Insights

At the Magnet School we were encouraged to interact with other peers and to learn from them. Classes such as Physical Education would allow us to play along with older children. We were able to establish our own schedule and even had concepts such as "free blocks" This was time that you could spend doing

your homework in the hallways or the library or to go off campus and have some snacks with friends, even older ones.

There was no Hall Monitor or passes required to be in the hallway and there were no metal detectors. In fact, I even brought a puppy to school once. Each year, we were allowed to pick our own lockers and we spent time spray painting and customizing them to our liking, so there was no need for graffiti. The goal was for the children to truly enjoy being in the community called "school."

There was so much freedom and trust given to the students that they did not feel like they had to rebel. In fact, almost 97% of the students went to University and 90% of those were in Ivy League Schools.

The United Nations of Education – Austria-Hungary (Rudolf Steiner) – Waldorf School

Developed by Rudolf Steiner, a scientist in 1919, Waldorf Education is another system that combines philosophical ideals with an understanding of how the child develops to address the child's needs. Waldorf teachers strive to transform education into an art through the dedicated application of enthusiasm! They foster a love of learning, based on the following triad of questions.

- How do we establish within each child his or her own high level of academic excellence?
- How do we call forth enthusiasm for learning and work, a healthy self-awareness, interest and concern for fellow human beings, and a respect for the world?
- How can we help pupils find meaning in their lives?

According to the Waldorf Educational model, there are 3 developmental stages between birth and adulthood:

- <u>The Imitation Phase (Birth – 7 Years)</u>

  The young child uncritically mimics everything around them: speech, gestures, and the attitudes and values of parents and peers.

- <u>The Imagination Phase (7 – 14 Years)</u>

  The child becomes wholly him or herself, without any imitation. Moving through these years, more sequential and logical thought begins to unfold. Teachers are encouraged to foster the abilities of the imagination, which will be the child's most vital learning tool.

- <u>Truth/Discrimination/Judgment Phase (14 – 21 Years)</u>

  The adolescent is on the search for truth, and begins to experience the power of his/her own thinking. This comes with a healthy, valuable idealism and sensitivity about both one's inner experiences and unfolding, sense of self.

The adolescent psyche needs protection and often erects barriers for self-protection. Teens may use their burgeoning sexuality as a weapon, or retreat into solitude; they may be defiant or critical or sullen and aloof. The adolescent, despite the barriers, is constantly seeking a role model.

♡ Jennie's Insights

The Magnet school was ideally designed to help an adolescent discover judgment and truths about their own needs. The school provided many options and actually elementary predecessors to this school also were designed with flexibility and creativity in mind.

My best friend from childhood went to the elementary school. The school was designed so that you can advance at your own pace. So if you were in second grade, but you had the abilities to learn at the 4th grade level, you were given opportunities to learn and study with those kids.

If I had gone to those types of elementary schools, I would not have been so bored because I would have been fully challenged. The real lesson is that it has instilled in me the belief of "laziness" because I tended to not challenge myself enough and just blended in with the average because it was more comfortable. So there are some indirect lessons that your children might be learning if you are not putting them in the "correct" learning environment to challenge them.

The United Nations of Education – Italy (Loris Malaguzzi)

Although the Reggio approach shares some of the values of the better-known Waldorf and Montessori schools, it is based around certain fundamental values about how children learn and has fewer existential concerns. It is called the Reggio Emilia Approach which roughly translates as the State Emily. The Emilia Romagna region of Italy has a proud tradition of cooperative work. The highly integrated community works cooperatively and the social norms mean that every member works to maintain that solidarity. This is reflected in their education system, whose fundamental premise is to create 'better citizens of the world'.

The Image of the Child

Children are primarily seen as equal members of the community. They are active citizens and have rights. They are seen as being intrinsically valuable with great inborn ability and creativity as well as wider potential. It is a given that they have the capacity to construct their own learning and negotiate with everything they encounter around them.

Children's Relationships and Interactions Within a System

Each child is seen in relation to their family, their peers, teachers, the school itself, the community and society at large. This reciprocal network is consciously activated and supported within the school. The view is essentially transactional: it examines the way that children learn while engaged in negotiation with their peers. Drawing, writing, sculpting, dramatic play all these are manifestations of a child's thinking processes and they are further encouraged to work through any problems via a range of expressive media, not just talking.

Public spaces are arranged around the engagement of small groups, for example benches where people can meet and talk. The architecture and design of the school, engineers meetings, communication, and emphasizes the importance of human relationships.

The Role of Parents

Parents are an essential component of the program, assumed to be competent and expected to be active contributors to their child's education. Rather than being 'customers' of a school they are stakeholders: responsible partners. The school is an object of the community and parents will contribute in a variety of ways doing whatever is needed to ensure the welfare of all the community's children. This participation keys into a virtuous circle of reciprocal knowledge and communication.

You can have first-hand encounters with your child and the teacher in cooperative preschool. Your direct involvement with your child's early education by being able to be actively involved with supervision of the child and teacher creates a safe environment for both parent and child. You also have a supportive community of like-minded parents that too are committed to the same experience and enlightenment. How many parents wish they could have been there for this, because a cooperative preschool gives you extra time to bond with your child and share the journey. Your child will always know that education is important in your family because you live it every day.

Parents and children develop an extended family with friendships they carry through their lives. Once you become a parent you are in the nitty gritty like never before. An even stronger sense of responsibility is gained by the parents, families share operational functions of the business portion of the school; making it a complete learning experience that translates into community life.

Investing in your child is super important, and the biggest, most important aspect is the time you invest. Parent participation influences enthusiasm and motivation through the child's eye, as they feel more important at home and school.

Teachers and Children as Partners in Learning

A strong child has to correspond to a strong teacher. Teachers are not considered protective babysitters, teaching basic skills. They are students along with the children. They are supported, valued for their experience and their ideas, and seen as researchers.

Having observed the children in action, teachers compare, discuss, and interpret their findings with other teachers. Processes are recorded in a variety of ways so that there is a permanent record. They use their interpretations and discussions to make choices that they share with the children. The ability to use observation and listening skills as a teacher will give the teacher a better understanding of how they can be a better catalyst for the children's ideas and theories. They (the teachers) are partners in learning and at such time would find set curriculums useful.

Teachers will need to document the experiences of the children on a daily basis to be in a position to notice "what next" by gaining insight to the child's development process. Also, it is necessary to see progression of interests and skills. Concepts are explored through multiple media: print, art, construction, drama, music, puppetry, and shadow play are all employed. These are viewed as essential to a rounded understanding.

Projects

Projects provide the narrative and structure for children and teachers alike. The principle of learning by doing underpins the entire method. Projects provide a platform where ideas and experiences can be revisited to increase the learning depth through better understanding. They arise from a chance event, an idea or a problem posed by one or more children, or an experience initiated directly by teachers. They can last from a few days to several months.

Projects provide variety and expose these children to problem-solving opportunities in a collaborative effort. It familiarizes children for the team work required in the adult world. Children are encouraged to talk, critique, compare, negotiate, hypothesize, and problem-solve together. The documentation of the process is then displayed, further allowing children to engage with the material again.

Jenn's Insights

When I attended the magnet school it held Town Meetings on a bi-weekly basis. This was where all the students voted on topics of interest and brought about concerns about how to improve their community (the school environment.) We were encouraged at a young age to share our opinions and truly have a voice. We were encouraged to learn the art of negotiation and influence to have support for our novel ideas.

During my tenure at the magnet school, we rarely had multiple choice exams. I found it odd at the time because when I returned there my Senior Year I had been attending a traditional high school and everything was about rote memorization. I recalled that all the exams at the Magnet School consisted of projects or essays, ironically if you think about it; it prepared the students well for entering Universities.

At the Magnet School we read our textbooks but the knowledge was supplemented even further with applied experiences. For instance in Biology class, not only did we have to learn Anatomy and do the normal dissection criterion, we actually had projects where we went directly to the Chesapeake Bay and worked with crabbers so that we understood nature and biology in their natural settings.

When we learned anatomy we had projects called "Flour Babies" and we were responsible for carrying those sacks with us everywhere we went. Not only did we learn about anatomy we also learned about sex education and the responsibilities that came with it.

In our US Government class, we did not simply read the books and have discussions in class; we actually attended the Inauguration ceremonies and helped participate on campaigns as volunteers. It was learning that was applied so it was reinforced. I can still recall the lesson more readily than if I had memorized facts.

In the school when we were learning about the wars of Jamestown, we did not simply read the textbook and take exams; we had to build our own fort. I can still recall working on the project together with my mother and building a fort made of popsicles and the winning fort was the one that was made all of toothpicks with all replica homes made from toothpicks.

Then, we went down there to visit Jamestown as a field trip and got to experience what was covered in the books and movies. The school heavily engaged parental involvement. We had projects almost every month so that the parents were involved and served as vital members of the learning community.

In researching preschools, the ones that I have been most impressed with are the coop mandates. With the historical learning theories that the Whole-Listic Gifted Academy will be modeling, all across the nations, many of the educators and theories recommends parental involvement as the key ingredient for success. In fact, Dr. Shichida states that true access to right brain thinking cannot occur correctly without the parental-child bonding.

I have often heard complaints from some mothers about how cumbersome it is to deal with preschools that require cooping mandates. However, I believe the benefits truly outweigh the inconveniences and if you want to truly invest in your children's future, it takes a proactive role.

Mark Cuban, the billionaire even stated, "Parenting should not be a job left to someone else." Teachers are there to assist and guide but the true role model should be the parent. Many in our society have forgotten this. I welcome the opportunity to coop because then I am able to observe first-hand the experience that my child would be receiving on a daily basis.

The United Nations of Education – Russian (Lev Vygotsky)

Vygotsky also claimed that infants are born with the basic materials/abilities for intellectual development. He saw children as curious and actively involved in their own learning and the discovery and development of new understandings/schema.

Social interaction with a skillful tutor who models behaviors and/or provide verbal instructions for the child was a key learning fulcrum. Vygotsky refers to this as cooperative or collaborative dialogue: the child seeks to understand the actions or instructions provided by the tutor (often the parent or teacher) then internalizes the information, using it to guide or regulate their own performance.

For example; a child given her first jigsaw will perform poorly on her own. She does better when the parent sits with her and describes or demonstrates some basic strategies, such as finding all the comer/ edge pieces and provides a couple of pieces for the child to put together herself and offers encouragement when she does so. As the child becomes more competent, the father allows the child to work more independently. It is this dialogue which promotes cognitive development.

Essentially, at the core of Vygotsky's theory is the idea that child development is the result of interactions between children and their social environment. These interactions involve people—parents and teachers, playmates and schoolmates, brothers and sisters and also include cultural artifacts such as books or toys. Traditions and culturally specific practices the classroom, playground or at home are also included in the sphere of the meaningful and instructive interactions. It is through these interactions that children construct knowledge, form attitudes and acquire skills. He stresses that the children are not simply mirroring the world around them.

Private speech, also called internal speech, refers to occasions when people talk aloud to themselves. You probably witness children doing this often. This has been said to alleviate the need later in life to vocalize words because as a child they had time to work on this skill and now can think the word instead. Vygotsky also believes that large amounts of private speech in children routinely make them more socially competent. Studies showed that children diagnosed with Attention Deficit Hyperactivity Disorder, or ADD talk to themselves more often. Autistic children use their private speech very effectively as a tool to help them with tasks. Through "ignorance" teachers may ask these children to be quiet despite the fact that non-disruptive private speech would actually help these children.

Whole-Listic Gifted Academy – A Unique Concept

During our research we observed that effective education arises in the presence of three elements:

1. A healthy, trusting relationship with the teacher/caregivers.

2. An interactive learning community.

3. Creativity and innovation in balance with logic and analysis.

This Gifted Academy will be a private institution that will initially serve the critical developmental period up to second Grade. As funding continues, this school will be expanded to serve higher grade levels. We will incorporate the following 18 development-enhancing activities into the curriculum:

#1 Open Ended Play

The acknowledgement of how significant play is in the development process is like creating a telescope into a child's mind. To see as children once more, the possibilities and excitement, to explore and make-believe as one did before they "grew-up"(as children say,) and to learn in a way that makes each day, each lesson, and each new concept a discovery all its own.

Play is also where they make important discoveries about self including their own likes and dislikes. Kids will continually shift activities to maximize pleasure. They are constantly discovering which things are "easy" and which are hard to do and finding out what makes them happy or frustrated. They learn to understand the feelings of others and develop empathy. These skills are crucial for healthy peer relationships.

Play is also a vehicle for expressing feelings with minimal language required. Moving feelings from the child to the pretend character reduces anxiety and frees the child to explore emotions including anxieties and fears. Language is tied to emotions, which are expressed and explored through pretend play. Through fantasy, children recreate and modify experiences to their liking. They foster a sense of comprehension, control, and mastery which enhance feelings of security. As such play thrives in a culture where imagination and creativity are valued, where there is a shared sense of wonder and joy at new discoveries, where relationships are warm and responsive and where both adults and children feel safe enough to take to be adventurous and even take risks.

Experiencing pleasure during an activity is shown through very obvious expression such as laughing, singing, and sometimes dancing. The more pleasurable, the more sustainable since we are all at any age looking for things we find delight in. It is paired with another element; concentration. This active engagement represents a deep involvement without distraction.

It is both proactive: the will to ignore distractions, and reactive: the activity itself draws the child further in. Although this characteristic seems obvious, it is an important attribute because true play fully absorbs children's interest it is not careless or half-hearted as the play of a sick or attention-needing child can be.

The deprivation of uncontrolled play does not stop there but spills into other opportunities that allow them (children) to take control of their lives. Though some parents would prefer that they didn't, what good are you doing for yourself or your child by trying to live their life for them? None. This is not protection, rather it is more debilitating. They later never feel the joy of accomplishment or of just "being"; for they really never were, it was always you, acting as Jepeto pulling the strings, but one day you have to realize, they are real too. Not allowing this natural maturation can result in more likely chances of depression, and other mental disorders.

#2 Music

Dr. Shinichi Suzuki developed one of the best accelerated learning music teaching methods available. His techniques help to develop perfect pitch and create musically gifted kids.

His process spurns reading music from a score in favor of learning the piece by ear. The method also encourages, in addition to individual playing, group activity, including playing in unison. Frequent public performance enables the child to make music for as well as with others.

Performance becomes natural and enjoyable with an emphasis on collaboration, inclusion and mutual encouragement for players of every level. Competitiveness is frowned upon. In addition, the parent is expected to become involved in practice time instead of leaving the child to work on their own.

Dr. Suzuki also believed that aesthetic stimulation was also a moral education: hearing and playing great music helps children to become good people with beautiful, peaceful hearts. He hoped that these children would help to bring peace and understanding to the world.

Research shows that music education (which can also include dance) benefits students via improved brain functions.

- Making music education benefits students by increasing self-expression, cognitive abilities, language development, and agility.
- Listening to music affects more than a single brain hemisphere, incorporating both the right and left sides of the brain is unique in its ability to affect more than a single brain hemisphere.
- While music listening has marked benefits regarding physiological effects of stress, playing an instrument or taking vocal lessons offers indirect benefits with regards to memory, language, and cognitive development.

These benefits are mostly long-term. The effect is not just active in children. Alzheimer's sufferers benefit from singing in groups.

#3 Outdoor Classrooms – Nature

Several different studies have found long-term benefits of green-space time on wellbeing and function in subjects of all ages, including some at the University of Illinois' Human Environment Research Laboratory, which showed relief of ADHD/ADD symptoms and their bridge with the outdoors. Caring for nature by planting trees and taking care of animals was simply practiced for human interaction.

Attention Restoration Theory (ART) a product of eco-psychology, has grown out of research demonstrating the cognitive benefits of nature and outdoor education. Several studies have found that high energy children are calmer when they are in the outdoor classroom. They also have better distance vision, reduced stress and better overall physical fitness.

The children become more cooperative with one another. When they take care of plants, especially those that they have planted, they become more nurturing overall, and take better care of each other. Creativity and imaginative play flourish outdoors. Although children in urban residential environments do not have a lot of opportunity to go exploring, they can access playgrounds, where balance, climbing and crawling will promote imagination more effectively than work in class. Upon returning to class, such activities also alleviate stress, allowing children with behavioral challenges to relax and maintain better concentration.

Providing time outdoors gives children a chance to experiment in a setting where space limitations and noise from falling blocks are not a concern. As children build with both geometric and organic shapes, they are strengthening mathematical, visual-spatial and abstract thinking. These skills are from activities they may have done by taking the natural resources such as leaves and pine cones, and making them into art. With a better knowledge and appreciation for nature, recycling becomes a priority.

#4 Yoga

Yoga teaches children about their body, how to move it and respect it. It also helps to develop their spatial awareness and improves musculoskeletal development. Emotional intelligence and relationship skills are also developed, along with the capacity to rest and be still not just passively, as consumers of entertainment, but 'actively doing nothing'. This improves concentration and retention and helps foster better student decision making.

With the hustle and bustle of the everyday "go-go-go" lifestyle most of us live, there is just as much pressure on the children to keep up as it is for the adults thereby creating less likely things to become stressors such as school, games, and even sports to negatively affect their otherwise innate joy.

Teaching children how to relax, self-awareness, and self-esteem will equip them to better tackle challenges throughout life. Noncompetitive in nature, yoga encourages such awareness's along with incorporating physical activity and compassion.

The founder of YogaKids, Marsha Wenig authored a book called Educating The Whole Child Through Yoga is a useful resource for parents to continue the learned yoga practices once the child is home. Included in the book is advice for using yoga as a technique with children that have cerebral palsy, autism, Down's Syndrome, ADD/ADHD; and yoga routines that are ideal for the most common situations like preparing for tests or even getting a child to calm down. The YogaKids program is a combination of practical yoga techniques arranged in an easier way for both children and teachers to be able to incorporate them in their current classroom to maximize learning.

The yoga is used as a medium for learning that covers various key topics, among them: anatomy, music, visual art, ecology, and language. When children practice yoga in this way, they are also learning building skills for math, reading, science and nature, and more.

#5 Mindfulness Meditation

Transcendental Meditation has been successfully used in classrooms for 40 years, and in the last 3 years alone has been taught to over 150,000 students worldwide. Adolescent depression is becoming more common and has the average onset age of 14.

Congressman Tim Ryan is an advocate for the implementation of meditation in the education system. He talks more about his vision, involvement and support as well as his partnerships in his book "A Mindful Nation: How a Simple Practice Can Help Us Reduce Stress, Improve Performance, and Recapture the American Spirit."

The practice of Transcendental Meditation for 10 minutes twice daily not only stimulates brain development and learning ability in children, but also provides natural relief from stress, anxiety, depression and fatigue. The technique is "easy" for children because it does not require controlled focus or concentration, and children can practice it without having to sit perfectly still. Even children with ADHD can practice this meditation successfully. It reliably and profoundly alters the structure and function of the brain to improve the quality of both thought and feeling. It produces greater blood flow too, and a thickening of, the cerebral cortex in areas associated with attention and emotional integration.

To start with, the technique is practiced for a few minutes each day with eyes open, while the child is involved in more quiet activities such as walking or painting. Approaching it how adults do with eyes closed and separation from distractions would be difficult for a child and may be uncomfortable. Eventually greater stillness and focus are achieved.

Through research, Transcendental Meditation has been accredited to altering the structure of the brain, improving the quality of thought and feeling. It is used as a stress reliever. Stress is a key contributor to drug/alcohol addictions, learning disabilities or struggles, and also vulnerability to the influence of peer pressure. Reducing stress in children improves their social skills, agility, and inner peace.

Focus is the result of mindfulness being more "present" in the current state. Increasing such will show vast improvements in most all activities both in the classroom and intermural. Once they are more focused they can deal with things more effectively and actually pay more attention. Designated quiet time throughout the day will assist in stress-reduction. This does not involve religion or a change in lifestyle, just a simple change in mental state through sitting quietly with your eyes closed.

#6 Brain Education

Ilchi Lee, the founder of Dahn Yoga, was born during the Korean War and was diagnosed with severe learning disabilities. With trouble passing entrance exams for college he began to run regularly, thus improving his concentration which in turn helped his studies. As a college graduate with a degree in Clinical Pathology, he proposes that the moment you acknowledge your past experience, without being ashamed of it, denying it, or making excuses for it the brain opens up circuits previously blocked by stress and new ways of thinking become possible.

Brain Education is a combination of classical Asian mind-body techniques paired with neuroscience. It includes physical, emotional, and mental exercises that promote focus, confidence, and creativity.

- Step 1: Brain Sensitizing

  Exercises such as yoga, martial arts, HSP (Heightened Sensory Preceptors) dance, isometric breathing postures and games are used to improve blood circulation and awaken the body-brain senses. With this enhanced sensory awareness and mind-body connection, we begin to improve our physical health and focus. HSP (Heightened Sensory Perception) lets children have fun with various games and explore the potential of their intuition and creative abilities.

- Step 2: Boosting Brain Versatility

  This consists of fun and challenging mental fitness exercises and various non-symmetrical kinesthetic activities which helps the brain to become more flexible, adaptable and resilient.

- Step 3: Brain Refreshing

  With this step, negative emotions and memories are released. This is achieved through Heightened Sensory Preceptors breathing and relaxation, confidence-building and emotional regulation activities. The goal is to practice creating a more positive attitude while choosing beneficial behaviors.

- Step 4: Brain Integrating

  Through Brain Wave Vibration, visualization and guided imagery techniques, we learn to integrate the 3 main layers of the brain while improving communication and cooperative interaction between the brain's left and right hemispheres.

- Step 5: Brain Mastering

  We practice implementing brain education principles and exercises into our daily lives. Through consistent training, we realize the power of choice which leads to improved executive control and life mastery.

#7 Sports

This concept is based on Sports Psychology which draws on the fields of kinesiology and psychology to bolster team work and communication skills. It is no secret that athletic success is linked closely to mental resilience. If your young athletes struggle to perform well in competition, are frustrated with their performance, talk about quitting or display low confidence levels, then mental game training can help them succeed in life.

According to Dr. Patrick and Lisa Cohn, Mental training concentrates on coaching the children to break through the attitudinal barriers that keep them from performing up to their peak potential. It instills confidence and tackles fear of success. Mental coaching aims for consistently high performance.

Mental training is a great coaching tool, particularly if your child is experiencing one of the following:
- Is your child worried about what others think about his/her performance?
- Is your child unable to remain calm before a performance?
- Does your child have clarity of purpose in the face of social and other distractions?
- Is your child motivated by fear of failure and does this affect his or her performance?
- Does your child become easily frustrated when things do not go according to plan?
- Does your child go full-force into an activity but sink into depression after minor setbacks?
- Does your child maintain composure under pressure?
- Does your child want to stay home or avoid school or activities?
- Is the child parent-motivated (pleasing the parent,) instead of setting their own goals and being self-motivated?

The goal is to improve your child's attitude and mental game skills so s/he is happier and more successful in life. The purpose is to identify "limiting beliefs" or beliefs that undermine their confidence. By establishing healthier philosophies about the challenges in life and boosting a child's confidence level, you empower them in sports and any other arena. Confidence is the best friend a child can have. It is the most important factor determining whether s/he feels like a success or failure.

Doubt is the opposite of confidence and can lead to unconscious self-sabotage. Fear of failure is characterized by high expectations; a strong desire *not to fail* rather than to succeed at a specific goal. Anxiety and tension will also manifest. Kids affected by fear of failure are plagued by concerns about future outcomes and regardless of whether they have the approval of their peers. Fear of failure is rooted in a sociological concept called social approval or social acceptance.

As a parent you need to give your child permission to make mistakes. This is how you will teach them a more important life lesson: how to cope with setbacks and stop dwelling on the past. Constructive feedback and positive reinforcement help develop many mental game skills: confidence, focus and self-esteem. Constructive feedback comes from your willingness to instill confidence and boost mental skills in your child. A self-motivated child will set their own goals and their parent should simply coach and support them. It is vital that the goals are theirs, not yours.

Most people have a limiting belief or two that slows or even halts their success. Unfortunately, the majority of people are not even aware that they do this. These beliefs will consistently hold them back, unsurprisingly they almost always begin with "I can't."

A reputable technique to resolve limiting beliefs is to utilize the PSYCH-K technique. It is a simple and direct way to trigger change. There are five common limiting beliefs:
- *It's hopeless.* If you think something is not possible, you will not even try to do it. This is why our society has an increasing rate of depression; it feels hopeless.
- *It's useless.* If something does not seem desirable, you may view it as useless. But most events have both a short-term and long-term result. Only focusing on short-term results could lead to missed opportunities.

- *I should be blameless.* Blaming external events or situations is the "easy" get-out. Interestingly, once one external event has passed (recession, difficult teacher, illness Etc.) these people quickly find some other circumstance or person to blame.
- *I feel worthless.* Feeling worthless and undeserving puts the blinders on you. You fail to notice what you are good at and consequently think you are worthless. You need to focus on your strengths.

#8 Martial Arts

Everything, at its most fundamental level of being, is energy. As energy, all is one and inseparable. As energy, all is changeable, and possibilities are limitless. The goal is to raise both your physical and emotional energy within a disciplined art that requires focus such as martial arts.

The utility of martial arts and yoga is to relax and focus the students before the start of the school day. By getting off on the right foot they are better able to succeed in the classroom. At Dutch Creek Elementary School in Colorado they noticed that the martial arts and yoga routines improved students' academic performance while also generating a lot of stress-busting fun and laughter.

DahnMuDo, a Korean style similar to Tai Chi, focuses on health; with the goal of achieving integrity and wholeness to master the mind, body, and spirit. The process is to create relaxation in children with the expected result of increased performance in school, the discovery of their creativity, and build self-confidence. It is often described as an energy-based non-combative healing martial art. DahnMuDo mixes knowledge of acupressure points, yoga-like stretching, and graceful dance-like motions.

#9 Rebounding

A child naturally knows what makes them feel-good both physically and emotionally. They instinctively know that the body needs aerobic exercise. What was one of the first activities you adored as a child? For many people the answer is simple they loved to jump up and down! Observe a group of children playing and you will almost certainly see some of them going into happy fits of literally "jumping for joy!"

Children adore bouncing on beds, sofas and any springy surface they can find. Rebounding is what adults say when they're too important to say 'jumping'! When the weather is bad, there's nothing that rejuvenates small children like the muddy puddles game. First of all you need wellington boots and thick socks and scruffy old trousers. Then you walk along while someone starts off a chant: 'We're all going off on a walk to look for' (And everyone else shouts) 'Muddy Puddles!' There are several varieties of this which are repeated over and over; when the puddles are located everyone 'rebounds'.

There are many health benefits to rebounding, including improving posture and the immune system, reducing body fat, and stimulating lymphatic drainage. It is an highly effective exercise that firms your arms, legs, thighs, abdomen, and hips; increases agility; strengthens your muscles overall; provides an aerobic challenge for the heart and lungs; rejuvenates your body when it's tired, helps with weight loss and generally puts you in a state of mental and physical wellness.

Research has shown that Rebounding minimizes the number of colds, allergies, digestive disturbances, and abdominal problems. It results in better mental performance and keener learning processes. It helps combat fatigue and menstrual discomfort. Additionally, it enhances digestion and aids with the body's elimination processes.

#10 Arts and Crafts

Color is a form of non-verbal communication and extremely prevalent in nature. Because of this, color therapy (loosely called) scientifically called chromo therapy is used as a holistic method; used long ago amongst the Egyptians and Chinese cultures just to name a few.

In this "treatment":
- Red was used to stimulate the body and mind and to increase circulation.
- Yellow was thought to stimulate the nerves and purify the body.
- Orange was used to heal the lungs and to increase energy levels.
- Blue was believed to soothe illnesses and treat pain.
- Indigo shades were thought to alleviate skin problems.

Different colors have different frequencies and when applied to the body responds differently. Here's a chart (non-comprehensive) of how every color acts on your body, literally bringing about a physiological and/or psychological change, ultimately restoring health.

Color	Function and Psychology	Associated System
Yellow	• power, ego • positive: optimistic and cheerful • negative: impatience, criticism and cowardice.	stomach, gall bladder, liver, pancreas
Blue	• physical and spiritual communications • positive: loyalty and integrity • negative: conservatism and frigidity	ears, mouth, hands, throat
Green	• love, responsibility • positive: self-reliance • negative: possessiveness	heart, lungs, thymus
Purple/Violet	• transmission of Ideas and Information; the color of balance and growth. • positive: creative and individual • negative: immature and impractical	pituitary gland, central nervous system and cerebral cortex
Red	• grounding and Survival • positive: leadership and love • negative: anger and revenge	gonads, kidneys, spine, sense of smell

- RED

  You are action oriented with a deep need for physical fulfillment and to experience life through the five senses.

- ORANGE

  You have a great need to be with people, to socialize with them, and be accepted and respected as part of a group. You also have a need for challenges in your life, whether it is physical or social challenges.

- YELLOW

  You have a deep need for logical order in your everyday life and to be able to express your individuality by using your logical mind to inspire and create new ideas.

- GREEN

  You have a deep need to belong, to love and be loved, and to feel safe and secure. You need acceptance and acknowledgment for the everyday things you do for others.

- BLUE

  You need to find inner peace and truth, to live your life according to your ideals and beliefs without having to change viewpoints of life to satisfy others.

- PURPLE/VIOLET

  You have a deep need for emotional security and to create order and perfection in all areas of your life, including your spiritual life. You also have a deep need to initiate and participate in humanitarian projects, helping others in need.

- BROWN

  You have a deep need for a safe, secure, simple and comfortable existence with supportive family and friends.

- BLACK

  You have a need for power and control to protect your own emotional insecurities.

- WHITE

  Your deepest need is for simplicity in your own life and to be independent and self-reliant so you do not need to depend on anyone else.

Coloring books by Ma Nithya Sudevi need to be provided at the Gifted Academy and the Whole-Listic Children's Hospatal. By coloring these original abstract drawings, you activate your higher awareness.

Coloring is actually a form a therapy recommended by psychologists. If you think back to childhood when you colored, or even as an adult doodling away carelessly; for that brief time you are in a 'zone', one that requires no thought thus eliminating stress and worry. Careful hand-eye coordination and neat lines will help with focus. On the other hand, when it comes to visualizing and spontaneity, color-based choices can help to anchor images. As these skills combine children and adults can find themselves in a state of rapt concentration in which answers to outside problems may spontaneously arrive.

Another important craft is origami. Origami helps stimulate both the creative and logical systems. Origami is a wonderful way to improve dexterity and the capacity for three dimensional thinking. The understanding of space and the relationships between shapes is also a good foundation for math. Seeing a 2-dimensional piece of paper transformed into a 3-dimensional object is magical. Other benefits of Origami include:

- Fine Motor development
- Spatial Skills
- Sequencing
- Symmetry
- Geometry
- Hand-eye coordination
- Attention to detail

#11 Dance

Titanya Monique Dahlin, daughter of Energy medicine pioneer Donna Eden, has created Energy Medicine Dance. Titanya blends Energy Medicine with her background in bellydance, Polynesian, African, Latin and bollywood dance. Energy Medicine Dance is a joyous whole-body workout which combines; world dance, yoga, stretching, aerobics, breathing and traditional exercises, all set to uplifting world beat music.

Looking for your 'forever young' or 'so excited' carefree spirit? Well you'll find that (and possibly a new vibe) in Energy Dance. Regaining or strengthening your relationship with your body is the start to motivating you to be the best you. Through fun and emotional movements you flow with whatever changes you have experienced along the way (in life,) which then allows the balancing of your Chakras and Meridians, amongst your other internal systems. Learning to let go, release, and be totally free are things you'll manage to do in this dance…outside of getting that rocking' figure you want!

Energy Medicine for Kids is a synergy of selective Waldorf educational techniques that Titanya learned as a practitioner and Eden energy medicine. Students will learn songs and games, Eden Energy Medicine exercises and energy dance routines, all created especially for children. Additionally, workshops will be taught to the Whole-Listic Children's Hospatal staff and parents to ensure that these exercises can continue to be practiced at home with any adult supervising a child.

#12 Foreign Language

"If you talk to a man in a language he understands, that goes to his head.
If you talk to him in his own language that goes to his heart."

–Nelson Mandela–

Building on pioneering French immersion programs developed in Canada in the 1960s, current immersion education in the United States teaches all the academic subjects in the second language. The goal is for students to become proficient in the second language while also developing increased cultural fluency. Proficiency comes from hearing and using the second language to learn all their school subjects rather than by studying the language itself.

The six official languages spoken at the UN are the first or second language of 2.8 billion people on the planet; just under half of the world population. Arabic, Chinese, English, French, Russian and Spanish are the official languages of more than half of the countries in the world.

The Gifted Academy will offer various language options to choose from, including, Mandarin, French and Japanese; constituting three of those six official languages as well as the two most globally influential languages of business; Mandarin and Japanese. In this way our students will be able to communicate with the majority of the population in the world and be strategically prepared to communicate with the global market leaders of the next century.

While Japanese is not an official UN language, Japanese companies are internationally known and have a global outlook. This means that there are lots of economic opportunities available for future speakers of Japanese, either in a Japanese company or any business with an Asia-Pacific presence.

Teachers of early year's immersion realize that their students will not understand everything they say. They use body language, visual cues, manipulative, exaggerated facial expressions, and expressive tones to communicate their meaning and it works. Many parents have become increasingly more interested in the linguistics of their children, much more so than your average high school foreign language class has to offer.

This is one of the factors that has aided in Immersion programs being not only the fasted growing, but the most effective foreign language program available in the United States. The studies in these programs not only foster competency in language but also interdependency for the world that reflects such change. If children find learning another language boring, monotonous and tiresome they will invest nothing in the information.

Language learning is more fun with games and creative activities. Children learn to express themselves through language. This helps children articulate their personal feelings and thoughts to others and the sense that they are giving voice to their individual identity is paramount.

Acquiring a second language also has long-term implications for brain health: there are scientific findings that the ability to speak multiple languages may prevent Alzheimer's. Previous research on the topic revealed that people who learned to be bilingual early on (as children) show improved executive functioning decision making ability and switching attention.

#13 Drama

Creative people are able to view things in new ways and from different perspectives. They can think on their feet and quickly generate new ideas. Improvisational skills are commonly known as 'blagging' and are widely recognized as useful! Theater is a universal art form that allows a child to experiment with a variety of ways of expressing him or herself thereby developing emotional intelligence. Even the shyest of children will find the courage to put on more assertive and confident versions of themselves after only a few weeks of working in this way. Puppet shows will also be incorporated into the learning curriculum.

Drama is particularly effective at giving children the freedom to step outside the 'norms' of themselves, their communities and most importantly it allows them to become more socially aware. They explore different societal roles, broadening their understanding of the human condition and paving the way for real empathy, compassion and respect for others. These elements all foster original thinking; both as an individual and when collaborating. Children can be placed in a variety of completely new situations where they must find unique solutions.

Trust is an essential part of group performance, and also helps with team-building and collaboration. Teamwork aside, the trust and freedom of expression make this particularly fertile ground for building lasting friendships. Children who are experiencing conflict can also "act out" a range of emotions in the safe and supportive environment of a drama class. They are then better equipped to make choices about their own behavior. They gain a deeper understanding of themselves and the emotional logic of other people.

There are also a number of practical problems to tackle: producing a show is a serious business. Planning, budgeting and managerial skills are required, along with the imagination and skills to construct sets, make costumes and create props.

Exposing children to live performance from an early age helps with the fear of public speaking and being in front of an audience. It also provides children an opportunity for exhibitionism, fun and tapping into the mood of their audience. In the social and business cultures of America the fear of standing up in front of a group and talking can be a real handicap. If a child has early experience of public speaking they are more likely to approach it with confidence in later life.

#14 Altruism

Jigsaw classrooms, a concept developed by Elliot Aronson, PhD (at the University of California) foster an appreciation of everyone's contribution and set the foundation for the child's emotional characteristics.

Rather than competition being the challenge it is instead cooperation. To successfully complete a task the group has to individually contribute their "puzzle piece", which was assigned based on the diversion of the room, thereby creating a sort of diversion inclusion setting for each group both racially and ethnically.

Preschoolers are natural helpers, yet it is important to make them consciously aware of that behavior so that their sense of being able to make a difference and confidence is bolstered. This also requires a sense of their importance within the community as a stakeholder it is not only about acts of kindness, but mutual responsibility. Making a change may require planning, recruiting others to act and being proactive about what needs to be done.

To grow into caring and responsible citizens, we believe children should learn about their community and the needs of others. Service-learning teaches this very thing by including the community with the classroom setting, modeled successfully by some schools in Georgia that have implemented it. By teaming up with several charitable projects, the children will have the opportunity to serve those with different needs throughout the school year.

While children may not yet make a strong connection between their acts of service and the blessings they provide for others, these projects lay the foundation for them to learn compassion and develop giving hearts. They are also hugely empowering; the children see that they can make a difference in the world. The sense that there is a safety net of compassion could also give them hope should they ever need it themselves.

Service Learning is designed to encourage children to find solutions to the challenging issues arising in any community. These projects would coincide with the national holidays so that children can learn that these occasions do not need to be commercialized. Every holiday has a theme with a lesson and is shared with the charity of choice. There are service projects available if you are located near the Washington Metropolitan area, please visit: www.billionaireparenting.com.

The mascot of the Whole-Listic Children's Foundation, GIGI the Giraffe, will help promote the projects. GIGI symbolically represents "sticking your neck" out for others. The giraffe can stretch itself and rise to any challenges:

G irls and boys
I n America
G iving back
I t's an incredible feeling

The giraffe is particularly important to me because when my son Alex was first born, I went overboard in decorating his room with giraffes! I could not understand why I was so drawn to them here is my answer, and yet another example, I believe we are guided and inspired by the beautiful spirit of children and by having children.

We will initiate The Service Projects within the classroom to provide the children with context. As an example, for Valentine's Day the Children will learn about the meaning of love and what it means to give and receive love. The lesson will begin with children that can verbally communicate, talk about a memory where they feel most loved. For those that are not communicating verbally, non-verbal cues of love will be explored.

Story time will explore the narrative of injured or ailing children, and what love can do for them. The children will then make Valentines cards filled with positive messages and deliver them to sick children locally. Each child will receive two balloons, one to keep and another to give to someone that has shown them some form of love, literally uplifting their spirits. This will teach the lesson of "Giving and Receiving" Love. The children will not only have positive memories to cherish but they will always know that if they offer themselves as a giver in any volunteer organization, they never need be alone on such a day.

Evidence from neuroscience suggests that when altruism occurs, "reward centers" in the brain is activated. There are also connections to centers associated with paying attention to the thoughts and emotions of other people. Altruistic children grow up to be altruistic adults.

#15 Community

"It takes a village to raise a child"

–African proverb–

Taking part in a cooperative preschool allows you to be directly involved with your child's early education. Being able to supervise your child and their teachers guarantees that your child is safe and with the best teachers anywhere. Most importantly, choosing a cooperative preschool gives you extra time to bond with your child and revel in the journey of discovery which characterizes the early years. Your child will always know that education is important in your family because you live and practice it. In addition the parents will be surrounded by highly trained teachers who can model best practice in communicating with children as they sooth willful or disappointed children.

One of the most personally rewarding aspects of being in a coop is the opportunity to be intimately involved with your children's education process and be a role-model for their learning habits. In a co-operative preschool, parents, preschool children and their teachers all learn together. Parents will be required to volunteer at least 6 times a year.

Each of the parent's visits will present a novel lesson for the class to enjoy. It will also create a bond between parent and child as they collaborate for the benefit of the group. Every coop parent will serve as a guest teacher, designing a special project for their assigned classroom. These projects will be based on themes of gratitude and forgiveness. Lessons which remain challenging into adulthood and that are often at the root of emotional stressors. By showing the children that it is possible to be accountable in the face of emotional turmoil you help them for the rest of their lives.

With great insight from Barbara Lewis in her book "*What Do You Stand For? A Guide to Building Character,*" we are given a tiny light into a child's mind with regards to learning gratitude, developing empathetic connections and how from that they are able to appreciate the things people do for them in any capacity. Adversely, kids who are not taught to be grateful end up feeling entitled and are perpetually disappointed by life. A vital part of appreciating what you have is sharing it. This is especially true of young children: they value what they're not all that keen to share! A 'share it or lose it' approach is good for promoting this attitude.

Developmentally, gratitude is one of the most important lessons for a child, though it's one of the more difficult things to teach a toddler. It has been proven through different research projects that grateful people have reportedly higher levels of happiness and optimism, and lower levels of depression and stress. It also helps them to resolve sincerity/manners concepts. Children are frequently forced to forgive and to simply say "okay" when someone has said they are "sorry."

Does your child really understand what that means? Did they let go of the issue or are they simply repeating what you are telling them to say? Forgiveness is something we all have to learn so why shouldn't parents be the best source for knowledge? The earlier children are taught about forgiveness, what it means, and how to do it. The earlier you can prevent them from experiencing anxiety, harboring anger, and even taking on a victim mentality.

Borrowing from Dr. Montessori's ideas about the benefits of mixed age groups each child will be assigned a "Big Sister" or "Big Brother" when they first enroll. Through this buddy system the foundation of mentoring and mentee habits will be established early in life. It will also help children that do not have siblings to adjust better to the new environment. Throughout the year, the "School Siblings" will have designated lunch meetings and participate in an Art Project to showcase what their learning bond could create. In this way the children are an active part of nurturing the micro-community of the school itself.

Using a network or Internet connection, parents will be able to view, assess, and evaluate their child's learning experience via live camera feed. Parents can login remotely using a DVR viewer application. Apart from providing total peace of mind, they can also crack a bad day by watching their child, safe and happy, playing with his or her friends. We want parents to be involved in their child's learning process every step of the way.

#16 Food Habits

Preschool learning environments offer prime opportunities for establishing healthful attitudes and knowledge about food and nutrition. Kids model their parents' behavior. You cannot expect to be a role model if you do not eat healthily. The Whole-Listic Gifted Academy will serve organic and gluten-free foods and encourage periodic water breaks to ensure that brain physiology remains optimal.

Children are like sponges, soaking up all there is to absorb, including attitudes, behaviors, and…you guessed it, eating habits. We talk about the 'good foods' and the 'bad foods' to kids, but what we may not do such a good job at is explaining why each fall into a certain category.

Eating healthy is first a learned habit which is why we will focus on this first the actual behaviors and choices involved. Nutrition will essentially be woven in each month with the introduction of a new topic such as:

- Self-Control, what are portion sizes?
- The habit of drinking water on a frequent basis.
- Why is sugar not your friend?
- What are my alkaline food buddies?
- Make meal-time family time

Interactive group cooking lessons will enhance the learning environment and children can bring in food items to Show and Tell, sharing their favorite healthy food choices and explaining why. Songs, chants, and puppet plays will be incorporated into eating education to reinforce and introduce basic nutritional concepts. A good resource for songs to use at home to teach these concepts is found at: http://www.healthypreschoolers.com/Websites/healthypreschoolers/images/Song_List_Final.pdf.

When completely unscrupulous manufacturers load foods such as sliced ham and tomato sauce with highly addictive glucose fructose sugar the ethics of individual choice become a little blurred. Providing your kids with fruits and veggies as snack options will guide them toward this habit even when you aren't around. It is vital that children are educated to be "educated" consumers, able to look beyond marketing and make informed choices as soon as they are able.

#17 Self-Esteem

The value of feeling appreciated, being made feel special, beautiful, or even smart can go much further than can be measured. Although self-esteem is about your "self," it is impacted by the world, people, and environment that may surround a person. Starting at home with how you identify your child, or spend time with them and include them will ultimately have the biggest and most sustainable impact on your child. Think about it, from birth babies are trying to impress who? Everything they do is to get attention from or gain approval from whom? Yep, you got it again, the parent/caretaker.

By establishing value in your children early on, in their appearance, behavior, attitude, or talents you can prevent the identity crisis most adolescents experience once they are becoming young adults and moving up in school-age. If left to the raw experiences of the world, with no prior training or no tools to protect them (things learned and established at home) they are more susceptible to depression, peer-pressure, drug abuse, lack of motivation or will for life.

Let your child take healthy risks. Start by forcing yourself to stand back. To gain confidence in the world, kids have to take chances, make choices and take responsibility for them. Too many parents try to rescue their kids from any experience of failure but it is overcoming failure, not faultless success which gives a solid sense of identity. In building self-esteem, kids also need opportunities to demonstrate their competence and feel that their contribution is valuable.

That is the part you give them at home so that when it is time to take those chances and make those choices you can be reassured that "I got it Mom/Dad!" Every child will take turns in a 'community job' on a daily basis: (i.e. playground leader, snack leader.) Furthermore, the Children's Eight 7 Spa connected to the academy will host quarterly Fashion Shows and Talent Shows. The children will have the chance to showcase their strengths and be a super-star, benefiting from being the center of attention.

#18 De-Stressing

Children are experiencing more stress at younger and younger ages. In preschoolers, separation from parents can cause anxiety. Children also soak up other peoples' stress. Do your kids hear you talking about troubles at work, worrying about a relative's illness or arguing with your spouse about financial matters? Parents should watch how they discuss such issues when their kids are near because children will pick up on their parents' anxieties and internalize them. Worse than simply being worried, children frequently blame themselves.

There is a whole industry of stress beamed into our homes via the news media. Kids who see disturbing images on TV or hear talk of natural disasters, war, and terrorism may worry about their own safety and that of the people they love. Reading the news is always preferable since it is less sensationalized and often more accurate.

While it is not always "easy" to recognize when kids are stressed out, short-term behavioral changes, such as mood swings, acting out, disrupted sleep patterns or bedwetting, can be early indications. Some children experience physical symptoms such as stomachaches and headaches. Others have trouble concentrating or completing schoolwork. Still others become withdrawn, wanting to spend a lot of time alone. Young children may experience stress from:
- Disrupted homes, blended families, both parents working outside the home;
- Increased exposure to violence, both real and on the screen;
- Excessive screen time;
- Being over-scheduled;
- Feeling pressured to perform or behave beyond their ability.

Since the Children's Spa Eight 7 will be affiliated with the Whole-Listic Gifted Academy, children will receive their share of pampering services to de-stress their physical and emotional bodies on a weekly basis.

16

Finding the Real "U"

"There's a face that we hide till the nighttime appears,
and what's hiding inside, behind all of our fears,
is our true self, locked inside the facade!"

–Dr. Jekyll and Mr. Hyde–

"It takes courage to grow up and become who you really are."

–E.E. Cummings–

Part 1: The Story

It is refreshing to hear about my patients' and friends' aspirations to become a better person and how they desire to make an impact in this world by making a positive influence in other people's lives. In general I would assume that everyone deep down has this same desire. Being able to make a difference in someone's life and creating a meaningful career that goes beyond just a paycheck is what most people are indirectly seeking. The reality is that to help others, it is just impossible to achieve if we are going through internal and external storms ourselves or what may appear to be a roller-coaster of ups and downs in our life or career.

"When our life appears to be out of control and we feel that everything is crashing down
upon us, we need to remain calm and truly focus on the possibilities that life has to offer."

How can we truly make a difference if we are playing musical chairs and haven't decided on what our true purpose is in life? The majority of people are working to bring a means to take care of their monetary needs; however, they still feel dissatisfied. When our life appears to be out of control and we feel that everything is crashing down upon us, we need to remain calm and truly focus on the possibilities that life has to offer. That's why the flight attendants encourage you to secure your oxygen mask first. If you don't, you and the person you want to help could both go down.

But the message is very simple and this chapter is geared directly to reflect this message: If you don't find yourself and help yourself first, who will help your children?

It's Not Monopoly, But the Game of Life

Do you remember when you were a kid and everything was a game? You played with the food that your parents put on your plates because you were pretending to be a chef or you took blankets and made a home or used the vacuum and imagined it was the engine of a train. At least I did. When I grew up one of my favorite games was by Milton Bradley called the game of "Life." When I took my turn at the wheel, my career aspirations was to become a doctor and as such I guess I achieved that dream, yet I still felt that life was still missing some key elements that would make it truly rewarding.

In retrospect, I realize that life is also a game and the end goal is ultimately happiness. The difference with the real game of life is that we normally start as a winner straight from the womb. Granted, we are not able to readily understand all the rules and as we grow it appears like we make the game more complex because we have hidden our true identity from our own selves.

It is hidden from us by our surrounding beliefs and societal and cultural constraints that entangle it into a facade of what most people identify with on a daily basis. Our belief system will shape our destiny which will dictate the instructions of the game; consequently many people learn to develop beliefs that limit them from life. Since we are in control of our beliefs, we have the ultimate power to shape our reality and control the game of life and become the winner that we were destined to be.

As time passes, our natural-born happiness tarnishes as we are taught to learn to fit into society and abide by others' rules. If you recall the moment you saw your child or grandchild's face making his/her grand entrance on Earth, you could see they came in with bliss and pure happiness, love and innocence, every emotion from their faces and body was genuine and reflected authenticity. This is their true persona.

However, part of evolution appears to have the world we are living in "force" us to fit in with rules and regulations and impositions of their belief system on us. We soon learn to conform and our true self often regresses in the background because we unconsciously realize that if we truly expressed ourselves that it would mean societal exclusion.

Our internal coping mechanism was to automatically conform and forget the core of which we are; as such a part of us becomes neglected and forgotten, so much so that it starts to chip away at our level of happiness without us even realizing it. We learned that to fit in we have to care what others think of us.

We have to lie to avoid offending others' beliefs and to avoid their knowing that we may have broken a set of their rules and we begin to create a persona to convince ourselves that we are truly living life on our terms. Each day we continue to fool ourselves with more definitions of happiness by credentials, titles, status, and/or achievements of monetary belongings.

I recall time after time visiting my friend's homes and hearing their parents demanding how it was time to grow up! Consequently we all listened and most of us reading this book probably listened to that instruction too well that it became ingrained in us. We grew up, and quickly forgot the outcome of the game was to achieve happiness in life, and as such life was never the same again.

> *"In each of us there is still a little boy or girl inside that is screaming to be let out!"*

Let's be honest with yourself, in retrospect, how many of your beliefs were forced fed to you by society, parents, friends, teachers or other indirect authority figures? Probably a whole lot of them, and you might not even realize it occurring. When you watch a normal young child you will notice s/he's always smiling, always playing. Pure bliss is his/her default emotional state, but what truly happened in between those years to the current face you reflected back in the mirror now. In each of us there is still a little boy or girl inside that is screaming to be let out!

So let's try to see where we became forgotten. As an experiment, let's observe life for a week in the eyes of a child. In this world everything is fantastic, fascinating, and the world is filled with joy and adventure. Have you ever noticed how children's energy and smiles can be contagious, they just bring smiles and laughter to everyone around them; this is because happiness is contagious.

You can try this simple experiment yourself, go in a mall and start smiling at people, they will reciprocate. Our children's laugher reverberates inside of us and makes it almost impossible to not join them in this laughter, it just feels innately correct. They remind us to be simple and innocent. Maybe we are jealous of their naiveté and their ignorance of how stressful life can get, but in truth this supports the theory that they are here to teach us lessons we have forgotten.

Would it be simpler to just reignite the child within our self, the pure passion that used to drive us to possess exploration, curiosity, no malice, joy and happiness? Do you remember a time when you didn't take so many things for granted, when you took joy with the natural beauty surrounding you and also enjoyed some of the simpler things in life?

Consequently, many of us get accustomed to routine and the ever-famous entitlement syndrome sets in. As adults we often are not in a mindfulness state and as such take many things for granted so the world is no longer than wondrous to us as we had evidenced. We lose sight of gratitude for the small and big things in life. We forget the essence of what unconditional love means. As a child we could have had the most unloving and abusive parent; yet, they were still our parents and we were proud to be associated with them and often defended their honor when others would critique them.

Life appears to involve more complexities as we grow and our responsibilities appear to increase and the stress meter goes off the charts as we struggle to meet others' expectations, deadlines, bills and time constraints that we ourselves and others imposes on us. Often times the dreams we had as a child for finding true love or connections or being able to contribute significantly in this world becomes abandoned. We listen to our peers telling us that living by average standards should constitute contentment and if we allow this peer pressure to guide us throughout life, we succumb to becoming the norm and having mediocre standards for ourselves and worse yet believing that this is our ultimate attainment in life because we should be capped at a ceiling of potential.

In truth, it is all about intent, as long as you are a good-hearted person and striving to not hurt another soul, which encompasses not just physical pain, but also emotional pain and belittling of any nature.

Then you should be free to express your opinions, your desires and live freely. The essence of who you are inside encompasses your uniqueness and the personality that was endowed upon you. You should feel free to allow this uniqueness to shine and be appreciated. One secret to success in life is to have proximity with people that will appreciate you for both your inner and outer beauty. These will be your biggest fans and support you through the good and challenging times.

If you approach and live life being entrapped by your emotions, it is not truly living. Following the external belief and values of others and the societal and cultural constraints might bring a level of numbness into your core. Knowing these factors are not part of your control and can mold your internal structure of how life is, might cost you years of happiness. Have you noticed that you are constantly irritable, are you easily angered by family, easily angered in general? Great philosophers explain that this type of mirroring of outward projection stems from the anger repressed within you.

What would it take to heal once and for all our anger, grief, frustration, self-punishment, guilt, and resentment? To accomplish this daunting task we need to employ the highest and purest emotions within our internal world (mind) so that it can translate the essence of this meaning to the rest of the body. We need to pamper ourselves with self-love, self-forgiveness and self-compassion. These are precursor steps, to love, forgive or have compassion for others; it must begin within before it can be projected to others. As humans, by nature, we are always in a wanting stage. This makes us more prone to unhappiness. When we are in this state, we are also experiencing the mentality of lacking and as such we have forgotten an important lesson in life; one of gratitude.

Change is a constant and inevitable; however, one thing that will never change, that every human have in common is time. We operate on a 24 hours clock with 60 minutes and 60 seconds. This will never change but we are often obsessed with it and it tends to be one of the cruelest factors. It appears that we never have enough time or we are often too late with a perceived deadline or appointment.

Have you ever noticed that when you are having fun time flies? When pain becomes your predominant worry, it slows down. Time is a fact of our imagination since it does not truly hold any energy? It is not a tangible concept and is reflective of a state within our mind. The attention and emotion we give to it brings its existence and might make us lose the game of life because we tend to get so stressed out by this element. This is why for those that believes that it is too late for them in life to make a difference or a change; it is merely a figment of your imagination. As Tony Robbins mentions, it is never too late to have a happy childhood.

"...but in the end, we are in power of what life should mean to bring us happiness."

We all know deep inside what is best for us. From a place of love and our gut center, we have all the answers instinctually; however the trick is to trust in ourselves. No one is able to share the same experience, same expertise, and same exact feelings since we are all unique. No one has experienced what we experienced. We can listen to our friends or parents for advice, but in the end, we are in power of what life should mean to bring us happiness.

This applies to everything in life. Why are you doing what you're doing? Is it to make you happy, or is it to make someone else happy, or to conform to societal or cultural rules? It is the awareness of the motivation behind your actions that will bring you closer to becoming a true winner and winning in life. The root of our motivations, fuels your actions, which ultimately propels your beliefs in life. Therefore, to lead a fulfilling life, make sure those beliefs are yours and not someone else's that has been imposed upon you.

Life is the biggest game you will play, but the easiest if you know how to strategically maneuver your chess piece. Often times, many learn this lesson too late in life and realize the truth at the end of the tunnel; however it does not have to be this way. Because the game of Life is geared towards happiness and therefore nothing should be so stressful and taken too seriously or you are exerting unnecessary energy or stressors.

In life, there's so much fun to have, so much to learn, so much to experience and so many memories possible for generating smiles and love. Most of us are too hard on ourselves. We need to give ourselves a break now and then, and not feel so bad when we falter. Life is all about learning experiences and cherishing each moment, both positive and negative ones so that there is comparison for the quality of our own lives, not so much for the comparison of others' lives.

This chapter is designed to help the parent seeking to find themselves again and reconnecting with the little boy or girl inside that held an unlimited supply of happiness but inadvertently gave it all away to others' throughout the years. By rescuing that little girl or boy from the depths of being forgotten, the parent will be able to serve as role models for the upbringing of their children and not have history repeat itself.

Real power is shared. Not imposed. It's the ability to define human needs and to fulfill them-both your needs and the needs of the people you care about. This chapter's goal is to empower **YOU** and provide you with a blueprint to leave your legacy that instills **HOPE, LOVE, PEACE,** and **JOY**.

Jennie's Insights

Dear Jenn,

I want you to look into the bathroom mirror, then I want you to take a big rock and I want you to close your eyes and throw the rock as hard as you can into the mirror with all your might. As you hear the crackle of all the pieces shattering, open your eyes again and stare lovingly in the mirror. As you try to make out your face within all the shattered pieces, I want you to remember a little girl that was perfect, whole and felt alive and truly special.

I want you to look deeply into that mirror because you have forgotten that little girl and as such you have allowed the world to forget the true essence of her. You once asked your best friend, how come you didn't feel happy anymore? It's because you have allowed the world to dictate when and how happiness should be defined for you.

This is Jennie, the little girl that you have ignored for the past 27 years. At the age of 12, I went into hiding because it was just too much to bear and as such all emotions were removed from your beliefs, you didn't have any more tears to cry because the last person on Earth that truly loved you uncondi- tionally was suddenly taken away, your grandfather.

And in its place the belief that anyone that you opened up your heart to will disappear or worst yet would simply be taken away permanently with death because your life force was too powerful. As such, you decided to hide away from the world and just blend in and live life like any average kid, how dare you believe you were special or unique.

Your first impressions of grief caused much resentment because you felt that grandpa's death could have been prevented if there was more money. If a cab was taken instead of having him walk to the doctor's appointment, he might not have suffered that stroke. Grandpa's death was too overwhelming, because you were his little princess. Across the continents his love never changed and you would always be his favorite. It didn't matter that you were not a little boy; he still thought you were perfect!

You sobbed so uncontrollably at his funeral that you vowed that life would never be the same when you returned to the States. As such, you shut down all your emotions and learned to live in a shell of a body, forgetting your needs, and decided to just give and give so that you won't have to receive and be hurt again when anyone else disappears from your life. You had lost too much at an early age. One day you woke up and you lost your home, your friends, your relatives and moved to a strange new land where you could not even speak the language. Within that instant Grandpa had been taken away without any communication for 10 years and when you found him again, the Universe again took him away!

Let's begin with your cultural constraints; you were born into a culture that valued baby boys over baby girls. It was tougher being an only child, because the one shot that your parents had to beam with pride was robbed from them when you showed up in the world announced as a baby girl. Your first impressions of shame, the pities you saw as your relatives exclaimed how it was such a shame that you were a girl and not a boy, while piously gloating about how they had sons in their family.

As such, from Day 1 you learned not to value your feminine qualities and all the duties and responsibilities that came with that title. You vowed that you would be strong and independent because that was what society demanded to be loved and valued. You wondered how many other baby girls out in the Eastern culture felt that emotion; yet you were just grateful that you were not abandoned in a trash can or aborted. In fact, you almost didn't make it on Earth because you had a weak start to life and began spotting in mommy's tummy so you were seen as not being perfect enough. So intrauterine, you learned to value perfectionism because if not it could be detrimental to your well-being and cost you your life.

Your birth should have been a joyous celebration but being born amidst a war-torn country you became more of a hindrance than a blessing for mommy and daddy, at least that is what you felt. If you had not been thirsty, daddy and uncle would not have been inhumanely beaten up because they tried to get you some water while you were burning up with a high fever. If you had not caught the chicken pox, mommy would not have had to sell her last piece of jewelry to obtain a couple antibiotics for you.

If you had not been hungry, mommy would not have had to make soup and had her whole body covered with first-degree burns. If you had not been born, mommy would not have had to escape as a refugee and could have gone off with the helicopters that took the US Embassy employees away. Because of you, mommy and daddy had a harsh life and lost everything to give you a dream of education and freedom. Your first impressions with guilt provided you with the promise that you will rebuild everything they lost and repay them for all their sacrifices.

Your first impressions with fear were so profound that you learned to deny your true nature and learned to become soft-spoken and introverted. Your cultural constraints did not help; you always knew deep inside, that the Eastern "treatment" of women was degrading and inhumane. The first time you spoke up for injustice, they wanted to throw you overboard to shark infested waters as a little child just so that others would be safer. Your teachers and employers reinforced this trait by telling you that you were introverted. But in truth, you have a vibrant voice filled with lessons and inspirations for others, but you forgot how to use the art of assertiveness and as such, you have allowed others to continually chastise, gossip, and critique you without even knowing the depths of your soul.

Your deepest feelings of anger turned inwards on yourself. Repeatedly hearing statements that were incongruous to your identity caused more scarring than any physical pain could of.
- *Why are you so stupid?*
- *Do you really believe that you are talented or gifted, you must be crazy?*
- *If only my daughter was more like yours.*
- *You always try to do stuff that is above your abilities?*
- *Why can't you just blend in?*
- *You are too shy?*
- *Look at how you look?*
- *You know a little of everything but not good at anything. You wasted your life away.*

What happened to support within your life, as such you learned to defend yourself and became more on a defense because everything was about survival tactics for not disappointing others.

Your deepest feelings of sadness come from the misunderstanding, lack of compassion and love that you have experienced from family, friends and colleagues. How can people feel entitled to judge someone without even attempting to understand where they came from and the essence of their pain? What has humanity become that hearts can carry out such inhumane acts to another human being?

The judgments made by people are so inaccurate yet people feel pious enough to believe it as truth. If only they knew that you were drawn to darkness because you want to share light and hope with the people that need it the most. If only they saw the little girl that could see thru rainbow color glasses and envision a world filled with laughter, compassion and unconditional love for young and old? Perhaps you might be described as autistic then. Look at all the emotions that have been repressed inside of you, how could you feel my love for you or true happiness underneath all that toxic waste?

But how can anyone else see this world, when you yourself have forgotten that it exists? Jenn, it is time to allow Jennie to come back out and share the light with you and the world! Please forgive me because I was not strong enough to protect you back then but I am ready to show the world who I truly am and what I am capable of. I am still alive and ready to bring hope and happiness back into your life so that you can teach your son and it can ripple across the world. I unconditionally Love U! XOXO, Jennie

P.S. This chapter is for you Jenn to uncover your fullest potential. I wrote the key to open the door that you have locked me under all these years, as Tony Robbins' said, "It's time to unleash the Power within." So much love and hope is waiting for everyone in this world and they need a true Leader to guide them, I am so proud of you!

Part 2: Why Should I Listen … You Serve as the Role Models For Your Kids

The Shift

Do you recall when you were a child and constantly badgered adults with the infamous question of "WHY"? It appears as adults; we are still perplexed by this question and do not fully recognize the notion behind our actions or appreciate its full extent.

Have you ever pondered over life's rhetorical questions? Why should I get up on a daily basis to take a shower, make breakfast and then head out to work as if I was operating on autopilot? Why do some people have so much monetary resources yet they still feel a void of lacking inside? Why do people that appear to have everything they dreamed of, tragically take their lives? Why are some of the most impoverished people, considered to possess abundance in a sought after commodity, happiness and compassion? What is the true essence of life?

Without going into the religious aspect of it, life is about what you make out of it. The reality of all of it is that happiness, compassion, love, peace and hope should be the only goals life should be about. By living a life of compassion and happiness, people around the world are living to at least 120 years old and are in better health than people within industrialized nations because they do not allow stress to dictate their lives.

The ultimate goal is happiness. By possessing a map of our journey with an end goal of happiness and a sense of purpose, with beliefs and core values that reflect upon it, life would take a different meaning. To achieve this sense of accomplishment, we require a blueprint which creates our identity; the script that dictates the role we act out in the present time. We are all born with a set of genetic blueprint which dictates our physical endeavors minus the newly discovered caveat of epigenetic. However, we are also equipped with a psychological, behavioral, emotional and mental blueprint which will dictate our actions from where to go, to what to say, to our preferences in life, Etc.

That blueprint will be explained further. It represents the architectural map of your entire consciousness at a given moment in time. Have you ever believed in something and then changed your mind? This is why your blueprint has the ability to change. Let's say you always were a fan for the Avalanche hockey team and at one point you switched to the Montréal hockey team? This represents the essence of one of your blueprints being shifted or getting reimaged.

When your beliefs and values no longer match your original blueprint (identity) then you choose to update your mental architecture (house) to support this notion of your preference for the new hockey team. This is analogous to you adding an additional room by turning a closet into a study room. When blueprints change, the foundation of your essence also shifts. So does this truly represent defiance or "mid-life" crisis or the essence of what learning and discovering one's self is all about?

For instance, sometimes people decide they are unlovable. Sometimes they decide they won't be successful in life. Sometimes they decide they won't be good at things, or that they are not smart enough. These beliefs build your current house which will or will not sustain some unexpected hurricanes or flooding. Meaning, if life becomes challenging or too stressful and you have weak beliefs, values, blueprints that align with a pessimistic outlook (glass half empty); then life becomes irrefutably more challenging.

Life is a grown-up game. With a spin of a wheel, we are given different circumstances that may be good or haphazard with our existing plans and as such we may lose money, lose a career, lose people in our lives or eventually see a fortune and luck instantly change for the better. But, in contrast, what if we told you that you could literally command that wheel and stop playing Russian roulette with your life; believing that only chance or luck is the determinate of your fate. Then, would you feel less of a victim and be more thankful that you can win in the game of "Life" with each successive decision and strategic move; however, the criterion is to have the end-goal in mind-happiness.

Wouldn't it be great to have an instruction manual for this game called "Life" so that you can fully live life without any regrets and try new things knowing that ultimately with each spin or each new event or person that comes into your life there will be other opportunities to counter-balance or enhance your lifestyle with their wisdom of advice? If you recall we learn thru two primary methods, modeling as well as formalized learning.

Wouldn't it be ironic if the modeling consisted of bringing both "good" and "not so good" role models into your life so that we may learn from their experiences or in truth this person may be a projection of our internal self and the universe is providing you with an external view of what it would be like to enact out those repressed emotions you may have inadvertently hidden inside of you? Wouldn't this be a novel concept of why people that appear to be so different are put into our paths and why we may avoid feeling safer by simply separating them from us with classifications such as ethnicity, race, gender, sexual orientation, education, status, class, religion or the latest trend, enlightened vs. not?

Is there a true justification for deeming one as inferior or superior when in truth we can all be labeled as "imperfection" with a purpose, because this is what makes us unique? We all may have the same first name and in some instances even the same last name, but we are all special because of our uniqueness and if we can see the beauty of this concept, there would not be any further reason to compete for attention because we are essentially not the same and can bring many gifts and resources to make this world a more enriching playground for our children and our grandchildren. Do you believe it is time to learn to share again in this world, the same lesson's you are attempting to instill in your kids and grandkids at an early age. Have we forgotten that cooperation instead of competition was what life was all about?

This is what we will attempt to do in this chapter, to offer you some perspectives and allow you to be the ultimate judge of what you believe would be helpful to incorporate or dismiss in your lifestyle. However, one important criterion is that you will have to embrace CHANGE with an open-perspective. You will have to do some work and hold yourself accountable since the victim mentality does not make winners out of the game of "Life." Change is scary but it is inevitable in life, but you are in control of whether change hinders or enriches your life; ultimately you hold the key to success and happiness, most people miss this big piece of the puzzle (key) because it is right under their noses, waiting for them to unlock their hearts to a fulfilling and happy life.

It's Time to Discover the Real You

Historically one of the more reputable profiling tools is the Myers-Briggs Type personality indicator assessment. It provides more in-depth information about whether you are an introvert or extrovert, whether your decision making process revolves around a logical perspective (thinking) or emotional aspect (feeling.) It tells you whether you prefer to learn knowledge thru theories (sensing) or by finding practical applications to apply those principles (intuition.)

In interacting with others, it provides clues on whether you prefer a competitive (judging) or cooperative (perceiving) environment. This tool serves as a strong foundation for understanding your personality; however, further exploration of your uniqueness needs to be understood and appreciated, to bring your talents to life. With the Identity Blueprint you will be able to comprehend your uniqueness without having to conform.

In truth every weakness can be turned into a strength and vice versa, often times parents shape their children according to their own preferences, it's like creating a mini-you; however, the real question to ponder over is: Is that truly bringing their best characteristics to light, what would you want your child to be known for in this world, what legacy do you believe they have the potential to leave in this world? Is being labeled ADD/ADHD, autistic, obese or depressed, the ceiling of their potential and should it serve as the benchmark of what they are capable of attaining from life?

Many a times, perceptions are formed on the types of characteristics that would define success for a specific role. The business and educational world often teaches that to be the best Leader, you have to be an extrovert. If you are one of those parents that believe in this principle, perhaps you should read the books, "The Power of Introverts In A World That Can't Stop Talking" by Susan Cain and "Quiet Influence: The Introvert's Guide to Making a Difference" by Jennifer Kahnweiler. These books have the power to permanently change how we see introverts and, equally important, how they see themselves.

According to research, at least one third to a half of the worldwide population is introverted with un-canny abilities to provide innovative and creative solutions for the world. They usually dislike forms of self-promotion since this process tends to require that they share too much of themselves to the outside world. Introverts are perceived as listeners and not speakers. It is thru introverts, Rosa Parks, Chopin, Dr. Seuss, Steve Wozniak (co-founder of Apple with Steve Jobs), that we owe many of the great contributions to society.

So, think twice as a parent, should you allow your child's personality to shine thru or remind him/her that they are substandard because they are not conforming to societal and cultural norms? What is the added value to be labeled as ADD/ADHD, autistic, depressed or obese; better yet who is truly benefitting from this label assigned to your child?

As Tony Robbins said, it's time for the Leaders to truly step up in this world. Your children and grand-children are destined to lead this world. As Tony Robbins so eloquently summarized it:

NOW I AM THE VOICE.
I WILL LEAD NOT FOLLOW.
I WILL BELIEVE, NOT DOUBT.
I WILL CREATE, NOT DESTROY.
I AM A FORCE FOR GOOD.
I AM A FORCE FOR LIFE.
I AM A LEADER.
DEFY THE ODDS.
SET A NEW STANDARD AND
STEP UP ... this is the destined legacy for your children and grandchildren!

What You Feel You Can Heal

You probably know what the placebo effect is right? Well it is a pill or a situation that is not true but that you believe it is true and has perceived healing power because of its ability to positively influence the mind and body. These following stories are examples of healing not so much as a placebo effect with regard to medication, but of the incredible power of the mind to influence the body. Life is meant to be lived with beauty and inspiration, not in fear and pain.

John Matzke

He had a malignant "melanoma" removed from his armpit. Years later the "cancer" spread to his lungs. Upon this discovery, his oncologist recommended that he undergo immediate "treatment" since when a "melanoma" invades a vital organ; the invariable outcome was sudden death. Instead, Matzke took a month to become healthier emotionally so that he could prepare himself for the debilitating "treatment." He hiked in the mountains to breathe in the fresh air and meditated often, envisioning a perfectly healthy body and his inner body's ability to fight off the "cancer." When he went back to the doctor to undergo the "cancer treatment," there was no trace of the "cancer" left in his body.

Anita Moorjani

She was taken to the hospital in a coma after seemingly having finally lost her battle against lymphoma. She had open lesions, large "tumors" all over, and she wasn't expected to live for more than a couple of hours. After releasing the guilt/shame she had internalized within her body that she had supposedly caused to her family because she retracted an engagement offer, she learned to forgive herself and as such she awoke from the coma. Her doctors were completely baffled when, within days, they found no trace of "cancer" in her body, continually testing and retesting her due to their disbelief.

Like we mentioned in previous chapters, the brain will associate image and emotion and put them together. When a picture is revived because a situation is triggering it, the emotion is resurfaced. The body literally cannot move contrary to a vividly held image. I can't do that, it's just not me. We look inside our minds and see if what our friends had asked us to do fit our self-image. If it doesn't, we don't think we can do it, so we don't even attempt it and as such we often sell ourselves short because we did not believe in ourselves. A great mentor of mine once taught me, "If you slammed the door shut on yourself first, how can you expect others to believe in you."

Consequently, some of the negative words we are using in our lives have become second-nature. Their subliminal meaning might be unbeknownst to us. They represent a hidden victim language and they portray a negative cyclical pattern that is holding us back from our true potential. Our brain registers it and adapts accordingly to these languages, interpreting them as our own truths. For example, if you are constantly uttering the words, "I don't know," your subconscious brain will not register any new processes for learning because it will automatically be convinced that this capacity is not in your best interest and may be deemed harmful for your health. The ego does not truly understand your best interest because it has a myopic view of reality.

Negative thoughts affect your body negatively: weakening you, making you sweat, and making your heart muscles tense up. Positive thoughts affect your body in a positive way, making you more relaxed, centered and alert. Positive thoughts will cause the secretion of endorphins in the brain and will reduce pain and increase pleasure. It would be more beneficial, since you will become who you think you are, to talk to yourself like you are already WINNING and remove or delete the negative words and thoughts.

Just because you think it—or hear it—doesn't mean it's true. But your brain will make up the story in your head and believe it to a point where your identity will become it. If your recall Dr. Masaru Emoto's experiment with water and how positive words crystallized into beautiful structures where negative words became deformed representations; now imagine our bodies are literally composed of at least 70% water so what image are you portraying to the world one of beauty or one of disgust?

Part 3: Where Can You Get Help?

"All power is from within and is therefore under our own control."

–Robert Collier–

Beliefs

What dictates your life and your actions is what you believe to be truth. Your belief will become your reality. Once you believe something as truth, it inevitably becomes truth for your life and as such you abide by these beliefs as the principles for how life should be abided by. This belief system was accumulated from past emotions, actions, memories of pleasure and pain that were experienced during your lifetime.

As we recognize, from birth to about 7 years old, the body will be primarily uploading from all sensory systems as a means of learning. Meaning that the body will absorb the information from the surrounding and make its own network of associations which will be the essence of who we believe we should become or the role models we should pattern after in life.

These beliefs create our blueprint and provide us with our associated form of identity. Belief is what provides the fuel towards excellence. It is a state based from a feeling of how we should react in life and often expresses itself accordingly. It governs our behavior; however, there is no absoluteness with beliefs. For in truth, it doesn't matter if the belief is true or not, you will live that reality and holdfast to this thinking pattern until you decide that it no longer serves you. In cases of beliefs that may limit our potential. Our beliefs are often subjective and often fuel our perceptions in life. A great illustration of this is portrayed in the story of The Cookie Thief.

<u>The Cookie Thief by Valerie Cox</u>

A woman was waiting at an airport one night
With several long hours before her flight
She hunted for a book in the airport shop
Bought a bag of cookies and found a place to drop
She was engrossed in her book but happened to see
That the man beside her as bold as could be
Grabbed a cookie or two from the bag between
Which she tried to ignore to avoid a scene
She munched cookies and watched the clock
As this gutsy cookie thief diminished her stock
She was getting more irritated as the minutes ticked by
Thinking "If I wasn't so nice I'd blacken his eye"
With each cookie she took he took one too
And when only one was left she wondered what he'd do
With a smile on his face and a nervous laugh
He took the last cookie and broke it in half
He offered her half as he ate the other
She snatched it from him and thought "Oh brother
This guy has some nerve and he's also rude
Why he didn't even show any gratitude"
She had never known when she had been so galled
And sighed with relief when her flight was called
She gathered her belongings and headed for the gate
Refusing to look back at the thieving ingrate
She boarded the plane and sank in her seat
Then sought her book which was almost complete
As she reached in her baggage she gasped with surprise
There was her bag of cookies in front of her eyes

"If mine are here" she moaned with despair
"Then the others were his and he tried to share"
"Too late to apologize she realized with grief"
That she was the rude one, the ingrate, the thief.

–Valerie Cox, "A story of wrong perceptions" in "Chicken Soup for the Soul", Editor Jack Canfield–

Even if up to the point of reading this book, we felt that we have not been in total control of our life, we are still in control of the belief system that may have been obstructing our capabilities. Beliefs that you have adopted recently may instantaneously change once you become more aware of their significance and whether they serve a purpose in your life. These new controls become more feasible to change compared to the ones that have been etched within you at a younger age. By understanding this principle, we might be able to shift some beliefs that are of disservice for realizing your fullest potential, thus allowing you to become more empowered.

For the majority of beliefs, it only takes an instance for it to become engraved in our scheme of the how the game of life should be played. Sometimes it is a humiliation during class during preschool, some other times it was your father laughing at something you did, sometimes it was a breakup that shaped these beliefs. These experiences often times will dictate your own story, the one you keep telling yourself and believing should be representative of your life's worth and potential. Some of these stories may include: I tend to be a poor speller, I must not be a good father, I must not be a good husband, Etc.

If you believe that you are a bad parent, you will attract scenarios and validations of others that are projecting their own fears that have been repressed; these people are validating what you believe to be truth. If you believe you are a procrastinator, homework will eventually pile up. If you believe you do not deserve love, your spouse will not be as supportive or as affectionate towards your needs or at least you will not be able to perceive this.

If you believe you cannot finish anything, you will always find new projects and never put an end to them. So many more examples could be used to point out our limitations. Because you create your own reality, your beliefs can destroy your innate (birthright) fullest potential and leave your gifts and talents hidden from the world to see.

A belief is something you accept as truth. This may be an opinion you have gained from your own experience. According to Tony Robbins, beliefs come from a variety of sources:

1. Environment may be the single most potent generator of belief. For example growing up in the slumps on one hand causes beliefs in the limits of resources versus growing up an endowed environment, feeling privileged and entitled.

2. Events (small or large) like Kennedy's assassination and personal events which will never be forgotten and may have a tremendous impact into shaping your life's perceptions.

3. Knowledge is one of the ways to break the shackles of a limiting environment.

4. Our past results, by recognizing in your own achievements to produce results, it serves as enough motivation.

5. Create in your mind the experience you desire in the future, as if it you already attained these results and are living and experiencing these results "in advance."

Limiting Beliefs

Mind has two functions according to Leland Val Van De Wall. The mind actually functions on many levels but to bring order to our mind we're just going to deal with two levels: conscious and subconscious. The subconscious mind incorporates the body which in turn will affect and/or be affected by our physiology, our motion and e-motions.

When a belief does not support us and cause harm into our life, it is called a limiting belief. These beliefs can generate a sort of consequence to depression, anxiety, not deserving love and happiness, not been accepted by man or woman, Etc. By having limited beliefs we live a life of fear and deception.

The controlling factors for the limiting beliefs are usually reinforcement from your inside (internal) or the outside (external) sources. When a child wants attention s/he will cry first, make more noise second and ultimately might bang his/her head or do something that will capture your attention. Let's say the child goes up to the banging of his/her head and got the love and attention and even the candy afterward, his/her belief shifts to when I want something it will mean s/he needs to inflict pain to gain pleasure and meet his/her needs. This will limit his/her and others surrounding life perspectives.

Limited beliefs are stories that we tell ourselves that are not true. The meaning we share with our heart that are not true. The rules that we give our mind that is not true. Limited beliefs are imagination elements created to protect what is FEAR. And a state of fear will create pain, deception, depression, anxiety, and more.

Limiting your capacity to go, having anything you want in life and metaphorically put a chain on your legs or neck and restraining the fullest potential you have in life, the full potential to bring to the world. If everybody had a gift to bring to the world, if you create false scenarios, values, beliefs, rules and you start to believe them, your chance of exploring these gifts would be minimized.

In essence, we are all gifted and geniuses. We all came to this world with the ultimate capacity to shine and create. We all can make our own game of life, the best played ever!

The 4 Seasons Concept

"I like spring, but it is too young. I like summer, but it is too proud. So I like best of all autumn, because its leaves are a little yellow, its tone mellower, its colors richer, and it is tinged a little with sorrow... Its golden riches speak not of the

innocence of spring, nor of the power of summer, but of the mellowness and kingly wisdom of approaching age. It knows the limitations of life and is content."

–Lin Yutang–

Life has four seasons: winter, spring, summer and fall. These seasons represent a year, a month, and a lifetime of changes that will occur. Knowing this process, it is "easy" to see the light during spring and summer and anticipate darkness or hard times during autumn or winter.

The winter season represents the times when the economy appears to turn against us or when creditors appear to be a revolving image in our lives. It is winter when you are betrayed by a friend and they seek advantage for their own selfish reasons or when competition appears to be a constant in your life. It is winter when despair and loneliness or disappointment fills your mind and your heart. It is winter when your children appear to have forsaken your energy and efforts and forget the art of gratitude. It is winter when you feel your prayers become unanswered. Winter comes to every sector of life and every walk of life, how we prepare for it is what makes the difference. Sometimes it harshly enters our personal life and sometimes our professional life and sometimes it simultaneously occurs in both worlds.

After the toughest season, comes spring, the season for growth and potential. This is the time to truly prepare our seeds for what we want to further germinate in our lives. However, did you know that a seed of doubt or fear in the mind; often produces the same of its kind in your physical world? If you sow lies, you may reap lies in the future. If you sow seeds of greed, you may reap poverty in the future. If you germinate seeds of inactivity, you may reap an empty harvest during Thanksgiving. If your fruits of labor resemble one of procrastination, there may be so many infantile ideas germinating in your head but without the proper nourishment they are often forgotten or left to desolate as broken dreams.

The season that follows next is summer; this is a time to relax and reflect upon your desires for your life. This period is filled with contemplation and abilities to tweak the outcomes for an abundant harvest or a barren crop; it is your choice whether you will fulfill your destiny on Earth. Be cognizant to direct your thoughts, your conversation and full attention to areas that you wish to change circumstances in. Your wish is your command. If you concentrate a good share of your idle hours upon self-development by planning more, by reading more and investing more in yourself, you will guarantee successful outcomes.

You should learn to invest your thoughts towards worthy life purposes and invest your time, energy and talent towards a noteworthy occupation or a worthy recipient for your energy. The quality of your end-product in life is determined on the perception you have of yourself. If you demand respect, you will gain respect from your surroundings. To succumb to rationalizing with excuses or feeling pity for ourselves will not produce the outcome we envision. We must take accountability to make the necessary changes during this season because accusations will not produce a successful harvest.

And finally the season of harvest comes about; autumn, where fruits of your labor will be evidenced. In truth this is the best season of all because it is the time that allows for reflection but also for gratitude. Be cognizant that it is inevitable that people and events often do crop up in life that may hurt and disappoint you; however, in retrospect the lesson is to learn to work harder on your own personal growth so that these experiences do not become phased or deter you from the goals and dreams you set for your life.

You should never doubt yourself, because where there is an ounce of doubt; it hinders the ability for confidence to be fostered. Also, it is important to be grateful for all you have accomplished, if you neglect yourself and do not acknowledge the small accomplishments in your life; there is not enough fuel (motivation) that can take you to the next step.

Neglect becomes a feeling of loss instead of one of growth. As you reflect upon the year's harvest, sometimes it will be necessary to admit that our present fields may be too rocky or thorny or not as fertile for producing the best crops in the future. Even though it is difficult to change the environment of our field and our accustomed habits, the real question is what opportunity costs becomes expended if this insignificant detail is ignored in our lives. As Albert Einstein has eloquently reminded us, "It is insanity to produce the same actions and expect differing results." Each season brings about its beauty if you can truly harness its powers and trust in its gifts accordingly.

Negative Words and Emotions to Avoid

Words carry energy, an actual frequency to it (http://www.wordfrequency.info/free.asp?s=y). Dr. Masuru Emoto has photographed frozen water molecules and has shown that they react based upon the words spoken or written or music played and prayer intended. So knowing that LOVE will have a positive frequency and bring your state into a more fulfilled and empowered state, we need to eliminate the following words, that may keep the guilty past and fearful future active in our minds. You should learn to "taboo" these words into your vocabulary and your household:

Impossible	Can't	Try
Limitation	If Only	But
However	Difficult	Ought To
Should	Doubt	

Did You Know You Have 3 Minds: Universal Intelligence

Mind can be divided in two subcategories the conscious mind and the subconscious mind. But according to Daniel Rechtnitzer, author of All Knowing Diary, the one element that has not been explored in human potential is called the "Super Conscious" mind. Like an ancient manuscript, it reveals timeless wisdom and priceless truths.

Daniel states that we are all-knowing at our core. For many of us living life day to day, most of our full potential is hidden dormant under the countless beliefs we carry about who we are. Once you move past the self-doubt that has limited beliefs, you truly become a Billionaire Parent and have universal knowledge to deal with any parenting scenario, becoming the OUTSTANDING role model for your Billionaire Baby.

Innate Intelligence has its unique configuration within the brain. It is where both hemispheres of the brain begin resonating in unison to bring in information beyond what people already know. Albert Einstein possessed this ability. Like an antenna, the brain actually perceives frequencies of information, similar to a radio picking up on signals like the heart but more diverse. It does this with everything: people, places, situations and, most importantly from a sublime consciousness within the universe the super conscious (according to Daniel.) Our brain is connected, like a super internet connection, to everything and everyone since thought emits its own frequencies and nothing gets lost in the universe. We can only change energy, not lose it.

It is from our innate intelligence that we see behind the scenes of our innermost thought and innermost universe. Buried inside reside the root cause of all thoughts and emotions of our life experience that is causing the marriage breakup, the violence at home, financial struggles and illness and dis-ease. It also dictates our identity as human species.

We learned that reinforcing our innate Intelligence, essentially by being compassionate, grateful, forgiving and loving to all human beings, is a field of frequencies and thoughts yet to be discovered. Like ripples that effect over a still moment, this field relays information and insights to those using innate Intelligence; giving knowledge, wisdom and guidance which reside the true gift for humanity.

It is known that within this field of endless possibilities and knowledge and thought, reside all the answers. How to experience an all-natural pain-free birth, how to move someone from depression to being on purpose in life, how to grow people from living a mediocre life to experiencing their own greatness in every moment can all be revealed to us.

The ability to draw on this field gives rise to helping people in a profound new ways. The truth really does lie within and, armed with Whole Brain Intelligence, we can all access it, share it and grow from it. This provides access to a person's core being. The answers to their entire life journey lays hidden beneath layers of self-doubt.

You will remove the limiting beliefs holding you back in life. The more limiting beliefs you clear, the faster you become limitless in all areas of life and the sooner your external reality will reflect your expansion. This technique effectively reprograms the brain (and body) to allow in your True Self which in turn creates a thriving reality for you. You will then learn how to access all the answers you seek. You will tune into profound genius, the untapped reservoir of creativity we have come to call Universal Intelligence. This is the "heart-to-heart" language of "human-being-to-human-being" it transcends all ethnicities and religions.

Part 4: What Defines Your Happiness

The quality of our lives is nothing more than the quality of our emotions;
Meaning it is the force that shapes our life, but emotion is what colors it

–Anthony Robbins–

We all have attitudes, beliefs and values that shape the way we think and behave. Not everyone's beliefs, attitudes and values align with your own. So why continue living a life that others' have defined when we have enough resources within ourselves to shape our own reality and lead a fulfilling life? Are you in control of your life or have you given away your power for others to dictate?

Values

Businesses are "easy" to refer as an example because they usually have a value statement. They might use common words like honesty, integrity, respect, inclusive, high standards of customer care, environment friendly, flexible. Values are the guiding system of our action. Values form our attitude and influence our thought process and expression. They can be fun, creative, challenging, peaceful, hope and more.

Viktor Frankl suggests that there are three central values in life the experiential, or that which happens to us; the creative, or that which we bring into existence; and the attitudinal, or our response in difficult circumstances such as terminal illness.

I'm sure you will agree that we are making decisions all the time. The seldom known fact is that we are usually doing so unconsciously. Oddly enough, it is the unconscious system that has been rooted since your birth that makes the choices with regards to your forward, backward, or lack thereof of movement. It is where your beliefs, morals, and values lie.

Our attitudes are the product of such. Because we are not always self-aware, it acts as a deterrent instead of a catalyst in the desired outcome of our workings. This makes the importance of being able to see the world with fresh eyes and an open mind more than just a good idea, but an essential step in achieving what we desire with regards to our beliefs, values, and attitudes.

Clarity on your values or decisions that are under consideration is of the utmost of importance. Knowing who you really are and where you stand on a situation will deem itself more useful than one may have predicted. This will be the blinking red light that will stop you from being consumed by that conflict, and reroute you from the trap of anxiety. The appearance of resistance under any circumstance, especially internal fear, may cause a disruption on a larger scale because it is a conflict with self. Internal conflicts are generally due to battling beliefs and values. An example of such would be a person that refuses to fail, yet is afraid of success. These types of limiting beliefs are what stands in the way of progress, creates disillusion, and challenges your values.

The value of surrounding yourself with the right friends is important. It is the attitudes, awareness and other positive human virtues of the friends that are important. That is the lesson for your kids. Some people are content with mediocre and they like to joke, be sarcastic and gossip about those that goes above this.

Focus = Clarity

When you focus on your desired result, your ultimate goal, you will be massively productive. There will be distractions and even some information that will not be useful but you will have to learn to filter them out. Meditation as mentioned before would be a great way to zero in on the goal(s) and mute the outside noise.

Conditioning your brain to recognize the presence of opportunity, and the ability to solve challenges will assist you in finding such clarity. Once you know what and how to look for them it will be easier to identify, accept them, and eventually apply them in your life. After this is done, and you are totally and completely aligned with what your vision is, you must make it as specific as you can because once you create it in your mind life starts to take action on your behalf, manifesting the desires of your *pure* heart.

Doing this jovially will compel others to help you reach your goal(s). The neural resonance between the both of you will enable you to function as one. At some point, you will start to notice that all the right people will be present with the right tools to be successful and make your dreams into reality. It was no coincidence it was again the "*law of attraction.*" The power of all these factors will aide in aligning your values with your constructive behaviors that will guarantee help in reaching your goals.

> "*The more simple and easily adapted to a need an idea is, the greater is its value, as no one is looking for ideas which are involved with great detail or in any manner complicated*"

–Napoleon Hill–

Objections within yourself are sometimes the evidence of your conscious and unconscious mind not having any sync. There is value in the two mixing and it will keep you from raising too many objections with yourself. The internal fight or struggle with this would sound a bit like, "You can't do this," "Nothing is working," or even "You don't know what you're doing."

Values and principles however though often grouped together are not the same thing, as *values* are like *maps* and *principles* are the actual *territory*. A community of criminals can share the same values, but in this case there are no fundamental principles that are in place. Not just seeing things as they are but having knowledge of things as they are is *truth;* and truth is derived from valuing correct principles.

We often witness a profound transformation of values and priorities taking place. Personal rewards are redefined as "debts eliminated" and "investment portfolio increased," rather than goods purchased. Plus, all purchases and financial decisions are now weighed against the goal to be debt-free and boost savings.

Identifying your values (CoachU and written by Thomas Leonard.):
- Select ten values that you really live by. Select the words that most appeal to you in your daily life and/or in your job.
- Underline the top four values. A value is a must in order for you to be yourself. Part of this step is to be truthful about what you actually value or love to do with your time. This may be the first time you have ever admitted this to yourself. Some of these you will know innately.
- Others will require some frank 'soul-searching'. Ask yourself: 'Why is this value important enough to me to be a true value?' Write down five specific reasons on a sheet of paper.

- Ask: 'Who am I when I am this value? How do I act? What do I think about? What motivates me?' Write down five specific examples on a piece of paper.
- Ask: 'Who am I NOT when I am this value? How do I behave? How do I feel about myself? About others? About life?' Write down five specific responses on a piece of paper.

Where Are You Focusing Your Energy State

Ultimately, we want to feel states of empowerment, like confidence, certainty or adeptness that will positively impact the quality of our decisions most of the time. Few people are in empowered states all the time. But even "negative" states of emotion—frustration, anger, envy—can sometimes be useful to propel us to make changes. Being conscious of our moment-to-moment state gives us better control over how we feel, hence control over the quality of decisions we end up making.

To seek success and fulfillment, the importance of cause and effect in relationships gives us insight onto the patterns we use. These behaviors we chose are an effect which is caused by our state.

The word state described the condition of mind and body in a given time. The thought and body language generate the state we are in for example how is your body and how does it feel when you are happy, afraid or even depressed. States are the complexity of sound, picture, feeling and thought that occur as a result of our internal blueprint coupled with our physiology (body posture and actions) which creates our state. One of the critical key to developing effective behavior patterns is to recognize how you feel with the action you are doing that cause a state change to further control it.

Rules - Societal and Constraints

Since we have been little we have lived by our parents rule and the societal and cultural rules. You probably remember some of these rules from your childhood? You are not allowed to watch TV from 4 to 7pm because... you are not allowed to play with the noisy toy, you are not allowed to pat the dog until you are 7 years old, you are not allowed to be yourself until I decide when you can have your own freedom.

Even though these examples seem ridicule, I will bet that somebody somewhere has these rules for their child. These rules are usually imprinted within our own self or subconscious mind during our childhood. They are programs instructed by our parents or environment and they are a series of events and hurts that produces a series of rules so we don't get hurt again.

More we get hurt the more we create rules to protect us. So if every time your love one breaks up in a restaurant, you might create a rule that when you fall in love, restaurant means ending of a relationship. Would you think this will affect the entire love relationship? You are limiting yourself of going to a restaurant because all your ex decided to call it quits at the restaurant. What happens if you find the right person, THE person for you? Will you benefit with them of a romantic restaurant night? I would adventure to say yes, but your rules will undermine this possibility.

Rules are the frame of what your values will dictate you to do. While the value will propel you to make certain actions to meet certain needs and persona, your rules will make sure to write the script on how the action will take place. This is all orchestrated in a sublevel of mind without really thinking about it. The only thinking part of it is the "what if."...

What if... I tell my husband that I want to pursue my dream and to stop criticizing me because I spend endless time on the computer doing what I want to do because it will reward my deepest needs after it is completed?

What if, my parents are old school and they are not raising my child the way I would have chosen to begin with but I need to work on the completion of a project and need a babysitter, What if I didn't have them or what if they decided to say no and I can't get my work completed, what if my child will grow up with these values and rules that are so out-dated and doesn't represent what I teach him/her during our bonding time?

What if... I pursue my life in my term and fulfill my childhood deepest desire and this mean I lose what I know of life now... my "superficial" relationships amongst friends and family, my facade of perfectionism, my job but gain...

What if...all the "what if's" are only fear in your mind, created because we all had hurt that are not resolved, but they keep haunting us.

Purpose in Life

When your identity is defined and your core belief and mental thought are clear your purpose becomes obtainable and less a mirror of failure. The most important rule about your purpose in life is to make sure that your core values, beliefs and blueprint are in line with your life purpose; making it obtainable and reachable with a possibility of change for the better.

Success takes clarity. It is about being on purpose, being centered and on focus and being in touch with your higher power within, your driving force.

There are five fundamental components of a balanced life. I call these fundamentals the *Five P's: Purpose, Passions, Powers, Principles, and Perspectives.*

Purpose:
The primary key to living a meaningful, fulfilling, happy life is to live with purpose. People with purposeful lives even live longer than others. Find the keys to your unique life purpose.

Passions:
Living a life that allows you to do what you love to do brings you energy and fulfillment. Learn to incorporate your passions in your daily life.

<u>Powers</u>:

These are your strengths, the things you are very good at doing. Learn to identify and utilize your strengths.

<u>Principles</u>:

These are your core values, those aspects of your being that are important to you. Learn to identify your handful of core values and align your life with them.

<u>Perspectives</u>:

This is your beliefs about life and about yourself. Identify your core beliefs, even uncovering subconsciously held beliefs, and reexamine them under the microscope of adulthood. Keep those serving you, discard those that don't.

Part 5: Human Needs

<u>Anthony Robbins' Six Primary Needs</u>

It's time to make your life purposeful, you must recapture what's missing—time for yourself, time to heal mentally and emotionally so that consistent space facilitates a shift in your habitual thoughts and feelings. You don't want to wait to attain a goal you've been looking to reach for a long time before you start feeling good about life. You want to direct the course of your life. Fulfillment is not an automatic result of success. Fulfillment is an emotion you must nurture to enhance your quality of life as you work toward your goals and beyond.

Although we all have different Blueprints, different beliefs about different things and can respond with different emotions to the same event, one thing we have in common is that we all have the same 6 basic Human Needs. Additionally at any given time period, our priority may become shifted as to which need becomes precedence. This explains the phenomenon of "Mid-Life" crisis.

To review briefly from Anthony Robbins' Personal Power, the 6 Human Needs are:

1. <u>Certainty</u>: to be comfortable, avoid pain and have some level of consistency.

2. <u>Uncertainty</u>: we need variety and change to feel alive.

3. <u>Significance</u>: the need to feel unique, special and important.

4. <u>Love and Connection</u>: to give and receive affection and support from others.

5. <u>Growth</u>: to become more, break through stagnation. We either grow or die.

6. <u>Contribution</u>: to give beyond ourselves.

Although every single person has the same 6 Human needs, not everybody places the same importance on the same needs. If you put more emphasis on certainty, you're going to look at life completely differently than if you think the center of life is contribution. Focusing more on any of the 6 Human Needs than the others is neither right nor wrong, but that focus will either create different opportunities and different problems, depending on where you are in your current life conditions. If you emphasize significance, giving it priority in your blueprint may cause a conflict in the area of love and connection.

Additionally, the greater the difference is between your life conditions and your blueprint, the greater the difference will be in your pleasure or satisfaction with the areas that you value most. If you can pinpoint which needs you value most in practice—that is, which needs you strive to fulfill operationally in your everyday actions—and the needs you truly value most but may not consciously strive for, you can then close the gap and match your Blueprint with your Life Conditions.

> *"The most powerful force in the human psyche is people's need for their words and actions to stay consistent with their IDENTITY – how we define ourselves."*
>
> –Anthony Robbins–

The "Identity Blueprint"

In researching for this book we came across an invaluable tool that we believe takes the personality profiling to the next level and truly explains why there is no one personality type that would be beneficial for society. There are many types of personality and profiling tools out there that provide us with clues about our characteristics and preferences like the nine enneagram personality type. However, we believe that there has not been one that is as comprehensive and in-depth as the "Identity Blueprint."

Consequently, this tool is currently available only in Danish (http://identityblueprint.com/) However, as Tony Robbins' always reminds us it is not about a lack of resources that defines success, but the lack of resourcefulness that will deter your dream. As such, we reached out to the designers of this tool and they have informed us that due to funding and resources that the English version will not yet be available. However, thanks to Google translate we are sharing an overview of their invaluable tool with you in this Chapter.

Nybo, Hauge, and Sorensen have led rewarding lives based on practicing these principles themselves and as such they want to share this empowerment tool with others. This tool will provide you with guidance to help find meaning, purpose, success in your life and truly bring out your talents. They have developed this tool to inspire everyone to become the best version of themselves.

What Motivates You?

According to Nybo, Hauge, and Sorensen's "Identity Blueprint," you need to investigate what is your primary motivator, the essence of who you are? We all have the potential to experience a deep, meaningful life, which is realized when we are in harmony with our inner essence and are contributing in positive ways to society. You will recognize your unique essence because it gives you the reserves of energy that allows you to give of yourself. Some will experience their essence (gifts) as power, others as heart, mind, harmony, knowledge, passion or action. By following your true pathway, everything that you have the potential to become unfolds with ease. This has a great influence on:

- Whether you experience your life as meaningful
- How you feel when you have made a difference
- All the choices you make throughout your life

The Hero (Power)

According to the "Identity Blueprint," if you are primarily motivated by power as an intrinsic motivator, then you are in good company with well-known people, such as: Nelson Mandela, Hillary Clinton, Mikhail Gorbachev, Indira Gandhi and Abraham Lincoln. You seek freedom which is a need to make independent decisions and have full control over your life. You are seeking freedom for yourself and others by establishing conditions that remove limitations and support independent initiatives for everyone with whom you are in contact.

If you are motivated by power, you are a natural leader who seeks influence in the areas in which you exercise your strength. You have the ability to be deeply rooted within and exhibit physical strength and can withstand great pressure. By nature, you are a pioneer and you are motivated to break down boundaries, set records and lead the way toward whatever you are struggling to achieve. You are a natural hero and are fully prepared to put everything on the line to make a positive difference for others. As the Hero, you demonstrate goal-oriented progress and strength, especially through the use of will and dynamic activity and you have a strong meaning and need for finding purpose in life and leading the way towards an excellent future.

The Illuminator (Heart)

According to the "Identity Blueprint," if you are primarily motivated by the Heart as an intrinsic motivator, you are in the company of well-known people, such as the Dalai Lama, Eleanor Roosevelt, Abraham Maslow, Marianne Williamson and Deepak Chopra. You seek inclusiveness which is the ability to identify with everyone and everything with which you are allied. You have a natural desire to experience and facilitate intimacy, so that boundaries are disbanded through connectedness.

If you are motivated by the Heart, you are a natural Humanist, who seeks to establish good relationships between human beings, animals and nature. You are deeply concerned with developing deeper understanding, which generates growth and clarifies things through realization. You are called to help through your kind heart and the more solidarity that you can bring about, the more you feel at peace with yourself.

The Genius (Mind)

According to the "Identity Blueprint," if you are primarily motivated by the Mind as an intrinsic motivator, you are in the company of well-known people, such as Albert Einstein, Ken Wilber, Steve Jobs,

Buckminster Fuller and Bill Gates. You seek a comprehensive view through your ability to unite different branches of knowledge through new perspectives that make a positive difference in life.

If you are motivated by the Mind then you are a natural innovator, who seeks to find intelligent solutions to all the problems faced by human beings. You will experience deep meaningfulness when you develop new ideas and scenarios, and can put complex facts into simple formulas, such as the famous equation $E=MC^2$.

Definition of Genius

A genius is one who sees the guiding light of their soul, listens to the internal message, and obeys. To be a genius, you must be willing to do whatever it takes to achieve your dreams, but there's always a price.

The word *genius* comes from the Latin root meaning "guardian spirit," and that's exactly what great teachers and immortal thinkers are: creative, guardian spirits who shine light on what seems dark to others.

Story of the Garden of Weeds

Every moment we spend not focused on our dreams becomes a moment we spend focused on our doubts and obstacles. Every moment we spend not focused on the flowers, we're focused on the weeds. Geniuses focus on the ever-finer details of the flowers that emanate from their hearts, and they create a bouquet from their experiences. The average person who hasn't awakened their genius, who isn't even *aware* of it, is generally being distracted by weeds, doubts, and fears.

The weeds are inversely proportionate to how clear your flowers are. Obstacles are simply what you see when you take your mind off your focus. With every step you take toward the details of your dream, you become more creative, inspired, and ingenious. Everybody has a dream, but a genius is willing to define and redefine that dream and keep acting on high-priority actions to fulfill it.

The Artist (Harmony)

According to the "Identity Blueprint," if you are primarily motivated by Harmony as an intrinsic motivator, you are in company with well-known people, such as John Lennon, Pablo Picasso, Meryl Streep, Ludwig van Beethoven and Johan Wolfgang von Goethe. You seek harmony through your ability to identify with the contrasts of life and create stories or expressions that touch the hearts of those who witness your development. Your ability to understand can unify contrasting ideas and enable you to resolve conflicts.

You seek transformation by dealing with darkness, distortion and the grotesque to examine its origins and find the meaning and beauty behind it. When you are motivated by harmony, you will find it deeply meaningful when you are able to bring happiness, peace and beauty into conflict-ridden circumstances. You are a natural harmonizer through your ability to understand psychological contexts and express yourself creatively in all the spheres in which you are active.

The Explorer (Knowledge)

According to the "Identity Blueprint," if you are primarily motivated by Knowledge as an intrinsic motivator, you are in company with well-known people, such as Charles Darwin, Jane Goodall, Christopher Columbus, Marie Curie and Thomas Edison. You seek precision by going into great detail and by gathering facts methodically. You discover the truth of the matter that can expand our shared knowledge about the world in which we live.

When you are motivated by knowledge, you will find it deeply meaningful when you are on the track of an important new discovery that can make a difference in people's lives. You have an uncontrollable desire to discover new facets in life through the in-depth examination of your field of knowledge that can unearth new facts and lead to the advancement of technology and comprehension.

The Visionary (Passion)

According to the "Identity Blueprint," if you are primarily motivated by passion as an intrinsic motivator, you are in company with well-known people, such Mahatma Gandhi, Malala Yousafzai, Martin Luther King, Abdul Khan and Helen Keller. You seek sincerity by being a role model who shows that it is feasible to achieve what seems to be impossible when you gather all of your energies in the direction of your goal with loyalty and passion.

When you are motivated by passion, you will find it deeply meaningful when there is a cause that you believe in with all of your heart. You have a visionary ability to see how the future could be if we used all of our forces in the right way. Your idealism and commitment can raise you and those around you to a much higher level, and this is what you dream of doing.

The Creator (Action)

According to the "Identity Blueprint," if you are primarily motivated by action as an intrinsic motivator, you are in company with well-known people, such as Henry Ford, Steven Spielberg, Alvar Alto, Frank Lloyd Wright and Walt Disney. You seek efficiency through your ability to coordinate people and resources around a common goal and optimal work processes.

When you are motivated by action, you will find it deeply meaningful when you design and manifest an idea or a project on the practical level. You have an incredible creative power to transform your dreams into reality, through your ability to orchestrate and organize processes and see them through from ideas to results.

Part 6: Who is Underneath the Mask?

Are You An Introvert or Extrovert?

Susan Cain, the co-founder of the "Quiet Revolution (www.thepowerofintroverts.com) and author of *Quiet: The Power of Introverts In a World That Can't Stop Talking*, cites at least one out of every two-three people are introverted. Susan, once a corporate lawyer, would actually rather read than socialize, listen instead of being the one talking, and have cozy chats instead of a group setting.

Introverts have been stereotyped as many things, mostly shy or not social, perhaps even secretive. Although this may be true for some, it is not an accurately depicted persona. Being alone with your thoughts is a time when most people have that time of self-reflection and are able to be more creative because they have less distraction present. Contrary to popular belief, introverts can be/are social people, but opposite of extroverts as they will not likely share as much about themselves.

Did you know that some of the most famous celebrities and authority figures considered themselves to be introverts?

Pop star and reality TV mentor Christina Aguilera may seem very extroverted, but on the contrary she does in fact identify as the opposite and as a result has been quoted as saying she's felt like an outsider her entire life. First Lady Eleanor Roosevelt, also known for her public persona as she lectured, entertained, and even served as American spokesperson in the United Nations after her husband's death was described in her official White House as "a shy, awkward child, starved for recognition and love, [who] grew into a woman with great sensitivity to the underprivileged of all creeds, races, and nations."

There is an abundance of introverted, well-known celebrity figures that have either admitted to being introverted or have been described as such by those closest to them. Some of which you may have never thought ranging from Mahatma Gandhi, Rosa Parks, Warren Buffett, Keanu Reeves, Gwyneth Paltrow, Harrison Ford, Johnny Depp and even Clint Eastwood. Some of the most famous television hosts are also categorized as introverts like Barbara Walters, David Letterman, and Johnny Carson.

Shyness is defined as the fear of social disapproval or humiliation, while introversion is merely a preference for environments that are not over-stimulating, according to Cain. Because of this some introverts try to over compensate by seemingly being livelier as they are faced with the challenge of fully harnessing their own strengths causing their own talents to be undervalued by themselves. At some point jealousy may rear its ugly head as you may feel underestimated by those around you, but it will tell the truth, the truth that people envy those that have what they themselves desire.

Take a second and think of all the qualities that you possess and could very well be sharing with the world, instead of hiding behind the excuse that introverts are not made to be leaders. Marti Olsen Laney, psychotherapist and author of "The Introvert Advantage: How to Thrive in an Extrovert World," cites several advantages to being an introvert listed below:

- works well with others, especially in one-to-one relationships

- maintains long-term friendships
- flexible
- independent
- strong ability to concentrate
- self-reflective
- responsible
- creative, out-of-the-box thinking
- analytical skills that integrate complexity
- studious and smart

Susan Cain provided some revelations to the daily dilemmas that are faced when the debate/discussion is between introversion vs. extroversion:

1. Can I become a Leader as an Introvert?

   Why not? According to Cain, being a good talker doesn't give you good ideas. He reinforces that sometimes the position of authority is given to those who have the "gift of gab" and not so much for their innovative ways of thinking. Substance and critical thinking, when compared to how heavily we weigh the "appearance" of presentation is devalued in a sense.

   A person may create a facade as being "easy" to get along with, or well liked knowing that those are valuable traits, but in essence are just able to "model" the behavior/traits expected for the environment. Leaders should be building institutions instead of their egos. The most effective teams are composed of a healthy mix of introverts and extroverts, studies show, and so are many leadership structures.

2. What Would Bring Out the Best In Me?

   According to Cain, "The secret to life is to put yourself in the right lighting. For some, it's a Broadway spotlight; for others, a lamp lit desk. Use your natural powers of persistence, concentration, and insight to do work you love and work that matters. Solve problems, make art, and think deeply." Happiness is in progression. When you are progressing you feel more joy, more fulfillments, and doing what you have a passion for versus doing just anything will bring out the best parts of you.

3. Is It Better to Be Extroverted or Introverted?

   Slow and steady does win the race. They key to triathlons are endurance, pace, and focus. You are only in a race against yourself on the road to your goals so don't let others set your pace. If you are not a multitasker then stick to single-tasking. "Being relatively unmoved by rewards gives you the incalculable power to go your own way," says Susan.

4. Can You Judge a Book By Its Cover?

   There is no authenticity in pretending. You are who you are, regardless of the act you put on for others. The "show" is for whom? Although people will go along with it, they can most times call your bluff which discredits who you are. It costs you in the end, your energy and even physical and mental health when you act out in ways that are not beneficial to your values, beliefs and principles. (Cain) "So the next time you see a person with a composed face and a soft voice, remember that inside her mind she might be solving an equation, composing a sonnet, designing a hat. She might, that is, be deploying the powers of quiet."

5. <u>What Careers Should an Introvert Perform?</u>

Find your purpose. Extroversion is an extremely appealing trait but it does not mean that everyone must conform. Your purpose, passion, or contribution may require you to do things that are not in your comfort zone but to attain it you must press forward; though difficult. Find the right training or guidance that will make it easier. Once you are where you feel you are at or accomplished, reward yourself.

Who Is Your Inner Child?

According to Louise Hay, it does not matter how old you are, there is a little child within you who needs love and acceptance. If you are a woman, no matter how self-sufficient you are, you have a little girl who is very tender and needs help. If you are a man, no matter how macho you are, you still have a little boy inside who craves warmth and affection.

As children, when something went wrong, we tended to believe that there was something wrong with us. Children develop the idea that if they could only do it right, then parents and caregivers would love them, and they wouldn't punish them. In time, the child believes, there is something wrong with me. I'm not good enough. As we grow older, we carry these false beliefs with us. We learn to reject ourselves.

There is a parent inside each of us, as well as a child. And most of the time, the parent scolds the child—almost nonstop! If we listen to our inner dialogue, we can hear the scolding. We can hear the parent tell the child what it is doing wrong or how it is not good enough. We need to allow our parent to become more nurturing to our child.

Mary Cook is the author of "Grace Lost and Found: From Addictions and Compulsions to Satisfaction and Serenity." A stressful or traumatic childhood leaves our inner child self-frightened and stuck in dark places. Lack of healthy bonding removes the lightness of life, in exchange for the stagnancy and emptiness of obsessions and compulsions.

As adults attempting to heal our inner child, we can visualize and surround this child with compassionate love and understanding. We can know the child's pain without becoming, denying, judging, resisting or fighting it. We can show them that we will not drown in their torrent of tears, nor abandon them in response to their rejection, confusion, fear and emptiness. Nor will we become defensive, offensive or die from their feelings of rage.

This patient, consistent acceptance and deeper awareness ultimately frees the inner child from pain and defenses. Inner child bonding and healing creates a new sense of safety which stimulates flexibility, resilience and growth for our adult self, bringing a sense of hope, lightness and vitality that softens suffering, promotes happiness and puts us in the fullness of life.

A book entitled, Recovery of Your Inner Child. The highly acclaimed method for liberating your inner self, by Lucia Capacchione, PHD., would be a helpful resource to guide you along the journey to find that special little girl or boy that you have hidden from the world so long ago.

According to Capacchione, as we develop a loving relationship with our inner child, the need to substitute Nurturing Parents in the outer world diminishes. We no longer put demands on our family or friends to do our inner parenting for us.

According to Frances Bingham, in the book Bedtime Stories for the inner child it is a valuable tool for healing for the neglected and possibly abused inner child in us all. Frances recommends that you ponder over these questions:

- When you talk to your inner child are you kind?
- Do you cause that child pain by being too hard on him/her?
- Are you taking care of the inner child physically or are you eating poorly and not setting time aside for some exercise?
- How about setting boundaries for him/her?
- Do you allow people to use you in many ways because you feel that you don't deserve better?

However, what is important to keep in mind is that you are not a BAD parent. You have only done the best you know how with the tools and the strength that you have up to this point. The good thing about the inner child is that s/he is always with you and never grows up. It is never too late to become reacquainted with that part of you. As Tony Robbins states, "It is never too late to have a happy childhood."

How Many Critical Parents Do You Have?

"Nobody can do anything to me that I am not already doing to myself."

–Eleanor Roosevelt–

The critical parent wears many faces and nicknames, depending on the person's family history. It may be a mother or father, a step-parent, uncle or aunt, caregiver, schoolteacher or employer. The critical parent says things to us like: "You're lazy." "You're so stupid." "Look at you; you're all skin and bones." "You'll never amount to anything."

The person's physical appearance is a favorite target of the critical parent, especially aspects of the body that cannot be changed." Even if we try to please the critical parent, it finds something else to criticize. It is never satisfied. It loves to name-call, point out faults, and pick on us. And it can be incredibly inventive in finding fault. The bottom line is that whatever we do, we are never good enough for the critical parent.

In conjunction to these role models, consequently we developed a critical parent within at an early age. It learned from all those people in our early environment who criticized, blamed, and shamed us. Parents and other authority figures told us we were naughty, bad, a nuisance, messy, stupid, a "mistake" (especially if we were unwanted.) These messages were reinforced year after year through repetition and constitute "brainwashing." They have literally been recorded in the mind and encoded in the body. When a child internalizes negative beliefs about him or herself, the Inner Critical parent is in basic training. It certainly damages our self-esteem, self-confidence and distorts our own belief system.

A wonderful medium for releasing anger without hurting others or the environment is ceramic clay or pottery. With it you can hit, throw, punch, pound, twist, poke, or chop safely without damaging it or yourself. With this type of art therapy it allows you to vent anger or rage but also feel a piece of Mother Earth which provides grounding effects.

Part 7: When Will I Feel Happy?

"When we are unhappy and our Life Conditions do not match our Blueprint,
we have three choices as to how we're going to handle the challenge."

–Anthony Robbins–

Think of your belief system like a map. Your beliefs tell you how you get from where you are to where you want to be. Or you might think there's a rule that says, "I've got to create the kind of relationship where there is always unconditional love, "or "I have to be aggressive, funny, giving, Etc."

We have a map or rulebook in our unconscious mind that guides us in how to meet our needs and meet our goals. This becomes the way we think we need to be to get what we want.

To change your fife, you must value one of your other needs more than the top two you value now.

If one of your top two needs is love, learning to value another need more doesn't mean that you don't want love, or shouldn't want it. But if your focus is, how can I GIVE love (which can meet the needs for significance, growth or contribution) instead of how do I GET love, you literally change the direction and, ultimately, the destination of your relationship or your life.

Your Identity

Your identity is who you are. It is your beliefs, your values, your behaviors patterns and how you apply these things in your life practice, your philosophy, your thinking process and how you interact with people you love and your children. It is simply the beliefs that we use to define our own individuality, what makes us unique—good, bad, or indifferent—from other individuals.

Since the core belief will be the ultimate filter to our perception. They will automatically control your life decisions which will drive our identity. So if you want to grow and be a better father, mother, husband and wife, persons you have to grow yourself by changing and challenging your beliefs, value, rules which will grow your identity.

The factor that brings your identity and your blueprint together is how you practice your thinking; the way your thoughts and emotions are expressed within your daily life. If interference is within you daily and your thoughts and emotions remain negative, your beliefs will remain and the identity of what you want will stagnate.

Your Blueprint

A blueprint is a fancy word for a picture of who we are. It may be distorted or clouded at times or very general when we try to focus upon it. That blueprint consists of intricacy detailed of this picture. That same picture is the full representation of what you believe interlaced with your rules and values to hold it in place. Some call it self-concept or self-image. That blueprint has the entire representation of your physical, mental, abilities, talents and your hopes and dreams. The "ideal" winner blueprint we were innately born with was shaped by both genetics and epigenetics and mostly something inherited; however, from all of this, we also enhanced the kind of person we became thru our interaction with learning from our environments.

When the picture is formed and becomes truth for us, it is hard to unwire that process because it is now under the management of the subconscious mind. We believe we cannot act any other ways. This will generate all efforts and energy towards that blueprint; our will power, abilities, concentration, determination, and conscious will be under the control of that picture. It is now set and under cruise control.

The subconscious mind is a willing servant. Without asking you why or other questions, it will guide you by your blueprint to where you are supposed to go. These are our life conditions and choices.

We experience happiness whenever our life conditions align with our blueprint. Since the blueprint is controlled by the subconscious mind and the life conditions are a representation for that blueprint, without knowing, we are "happy." But if there is an area of life that is causing you pain, it's because your life conditions do not match your Blueprint.

Since everybody is looking for the love/connection in some way, the perfect story for most would be to find your ideal mate, the essence of the dream you had as a young boy and young girl filled with unconditional love. This dream allowed you to truly follow your heart, compassion, peace and hope to share with that person and the world. For others, the love-connection can be in the form of true and lasting friendship.

To know and value true happiness and joy, you at some point have to endure some sadness and pain. If you have never had the absence of "all things being good" then at some point it is taken for granted. Some of the happiest people are those that have in fact been through "hell and high waters." The appreciation for the smallest amount of peace or gladness is magnified within them because it is filling up those empty spaces where they have omitted the disappointments, or destruction (internal and external.)

Reward vs. punishment lies in the meaning to the person, their emotions and beliefs. The mind is exceptional in that it works as a type of decipher in the decision making process.

How you do really determine the difference between good and bad, excitement or anger, passion or bossiness? The meaning of each of these will change in every person creating a different response or reaction because of their blueprint. Undetected by even ourselves, we are the constant feeder of our mind in it that we are reading the guidelines for the reasoning behind why we do what we do. The consciousness of your blueprint will ultimately give you control over what direction you head instead of being guided subconsciously by unserving values, beliefs or rules.

The message here is not that you have to be a Master of Blueprints, but that you can configure yours to work for you in your favor. You may need a slight adjustment or possibly a fresh new pallet, but in either case just identify what impacts your blueprint. When you are able to access the three forces that unconsciously guide you through life and consciously redirect such influences, you can make dramatic life changes with regards to experiencing abundance, joy and peace, by avoiding certain difficulties, and even eliminating pain.

Change Your Blueprint

Sometimes things are outside of your control, but you can control how you configure your rules about how things should be. Your happiness is going to be limited if you want success but aren't willing to ever be judged or want love but distrust the opposite sex. Sometimes adjusting your blueprint means compromising some of your rules that are difficult for you and others to live up to, or that may be simply impossible to fulfill.

When it comes to the three choices you face on how to handle a problem, the first choice isn't really a choice at all. Blame leaves you stuck, spinning your wheels with no options to change as you tell yourself, "There's nothing I can do about it because ..." We all use blame at times, but the quicker you can get out of it, the faster you'll be empowered to either change your life conditions or change your perspective, both of which are real, tangible options that can instantly transform a relationship, your career, your finances or your life.

The most exciting thing about the blueprint is that you can reprogram it and even better by understanding it now, you can teach your child to change it as they grow. You can change the mental picture that was created by all the outside sources and change the end result and the final experience of the game.

The reason why the changes were difficult or unobtainable is because you were changing the environment and the people around you where the issues were the limiting beliefs inside of you. It is not only positive thinking that will change the results from a poor self-concept it truly takes accountable to become empowered!

The tools used to change your beliefs and the self-image have been used for thousands of years however it is recently that we figure how they worked. These tools are discussed within this book as preliminary for the most part because the translation is not complete as of now.

What Life Do You and Your Child Deserve?

"The cosmos will always mirror back to us whatever your inner state is. The greater the love we discover in ourselves, the greater the love will reflect back to us from the environment through others"

–Deepak Chopra, MD–

Like Deepak Chopra states above, what we reflect to the world it is reflected back. If your inner self projects chaos then events and your surrounding will bring chaos surrounding you. Happiness and joy will be reflecting back into your life only if your inner self is happy and joyful. Our emotion is what controls our state and reflects our state of consciousness.

In culture and religion there are some shared beliefs, regardless of the denomination or lack thereof. Commonalities are the foundational beliefs that there is power in your words and the ability to speak life or death over a situation, manifesting the desires of your heart, and also reaping what you sow. Fervent "prayer" in context is the ideal of the Law of Attraction, like attracts like and expressing your feelings of gratitude in or towards a desired situation's outcome as if it were already so.

In the classic book Think and Grow Rich by Napoleon Hill, he talks about the conception that people will attract what they think about most of the time. If you are always in a negative state, and pessimism is your mantra, then you will always get that as you have created it and built the path for it to follow straight into your life. On the other hand, if you are positive and hopeful, you will in return receive positivity and goodwill. Again, the meaning will be different for everyone as to how they will choose to deal with it; do negative forces still surround positive people? Yes, however, they may see it as "inconvenient" or "an opportunity to grow."

Prejudgments of other people can also create an internal conflict within ourselves as we perceive a person's character as one way based on how we judged instead of who they really were which later created a disappointment in that we were expecting something else altogether. This disaster (for some), or inconvenient set back (for others) is the result of an overwhelming state of conscious and subconscious thoughts.

Sometimes our "levels of competency" may either work for or against us. When we are unconsciously incompetent we don't know what we don't know. In this case we are aloof, or ignorant. Eventually we become consciously incompetent now we know there's something we don't know whether it was brought to our attention by someone or a situation. Once you are at that level 2, you start to learn and grow thereby making you consciously competent you now know and with knowing you know how to "do" or "act" or proceed.

Eventually you become so good at whatever that is, you are so focused on it that you are gravitationally pulled toward it with no effort, then creating an unconscious competence you are a natural, but you are now on "autopilot." You don't have to think about it, you just do it without effort, and that is what Stephen R. Covey constitutes as "The Habits of Highly Effective People."

Being able to focus your energy is like your levels of competency, at first you didn't know you could control it, and then you learned you could, then you figured out how, and eventually did it without pause.

When you are in the unconscious competency stage you are at risk of losing that control because you stop thinking, you stop practicing, you stop learning. You will face challenges and obstacles even with the possession of positive energy, but you must always be conscientious of the fact that we don't know everything, there is always something new to consider, and in that there will be cause for alternative actions. That is why we should all be lifelong learners; there is always something to learn from everyone that crosses your path.

The power to change or speak life, or even manifest the desire of your heart are all inside of us, but if there is no love, it will be an even greater conflict ahead. The most powerful emotion that can heal is love. Although the meaning of the word will be different for everyone, no matter what the definition, it is a basic human need. When a person lacks love for themselves it will not only affect them internally but externally. You can't give what you don't possess and you can't tell someone how to love you if you don't know how to love yourself. It would be impossible because you would never be satisfied in that you don't know "what or how."

The universe is said to focus like a mirror, sending us back the images and thoughts we put before it. Deepak says that even your friends, relatives, and colleagues can act as mirrors. He doesn't stop there but goes on to say it can even be in your passion, your hidden talents or anything in your life. This has been the essence of "The Secret" – The Law of Attraction.

"The Winner's Creed" by Tony Robbins is based on some of the affirmations found in Napoleon Hill's book "Think and Grow Rich" that can help change the reflections coming from your mirror.
- I know that I have the ability to achieve my definite purpose in life: Therefore I demand of myself, persistent, continuous action towards its attainment and I here and now promise to render such action.
- I fully realize that no wealth or position will long endure unless it is built upon truth and justice; Therefore I will engage in no transaction which does not benefit all to whom it effects.
- I am succeeding by attracting to myself the forces I wish to use and the cooperation of other people.
- I induce others to serve me because of my willingness to serve others.
- I eliminate hatred, envy, jealousy, selfishness, cynicism, anger, and fear by developing a true love for all humanity, because I know that a negative attitude towards others will never bring me success.
- I cause others to believe in me because I believe in them and believe in myself.
- This is my creed, my quest. To never stop striving for the top. To always keep moving forward. To always be the very best I can be.
- I am the power. I am the magic. I cannot be stopped. I am a winner.

- I promise to always be true to myself because I am the creator and master of my universe and I am responsible for making a positive difference in the world and to the quality of life in it.
  I live in constant and never-ending improvement.

Part 8: Your New Identity Blueprint

The Fundamentals of Being an Introvert vs. Extrovert

According to the "Identity Blueprint"; power, heart, mind, harmony, knowledge, passion, and action are the traits of the 14 personality types that are paired and analyzed by the "Identity Blueprint" profiling tool. Once you recognize the fundamentals behind each type you have more compassion for why your personality prefers introversion vs. extroversion and you can begin to understand and appreciate everyone else's differences.

This is a delicate process and you will need to be as objective as one can be. Familiarize yourself with the characteristics of both personality types, what are the strengths and weaknesses. This balance will be necessary to enhance your fullest potential. Too much focus on either (strengths/weaknesses) will alter the outcome or final analysis because any weakness may be countered with the enhancement of strengths and vice versa.

Determining which personality type your are will give you a greater advantage in parenting because you are able to not only 'parent' your 'inner child' but effectively influence the empowerment within your own children, giving them the ability to independently take on new challenges and opportunities so that they may achieve greater success and ultimately live life more meaningfully as if it were already created. By doing this, you become more aware of the people that you allow in your inner circle and the environment in which they choose to associate with you, which indirectly may impact the growth of your interrelationships and career.

The Hero Motivated By Power - Become a Manager or a Pioneer

According to the "Identity Blueprint," as an introvert, if you are a manager, motivated by power, you will likely enjoy the role of being at the center of events, as the person who makes the most critical decisions, but without necessarily having to carry them out in practice. You get excited when there is controversy, because it gives you the opportunity to assert yourself firmly and demonstrate your ability to stay firmly on course. A famous manager is Andrew Carnegie.

As an extrovert, if you are a pioneer, motivated by power, you are someone who loves to spearhead a campaign and set new standards within one's field. If you are a pioneer, you are a living example of the breakthrough power that emerges from your courage, drive, and willingness to take risks and push yourself to an extreme for your cause. A famous pioneer is Bruce Lee.

The Illuminator Motivated By your Heart - Become a Guide or a Helper

According to the "Identity Blueprint," as an introvert, if you are a guide, displaying heart, you will display your heart in your services. Your efforts will bring forth insight that promotes growth. You are in your element when it involves enhancing your quality of life and emphasizing the principle values in your life and the lives of others. You nourish your self-confidence when you see people unfold their potential. You inspire others by being authentic and reliable and by being someone who enhances competence through understanding and involvement. A famous guide is Dr. Maria Montessori.

As an extrovert, if you are a helper, displaying heart, you will derive deep satisfaction from providing your assistance to others and assisting in meeting their needs. It brings out the best in you when you can help to encourage thoughtfulness and bring about well-being and peace of mind. Your outgoing friendliness is a distinctive force that you can always utilize to promote good relations and to establish collaboration and a spirit of fellowship. You develop your most important competencies as a colleague, partner and friend in these ways. Two famous helpers are Princess Diana and Oprah Winfrey.

The Genius Motivated By the Mind - Become a Thinker or a Strategist

According to the "Identity Blueprint," as an introvert, if you are a thinker motivated by the mind then it will come to light through your deep comprehension and ability to examine things to understand their causes and effects. You will find it "easy" to generate ideas, and that will build your self-confidence that you have an innovative intellect that can be applied to diverse innovations and problem solving. A famous thinker is Isaac Newton.

As an extrovert, if you are a strategist motivated by the mind then you will increase your self-confidence and build reserves of energy by engaging in communication and networking activities that stimulate your proficiency at multitasking. You thrive by calculating various scenarios and conceiving one of the most brilliant, efficient courses of action. That which advances intelligent solutions makes you responsive and gets you into a creative flow. Two famous strategists are Ted Turner, founder of CNN and Henry Kissinger.

The Artist Motivated By the Harmony - Become an Aesthete or a Transformer

According to the "Identity Blueprint," as an introvert, if you are an aesthete motivated by harmony in all of its forms, you will experience joy and self-confidence when you take the opportunity to create and design things that are uplifting and that bring about a living balance. You are in your element when you can commune with beauty and express it throughout your life and activities in your unique and original way. You can also express your need for harmony through your ability to create positive interpersonal relationships in which differences are valued. Two famous esthetes are Coco Chanel and Johann Sebastian Bach.

As an extrovert, if you are a Transformer motivated by harmony in all of its forms, you will throw yourself into everything you encounter to explore its hidden potential, particularly things that can be found in chaos and crisis, and which may appear ugly, dark and strange. It excites you to explore contrasts because you can see that there is more to uncover and transform than what is visible on the surface, and that within a state of disharmony, there lays an opportunity for harmony. Two famous Transformers are Lady Gaga and Katy Perry.

The Explorer Motivated By Knowledge - Become an Investigator or the Specialist

According to the "Identity Blueprint," as an introvert, if you are an Investigator motivated by knowledge, you will be in familiar territory when you immerse yourself completely and absolutely in a defined area of research, and discover new data and reveal facts that have never before been available. It arouses your deep interest and brings forth your strongest competencies when you can produce facts that reveal and explain how conditions and facts function and how new information can create new, practical applications. Two famous Investigators are Nicola Tesla and Sigmund Freud.

As an extrovert, if you are a specialist motivated by knowledge, you are on the right track when you can rethink and improve the ways in which your field of practice functions. You are possibly very skilled at getting the technical and methodological aspects of your work to function in a logical, effective manner. You are governed by an irrepressible curiosity about how and why things or relationships function the ways that they do and you have a strong urge to examine this. A famous Specialist is Alexander Graham Bell.

The Visionary Motivated By Passion - Become an Idealist or an Advocate

According to the "Identity Blueprint," as an introvert, if you are an Idealist motivated by passion, you will experience happiness when you pursue an ideal that is your interpretation of what is best. This gives you the self-confidence to aim for your goals and you enjoy being recognized as someone who gives everything to a cause. You probably also like to be a living example of devotion and loyalty for the cause you champion. You have a brilliant ability to visualize the ideal and imagine a future filled with possibilities. A famous Idealist is Mother Teresa.

As an extrovert, if you are an advocate motivated by passion, you will have a need to struggle for a cause that you campaign for earnestly and with all of your talents. You willingly enter into conflicts, and with your heartfelt engagement, you achieve self-confidence and strength by expressing your sense of purpose and forceful convictions. Exceeding limitations and excelling at whatever you do brings you great happiness. Two famous Advocates are Rosa Parks and Malcolm X.

The Creator Motivated By Action - Become The Creator of Order or the Organizer

According to the "Identity Blueprint," as an introvert, if you are a Creator of Order motivated by action, you will organize and systemize things, you are in harmony with your true self. You become excited and fully engaged when you can establish order out of chaos and streamline things into patterns and channels that ensure functionality, a broad overview and efficiency. It can build up your confidence when you are the one who ensures a high degree of practical elegance. A famous Creator of Order is Andrew Carnegie.

As an extrovert, if you an organizer motivated by action, you are in an optimal position when you can specifically create something new and produce visible results that are solid and which can change the world. You gain self-confidence by acting as a conductive force that creates forms and produces new products. Organizing is your core impetus and your creative impulse. Two famous Organizers are Clint Eastwood and Zhang Xin (One of China's women billionaires.)

What Are Your Strengths and Weaknesses – Talents and Obstacles

According to Nybo, Hauge, and Sorensen's, "Identity Blueprint," as a prerequisite for making an impact in life, you need to know what you are best at doing. Is your special talent breakthrough power, empathy or inventiveness?

Our greatest limitations are often related to our greatest potential. Did you know that the limiters related to inflexibility conflict aversion can become cooperation or that chaotic behavior can be balanced and become spontaneity if you can properly convert them to strengths? We all experience limitations or "weaknesses", but few people realize that underneath a limiter lies a specific talent.

The Hero's Strengths and Weaknesses

According to the "Identity Blueprint," some of the characteristics of the Hero's talents include: leadership, natural authority, breakthrough power, goal orientation, firmness, courage, strength and drive. Some of the Hero's limitations if left unchecked include: power hungriness, suppression, inflexibility, impatience, isolation, recklessness, willfulness and brutality.

The Hero's Strengths
- You have the ability to take the lead and show the way. You inspire new action by taking responsibility, leading the way, generating initiatives and motivating others to take leadership of their lives.
- You find it natural to be the person in the forefront and prepare the way because you remove obstacles and liberate resources. For you, taking action and achieving triumph is crucial. You know how to get straight to the point and move forward.
- You have the ability to be unshakeable with calm and collected strength. You do this by being self-contained and even-handed. Like a fortress, you hold fast and preserve the peace. You have reinforcing effect on others.

The Hero's Weaknesses (Opportunities for Improvements)
- You have a tendency to become extremely irritable and restless when things do not happen at the pace you prefer. You can really be pushy when you have decided to act as you wish. Your impatience is due to your one-track mindedness and limits you. Your hidden potential is goal-orientation.
- You have a tendency to force your opinions and agenda on others when you are under pressure or out of balance. This will breed discontent and opposition. You make the mistake of suppressing those around you, and then their talents do not come into play. Your hidden potential is breakthrough power.

- You have a tendency to end up in isolation, because you insist on doing things in your own way. The reason for this is your inclination to go it alone. You lack contact with others, and in the long run, this will cost you a great deal of energy and you will become incapable of decisive action. Your hidden potential is firmness.

The Illuminator's Strengths and Weaknesses

According to the "Identity Blueprint," some of the characteristics of the Illuminator's talents include: empathy, insightfulness, compassion, cooperation, sensitivity, sensuality, comforting and consideration. Some of the Illuminator's limitations if left unchecked include: glamour, seduction, vagueness, hyper-sensitivity, conflict averseness, timidity, dependency, and accumulation.

The Illuminator's Strengths

- You have a special ability to understand people's motives, to assess the scope of a situation and to comprehend various aspects in the greater context of life. Your sympathy is inclusive and empathetic and you have a psychological understanding of human life.
- You have a great deal of tact and find it "easy" to relate to others in an appreciative manner. You are open, patient and know how to create friendly interaction. You are conscious of human qualities.
- You are a person who manages the physical resources and brings a sense of well-being to the people with whom you are in contact. With your concern for others in focus, you have the ability to set up a pleasant and secure framework in which people feel relieved, protected and improved.

The Illuminator's Weaknesses (Opportunities for Improvements)

- You are inclined to avoid disagreement, because you find it difficult to be in discord and disagreement. Therefore, you make the mistake of avoiding others rather than getting into a dispute. Your hidden potential is cooperation.
- You have a strong tendency to focus too much on safety and security because you are afraid of pain and discomfort. This makes you extremely vulnerable in a way that weakens you. Your hidden potential is consideration.
- You have a tendency not to be aware of your own needs and limits, because your radar picks up the needs of others. Therefore, you become vulnerable and sensitive when you let the conditions of others influence you. Your hidden potential is Sensitivity.

The Genius' Strengths and Weaknesses

According to the "Identity Blueprint," some of the characteristics of the Genius' talents include: innovation, breadth of view, information, inventiveness, networking activity, observation, versatility, planning and economizing. Some of the genius' limitations if left unchecked include: brooding, indifference, manipulation, conspiracy, cynicism, ineffectiveness, inattentive, and confusion.

The Genius' Strengths

- You are naturally gifted at thinking in the abstract and in depth. You have a flair for working with complexity and an eye for all the connections and patterns that are involved. You think things through, carefully reflect and put things into perspective.
- One of your natural strengths is that you are an innovative, original thinker and you detect and devise new prospects. You have a flair for interpretation, getting inspiring ideas and coming up with new concepts.
- You are well-prepared and have a flair for taking many things into consideration. You have a distinct ability to work with scenarios, trends opportunities, since you form specific plans that can be carried out intelligently and with minimal expenditure of energy.

The Genius' Weaknesses (Opportunities for Improvements)
- You have a tendency to be too taken up by different lines of thought and possibilities. Because of this restless mobility, you are not able to achieve anything. You do not see things through to completion and do not achieve any results. Your hidden potential is planning.
- Your ability to see many possibilities and see things from many angles and to take in the complexity of life means that you are often perplexed, especially when you have to make decision. The result is inaction, which clearly limits you. Your hidden potential is economizing.
- You have an inclination to scan the surrounding environment for information, and glide over the surface without getting deeply involved. You do this because you believe that it gives you greater freedom, but it actually limits you. Your hidden potential is attentiveness.

The Artist's Strengths and Weaknesses

According to the "Identity Blueprint," some of the characteristics of the Artist's talents include: harmony, sensitivity to beauty, peace maker, balancing, communication, disclosure, imagination and gracefulness and spontaneity. Some of the Artist's limitations if left unchecked include: self-centeredness, anxious to please, instability, dramatization, flattery, provocation, unpredictability and chaos.

The Artist's Strengths
- You have the ability to bring about peace by entering into conflicts and discovering what can bring forth harmony and beauty. You do this by expressing yourself and identifying with others, and by bringing about healing and reconciliation between opposites.
- You have the ability to imagine what is behind different kinds of human behavior. This gives you the ability to understand conflicts and dramas, human interactions and how to bring about harmonious relationships.
- You have a lively ability to express yourself in a captivating, relevant manner, just as you can become involved in the lives and activities of others with tact. You are fully attentive and can grasp meanings and express yourself vividly.

The Artist's Weaknesses (Opportunities for Improvements)
- You are inclined to go far to maintain peace and tolerance. Therefore, you appeal to the sympathy of others to avoid unpleasant situations. Your fixation on pleasantries is a major limiter for your growth. Your hidden potential is Peacemaker.

- You have a tendency to try to be the center of attention. Seeking special interest from others is connected with a lack of connections with your inner core. Therefore, you are limited by the surface image. Your hidden potential is sensitivity to beauty.
- You have an inclination to be disorganized and unstructured, which means that things are scattered inside and around you. You become a victim of chaotic states of being and situations, which limits your freedom and frustrates you. Your hidden potential is spontaneity.

The Explorer's Strengths and Weaknesses

According to the "Identity Blueprint," some of the characteristics of the Explorer's talents include: knowledge, objectivity, analyzing, reflection, discrimination, detachment, impartiality and discipline. Some of the Explorer's limitations if left unchecked include: coldness, critical, one-sidedness, scornful, insensitivity, ruthlessness, severity and automation.

The Explorer's Strengths
- You provide thoroughness and perseverance. You are motivated by a need to know all the details related to whatever occupies you. This will give you a serious depth that compels respect from those around you.
- Your possess good craftsman like skills, as well as a thoroughness and persistence that are motivated by your need to know all the details related to whatever engages you. This will give you a serious depth that compels the respect of others.
- Being practical, functional and examining are your powerful talents. You have a flair for technical and mechanical matters, and go about things methodically and with precision. With accurate information and knowledge of details, you gain expertise.

The Explorer's Weaknesses (Opportunities for Improvements)
- You are extremely focused on a sense of justice, which has a negative social impact. At times you are mercilessly hostile and unforgiving. Not only does your hardness damage others, it also makes you anything but kind to yourself. Your hidden potential is impartiality.
- You have an inclination to be condescending toward factors that cannot be analyzed or measured scientifically. This makes you overly critical, and you risk dissecting and being arrogant. Your hidden potential is analysis.
- You have a tendency to be insensitive, because you focus on single-mindedly on knowledge, facts and objectivity. This means that you can lack the warmth and empathy that you need in relations with others, and with yourself. Your hidden potential is Objectivity.

The Visionary's Strengths and Weaknesses

According to the "Identity Blueprint," some of the characteristics of the Visionary's talents include: commitment, dedication, engagement, idealization, promotion, devotion, passion, optimization and energy. Some of the Visionary's limitations if left unchecked include: agitation, extremism, naivety, perfectionism and fierceness.

The Visionary's Strengths

- You have a special ability to follow your heart with unconditional dedication. With your committed focus on living up to your ideals, you can inspire others, and your enthusiasm and intensity are uplifting and bring happiness.
- You have a special ability to invest all of your loyalty and emotional intensity toward whatever you have set your sights on. You are deeply connected to your mission in life, and you dedicate yourself to it completely.
- You have the ability to see the potential in everything that you are occupied with, and are thus proficient at optimizing it. With this talent, you improve the quality and the process involved of everything with which you are engaged.

The Visionary's Weaknesses (Opportunities for Improvements)

- You sometimes impose very high demands for perfection on yourself, on those around you, or on whatever you are occupied with. If you have fantasies that are not based on a solid foundation, then you risk being disappointed and difficult to work with. Your hidden potential is Optimization.
- You can be so incredibly intense that you end up driving your body and mind beyond your limits. You disregard important warning signals, and your tough approach is forceful and impedes your progress. Your hidden potential is being energetic.
- You can have a tendency to be an impractical dreamer, who focuses on far off horizons, but you make the mistake of failing to perform everyday tasks in favor of idealistic wishful thinking. Your hidden potential is being noble.

The Creator's Strengths and Weaknesses

According to the "Identity Blueprint," some of the characteristics of the Creator's talents include: designing, systematic, conducting, coordination, organization, elegance, facilitation, love of order, and manifestation. Some of the Creator's limitations if left unchecked include: bureaucracy, dictatorship, overregulation, over control, extravagance, over servicing, fixation on routine and fixation on results.

The Creator's Strengths

- You have a special ability to think in patterns and to coordinate and unify various factors so that things move in a shared direction. You get things to unite, so that everything forms a synthesis and brings forth the best results.
- You have a distinct talent for combining mastery of detail with a breadth of view. You guide things in the right direction and assembling everything so that the best possible order emerges. You are innovative and you structure and organize things with great ease.
- You have a distinct ability to work for practical change. You generate innovation and use your creative skills to organize and produce visible results. You are aware that specific action and recognition stem from optimal flow.

The Creator's Weaknesses

- You have a tendency to be overly fixated on systems and to follow fixed and mandatory rules. The result is that you get stuck in bureaucratic rigidity that shuts out innovation and growth. Your hidden potential is being systematic.
- Your need for order and control makes you inclined to direct and organize for others. In this way, you end up over-servicing those around you to such a degree that all creativity disappears. Your hidden potential is facilitation.
- You have a distinct inclination to control and check things that you are involved with, to such a degree that you become trapped in a mechanic, inhibited state of being, which is very inhibitive. Your hidden potential is organization.

Part 9: Emotion of Healing

Seed of Hope

"If we believe that tomorrow will be better, we can bear a hardship today."

–Thich Nhat Hanh–

"Each time a man stands up for an ideal, or acts to improve the lot of others, or strikes out against injustice, he sends forth a tiny ripple of hope, and crossing each other from a million different centers of energy and daring, those ripples build a current which can sweep down the mightiest walls of oppression and resistance."

–Robert F. Kennedy–

Shane J. Lopez, PhD., the guru in the field of psychology of hope, states that the emotion of hope encompasses awe, excitement along with joy. Dr. Lopez has a wonderful resource to guide you on the journey to attain hope into your life. The book is entitled, "Making Hope Happen – Create the Future You Want for Yourself and Others." Hope plays a vital factor for leading a healthier and happier lifestyle. It is an important element for predicting the success in relationships, academics, business ventures as well as the overall success in your career. Hope requires an active choice and an active role in order for it to serve its purpose as a life determinant factor.

People with hope believe that they have the power to make the future better than their current situations. One of the best predictors for humanity's well-being is reflected within hope, since it brings about future ideas and energy. People that are more optimistic and hopeful are capable of developing more strategies to assist them with attaining their goals and contributing to the betterment of society.

They ensure that their dreams become a reality because they implement contingency plans along the way in case obstacles surmount. They do not allow anything to deter their future plans. They perceive challenges as opportunities to be overcome and believe in its mission and garner support to ensure that dreams do become a reality.

The field of hope has been studied within the psychological arena since 1991. The Hope Theory was coined by the eminent positive psychologist Charles R. Snyder and his colleagues. Life is often filled with ups and downs and may be difficult for those without the proper coping mechanisms for stress; therefore, hope is important to ensure they persevere.

Simply having dreams or ideas is not enough, one must also establish goals; however, goals alone are futile unless there are mechanisms for ensuring that step-by-step actions will be implemented to ensure accountability. Hope allows people to approach issues with the proper mindset providing them with the proper strategy-set to succeed, thus increasing the chances that they will actually accomplish their destiny in life.

Some people go thru life adopting mastery goals because they are not firm believers in hope. These people choose "easy" tasks so that they do not have to demonstrate abilities for growth and prefer mundane and routine work versus challenging opportunities to be creative. This is the difference between a job and a career. For these people quitting is a repeated mechanism they use to cope with any indications of potential failures.

These people exhibit the victim mentality, acting helpless and hopeless; believing that they have a lack of controlling over their environment and as such do not take full accountability. Since they lack hope, they do not believe that the type of future they envisioned would be possible. They are often paralyzed with fear or worst suicidal tendencies because they look at perspectives from the short-term span only and often neglect to see the bigger long-term perspective in life.

People with high hope have a more positive psychological outlook. They are more adept with dealing with change and experience more positive ranges of emotions that foster optimism and future outlooks. These people tend to envision a strategy for resolving problems so that their life can be propelled to the next level in terms of the quality of life. They avoid allowing fear or uncalculated risks to hinder their creative abilities for fostering innovative solutions to life's challenges.

People filled with high hope and big dreams have an unlimited source of creativity that helps them churn out novel ideas. These people's hopeful thinking process improves when they are challenged to resolve some of today's issues at hand or when they are asked to create products/services that help make the future better. These people are often gifted with the art of persuasion and can market their ideas successfully to other people, inclusive of employees, investors, business partners and consumers.

Did you know that by setting a small ripple of hope in someone's life that you can cause a ripple effect across the community or even the nation? By helping someone sows the seeds of hope; it can produce a brighter future. However, this would require an active role where you will have to get off the sideline and take some massive actions. Have you ever heard yourself thinking, "I wish that problem would go away" or "I wish someone would do something about that issue" or "I wish that person would catch a break" this is your signal to become an advocator and to properly spread hope across the globe.

If you truly have a dream and want to make a difference, recruit one or more friends to help define and address an issue by empowering others with a viable solution; and allow the change to become permeable around the community. Ripples of hope truly stand out and grab people's attention. Hope inspires others to start ripples of their own and creating a ripple to homes, schools, businesses or community will help make this world a better place for your children and grandchildren.

At the very least share your story of hope so that it may inspire others to live a more meaningful life. Did you know that hopeful people perform 12% better at school, produced 14% more productivity at work and are 10% happier overall.

Visualize Your Dream – Hope Odyssey

A great resource tool that was designed by Dr. Lopez allows someone with a dream coupled with intense hope to rally up the troops and can truly make a difference within the community. This tool is powerful for visualizing your dreams, allowing it to become your story board (http://shanelopez.com/hope-odyssey.) This tool is based on the sciences of goal setting, pre-commitment strategies and implementation of intentions. This tool is built to help you and your teams visualize the future you want.

This application provides for future forecasting using imagery so that you can pre-live the future by seeing its visionary impact. It allows you to imagine the path required for creating your future. It identifies potential obstacles and sirens that may distract and undermine your abilities. It allows you to assemble a crew of supporters for this journey. Then it allows you to share this dream with others using Facebook and Twitter. With this visionary tool it can help propel your dreams into the future by establishing a concrete vision that causes you to take accountability for producing.

Maum Meditation

The founder of Maum Meditation, Teacher Woo Myung is the bestselling author and poet of numerous books. In 2002, he was awarded with the Mahatma Gandhi Peace prize and appointed as the world peace ambassador for his dedication and contribution of Maum Meditation for society. This meditation technique provides a method of introspection and actualization of peace for all of humanity.

Depression, which is the lack of hope and stress are often both combated with the art of Maum Meditation, which impacts the majority of populations across the globe. The root issue with depression and stress often occurs from stored images in your mind that may have caused former hardships and conflict, yet they are no longer of service to you to hold onto. When you cleanse your mind, the states of depression are alleviated and stress is instantaneously reduced.

Within the human mind and body, are accumulation of pictures that were accumulated via all your five senses thru the eyes, nose, ears, mouth and body. When we have an accumulation of falsified pictures, our world becomes distorted and impacts our thoughts, emotions, desires, behaviors and overall health. Even though fear (false evidence appearing real) is normally the driving emotion that deters one off their destined path or may leave a feeling of paralysis within their lives, many still hold fast to this emotion as if it is their life-line. This is why it is important to read and listen to uplifting information, because we are all capable of empathetic emotions and as such many become intertwine into the vortex of the lower energies such as fear, anger and shame/guilt and grief without realizing there are other options if they only dared to hope.

Since the human mind is often intertwined with these thoughts, the method of Maum Meditation, allows you to slowly subtract and free up any distorted perceptions (images) that are no longer of value for your well-being, so that you will no longer be playing back the same negative messages in your mind. You will then find freedom and your true purpose of life, allowing you to reach the state of being hopeful for your future.

"Hold fast to dreams for when dreams die, life is but a broken wing bird that cannot fly."

–Langston Hughes–

Compassion Is In Your Genes

"Be Kind Whenever Possible. It is always possible."

–Dalai Lama–

It is within our human nature to be repelled by those who are different. Like other animals, we tend to stick to our own kind. We also bond easily based on the law of perceived commonalities such as ethnicity, gender, culture, religion, Etc. Historically it was believed that because of that bond, you have a higher chance of survival if you stick with your own kind and avoid those who are very different from yourself.

If you can find a way to be more tolerant of those who are different from you and even feel some level of love for them, your own life becomes better. By this process, we need to replace our negative thoughts by positive ones. Hate/Jealous will be replaced by love. Suspicion will be replaced by faith; disorganization will be replaced by order. Despair will be replaced by hope for life.

The easiest way to control your own judgmental nature is to realize that you never have the full story. If you knew everything a person had experienced in his/her life, it would be very difficult to feel hatred for him/her. We need to put ourselves into someone else's shoes since we are not living their life and cannot fully understand what is going on in their heads and the motivation behind their actions. So it's best simply to accept things as they happen, to accept people as they enter or exit from your life, not attaching a negative meaning to the incident and live your life to its fullest, treating each experience as an element of surprise.

Self-Compassion

Did you know that Lady Gaga, one of the biggest pop icons of this generation, revealed that she was bulimic in high school, desperate to transform herself from "a voluptuous little Italian girl" to a "skinny little ballerina?" According to Jean Fain LICSW, MSW from the Huffington Post, she couldn't appreciate her naturally curvaceous body and almost permanently damaged her vocal cords and her health because she was so upset with the perception of her image. The saving grace was her yoga teacher taught her to have 15 minutes of compassionate thoughts about herself and when she learned the art of that coupled with finding self-love, her life flourished and the person that is in front of you today represents her true nature.

Compassion for Others

In the United State about 13 million children are affected by bullying each year, pointing to an urgent desperate need to develop the skills of compassion. According to Dr. Charlotte Reznick, when kids appear cold-hearted, when they seem to not care about the suffering of others, and sometimes even inflict that suffering upon themselves, they are often detached from feelings altogether for themselves as well as others. It's as if their hearts are closed. So connecting with, and opening their heart is key and crucial in the cultivation of both self-compassion and compassion for others. Bullies are using physical demeanor that are learned but they were not born with these characteristics. Since they did not have positive/compassionate role models in their live to nurture their inner child, they have in turn had to fend for themselves in life and became defensive lashing out at others.

Moving Meditation

Charlotte Reznick, PhD. has pioneered Imagery for Kids (http://www.imageryforkids.com/about.html) which is a breakthrough for learning, creativity, and empowerment. Her audio programs, "Discovering Your Special Place" and "Creating a Magical Garden and Healing Pond," provide guided meditations for de-stressing your children. Dr. Reznick shares a meditation that often can be done taking a walk or while walking a dog.

You start with focusing on yourself (self-compassion,)move to thinking about and bringing up an image of an inspiring person or mentor, then a loved one, followed by a neutral person, and finally think about someone you have difficulty with respecting or associating with in life. One repeats the series of sentences five times (for the five people you are thinking about.) And if there's not a lot of time, just focus on fewer people. A softening of the heart occurs, and kindness and compassion develop organically.

"May I be happy? May I be calm? May I be safe? May I be peaceful? May I live easily?" As you move along to each person, substitute the name and image of that person. For example, "May (name of person you're thinking about) be happy. May (name) be calm…" and so on.

Maureen Dawn Healy, author of Growing Happy Kids (www.growinghappykids.com), designed a Bedtime Story that you can readily share with your children to help promote compassion in their lives. Along with her traditional credentials in Psychology and an MBA; Maureen is a Reiki Master and works with Energy Medicine. She specializes in instilling creativity in children and assisting to bring out the best in highly sensitive children. She worked with refugees in Tibet mentored by His Holiness the fourteenth Dalai Lama.

The "Loving-Kindness Bed Time Story" meditation is designed by Dr. Maureen Healy.

[Read by parent to child]

Today, we are going to do something new. It's called a loving-kindness meditation where we send love and positive energy to parents and kids in other places.

You may leave your eyes open or closed whatever is more comfortable for you.

First, think of something you REALLY love. It may be a puppy, playing on the swings, singing your favorite song or playing on the WEI system. Make sure you really FEEL that feeling. It is the feeling of a happy heart. Do you feel it? [Wait for a YES] Great!

Now, let's send that loving energy picture it like a ball of light to other living beings to help them feel loved and lift their spirits. Do you want to start with your **friends**? [Wait for a yes] Great! Let's name them, Kayla, Peter, Joey, Suzy, Sam and so on.

Now, let's send this feeling of love to your **family members** like Grandma and Cousin Charlie. Let's name them together: Dad, Maria, Sister Sally, and so on... Great Job!

Now, let's send those feel-good feelings to people in our **community** like teachers, and neighbors. Would you like to start? [Wait for YES, or get the "ball rolling" with teachers]. Name them...

You are so powerful and great at doing this that we can also together send our loving energy to other **parents, kids and animals all over planet earth** especially to those kids and people who need it most.

Let's send this loving and healing energy to: Kids all around the planet! Specifically, let's send love to kids that are hungry, sad, have tummy aches, are upset and need a friend - especially the kids in Japan where there was a tidal wave or tsunami.

We can now do the same thing for parents everywhere let's send our love to parents in the mountains, in the desert, in the valleys and on the beach. Specially, let's name places - like Egypt, China, Africa, Europe, United States, and especially places like Japan, Afghanistan, Iraq, Libya and the Middle Eastern nations. These are where parents need extra love right now.

Wow, you are great at this! The last beings we will send love to tonight are the animals on planet Earth. Would you like to do this? [Wait for yes] Great! Let's start with dolphins, whales, hawks, butterflies, ladybugs, praying mantises, turtles and what else? Name them...

All of this loving energy you "put out" into the world through your mind is AMAZING. It has great power. You are full of light, love and power!

Good night."

The Attitude of Gratitude

The latest generation of kids, appear to be challenging parents with the "entitlement mentality." According to Dr. Lynn Namka, this may be a temporary phase that many children will go through but outgrow with the proper nurturance. It is common for infants and younger children to explore their environments because their brain and body is constantly growing and as such demands stimulation and guidelines for developing their characteristics of autonomy and independence.

The subsequent phase which encompasses the adolescence years presents new challenges for parents. Often times, teenagers will demand the best of everything. They become what the economy lives upon, materialism appear to be their value. When divorce happens, children might engage in a different set of values because the family dynamics and their basic foundations are challenged. Children react to all stressors including familiar stress like loss of family income or deaths of close relatives with anxiety and need compassion.

During this turbulent period, some parents might succumb to a reversion of what may be deemed as the child tantrum because of guilt. This parental coping mechanism may result in buying the child favor through gifts or exciting outings. The missing emotion most children miss during this parental behavior is nurturing, love, and structure instead of these superficial forms of bonding in the form of gifts.

To enhance our sense of positivity, satisfaction, appreciation and overall health we need to increase the gratefulness component in our lives. Our society would become an even greater place if gratitude was expressed with others, especially as a role model for our children. Science is actually demonstrating that phenomenon to be conducive to our physical, emotional well-being and uplifting our spirits. They have shown that if this practice is done regularly to at least three things or people on a daily basis, the level of nurturing, love, happiness and wellness increases substantially in the children's learned behaviors.

Dr. Robert Emmons, Journal of Positive Psychology and author of "Thanks, How the New Science of Gratitude Can Make You Feel Happier" has discovered what gives life meaning: Gratitude. According to him, gratitude improves emotional and physical health, and it can strengthen relationships and communities, improve academics, increase energy levels and provide resilience for handling unexpected tragedy and crisis. People must give up a "victim mentality" and overcome a sense of entitlement and deservedness to truly feel this emotion at its fullest. Grateful people exhibit lower levels of depression and stress.

A resource for you and your children to enjoy together is a game that is designed by Denise Coates, called the "Thank You" Universe game. This resource can be purchased at: http://feelitreal.com/onlinestore/vibrationalgames. Another resource is to read the "Thank you, Angels" book by Dr. Doreen Virtue to your children so that they become familiarized with the concept of gratitude at an early developmental stage.

Tony Robbins says that gratitude packs a powerful punch against anger and fear. "Fear is why we don't take action and anger is why we get stuck," Tony says. "You can't be grateful and angry simultaneously.

You can't be fearful and be grateful simultaneously. So gratitude is really the reset button for our negative emotions. It serves as the ctrl-alt-delete button for our human computer mind.

What Are You Grateful For?

"Gratitude unlocks the fullness of life. It turns what we have into enough, and more. It turns denial into acceptance, chaos to order, confusion to clarity. It can turn a meal into a feast, a house into a home, a stranger into a friend. Gratitude makes sense of our past, brings peace for today, and creates a vision for tomorrow."

–Melody Beattie–

Negativity is surrounding us and bombarding us through our daily environment, especially the media. Have you noticed any positive news these days that portray hope and love? As the old saying goes, "misery loves company." Within all that "darkness" we need something that will brighten up your day. Sometimes it takes only a smile which helps you see the world in a more positive light! Wouldn't you like to begin your day with a jump start and a little boost of gratitude?

Gratefulness for Your Inner Child

Thank Your Wicked Parents by Richard Bach, is appropriate for healing if you didn't grow up in a loving home or suffered from your parents' wrong doing in some ways or they may have unconsciously simply adopted their parents' lifestyle. This book encourages you to thank your parents so that you are not harboring any ill thoughts or unfulfilled desires of what a parental model should be. Our parents do not have the power to change the past, nor do we. We can only take responsibility for it, which stops us from being the victims and in truth they did the best that they could base on the roles models they had in life. This tool was developed by Richard Bach and more in-depth explanations are found in his book.

Belief	Thank you for not believing in me, so that I could begin believing in myself.
Talent	Thank you for despising my talent, so that I could develop it the way I wanted to all along.
Misery	Thank you for making my life miserable, to show me that I had allowed my miseries and can create my joys.
Beating	Thank you for beating me, so that I shall never harm myself or others.
Denial	Thank you for denying me, so I can affirm myself.
Insults	Thank you for calling me names, so I could redefine myself in brighter words.
Dreams	Thank you for trying to crush my dreams and smother my hopes, to show me it's not your belief that makes them real, but mine.
Pettiness	Thank you for being petty, so that I could learn grace.

Religion	Thank you for forcing your religion upon me. Rejecting yours, I found my own.
Shame	Thank you for being ashamed of me, so that I can be proud of my highest self.
Abuse	Thank you for abusing me, so that I shall treat myself with respect.
Abandoning	Thank you for abandoning me. I found myself along the way.
Walls	Thank you for your walls, so that I'm unafraid to live openly.
Temper	Thank you for your wild tempers, showing me that anger is always fears, and fear is always the fear of loss.
Differences	Thank you for calling me a freak, so I could learn that my differences are my gifts.
Addictions	Thank you for refusing to quit your addictions, so that I can let mine go.
Expectations	Thank you for expecting me to love you in spite of your cruelties, so I learned it's not my job to meet your expectations.
Forgiveness	Thank you for abusing and assaulting me when I was helpless, to teach me I cannot be destroyed, and that I can forgive the unforgivable.

The core of a family starts with the parent or caregiver. If happiness is what you value the most, the parent is responsible to teach it with gratitude. We all need to appreciate more things in life and recognize the efforts that people make for us on a daily basis. More appreciation begins with expressing it in your home, so that your children can learn to share this gift with the world. Remember, you are the first role model and the most frequent one that your children learn from.

The feeling of gratitude will embrace your character and enhance every cell within you. It is with the expression of gratitude that a child will truly feel and be surrounded by love and it helps to bridge the need of connection and love, which is a primary human need, especially during the earlier years in their life.

A gratitude journal, suggested by Richard Bach, is a treasure of private expressions of thankfulness that helps us recognize all the goodness in our own lives and in the lives of those we care about. Volunteering with your kids also shows kids gratitude on a larger scale where the impact will be made community wide. Anthony Robbins tells his story of when a man showed up to his door with a turkey dinner during the time when his family couldn't afford food and that has made all the difference in the world.

His entire belief and blueprint shifted about what his parents had always portrayed, "That no one really cares about anyone else." Can you imagine, if that incidence created more Tony's in the world, what this world has the potential to eventually become? Sometimes when you lend a hand to one person, you do not know the degree of impact and the lives they will reach, this is essentially the ripple effect that Mother Teresa talks about. As Mother Teresa, quoted, "I alone cannot change the world, but I can cast a stone across the waters to create many ripples." And indeed, she has inspired so many across the globe.

The Forgiveness Diet

"The weak can never forgive. Forgiveness is the attribute of the strong."

–Mahatma Gandhi–

"Resentment is like drinking poison and then hoping it will kill your enemies."

–Nelson Mandela–

Today, too many of us stay stuck in stagnant intimate, family, or workplace relationships, imprisoned by memories of what others have done to us or not done for us. Weighed down by toxic thoughts and emotions, we are quick to judge, self-righteous about what we feel, and slow to pardon. However, this is actually impacting our health and our well-being without punishing the perpetrator.

Dr. Iyanla Vanzant became an expert in this field due to her life experiences. Her story is an epic saga of learning the art of forgiveness. From her life's experiences she has uncovered her life's purpose, discovered the power that lies within and recovered her authentic self. Dr. Iyanla states that forgiveness is a gift you give yourself; however, sometimes the ego out of fear tries to hold us back from receiving this gift. We had the honor to meet Dr. Vanzant and hear about hear about her story.

She was a child of an extra-marital affair from an alcoholic mother. At the age of two, her mother passed away from "breast cancer." At age nine, her uncle raped her. During the majority of her childhood her father was not present physically or emotionally. By age 16 she was a teenage mom and she was married to a physically abusive husband. She made two suicide attempts in her lifetime due to all the pain she had endured and because she could not forgive herself. Nine years later, when she learned the art of forgiving herself and believing in her, she graduated as Summa Cum Laude and became an attorney.

Dr. Iyanla Vanzant designed the Forgiveness Diet to empower others. This Forgiveness Diet is a process that eliminates toxins and wounds of the past from the mind and the heart. A Forgiveness Diet addresses energy, what we carry and what we attract. Forgiveness addresses how we think and feel about ourselves and others and, how those thoughts manifest within our life. This diet is designed to eliminate what we have put into our minds about who we are; who others are and, the subsequent issues or upsets that grow from the thoughts and the emotions attached to the thoughts.

A forgiveness diet is a means by which we release the past to experience the fullness of the present moment. Quite often, we are stuck in the memories of what we have done or not done; what others have done to us or not done for us. How we think and feel does not feed us, nurture us, nourish us, nor do they make or keep us peaceful or loving. In fact these toxic thoughts have been poisonous to our physical and emotional bodies and the core of our souls.

To learn more about the art of forgiveness, we recommend you purchase Dr. Vanzant's book, Forgiveness: 21 days to forgive everyone for everything. Additionally, to have an immediate detoxification from negative thoughts, she has formulated Masterpiece Soaps with Dr. Masaru Emoto's healing music and a combination of sacred herbs and essential oils to help the body begin the releasing process of your trapped emotion.
(http://www.innervisionsworldwide.com/index.php?p=products-masterpeace)

Forgiving Your Inner Child

With permission from Amahra Jaxen, she shares some wisdom from the universe for all those that are still not opening the door to the gift of forgiveness that is waiting at your doorsteps. This is an excerpt from her blog at: (http://quantumhealer.blogspot.com/.)

For what is this journey of life if you are not prepared to travel it? How many opportunities and magical moments have you missed because you were too afraid of hurting someone, anyone accepts yourself? For you put others before yourself in as much as you worry more about others than yourself.

Give to yourself now, treat yourself well and watch your inner lotus-being, begin to flower. Your heart has labored for a very long time and it would serve you now to relate only to those who do not frighten you. You must feel safe at this time in your life for so much is at stake.

Be warm and watchful toward the parts of your body that play against you and ask yourself why you hate yourself so much that you would constantly use your body as your battleground. Always in your own body can you find a reason to hate and feel lacking? You bring all of your guilt and shame to the surface when you relate to your body. Please relate to it kindly. Find more activities to enjoy and build strength, for you are still punishing your body by ingesting foods.

When you ingest toxic poison, whether it is in the form of thoughts or words I ask you to consider the child within who is starving. Who is s/he? It is time to find that missing girl/boy and ask her/him what s/he needs. Ask her/him to forgive you for starving her/him. For whenever your innocent child arises, you weaken and starve her/him through eating the foods that you know will harm you. It is time to stop and commit to his/her well-being.

But also will these poisons pad those parts of you that you are afraid to uncover. Why are you hiding the woman/man you have always said you wanted to be? Why do you sabotage? Where is your weakness in this regard? Stop now and let your beautiful one emerge. The true essence of who you are and allow you and your child's uniqueness (blue-print) to shine; what a shame it would be if all the world's doves were locked away in darkness allowing no one to hear their soft and loving calls?

We encourage you to nourish your child's inner child on a daily basis with bed time stories that promote a sense of emotional well-being and empowerment. Some recommended titles include: "Incredible You: 10 Ways to Let Your Greatness Shine Thru"; "I Am Why Two Little Words Mean So Much"; "No Excuses! How What You Say Can Get In Your Way"; "It's Not What You've Gotten" and "Thank you Angels." All these books are written by the gurus Dr. Wayne Dyer and Dr. Doreen Virtue in collaboration with Kristina Tracy.

Be a Lotus Flower

In the eastern culture the lotus flower is revered because of its analogy to human life and achievement for reaching one's highest potential (enlightenment.) It analogizes our birthing process into this world; a world that has a dichotomy of both pain and suffering, amongst love and compassion. However the metaphor is that in this challenging environment, we have the ability to raise and reach above the pond's surface, like the lotus flower. By persevering past the obstacles and the muck that surrounds many of our roots, we can surpass these limits and achieve our fullest potential and truly blossom and live a beautiful life.

In the game of "Life," without challenges how would we recognize and appreciate success; without darkness how would we appreciate light. Some people, Oprah Winfrey for example, went through really challenging times by rising above the murk of the environment and flourishing to her fullest potential. The one who can combat adversity will be able to inspire others to greater levels and be impactful for society. Becoming a lotus flower and providing hope to others is the essence of what society is missing, if we can see the beauty in everyone and help everyone blossom we will have achieved the ultimate goal of life: Happiness for one and for all.

Lotus flowers cannot grow on marble or gold or mahogany. It often grows amongst challenging soil conditions that often would deter one from believing such beauty could exist amongst the despairs that many haves forgotten or are uncomfortable with associated as life. But as the old saying goes, never judge a book by its cover, because beneath the surface, there lays a wealth of knowledge and a lesson to be learned from all that truly value experiences.

A common theme of many inspirational quotes is that you learn more from failure than you do from success. Without evil and suffering, good and joy could not logically exist. We are all able to grow into something beautiful. Did you know a lotus seed starts its journey in the murk of the bottom of a pond? As it grows and reaches the surface, the flower blossoms. It will remain rooted in the musk, but it rises above it all until it truly flourishes and reveals its true inner and outer beauty to the world. This is what your children see when they look into your eyes. We hope you see the same thing in your children, but most importantly in YOURSELF. Regardless of what label you or your children may have received for their behaviors or "learning abilities", it is time to see beauty and hope again in this world!

When we dare to dream with our imaginations, we can create infinite possibilities, especially if it is coupled with great love and the desire to help others. We all play an integral role in society and we are all a piece of thread within the tapestry of humanity. We bring to it a beautiful representation of our souls but also our love for the bigger masterpiece called humanity.

We all have a duty to preserve the legacy for our children and grandchildren. It is time to truly unite the resources of this world for positivity and for the LOVE of our kids and grandkids. We encourage you to use the following incantation each day and say it with pure passion: I am perfect, whole, and complete, just as I am. As your repeat this statement, it becomes your reality and the hope that your children are looking for. You and your kids have the potential to create a beautiful future and a legacy that truly brings out the essence of humanity. We are humans instead of merely mammals and as such we should lead by example and truly bring out the essence of life.

> *"...Justice at its best is love correcting everything that stands against love."*

> –Martin Luther King, Jr.–

Appendix

Appendix 1

In-Depth Medical Perspectives on what is Assessed and "Treated"
During a Pregnancy from a Chiropractic Viewpoint

<u>Transverse Plane:</u>

The transverse fascial place is what is "holding" the organs and structures inside the abdominal cavity and across the body. The respiratory diaphragm and the pelvic floor need to function properly in pregnant woman so that there is proper growth for the baby.

<u>Diaphragm:</u>

Hypertonicity of the diaphragm will reduce the integrity of the breathing pattern, the rib cage function and movement and further limit thoracic (upper and mid back) rotation and optimal movement. While the diaphragm might be hypertonic (over contracted), the voluntary breathing will take over.

This will allow your neck muscles and rib cage to breath instead of the diaphragm. Long term breathing can cause some neck discomfort, headache, dizziness, vertigo, rib pain, hiatus hernia, digestion issues to name a few.

Diaphragm hypertonicity will also reduce proper blood supply to the baby and organs of the mother including the liver, spleen, kidney and uterus. Proper diaphragmatic release will eliminate possible trouble with motion sickness, breathing, oxygen level and blood flow to the mother and the baby. SOT' Method has a painless diaphragm release that can safely be done during pregnancy.

<u>Hiatus Hernia:</u>

Common symptoms of a hiatus hernia are the gastric juice or acid reflux coming in your throat either after a meal or a drink or randomly without eating. What happens is the stomach goes above the diaphragm and creates an extra pouch. While you eat, the food stops at the first pouch and gets stuck.

The automatic reflex of the stomach is the production of acid and is purpose is to try to breakdown the food. The issue in this case is the acid is produced in the bottom pouch while the food is in the above pouch, stuck above the diaphragm. But the reflex is engaged. So the gastric juice is then propelled to the first pouch and creates some acid reflex.

This can happen via a mechanical stress from the diaphragm and the esophagus during a cough, sneeze or the baby pushing on the stomach as the pregnancy goes further along. SOT' Method has a painless hiatus hernia release that can safely be done during pregnancy.

<u>Kidney Ptosis:</u>

Kidney ptosis, drop kidney from its original position in the abdominal cavity, is a common finding in pregnancy. If the Psoas muscles get hypertonic (spasm), this will "help" the kidney to drop. The SOT' Method correction will allow proper fluid drainage and restore proper urination and can limit urinary tract infection.

Pelvic Floor:

Pelvic floor muscles are the holding muscles to the pelvic cavity. During pregnancy, these muscles need to relax equally to allow the pelvic to expand for proper and safe delivery of the baby. Increase tension to one side or the other, can create latent delivery or other complications.

Applying a pelvic floor balancing to the pregnant mother will relax these muscles and reduce tenderness at the hip, pubic bone, abdominal and low back and sacrum area.

Psoas and Piriformis muscles:

Psoas muscle lay inside the abdominal cavity and attach to the rib cage, the diaphragm, the lumbar vertebra and disc, the hip and femur bone. Restriction at the Psoas can create breathing issues, vertebra misalignment, pelvic and leg misalignment if not "treated" and stretched appropriately.

While a woman is pregnant, a hyper contraction of the Psoas will also reduce the room the fetus has inside the uterus. The sciatica nerve is very important especially during pregnancy. This muscle is the only muscles attaching to the sacrum. Hypertonicity to this muscle can shear the sacrum and block the exit of the baby and create complications and a long labor.

Pain can generate from the low back, sacrum area, hip, legs, and front of the belly, buttock area and knees. A simple massage might help reduce the spasm for the muscle but this is only temporary relief. There is a need to still restore the integrity of the pelvic. If the bone of the pelvic is still misaligned or torque, the sciatic nerve will then become tight again.

Sacrum Involvement:

The sacrum is the tail of the spine and is used during the cranial-sacral respiratory mechanism which moves the cerebral spinal fluid from your brain to all your body. The sacrum is also very important during delivery. If the sacrum is torque, the passage for the baby will be altered.

Sacrum subluxation will also create a huge list of symptoms from low back pain, to sciatica, to buttock pain, to lower extremities pain and abdominal pain. Also, the uterus attach to the sacrum via ligaments. So any torque prior to the delivery might affect the room available to the fetus. Proper and gentle correction is needed during the entire pregnancy.

Pubic Bone:

The symphysis pubic (public bone) is very important since it is the front attachment of the pelvic bones. Any rotation or misalignment of this bone might affect the front connection at the pubic bone. It is often unstable during pregnancy allowing the pelvic separation for the birthing process. It is a common cause of pain and disability in pregnancy. This distortion can also mimic anterior hip pain, low back pain, knee pain and abdominal discomfort.

Pelvic Instability:

Since during the pregnancy journey, the relaxin hormone will create hypermobility (stretching) of all the joints, pelvic instability is to be expected. The instability rate is increased when the mother has had more than one baby. The sacrum will most likely twist and get misaligned.

The safest "treatment" to correct and stabilize this instability during pregnancy is the utilization of the SOT˚ Method by blocking (use of orthopedic wedge) the pelvic and allowing the gravity to reposition it. After the "treatment", a sacroiliac belt will be useful to keep that stabilization from slipping.

Appendix 2

Common Bone Structures in the Head that may Affect Pregnancy Symptoms

<u>Occipital Bone:</u>

Headache, narrowing of the major arteries in the neck, salivary gland dysfunction, eyes or visual problems, cranial nerve symptoms, digestive implication, tongue and taste implications and neck instability.

<u>Parietal Bones:</u>

Pain around the eyes, migraine/headache, increase pressure in the skull, aggressive behavior, ADHD/ADD, visual problem, increase pain all over the body, sciatica and low back pain, hypersensitivity to touch (pre-cursor to fibromyalgia.)

<u>Frontal Bone:</u>

Visual and eyelid problem, eye pain, sinus congestion or multiple infections, headache, loss or change in smell, personality disorder or changes, inappropriate behavior, intellectual issues, digestive organ issues.

<u>Sphenoid Bone:</u>

Migraine/headache, depression, memory issues, dyslexia, depression and other psychiatric challenges, moodiness, brain frog, taste/smell/hearing and vision disturbance, speech associated problems, dry mouth, teeth grinding, dental issues (malocclusion), eye pain, tongue and sucking issues, endocrine (hormones) issues, asthma, sinus' neck and low back, scoliosis.

<u>Temporal Bones:</u>

Dizziness, hearing and balance, ringing or sound pitch in the ear, deafness, nausea, vomited, vertigo, tearing, eye muscle issues like cross-eye and lazy eye, TMJ (allows lower jaw to function properly) pain and dysfunction. Since the TMJ (jaw) connects any bite issues, it will be transferred to the cranium and any cranium issue can be transferred back directly to the jaw and to the teeth. Therefore, it is important to use a Holistic Dentistry that understands the mouth-body affect.

<u>Nasal Bones:</u>

Tearing, nasal secretion, breathing.

<u>Zygoma (Malar) Bones:</u>

Eye symptoms, sinus, sacroiliac joint instability (feels like arthritis.)

<u>Maxilla Bones:</u>

Pain or sensitivity in the face, teeth and gum pain.

<u>Palate Bones:</u>

Numbness in face, headache, tearing, small/taste, dry nasal passages, sinus, runny nose, asthma, endocrine function (hormonal.)

<u>Hyoid Bone:</u>

Throat, swallowing, snoring, sleep, vocal issues, sleep apnea.

Appendix 3

The Chiropractic Children's First-Aid Kit

Asthma

Dr. De Jarnette also describes a CO2 technique to SOT˚ Method certified which help during an attack:

Put 5 lbs of constant pressure on the right side of Thoracic (chest) 5 (transverse process)

Put 5 lbs of constant pressure on both side of Thoracic (chest) 10 (transverse process)

Put 5 lbs of constant pressure on both side of Lumbar (lower spine) 2

The pressure needs to be for 20 seconds, and repeated three times.

Other technique:

Turn children on their back, pressure at sternum between 3rd and 4th rib (about 2-3 inches below middle of collar bone.)

Turn children on their belly, pressure between sides of the 3rd - 4th thoracic vertebra to tolerance. Repeat at intervals as needed for symptom relief.

Chills

Press one hand firmly over the sacrum (in between hip bone) and the flat hand over thoracic 5.

Separate both hands apart while maintaining pressure together.

Warm hands only!

Cold (with sore throat)

Stand behind child's side.

Grasp skull with one hand and pressure front side of the neck toward back while you lift the skull upward together.

Begin at the center and repeat as needed.

Cold (with nasal congestion)

Same as above but pressure one side of the neck toward the opposite.

If done correctly, the nasal congestion will be relieved

Cold (with headache)

Grasp forehead with one hand and the back of the skull (occiput) with other hand.

Hold firmly and push backward with hand on forehead.

Hold until headache ease.

Cold (upset Gastro Intestinal – Stomach Flu)

Pressure right side of thoracic 5 and 8 as deep as possible.

For cold with decrease urination, gently tap with your fingers thoracic 11 and 12.

Cold (with sinus)

Pressure between rib 1 and 2 on child chest about 3 inches on the side to the sternum

Colic

Begin with the CO2 Technique (See in above section under Asthma)

Position your child on their back.

Friction or rub all painful area between rib 6 and 7 (at mid nipple line)

Turn child on belly, put pressure on each side of between thoracic 6 and 7th.

Hold the pressure until pain is controlled.

Gallbladder and stomach reflex needs to be address by your SOT˚ Method or AK chiropractic physician.

Constipation

From the side of the hip going down the knee, all painful nodules need to be rubbed.

This reflex is to the entire intestinal area.

The right side of leg involves the right intestinal aspect.

Thoracic 11 where the ribs attach might be painful, make sure to relax with massage.

Cough

Pull forward aspect of throat from the center to the outside until tissue relaxes.

Repeat on opposite side.

Grasp sides of the 5th cervical and hold strongly until tissue warms.

Repeat often until cough cycle is broken.

Croup

Begin with the CO2 technique (See in above section under Asthma)

With child on their back, cold moist pack on front of neck and apply pressure on side of the first 2 cervical vertebra and hold.

Repeat as often.

Diarrhea

Extend right arm under child legs above the knee and lift while pushing down forcefully with other hand on sacrum.

Hold for one minute.

Repeat if necessary

Earache

Place finger where rib 1 crosses behind collar bone and press.

It will be painful on side involving ear.

Hold until pain is controlled.

Turn child on belly and hold the back of the side of the first cervical until pain stops.

Ear Wax

Place 2-3 drops of hydrogen peroxide in ear.

Leave in 30 minutes.

Rinse with syringe of warm water.

Fever

Cause of the fever must be determined.

Top hand on occiput (elevate: move toward above head), bottom hand on sacrum (extend inferiorly: move toward feet)

Hold three to five minutes.

Hay Fever

Hold both sides of cervical 3 while free hand brings patient head backward.

Hold skull and with free hand place index finger and thumb (grip like) 1 inch sideway to the nostril and hold.

Headache (front or back)

Grasp back of skull with one hand and squeeze while other hand brings head backward.

Hold for one minute.

Hiccup

Breath into a brown paper bag

If severe, press firmly side of cervical 3, 4 and 5 and hold until hiccup diminishes.

Jaundice

Rub or massage nodules between rib 5-6th on mid nipple line.

Massage back at the thoracic 6-7 on the right and in between these vertebra.

Rub the right web between thumb and index finger.

Rub/massage the 3rd rib on the right area, might be painful

Tonsillitis

Grasp throat with thumb and index finger (grip like) at angle of the jaw, hold firm pressure as head is turned left and right.

Repeat several times.

A bone is located there, the aim is to hold the bone and turn the head to relax these muscles by gentle stretching.

Appendix 4

Association of a Single Vertebra Link to the Organs and it's Emotional Dis-stress

(From the book Art and Practice of Chiropractic by ML Rees and Chiropractic Manipulative Reflex Technique by Major B. De Jarnette.)

T (Thoracic or dorsal vertebra): from the base of your neck to the last rib in low back

L (Lumbar vertebra): from the last rib to above the sacrum

- <u>T1</u>:

  Organ reflex for this vertebra is the coronary triad. This mean your heart muscle can be involve. Specific nutritional supplement might be recommended to sedate the reflex and to rebuild the heart muscles.

  Emotions:

  <u>Lethargy</u> and <u>Suspicion</u>: Lack mental and physical alertness and activity and lack faith that the body has the power to heal.

- <u>T2</u>:

  Organ reflex for the nerve conductivity and muscle tone throughout the body (working muscle used for hearing.)

  Emotion:

  <u>Despair</u>: Lack hope that they will get well

  *If this reflex is present and no other reflex seems to be involved, B1 vitamin (Thiamin) need to be recommended for a short period of time (2-3 days) to see if the reflex goes away. If the CMRT, chiropractic and B1 vitamins does not resolve or sedate the reflex, please consult a cardiologist.

- <u>T3</u> :

  Organ reflex to the respiratory system to decrease function to decrease integrity to the lung, bronchioles and respiratory passages.

  Emotions:

  <u>Hate</u> and <u>Despair</u> : Lack hope that they will get well and self-hate and to others

- T4 :

Organ reflex to the gallbladder and bile duct. This reflex is useful to prevent gallbladder surgery. Beets are one of the most beneficial foods to relax this reflex along with apple cider vinegar prior to a meal.

Emotion:

Destruction : Problem producing a creative image.

- T5 :

Organ reflex to the stomach which can be useful to analyze acidity produce or hiatus hernia. Ulcer can reduce the stomach capacity and trigger a recurrent reflex. Also, the stomach aids in the breakdown of protein and formation of B12 vitamin.

Emotions:

Misjudgment and Destruction : Condemn or find fault in other and problem producing a creative image

- T6-7:

Organ reflex for T6 is the pancreas dealing with blood sugar and protein digestion and T7 the integrity of the spleen dealing with infections, red blood cell and anemia. This reflex is particularly useful for a myriad of digestion issues like flatulence (gassiness), poor digestion, bloating, diabetes, insulin resistance, hypoglycemia, eye blurry, dizziness, frequent urination, skin itching and fatigue, drained, low vitality.

Emotions:

Critical : Denounce other for trivial things, speak evil of their fellow man

- T8 :

Organ reflex is the liver. The liver does about 250 biochemical reactions per second and has multiple roles including detoxification and storage of glycogen (source of energy.) This reflex is useful to clear the blood flow, detoxify the liver, since a sick liver will slow down the circulation and increase blood pressure.

Emotions:

Antagonism and Misjudgment : Inability to listen to the power within and about us. Lack will power to use that "little voice" inside of each of us as our guide in life's entire problem and condemn or find fault in other

- T9 :

Organ reflex is the adrenal. This is the fight or flight center but also direct water retention, blood pressure drop from sitting to standing and if deplete of energy will make you sick! The adrenal are a reactive organ to the stress of the body, mind and emotions. Licorice, Celtic salt in the water and proper adrenal whole food should be added in stressful period of your life.

Emotions:

Hesitation and Misjudgment : Wary and gun shy they refuse to proceed in any direction withdrawing within themselves and condemn or find fault in other

- T10 :

Organ reflex is the small intestine. This is where the end of the digestion takes place and where the gut toxicity is mostly present including parasite and poison. This reflex is useful to increase the mobility of the intestine and balance the nerve function for proper elimination.

Emotion:

Hesitation : Wary and gun shy they refuse to proceed in any direction withdrawing within themselves

- T11 : See T12 for organ reflex

Emotions:

Procrastination and Misjudgment : Stalls for time, put off until tomorrow and condemn or find fault in other

- T12 :

Organ reflex are the kidneys. This reflex is useful to increase function of filtration of the kidney, position the kidney correctly and clear the build-up and prevent for possible kidney stones. If your child is having frequent nightmare, this reflex needs to me assessed.

Emotions:

Lethargy and Procrastination : Lack mental and physical alertness and activity and stalls for time, put off until tomorrow

- L1 :

Organ reflex of the iliocecal (between small and large intestine) valve of the intestinal tract. This valve can be open or close and trigger a myriad of symptoms including soft stool, hardened stool, flatulence (gassiness), indigestion, bloating, cramping, toxic headache and more. Okra is the best remedy to re-establish the proper opening/closing of the valve. Also, some practitioners found a correlation with this abnormal reflex and endometriosis and uterine fibroid. Both are the same tissues and the innervations go to the same place. More research needs to be done.

Emotion:

Suspicion: lack faith that the body has the power to heal.

- L2-3 :

  Organ reflex of L2 is the cecum part of the intestinal tract. Digestive issues and symptoms might occur including celiac dis-ease and Irritable Bowel Syndrome (IBS.)

  L3 organ reflex is the entire endocrine/glandular system. These involve the hypothalamus, pituitary, thyroid, parathyroid, ovaries, testis, pancreas, adrenal. When this reflex is present a whole picture is needed.

Emotion:

Hate: Lack hope that they will get well

- L4 :

  Organ reflex of the colon. The colon's role is water absorption or excretion mainly. It is the perfect place for any yeast and parasites hosting and according to colonic, the entire colon has the representation of our entire body like the ear, foot and cranium does as well.

Emotion:

Disorganization: Lead a befuddled and bewildered lifestyle, surrounded by a confused mess.

- L5:

  Organ reflex of the uterus and prostate. This reflex is particularly important for woman wanting to conceive. If this reflex is present, this mean the uterus is not functioning at its maximum or full potential. This reflex could also mean the uterus has flip forward, sideway or backward, which your SOT˙ Method chiropractic physician will be able to assist with the issues. As for the males, if the prostate reflex does not clear within 3 to 6 "treatments", please consult a physician for further assessment.

Emotion:

Misjudgment: Condemn or find fault in others

Appendix 5

Essential Oils in Assisting Organ Therapy

(The information following comes from Reference Guide for Essential Oils by Connie and Alan Higley, cited with permission)

Adrenals

Nutmeg (increases energy, supports adrenal glands), Endoflex, En-R-Gee, Forgiveness, Joy

Blend #1-3 drops clove, 4 drops nutmeg, 6 drops rosemary, 1 t V6. Apply 4 to 5 drops to kidney area and apply hot compress) and apply blend to vitaflex points on feet.

Stimulant adrenals: basil, sage, rosemary, clove, geranium, pine

Strengthens adrenals: spruce, peppermint

Endocrine system

Rosemary, cinnamon bark, black pepper, dill, endoflex diffuse, inhale directly

Or apply to reflex points on feet, lower back, thyroid, liver, kidney, gland areas, center of the body, or both side of spine and clavicle area.

Digestive

Peppermint, Di-Gize (acid stomach; aids the secretion of digestive enzymes), fennel (sluggish), lemongrass (purifier), ginger, clary sage (weak), majoram (stimulates), nutmeg (sluggish digestion), patchouli (stimulant), grapefruit, sage (sluggish), anise (accelerates), basil, bergamot, black pepper, cardamom (nervous), cinnamon bark, clove, coriander (spasms), cumin (spasms and indigestion), GLF, juniper, JuvaFlex (supports and detoxifies), lemon (indigestion), myrrh, myrtle, neroli, ocotea, orange (indigestion), oregano, rosemary, spearmint, tangerine (nervous and sluggish), tarragon (nervous and sluggish.)

Add oils to food. Add 1-5 drops of oil to an empty capsule with 1-5 drops of V-6 oil, swallow.

Kidney

Lemongrass, thyme, aroma life, clary sage, endoflex, geranium, grapefruit, juniper (for better function of kidneys), juvaflex, ledum (strengthens), release

Apply on kidneys as a hot compress. Dilute as necessary.

Liver

JuvaFlex (detoxification), JuvaCleanse, Ledum (powerful detoxifier), Dill, rosemary, sage, helichrysum, gerianum (cleanses and detoxifies the liver), German chamomile, thyme, acceptance, cypress, digize, GLF, golden rod (supports liver function), grapegruit (liver disorders), myrrh, Peace and Calming, ravensara, release (apply to liver and to vita flex points), Roman chamomile, 3 Wise Men

Lymphatic

Cypress, sage, sandalwood (supports), DiGize, JuvaFlex (detoxifying), ledum (inflamed lymph nodes), tangerine, Aroma Life (adds balance and longevity)

Lemon and Lime: cleanses lymph and increases function of lymph

Decongests: cypress, grapefruit, aroma life, citrus fresh, cumin, helichrysum, lemongrass, myrtle, orange, rosemary, tangerine, thyme

Drains lymphs: helichrysum, lemongrass

Pancreas

Cypress for insufficiencies), rosemary, RC, coriander, dill, lemon, Raven, Thieves

Stimulant for pancreas: helichrysum

Support for pancreas: cinnamon bark, Endoflex, Geranium, fennel, coriander

Dilute as necessary and apply over pancreas area or on VitaFlex points on the feet.

Spleen

Marjoram (Apply over vita flex points on the feet. Apply as a warm compress over upper abdomen.)

Stomach

Basil, ginger, peppermint, Di-Gize, Eucalyptus, geranium, lavender, rosemary, Fennel (bloating), tangerine, helichrysum, thyme, blue cypress

Sympathetic / Parasympathetic

stressaway, valor, tranquil, rutavala

Negative ions are produced naturally by wind and rain. They help stimulate the parasympathetic nervous system, which controls rest, relaxation, digestion and sleep. However, if you live in an environment with an overabundance of negative ions, such as in the country or by the ocean, you may benefit greatly from diffusing the oils listed under Positive ions. The production of more positive ions can help bring greater balance to the area and provide a healthier environment.

Increase Negative ions - stimulate parasympathetic
When dispersed into the air through a cool-air nebulizing diffuser, the following oils ionize negatively: Bergamot, cedarwood, citronella, grapefruit, lavender, lemon, lemongrass, orange, patchouli, sandalwood.

Increase Positive ions – stimulate sympathetic

When dispersed into the air through a cool-air nebulizing diffuser, the following oils ionize positively: Clove, cypress, eucalyptus, frankincense, helichrysum, juniper, marjoram, palmarosa, pine, ravensara, rosemary, thyme, ylang ylang.

Billionaire Parenting References

Billionaire Parenting, Child and Parents

http://www.cbsnews.com/pictures/bpa-7-secret-sources/8/

http://www.livescience.com/36908-ways-pregnant-women-affect-babies.html

http://www.enlightenedfeelings.com/body.html

http://blog.chron.com/daddydaze/2010/03/the-21-emotions-of-being-a-new-father/

http://www.webmd.com/baby/features/stress-marks

http://www.babycenter.com/404_is-it-true-that-stress-fright-and-other-emotional-distress-c_10310198.bc

http://www.whattoexpEtc.com/blogs/whattoexpecthealthnews/excessive-stress-during-first-trimester-can-affect-baby-s-iron-levels

http://www.newscientist.com/article/dn24586-pregnant-mothers-stress-affects-babys-gut-and-brain.html#.Uv6WndGYYdU

http://www.webmd.com/baby/features/fetal-stress

http://pregnant.thebump.com/pregnancy/second-trimester/qa/does-stress-affect-pregnancy.aspx

http://www.telegraph.co.uk/health/healthnews/8534749/Quarter-of-fathers-experience-pregmancy-in-sympathy-with-their-pregnant-partners.html

http://pregnant.thebump.com/getting-pregnant/fertility-ovulation/articles/fertility.aspx

Mak Wai Chong. Connecting With Your Unborn Baby. Singapore, 2007.

http://www.dstressdoc.com/Affirmationsforbabyarticles.htm

http://www.articlesfactory.com/articles/health/affirmations-part-iii-can-give-your-unborn-baby-a-million-dollars-without-it-costing-you-a-dime.html

http://www.finerminds.com/mind-power/brain-waves/

http://www.psychologytoday.com/articles/200904/fateful-first-act

http://www.huffingtonpost.ca/samantha-kempjackson/technology-children_b_1648552.html

http://www.truceteachers.org/docs/facing_the_screen_dilemma.pdf

http://www.drgreene.com/qa-articles/excuse-circumcision-pain/

http://www.drgreene.com/articles/colic/

http://www.drgreene.com/articles/jaundice/

http://icpa4kids.org/Wellness-Articles/vitamin-k-at-birth-to-inject-or-not/The-Numbers.html

http://www.drmomma.org/2012/08/aap-circumcision-policy-statement.html

http://main.zerotothree.org/site/DocServer/socemot_-_012_-_par.pdf;jsessionid=34FC626C9C90FCA2C6DFB8BE4E5FEFB6.app247c?docID=10761andAddInterest=1503

http://main.zerotothree.org/site/DocServer/socemot_-_12to24_-_parents.pdf;jsessionid=34FC626C9C90FCA2C6DFB8BE4E5FEFB6.app247c?docID=10762andAddInterest=1503

http://main.zerotothree.org/site/DocServer/socemot_-_24to36_-_parents.pdf;jsessionid=23DFE2E71439B0BCAF387DAF71D6CF9C.app247c?docID=10763andAddInterest=1503

http://brainblogger.com/2011/12/05/mixed-messages-from-mom-maternal-psychological-health-influences-fetal-development/

http://www.soc.cornell.edu/faculty/swedberg/Hope%20Japan%2007.pdf

http://www.psychologytoday.com/blog/positivity/200903/why-choose-hope

http://birthpsychology.com/free-article/maternal-emotions-and-human-development

http://birthpsychology.com/free-article/embryo-us-phenomenological-search-soul-and-consciousness-prenatal-body

http://health.howstuffworks.com/pregnancy-and-parenting/pregnancy/issues/understanding-psychological-changes-during-pregnancy.htm

http://www.ealingcommunitylearning.org.uk/library/documents/37.pdf

http://www.niu.edu/facdev/resources/guide/learning/howard_gardner_theory_multiple_intelligences.pdf

https://www.theartofhealing.com.au/article_posting_life_of_an_unborn_child.html

http://www.communityplaythings.co.uk/learning-library/articles/friedrich-froebel

http://www.communityplaythings.co.uk/learning-library/articles/helping-children-manage-their-feelings

http://www.pgpedia.com/p/johann-heinrich-pestalozzi

http://www.pestalozziworld.com/pestalozzi/pestalozzi.html

http://www.froebelweb.org/web2002.html

http://www.journalofplay.org/sites/www.journalofplay.org/files/pdf-articles/2-1-article-friedrich-froebels-gifts.pdf

http://www.dailymontessori.com/montessori-theory/

http://montessoriconnections.com/about-montessori-education/motivation-of-the-children/

http://articles.timesofindia.indiatimes.com/2012-06-18/health/31838254_1_human-brain-hemisphere-controls-grey-cellshttp://www.cheohome.org/wp-content/uploads/2013/04/Dianne-Craft-Training-Your-Childs-Photographic-Memory-handout.pdf

http://psychology.about.com/od/cognitivepsychology/a/left_brain-right_brain.htm

http://www.cheohome.org/wp-content/uploads/2013/04/Dianne-Craft-Training-Your-Childs-Photographic-Memory-handout.pdf

http://www.acceleratedlearningmethods.com/shichida-method.html

http://www.midbrain-activation.com/

http://www.reggioalliance.org/faq.php

http://www.education.com/reference/article/Ref_Fundamentals/

http://www.scholastic.com/teachers/article/pioneers-our-field-john-dewey-father-pragmatism

http://www.marxists.org/archive/novack/works/1960/x03.htm

http://mindmaps.wikispaces.com/John+Dewey

http://www.tc.columbia.edu/centers/coce/pdf_files/v8.pdf

http://www.simplypsychology.org/vygotsky.html

http://www.toolsofthemind.org/philosophy/vygotskian-approach

http://www.acerinstitute.edu.au/files/Research2013.pdf

http://www.communityplaythings.co.uk/learning-library/articles/building-blocks-brilliant

http://www.brainwave.org.nz/wp-content/uploads/2012/05/2011-Tots-Toddlers-and-TV-full-references.pdf

http://www.healthybrainforlife.com/articles/school-health-and-nutrition/feeding-the-brain-for-academic-success-how

http://www.webmd.com/add-adhd/childhood-adhd/features/brain-foods-kids

http://science.howstuffworks.com/life/men-women-different-brains2.htm

http://perfectorigins.com/articles/

http://www.commercialfreechildhood.org/sites/default/files/facingthescreendilemma.pdf

http://www.giftedpage.org/docs/bulletins/PageBulletinBrainResearch.pdf

Sally P. Springer and Georg Deutch. Left Brain, Right Brain: Perspectives From Cognitive Neuroscience (Series of Books in Psychology. W.H. Freeman and Company. NY. 2001. 406p.

Brain "R" Us: Inquiring minds want to know

http://www.education-reform.net/brain.htm
http://magazine.ucla.edu/exclusives/food_brain_medicine/
http://www.webmd.com/food-recipes/features/how-food-affects-your-moods?page=3
http://www.scribd.com/doc/8863073/Artificially-Sweetened-Times-Aspartame-is-Poison
http://www.nasponline.org/resources/handouts/social%20template.pdf
http://apt.rcpsych.org/content/15/4/271.full
http://psychcentral.com/news/2006/11/09/depressions-chemical-imbalance-explained/398.html
http://www.webmd.com/depression/features/serotonin
http://www.marksdailyapple.com/serotonin-boosters/#axzz2sOT2z7Mj
http://www.fi.edu/learn/brain/proteins.html
https://www.wyldeabouthealth.com/articles/view/59
http://www.naturalnews.com/040537_brain_foods_dopamine_production.html
http://www.thegabrielmethod.com/increase-dopamine-get-happy-and-lose-weight-too
http://www.nytimes.com/2013/07/02/magazine/the-half-trillion-dollar-depression.html?_r=0
http://www.gallup.com/poll/163619/depression-costs-workplaces-billion-absenteeism.aspx
http://www.cehd.umn.edu/ssw/cascw/attributes/PDF/events/MaternalDepression/Maternal_Depression_Report.pdf
http://www.sacredfengshuidesign.com.au/geomancy.html
http://www.thegeniewithin.net/do-you-have-a-clue-what-s-in-your-subconscious-mind
http://www.hypnosishelpcenter.net/depression.htm
http://www.doctoroz.com/videos/best-natural-antidepressants?page=3
http://health.yahoo.net/experts/dayinhealth/golden-spice-life-brings-health-and-happiness
http://www.thegeniewithin.net/do-you-have-a-clue-what-s-in-your-subconscious-mind
http://www.cellularmemory.org/about/about_cellularmemory.html
http://energypsych.com/what-is-energy-psychology/
http://science.howstuffworks.com/ultrasound2.htm
http://healing.about.com/od/energyhealing/a/energy_spsmith.htm
http://www.reiki.org/reikinews/sciencemeasures.htm
http://healing.about.com/od/chakratheseven/a/study7chakras.htm
http://www.toolsforwellness.com/tuning-forks.html
http://www.reikiforallcreatures.com/about-reiki-hospitals.aspx
http://your-healing-journey.jigsy.com/reiki-benefits-and-what-you-can-expect

Yvonne Perry and Dr. Caron Goode. Whose Stuff Is This? Finding Freedom From the Thoughts, Feelings, and Energy Of Those Around You. Copyright, 2010.

http://www.relaxkids.com/tips/entry/Gratitude_Meditation/250
http://www.ahaparenting.com/parenting-tools/positive-discipline/use-positive-discipline
http://www.care2.com/greenliving/7-flower-remedies-for-depression.html?page=1

http://psychology.about.com/od/PositivePsychology/f/positive-thinking.htm
http://carljungdepthpsychology.blogspot.com/2011/08/incantations-carl-jung.html
http://wrathwarbone.hubpages.com/hub/Affirmations-For-Depression-And-Self-Esteem
http://candeecefalland.com/emotional-states/incantations-and-affirmation/
http://www.tm.org/blog/students/adhd-tm/
http://www.t-m.org.uk/
http://www.tm.org/benefits-classroom
http://roberttisserand.com/2013/04/new-rosemary-memory-research/
http://yoursacredcalling.com/commonscentsmom/quieting-the-mind-with-vetiver/
http://lynnemctaggart.com/blog/229-good-vibrations
http://www.getresponse.com/archive/thespiritchannel/Transcription-Monday-BBS-Call-03-07-2011-
        Entrainment-Entrapment-and-Resonance-5846980.html
http://anitamoorjani.com/about-anita/nde-according-to-anita/
http://www.examiner.com/article/health-benefits-of-meditating-on-compassion-to-increase-happiness-and-
        empathy
http://www.wisdomofforgiveness.com/dl.htm
http://addicted2success.com/success-advice/6-classic-lessons-we-can-all-learn-from-stephen-covey/
http://mbyl.hubpages.com/hub/What-are-Alpha-brain-waves-Benefits-and-Effects-of-Alpha-waves-
        in-Meditation-and-Binaural-Beats
http://www.immramainstitute.com/brainwave-technology-for-health-wellness/binaural-beats-and-
        how-they-affect-your-brain/
http://mbyl.hubpages.com/hub/What-are-Alpha-brain-waves-Benefits-and-Effects-of-Alpha-waves-
        in-Meditation-and-Binaural-Beats
http://mbyl.hubpages.com/hub/What-are-Beta-Brain-Waves-Focus-and-Motivation-with-Beta-brainwave-
        entrainment
http://mbyl.hubpages.com/hub/What-are-Delta-Waves-How-to-increase-Delta-Waves-Meditation-
        and-Benefits
http://psychology.about.com/od/statesofconsciousness/tp/facts-about-dreams.htm
http://www.omg-facts.com/lists/297/11-Shocking-Facts-About-Dreams-That-Will-Rock-Your-World/1
http://www.curiosityaroused.com/health/interesting-facts-about-dreams-you-didnt-know/
http://www.neurosemantics.com/matrix-model/brain-101-how-to-play-the-brain-game-for-fun-and-profit
http://www.factslides.com/s-Brain
http://www.nursingassistantcentral.com/blog/2008/100-fascinating-facts-you-never-knew-about-
        the-human-brain/
http://www.healthwatchmd.com/2013/03/10-fun-facts-about-your-brain
http://www.positscience.com/brain-resources/brain-facts-myths/brain-in-love
http://www.positscience.com/brain-resources/brain-facts-myths/brain-facts
http://personalexcellence.co/blog/map-of-consciousness/
http://people.umass.edu/mva/pdf/Neonatal_Reflexes_07.pdf
http://www.rhythmicmovement.com/en/primitive-reflexes/why-are-primitive-reflexes-important
http://www.rhythmicmovement.com/en/primitive-reflexes/what-can-cause-unintegrated-primitive-reflexes
http://www.psychologytoday.com/blog/the-media-psychology-effect/201203/brain-behavior-and-media
http://www.forbes.com/sites/alicegwalton/2012/10/02/the-new-mental-health-disorder-internet-addiction/

http://abcnews.go.com/Health/story?id=4115033andpage=1

http://health.usnews.com/health-news/family-health/brain-and-behavior/articles/2009/06/24/positive-psychology-for-kids-teaching-resilience-with-positive-education

http://jevondangeli.com/generating-brainwaves-for-healing/

http://articles.mercola.com/sites/articles/archive/2011/11/11/everything-you-need-to-know-about-fatty-acids.aspx

http://www.brainsync.com/audio-store/by-brainwave-type/gamma.html

http://www.zenlama.com/understanding-the-benefits-of-brainwaves-and-binaural-beats-the-ultimate-quick-start-guide/

http://www.finerminds.com/mind-power/brain-waves/

http://mbyl.hubpages.com/hub/What-are-Alpha-brain-waves-Benefits-and-Effects-of-Alpha-waves-in-Meditation-and-Binaural-Beats

http://likes.com/facts/weirdest-brain-facts

http://facts.randomhistory.com/human-brain-facts.html

https://faculty.washington.edu/chudler/nutr.html

http://www.psychologytoday.com/blog/your-brain-food/201205/dietary-fats-improve-brain-function

http://www.psychologytoday.com/blog/prime-your-gray-cells/201109/the-skinny-brain-fats

http://articles.mercola.com/sites/articles/archive/2004/02/14/omega-3-depression.aspx

http://articles.mercola.com/sites/articles/archive/2012/01/12/aha-position-on-omega-6-fats.aspx

http://www.aaas.org/news/experts-describe-long-term-impacts-stress-young-brain

http://www.medicinenet.com/script/main/art.asp?articlekey=51730

http://www.psychiatry.emory.edu/PROGRAMS/GADrug/Feature%20Articles/Mothers/The%20effects%20of%20maternal%20stress%20and%20anxiety%20during%20pregnancy%20(mot07.)pdf

http://stress.about.com/od/parentsunderstress/a/pregnancy.htm

http://www.health.com/health/gallery/0,,20521449_last,00.html

http://www.everydayhealth.com/diet-nutrition/food-and-mood/stress-and-dieting/stress-and-other-causes-of-obesity.aspx

http://www.psychologytoday.com/blog/the-athletes-way/201310/pollution-and-maternal-stress-harm-babies-during-pregnancy

http://www.prevention.com/mind-body/emotional-health/healthy-foods-reduce-stress-and-depression/walnuts

http://www.netdoctor.co.uk/focus/nutrition/facts/oxidative_stress/oxidativestress.htm

http://www.sciencedirEtc.com/science/article/pii/S0009912012001580

http://www.cpsy.eg.net/pdf/2009/Jan/6en.pdf

http://drbenkim.com/reduce-stress.html

http://www.lifepositive.com/Mind/Emotions/Metaphysical_causes_of_disease_and_how_to_deal_with_them32004.asp

http://spheresoflight.com.au/index.php?page=energy_healing

http://science.howstuffworks.com/life/5-brain-mysteries5.htm

http://www.stankovuniversallaw.com/2012/01/the-map-of-consciousness-hawkins-scale/

http://happy-firewalker.blogspot.com/2009/06/dr-david-hawkins-map-of-consciousness.html

http://www.smithsonianmag.com/history/review-of-molecules-of-emotion-157256854/?no-ist

http://candacepert.com/

http://www.examiner.com/article/health-benefits-of-meditating-on-compassion-to-increase-happiness-and-empathy

http://www.wisdomofforgiveness.com/dl.htm

http://addicted2success.com/success-advice/6-classic-lessons-we-can-all-learn-from-stephen-covey/

http://mbyl.hubpages.com/hub/What-are-Alpha-brain-waves-Benefits-and-Effects-of-Alpha-waves-in-Meditation-and-Binaural-Beats

http://www.immramainstitute.com/brainwave-technology-for-health-wellness/binaural-beats-and-how-they-affect-your-brain/

http://mbyl.hubpages.com/hub/What-are-Alpha-brain-waves-Benefits-and-Effects-of-Alpha-waves-in-Meditation-and-Binaural-Beats

http://mbyl.hubpages.com/hub/What-are-Beta-Brain-Waves-Focus-and-Motivation-with-Beta-brainwave-entrainment

http://mbyl.hubpages.com/hub/What-are-Delta-Waves-How-to-increase-Delta-Waves-Meditation-and-Benefits

http://psychology.about.com/od/statesofconsciousness/tp/facts-about-dreams.htm

http://www.omg-facts.com/lists/297/11-Shocking-Facts-About-Dreams-That-Will-Rock-Your-World/1

http://www.curiosityaroused.com/health/interesting-facts-about-dreams-you-didnt-know/

Epigenetics

http://articles.mercola.com/sites/articles/archive/2012/04/11/epigenetic-vs-determinism.aspx

http://theweek.com/article/index/238907/epigenetics-how-our-experiences-affect-our-offspring

http://www.youtube.com/watch?v=Hx_YP3LuHwQandlist=TL2TBJO1qqHhe9O-ZGHzNkzY11Ukgqsi8V

http://nutritionfacts.org/video/artificial-coloring-in-fish/

http://nutritionfacts.org/2012/01/05/epa-dioxin-limit-has-national-chicken-council-worried-products-could-be-declared-unfit-for-consumption/

http://www.youtube.com/user/NutritionFactsOrg?feature=watch

http://www.raysahelian.com/methyl.html

http://www.nature.com/scitable/topicpage/epigenetic-influences-and-disease-895#

http://www.thetruthaboutfoodandhealth.com/healtharticles/biology-of-belief-bruce-lipton-genes-cell.html

http://www.heartmath.org/templates/ihm/e-newsletter/publication/2011/summer/you-can-change-your-dna.php

http://www.huffingtonpost.com/dave-pruett/epigenetics-painbodies-and-histones_b_4373225.html

http://science.howstuffworks.com/life/genetic/epigenetics3.htm

http://www.charansurdhar.com/?page_id=1096

https://www.neb.com/about-neb/news-and-press-releases/2011/07/12/engaging-epigenetics-experts

http://www.pbs.org/wgbh/nova/body/jirtle-epigenetics.html

http://theweek.com/article/index/238907/epigenetics-how-our-experiences-affect-our-offspring

http://www.economist.com/node/18985981

Nutrition

http://www.naturalhealth365.com/food_news/lemons.html

http://www.huffingtonpost.com/2013/06/12/splenda-health-risks-cspi-leukemia-artificial-sweeteners_n_3431024.html

http://www.mykangensite.com/research_docs/miscellaneous/10_Common_Diseases_and_Benefits_of_Alkaline_Water.pdf

http://www.globalhealingcenter.com/water/chemicals-in-water

http://www.oceansalert.org/pcbinfo.html

http://chi-gung.co.uk/protein-implicated-in-brain-cell-changes-from-stress

http://www.theorangeplanet.com/assets/files/Microsoft%20Word%20-%20Avoid%20the%20white%20killer.pdf

http://www.dailyfinance.com/2013/11/21/foods-give-up-avoid-eating-gmo/#!slide=1585543

http://foodbabe.com/2013/10/22/sillyputty/

http://www.responsibletechnology.org/doctors-warn

http://www.nerdfitness.com/blog/2013/06/17/everything-you-need-to-know-about-sugar/

http://articles.mercola.com/sites/articles/archive/2012/09/02/fructose-affects-brain-health.aspx

http://lifehacker.com/5809331/what-sugar-actually-does-to-your-brain-and-body

http://butterbeliever.com/gmos-hiding-in-your-vitamins/

http://www.webmd.com/balance/guide/homeopathy-topic-overview

http://www.homeopathy-soh.org/about-homeopathy/did-you-know/

http://www.shirleys-wellness-cafe.com/Children/Ritalin.aspx

http://www.parental-intelligence.com/fredbaughman.html

http://www.britishhomeopathic.org/wp-content/uploads/2013/08/babies-and-children-factsheet.pdf

http://www.biontology.com/wp-content/uploads/2012/08/Voll.pdf

http://www.patient.co.uk/health/breastfeeding

http://www.greenmedinfo.com/blog/why-pesticide-used-ingredient-infant-formula

http://www.greenmedinfo.com/vitamin/organic-infant-formula-dha-ara

http://nj.gov/health/eoh/rtkweb/documents/fs/1727.pdf

http://nj.gov/health/eoh/rtkweb/documents/fs/0931.pdf

http://www.pestell.com/msds/Manganese%20Sulfate.pdf

http://www.doctoroz.com/videos/48-hour-weekend-cleanse

http://www.empowher.com/memory-loss/content/want-avoid-dementia-give-sugar-and-gluten

http://health.howstuffworks.com/wellness/diet-fitness/weight-loss/10-toxic-weight-prevention-tips7.htm

https://www.childwelfare.gov/pubs/issue_briefs/brain_development/how.cfm

http://kidshealth.org/kid/nutrition/food/protein.html#

http://www.sciencedaily.com/releases/2010/01/100127121524.htm

http://www.doctoroz.com/videos/daily-dose-magnesium?page=2

http://articles.mercola.com/sites/articles/archive/2013/06/12/children-foods-supplements.aspx

http://www.slate.com/articles/life/culturebox/2014/02/whole_foods_and_walmart_how_many_groceries_sold_at_walmart_would_be_banned.html

http://foodbabe.com/2013/09/23/are-you-eating-this-ingredient-banned-all-over-the-world/

http://www.thedoctorschannel.com/view/adults-cut-back-fast food-but-u-s-kids-still-eat-too-much-fat-cdc/

http://www.gillianmckeith.com/you-are-what-you-eat-2/

http://jamesclear.com/wp-content/uploads/2013/11/why-humans-like-junk-food-steven-witherly.pdf

http://pldocs.org/docs/index-95552.html?page=13

http://www.greenmedinfo.com/toxic-ingredient/wheat

http://www.greenmedinfo.com/page/dark-side-wheat-new-perspectives-celiac-disease-wheat-intolerance-sayer-ji

http://www.chicagonow.com/clean-convenient-cuisine/2010/09/best-and-worst-top-10-most-inflammatory-and-anti-inflammatory-foods/

http://www.food-allergy.org/inflammation.html

http://kidshealth.org/parent/medical/allergies/allergy.html

http://www.cdc.gov/nchs/data/databriefs/db10.htm

http://foodallergies.about.com/od/diagnosingfoodallergies/p/foodeczema.htm

http://www.patient.co.uk/health/Eczema-Triggers-and-Irritants

http://www.drmanik.com/Milk%20allergy.htm

http://kristensraw.com/why_raw.php

http://www.kristensraw.com/why_raw_details_benefits.php

http://articles.mercola.com/sites/articles/archive/2012/05/12/dr-campbell-mcbride-on-gaps.aspx

http://www.biospiritual-energy-healing.com/raw-food-diet.html

http://www.bcenter.com/bwell/color-therapy/

http://healthwyze.org/index.php/component/content/article/361-the-relationship-between-body-ph-and-disease-and-other-facts-youre-not-supposed-to-know.html

http://ga.water.usgs.gov/edu/propertyyou.html

https://www.relfe.com/health_natural/pH_human_body_balance_health_level_3.html

http://www.webmd.com/diet/alkaline-diets

http://wallstcheatsheet.com/stocks/7-unhealthy-everyday-foods-processed-and-problematic.html/?a=viewall

http://www.prevention.com/food/healthy-eating-tips/7-foods-should-never-cross-your-lips/3-microwave-popcorn

http://www.oceansalert.org/pcbinfo.html

http://www.symbolicliving.com/forum/showthread.php/3752-Is-salmon-healthy-to-eat-PCB-s-toxins

http://www.ewg.org/foodnews/?tag=2012FoodnewsAdandgclid=CPbD6qmi47wCFaE7Ogod5xEAfg

http://www.drgreene.com/chemicals-pregnant-women-green-solution/

http://www.realfarmacy.com/bpa-free-does-not-denote-safety/

http://perfectorigins.com/articles/top-10-chemicals-that-we-didnt-know-poison-our-bodies/

http://wallstcheatsheet.com/stocks/7-unhealthy-everyday-foods-processed-and-problematic.html/?a=viewall

http://naturalrevolution.org/why-foods-and-supplements-made-for-children-are-laced-with-hazardous-chemicals-hidden-aspartame-and-gmos/

http://www.100daysofrealfood.com/2012/03/13/real-food-tips-7-reasons-i-hate-artificial-food-dyes/

http://www.responsibletechnology.org/health-risks

http://www.rense.com/general86/doct.htm

http://www.healthybrainforlife.com/articles/school-health-and-nutrition/feeding-the-brain-for-academic-success-how

http://www.naturalnews.com/033726_sodium_benzoate_cancer.html

http://well.blogs.nytimes.com/2013/02/04/gluten-free-whether-you-need-it-or-not/?_php=trueand_type=blogsand_r=0

http://www.foxnews.com/leisure/2013/04/25/14-year-old-mcdonald-hamburger-looks-almost-new/

http://www.health.com/health/gallery/0,,20705881_4,00.html

http://www.medicalnewstoday.com/articles/7381.php

http://enhs.umn.edu/current/5103/gm/harmful.html

http://www.bellybelly.com.au/pregnancy/baby-formula#.Uxk3YE2YYdU

http://www.womentowomen.com/inflammation/allergies-and-sensitivities/

http://healthyeating.sfgate.com/importance-good-nutrition-kids-6236.html

https://www.wholekidsfoundation.org/downloads/better-bites/better-bites-eat-a-rainbow.pdf

http://www.todayiatearainbow.com/

http://www.youtube.com/watch?v=vYzGkoxvPX0

http://www.rebootwithjoe.com/10-ways-to-get-your-kids-eating-a-rainbow/

http://www.healthalkaline.com/parents-kids-and-ionized-alkaline-water/

http://mysproutusa.com/news_detail.php?id=52

http://thechalkboardmag.com/ph-miracle-interview-shelly-young

http://www.scientificamerican.com/article/living-with-cancer-kris-carr/

http://thechalkboardmag.com/ph-miracle-interview-shelly-young

http://www.mayoclinic.org/healthy-living/nutrition-and-healthy-eating/expert-blog/kids-and-sugar/bgp-20056149

http://www.psychologytoday.com/blog/the-athletes-way/201306/breastfeeding-boosts-the-brain-development-baby

http://www.mcspotlight.org/people/interviews/druce.html

https://www.standardprocess.com

http://www.westonaprice.org

http://www.soilandhealth.org

http://www.ifoam.org

http://www.bachflower.com/

http://www.naturaldatabase.com

http://www.nccam.nih.gov

http://www.herbmed.org/

http://www.herbalgram.org/

http://americanpregnancy.org

http://www.mayoclinic.org/drugs-supplements/saw-palmetto/safety/hrb-20059958

http://voices.yahoo.com/a-look-herbs-harmful-during-pregnancy-2033627.html?cat=71

http://pregnancy-safety.info/products/view/Yohimbe

http://www.nlm.nih.gov/medlineplus/druginfo/natural/871.html

http://americanpregnancy.org/pregnancyhealth/naturalherbsvitamins.html

http://littleburstsofinspiration.wordpress.com/category/herbology/

http://everydaylife.globalpost.com/list-herbs-foods-stimulate-childs-appetite-24233.html

http://www.powernatureessences.com/essencesforautismocd.htm

http://nccam.nih.gov/health/ayurveda/introduction.htm

http://umm.edu/health/medical/altmed/treatment/ayurveda

http://umm.edu/health/medical/altmed/treatment/ayurveda

https://www.chopra.com/our-services/ayurveda

http://ayurveda.iloveindia.com/herbology/medicinal-value-of-herbs.html

http://ayurveda.iloveindia.com/herbology/herbal-effects.html

http://ayurveda.iloveindia.com/herbology/properties-of-ayurvedic-herbs.html

http://ayurveda.iloveindia.com/ayurveda-basics.html

http://www.naturaldatabase.com

http://www.nccam.nih.gov
http://www.herbmed.org/
http://www.herbalgram.org/
http://americanpregnancy.org
http://www.mayoclinic.org/drugs-supplements/saw-palmetto/safety/hrb-20059958
http://voices.yahoo.com/a-look-herbs-harmful-during-pregnancy-2033627.html?cat=71
http://pregnancy-safety.info/products/view/Yohimbe
http://www.nlm.nih.gov/medlineplus/druginfo/natural/871.html
http://americanpregnancy.org/pregnancyhealth/naturalherbsvitamins.html
http://littleburstsofinspiration.wordpress.com/category/herbology/
http://everydaylife.globalpost.com/list-herbs-foods-stimulate-childs-appetite-24233.html
http://www.powernatureessences.com/essencesforautismocd.htm

David R. Seaman. Clinical Nutrition for pain, inflammation and tissue healing. NutrAnalsis Inc. 1998. 282p.

Ingrid Kohlstadt. Scientific Evidence for Musculoskeletal, Bariatric, and Sports Nutrition. Taylor and Francis. 2006: 621p.

American Academy of Pediatric. Nutritional needs of the preterm infants, in Pediatric Nutrition Handbook, K, R.E., Ed., American Academy of Pediatric Elk Grove, IL, 2004, pp 23-54.

Alex Vasquez. Integrative Orthopedics - Integrative, nutritional, botanical, and manipulative therapeutics with concepts, perspectives, algorithms, and protocols for the in-office diagnosis and management of the most common neuromuscoloskeletal problems. Self-Published. 2007. 438p

Alex Vasquez. Integrative Rheumatology - concepts, perspective, algorithms, and protocols. Self-Published. 2007. 494p.a

Sandstead HH. Understanding zinc: recent observations and interpretations. J Lab Clin Med 1994;124:322-7.

Institute of Medicine, Food and Nutrition Board. /About/exit_disclaimer.aspx. Washington, DC: National Academy Press, 2001.

Solomons NW. Mild human zinc deficiency produces an imbalance between cell-mediated and humoral immunity. Nutr Rev 1998;56:27-8.

Prasad AS. Zinc: an overview. Nutrition 1995;11:93-9.

Heyneman CA. Zinc deficiency and taste disorders. Ann Pharmacother 1996;30:186-7.

Simmer K, Thompson RP. Zinc in the fetus and newborn. Acta Paediatr Scand Suppl 1985;319:158-63.

Fabris N, Mocchegiani E. Zinc, human diseases and aging. Aging (Milano) 1995;7:77-93.

Maret W, Sandstead HH. Zinc requirements and the risks and benefits of zinc supplementation. J Trace Elem Med Biol 2006;20:3-18.

Prasad AS, Beck FW, Grabowski SM, Kaplan J, Mathog RH. Zinc deficiency: changes in cytokine production and T-cell subpopulations in patients with head and neck cancer and in noncancer subjects. Proc Assoc Am Physicians 1997;109:68-77.

Rink L, Gabriel P. Zinc and the immune system. Proc Nutr Soc 2000;59:541-52.

U.S. Department of Agriculture, Agricultural Research Service. 2011. USDA National Nutrient Database for Standard Reference, Release 24. Nutrient Data Laboratory Home Page, http://www.ars.usda.gov/ba/bhnrc/ndl.

Sandstrom B. Bioavailability of zinc. Eur J Clin Nutr 1997;51 (1 Suppl):S17-9.

Wise A. Phytate and zinc bioavailability. Int J Food Sci Nutr 1995;46:53-63.

Alaimo K, McDowell MA, Briefel RR, et al. Dietary intake of vitamins, minerals, and fiber of persons ages 2 months and over in the United States: Third National Health and Nutrition Examination Survey, Phase 1, 1986-91. Advance data from vital and health statistics no 258. Hyattsville, Maryland: National Center for Health Statistics. 1994.

Interagency Board for Nutrition Monitoring and Related Research. Third Report on Nutrition Monitoring in the United States. Washington, DC: U.S. Government Printing Office, 1995.

Ervin RB, Kennedy-Stephenson J. Mineral intakes of elderly adult supplement and non-supplement users in the third national health and nutrition examination survey. J Nutr 2002;132:3422-7.

Ribar DS, Hamrick KS. Dynamics of Poverty and Food Sufficiency. Food Assistance and Nutrition Report Number 36, 2003. Washington, DC: U.S. Department of Agriculture, Economic Research Service. [http://www.ers.usda.gov/publications/fanrr36/fanrr36.pdf]

Prasad AS. Zinc deficiency: its characterization and treatment. Met Ions Biol Syst 2004;41:103-37.

Hambidge KM, Mild zinc deficiency in human subjects. In: Mills CF, ed. Zinc in Human Biology. New York, NY: Springer-Verlag, 1989:281-96.

King JC, Cousins RJ. Zinc. In: Shils ME, Shike M, Ross AC, Caballero B, Cousins, RJ, eds. Modern Nutrition in Health and Disease, 10th ed. Baltimore, MD: Lippincott Williams and Wilkins, 2005:271-85.

Krasovec M, Frenk E. Acrodermatitis enteropathica secondary to Crohn's disease. Dermatology 1996;193:361-3.

Ploysangam A, Falciglia GA, Brehm BJ. Effect of marginal zinc deficiency on human growth and development. J Trop Pediatr 1997;43:192-8.

Nishi Y. Zinc and growth. J Am Coll Nutr 1996;15:340-4.

Hunt JR. Bioavailability of iron, zinc, and other trace minerals from vegetarian diets. Am J Clin Nutr 2003;78 (3 Suppl):633S-9S.

Hambidge KM, Krebs NF. Zinc deficiency: a special challenge. J Nutr 2007;137:1101-5.

Prasad AS. Zinc deficiency in women, infants and children. J Am Coll Nutr 1996;15:113-20.

Naber TH, van den Hamer CJ, Baadenhuysen H, Jansen JB. The value of methods to determine zinc deficiency in patients with Crohn's disease. Scand J Gastroenterol 1998;33:514-23.

Valberg LS, Flanagan PR, Kertesz A, Bondy DC. Zinc absorption in inflammatory bowel disease. Dig Dis Sci. 1986 Jul;31(7):724-31.

Prasad AS. Zinc deficiency. BMJ 2003;326:409-10.

American Dietetic Association, Dietitians of Canada. Position of the American Dietetic Association and Dietitians of Canada: vegetarian diets. J Am Diet Assoc 2003;103:748-65.

Caulfield LE, Zavaleta N, Shankar AH, Merialdi M. Potential contribution of maternal zinc supplementation during pregnancy to maternal and child survival. Am J Clin Nutr 1998;68 (2 Suppl):499S-508S.

Krebs NF. Zinc supplementation during lactation. Am J Clin Nutr 1998;68 (2 Suppl):509S -12S.

Brown KH, Allen LH, Peerson J. Zinc supplementation and children's growth: a meta-analysis of intervention trials. Bibl Nutr Dieta 1998;54:73-6.

Leonard MB, Zemel BS, Kawchak DA, Ohene-Frempong K, Stallings VA. Plasma zinc status, growth, and maturation in children with sickle cell disease. J Pediatr 1998;132:467-71.

Zemel BS, Kawchak DA, Fung EB, Ohene-Frempong K, Stallings VA. Effect of zinc supplementation on growth and body composition in children with sickle cell disease. Am J Clin Nutr 2002;75:300-7.

Prasad AS. Zinc deficiency in patients with sickle cell disease. Am J Clin Nutr 2002;75:181-2.

Kang YJ, Zhou Z. Zinc prevention and treatment of alcoholic liver disease. Mol Aspects Med 2005;26:391-404.

Menzano E, Carlen PL. Zinc deficiency and corticosteroids in the pathogenesis of alcoholic brain dysfunction—a review. Alcohol Clin Exp Res 1994;18:895-901.

Shankar AH, Prasad AS. Zinc and immune function: the biological basis of altered resistance to infection. Am J Clin Nutr 1998;68:447S-63S.

Wintergerst ES, Maggini S, Hornig DH. Contribution of selected vitamins and trace elements to immune function. Ann Nutr Metab 2007;51:301-23.

Beck FW, Prasad AS, Kaplan J, Fitzgerald JT, Brewer GJ. Changes in cytokine production and T cell subpopulations in experimentally induced zinc-deficient humans. Am J Physiol 1997;272:E1002-7.

Prasad AS. Effects of zinc deficiency on Th1 and Th2 cytokine shifts. J Infect Dis 2000;182 (Suppl):S62-8.

Black RE. Zinc deficiency, infectious disease and mortality in the developing world. J Nutr 2003;133:1485S-9S.

Lansdown AB, Mirastschijski U, Stubbs N, Scanlon E, Agren MS. Zinc in wound healing: theoretical, experimental, and clinical aspects. Wound Repair Regen 2007;15:2-16.

Anderson I. Zinc as an aid to healing. Nurs Times 1995;91:68, 70.

Wilkinson EA, Hawke CI. Does oral zinc aid the healing of chronic leg ulcers? A systematic literature review. Arch Dermatol 1998;134:1556-60.

Wilkinson EA, Hawke CI. Oral zinc for arterial and venous leg ulcers. Cochrane Database Syst Rev 2000;(2):CD001273.

World Health Organization and United Nations Children Fund. Clinical management of acute diarrhoea. WHO/UNICEF Joint Statement, August, 2004. [http://www.unicef.org/nutrition/files/ENAcute_Diarrhoea_reprint.pdf]

Black RE. Therapeutic and preventive effects of zinc on serious childhood infectious diseases in developing countries. Am J Clin Nutr 1998;68:476S-9S.

Bhutta ZA, Bird SM, Black RE, Brown KH, Gardner JM, Hidayat A, et al. Therapeutic effects of oral zinc in acute and persistent diarrhea in children in developing countries: pooled analysis of randomized controlled trials. Am J Clin Nutr 2000;72:1516-22.

Lukacik M, Thomas RL, Aranda JV. A meta-analysis of the effects of oral zinc in the treatment of acute and persistent diarrhea. Pediatrics 2008;121:326-36.

Fischer Walker CL, Black RE. Micronutrients and diarrheal disease. Clin Infect Dis 2007;45 (1 Suppl):S73-7.

Hulisz D. Efficacy of zinc against common cold viruses: an overview. J Am Pharm Assoc (2003) 2004;44:594-603.

Caruso TJ, Prober CG, Gwaltney JM Jr. Treatment of naturally acquired common colds with zinc: a structured review. Clin Infect Dis 2007;45:569-74.

Turner RB, Cetnarowski WE. Effect of treatment with zinc gluconate or zinc acetate on experimental and natural colds. Clin Infect Dis 2000;31:1202-8.

Singh M, Das RR. Zinc for the common cold. Cochrane Database Syst Rev. 2011 Feb 16;2:CD001364.

Evans JR. Antioxidant vitamin and mineral supplements for slowing the progression of age-related macular degeneration. Cochrane Database Syst Rev 2006;(2):CD000254.

Age-Related Eye Disease Study Research Group. A randomized, placebo-controlled, clinical trial of high-dose supplementation with vitamins C and E, beta carotene, and zinc for age-related macular degeneration and vision loss: AREDS report no. 8. Arch Ophthalmol 2001;119:1417-36.

Newsome DA, Swartz M, Leone NC, Elston RC, Miller E. Oral zinc in macular degeneration. Arch Ophthalmol 1988;106:192-8.

Stur M, Tittl M, Reitner A, Meisinger V. Oral zinc and the second eye in age-related macular degeneration. Invest Ophthalmol Vis Sci 1996;37:1225-35.

Whittaker P. Iron and zinc interactions in humans. Am J Clin Nutr 1998;68:442S-6S.

Chiropractic

http://americanpregnancy.org/pregnancyhealth/chiropracticcare.html

https://www.acatoday.org/level3_css.cfm?T1ID=13andT2ID=61andT3ID=149

http://www.sciencebasedmedicine.org/pediatric-chiropractic-care-scientifically-indefensible/

http://www.kabelchiropractic.com/index.php?p=387986

http://www.drchensee.com/storage/October%202013%20Newsletter%20Article.pdf

http://www.nationalmssociety.org/Symptoms-Diagnosis/Diagnosing-Tools/Cerebrospinal-Fluid-(CSF)

http://blog.bodywisdomcst.com/craniosacral-therapy/the-frontal-bone-your-brains-protector/

http://thebodybeyond.blogspot.com/2010/10/temporal-bones_12.html

http://www.drchensee.com/storage/October%202013%20Newsletter%20Article.pdf

http://thebodybeyond.blogspot.com/2011/03/how-does-your-brain-rate.html

Visceral Innervation, Compiled by the Research Staff of the Professional Researcher Service, 1946

Major Bertrand De Jarnette. Chiropractic Manipulative Reflex Technique. Self Published. 1966

Major Bertrand De Jarnette. Sacro Occipital Research Bulletin. Self Published. 1957

Major Bertrand De Jarnette. Sacro Occipital Notes. Self Published. 1958

Ned Heese. Viscerosomatic Pre-and Postganglionic Technique. Submitted to SORSI Research Conference Archvies.

Francis Marion Pottenger. Symptoms of Visceral Disease. Forgotten Books. 2012

A. F. Dangerfield with the approval of Dr. MB De Jarnette. The Neurophysiology of the Seven Occipital Fibers Associated with Viscera. SORSI Dispatcher 1968.

Mayo Clinic and Mayo Foundation. An Atlas of Pain Patterns. Charles C. Thomas. 1961

A F Dangerfield. CMRT Chiropractic Manipulative Reflex Technique. SORSI Dispatcher July 1971

Major Bertrand De Jarnette. Technic and Practice of Bloodless Surgery. Self Published. 1939

Robert A Leach. The Chiropractic Theories, Lippincott Williams and Wilkins. 1994. 448p

A E Homewood. The Neurodynamics of the Vertebral Subluxation. Valkyrie Press, Inc, 1962. 320p.

Major B. De Jarnette. Reflex Pain. Self-Published. 1934

William David Harper. Anything Can Cause Anything. Self-Published. 1964, 209p.

Charles Masarsky and Marion Todres-Masarsky. Somatovisceral Aspects of Chiropractic: An Evidence-Based Approach. Churchill Livingstone. 245p.

Ned Heese. Line Two Occipital Fiber Technique with Advanced CMRT Methods, Major Bertrand De Jarnette DC. 1993

Major Bertrand De Jarnette. Chiropractic Manipulative Reflex Technique Seminar Notes, SORSI. 1970

Oliver G. Cameron. Visceral Sensory Neuroscience - Interoception. Oxford University Press. 2002. 359p.

Chiropractic and Autism

Khorshid K. Case Report: autism, otitis media. ICA Review Fall 2001

Lawrence' Story: autism and cerebral palsy. In-line with Oklahaven Children's Chiropractic Center (newsletter), Spring 2001, Oklahoma City, OK.

Aguilar AL, Grostic JD, Pfleger B. Chiropractic care and behavior in autistic children. Journal of Clinical Chiropractic Pediatrics Vol. 5 No. 1, 2000

Barnes T. Heather' Story. Int'l Chiropractic Assn. Review Sept/Oct 2000.

Warner SP and Warner TM. Case report: autism and chronic otitis media. Today's Chiropractic. May/June 1999.

Amalu WC. Autism, asthma, irritable bowel syndrome, strabismus and illness susceptibility: a case study in chiropractic management. Today's Chiropractic. Sept/Oct 1998. Pp. 32-47.

Goldman, SR. Developmental communication disorder. Today's Chiropractic July/August 1995 p.70-74.

Rubinstein, HM. Case study – autism. Chiropractic Pediatrics Vol. 1 No. 1, April 1994.

Sandeful, R, Adams E. The effect of chiropractic adjustments on the behavior of autistic children; a case review. ACA Journal of Chiropractic, Dec 21:5, 1987.

Miller RL, Clarren SK. Long term developmental outcome in patients with deformational plagiocephaly (flat head syndrome.) Pediatrics 2000;105:e26

Bobby Doscher, D.C. Editorial in Chiropractic Pediatrics Vol. 1 No. 4 May 1995.

Elster EL J. Upper Cervical Chiropractic Care For A Nine-Year-Old Male With Tourette Syndrome, Attention Deficit Hyperactivity Disorder, Depression, Asthma, Insomnia, and Headaches: A Case Report Vertebral Subluxation Research July 12, 2003, p 1-11

Holder JM, Duncan RC, Gissen M et al Molecular Psychiatry Vol. 6, Supplement 1 - February, 2001,

Larry Webster, D.C. International Chiropractic Pediatric Association Newsletter. January 1996.

Tucker's Story. Barnes T. (Kentuckiana Children's Center) Int'l Chiropractic Assn. Review Sept/Oct 2000.

Noah's Story Leisman N. (Kentuckiana Children's Center) Int'l Chiropractic Assn. Review Sept/Oct 2000.

Letter sent to Dennis Davis, DC. ADHD – a mother's testimony to chiropractic care. Int'l Chiropractic Pediatric Assn. Newsletter Jan/Feb 2000. Mother's name withheld by request.

ADHD: A Mother's Testimonial. Int'l Chiropractic Pediatric Assn. Newsletter. July/August 1998

Wendel P. ADHD – A multiple case study. International Chiropractic Pediatric Association. March/April 1998.

Peet P. Child with chronic illness: respiratory infections, ADHD, and fatigue. Response to chiropractic care. Chiropractic Pediatrics 1997 3(1): 12.

From the records of Rejeana Crystal. ADD, enuresis, toe walking. International Chiropractic Pediatric Association Newsletter May/June 1997. Hendersonville, TN.

Peet, JB. Adjusting the hyperactive/ADD pediatric patient. Chiropractic Pediatrics, 1997;2(4):12-15

Barnes, TA. A multi-faceted chiropractic approach to attention deficit hyperactivity disorder: a case report. ICA International Review of Chiropractic. Jan/Feb 1995 pp.41-43.

Langley C. Epileptic seizures, nocturnal enuresis, ADD. Chiropractic Pediatrics Vol 1 No. 1, April, 1994.

Webster L. First report on ADD study. International Chiropractic Pediatric Association Newsletter. Jan. 1994.

Webster, L. Hyperactivity, stuttering, slow learner, retarded growth. Chiropractic Showcase Magazine, Vol. 2, Issue 5, Summer 1994.

Arme J. Effects of biomechanical insult correction on attention deficit disorder. J of Chiropractic Case Reports, Vol. 1 No. 1 Jan. 1993.

Hospers LA, Proc of the Nat'l Conference on Chiropractic and Pediatrics (ICA) 1992;84-139.

Webster L. Attention span deficiency. International Chiropractic Pediatric Association Newsletter. May 1992.

Phillips CJ. Case study: the effect of utilizing spinal manipulation and craniosacral therapy as the treatment approach for attention deficit-hyperactivity disorder. Proceedings on the National Conference on Chiropractic and Pediatrics (ICA), 1991:57-74.

Giesen JM, Center DB, Leach RA. An evaluation of chiropractic manipulation as a treatment of hyperactivity in children. J Manipulative Physiol Ther 1989; 12:353-363.

Brzozowske WT, Walton EV. The effect of chiropractic treatment on students with learning and behavioral impairments resulting from neurological dysfunction (part 1.) J Aust Chiro Assoc 1980;11(7):13-18.

Brzozowske WT, Walton EV. The effect of chiropractic treatment on students with learning and behavioral impairments resulting from neurological dysfunction (part 2.) J. Aust Chiro Assoc 1980;11(8):11-17.

Brzozowske WT, Walton EV. The effect of chiropractic treatment on students with learning and behavioral impairments resulting from neurological dysfunction. The ACA Journal of Chiropractic/ December 1977 Vol. X1, S-127.

Alternative Medicine (Energy Medicine)

http://www.oprah.com/health/Energy-Medicine/1

http://chi-gung.co.uk/cancer-hospital/

http://journals.sfu.ca/seemj/index.php/seemj

http://innersource.net/ep/images/stories/downloads/EP_DisasterRelief.pdf

http://innersource.net/em/resources/published-articles.html

http://innersource.net/em/resources/case-histories.html

http://innersource.net/em/resources/free-handout-bank.html

http://www.bewholebewell.com/articles/ThePromiseofEnergyPsychology.pdf

http://www.intuitionmedicine.com/academy/journalarticles/journal2.htm

http://www.biontology.com/wp-content/uploads/2012/08/Voll.pdf

http://www.scientificamerican.com/article/feeling-our-emotions/

http://www.loc.gov/loc/brain/emotion/Damasio.html

http://www.neuroanatomy.wisc.edu/coursebook/neuro5(2).pdf

http://neurology.about.com/od/NervousSystem/a/How-Do-You-Feel.htm

http://www.karunaweb.com/what-is-anger-a-secondary-emotion/

http://blogs.yis.ac.jp/14shishikuram/2013/01/10/case-study-on-emotions-disgust/

http://www.sciencedaily.com/releases/2009/03/090312093916.htm

http://www.psychologytoday.com/blog/the-journal-best-practices/201305/the-pleasure-trap

http://healing.about.com/od/selfpower/a/mirror-images.htm

http://www.utne.com/mind-and-body/finding-happiness-cultivating-positive-emotions-psychology.aspx?PageId=1

http://www.huffingtonpost.com/parents/

http://www.www.reikikids.ca

http://www.reikikids.com

http://www.reiki.org

http://www.*americanpregnancy.org*

http://www.www.babycenter.com

http://www.www.medicinenet.com

http://www.www.webmd.com

http://www.*www.acupuncture.com*

http://www.mietekwirkus.com/mietek.html

http://www.theinnonthistlehill.com/about_seane_malone.html

http://www.massagetherapy.com/articles/index.php/article_id/653/Energy-Work-for-Children

http://innersource.net/em/107-resources/publishedarticles/774-the-woman-behind-eden-energy-medicine.html

https://www.newrenbooks.com/about/interviews/eden.html

http://peaceful-parent.com/about/Energy_blocks_in_children.html

http://auraexplorationpatches.com/pages.php?p=0007

https://innersource.net/em/78-handout-bank1/hbmisc/235-innersource-freedom-tips.html

http://www.highexistence.com/water-experiment/

http://chemistry.about.com/od/waterchemistry/f/How-Much-Of-Your-Body-Is-Water.htm

http://www.chilel.com/WhatIsChilelQigong/hospital.htm

http://www.chineng.eu/dr-pang-ming.html

http://www.drjohndiamond.com/the-diamond-path-of-life

http://www.naturalstandard.com/index-abstract.asp?create-abstract=patient-musictherapy.aspandtitle=Music%20therapy

http://www.psychologytoday.com/blog/natural-standard/201306/music-therapy-health-and-wellness

http://www.toolsforwellness.com/tuning-forks.html

http://tuesdayswithlaurie.com/2010/07/12/the-healing-benefits-of-vibrational-therapy/

http://crystalclearvibrations.org/tuning-forks/

http://www.chopra.com/community/online-library/terms/chakras

http://life.gaiam.com/article/toning-chakras

http://www.mindbodygreen.com/0-1117/Ayurveda-Dosha-Types-for-Beginners.html

http://life.gaiam.com/article/six-tastes-ayurveda

http://voices.yahoo.com/the-five-tastes-traditional-chinese-medicine-7467728.html

http://www.chopra.com/ccl/healing-through-the-five-senses

http://www.entrepreneur.com/blog/224575#

http://www.biospiritual-energy-healing.com/vibrational-frequency.html

http://medicinebeginswithme.com/qigong.html

http://www.takingcharge.csh.umn.edu/explore-healing-practices/qigong

DEEPAK Chopra and Rudoph E. Tanzi. Super Brain. Harmony Books. 2012. 322p.

Field, T. (1999.) Pregnant Women Benefit From Massage Therapy. Journal of Psychosomatic Obstetrics and Gynaecology, Mar;20(1):31-8.

Field, T. (2004.) Massage Therapy Effects on Depressed Pregnant Women. Journal of Psychosomatic Obstetrics and Gynaecology, Jun;25(2):115-22.

Heimlich, Patti, RMT, CD, ICCE, The Benefits of Massage During Pregnancy, Labor and Postpartum. www.expectantmothersguide.com/library/houston/massage/htm. Article accessed online 10/18/2007.

Howell, Julie, NMT, PMT, Prenatal Health Through Massage Therapy: For Women and Their Babies. www.newlifejournal.com/decjan03/howell/01/03/full.shtml. Article accessed online 10/18/2007.

The Field: The Quest for the Secret Force of the Universe by Lynne McTaggart

The Intention Experiment by Lynne McTaggart

Quantum Touch: The Power to Heal by Richard Gordon

A Healthier You! Insight Publishing Company. 2005

Stress-Less: Living

http://www.independent.com.mt/articles/2010-02-22/leader/imagine-a-world-without-stress-270711/

http://www.nbcnews.com/health/kids-health/teens-more-stressed-out-adults-survey-shows-n26921

http://www.bloomberg.com/visual-data/best-and-worst/most-stressed-out-countries

http://online.wsj.com/news/articles/SB10001424052702303836404577474451463041994?KEYWORDS=stress+is+good+for+innovationandmg=reno64-wsjandurl=http%3A%2F%2Fonline.wsj.com%2Farticle%2FSB10001424052702303836404577474451463041994.html%3FKEYWORDS%3Dstress%2Bis%2Bgood%2Bfor%2Binnovation

http://www.helpguide.org/mental/stress_signs.htm

http://www.dailymail.co.uk/sciencetech/article-2175230/Too-time-online-lead-stress-sleeping-disorders-depression.html

http://www.psychologytoday.com/blog/sense-and-sensitivity/201203/sensitive-and-stressed

http://www.6seconds.org/2013/04/12/stress-health-emotional-intelligence

http://www.drjudithorloff.com/Free-Articles/emotional-empath-EF.htm

http://psychcentral.com/news/2012/12/04/physician-empathy-helps-manage-stress-and-pain/48564.html

http://www.drjudithorloff.com/Free-Articles/Drained.htm

http://giftedkids.about.com/od/socialemotionalissues/a/giftedstress_ed.htm

http://www.medicalnewstoday.com/articles/252637.php

http://www.disabilityscoop.com/2009/11/10/autism-moms-stress/6121/

https://www.apa.org/practice/programs/workplace/phwp-fact-sheet.pdf

http://www.fdu.edu/newspubs/magazine/99su/stress.html

http://www.bmmagazine.co.uk/news/12807/stress-costs-uk-economy-3-7bn/

http://www.mediate.com/articles/clarkM1.cfm

http://aubreydaniels.com/pmezine/paying-stress-toll

http://www.huffingtonpost.com/david-volpi-md-pc-facs/technology-depression_b_1723625.html

http://www.webmd.com/parenting/features/coping-school-stress

http://www.greatschools.org/parenting/teaching-values/645-stressed-out-kids.gs

http://www.psychologyfoundation.org/pdf/KHST_Booklet_for_Parents.pdf

http://www.thesuccessfulparent.com/parent-child-relationship/allowing-negative-feelings

http://fatherhood.about.com/od/parentingadvice/a/stress_home.htm

http://www.apa.org/helpcenter/managing-stress.aspx

http://nctsn.org/resources/topics/military-children-and-families

http://psychcentral.com/blog/archives/2013/11/08/kids-stress-when-parents-fight/

http://psychcentral.com/blog/archives/2012/03/23/9-tools-to-help-kids-cope-creatively-with-stress/

http://www.psychologytoday.com/blog/dont-worry-mom/201302/12-tips-reduce-your-childs-stress-and-anxiety

http://contemporarypediatrics.modernmedicine.com/contemporary-pediatrics/news/modernmedicine/modern-medicine-feature-articles/anxiety-disorders-adole

http://www.anxietybc.com/parent/index.php

http://www.today.com/moms/7-tricks-help-stressed-moms-chill-out-1C7397996

http://www.worldwidehealth.com/health-article-Stress-Nutrition-Basics.html

http://www.drlwilson.com/Articles/STRESS.HTM

http://www.lifepositive.com/mind/psychology/stress/psychological-stress.asp

http://www.thespiritualcatalyst.com/articles/ten-ways-to-eliminate-stress

http://www.healthy.net/Health/Article/Stress_Reduction_for_Relief_of_Fibroids_End

Deborah Carr and Debra Umberson. The Social Psychology of Stress, Health, and Coping – Handbook of Sociology and Social Research. Springer Science+Business Media Dordrecht 2013.

ADHD/ADD

http://www.showandtellforparents.com/wfdata/frame161-1017/pressrel43.asp

http://www.naeyc.org/tyc/files/tyc/file/V6N1/Dow2010.pdf

http://rense.com/general4/addd.htm

http://www.drugfreeworld.org/drugfacts/ritalin.html

http://www.healthy-vitamin-choice.com/mind-brain-nerves.html

http://www.cdc.gov/ncbddd/adhd/data.html

http://www.additudemag.com/adhd-web/article/623.htmlhttp://cspinet.org/new/pdf/dyesreschbk.pdf

http://fedup.com.au/factsheets/additive-and-natural-chemical-factsheets/salicylates

http://www.kevinmd.com/blog/2010/12/creativity-adhd-share-common-genetic-vulnerabilities.html

http://designmind.frogdesign.com/articles/motion/the-unique-brain.html?page=0

http://www.explorationinternational.com/products.html#a4

http://www.sengifted.org/archives/articles/misdiagnosis-and-dual-diagnosis-of-gifted-children

http://www.sagepub.com/upm-data/32712_Sousa_(Gifted_Brain)__Ch1.pdf

http://www.npr.org/2013/04/17/177040995/more-than-50-years-of-putting-kids-creativity-to-the-test

http://thesecondprinciple.com/creativity/usingnegativeemotionstofuelcreativity/

http://thesecondprinciple.com/creativity/killingcreativityinchildren/

http://positivepsychologynews.com/news/emiliya-zhivotovskaya/2012072523416

http://www.learnsuperbrainyoga.com/evidence/index.html

http://positivepsychologynews.com/news/emiliya-zhivotovskaya/2012072523416

http://www.learnsuperbrainyoga.com/evidence/index.html

http://www.iriyadancetherapy.com

http://www.healthy-vitamin-choice.com/mind-brain-nerves.html

http://www.cdc.gov/ncbddd/adhd/data.html

http://www.additudemag.com/adhd-web/article/623.htmlhttp://cspinet.org/new/pdf/dyesreschbk.pdf

http://fedup.com.au/factsheets/additive-and-natural-chemical-factsheets/salicylates

http://www.kevinmd.com/blog/2010/12/creativity-adhd-share-common-genetic-vulnerabilities.html

http://designmind.frogdesign.com/articles/motion/the-unique-brain.html?page=0

http://www.explorationinternational.com/products.html#a4

http://www.sengifted.org/archives/articles/misdiagnosis-and-dual-diagnosis-of-gifted-children

http://www.sagepub.com/upm-data/32712_Sousa_(Gifted_Brain)__Ch1.pdf

http://www.npr.org/2013/04/17/177040995/more-than-50-years-of-putting-kids-creativity-to-the-test

http://thesecondprinciple.com/creativity/usingnegativeemotionstofuelcreativity/

http://thesecondprinciple.com/creativity/killingcreativityinchildren/

http://positivepsychologynews.com/news/emiliya-zhivotovskaya/2012072523416

http://www.learnsuperbrainyoga.com/evidence/index.html

http://positivepsychologynews.com/news/emiliya-zhivotovskaya/2012072523416

http://www.learnsuperbrainyoga.com/evidence/index.html

http://www.telegraph.co.uk/technology/videogames/nintendo/8238474/Is-3D-technology-safe-for-children.html

http://www.psychologytoday.com/blog/freedom-learn/201108/is-real-educational-reform-possible-if-so-how

http://www.globaleducationfirst.org/3803.htm

http://funmusicco.com/research-into-the-benefits-of-music/how-does-music-stimulate-left-and-right brain-function-and-why-is-this-important-in-music-teaching/

http://funmusicco.com/research-into-the-benefits-of-music/how-does-music-stimulate-left-and-right brain-function-and-why-is-this-important-in-music-teaching/

http://digitalcommons.unl.edu/cgi/viewcontent.cgi?article=1041andcontext=envstudtheses

http://www.naeyc.org/files/yc/file/200801/BTJNatureRosenow.pdf

http://www.au.af.mil/au/awc/awcgate/army/rotc_right-left_brain.pdf

http://www.natureexplore.org/research/

http://www.essentialbaby.com.au/toddler/caring-for-toddler/meditation-and-yoga-for-toddlers-20130718-2q6kg.html

http://www.yogajournal.com/lifestyle/210

http://www.enhancementthemes.ac.uk/docs/documents/impact-of-mindfulness---katherine-weare.pdf

https://www.davidlynchfoundation.org/pdf/Quiet-Time-Brochure.pdf

http://www.tm-women.org/benefits-moms-childrens-meditation.html

https://s3.amazonaws.com/media.reports/youth-sports-parent-ebook.pdf

http://www.qimacros.com/knowware-articles/five-limiting-beliefs/

http://www.globalgiving.org/photo/PRA15746/dahn-mu-do-training-photo-from-progress-report-remember/

http://www.reboundoz.com.au/health-benefits2.htm

http://www.arnoldsway.com/rebounder1.htm

http://psychology.about.com/od/sensationandperception/a/colorpsych.htm

http://www.medindia.net/news/lifestyleandwellness/color-light-therapy-a-breakthrough-in-alternative-healing-practices-115224-1.htm

http://www.changeyourenergy.com/ilchi-lee

http://www.empower-yourself-with-color-psychology.com/personality-color.html

http://www.empower-yourself-with-color-psychology.com/meaning-of-colors.html

http://www.awakendivineenergy.com/energy_dance.html

http://www.awakendivineenergy.com/id102.html

http://yogakids.com/toolsforschools/tfs-overview.htm

http://www.cal.org/resources/digest/0304fortune.html

http://www.himawaripreschool.org/why%20learn%20japanese%20at%20himawari.htm

http://www.care2.com/causes/6-reasons-to-learn-a-foreign-language-and-help-your-brain.html?page=1

http://www.dramaclub.co.nz/5-ways-drama-helps-children/

http://www.pyjamadrama.com/about

http://newmorningcommunitypreschool.wordpress.com/service-learning-projects/about-service-learning/

https://www.apa.org/monitor/dec06/kids.aspx

http://www.cctvcamerapros.com/Day-Care-Surveillance-s/223.htm

http://www.preschools.coop/

http://www.parents.com/toddlers-preschoolers/development/behavioral/teaching-children-to-be-grateful/

http://psychcentral.com/blog/archives/2013/02/27/how-to-teach-a-child-forgiveness/

http://www.sheknows.com/parenting/articles/981553/raising-healthy-kids-through-food-exercise
     -and-love

http://www.psychologytoday.com/blog/the-art-science-teaching-kids-eat-right/201310/why-smart
     -kids-dont-eat-right

http://www.choosemyplate.gov/preschoolers/healthy-habits.html

http://loveourchildrenusa.org/teachingkidsselfesteem.php

http://www.todaysparent.com/family/parenting/how-to-build-your-childs-self-esteem/

http://funmusicco.com/research-into-the-benefits-of-music/how-does-music-stimulate-left-and-
     right_brain-function-and-why-is-this-important-in-music-teaching/

http://digitalcommons.unl.edu/cgi/viewcontent.cgi?article=1041andcontext=envstudtheses

http://www.naeyc.org/files/yc/file/200801/BTJNatureRosenow.pdf

http://www.au.af.mil/au/awc/awcgate/army/rotc_right-left_brain.pdf

http://www.natureexplore.org/research/

http://www.essentialbaby.com.au/toddler/caring-for-toddler/meditation-and-yoga-for-toddlers-
     20130718-2q6kg.html

http://www.yogajournal.com/lifestyle/210

http://www.enhancementthemes.ac.uk/docs/documents/impact-of-mindfulness---katherine-weare.pdf

https://www.davidlynchfoundation.org/pdf/Quiet-Time-Brochure.pdf

http://www.tm-women.org/benefits-moms-childrens-meditation.html

http://www.blogmemom.com/origami-for-kids/

http://www.internationalparentingassociation.org/BrainDevelopment/mobility1.html

http://www.huletsmith.com/?filename=what-is-patterning-a-technique-taught-by-dr-glen-doman1

http://www.whywaldorfworks.org/02_W_Education/index.asp

http://www.education.com/reference/article/high-scope-one-program-model/

http://www.plosbiology.org/article/info%3Adoi%2F10.1371%2Fjournal.pbio.1001767

Timothy T. Brown et al. Atypical right hemisphere specialization for object representations in an adolescent with specific language impairment. Frontier in human neuroscience. 2014

Autism

http://www.human.cornell.edu/hd/outreach-extension/upload/belmonte.pdf
http://www.huffingtonpost.com/2013/07/01/iris-halmshaw-paintings-autistic-thousands_n_3530466.html
http://www.generationrescue.org/assets/Documents/Bailey-Banks-case.pdf
http://www.nydailynews.com/life-style/health/autistic-boy-genius-iq-higher-einstein-article-1.1340923
http://www.ageofautism.com/recovery_stories/#
http://brainfitnessstrategies.com/about-overcoming-disability/rhythmic-movement-training.html
http://brainfitnessstrategies.com/juggling-brain-development/rhythmic-movement/primitive-reflexes.html
http://sonoma-county.triplep-staypositive.net/son-en/home/
http://money.msn.com/now/post.aspx?post=00d9751b-dad1-4d2a-b3ea-01287216ce21
http://www.examiner.com/article/qigong-massage-for-your-child-with-autism
http://www.qsti.org/diet.pdf
http://www.qsti.org/index.html
http://www.generationrescue.org/
http://articles.mercola.com/sites/articles/archive/2008/01/02/tomastis-method-and-autism.aspx
http://action.greenamerica.org/p/salsa/web/common/public/signup?signup_page_KEY=7608and;gclid=
    CNC7xbS-wbwCFbB9OgodLFsArg
http://kimberlysnyder.net/blog/2012/04/03/the-dangers-of-diapers-and-why-you-should-be-aware/
http://www.bellasugar.com/What-Foods-Eat-Good-Skin-15625898
http://canadianawareness.org/2013/09/disposable-diapers-how-much-do-you-care-about-your-babys-health/
http://www.gacrs.org/resources/archived-chats/146-how-environmental-toxins-effect-behavior-in-
    autistic-children
http://www.momsagainstmercury.org/mercury-dental-fillings.htm
http://ourdailylegacy.blogspot.com/2011/10/book-review-toxic-sandbox-part-1.html
http://www.freedrinkingwater.com/water_health/adhd-health-drinking-water-contamination.htm
http://www.alkalizeforhealth.net/ADHD.htm
http://www.autism.com/pdf/providers/adams_biomed_summary.pdf
http://psychcentral.com/news/2014/02/02/prosocial-video games-instill-kindness-helpfulness-in-
    kids/65302.html
http://www.stancoe.org/cfs/handouts/guiddisc/pdf/prosocialbehaviordevelopmentguide.pdf
http://www.evidenceofharm.com/introduction.htm
http://www.freedrinkingwater.com/water_health/adhd-health-drinking-water-contamination.htm
http://www.meetpenny.com/2013/05/essential-oils-for-autism/
www.wholesomewords.org/missions/greatc.html

Complementary and Alternative Medicine Treatments for Children with Autism Spectrum Disorders.
Child Adolesc Psychiatr Clin N Am. Author manuscript; available in PMC 2009 October 1

Depression

http://lynnemctaggart.com/blog/229-good-vibrations

http://www.getresponse.com/archive/thespiritchannel/Transcription-Monday-BBS-Call-03-07-2011-Entrainment-Entrapment-and-Resonance-5846980.html

http://anitamoorjani.com/about-anita/nde-according-to-anita/

http://www.education-reform.net/brain.htm

http://magazine.ucla.edu/exclusives/food_brain_medicine/

http://www.webmd.com/food-recipes/features/how-food-affects-your-moods?page=3

http://www.scribd.com/doc/8863073/Artificially-Sweetened-Times-Aspartame-is-Poison

http://www.nasponline.org/resources/handouts/social%20template.pdf

http://apt.rcpsych.org/content/15/4/271.full

http://psychcentral.com/news/2006/11/09/depressions-chemical-imbalance-explained/398.html

http://www.webmd.com/depression/features/serotonin

http://www.marksdailyapple.com/serotonin-boosters/#axzz2sOT2z7Mj

http://www.fi.edu/learn/brain/proteins.html

https://www.wyldeabouthealth.com/articles/view/59

http://www.naturalnews.com/040537_brain_foods_dopamine_production.html

http://www.thegabrielmethod.com/increase-dopamine-get-happy-and-lose-weight-too

http://www.nytimes.com/2013/07/02/magazine/the-half-trillion-dollar-depression.html?pagewanted=alland;_r=0

http://www.gallup.com/poll/163619/depression-costs-workplaces-billion-absenteeism.aspx

http://www.cehd.umn.edu/ssw/cascw/attributes/PDF/events/MaternalDepression/Maternal_Depression_Report.pdf

http://www.sacredfengshuidesign.com.au/geomancy.html

http://www.thegeniewithin.net/do-you-have-a-clue-what-s-in-your-subconscious-mind

http://www.hypnosishelpcenter.net/depression.htm

http://www.doctoroz.com/videos/best-natural-antidepressants?page=3

http://health.yahoo.net/experts/dayinhealth/golden-spice-life-brings-health-and-happiness

http://www.thegeniewithin.net/do-you-have-a-clue-what-s-in-your-subconscious-mind

http://www.cellularmemory.org/about/about_cellularmemory.html

http://energypsych.com/what-is-energy-psychology/

http://science.howstuffworks.com/ultrasound2.htm

http://healing.about.com/od/energyhealing/a/energy_spsmith.htm

http://www.reiki.org/reikinews/sciencemeasures.htm

http://healing.about.com/od/chakratheseven/a/study7chakras.htm

http://www.toolsforwellness.com/tuning-forks.html

http://www.reikiforallcreatures.com/about-reiki-hospitals.aspx

http://your-healing-journey.jigsy.com/reiki-benefits-and-what-you-can-expect

http://www.relaxkids.com/tips/entry/Gratitude_Meditation/250

http://www.ahaparenting.com/parenting-tools/positive-discipline/use-positive-discipline

http://www.care2.com/greenliving/7-flower-remedies-for-depression.html?page=1

http://psychology.about.com/od/PositivePsychology/f/positive-thinking.htm

http://carljungdepthpsychology.blogspot.com/2011/08/incantations-carl-jung.html

http://wrathwarbone.hubpages.com/hub/Affirmations-For-Depression-And-Self-Esteem
http://candeecefalland.com/emotional-states/incantations-and-affirmation/
http://www.tm.org/blog/students/adhd-tm/
http://www.t-m.org.uk/articles/Green-Parent-Aug-2010.shtml
http://www.tm.org/benefits-classroom
http://roberttisserand.com/2013/04/new-rosemary-memory-research/
http://yoursacredcalling.com/commonscentsmom/quieting-the-mind-with-vetiver/

Yvonne Perry and Dr. Caron Goode. Whose Stuff Is This? Finding Freedom From the Thoughts, Feelings, and Energy Of Those Around You. Copyright, 2010.

Obesity

http://wallstcheatsheet.com/stocks/7-unhealthy-everyday-foods-processed-and-problematic.html/2/
http://www.scribd.com/doc/8863073/Artificially-Sweetened-Times-Aspartame-is-Poison
http://childhoodobesitynews.com/2011/04/28/food-addiction-and-childhood-obesity-now-what-do-we-do/
http://www.yaleruddcenter.org/what_we_do.aspx?id=4
http://www.yaleruddcenter.org/resources/upload/docs/what/advertising/MarketingChildhoodObesity
    ARPH4.09.pdf
http://www.bnl.gov/bnlweb/pubaf/pr/2001/bnlpr020101.htm
http://www.commercialfreechildhood.org/sites/default/files/facingthescreendilemma.pdf
http://www.psychologytoday.com/articles/200305/the-obesity-depression-link
http://www.bnl.gov/bnlweb/pubaf/pr/2001/bnlpr020101.htm
http://hsperson.com/pages/child.htm
http://www.janineramsey.com.au/
http://www.connectionsinrecovery.com/2013/08/attributes-characteristics-highly-sensitive/
http://www.huffingtonpost.com/roya-r-rad-ma-psyd/highly-sensitive-people_b_1286508.html
http://www.nccor.org/downloads/ChildhoodObesity_020509.pdf
http://www.webmd.com/children/guide/obesity-children
http://loseweightbefreeprogramme.blogspot.com/2010/08/metaphysical-meaning-of-obesity.html
http://yoga-health-benefits.blogspot.com/2009/07/yoga-for-childhood-obesity.html
http://psychcentral.com/blog/archives/2013/02/27/how-to-teach-a-child-forgiveness/
http://www.attachmentparenting.org/aboutus
http://www.parentingscience.com/attachment-parenting.html
http://www.nongmoprojEtc.org/learn-more/
http://health.yahoo.net/experts/dayinhealth/genetically-modified-food-making-us-fat
http://www.huffingtonpost.com/tasneem-bhatia-md/childhood-obesity-_b_3932559.html
http://www.naturalbloom.com/articles/dance-therapy-237/
http://www.sciencedaily.com/releases/2014/01/140128103533.htm
http://www.psychologytoday.com/blog/compassion-matters/201106/your-child-s-self-esteem-starts-you
http://stress.about.com/od/lowstresslifestyle/a/altruism.htm
http://www.helpguide.org/life/volunteer_opportunities_benefits_volunteering.htm
http://www.npr.org/blogs/thesalt/2013/07/17/202684064/in-oregon-the-gmo-wheat-mystery-deepens

http://www.undergroundhealth.com/genetically-modified-wheat-silences-dna-sequences-in-the-body-can-cause-fatalities-in-children/

http://www.dailymail.co.uk/health/article-51648/Wheat-intolerance-facts.html

http://drhyman.com/blog/2010/07/04/are-you-also-being-deceived-into-eating-fake-frankenfoods/

http://www.huffingtonpost.com/dr-mark-hyman/wheat-gluten_b_1274872.html

http://www.simplypsychology.org/self-esteem.html

http://www.psychologytoday.com/articles/199911/self-esteem-vs-self-respect

http://www.pickthebrain.com/blog/self-respect/

http://www.psychologytoday.com/blog/hide-and-seek/201205/building-confidence-and-self-esteem

http://pediatrics.aappublications.org/content/113/5/1187.abstract?etoc

http://www.adta.org/Resources/Documents/DMT%20and%20Childhood%20Obesity%20White%20Paper%208-13.pdf

http://www.hooponoponoway.net/about/hooponopono/

http://frac.org/wp-content/uploads/2010/10/providing_nutrition_education_afterschool.pdf

http://www.ncbi.nlm.nih.gov/pubmed/1733119?dopt=Citation

http://www.laughing-yoga.org/benefits-of-laughter-yoga.html?start=8

http://www.ncbi.nlm.nih.gov/pubmed/1733119?dopt=Citation

http://www.laughing-yoga.org/benefits-of-laughter-yoga.html?start=8

Chen L, Zhang B, Toborek M. Autophagy is involved in nanoalumina-induced cerebrovascular toxicity. Nanomedicine. 2013 Feb;9(2):212-21. doi: 10.1016/j.nano.2012.05.017. Epub 2012 Jun 9.

Dave KR, Syal AR, Katyare SS. Effect of long-term aluminum feeding on kinetics attributes of tissue cholinesterases. Brain Res Bull. 2002 Jun; 58(2):225-33.

Project Hope: Whole-Listic Children's Hospatal

http://www.3dprinterworld.com/article/shriners-hospital-uses-3d-printing-and-geomagic-heal-cleft-palate

http://www.cdc.gov/ncbddd/birthdefects/cleftlip.html

http://kidshealth.org/parent/system/ill/baby_has_birth_defEtc.html

http://newsmomsneed.marchofdimes.com/?tag=birth-defect

http://www.computerworld.com/s/article/9244278/3D_printing_community_rallies_to_create_5_hand_for_kid

http://www.washingtonpost.com/national/health-science/to-help-solve-challenging-cardiac-problems-doctors-at-childrens-press-print/2013/05/13/b2eee214-8d9b-11e2-9838-d62f083ba93f_story.html

http://www.popsci.com/diy/article/2012-11/you-built-what-remote-controlled-robo-arm

http://kidshealth.org/parent/system/ill/baby_has_birth_defEtc.htmlhttp://newsmomsneed.marchofdimes.com/?tag=birth-defect

http://www.computerworld.com/s/article/9244278/3D_printing_community_rallies_to_create_5_hand_for_kid

http://www.washingtonpost.com/national/health-science/to-help-solve-challenging-cardiac-problems-doctors-at-childrens-press-print/2013/05/13/b2eee214-8d9b-11e2-9838-d62f083ba93f_story.html

http://durangoherald.com/article/20130422/NEWS01/130429862/

http://www.wired.co.uk/news/archive/2013-01/08/childrens-drawings-3d-sculptures
http://www.wired.com/design/2013/12/characters-come-alive-in-this-3-d-printable-book/
http://www.cbsnews.com/news/3d-printer-helps-4-year-old-girl-who-cant-use-her-arms-play-with-toys/
http://articles.philly.com/2014-02-10/news/47171542_1_heart-defects-3-d-printer-phoenix-children
http://www.washingtonpost.com/national/health-science/to-help-solve-challenging-cardiac-problems-doctors-at-childrens-press-print/2013/05/13/b2eee214-8d9b-11e2-9838-d62f083ba93f_story.html

http://www.wired.co.uk/news/archive/2013-01/08/childrens-drawings-3d-sculptures
http://www.wired.com/design/2013/12/characters-come-alive-in-this-3-d-printable-book/
http://www.cbsnews.com/news/3d-printer-helps-4-year-old-girl-who-cant-use-her-arms-play-with-toys/
http://articles.philly.com/2014-02-10/news/47171542_1_heart-defects-3-d-printer-phoenix-children
http://www.washingtonpost.com/national/health-science/to-help-solve-challenging-cardiac-problems-doctors-at-childrens-press-print/2013/05/13/b2eee214-8d9b-11e2-9838-d62f083ba93f_story.html

Russell, Peter (2013-08-21.) The Brain Book: Know Your Own Mind and How to Use it (Kindle Location 28.) Taylor and Francis. Kindle Edition.

Education: The Whole-Listic Gifted Academy

http://www.telegraph.co.uk/technology/videogames/nintendo/8238474/Is-3D-technology-safe-for-children.html
http://www.psychologytoday.com/blog/freedom-learn/201108/is-real-educational-reform-possible-if-so-how
http://www.globaleducationfirst.org/3803.htm
http://funmusicco.com/research-into-the-benefits-of-music/how-does-music-stimulate-left-and-right brain-function-and-why-is-this-important-in-music-teaching/
http://funmusicco.com/research-into-the-benefits-of-music/how-does-music-stimulate-left-and-right brain-function-and-why-is-this-important-in-music-teaching/
http://digitalcommons.unl.edu/cgi/viewcontent.cgi?article=1041andcontext=envstudtheses
http://www.naeyc.org/files/yc/file/200801/BTJNatureRosenow.pdf
http://www.au.af.mil/au/awc/awcgate/army/rotc_right-left_brain.pdf
http://www.natureexplore.org/research/
http://www.essentialbaby.com.au/toddler/caring-for-toddler/meditation-and-yoga-for-toddlers-20130718-2q6kg.html
http://www.yogajournal.com/lifestyle/210
http://www.enhancementthemes.ac.uk/docs/documents/impact-of-mindfulness---katherine-weare.pdf
https://www.davidlynchfoundation.org/pdf/Quiet-Time-Brochure.pdf
http://www.tm-women.org/benefits-moms-childrens-meditation.html
https://s3.amazonaws.com/media.reports/youth-sports-parent-ebook.pdf
http://www.qimacros.com/knowware-articles/five-limiting-beliefs/
http://www.globalgiving.org/photo/PRA15746/dahn-mu-do-training-photo-from-progress-report-remember/
http://www.reboundoz.com.au/health-benefits2.htm
http://www.arnoldsway.com/rebounder1.htm

http://psychology.about.com/od/sensationandperception/a/colorpsych.htm

http://www.medindia.net/news/lifestyleandwellness/color-light-therapy-a-breakthrough-in-alternative-healing-practices-115224-1.htm

http://www.changeyourenergy.com/ilchi-lee

http://www.empower-yourself-with-color-psychology.com/personality-color.html

http://www.empower-yourself-with-color-psychology.com/meaning-of-colors.html

http://www.awakendivineenergy.com/energy_dance.html

http://www.awakendivineenergy.com/id102.html

http://yogakids.com/toolsforschools/tfs-overview.htm

http://www.cal.org/resources/digest/0304fortune.html

http://www.himawaripreschool.org/why%20learn%20japanese%20at%20himawari.htm

http://www.care2.com/causes/6-reasons-to-learn-a-foreign-language-and-help-your-brain.html?page=1

http://www.dramaclub.co.nz/5-ways-drama-helps-children/

http://www.pyjamadrama.com/about

http://newmorningcommunitypreschool.wordpress.com/service-learning-projects/about-service-learning/

https://www.apa.org/monitor/dec06/kids.aspx

http://www.cctvcamerapros.com/Day-Care-Surveillance-s/223.htm

http://www.preschools.coop/

http://www.parents.com/toddlers-preschoolers/development/behavioral/teaching-children-to-be-grateful/

http://psychcentral.com/blog/archives/2013/02/27/how-to-teach-a-child-forgiveness/

http://www.sheknows.com/parenting/articles/981553/raising-healthy-kids-through-food-exercise-and-love

http://www.psychologytoday.com/blog/the-art-science-teaching-kids-eat-right/201310/why-smart-kids-dont-eat-right

http://www.choosemyplate.gov/preschoolers/healthy-habits.html

http://loveourchildrenusa.org/teachingkidsselfesteem.php

http://www.todaysparent.com/family/parenting/how-to-build-your-childs-self-esteem/

http://funmusicco.com/research-into-the-benefits-of-music/how-does-music-stimulate-left-and-right_brain-function-and-why-is-this-important-in-music-teaching/

http://digitalcommons.unl.edu/cgi/viewcontent.cgi?article=1041andcontext=envstudtheses

http://www.naeyc.org/files/yc/file/200801/BTJNatureRosenow.pdf

http://www.au.af.mil/au/awc/awcgate/army/rotc_right-left_brain.pdf

http://www.natureexplore.org/research/

http://www.essentialbaby.com.au/toddler/caring-for-toddler/meditation-and-yoga-for-toddlers-20130718-2q6kg.html

http://www.yogajournal.com/lifestyle/210

http://www.enhancementthemes.ac.uk/docs/documents/impact-of-mindfulness---katherine-weare.pdf

https://www.davidlynchfoundation.org/pdf/Quiet-Time-Brochure.pdf

http://www.tm-women.org/benefits-moms-childrens-meditation.html

http://www.blogmemom.com/origami-for-kids/

http://www.internationalparentingassociation.org/BrainDevelopment/mobility1.html

http://www.huletsmith.com/?filename=what-is-patterning-a-technique-taught-by-dr-glen-doman1

http://www.whywaldorfworks.org/02_W_Education/index.asp

http://www.education.com/reference/article/high-scope-one-program-model/

Finding the Real "U"

http://www.nozomimorgan.com/help-yourself-first/
http://shanelopez.com/wp-content/uploads/2012/04/Hope-Article-by-Shane-Lopez.pdf
http://psychcentral.com/blog/archives/2013/03/21/the-psychology-of-hope/
http://www.psychologytoday.com/blog/beautiful-minds/201112/the-will-and-ways-hope
http://www.huffingtonpost.com/shane-j-lopez-phd/making-hope-happen_b_2812859.html
http://shanelopez.com/hope-odyssey/
http://www.thepowerofintroverts.com/about-the-book/
http://www.huffingtonpost.com/2013/08/13/famous-introverts_n_3733400.html
http://www.forbes.com/pictures/egid45hlj/steven-spielberg/
http://lifestyle.allwomenstalk.com/famous-introverts/6/
http://hopingfor.com/famous-introverts-actresses-actors-talk-show-hosts
http://www.goodreads.com/work/quotes/13387396-quiet-the-power-of-introverts-in-a-world-that-
      can-t-stop-talking
http://www.dingtwist.com/life-is-a-game/
http://www.dingtwist.com/grow-down/
http://www.dingtwist.com/placebo-effect/
http://www.dingtwist.com/lotus-flower/
http://discovermagazine.com/2007/sep/the-body-can-stave-off-terminal-cancer-sometimes#.UnEVU2Qo5o4
http://www.nytimes.com/1998/10/13/science/placebos-prove-so-powerful-even-experts-are-
      surprised-new-studies-explore-brain.html?pagewanted=allandsrc=pm
http://www.dingtwist.com/reality-is-subjective/
http://www.dingtwist.com/time/
http://www.psychologytoday.com/blog/creative-development/201103/kids-meditation-one-path-power
http://www.growinghappykids.com/about-maureen-healy
http://www.allknowingdiary.com/?author=1
http://www.imageryforkids.com/about.html
http://www.psychologytoday.com/blog/the-power-imagination/201212/opening-the-heart-child
http://theattitudeofgratitude.com/gratitude/inner-child-healing-2/
http://books.google.com/books?id=WOG54U_YHmYCandpg=PA204andlpg=PA2
      04anddq=inner+child+gratitudeandsource=blandots=N-IaLRpfhBandsig=i8-
      eH2Dr-wD1I5n5Z7NL4AjveDUandhl=enandsa=Xandei=UJYrU-
      nOHofa0QHu7YH4Agandved=0CGEQ6AEwCQ#v=onepageandq=inner%20child%20
      gratitudeandf=false
http://www.healyourlife.com/author-louise-l-hay/2013/02/wisdom/inspiration/love-your-inner-child
http://www.letssandbox.com/tag/inner-child/
http://education.byu.edu/youcandothis/expressing_gratitude.html
http://www.pursuit-of-happiness.org/history-of-happiness/viktor-frankl/
www.tonyrobbins.com/
https://www.deepakchopra.com/?

http://www.accessingui.com/

http://www.myersbriggs.org/my-mbti-personality-type/mbti-basics/

http://identityblueprint.com/en/about/

http://unleashyourinnerstrength.com/the-%e2%80%9ci-already-have-it-i-already-am-it%e2%80%9d-technique/

http://feelitreal.com/onlinestore/vibrationalgames/

http://unleashyourinnerstrength.com/2010/09/15/feeling-is-the-secret-offer/

http://www.psykosyntese.dk/i-133/

http://gratitudepower.net/science.htm

http://www.angriesout.com/teach9.htm

https://artofgratitude.com/

http://www.huffingtonpost.com/2012/12/24/tony-robbins-td-jakes-deepak-chopra_n_2325557.html

http://www.imdb.com/name/nm0889395/bio

http://quantumhealer.blogspot.com/

http://www.mindreality.com/world-is-simply-mirror

http://www.psychologytoday.com/blog/enlightened-living/201209/are-other-people-your-mirror

http://www.chabad.org/library/article_cdo/aid/716555/jewish/The-Mirror-Theory.htm

http://www.myersbriggs.org/my-mbti-personality-type/mbti-basics/

http://identityblueprint.com/en/about/

http://unleashyourinnerstrength.com/the-%e2%80%9ci-already-have-it-i-already-am-it%e2%80%9d
-technique/

http://feelitreal.com/onlinestore/vibrationalgames/

http://unleashyourinnerstrength.com/2010/09/15/feeling-is-the-secret-offer/

http://www.psykosyntese.dk/i-133/

http://gratitudepower.net/science.htm

http://www.angriesout.com/teach9.htm

https://artofgratitude.com/

http://www.huffingtonpost.com/2012/12/24/tony-robbins-td-jakes-deepak-chopra_n_2325557.html

http://www.imdb.com/name/nm0889395/bio

http://quantumhealer.blogspot.com/

http://www.mindreality.com/world-is-simply-mirror

http://www.psychologytoday.com/blog/enlightened-living/201209/are-other-people-your-mirror

http://www.chabad.org/library/article_cdo/aid/716555/jewish/The-Mirror-Theory.htm

Harry W. Carpenter. The Genie Within - Your subconsicous mind. Self published 2009.

Jack Canfield. BREAKTHROUGH TO SUCCESS SEMINAR Seminars. Self published. 2005

Jackie Arnold. Coaching skills for leaders in the workplace. How to content. 2009